H. A. Tupper

Foreign Missions of the Southern Baptist Convention

H. A. Tupper

Foreign Missions of the Southern Baptist Convention

ISBN/EAN: 9783743327153

Manufactured in Europe, USA, Canada, Australia, Japa

Cover: Foto ©ninafisch / pixelio.de

Manufactured and distributed by brebook publishing software (www.brebook.com)

H. A. Tupper

Foreign Missions of the Southern Baptist Convention

THE FOREIGN MISSIONS

OF THE

Southern Baptist Convention.

BY

H. A. TUPPER.

PHILADELPHIA:
AMERICAN BAPTIST PUBLICATION SOCIETY.
NO. 1420 CHESTNUT STREET.

RICHMOND, VIRGINIA:
FOREIGN MISSION BOARD OF THE SOUTHERN BAPTIST CONVENTION.

INSCRIPTION.

I WRITE ON THIS PAGE THE NAME OF THE MAN OF GOD,
WHO, FOR MORE THAN A SCORE OF YEARS,
SAT AT THE HEAD OF OUR BOARD;
WHOSE ZEAL FOR THE WORK WHICH IT AIMS TO DO
HAS RUN THROUGH SOME THREE-SCORE YEARS; AND WHO, IN
HALE AND WISE OLD AGE, GIVES HIS LAST STRENGTH TO THE BOARD OF
WHICH HE HAS BEEN FROM THE FIRST A STRONG PART,

THE REVEREND JEREMIAH BELL JETER, D.D.

FOR HIS GOOD AND GREAT LIFE I THANK GOD;
AND, WITH NO LEAVE, BUT WITH MUCH LOVE, I PUT HIS
NAME HERE TO DECK AND GRACE MY BOOK.

H. A. T.

Richmond, Virginia, January 1st, 1880.

WHY THIS BOOK?

ACTION OF THE SOUTHERN BAPTIST CONVENTION.

"RESOLVED, 1. That we recognize in the series of articles lately published in the various papers of our denomination, over the signature of "T," on the History of our Foreign Missions and Foreign Missionaries, an efficient means of extending missionary intelligence among our churches, and of arousing a more general and lively interest in the work of evangelization in heathen lands.

RESOLVED, 2. That we hereby express our deep conviction that said articles should be put into a more convenient and durable form, and our earnest wish that an arrangement to this end be at once made.

RESOLVED, 3. That we hereby pledge ourselves to aid, to the full extent of our ability, in the circulation of these articles, should it be practicable to carry out the idea expressed in the second resolution."

ACTION OF BOARD FOR FOREIGN MISSIONS.

"RESOLVED, That the Corresponding Secretary, in the publication of his forthcoming work on Missions, be permitted to use the imprint of this Board."

Minutes of Board, August 4, 1879.

WHENCE THIS BOOK?

GENERAL ACKNOWLEDGMENT.

The work of one who longs to do all he can for the cause to which he gave his life when he gave his heart to him that died to save the world, and, who, when he first put in print the most of what is found in this book, said once for all: "I only aim at a compilation, which may aid my ministering brethren, stimulate the churches, and furnish material somewhat prepared for future history."

AUTHORITIES FREELY USED.

RECORDS OF THE BOARD OF FOREIGN MISSIONS; PROCEEDINGS OF SOUTHERN BAPTIST CONVENTION; *Southern Baptist Missionary Journal; The Commission; Home and Foreign Journal; Foreign Mission Journal; Unpublished Letters of the Foreign Mission Rooms;* FRIENDS AND RELATIONS OF OUR MISSIONARIES.

Gammel's *History of American Baptist Missions;* Tracy's *History of American Missions; Foreign Missions,* by Dr. Rufus Anderson; *Go or Send,* by Dr. Hagood; *The Foreign Missions of the Presbyterian Church,* by Dr. I. C. Lowrie; Bowen's *Central Africa;* Livingstone's *Explorations;* Barth's *Discoveries of North and Central Africa; Western Africa,* by Dr. J. L. Wilson; *The Middle Kingdom,* by S. Wells Williams; *An Exploratory Visit to the Consular Cities of China,* by Rev. George Smith, M. A.; *The Chinese,* by Sir John Francis Davis, Esq., F.R.S.; *The Great Commission,* by Harris; Knowlton's *China, as a Missionary Field;* Biographies of *Judson, Mrs. Shuck,* and *Rev. J. B. Taylor, D D.;*

Letters of Dr. G. B. Taylor; The Cyclopedia of Missions, by Harvey Newcombe; Dr. Wm. Williams' *Historical Sketch;* Dr. Coxe's *History of the Baptist Mission; Our Life in China*, by Mrs. Nevius; *The Missionary World*, by Boyce, Mullens, and Underhill; Perry's *Expedition to Japan; Japan*, by Charles MacFarlane, Esq.; *Brazil and the Brazilians*, by Kidder and Fletcher; Ranke's *History of the Popes;* Lord's *Theological and Literary Journal; The Missionary Magazine*, by R. G. Wilder, D. D.; *The Baptist Missionary Magazine;* many other Missionary periodicals and religious papers.

SPECIAL OBLIGATIONS.

THANKS ARE DUE TO FRIENDS, IN FAR OFF LANDS AND AT HOME, UNDER WHOSE EYE THE WORK WAS PUT, ERE IT SHOULD GO OUT IN BOOK FORM.

IN MEMORIAM.

Rev. JAMES B. TAYLOR, D. D.

The first words which the present Corresponding Secretary, who entered upon his office in February, 1872, wrote to the Southern Baptist Convention, were these words of sadness:

"This report might well be draped in mourning. The prospect of the future and the retrospect of the past are gloomed by the remembrance that the moving spirit of our Foreign Mission Cause—to whom, under God, more perhaps than to any other agency, was due its deep imbedding in the hearts of our people, and its vigorous prosecution in its various fields of labor—is passed away, and the ponderous work, which he so meekly and successfully carried forward, is transmitted to other and untried shoulders. The history of Foreign Missions, under the patronage of the Southern Baptist Convention, is the monument of our late Corresponding Secretary, Dr. James B. Taylor. They were founded with his counsels, reared under his superintendence, and cheered by many triumphs of grace, in accordance with his strong faith, his earnest prayer, and his indefatigable labor. His life was missions, and his death the missionary's crown.

"Anticipating this event, he resigned the Secretaryship on the 11th of December, 1871, when the Board, submitting to what seemed the hand of Providence, made the following record:

Rev. J. B. Taylor, D. D., has been the only acting Corresponding Secretary of this Board. During the whole period of its existence, extending through twenty-six years, he has performed the duties of his office with a diligence, fidelity, and disinterestedness never excelled, and with a judgment, prudence, and efficiency rarely equalled. He has been, in truth, the life and motive power of the Board.

IN MEMORIAM.

"The wisdom of his resignation was justified by his translation, on the twenty-second day of the same month, to his Heavenly Lord, whose kingdom he had so faithfully served. With afflicted hearts the ensuing action was adopted by the Board:

Resolved, That in the death of our venerated brother, Rev. James B. Taylor, his family, the Baptist Denomination, and the Foreign Mission Board have sustained a great loss, to which, thankful that his life was so long spared, and so fruitful of good, and deeply impressed with the wisdom and kindness of the Supreme Disposer of all events, we humbly and adoringly submit.

Resolved, That the example of our deceased brother, distinguished, as it was, by the disinterestedness of his motives, the fervor of his piety, the blamelessness of his conduct, the diligence of his labors, the symmetry of his character, and the benefits of his influence, is worthy of all commendation, and should be held up for the imitation of his survivors.

Resolved, That a suitable and permanent record of a life so exemplary and beautiful, so enriched by the fruits of the Spirit, so abundant in labors, so pleasing in results, and so consecrated to the cause of Foreign Missions, as was that of Dr. Taylor, could not fail to be an acceptable offering to the public, and promotive of the ends to which that life was devoted; and that Rev. George B. Taylor, son of our deceased Secretary, is peculiarly fitted to prepare such a work.

        J. B. JETER,
        N. W. WILSON,
        W. H. GWATHMEY."

As may be suggested by the table of "Contents," our book is arranged to bear upon the interest of Foreign Missions "under the patronage of the Southern Baptist Convention." In the successful past of the Convention, this work has been "the monument of our late Corresponding Secretary." In its more successful future, may our advancing enterprise be a grand memorial of the grace of God, and of the spirit of Missions in our Southern Zion.

CONTENTS.

	PAGE.
INSCRIPTION...	iii
WHY THIS BOOK?...	v
WHENCE THIS BOOK?...	vii
IN MEMORIAM...	ix

SOUTH AMERICAN AND EUROPEAN MISSIONS.

SOUTH AMERICAN...	3
BRAZIL MISSION...	3
EUROPEAN...	15
REV. W. N. COTE, M.D...	15
GEO. BOARDMAN TAYLOR, D.D...	30
A YOUNG MAN FOR ITALY...	64

CHINA MISSION.

CANTON MISSION...	77
CITY OF CANTON...	77
REV. JEHU LEWIS SHUCK...	79
REV. ISSACHAR JACOX ROBERTS...	83
MISS HARRIET A. BAKER...	90
REV. SAMUEL CORNELIUS CLOPTON...	94
REV. GEORGE PEARCY...	99

CONTENTS.

	PAGE.
Rev. Francis Cleveland Johnson	108
Rev. Bayfield Waller Whilden	116
Rev. Charles Washington Gaillard	123
Rev. John Griffith Schilling	129
Rev. Nicholas Butt Williams	132
Rev. Yong Seen Sang	135
Rev. Ezekias Z. and Mrs. Simmons	138
Rev. Roswell Hobart Graves	143
WOMEN AND WOMEN'S WORK	150
Mrs. Jane Wormeley Graves	150
Mrs. Jumelle Williams	150
Mrs. Louisa Whilden	151
The Mite Box	152
SHANGHAI MISSION	160
City of Shanghai	161
Matthew Tyson Yates, D.D.	163
Mrs. Eliza Yates	167
Thomas William Tobey, D.D.	168
George Washington Burton, M.D.	170
Rev. Asa Bruce Cabaniss	172
First Decade, 1846-1856	175
Second Decade, 1856-1866	186
Third Decade, 1866-1876	191
SHANTUNG MISSION	199
Province of Shantung	199
Tarleton Perry Crawford, D.D.	202
Jesse Boardman Hartwell, D.D.	204
Rev. James Landrum Holmes	208
Mrs. S. J. Holmes	212
Miss Edmonia Harris Moon	215
Miss Charlotte Moon	217
Origin of the Mission	221
Tung Chow Mission	223

	PAGE.
Monument Street Interest	233
North Street Interest	237
Chefoo Mission	239
Proposed Union of the Tung Chow Interests	243

JAPAN MISSION AND OUR LOST MISSIONARIES.

Japan	244
Our Lost Missionaries	247
Rev. John Quincy Adams Rohrer and Mrs. Sarah Rohrer.	247
Rev. Alfred Luther Bond and Mrs. Helena Dameron Bond.	250
Dr. John Sexton James and Mrs. Anne Price James	254
Does it Pay?	258

AFRICAN MISSIONS.

Africa and Liberia	265
Africa	265
Western and Central Africa	269
Liberia	272
Other Missions	276
Origin of our Mission in Liberia	279
Bird's Eye View	283
Rev. Eli Ball and Rev. John Kingdon	289
Liberia and Sierra Leone Missions	293
Our Colored Missionaries	293
Rev. John Day and Rev. A. L. Jones	293
Extracts from Prof. E. W. Blyden's Eulogy	302
Rev. Frederick S. James	305
Rev. J. H. Cheeseman	310

	PAGE
REV. A. P. DAVIS	317
REV. BOSTON J. DRAYTON	321
REV. J. T. RICHARDSON	328
REV. R. E. MURRAY	333
REV. JOSEPH M. HARDEN	336
REV. J. J. FITZGERALD	339
W. W. STEWART	341
REV. ISAAC ROBERTS AND REV. CÆSAR FRAZER	342
REV. LEWIS KONG CROCKER	343
REV. MELFORD D. HERNDON	344
B. P. YATES	345
REV. J. JAMES CHEESEMAN	349
OUR COLORED MISSIONARIES OF SIERRA LEONE:—H. P. THOMSON AND J. J. BROWNE	353
TROUBLES AND CLOSE	357
STATISTICS OF MISSIONS	357
LIBERIAN MISSION	358
DURING THE WAR	358
DISMAL INTERREGNUM	359
BASE OF OPERATIONS IN LIBERIA	361
MISSIONARIES AND STATIONS	362
YORUBA MISSION	369
YORUBA	369
FIRST DECADE, 1848–1858	373
THOMAS JEFFERSON BOWEN AND HENRY GOODALE	373
MESSRS. DENNARD, LACY, AND CLARKE	387
MESSRS. TRIMBLE, PRIEST, CASON, AND BEAUMONT	392
REV. A. D. PHILLIPS	407
REV. T. A. REID	409
SECOND DECADE, 1858–1868	412
REV. R. H. STONE	413
THIRD DECADE, 1868–1878	425
REV. WILLIAM J. DAVID	427

	PAGE.
Rev. W. W. Colley	427
Moses L. Stone	428
1878 and 1879	438

MISSION TO THE JEWS.

Anti-type of Judaic Typology	442
Jesus—The Messiah of the Jews and the Desire of all Nations	442

ORIGIN AND FOREIGN WORK OF SOUTHERN BAPTIST CONVENTION.

Its Origin	460
Sundry Items	472
Resumé of Operations of the Board	474
From 1845–1863	474
From 1863–1872	475
Supplement, 1872–1879	476
Views North and South	479
Receipts of Foreign Board from 1845–1879	481

PROTESTANT MISSIONS.

Summary of Missions	488
Synopsis of Foreign Missions of Southern Baptist Convention	490
General Index	496

FOREIGN MISSIONS

OF THE

SOUTHERN BAPTIST CONVENTION.

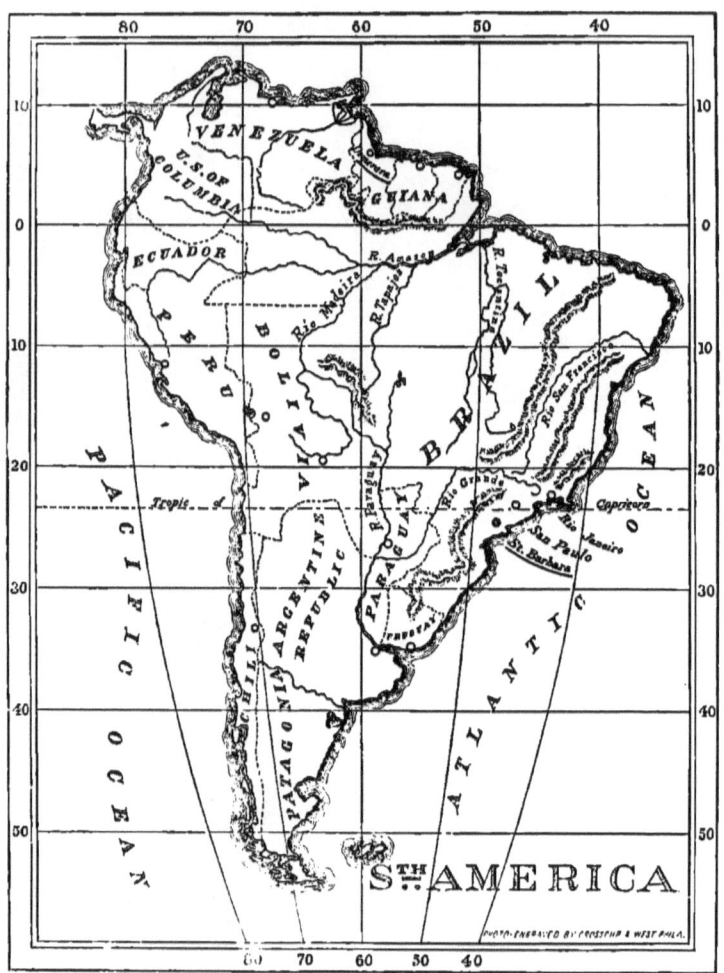

SOUTH AMERICAN AND EUROPEAN MISSION.

SOUTH AMERICAN.

BRAZIL MISSION.

IN accordance with the recommendation of our Board, the Southern Baptist Convention, at its meeting in 1879, expressed the hope that "the Board will feel authorized to enter Brazil at as early a day as its means may justify." A station has been opened at Santa Barbara, in the province of San Paulo, which adjoins the province of Rio de Janeiro. Elder E. H. Quillin is in charge of the mission.

Hoping that the hearts and prayers of our people are enlisted in this new enterprise, we presume that some account of the country and people, derived mainly from the admirable work, "Brazil and the Brazilians," will not be uninteresting.

NAME OF BRAZIL.

Every one who visited, in 1876, "the Centennial," in Philadelphia, was struck with the department of South America, conspicuous as it was for its rich and gorgeous articles, arranged with exquisite skill and taste, and for the rare and beautiful specimens of wood produced in that country of boundless forests and wonderful resources. From the dye-wood *Cæsalpinia Braziliensis*, called in the Portuguese language,

Panbrazil, on account of its resemblance to *Brazas*—" coals of fire,"— the country which was formerly known as Vera Cruz, or Santa Cruz, derived its present name, Brazil.

DISCOVERY.

" In 1498, Columbus landed near the mouth of the Orinoco. He recorded in enthusiastic terms 'the beauty of the new land,' and declared that he felt as if 'he could never leave so charming a spot.' The honor, however, of discovering the Western Hemisphere, south of the equator, must be awarded to Vincent Yanez Pinzon, who was a companion of Columbus, and had commanded the Nina in that first glorious voyage which made known to the Old World the existence of the New."

VASTNESS.

Brazil, which lies between the lines of 5° north and 33° south latitude, and contains an area of 3,500,000 square miles, is by far the most highly-favored portion of South America, which boasts the mines of Peru, the highest mountain of the Western Hemisphere, and the mightiest river of the world. The Amazon, which rises in the Andes, and flows from west to east through the whole extent of Brazil, waters, with its tributaries, a country of unsurpassed beauty,— filled with birds of brilliant plumage, and animals of rare kinds, and in extent no less than 2,330,000 square miles,—and sends into the Atlantic, through the Narrows at Obidos, 550,000 cubic feet of water every second. The ebb and flow of the ocean may be seen five hundred miles above the mouth of this "Father of Waters."

PEOPLE, LANGUAGE, AND RELIGION.

The Brazilians are descended from the Portuguese, but are a very superior people to their progenitors. They are described as mild, generous, courteous, intelligent, aspiring, and hospitable. Their self-possession is said to be remarkable. A resident of the country once told us that a Brazilian gentleman was superior to receiving or resenting an insult. The daughter of a distinguished gentleman of Virginia who, with his lady, spent some time at Rio Janeiro as U. S. Minister, and to whom we repeated this remark, replied somewhat *piquantly*, " Too lazy to fight! " The Portuguese language is universally spoken in Brazil. This is not a dialect of the Spanish, but as Viey says, is "the eldest daughter of the Latin." It is more masculine than the Castilian; and in its strength, compactness, and expressiveness, clearly indicates its Roman parentage. The religion is Roman Catholic; and, perhaps, in no Roman Catholic country is the priesthood more debased and despised. Their wickedness is notorious and avowed. But, by the liberal Constitution of the government, and by the equally liberal sentiments of the Brazilians, all other denominations have the right to worship God as they choose, * * with the single limitation that the church-edifice must not be in the form of a Temple, which has been defined by the Supreme Judges to be a building " with steeple or bells."

CLIMATE AND PRODUCTIONS.

The climate of Brazil is varied and delightful. " Cool breezes, lofty mountains, vast rivers, and plentiful pluvial irrigation are treasures far surpassing the sparkling gems and rich minerals which abound within the borders of this extended territory." Why Brazil is blessed in climate above other lands in corresponding latitudes is shown by Commodore Maury: "South America is like a great irregular triangle, whose longest side is upon the Pacific. Of the two sides which lie upon the Atlantic, the longest—extending from Cape Horn to Cape St. Roque—is 3,500 miles, and looks out upon the south-east, while the shortest, looking north-east, has a length of 2,500 miles. This configuration has a powerful effect upon the temperature and irrigation of Brazil. The La Plata and the Amazon result from it and from those wonderful winds called the Trades, which blow from the two Atlantic sides of the great triangle. Hence, winds which sweep from the northeast and from the south-east come laden with humidity and with clouds. They bear their vapory burdens over the land—distilling as they fly refreshing moisture upon the vast forests and the lesser mountains, until they are finally caught up by the lofty Andes, in whose rarefied and cool atmosphere they are wholly condensed, and descend in the copious rains which perpetually nourish the sources of two of the mightiest rivers of the world."

No other tropical country is so generally elevated as Brazil. The whole Empire has an average elevation of 700 feet above the level of the sea. The missionary does not have his first months of usefulness thrown away or his constitution injured by acclimating fevers. The mean temperature of Brazil is from 81° to 88° F., according to the different seasons of the year.

The culture of coffee is immense. Its principal growth is in San Paulo. This plant, whose home is Abyssinia, whence it was carried into Arabia, was taken to South America early in the present century. The annual exports of this commodity are 457,000,000 pounds; the product, 570,000,000 pounds.

GOVERNMENT.

During the war between Portugal and France the royal family of the former country fled to Brazil, and entered the harbor of Rio Janeiro on the 7th of March, 1808. In 1821, King Dom John VI. conferred the regency on his son Dom Pedro I., and returned to Portugal. On the 7th of September, 1822, in sight of San Paulo—a city which had ever been, as it is now, celebrated in Brazil for the liberality and intelligence of its inhabitants—Dom Pedro I., made that exclamation, *Independencia au morte*, (independence or death,) which became the watch-word of the Brazilian revolution. During a reign of ten years, under Dom Pedro I., the country made more advancement in intelligence than it had done in the three centuries which intervened between its first discovery and the proclamation of the Portuguese Constitution in 1820. On 7th of April, 1831, Dom Pedro I., abdicated in favor of his son, Dom Pedro II., the present enlightened, liberal, and gifted Emperor, whom many of us had the pleasure of seeing a few years ago in our country. The government is described as monarchical, hereditary, constitutional, and representative. The legislative power answers to the Parliament of England or the Congress of the United States. The senators are elected for life; the representatives for four years.

The presidents of the provinces are appointed by the Emperor. The press is free. There is no proscription on account of color. The Constitution thus formed was accepted by the Emperor, and on the 25th of March, 1824, was sworn to by his Imperial Highness, and by the authorities and people throughout the Empire. African slavery exists; but such is the spirit of freedom, that by industry and intelligence the slave may rise to any position in society or government. In 1871, the following act was passed: "All slaves shall remain slaves during life. Those born after the passage of this act shall be freed at the age of twenty-one years."

COMMERCE.

The great interests of Brazilian commerce draw an immense number of vessels from all parts of the globe. Brazil possesses the second navy of the world. * * Eight lines of steamers ply between her ports and other countries. In 1856, the United States exported to Brazil $5,000,000, while the United States imported from Brazil $19,000,000, leaving a cash balance in favor of Brazil of $14,000,000.

In 1874 the United States imported . . . $ 43,899,647
"   "   exported . . .   7,560,502
In 1875   "   imported . . .   42,028,863
"   "   exported . . .   7,631,865
In 1876   "   imported . . .   45,446,381
"   "   exported . . .   7,252,218
In 1877   "   imported . . .   43,498,041
"   "   exported . . .   7,497,118
Imported from June, '71, to June, '77 . . $274,148,500
Exported   "   "   "   . .   48,853,555

Balance of trade against the United States . $225,294,945
Total trade of Brazil, 1871 to 1877—
   Exports $579,041,492
   Imports 471,570,859

RIO DE JANEIRO.

This name of the political capital and commercial emporium of the nation, signifies the "River of January," from the month in which De Souza sailed into the river on which the city is located. It is the third city of the Western Continent, and boasts an antiquity greater than any city of the United States. Its harbor is said to surpass in beauty "the Golden Horn of Constantinople," or the universally-lauded Bay of Naples.

FIELD OF MISSIONARY LABOR.

Here is a free scope for doing good. Strong friendships have been formed between missionaries and the most elevated natives. "It is my firm conviction," says one of high authority, "that there is not a Roman Catholic country on the globe where there prevails a greater degree of toleration or a greater liberality of feeling toward Protestants than in Brazil." And where is there greater need of the gospel? While visiting Brazil, Henry Martyn said, "Crosses there are in abundance; but when shall the doctrine of the Cross be held up?" Some one remarks, " Shall the prayers of Henry Martyn be forgotten before the Lord of Hosts? We love to regard the petitions of the early Huguenots at Rio de Janeiro, those of the faithful missionaries of the Reformed Church of Holland at Pernambuco, and the prayers of Henry Martyn at Bahia, as not lost, but as having already descended and as still to descend in rich blessings upon Brazil." Messrs. Kidder and Fletcher say: "At the present time Brazil is in want of nothing so much as pious, self-denying ministers of the gospel—men who, like the Apostle of the Gentiles, will not count their lives dear unto themselves that they may win souls to Christ."

LONG DELIBERATION AND SHORT WORK.

Our present work in Brazil is not a new idea. For many years the Board have had their eyes on the southern and equatorial lands of our hemisphere. In 1850, the Convention selected, among other fields, "Central and South America, as important points to which the attention of the Board might be profitably directed." In 1851, the Convention "*Resolved*, That our Board of Foreign Missions be recommended to establish missions * * in any or all of the cities of Havana, Mexico, Rio Janeiro, Valparaiso, and Panama, or in any other part of South America." In 1852, the Board reported, with regard to South America, that "the occupation of this field is rendered specially difficult

SOUTH AMERICAN MISSION. 9

by the rigorous civil enactments of the various States, all of which are under the control of the Roman Catholic religion." In 1853, the Convention recommended "the occupation of British Honduras, with special reference to missionary labor among the Maya people, among whom Baptist missionary labor has already been expended, and into whose language several portions of the Sacred Scriptures have been translated." The next year the Board reported against ."the expediency of occupying British Honduras as a mission station." In 1859, the Board said that they had sought to comply with the direction of the Convention in 1857 " to watch the providence of God, as it now points to Japan and South America, as important and promising fields of missionary labor." An elaborate report on the subject was presented by the Board, in which the claims and prospects of Brazil were strongly emphasized. The Convention adopted the following sentiment: "Perhaps the missionaries of no other part of Christendom can operate so effectively in that region as the missionaries that might be sent from the Southern churches. A mission should be opened there the coming year, if possible." In 1860, the Board reported: " A distinct offer of himself to the Board having been made by our esteemed brother, Rev. T. J. Bowen, he was transferred from the Yoruba Mission * * to bear the message of salvation to Brazil. He feared a return to Yoruba in the shattered condition of his nervous system." Mr. and Mrs. Bowen, with their little daughter, sailed from Richmond in the bark Abigail on Friday, the 30th of March, 1859. In four or five weeks they were happy to land at the city of Rio Janeiro, where for a season and perhaps permanently they expected to be located. In 1861, the dismal tidings were communicated to the Convention : ":The mission begun by Brother Bowen at Rio Janeiro has been abandoned. The complete prostration of his health compelled him to return. He arrived about the 1st of April. May God graciously restore his health and grant him prolonged and great usefulness at home, and may our sister feel the support and consolation of the divine presence. * The obstacles were found so great, and the probability of surmounting them so small, that before the health of Brother Bowen necessitated his return the Board had decided to submit to the Convention the question of his recall. The Board do not deem it advisable to re-open this mission."

APPLICATION FROM SANTO PAULO.

Thus the matter stood for twelve years, when the following letter was received by the Board:

PROVINCE SAO PAULO, ST. BARBARA, }
BRAZIL, January 11th, 1873. }

To the Corresponding Secretary F. M. Board:

Allow us to state to you that since the year 1865, a number of citizens from the Southern United States have removed to the Empire of Brazil, and are located in this province—viz: Sao Paulo and in the District of Santa Barbara, most of whom are farming, (owning lands, &c.,) and permanently settled here. That on the 10th of September, 1871, a number of them, with letters from various Baptist churches of the States above named, did unite and organize a church under the style and name of the First North American Baptist Missionary Church of Brazil, which at this writing contains twenty-three (23) members, with a pastor and such other officers as Baptist churches usually have. That on the 12th of October, 1872, the church in conference did adopt the following resolution—viz:

Resolved, That Brethren R. Meriwether, R. Brodnax, and D. Davis, be appointed to communicate with the Baptist Board of Foreign Missions at Richmond, Va., in regard to sending missionaries to this country.

Done in church conference, 12th October, 1872.

Signed, R. RATCLIFF, *Pastor.*
W. H. MERIWETHER, *Sec.*

Rev. John L. Underwood, of Georgia, in forwarding the above letter to the Board, says of one of the committee, whose communication, in part, is given below: "Major Robert Meriwether is a stirring man and has a pious wife. I thank God for their usefulness in Brazil. We have been praying that they may be lights in that land. He writes privately that the prospects of the church are bright, and the colonies are enjoying some prosperity."

COMMUNICATION OF COMMITTEE.

Perfect religious toleration is accorded to all sects and denominations, (except to Jesuits, who are banished by law, although, in fact, many officiating priests are Jesuits.) The state religion is the Catholic. Five or six years experience and intercourse with citizens of this country enables us to state that now is a propitious time to set forth the religion taught in God's word to this people. Generally, they do not like their religion, saying "it begins and ends with money for the priesthood." Really many intelligent Brazilians have a contempt for their practices. "The Baptists," say they, "practice as did the Saviour and his Apostles; they baptized only believers and immersed; who has a right to alter their modes and practices?" The Portuguese translation of the New Testament is, if possible, more emphatic in describing baptism than the English translation. The presence of our people here has had, and is having, a salutary influence upon the feelings and opinions of this people.

Now, as a church, we ask no moneyed assistance to build a house of worship or to pay our preacher; we are able to keep our own house under the blessing of Providence. But we are not able to send out men to preach to others; we have neither the men nor the means for that purpose. Like the man of Macedonia, we "pray you to come over and help us." If you do come, your reception shall not be like the great Apostle's was, but our homes shall be open to you, our progress, our influence and labors will be for and with you. We hope a large Baptist community in this country will be added to the great Baptist family of the world, teaching, preaching and practicing the faith once delivered to the saints. The pastor of the church, (Rev. Richard Ratcliff,) has been in this country five years or more, hailing from Louisiana, and having been a pupil of the late Rev. Mr. Hartwell. He is well qualified for his position and very acceptable to the members; preaches once a month, with one hundred and fifty dollars salary per annum. Another Baptist preacher, Rev. R. Thomas, from Arkansas, has been here more than one year, and preaches without charge. These, with Mr. Piles, of Florida, some seventy-five or a hundred miles from here, surrounded entirely by Brazilians, are all the Baptist preachers in this country as we believe. We may add that many priests here are men of great ability and learning.

Respectfully and truly in Christian love,

ROBERT MERIWETHER,
ROBERT BRODNAX, } *Committee.*
DAVID DAVIS,

Address, Provincia de Sao Paulo, St. Barbara.

OTHER APPLICATIONS AND REPORT.

As favorable as this application seemed, the Board, not forgetful of its sad experience in 1860, were loth to give the subject more than a respectful consideration. Several further communications were received. Among them was the following letter:

MINDEN, LA., Oct. 1st, 1878.

Elder H. A. Tupper:

Dear Brother—In behalf of Foreign Missions, I would ask the Board to consider Brazil, S. A., as a very important field.

The recent changes in her laws respecting the toleration of Free Masonry, and the civil right of marriage, are some of the fruits of the rapid growth of the "Liberal" party, who wish to separate the Roman Church from the Empire.

The majority of that people would rejoice to be relieved from the dogmas of Rome, that they might exercise their own opinions in matters of religion. They are more than anxious to hear what they call "Protestantism." I speak from an experience of eleven years with them, while a self-sustaining missionary.

The first missionary Baptist Church in St. Barbara, Sao Paulo Province, is composed of English-speaking people. And it is the opinion of that church, as they have told you time and again, that if the Board would use them as a nucleus, or an aid, the Board could accomplish more with the same amount of means than in any other field.

They have never asked you for money for themselves, but that you help them preach the gospel to the natives. Their present pastor authorized me to say to the Board, that he would accept an appointment to the Brazilians, (he is a teacher of their language,) and make quarterly reports to the Board, without charging one cent.

I ask the Board to open correspondence with him at once—Elder E. H. Quillin, St. Barbara P. O., Sao Paulo Province, Brazil.

Yours in hope,
RICHARD RATCLIFF.

P. S. My motherless children constrained me to return. If the Board wish, I can give some of the causes why Brother T. J. Bowen in 1860 did not recommend Brazil as a favorable missionary field.

My address will be Mexia P. O., Limestone County, Texas.

R. R.

SOUTH AMERICAN MISSION. 13

In 1879, the Board made to the Convention the following report, which resulted in the establishment of the mission:

More prominent, in our consideration, have been the repeated applications of the " First Baptist Church of Brazil, near Santa Barbara, in the Province of Sao Paulo," who desire to be received by the Board as a self-supporting mission, because of the moral aid which the church would receive from the Board, and the material aid which the Board would receive from the church. They say: " We neither ask nor desire any disbursement of the finances of the Board for our support. We consider that we are self-sustaining in every relation connected with the temporal duties and responsibilities of the church." Their pastor, Elder E. H. Quillin, writes: "I am well acquainted with the church, and am assured that she has the ability to aid the Board. The members are prosperous in their basket and in their store, and are on the highway to wealth. * * * I am fearful that prosperity will make us worldly-minded." Rev. Richard Ratcliff, of Minden, La., to whom the church and pastor are intimately known, urges importunately the favorable consideration of the Board. Under these conditions the Board are disposed to think well of the application; and should the Convention have no definite instructions to give, they will decide the matter, with all the lights before them, and agreeably to their most deliberate judgment.

RESOLUTIONS OF THE CHURCH.

In a series of twenty-one resolutions, adopted by the church, of which the following are a specimen, there is a florid tinge, which suggests the warmth and exuberance of their equatorial and picturesque country:

1. *Resolved*, That in the providence of God we are called to dwell far from the scenes of our childhood, amid a vast moral waste, widely severed from the ineffable pleasures of church associations and the endearing influences of a wide-spread Christian intercourse; and that a consciousness of this loneliness at times hangs heavily upon the heart, and plays rudely with the tender sympathies of the soul, weakening the nerve of moral energy, and fringing the horizon of hope with the mist of a doubtful future.

2. *Resolved,* That we believe that some relational recognition on the part of the Foreign Mission Board would dispel our gloom, give confidence to our existence, inspire new life, and establish the unwavering conviction that we do in reality belong to the great Baptist family.

3. *Resolved,* That we ask the Board to receive us as an affectionate adopted daughter, in the great mission-field; and that we shall endeavor to be respectful to our relations, faithful to our obligations, pure in our attachments, and operative in our benevolence.

4. *Resolved,* That any minister, whether single or married, coming to Brazil, recommended by the Board, we shall identify his interest with our own, and see that he is pleasantly situated, with the prospect, at least, of an ample support.

5. *Resolved,* That any Baptist family or families, recommended by their church, emigrating to Brazil, on their arrival here we shall endeavor to make them feel that they are with their brethren; and that we will not withhold in their behalf until we shall have them agreeably located, where industry and economy, without some inconceivable misfortune, will ere long accumulate an ample competency to shadow the eventide of life.

ANOTHER BAPTIST CHURCH IN SOUTH AMERICA.

The following is from the pen of our missionary, Rev. R. H. Graves, of Canton, China:

This church is composed of Chinese immigrants, and is efficiently presided over by Brother Lough Fook. This brother is a member of the Canton Baptist Church, who went to Demerara in 1861. After serving some time as a coolie, some Christian friends bought out his time, and enabled him to devote himself entirely to Christian work. He soon gathered around him a little company of converts, and through God's blessing this body of believers has now grown to a church of 156 members. (These are their statistics in the annual letter for 1878; since then we have heard of the baptism of sixteen more converts.)

This church is a living, active body. They have built several chapels for themselves, and have of late taken steps toward the carrying on of mission work in China. One of their number, Brother *Tso Sune,* is a self-supporting missionary in China. Recent letters inform us that these Demerara brethren have raised $400, which they have invested in a paying business, where they expect it to yield 15 or 30 per cent. per annum. These proceeds they intend to send to China every year. The Chinese are traders by instinct, and show their practical wisdom

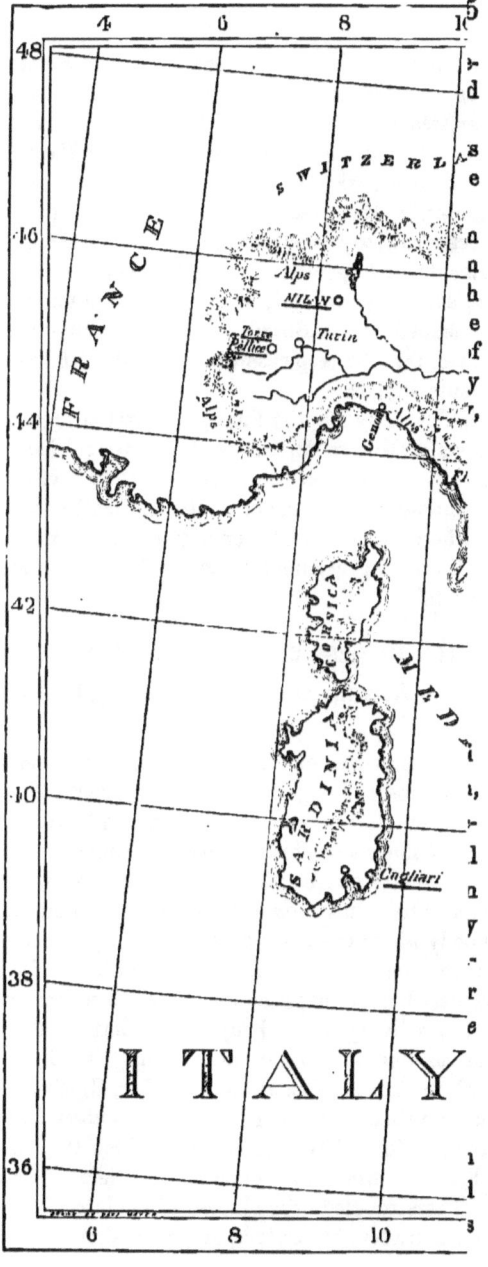

2. *Resolved,* That we believe that some relational recognition on the part of the Foreign Mission Board would dispel our gloom, give confidence to our existence, inspire new life, and establish the unwavering conviction that we do in reality belong to the great Baptist family.

3. *Resolved,* That we ask the Board to receive us as an affectionate adopted daughter, in the great mission-field; and that we shall endeavor to be respectful to our relations, faithful to our obligations, pure in our attachments, and operative in our benevolence.

4. *Resolved,* That any minister, whether single or married, coming to Brazil, recommended by the Board, we shall identify his interest with our own, and see that he is pleasantly situated, with the prospect, at least, of an ample support.

5. *Resolved,* That any Baptist family or families, recommended by their church, emigrating to Brazil, on their arrival here we shall endeavor to make them feel that they are with their brethren; and that we will not withhold in their behalf until we shall have them agreeably located, where industry and economy, without some inconceivable misfortune, will ere long accumulate an ample competency to shadow the eventide of life.

ANOTHER BAPTIST CHURCH IN SOUTH AMERICA.

The following is from the pen of our missionary, Rev. R. H. Graves, of Canton, China:

This church is composed of Chinese immigrants, and is efficiently presided over by Brother Lough Fook. This brother is a member of the Canton Baptist Church, who went to Demerara in 1861. After serving some time as a coolie, some Christian friends bought out his time, and enabled him to devote himself entirely to Christian work. He soon gathered around him a little company of converts, and through God's blessing this body of believers has now grown to a church of 156 members. (These are their statistics in the annual letter for 1878; since then we have heard of the baptism of sixteen more converts.)

This church is a living, active body. They have built several chapels for themselves, and have of late taken steps toward the carrying on of mission work in China. One of their number, Brother *Tso Sune,* is a self-supporting missionary in China. Recent letters inform us that these Demerara brethren have raised $400, which they have invested in a paying business, where they expect it to yield 15 or 30 per cent. per annum. These proceeds they intend to send to China every year. The Chinese are traders by instinct, and show their practical wisdom

14

2.
part
denc
convi

3.
adop
deav
in ou

4.
Braz
our
least

5.
their
deav
we w
ably
misf
the

Tl
of C

Tl
pres
Cant
some
enab
gath
bless
bers.
then

Tl
els f
of m
self-
thes
in a
per
The

by making the profits of trade contribute to the promotion of the Redeemer's kingdom. We shall watch the experiment with interest, and hope it will be wisely managed and result in great good.

Let me ask the prayers of the churches for this company of converts from heathenism on the shores of South America, just opposite those of our own southern country.

How different the plans of God's providence are from those we form in our own minds. God has answered the prayers of old Brother William Crane and others that Baptist churches might be raised up in South America, but who would have conceived that these churches would be composed of men driven from our midst by civil convulsions, and of converted heathen brought from the ends of the world. Let us pray and wait, and God will assuredly answer our prayers, though in a way, perhaps, that will fill us with surprise. R. H. G.

Canton, China.

EUROPEAN MISSION.

Rev. W. N. COTE, M. D.
1870–1873.

ONE of the pleasant recollections of our student-life at Madison University was a visit there of Madame Feller, of the Grand Ligne Mission, of Canada. This lady was accompanied by C. H. O. Cote, M. D., previously a priest, who was associated with her in her noble and successful enterprise. Though contemplating at that time going into the Foreign field, and being, for a while, Corresponding Secretary of the "Society for Inquiry," we little thought that in after life we should be so intimately related to the son of this reverend gentleman. The elder Doctor was the author of "*Un Mot en Passant a ceux Qui ont abandonné l'Eglise Romaine.*" His Memoirs have been given to the public.

DR. COTE AND A SUPERINTENDENT.

As early as 1850 the Board turned their attention to Europe. On the 7th of October of that year the "Rev. John Eschman was requested to appear before the Board in reference to his going to Switzerland as an agent of the Board." The same day the Board resolved "to adopt France as a field of missionary labor," and Rev. E. Kingsford, who was about to visit that country, "was requested to make such inquiries * * as would afford necessary information to the Board." In 1869, the Board reported to the Convention on "the obligation of Baptists to give the pure gospel to Catholic Europe, some parts of which are in as great need of the gospel as the Pagan world, and also on the wonderful openings of these fields by the hand of Providence." In 1870, this language of an intelligent brother was quoted to the Convention: "I believe Italy is the best place for a new mission. Other *denominations* are at work there; but Baptist principles are particularly needed, and will be likely to find a response in many a heart. * * * It is also important to know that some of our brethren, who will be large contributors, are feeling a special desire to see our Board entering and occupying some European field." On the 13th of June, Rev. Wm. N. Cote, M. D., who was Secretary of the Young Men's Christian Association of France, and was engaged to work in the Latin quarter of Paris, was present with the Board, whose attention had been called to him, as a suitable missionary by Rev. Drs. F. Wilson, G. W. Samson, and A. D. Gillette. Dr. Cote addressed the Board. Five days later it was resolved: "1. That the Board proceed at once to establish a mission in Southern Europe, to be located at Marseilles, or Milan, or Chamberry, or such other point as shall, after investigation, be considered the most advisable. 2. That Dr. W. N. Cote, of Paris, be appointed as a missionary to the Southern Baptist Convention, with authority to appoint two or more pious young Baptists to labor under his supervision, as colporteurs and missionaries. 3. That the young men so appointed, and others, shall be trained and instructed by Dr. Cote for other and more important labors as full ministers of the gospel." Three thousand dollars were appropriated for the work. Dr. Cote having accepted the position June 22d, sailed soon after to Europe. On the 23d of September, 1870, the army of Victor Emanuel, King of Italy, entered and took possession of Rome, and freedom for Missionary work was secured. On reading letters from Dr. Cote and Dr. John A. Broadus, from Rome, after its occupation by the

King's forces, the Board instructed a committee, March 6, 1871, "to consider the expediency of enlarging our operations in Italy; and specially to inquire into the propriety of securing a suitable brother from this country to superintend our missions in Southern Europe."

IMPRESSIONS AND EXPRESSIONS.

Dr. Cote wrote: Rome is now open to the gospel. The temporal power of the anti-Christ has come to an end, and his spiritual power is fast decreasing. A bountiful harvest in Rome and the provinces awaits the diligent sowers of the truth. Let Baptists be up and doing. Let them reclaim from error and perdition the fallen descendants of the primitive Roman Church, whose faith and sufferings for the cause of Christ had earned the commendation of the Christian churches of the whole world. * * * God be praised! Our room in Via della Croce was crowded last Thursday and Sunday evenings. We propose, when the King shall have made his entry into Rome, and the union of the Roman Provinces with Italy is formally sanctioned by Parliament, to hold, by way of experiment, one or two large meetings in the Music Hall. By doing so, we hope to complete the work already begun by our district meetings. * * We succeeded in distributing about fifteen hundred portions of the word of God. * * There seems to be a remarkable preparation in Rome for the reception of the gospel. The licentious habits of the clergy have divested them of all respect in the eyes of the people. * * Outside of Rome itinerant evangelists and colporteurs should be employed along the lines of railways from Turin to Milan and Venice; Turin to Bologna; Bologna to Ancona and Brindisi; Bologna to Pistoia and Florence; Florence to Rome and Naples; Rome to Civita Vecchia and Leghorn, and then along the coast to Genoa and Nice.

Dr. J. A. Broadus wrote, January 30th, 1871: The field is interesting in a high degree. There are but two essentially distinct types of Christianity—Church Christians and Bible Christians.—These people have seen the evils of the first, and it seems a refreshing and inviting contrast to present them the other. You will see presently that there have already been encouraging results. I had no idea beforehand how interesting and promising a field Rome would be, and had not thought much about this mission. I am now thoroughly satisfied that the Board has acted wisely in establishing this mission, and I should exclaim vehemently against any idea of abandoning it.

"Rev. J. Wall, of England, who came here from Bologna the day before Brother Cote arrived, has been eight years in Italy—supported for five years by a single man in England, and since by private contributions. He wants to be independent, and to go about as an evangelist, so as to be, as he expresses it, a *franc-tireur*, or free-shooter. He is a deeply devout man, with true missionary fervor; has become fluent in Italian, and speaks quite impressively. He is unselfish and does not seem sensitively ambitious.

"Last evening five men were baptized (in a bath-house, the Tiber being very swift, very muddy, and popularly regarded as very unhealthy,) and this morning three more. All, except the colporteur, are Romans and new converts; some of them with very interesting faces, and all regarded by Brethren Cote and Wall as giving good evidence of conversion. This morning these eight, with the other colporteur and Brother Giannini, and Brethren Cote and Wall and their wives, were constituted a church. Brother Cote had urged me to stay and be present. I was to have left yesterday, but I remained and found it a very interesting occasion. Dr. Warren Randolph of Philadelphia, and myself witnessed the baptisms, and this morning briefly addressed the church, (through Brother Wall,) and gave them the hand of fellowship, assuring them of the sympathy and prayers of baptized believers in America. Afterwards they observed the Lord's Supper—we partaking. The idea of forming a church was not suggested by me, but originated with the missionaries themselves."

Thirty thousand copies of portions of the Scriptures had been furnished by the Bible-stand of the Crystal Palace, and tracts and Bibles by the American Tract Society and the American Baptist Publication Society. The Board reported that "twenty-five thousand copies of parts of the word of God have been put in circulation, which is marvellous in our eyes."

Dr. Cote wrote: "These were gladly received—indeed, crowds of men, women and children would, at times, hold out their hands for the books.

Priests passing by would scowl at us, but did not dare to say a word, for fear of the people. They act with great caution now, for they well know that the least interference on their part might place their lives in jeopardy, so much are they hated and distrusted by the whole people. We went as far as the magnificent church of St. Peter, and distributed the word of God. The work of distribution, far from being interfered with by the police, is approved. A city guard, to whom one of our colporteurs gave a book, said to him, 'Go on with your work; Rome has great need of those books.'"

The statistics of the mission, as announced to the Convention in 1871, were "W. N. Cote, M. D., Signors Rosa, Gardiol, Pinelli, who are laboring in the city of Rome; one church; twelve baptisms, and eighteen as the total membership."

The Convention said: "The opening of Rome has permitted the preaching of the gospel, the conversion and baptism of several promising young men, and the organization of a Christian church, after the model described in Paul's Epistle to the Romans, in that ancient city," and the body resolved "that the Foreign Mission Board be desired to consider the expediency of the appointment of a General Superintendent of European Missions," and "that our churches be urged to take means for providing the support of the young brethren already gathered by Dr. Cote, of Rome."

ROME-CHAPEL ENTERPRISE.

On March 4th, 1872, the Board, being informed that "adverse litigation had dispossessed Dr. Cote of the premises he was using in his mission work," recorded "that if we hope to establish permanently a Baptist Church in the capital of Italy, it seems necessary that we shall control a building free from any vexatious claims that cupidity or craft may instigate. * * Four Christian denominations are also at work, and one of them has secured a house of worship. As in the providence of God we were the first to occupy the field, and our type of New Testament Christianity is pronouncedly antipodal to Romanism, it seems evidently proper that we should take steps to place our interests beyond the contingencies of faction, or covetousness, or revolution.

* * That the Corresponding Secretary be authorized to adopt such measures as may be needful to secure a house and lot in Rome that shall be, for a term of years, or in fee, under the control of the Southern Baptist Convention."

Strange enough, at the same meeting of the Board was read "a letter from Dr. A. D. Gillette, stating the purpose of Mrs. Gillette, of New York, and Mrs. Patton, of Philadelphia, to obtain funds to erect or purchase a house of worship for the Baptist Church recently formed in Rome, Italy, under the patronage of this Board." Whereupon it was resolved "that the thanks of the Board be tendered to the ladies for their generous offer; and that the Corresponding Secretary be requested * * to co-operate with them in any way desired by them in their noble effort."

It was deemed advisable that one-half ($20,000,) of the amount supposed to be needed for the chapel should be raised at the South; and that the return of Dr. Cote to this country to collect funds for the chapel, as had been proposed by him, was unnecessary. Not awaiting, however, the views of the Board, Dr. Cote appeared at their meeting of the 19th of April. "He presented letters from the church in Rome of which he is pastor, and the church in the Waldensian Valley, addressed to the Board; also a communication from Rev. Drs. H. H. Tucker and M. T. Yates, now in Rome. It was resolved that having heard the reasons which caused Brother W. N. Cote to return to this country, we heartily approve of his course and extend to him a cordial welcome." Also, "*Resolved*, That the churches of this city be requested to take up collections in the month of June next for the erection of a Baptist house of worship in Rome."

In the proceedings of the Southern Baptist Convention of 1872, the following appears, under date of May 10th:

"Brother H. A. Tupper, of Virginia, introduced Brother W. N. Cote, missionary to Rome. Brother Cote addressed the Convention in the interest of the mission in Rome. Brother H. A. Tupper, of Virginia, Corresponding Secretary of the Foreign Mission Board, called for pledges to build a house of worship in Rome, to be the property of the Southern Baptist Convention. Pledges to the amount of $20,190 were made."

EUROPEAN MISSION. 21

Dr. Tucker, writing from Rome, said: "The great question here is a question of *Place*." Dr. Yates, of Shanghai, wrote from the same city: "The great want of the mission—one absolutely necessary, and which must be supplied—is a proper house of worship." A committee of the Convention reported: "A Baptist chapel in Rome will now, beyond doubt, be supplied, through the generous pledges made at this meeting, and the kindness of our friends in other States," * * and "that the thanks of this Convention be tendered to the Christian brethren and sisters of the Northern States, who have so nobly and kindly volunteered to aid us in the great enterprise of building a Baptist chapel in Rome."

PROGRESS OF THE WORK.

The Board reported to the Convention six stations, six missionaries and evangelists, with an aggregate church membership of two hundred and seventy-one. Brother Cote wrote: "Almost every Sunday morning it is my privilege to baptize converts. What a large and effectual door is opening before us on all sides! In the Trastevere the attendance is so great that I find myself compelled to enlarge the room. Thieves broke into the Hall and carried away several Bibles and Testaments. This affair may lead to interesting disclosures, as to the part taken by the priests to hinder the distribution of the Scriptures among the people. I was in Bologna the evening when the church were considering an organic union with the Congregationalists. I urged them not to sacrifice the truth. They unanimously decided to maintain their separate organization, and dispense the ordinances of the gospel in their own *Locale*. While the formal proceedings of forcible occupation of my hall on Piazza Navona were going on, the Piazza was full of people who loudly and unequivocally expressed their disapproval, and denounced the sentence of the court as one of outrageous injustice."

Martinelli, the pastor at Bari, wrote November 23, 1871: "Rejoice with us, for the work of the Lord progresses powerfully in this city. It is pleasing to see each member of the flock doing his best to spread around him the light of the gospel, and sow the good seed of the truth, which will eventually bear fruit of holiness and righteousness to the glory of our Divine Lord and Master." The Board referred to this church at Bari coming over to us in this language: "The glorious news of a church of seventy-five members being born in a day at Bari, a city of 80,000 souls, on the Adriatic, has thrilled the heart of our Zion."

BAPTISM AND ORDINATION OF SIGNOR GIOJA.

The following is extracted from a communication from Dr. H. H. Tucker, under date of Rome, Italy, March 25, 1872:

"Brother Cote, Brother Yates, the candidate and myself, repaired to the banks of the Tiber near the city of Rome, and there, in broad daylight, under the very shadow of the Vatican, on Thursday, the 21st of March, 1872, in the river Tiber, Giovanni B. Gioja, on a profession of his faith in Jesus Christ, was scripturally baptized in the name of the Father and of the Son and of the Holy Ghost. As the candidate rose from the water he exclaimed 'I thank God that I have been buried with Christ in baptism.' God's name be praised, echoed our hearts, and the very waves seemed to kiss the banks as if they were glad. Certainly this was the first time for many centuries, and perhaps since the days of the Apostles, that the Tiber has been stirred as the Jordan was by John the Baptist.

* * * * * * * *

"Brother Gioja was ordained to the work of the gospel ministry on the following Sunday. * * * The Presbytery consisted of Rev. W. N. Cote, of the Rome Mission, Rev. M. T. Yates, of the China Mission, Rev. Dr. Geo. W. Anderson, of the American Baptist Publication Society, and the writer.

"Brother Gioja is about thirty-four years of age, and is a man of talents and accomplishments; a native of Rome, the Italian is, of course, his vernacular tongue; but in addition to this, besides a good knowledge of Latin and a fair knowledge of Greek, he speaks and writes correctly and fluently, the English, French, and Arabic languages, and I, believe, also the Spanish language."

GIOJA AND THE CHURCH.

On his return to Rome from America, Mr. Cote wrote, June 20th, 1872: "I am glad to find that, during my absence, the work has been going on with uninterrupted success. My excellent assistant, Brother Gioja, has faithfully discharged his duties, and the church has flourished under his care. * * With the exception of about half a dozen, all the members of the First Church have joined our organization."

Mr. Gioja wrote October 28th, 1872: "I will tell you summarily that, through grace from above, this small Baptist Church at Trastevere, of which I have the privilege to be the pastor, has become the sparkling spot of that most dark quarter of Rome. In fact, if the erroneous teachings of the Catholic priests have, in the course of many centuries, formed of the Roman population a mass of ignorant and superstitious persons, (I am speaking in regard to Christ's holy religion only,) nowhere in Rome have those same venomous teachings so much injured and spoiled both the heart and the mind of the people as in the quarter of Trastevere. Hence, the dangers of preaching the gospel of Christ are greater there than in any other part of Rome, except, perhaps, close by the Vatican, where Mr. W. C. Van Meter is going to establish a school, and where, God helping me, I will often preach."

DR. LORIMER.

The Board recorded thus: "May 20, 1872. A telegram having been received from Dr. Tupper," (who had gone to Boston to see Dr. Lorimer,) "1. *Resolved*, That Rev. G. C. Lorimer, D. D., be appointed a missionary to Italy, with authority to raise the means of erecting a house of worship for the mission church of this Board in Rome, and to superintend its construction. 2. *Resolved*, That Dr. Tupper be authorized to make such arrangements with Dr. Lorimer as shall secure his services to our Board in Italy."

In New York City, at the Northern Anniversaries that year, the appointment of Dr. Lorimer was announced in a talk by the Corresponding Secretary of our Board. After a speech of great power by Dr. Lorimer, the body rose in their expression of God-speed to his twofold work of raising $20,000 at the North for the chapel, and of rearing the building at Rome.

The following records of the Board explain themselves:

June 6th—" Dr. G. C. Lorimer having declined the superintendency of our Italian Mission, and having accepted the appointment to raise funds for the chapel in Rome, therefore, *Resolved*, That Dr. Lorimer be fully empowered to act in the name of this Board, in raising said funds, and on the conditions prescribed by him."

January 6th, 1873: "*Resolved*, That the grateful acknowledgments of this Board are due and are hereby extended to Dr. G. C. Lorimer for his valuable services, gratuitously rendered, in collecting funds for the Roman Chapel."

COMMISSION AND CAUTION.

On the 21st of June, 1873, Dr. J. B. Jeter was appointed a Special Commissioner to Rome. The same day the Board adopted a report: "That Dr. Cote should be cautioned against the collection of money for the purposes of the mission, except through the medium of the Board." * * And that there is an "indispensableness for an American missionary on whose piety, discretion, ability, and business-qualifications the Board can implicitly rely."

TROUBLES.

"The Corresponding Secretary having presented in full," March 28th, 1874, "the testimony with regard to the troubles of the church at Rome, the following report was adopted:

"*Whereas*, Dr. Jeter having advised the discontinuance of Brother G. B. Gioja as our missionary at Rome; and, *whereas*, grave considerations seem to demand other and radical changes in this mission, therefore,

"*Resolved*, 1. That, * * Brother G. B. Gioja be dismissed from the service of the Board of Foreign Missions. * * *

"*Resolved*, 2. That the family of our Brother, Dr. Cote, being so seriously involved in the troubles which have caused the dismissal of Brother Gioja, it is the conviction of the Board that for Dr. Cote's sake, as well as for the future peace and best interests of our Italian Mission, Brother Cote should be counselled to withdraw from the mission and service of the Board, as the simplest solution of the perplexed and endangered state of our church in Rome. * * *

"*Resolved*, 4. That our sympathy is due and is hereby extended to our little church at Rome in their present afflicted and trying circumstances, and to our venerable brother, Dr. Jeter, in the arduous and delicate work which he is seeking prudently and patiently to execute; and that he be assured that should he not secure a house of worship, either through lack of opportunity or from providential considerations, his special mission to Italy may be still regarded as of incalculable value; and may be so presented and demonstrated to the intelligence and piety of the Convention and the denomination."

DR. JETER'S REPORT.

My impressions are favorable concerning the Provincial Evangelists. I have seen three of them, Basile, Gardiol, and Mollo. The former two seem to be earnest, warm-hearted men, and the latter is a promising young man.

Modena.—This city contains 32,000 inhabitants. Martinelli has recently been sent there. The church is composed of thirteen members, who are walking in a manner satisfactory to the Evangelist. Several persons are ready to be baptized. On Sunday morning the attendance is not less than thirteen; commonly more attend the service. The evangelist labors part of his time at Carpi, a short distance from Modena, where there is a church of ten members, walking uprightly.

Civita Vecchia, about sixty miles from Rome, on the Mediterranean Sea, has a small church, gathered within the last eighteen months by Evangelist Gardiol. It is a little vine, but seems to have been divinely planted. I was encouraged by its appearance and its promise of fruitfulness. The Evangelist Mollo is highly commended by citizens of the town as a teacher, but has been compelled to discontinue his school for want of a license for teaching, which he hopes to obtain at the next session of the examining board. Meanwhile he is teaching from house to house, conducting a Sunday-school, and preaching, against which there is no law. He is a licentiate, and inspires hope of future usefulness. The church contains twenty-two members, all of whom, it is stated, are steadfast in their profession and attentive in their duties. They are mostly males, and have the appearance of being substantial, earnest church-members.

"The *Waldensian Valleys,* in the north of Italy, contain a population of 25,000. Ferraris, the missionary, reports forty-three persons baptized. Twenty are at La Tour, whom the Lord enables to walk consistently. The evangelist is a mechanic, and supports himself by his labors.

"*Bari*, on the Adriatic sea, has a population of 70,000 or 80,000. Basile has recently gone to this station. His letter, from which I give the following extract, has a more scholarly appearance than those of the other evangelists:

"According to the church register, the number of communicants is seventy-six. During a year, the church was without a pastor, and several strayed away, and others are gone from the city. The first Sunday that the Lord's Supper was celebrated, about forty communed. As a general rule the brethren give proof of their faith in Christ. As regards baptism, I hold it of absolute necessity to every believer in Jesus: therefore, every one, desiring to participate in the Lord's Supper must be immersed. Better be few and faithful, than undisciplined and scandalous."

Dr. Jeter continues: "Basile recommends the formation of what is substantially a Baptist Association.

"*Bologna*, in the north of Italy, contains 109,000 inhabitants. Giannini is the evangelist. He is well reported for his piety and faithfulness. The church numbers sixty-eight members, all obedient to Christ. Sunday morning, the congregation is about thirty-five, with six or eight catechumens; and at night from eighty to one hundred and fifty. The week-night attendance is from forty to seventy. Prospects are very encouraging. Evangelist Giannini has added thirteen members to the church. No other church has been so much prospered. On the whole, after all deductions from sanguine reports, the provincial churches, I think, are in a very promising condition. Mr. Wall says that the success of our mission in Bologna alone, would abundantly compensate for all our sacrifices and toils. I am more and more deeply convinced of the importance of Italy as a field of evangelical labor. I need hardly repeat my oft expressed and well confirmed opinion that some minister, discreet, able, and energetic, should be sent promptly to labor in Rome.

"*Rome*—The church in Trastevere is capable, when crowded, of accommodating one hundred persons. It has recently, through the liberality of Brother Preble, of New York, been supplied with a baptistery, which is a great improvement on the arrangement first used for the administration of the ordinance. The congregation last Sunday numbered about sixty. At the close of the sermon the Lord's Supper was administered. In the commencement of our mission here, Dr. Cote and Mr. Wall, the English Baptist missionary, were in full co-operation. They have together baptized between seventy and eighty persons. After their ejection from the Central Hall, and at the time of Dr. H. H. Tucker's visit, it was deemed proper to divide the church— one part following Dr. Cote beyond the Tiber, and the other adhering to Mr. Wall. The part accompanying Dr. Cote adopted, as you are aware, articles of faith prepared by Dr. Tucker.

There have been on the register forty-five members. The members whom I have met seem devout in spirit, and certainly grasped my hand with fraternal cordiality. That we should be allowed to preach the gospel in Rome at all is one of the wonders of the present age. That any have been converted from the thraldom of Popery is cause for gratitude to God. That we were one of the first, if not the first, to commence a mission in Rome, has committed us to the work; and we should sustain it vigorously. Another American missionary is immediately and pressingly needed to carry on the Mission. Gardiol has been called here from Velletri. He is a good man, and will be able to take care of the church."

FROM BOARD'S REPORT.

ROME CHAPEL.

"The gross amount collected for this chapel is $22,363.10; of which $3,165.96 were given by the North, $1,240.29 by Great Britain, and $17,956.85 by the South. As the purchase of an eligible site would probably consume most of our available means for the chapel, and as the Board deemed it prudent to contract no debt on the hope of future collections, Dr. Jeter was authorized, provided any present investment was thought advisable, to purchase a building which might be adapted to our purpose. No less than fifty houses have been examined; but, on account of sundry obstacles relating to titles, location, and price,—though deeds of conveyance have been drawn out ready for execution,—no purchase has been effected. This delay is not regretted by the Board, in view of the internal state of the Roman Church, with regard to which Dr. Jeter was sent to Italy, as well as to obtain a house of worship.

DR. JETER AND TROUBLES.

"Complications and dangers in the church at Rome and imposed conditions of aid in this country rendered imperative the appointment of a Superintendent. * * * * Extensive correspondence was opened, but before a permanent missionary could be secured, the immediate demand for a man of eminent prudence and piety, of widespread reputation, and of commanding powers and controlling influence, was met by the election of Dr. Jeter, of Virginia, to the responsibility and toil of a delicate and difficult commission. His salary was fixed at the rate of $2,500 per annum and ten per cent. on funds collected in Great Britain. * * This was the pecuniary cost of augmenting and guarding our funds, and of encountering troubles, the most painful and perilous which have ever tried the Board of Foreign Missions. The gravity of these troubles may be suggested by the fact, that they have involved the separation, from our employment of Brethren W. N. Cote and G. B. Gioja. Should the Convention investigate the matter, the Board recommend that, for the good of the cause, the investigation be conducted through a committee of one from each State, and of the most enlightened and experienced brethren, to whom this part of our report may be referred.

"In reference to the subject Dr. Jeter writes: 'In the whole course of my experience I have never found myself more painfully perplexed than I have been in regard to the matters of the Rome Church.'"

FROM REPORT OF CONVENTION.

"Fortunately all the evidence bearing on the questions involved is documentary, and the Secretary of the Board of Foreign Missions placed in the hands of your committee all the papers systematically arranged and appropriately labeled.

EUROPEAN MISSION. 29

" * * In the opinion of the committee, the action of the Board has been wise and judicious, and the report prepared by the Corresponding Secretary gives a fair and satisfactory view of the facts. * * * Many of the details which have come before this committee have not been embodied in that report, * * * for the publication of these details could, to say the least, do no good, and in the opinion of your committee could not possibly affect any action, nor modify in any way the opinions of this Convention. * * *

"It was imperative on the Board to send to the field some man of great wisdom and wide experience, and to the end that his action might command universal confidence, it was needful that it should be one whose praise is in all the churches. The providence of God seemed to supply the Board with just such a man in the person of our well-known, time-honored, and much-loved Brother Jeter.

" In regard to the dismissal from the service of Brethren Cote and Gioja, your committee have to report that serious difficulties arose between those brethren, the relative merits of which it is not necessary to our purposes to discuss or decide upon; still less is it needful that the details should be made public. Suffice it to say, that your committee, after having examined the facts, are unanimously of the opinion that in dispensing with the services of these brethren, the Board has acted with characteristic discretion."

DEATH OF REV. W. N. COTE, M.D.

The following, from the pen of Dr. Jeter, appeared in the *Religious Herald* of May 3, 1877:

"We learn from the *National Baptist* the death of this esteemed missionary. He died in Rome of a disease of the heart, supposed to have been aggravated by the troubles which befel him and bore heavily upon him. He was a son of Dr. Cote, long and honorably associated with Madame Feller, of the Grand Ligne Mission, in Canada. Dr. W. N. Cote, under the patronage of the Foreign Mission Board, Southern Baptist Convention, was the first Protestant missionary to enter Rome after it was opened to evangelical labor by the army of King Emanuel. For a time his success was quite surprising, and inspired high hopes of the rapid spread of the gospel in the pontifical city. Difficulties, however, soon arose in the mission, and its bright prospects were beclouded. The Board deemed it best, under the circumstances, to dissolve its connections with Dr. Cote, from no charge affecting his moral character or his capacity as a missionary. This was a sore trial to him, but he did not leave his post, or entirely abandon his work. He devoted himself partly to literary and partly to evangelical labor. Aided by friends in England, he made extensive researches among the baptisteries of the East, and prepared a work on the subject, illustrating the ancient manner of baptizing, which has been published, and must long remain as a proof of his laborious investigations.

"We knew Dr. Cote well, and considered him an earnest, faithful, diligent missionary, of highly respectable gifts. His knowledge of the French language enabled him very soon to speak Italian with facility; and he preached in this tongue with seeming fluency and power. His work was not lost. The seed of the kingdom which he sowed is not likely to perish. A hundred years hence his name and his labors may be better known than they now are. He left a wife who was devoting her energies to the support of her family, and two very interesting little daughters. A sad breach has been made in the household; but we trust that the constant God of the deceased husband and father will be their friend and protector."

GEORGE BOARDMAN TAYLOR, D. D.

1873 to 1878.

HIS NATIVITY AND APPOINTMENT.

Dr. Taylor is a son of the late James B. Taylor, D. D. He was born in Richmond, Va., and studied at Richmond College. He was also a student of the University of Virginia. Mr. Taylor is the author of several works, beside "The Life and Times," of his honored Father. In Baltimore and Staunton he held successful pastorates, and was a beloved Chaplain of the University of Virginia. He was pastor in Staun-

EUROPEAN MISSION. 31

ton, and in the midst of the "Memorial movement" for the endowment of Richmond College, when he was called by our Board to go as a missionary to Italy. In regard to the qualifications and work of such a missionary, a committee, on February 10th, 1873, reported that " vigorous health, willingness to labor, discretion, firmness, business capacity, a missionary spirit, scholarship, aptitude for acquiring foreign languages, and some acquaintance with European manners and modes of thought, are very desirable for this position. * * Papacy will not consent to be throttled in the Vatican, without a desperate and gigantic struggle. A mistake in the selection of a missionary, might, to all human appearance, be fatal. * * If not grossly mistaken in our judgment, Baptists have a great and pre-eminent work to do in the death encounter with Papacy."

In their report to the Convention of 1873, the Board say:

"On the 3d of March, after much prayer and consideration, Brother G. B. Taylor, of Virginia, was unanimously appointed our missionary to Italy, and expects to sail at an early day for Europe. The practical sagacity, the broad cultivation, the elevated character, and missionary spirit of this brother, render him, in the opinion of the Board, eminently qualified for succession to the troubled things at Rome, for training native preachers and undisciplined churches, and for pressing forward the work of the Lord by the pulpit and press, and by his personal consecration to the holy cause."

The Convention declared that "Providence has singularly supplied our wants in time of need; * * that Brother George B. Taylor, happily combining the opposite qualities of youth and age, * * is the man."

1873—1874.

GENERAL INSTRUCTIONS AND FIRST REPORT.

In July, Mr. Taylor, with his family, arrived in Italy. On the 22d of September the Board, replying to Mr. Taylor's request for some instructions, "*Resolved,* That Brother Taylor be authorized to make such changes in the stations and the Evangelists, and to adopt such a course, in reference to the Italian Mission, as he may deem proper, provided, that all important changes of this character shall be promptly reported to this Board, and shall be subject to its revision; and provided, that in no case the aggregate amount expended shall exceed the sum annually appropriated by the Board, and that Brother Taylor be directed to consult, as far as practicable, the wishes of the evangelists, and, in no case, to interfere with the independence of the churches, in his arrangements." Mr. Taylor wrote, " Rome is my headquarters, and Italy my field of labor. I am not, and would not be a Superintendent to lord it over God's elect, over Christ's ministers; but my work is, and for the present must be, general, and I must for the most part operate through others. * * I am, December 17th, just in receipt of letters from all five of our evangelists. I think that we may now feel that the old troubles are well over, and that things are moving on with fair prospect of gratifying results. * * I can correspond without difficulty with our evangelists, and have not much trouble in catechising and lecturing our school, and conducting its exercises. * * I preach in broken Italian indeed, but with as much earnestness as I ever did in my life."

NEW STATION AND LABORERS, AND THE CHURCHES.

Milan—Professor Cocorda, of Milan, who had labored successfully with the Waldenses, and with the Free Church, but who had adopted Baptist views, and was baptized, offered to work in the employ of our Board.

Our missionary visited Milan, and succeeded in convincing him of the scripturalness of our views in regard to the Lord's Supper, and subsequently employed him as our evangelist. A letter from the Professor says: "Some begin to give signs of awakening. The brethren are studying the subject of baptism. We shall proceed to administer the ordinance."

Mr. Taylor wrote: " I made an address, explaining and defending our peculiar views. I was followed by Professor Cocorda, who declared the accord of the majority with us, not only in feelings but in convictions, and added, ' we hope in a few days to be practically, as well as theoretically, with American Baptists.' He then made a noble address on baptism, repudiating with manly earnestness the egotism and indifferentism which asks, ' Is baptism essential to my salvation ?' "

The brethren organized themselves into a regular Baptist church.

Count Torre.—The Count, who was recently baptized at Modena, is much exercised as to the work of the ministry. Mr. Taylor says: "I explained to him the scriptural doctrine of a call to the ministry. He avows himself ready, with God's help, to make the needed sacrifices, and he expresses a burning desire to preach the gospel. Already he has, at the risk of losing his situation, spoken in the meetings in Modena."

Cocorda.—The Professor is a man of vigorous mind and thorough training, having been taught by Gaussen and D'Aubigne. He is an experienced teacher, both classical and theological, and is instructive and impressive. It is an important point thus to occupy Milan, which is really the intellectual capital of Italy, and sends forth more from the press than all the other cities combined. In answer to my prayers the Lord has sent to our aid Signor Revelli, of Turin, who is official reporter to the Italian Parliament, and a member of the Trastevere Church. This brother is well acquainted with the gospel, an intelligent and decided Baptist, and though not eloquent, an acceptable speaker. His work is entirely gratuitous—a labor of love. Sunday mornings half a dozen brethren and sisters spend an hour in prayer and singing, and studying a chapter of God's word. At night Signor Revelli addresses a company, generally consisting of from ninety to ninety-five persons, besides the forty or fifty children and youths of the school. We see signs of increase in the congregation, and are hopeful. I generally say a few words after he finishes his discourse.

"*In Rome*—we have a flourishing evangelical school, which is substantially like our Sunday-schools in America, with an average attendance of from forty to fifty. Rosa Guerrini, our Bible-woman, conducts very efficiently the female department of the school, and visits from house to house in the neighborhood. The field in the Trastevere is, in this respect, peculiarly interesting—'the poor have the gospel preached to them.' Our colporteur teaches regularly, four times a week, a Bible class of young men. I do not suppose that the church is more depressed than a church in America would be which had been subjected to similar experiences. Nor do I despair of a living church being gathered here, composed in part of old materials. A suitable place of meeting we probably could purchase, but not, as far as I am at present advised, with the sum to which I am restricted. Moreover, it seems wisest in purchasing to use great deliberation.

"*In the Provinces*—The churches are generally in a healthy state, and the work is making progress, if slower than we hoped, yet as fast as he wills who loves his cause infinitely more than we do."

Subdued Tones.—The Convention, catching the subdued tones of Mr. Taylor, adopted the following, which is taken from an able report presented by Dr. T. G. Jones:

"We must not be over-eager to see great results. Before he left us on his great enterprise, our beloved Brother Taylor gave us a well-timed caution against this. Let us heed the caution. Our faith and patience will doubtless yet be severely tried. Bravely bearing the trial, we shall be strengthened and sustained. While comparatively little has so far been accomplished, we trust that a firm, broad base is being laid for further and more effective operations. The work of the Board, though for a time embarrassed and obstructed by untoward circumstances and occurrences, from which it is now happily in great degree relieved, seems to us to have been, in the main, conducted with great prudence and sagacity, and we cordially congratulate our brethren, and heartily bid them God speed."

1874—1875.

IN FRANCE AND SWITZERLAND.

Besides his labors in the Valleys, our Evangelist Ferraris made two journeys into France and Switzerland, where he did much to spread gospel truth, and our distinctive principles. In one of these journeys he had his Testaments and tracts taken from him by the official, and narrowly escaped imprisonment. Under date of March 8th, he writes: "Forty-six have been baptized, but some are in France, and others scattered over Italy, so that less than half that number now come to the communion table."

BAPTISM.

Since the organization of the church in Milan, twenty-four have been baptized. In August, Dr. Taylor baptized Enrico Paschetto, a young minister of good education, and just finishing his course at Geneva. Prof. Cocorda baptized Mr. Cossù, who had been in the service of the Free Church Committee. Brother Taylor sent him to Civita Vecchia. On the 1st of October, Prof. Cocorda, going to Rome as native pastor, Signor Paschetto succeeded him as pastor at Milan. Prof. Cocorda writes, March 20th, with regard to the church: " I noticed in the members a more lively sentiment of duty and of the necessity of sanctification, and I believe that this proceeded from having fulfilled with courage and joy their obligation in regard to baptism. I noticed also an increase in the beneficence of the church, and evident development of Christian character. I hope in the Lord that with their new minister they will continue to increase, both in numbers and in spiritual force."

WOLF! WOLF!

On the 16th of February, Martinelli writes: "The work of evangelization in Modena, Carpi, and San Passidonio is thorny. But the Lord draws souls to himself which Satan cannot draw away. Blessed be God, while, a few months since, only ten had been baptized in Modena, nearly twice that number are now seen at the Lord's Table. The Lord has called to his service an entire family of eight, the father being a major, who served under the King of Italy. At Carpi, the bishop makes great war against us, and our brethren are despised by friends, renounced by relatives, and held aloof by society, and have had to claim the protection of the Carbineers. The membership is about the same as at Modena. Peace, order, and fraternal love reign in the church. From the moment 1 entered San Passidonio, Satan filled the priests with such fury that they have hunted for, and bought Bibles and tracts to burn them. They call us, from the pulpit, worse than 'damned heretics.' The boys are instigated to howl at us in the street, and cry, 'Wolf! Wolf!' Yet we have never less than 150 to hear us, and many are wounded by the word of God. A dear octogenary brother has been greatly injured in his estate for the sake of the gospel; but he waxes stronger in the faith by the persecution. He says: 'It is only my duty to confess Christ, who, in my old age, made me to know his grace, and not to fear what the evil one can do against me.'"

Mr. Taylor writes that since the above was communicated, the priestly party have succeeded in closing Martinelli's meetings in the hall of the hotel. They made disturbance, and then reported to the Sub-Prefect that the peace was endangered. Brother Taylor has authorized our evangelist to rent another *Locale*

PROTEST.

After the death of their pastor, Giannini, the Baptist Church at Bologna, went over to the Plymouth Brethren, with whose doctrines their pastor himself was not a little tinctured. Mr. Taylor made a solemn and public protest against their unscriptural views and practice on a communion season, and declined to partake with them of the Lord's Supper. Yet he thought it wise to let them go as a body rather than split them by dissension. Since that time, several of the brethren have been baptized, and Brother Taylor writes: "I cannot but think that the testimony I rendered on that occasion helped to produce this result; and I am consoled in believing that the church will remain not less baptistic than heretofore."

PERSECUTION.

Basile writes, December 4th: "Never have I experienced similar persecutions. And not only I, but all the faithful brethren and sisters, have suffered at the hands of the false brethren. The blackest calumnies have been hurled against us. In former years I have been stoned by the wayside and in the *Locale*, but this was done by fanatical clericals, and was the more supportable because predicted in Scripture. By the Lord's aid and consolation, I have not died of grief. The brethren accompany me from meetings for protection."

January 18th, he writes: "Some brethren, scandalized, have withdrawn, so that only fourteen remain. Observe, however, that many brethren are absent from Bari, seeking work. I hope, that with patience, the Lord will permit us to see the plague removed, and things change for the better. We baptized eight in 1874, and have two demands for baptism."

February 12th. "We have five applying for baptism. Four of these are students at the Lyceum. They go to Naples to pursue their studies, but they will be in the Lord's hands."

A NEW CHURCH AND A JOURNAL.

From a very interesting communication of Prof. Cocorda, to Brother Taylor, under date of March 20th, we extract the following: "I have come, like yourself, to the conclusion that we cannot count much on the old element of the Trastevere Church. * * I believe that we must labor to form a church, in fact new, and to educate it seriously according to our principles. * * The Sunday-school is composed of half a dozen intelligent youths; the meetings for evangelization are attended by a variable and encouraging number; the meetings of the church for worship leave something to be desired, both as regards the regularity and activity of the members: but we hope for improvement with the progress of time. In pastoral visiting, I meet everywhere with affection. We have some six who desire baptism. * * * As regards the difficulty growing out of our position on the 'communion question,' it is not impossible to overcome it." But the subject should be explained publicly, to scatter the many calumnies circulated against us; and I think we ought to establish immediately a little journal for the defence of our principles."

CHAPEL.

Mr. Taylor wrote: "I am satisfied that a neat, church-like chapel is, under all circumstances, essential to an enlarged and permanent success in Rome; and the expenditure of what may be necessary for such an edifice, will be, in the long run, true economy. I address myself to this enterprise convinced of its difficulty, but hoping to derive some advantage from the observation and experience of the past two years. As many months may be necessary to complete the work, there should be no needless delay in beginning."

THE GREAT NEED.

"In all the stations, forty-four persons have been baptized. I hope we may do something to educate students for the ministry. It is important to publish tracts and small volumes on our distinctive views. But the great need of this land is an outpouring of the Holy Spirit, to awaken in the infidel, the indifferentist, and the superstitious Roman Catholic, that profound sense of need which can find satisfaction only in the pure and simple gospel. For this, let all God's people send up their cries to his Throne."

COMMENDATION AND RESTRICTION.

The Convention said: "'The appointment of Dr. Taylor to the general direction of this delicate and difficult work in Italy has secured for us at Rome a representative upon whose zeal and discretion we can fully rely. He has inspired new confidence in the enterprise among good men everywhere, and the missions under his charge are making steady progress."

The Board recorded July 5th, 1875, "That they find the accounts of G. B. Taylor full, accurate, and entirely satisfactory, and calling for the express commendation of the Board."

Dec. 6th. "*Resolved*, That the Board would be unwilling to consider any proposition, looking to their obligation for a chapel, for an amount exceeding twenty thousand dollars."

1875—1876.

VIEWS OF VISITORS.

"Dr. Taylor is doing stalwart work in Rome."—*Dr. Wayland Hoyt.*

"Dr. Taylor has been highly favored in securing a pleasant room, centrally situated, for occupation as a chapel; and especially favored in obtaining the services of an excellent coadjutor, a trusty 'fellow helper to the truth,' in Mr. Cocorda, an eloquent Italian preacher, who was in his youth a student of the celebrated Dr. Merle D'Aubigne, at Geneva. He speaks English quite fluently, and it is to be hoped that he may have the opportunity in due time to visit America, and by the power of personal presence cheer onward to patient and determined effort the friends of evangelization in Italy. * * * * *

" It may be safely affirmed, that unless the case be 'studied up' and understood by those who have started hopefully in support of the work, the issue will be discouragement, despondency, and utter abandonment. The American Board, the leading missionary organization of the United States, has already withdrawn from Italy as an unremunerative field of labor; and every intelligent American who comes into communication with the Italian people is shocked by fresh discoveries of that impenetrable ignorance which renders his expressions on religious matters quite meaningless, in the view even of educated persons in the higher classes of society."—*Dr. Wm. Hague.*

Dr. Taylor's attention being called to Dr. Hague's letter he replied:

" Yes, I quite agree with the sober views expressed by Dr. Hague as to the Italian work. * * Mr. Ashmore, who has been for a quarter of a century missionary of the American Baptist Missionary Union in China, and who spent some weeks in Rome, * * said to me 'that extravagant statements had been the bane of Eastern missions, and added that the field in Italy was harder and less hopeful than that in China.' * * *But while I thus write, I am far from feeling discouraged. On the contrary, I feel that though all of us are doing little, God is working, and that there is a forward movement in the public mind difficult to describe, but real.* It would be an error to estimate results by the number of converts and churches."

Dr. J. L. M. Curry, President of our Board, wrote:

" The evangelists of the Southern Baptist Convention have been in Rome for several days in conference on matters pertaining to their respective fields of labor, and the work of evangelization in Italy. The brethren as they met, after a year's separation, greeted one another with kisses on the cheeks. The exercises consisted of reports of their work, encouragements and discouragements, familiar talks on passages of Scripture, discussions on methods of reaching the people, essays on assigned topics, and prayers and singing. The spirit of the meeting was unexceptionable. In Italy, a few artful appliances can secure a large nominal membership in churches. These evangelists seem to think that genuine conversion is a prerequisite of membership. I have only time to say that Cossù is a patented teacher in the public schools; Martinelli was once the Superior of a Romish convent; Basile is warm-hearted and enthusiastic; Ferraris is well acquainted with the Bible; Paschetto is a graduate of both literary and theological institutions in Geneva, and is a young man of much promise; Gardiol is less intelligent, but is zealous. I have written of Cocorda and Taylor. The Conference was attended one day by Count Pappengouth, a Russian Prince, who, since his baptism in England by Baptist Noel, has consecrated time, and talents, and treasure to missionary work. He is a very decided Baptist, and is exerting a potential influence for good in Italy and elsewhere. Full of zeal and faith, his address and prayers made a most favorable impression on the Conference."

ITEMS FROM DR. TAYLOR.

Interesting baptisms and good baptistery—"I had the pleasure of baptizing near Pozzuoli (Puteoli) fifteen persons.   *   *   At Modena I witnessed the baptism of four persons—three of them quite interesting.   *   *   A promising young brother of eighteen, who spoke well in the meeting, desires to study for the ministry.

"Yesterday, May 23d, Mr. Cocorda baptized in an excellent baptistery, which we have constructed in the basement of our *Locale*, five persons.   *   *   *   I was reminded of the baptisms in the Catacombs, but all was 'done decently and in order.' Two other candidates have been received for baptism. If we find it difficult or inexpedient to buy property, the having this baptistery makes us more contented to remain in rented premises. But I believe all the other denominations are moving forward vigorously as regards chapel edifices."

Our church at Rome—"After the baptisms referred to above," continued Dr. Taylor, "a covenant, which we had prepared, was signed by six of the original members, by the five just baptized, and by Mr. Cocorda, and his wife, and by myself. There are three or four more to sign. Thus we begin almost anew, and the little church is very feeble; but I am not without hope that God will make it to increase in numbers and in spiritual force. Mr. Cocorda has just concluded a course of three controversial (not denominational) lectures, which were listened to by good audiences."

"Mr. Cocorda writes in good spirits. The congregations are good, and three more have been baptized." * * * *

"I am rather encouraged about our little church in Rome. * * I hope for a good time this winter, but I hope very *soberly*." * * *

"Of the twenty-three uniting at the time, or since the new start in May last, eight were old members, fifteen were new members, and of these last, ten have been added by baptism. Even this small number has suffered diminution. Of the little handful who now compose our church, the most are regular in attending the meetings, and apparently firm in their convictions. I should add that this church is not only small absolutely, but relatively, being probably the smallest and weakest in the city, the others having maintained an uninterrupted existence since their formation, soon after Rome was opened for evangelical work."

Sunday and sundry services—"We have three services on Lord's Day, and preaching two evenings in the week. The congregations range from twenty-five to seventy persons. The Sunday morning meeting partakes of the nature of a Sunday-school and of a prayer meeting. We celebrate the Supper every Lord's Day morning. * * My part is limited to brief addresses at the Sunday morning and afternoon services. Our good Brother Cocorda preaches, sometimes too profoundly, but always instructively and forcibly; and since his severe illness last summer, his sermons have been peculiarly evangelical and full of unction. * * * At night, each of us has some fifty young men—he teaching the French and I the English language. The New Testament is the principal text book. Bible classes of ten or fifteen persons each, in French and English, meet on Sunday morning at 10 o'clock. These two classes, with one of children, taught by my son, constitute our Sunday-school.   *   *   The young men in the night school generally seem to be of a very good class, some of them being students at the University."

Trastevere work closed—The Trastevere is where our church was originally located, and where, until recently, we had an out-station, conducted by a native—Guerreni—who has behaved badly. Dr. Taylor informs us:

"The out-station in Trastevere has been abandoned. I was very glad that Mr. Wall was ready promptly to enter that field."

Summer recreation—From Bagna di Lucca, in July, Dr. Taylor wrote:

"I spend my mornings in study, and many of my afternoons in evangelistic labors in the numerous villages among the mountains, distributing tracts and Scriptures, and talking to the simple people, generally not in the controversial style. In this work I have been deeply interested, and have met at the same time much encouragement and much opposition. In some of my encounters with the priests, I found that my recent studies stood me in good stead."

Training Students.—"'Though we are retrenching,' says Brother Taylor, 'I feel that I must take three young brethren to study for the ministry; and hope, in one way or another, to pay or raise the necessary means myself.'"

Vatican adult school—"I may appropriately refer to the weekly gospel addresses which Signor Cocorda delivers to seventy-five or one hundred persons in the Vatican adult school of Mr. Van Meter, as an important and interesting feature of our own Mission work in Rome. I have not unfrequently attended that meeting myself, and in my own very imperfect way proclaimed to that congregation the blessed gospel."

Monthly Journal—"With the new year we commence the issue of a small monthly journal. We have chosen as our modest title '*Il Seminatore*' (*The Sower*,) which well describes the work we are trying to do in Italy—a work which makes little show at present, and demands much faith and patience; but which may be fraught with great and blessed results in the future."

THE "WELL DONE" OF THE CONVENTION.

"There is cause for devout thankfulness to God," reported Dr. N. K. Davis, "that prosperity has attended our mission in Italy during the year; that we are holding seven stations where the pure gospel is preached by eight earnest and devoted men of God; that in Rome a Baptist Church is now planted and ministered to by Brother G. B. Taylor and Signor Cocorda; that by his untiring labor and judicious management of the delicate and exceedingly difficult trust committed to him, Dr. Taylor has proved himself so eminently worthy of our Christian confidence and affection, and of our continuous and liberal support.

"The work which has been done by the Foreign Mission Board receives our hearty and grateful approbation. Its immediate results and promising condition encourage us to greater exertions in its support, to larger projects and larger contributions. It is manifest from the facts now before us that the firm and fruitful establishment of Baptist churches in Italy is a work of far greater difficulty and magnitude than had been anticipated by the least hopeful among us."   *   *   *

Resolved, That the Convention has heard, with great satisfaction, the statements of the President of the Foreign Mission Board respecting the present state of the Mission in Italy, as observed by him during his presence there, and respecting the fraternal conference held by him with our evangelists in Rome; that we hereby most cordially respond to their Christian salutations, that we exhort them to be courageous in God, and faithful, and that we pledge to them our heartfelt sympathy in their great difficulties, and our support to the gospel in their hands."

1876—1877.

DR. TAYLOR AS A TRAVELER.

"The train was nearing Dieppe, and it was midnight when the conductor came for tickets. I, who had traveled so many thousand miles without any mishap, and who rather prided myself upon being a good traveler, searched my pockets in vain for my ticket. What was worse, it was a round-trip ticket, and I had my son's as well. It was bad enough to have to suffer such a loss, but to be regarded by conductor and passengers as a rascal trying to steal a ride, was even more trying; but I proved myself a good traveler at least, by preserving a philosophic calmness in circumstances so annoying, paying the money without a word. Dieppe reached, and the crowded car cleared of its passengers, I made a careful search, which was rewarded by finding the tickets upon the floor. My reputation as a gentleman being thus re-established, it remained to recover my money, which was effected, though not without a disagreeable walk of a mile around the harbor in the darkness and falling rain. Fortunately, the boat was waiting for the tide, or I should have been left. Or, shall I say unfortunately? Certainly that channel trip was not a thing to be desired. It was what our English friends, more expressively than elegantly, call a 'nasty night,' and I, in eight or ten hours, suffered more from sea-sickness than in three Atlantic voyages. Various preventives and remedies were tried in vain. As for toothache, the only sure cure is to extract he discontented member, so against sea-sickness, the only absolute security is to stay at home. * * * *

"I cannot say I sympathize with those who find travel unfavorable to religious life. It may be so when the travel is for mere pleasure and with lively company, though even then it would seem that a life so varied and changeful would nourish the sense of constant dependence upon divine care; but certainly the lonely Christian traveler, mid scenes and company not in sympathy with him, should find himself driven closer to the one ever-present Friend. This, at least, is my experience. I find it easier to be spiritual in my long, lonely journeys than in the routine of home life; and often on rail-car or in a hotel, prayer and the word of God have a new sweetness. It is, on the other hand, a great error to think that any track is so beaten that one does not need divine guidance and support, or that any home life is so delightful and consoling that one can afford to walk less near to God. Who has not found himself in the most familiar circumstances surprised by temptation, and his soul in the most endearing scenes starving for an absent, because neglected, God? * * * * *

"Traveling in first-class cars, one comes in contact with another sort of people, and has the chance to speak of the gospel to persons who are not so apt to have been reached by it as are those of plainer condition. This was certainly my experience, and I had interesting religious conversations with sundry persons, among whom was a member of the Italian Parliament, with whom I spoke also of religious liberty and of the important bill which was then pending, which has since passed, to repress the abuses of the Roman Catholic clergy. As usual, I was well provided with tracts, which were read by many with whom I had no opportunity of much conversation. Indeed, after nearly four years of experience in Italy, I have come to regard a railway journey as offering excellent opportunities for evangelistic and colporteur work.

SUNDRY PLACES AND PERSONS.

"Earth has no joys like those of friendship, and rich as London is in attractions, my pleasantest hours there are those spent with dear Christian friends. Prominent among these is Mr. Oliver, an old-fashioned gentleman and Baptist, for many years, as now, the treasurer and main-spring of the Baptist Tract Society, which takes a deep and practical interest in our Italian mission-work. He is eighty-eight years old, but he has the vivacity of a child, and attends all his committee meetings, and performs all the duties of his office with punctual assiduity. He affords a beautiful practical illustration of the Psalm, and is, indeed, like the palm-tree, bringing forth fruit in old age, while his cheerful face and words always do me good like a medicine, or, better still, as a cordial, alike pleasant and refreshing. In his house I feel as with a good Virginia Baptist; while he honors me, as such men as Wm. F. Broaddus have done, by treating me as a dear son, I feel sad in thinking that if I continue from time to time to visit London, I cannot hope much longer to see his face; but, as I wrote him, we hope to meet in another city, bigger and brighter than London. * *

"I have never entered into the rather profane remark often made to express the American fondness for the capital of France, that 'good Americans, when they die, go to Paris.' Besides its utter irreverence, it does not express my conception of that gay metropolis, which, to me,

seems the embodiment of a high material civilization, dissevered from what is tenderest, dearest, and most sacred to our spiritual nature. Other graveyards may be sad, but the famous one of Pere la Chaise, with its splendid monuments of the rich, and tawdry offerings upon the graves of the poorer dead, the common pit for the pauper, and the heartless, semi-heathenish ceremonies I have witnessed there, has to me a dreariness which I have no language to express. Even the beauty of Paris half revolts me, for I see everywhere vice gilded, and made to appear less hideous than she is; whereas in London and New York she stalks forth bold and defying indeed, but in her true character.
* * * * * * * * * *

"I made a very pleasant visit to Signor Bracchetto, pastor of the Free Italian Church in Turin. This dear brother was my traveling companion for a short time in England last summer, and impressed me favorably. * * * * * * *

"The work in Turin, in connection with the Free Church, was commenced several years ago by Signor Bracchetto. At the first meeting only five persons were present besides himself and his wife; but these five brought a few more the next evening, and at the third meeting there were about forty present. Now there are, I think, 140 communicants. * * * * * *

"After such testimony as to the work in Turin, and as to the pastor, Signor Bracchetto, and his able coadjutor, the physician and professor, Signor Secundo Laura, you will be pleased to hear that these two brethren, having become fully convinced of the duty of believers' baptism, were, on the 26th of July, baptized in the river Po. In their investigations, the '*Seminatore*' was useful to them; but their conviction was mainly produced by the study of what I regard the best text-book on baptism, and which, I am happy to say, has been well translated into the Italian language. Need I say that I refer to the New Testament? * * * * * * *

"At Milan I passed two pleasant days with Paschetto and his family. He is full of plans for pushing forward the work. * * He is working away at a Hebrew-Italian Lexicon, a book which does not exist. But he is not without a certain practical vein, and I was much interested in the Sunday-school—which is composed of fifteen or twenty bright youths—and is well conducted by him. * * * *

"Modena scarcely seemed like Modena, with the dear Martinelli and his Brigida away. * * * Professor Count Torre would not allow me to remain at the hotel. * * * On Sunday morning we had the usual meeting, at which he took part, and also Garuti, who in Martinelli's absence comes from Carpi for the purpose. In the afternoon we three went to Carpi, half an hour distant by rail. Torre more and more impresses me as a man of guileless, generous heart and fine mental powers. He willingly got with Garuti in the third-class train, and showed that he knew how to 'condescend to men of low estate.' He seems anxious to preach the gospel, making the sacrifices which will be necessary, and his wife, who was opposed, seems cordial. I trust the Lord means to use him as a chosen vessel. Garuti, who is a teacher in the municipal schools, is suffering for his faith. He and the church in Carpi have been more or less under the influence of the excellent Count Guicciardini of Florence and other so-called 'Plymouth Brethren,' who, partly from the principles they hold and partly from misunderstanding, have, to state it very mildly, little use for American Baptists.

"Sitting in the station awaiting the train, I occupied myself by reading a chapter in the Bible. As I was doing so, a stout, pleasant old lady came up to me and began to talk very sociably, beginning by saying how refreshed she felt by meeting a fellow-Christian, which she supposed me to be from my employment. We got into the same compartment and had a very delightful religious conversation. * * * * When we parted, I handed her my card, and as she gave me hers, I read with surprise and pleasure the name 'Anna Shipton.' 'What!' said I, 'the Anna Shipton whose little books have been such a pleasure and a help to me?' It was even so, and this interview was one of the pleasantest episodes in my journey. * * * *

"In Venice the Lord seems to have opened the way for us to begin a new work. I had the opportunity of cultivating the acquaintance of the evangelist Signor Bellondi, whom I now introduce to your readers. He is a tall, fine-looking man of thirty-two or three, and seems zealous for the Master's cause. He was formerly with the Free Church, but has been for two or three years supported as an independent missionary, principally to the Jews. He now has a little nucleus of converted persons, who will probably unite with him in forming a Baptist Church. His work has been conducted on a very generous scale. He has had a magnificent hall, a piano, and a master of music, and has used gospel songs composed by himself and set to music by the master. Certainly the singing was magnificent. I thought almost too fine. But it is an important means in so artistic a city as Venice. The independent work in which Signor Bellondi has been engaged will now close, but he comes to us, not because of need, but because he is and has for some time been in sympathy with our principles. I have been much influenced in my action in the case by the strong recommendation coming from Signor Cocorda, who has known him many years. I spent a few days in Venice looking for a new *Locale*, and finally left the matter in the evangelist's hands.

"Behold me in Bari; still on Horace's route, but now-a-days we travel faster, having railroads; and besides, the poet was a trifle lazy. * * * *

"I have now ascertained, with the aid of Basile and an accomplished clerical of Bari, that there formerly existed in this city a baptistery for the immersion of adults, with rooms for preparing the candidates of both sexes; so that this baptistery must be added to the list of those hitherto mentioned by modern writers on this subject. * *

"From Bari to Taranto it is only four hours. I could not resist the temptation to visit that little city, unique for its position upon a rock in the sea. * * * * *

"With Signor Columbo, the minister of the Free Church, who, soon after my visit, was baptized by Basile in the Adriatic, I had an interesting conversation, in the course of which he narrated to me the opposition 'he had encountered in that city, and also the remarkable work which he had accomplished in Rocca Imperiale, where the chief priest has embraced the evangelical cause, and has been followed by a large part of the population. Great results may come if the error is avoided of forming a church of persons converted to Protestantism, but not converted to Christ. * * *

"My first halt was at San Germano, the seat of the famous and loftily perched monastery of Monte Casino. I had the pleasure of making the acquaintance of Tosti, the illustrious historian, who is to literature what Father Secchi, of Rome, is to science. He was very courteous. His black hair and fresh appearance show how conducive to health and longevity is a tranquil literary life in the free air of the mountains."

From Naples, Mr. Taylor wrote: "The evangelical movement here, so far as the Baptists are concerned, is almost entirely due to the labors of one man, Count Oswald Papengouth, of Russia, and connected by marriage with a noble English family. This gentleman had received a liberal education, but was living in sin and vice when arrested by the grace of God. His pious housekeeper often gave him tracts, which he, instead of reading, threw into the waste basket. One day, seeking a scrap of paper, he had his attention arrested by one of these tracts. He read it, was convicted of sin, and in this state of mind sallied forth. His steps were directed to where Baptist Noel was preaching in the open air, and the sermon completed what the tract had begun. * * He has preached the gospel very effectively in France and Switzerland, and I believe also in other countries in Europe.

"He came to this city rather more than two years ago and began operations. * * * In the autumn of 1874, he opened a hall for meetings, and, though he had Italian aid, commenced himself to read and explain the Scriptures. In April, 1875, several persons were seeking baptism, some being converts from Romanism, and others being from the other denominations. Mr. Wall came and baptized some of these candidates. A few weeks later I tarried in Naples for a day, and called on Mr. Papengouth, who had expressed a desire to make my acquaintance. I found him in many particulars in substantial agreement with American Baptists as to church polity. He gave me a most cordial reception, and begged me to remain and baptize several who were awaiting the ordinance. It seemed like the finger of Providence, so I consented, baptized several persons, and labored with him for several days. * * * *

PUBLIC DEBATE.

"Reaching Rome, I took a room with Mr. Cocorda, whose family is with mine in the Valleys. My arrival was opportune, as he needed to devote much time to the examinations in Mr. Van Meter's schools, and I was able to relieve him in our theological class, and in other ways. The students had made progress, and their recitations, specially in Greek, were very good. Two of them will probably engage in colporteur work during the vacation.

"For several weeks we have had very interesting meetings at our *Locale* in Rome. We offered free discussion to any opposers of evangelical truth. The offer was accepted by sundry gentlemen, who presented various infidel objections. Advocates of the gospel were not wanting in two of our students, two of our new members, a gentleman from another denomination, (who had, however, been converted from infidelity through Mr. Cocorda's instrumentality,) a professor of philosophy who is half in sympathy with the clerical party, not to speak of Mr. Cocorda and myself. Great metaphysical acuteness was shown by some of the Italian speakers on both sides. Indeed, I more and more respect the Italian mind, in which the reasoning faculty seems to predominate. Among the questions discussed were The Inspiration of the Scriptures, The Divinity of Christ, The Atonement. Our infidel friends would, doubtless, have preferred the cool style of a mere dialectic exercise, but I felt my spirit often stirred within me, and spoke much of the internal evidences of the gospel, of the great fact of sin, making home thrusts at the conscience. Unable to follow all that was said on the other side, I, for the most part, left the reply proper to Mr. Cocorda, who generally had the closing address, and it was in safe hands. Some of his addresses were masterly, at times with keen wit exposing the fallacies and absurdities of his opponents so, that he seemed to flay them, and at others, solemnly testifying to the verities of the gospel, and warning his hearers against being led away by the delusions of the devil to the ruin of their country and their own souls. The hall was almost always crowded, and often the people remained willingly till a late hour. On one occasion, Mazzarelli, who is a member of Parliament, entered and took the floor. It was late, but the audience rose from their seats and crowded around him, listening with wrapt attention as, in his calm, philosophical way, he pleaded for the gospel. He is a dear old man, and as he tenderly grasped my hand, the day that the Chamber of Deputies adjourned, and said, 'Courage! in twenty years we shall see great progress,' my heart 'thanked God and took courage.'"

CHEERING WORDS.

The Board, after reporting to the Convention that a station had been opened at Cagliari, the Capital of the Island of Sardinia; that Columbo was laboring for us with Count Papengouth in Naples: that Bellondi was employed in Venice: that the Vatican school had been put under our charge; that *Il Seminatore* was circulated even in Egypt; and that some twenty had been baptized, recapitulated thus:

"A few years ago a solitary colporteur entered the gates of Rome, forced ajar by a conquering army. To say nothing of the progress of other evangelical denominations, our own tenets are proclaimed from the North to the extreme South of Italy. Baptisms have agitated the Po and the Tiber, and have been administered in the Gulf of Taranto, and in the Adriatic and Mediterranean Seas. In the most important places we have churches or stations. Not only the obscure have come to the truth, but such men as the scholarly Paschetto, the astute Cocorda, the nobleman Papengouth, Columbo, an honored evangelist at Taranto, Signor Bellondi, late missionary to the Jews in Venice, and Barnardo Brachetto, and Secondo Laura, respectively pastor of the Free Church and Professor in the College at Turin. By the wise measures of Dr. Taylor, whose judicious management has dispelled the last vestige of our old troubles in Rome, and whose missionary tours have scattered by the way the good seed, strengthened the feeble hands of God's elect, and enlarged the borders of our church-views and practices in Italy, a tongue has been given to our principles through the distribution of the Baptist publications in adjacent France and in far-off Africa." * * *

"No wonder," said Dr. Winkler in a grand speech on the report of the Board, "that the evangelical Christians of the world resolved to press into that vast city, when once her gates were thrown ajar, and to publish the gospel of salvation to her people. For sore, sore is her need. The Paganism of Rome is condemned by God, who established the Old Dispensation as a perpetual warning and protest against the multiplication of gods, and the adoration of images. The Judaism of Rome is condemned by God, who sent his own Son to fulfil its types and prophecies, and to scatter its misty shadows forever by the sunburst of grace and of truth. The Romanism of Rome is condemned by God, to whom the blood of the martyrs has been appealing for a thousand years. There the long conflict of the centuries must be ended, by the preaching of that same gospel, which vanquished Rome in the days of the Cæsars."

1877—1878.

IMPORTANT BAPTISMS AND CHANGES.

Dr. Taylor reported: "On the night of June 3d, 1877, I baptized Signor Bellondi, in the locality where so many Christians were drowned, * * * Aug. 28th. In Bari, Signor Volpi, the minister of the Free Church, has, with his deacon, been baptized, and will take Basile's place, who has long desired to go elsewhere. It is pretty certain that all of Volpi's members will go with him. Signor Volpi is regarded as a laborious and successful evangelist. * * * Oct. 6th, 1877: I now write principally to say that I have accepted the proposition of Count Papengouth to turn over to us one-half of the work, we assuming all the responsibility of one of the *Locales*, and conducting a mission entirely independent, but with the most harmonious relations with that conducted by Mr. Papengouth. Colombo is very happy to remain in Naples under this arrangement, and I feel thankful for such a solution of the problem. The only trouble is an increase of expense. But in this, as in the case of Signor Volpi, the advance movement seemed necessary; and, moreover, there was no time to write and consult the Board. Cocorda is in Northern Italy. His place is partly supplied by Brother Berruatti, of whose baptism I wrote you last May. The Vatican school is opened well. The congregations at Monte Citorio are very fair. But we lack the life-giving Spirit. * *

"We fixed upon Barletta as a new station for Basile. Twelve years ago an interesting work was begun there by our Brother Giannini, which was broken up by cruel massacre.

"On the 15th October, Basile thus wrote me from Barletta: 'I came here day before yesterday, and having religiously preserved some names, given me by Giannini, of the survivors of that slaughter of March 19, 1866, I betook myself to one of these dear brethren, Signor Salminici, who received me cordially, and introduced me to some others whom I found to be faithful. I explained the object of my visit, and expressed my interest in them and my desire to labor for and with them. They approved my sentiments, but, jealous of their liberty in Christ, feared that I was coming to impose some human rules or systems upon them. I declared that such was not the wish either of our Board or myself, adding that I desired order for the sake of liberty.'

"Soon after this visit, Basile established himself in Barletta, and wrote me as follows: 'We have had a meeting of eight persons, all brethren tried in the furnace from the 19th of March, 1866, until to-day. They live in an element of martyrdom, but have not abandoned their Saviour. Others are dispersed, or absent in the country, but we hope the good example of these will recall them. Oh, what shakes of the hand! What welcomes! What joy shone on the faces of these modest heroes of the gospel! An aged brother, one of the most pious I have ever met, concluded the meeting with a simple and fervent prayer. We have need of Bibles and Testaments, for many of these brethren remain without them, the priests having, by means of wives and relatives, sequestered them. The priests and friars, always enemies of Christ, know of my arrival, and have ordered prayers for the undoing of the heretics. We will use prudence, but will not play the coward. We have need that the brethren fight for us at a throne of grace. It is morally impossible that the old scenes can be renewed; but it is not for the want of will on the part of those butchers. Until we have a regular *Locale*, the meetings will be held in my house."

The Board appropriated to the mission, for the year, $8,500.

DR. TAYLOR AND HIS WORK.

Our missionary to Africa, Rev. W. J. David, visiting Italy for his health, wrote:

"I am grateful to God for the privilege of meeting and conversing with Brother Taylor. Oh! how my soul has been longing and thirsting for Christian communion with a sympathetic heart. I feel strengthened and encouraged for the physical and spiritual trials on which I am about to enter."

Dr. Prime, of the *Observer*, wrote: "Rev. Dr. Taylor is a man of decided character; with a clear and vigorous intellect, a tender and glowing heart, and such a sound judgment as secures for him the respect and confidence of all who represent Protestant missions in Rome. By his invitation I attended his Sunday-school,* and found four or five different rooms filled with children of various ages, from the infant class to the youth of sixteen. An efficient corps of teachers were giving instruction in the Scriptures. They were all assembled in the largest hall, and engaged in singing hymns; and the parents of some of the children coming in, addresses were made to them and to the schools. The walls were hung with the American and the Italian flags. Texts of Scripture were inscribed. These rooms are filled every day of the week with scholars. In the evening they are occupied by young men studying the Bible. In another part of the town is the Baptist Church, where the gospel is faithfully preached by the Rev. Mr. Cocorda, and in at least seven other places in Italy preaching stations are maintained under the superintendence of Dr. Taylor. * * * * * * *

"These missions form an important part of the great work now in progress for the spread of evangelical religion in this land of Papal darkness. To the eye of unbelief it may seem the day of very small things. But it is enough to plant the seed, and the rains of heaven will descend upon it to the redemption of Italy. Now is the time to sow the seed of the word. Dr. Taylor is able to extend his missions and multiply the number of laborers just as fast as he has the means of supporting them. And you may be certain that he is judicious, careful, and wide-awake."

---

* The Sunday-school referred to above, is the one which had been left in Dr. Taylor's hands by Mr. Van Meter, when he came to this country.

ROME CHAPEL.

Among other trials, the perplexities attending the purchase of this chapel bore heavily on Dr. Taylor. He said: "The past year has been to me one of anxiety. Often, had I consulted the flesh, would I have sought a field involving less care and responsibility." On November 6th the Board, unwilling longer to restrict our missionary rigidly to the funds collected for the chapel, "resolved that * * if Brother Taylor, at an expense of not more than $25,000, can obtain a house and lot, such as our mission needs, he be authorized to make the purchase." The following communications from Dr. Taylor were reported to the Convention: "On March 17th, after much treating, I made a definite offer of 129,000 *Lire* ($25,800) *cash* for the house in Via Theatro della Valle, which has been before us for more than a year. * * * April 30th.—Yesterday I drew on the Treasurer of the Board for $5,000, gold, fifteen days after sight, and for $20,000, gold, three months after sight. * * By God's great mercy the affair seems happily terminated. * * I trust God will continue to smile upon us, giving us by the approaching autumn a complete chapel." A report presented by Dr. B. Manly and adopted by the Convention, held this language: "Our hearts are cheered by the evidence of good accomplished, of souls converted, of three native ministers raised up in God's providence during the year, and of the thirty-two baptisms, and over fifty hopeful inquirers at our ten centers of labor and influence throughout Italy. We are strongly impressed with the prudence, as well as the earnestness and zeal, with which our work has been conducted amid multiplied embarrassments and discouragements. * * *

"The long-wished-for *Locale* in the city of Rome has been purchased, and we are now able to enjoy the advantage of a settled habitation for our mission work there. The delay in purchasing has given us the advantage of securing what is thought by competent judges, familiar with the spot, to be "the finest place" in the whole city for our mission premises. It is on one of the great thoroughfares, two hundred yards from the Pantheon, a hundred yards from the University of Rome. Its cost is about five thousand dollars more than the sum already collected and on hand for that purpose. That amount, we trust, will be provided for before the close of this Convention. It is impossible to over-estimate the importance of this movement. It is the crisis in the history of our missions in Italy. Let us meet it manfully, liberally, and at once."

The report was followed by a thrilling speech by Dr. Henry McDonald, of Virginia. The proceedings record the result. "At the close of Brother McDonald's address, H. A. Tupper, of Virginia, the Secretary of the Foreign Mission Board, asked for subscriptions by States, and also by individuals, to the Rome-chapel-fund, when the sum of $7,300 was pledged."

1878–1879.

NORTHERN ANNIVERSARIES.

Five thousand dollars, beyond the $25,000 purchase money, were needed for the improvement of the chapel. The following action was taken by the American Baptist Missionary Union, at the anniversaries at Cleveland, Ohio, which were attended by W. T. Brantly, J. A. Broadus, C. E. Dobbs, and H. A. Tupper, as messengers from our Convention:

"WHEREAS, we have heard from the Southern Baptist Convention that they have bought an eligible building in Rome, Italy, for their long-wished-for chapel, and that after having secured some $20,000, about $10,000 are still needed to cover the cost of the house and the improvements necessary for a chapel; therefore,

"*Resolved*, That we commend this object to the liberality of our people, and will welcome any suitable representative of the Southern Baptist Convention who may be appointed to raise funds at the North for this purpose."

Dr. Lorimer, now of Chicago, in presenting the above preamble and resolution, which were heartily adopted, stated that Dr. Hague, of New Jersey, would no doubt be "the representative" of the Southern Baptist Convention. On hearing of this movement of the Missionary Union, our Board adopted the following:

"That our grateful acknowledgments are due, and are heartily extended to, the American Baptist Missionary Union for the action taken at their recent Anniversary, in reference to our Rome chapel; and that agreeably to that action, your committee recommend the appointment of Rev. Wm. Hague, D. D., as our representative to collect at the North for the chapel."

The ensuing report was adopted at the next meeting of our Convention:

"The Committee appointed at the last meeting of the Southern Baptist Convention to bear fraternal greetings to the American Baptist Home Missionary Society, at Cleveland, Ohio, report that they were received by their Northern brethren with the utmost cordiality. Profound interest was expressed in the work of the Convention, and, as a matter of practical sympathy, Rev. Dr. Hague was unanimously requested to appeal to Northern churches in behalf of our work in Rome. Our Secretary, Dr. Tupper, was requested to address their society on the Foreign Mission work of our Convention, and was heard with great attention and respect. W. T. BRANTLY, *Chairman*."

VATICAN MISSION.

An intelligent visitor at Rome reports: "When Mr. Van Meter left Rome, Dr. Taylor took his Vatican school. Although already overworked, rather than suffer the lambs to be scattered without a shepherd, he willingly added the care of it to his other burdens, and nobly did he watch them. I was at the school at Christmas, during his administration, and not a whit of the enthusiasm that Mr. Van Meter's presence inspired was wanting then." Mr. Van Meter, returning to Rome, resumed the charge of his mission. On October 7th, 1878, Dr. Taylor wrote:

."Yesterday I formally handed over to Mr. Van Meter his Vatican Mission, which, I think, has not grown less in my hands. I am glad to be free from the care of managing it, while I expect to be often there to speak of the gospel."

OUR EVANGELISTS.

Professor H. H. Harris, of Richmond College, visiting Italy, wrote: "Our excellent superintendent of the Italian work seems to have used the utmost prudence, and to have been guided by a good Providence in his selection of men. * * * Our corps of evangelists, so far as I have seen them, impress me very favorably. Like our preachers at home, they have their peculiarities, their weakness, their faults—they need our prayers for themselves personally and for their work—but they also deserve at our hands a more liberal support than the present rate of contributions will allow. One of them is a born poet; another gives his spare time to Hebrew and Arabic. Signors Paschetto and Cocorda both speak English—the latter well."

Another visitor writes: " Rev. Mr. Cocorda, who preaches at his chapel, is a very learned and eloquent man. I am not sufficiently *au fait* in the Italian language to judge critically as to the quality of his preaching, but a gentleman who is, and who hears him very often, says that every sermon he has heard is worthy of being reported and published. Judging from his earnestness and his action in the pulpit, so natural, so easy, so fluent, I should think no one who hears him and understands him would be unaffected."

NOTES ON STATIONS.

Torre Pellice.—Ferraris has baptized eight joyful converts.

Milan—Paschetto reports three baptisms, and five catechumens, who "are studying the word of God, and who are almost convinced of Baptist principles." The meetings of the church for the study of God's word the evangelist describes as "very edifying." The Sunday-school numbers twenty-one pupils, "punctual and studious."

Venice—Bellondi is popular as a preacher, and continues to compose hymns, "some of which will form a part of the permanent psalmody of Italy. A rare opportunity offers itself to buy a church-like edifice for $12,000." Brother Taylor exclaims: "Oh that we could do so!"

Modena—Martinelli applying for Basile to go to the neighborhood of Modena, Brother Taylor has consented. Count Torre wishes to give himself to the ministry, and has been preaching gratuitously at Carpi and Bologna. Basile has been located at Bologna and a church edifice has been rented for $200 per annum.

Barletta—Volpi, who is stationed at Bari, will "take Barletta in his circuit. Great progress in public sentiment has been made toward evangelical views."

EUROPEAN MISSION. 59

Bari—Volpi has baptized six, and three are awaiting baptism. He preaches at Grumo and Acquaviva. At the latter place was opened last month a *Locale*, and eighty persons were present. On his return from the Rome chapel dedication Volpi was arrested, and ironed, and imprisoned, as a "socialist." "It was a clear case of persecution for the gospel." Brother Taylor testified in his favor. Reparation was demanded of the government, and it was given.

NAPLES.

The *Locale* has been secured for another year. Colombo is not sanguine of great results, yet his report is encouraging in its tone.

CAGLIARI, ISLAND OF SARDINIA.

Cossù has baptized three. He says one of them can "repeat the whole New Testament, and supports every doctrine of his faith with appropriate passages." The evangelist preaches in other cities. He circulates tracts at his own expense. Brother Taylor says: "He is the right man in the right place."

ROME.

Three baptisms. With regard to Rome chapel troubles, Brother Taylor says: "You know all our troubles before the courts, and how God gave us the victory. Our adversaries were condemned to pay costs. * * * The Southern Baptist Convention has been 'recognized' as a corporate body." Brother Taylor assists Cocorda at the chapel, and preaches once a week at the Vatican Mission. Mrs. Taylor and Mrs. Cocorda hold a woman's meeting. Brother Taylor has complete charge of *Il Seminatore*.

In all the stations there were twenty-three baptisms during the year.

DEDICATION OF ROME CHAPEL.

The chapel was dedicated in November. The opening services on the second day of that month were participated in by all the ministers in Rome. Our evangelists continued for a week a nightly meeting in the chapel. The day-time was given to business conference. The organ of the Vatican referred to the dedication as the "opening of an Infernal Hall." Brother Taylor wrote: "The chapel is beautiful, and with its furniture is exquisitely simple and neat." The building is so constructed that it furnishes comfortable homes for Brother Taylor and Signor Cocorda, and their families. There are rooms on the ground floor, which may be either rented or used for some purposes connected with the Mission."

The Treasurer paid drafts for the chapel and improvements amounting to $31,838.26. The amount realized for the Rome chapel U. S. securities was $19,072.78. Receipts for the chapel during the year, $8,407.12; making the difference to be provided for $4,358,36.

That the chapel should be finally and legally secured after so many disappointments and perplexities, is a source of sincere congratulation. After the dedication, Brother Taylor wrote:

"Despite all difficulties, we were enabled to open the chapel according to appointment. The opening services continued just one week. Every thing passed off satisfactorily, and I cannot be thankful enough for God's great goodness. Indeed that we have actually entered and are worshipping and preaching the gospel in our beautiful chapel, after so many fears on my part, and so many actual obstacles and dangers, seems too good to be true."

DR. TAYLOR AND HIS RETURN.

Brother Taylor has been enfeebled by something like sun-stroke. His mission, however, absorbs his mind and heart. The Hon. Charles Thurber, of New York, who has visited Italy more than once, says with regard to our missionary:

"He is self-sacrificing, even to a fault, and indefatigable in his labors for his missions, both in sickness and health. A gentleman who has worked with him a good deal, and who has been to his house habitually, has often told me that in his sick bed he has always found him and his mission together and in conference. I have seen him myself on his way to his work so ill, that I used to think if the Master had been with him, he would have said, 'Sleep on now and take your rest,' 'the spirit indeed is willing, but the flesh is weak;' but he would not deign to plead this as an apology for not working. Almost every evening in the week demanded his presence at his mission, and sometimes every evening."

He also wrote:

"Dr. Taylor has a number of out-stations in Italy, which he visits periodically, and is almost daily receiving reports from some of them. Those who have charge of the stations, however honest and earnest, are yet so inexperienced that they need counsel and assistance given inconveniently often; but they receive it unmurmuringly on the part of Dr. Taylor."

Rev. Dr. Hague, who, agreeably to an action of the American Baptist Missionary Union, at its anniversary in Cleveland, consented to collect funds for the chapel at the North, having accepted a pastorate, the Board fearing that serious embarrassment might ensue from the obligations for the chapel as well as for the improvements having to be met by the Board,—especially as the contributions for the chapel, at the South, were lessening so greatly the contributions for the general work,—directed Brother Taylor to return to this country to collect principally at the North, so soon as he could do so without detriment to his mission. Shortly after his arrival, on the 24th of March, he began his labors among our Northern brethren, in behalf of his chapel. With regard to his return, the Convention, at which Dr. Taylor was present and made two admirable addresses on his work, "cordially endorsed and approved the action of the Board."

Rev. D. E. Butler reported on the Italian Mission: "In some points of view, this field is the most important now opened to us, * * * and the Convention should congratulate itself, and thank God for the good work so soon accomplished by the Foreign Mission Board in Italy, and in the city of Rome especially.

"The narration of facts made by Brother George B. Taylor at this session of the Convention is evidence on which to build a lively hope of larger and more abundant success by the proclamation of the gospel for the salvation of that people.

"The house of worship lately bought, put in order, and now the property of this Convention, is a home for our missionaries, and 'a dwelling-place for our God.' May it be, that from it unceasing prayer, inspired by the Holy Spirit, shall always go up to the Throne of Grace, and be daily answered in blessings and mercies from 'our Father in heaven.'"

Mr. Taylor attended the Northern Anniversaries at Saratoga as one of the messengers of the Southern Baptist Convention. He was also present at the "June Meeting" of the General Association of Virginia. At both assemblages he made a fine impression. At the latter meeting he was taken seriously ill. Dr. J. Staige Davis, of the University of Virginia, wrote: "I have never seen so little vitality in a man doing the work that Dr. Taylor is performing. I know his deep interest in his mission. But, if he goes to the North, as he proposes, to collect funds, it may be at the expense of his life. He needs perfect rest." On reading this letter the Board directed our brother to desist at once from his work, and gave him a "leave of absence" from his field until January, 1880. During the summer he rested in the mountains of his native State, accompanied by his accomplished and devoted wife.

Early in the fall he resumed his collections at the North, but was soon recalled by a severe domestic affliction. Many prayers ascend for his perfect restoration to health. At this writing, December, 1879, though still feeble, he is again pleading among our Northern brethren for his chapel. In the meantime Signor Cocorda has charge of the work in Rome, and the provincial churches when last heard from, are "doing well."

TOO MUCH.

"We see," says the *Missionary Review* of July–August, 1879, "that the Rev. Dr. G. B. Taylor, the indefatigable missionary of the Southern Baptist Convention, reached New York, March 24th, called home from Italy to collect funds for the chapel and work in Rome. Is it not putting double duty on a man to make him responsible for the work abroad, and at the same time constrain him to come home to gather his own forage? Our Southern Baptist brethren are expending a very large proportion of their strength, given to foreign missions, on Rome and Italy—more than $27,000 for the chapel at Rome. Is not Italy getting more than her due proportion from this branch of the church? We

EUROPEAN MISSION. 63

raise the question without presuming to decide it, for a recent tour from Naples through Rome and the chief cities of the kingdom gave us very vivid as well as deep and abiding impressions of the wonderful facilities and possibilities of wisely planned and executed evangelistic work in that sunny and most beautiful land, unsurpassed in art-treasures and historic memories. God grant her interesting people may soon share the full blessings of the Protestant faith."

EVANGELISM IN ITALY AND EUROPE.

"The eighth report of this evangelistic work in Italy gives brief details of deepest interest in some dozen of the chief cities, and in his preface Dr. McDougall well says:

'It affords abundant proof that the death struggle between Popery and the gospel continues as earnest as ever all over the Italian mission-field. * * * The evangelicals are still subjected to the liveliest persecution in their places of worship, in their worldly callings, in the bosom of their families, on their death-beds at home or in the hospital, and even at the cemetery, except where the popular feeling is sufficiently enlightened or the gospel cause sufficiently strong to prevent such occurrences.'

"Dr. McDougall gives the statistics of the general work of the Free Italian Church as follows, viz:

```
Ordained ministers . . . . . . . . . . . . . . . . 12
Evangelists . . . . . . . . . . . . . . . . . . . 13
Elders . . . . . . . . . . . . . . . . . . . . . 37
Deacons . . . . . . . . . . . . . . . . . . . . 65
Deaconesses . . . . . . . . . . . . . . . . . . 14
Communicants . . . . . . . . . . . . . . . . 1,635
Catechumens . . . . . . . . . . . . . . . . . 183
Regular hearers . . . . . . . . . . . . . . . 1,465
Occasional hearers (additional) . . . . . . . . 1,694
Churches, large and small . . . . . . . . . . . . 33
Out-stations . . . . . . . . . . . . . . . . . . 30
Contributions for all objects . . . . . . . . . $1,747
```

There are in Europe, exclusive of Denmark, Switzerland, Portugal, Greece, and Turkey, 64,752,000 Evangelical Christians; 136,466,000 Roman Catholics; and 63,478,000 Greek Christians. In all, about 264,000,000 Christians."

A YOUNG MAN FOR ITALY.

RICHMOND, VA., *November 20th*, 1879.

MY DEAR BROTHER:—At the Convention of 1877, our Board reported that Dr. G. B. Taylor urges that "a young man" be sent to Italy. He writes: "One who begins young enough finds no difficulty as to the language, and for zeal and earnestness, the Anglo Saxon excels the Latin nations. The right sort of a man can be of great help, and would be prepared, if the necessity arose, to take my place."

On the 17th of November, 1879, the Board adopted the following:

Resolved, That the Board are not unmindful of the request of our Brother Taylor that a young man be sent to aid him in his field; and, that, the Board will make it a subject of prayer that the proper man may be found, and that the Board may be furnished with the means to send him to Italy.

Knowing your missionary spirit and peculiar qualifications, as to scholarship and discipline, I invite your attention to this field of labor, which is well-fitted to kindle your enthusiasm, and to test the heroism of your nature, while it inspires strong hope of ultimate and triumphant success.

Carlyle says that we live in an unheroic and un-religious age; that, overlooking the dynamic forces of man's moral and spiritual nature, we give ourselves to materialism and machinery. But there seems to be something which calls forth the deep and holy sentiments of our being, and which savors somewhat of the heroic, in this enterprise of Baptists who have been battered through the ages by the Roman Catholic Church, to set themselves up in Rome—in Papal Rome—more venerable in antiquity; more unified in government; more fruitful in resources; more far-reaching in rule; more beloved by subjects; more sensitive about encroachments; more determined for universal empire than was ever the Rome of the Cæsars; and scarcely less essentially and irreconcilably opposed to the polity and the principles of our churches, than ancient Rome was to the religion of Barbarian, Jew, or Christian; and not less disposed to visit extreme retribution on all who question her authority, disregard her behests, or antagonize her progress.

If Rome shows no uneasiness, it is because she disdains the power she does not understand. When Scipio and Hannibal met before the walls of Carthage, they gazed on each other in mute admiration; but George B. Taylor, confronting Leo XIII. would be as Paul before Festus, or the shepherd boy of Israel before the hero of Philistia! But Baptists have a mission which burns in their bones; and the day may come when anathemas shall be hurled against them as hotly as those which fell upon Luther and Melancthon, Zwingle and Calvin. Let our people prepare for the worst, and may you covet to follow the example of that grand champion of the faith who said: "I am ready to preach the gospel to you that are at Rome also," and whom I present as your encouragement and inspiration.

Paul was possessed of the two grand ideas that the gospel was "the power of God unto salvation," and that he was a debtor to the world. Not satisfied with preaching in Palestine, and Asia Minor, and Eastern Europe, he, like Luther, who would go to Worms though opposed by as many devils as there were tiles on the house-tops, resolved to go to "Rome also," although there the Jew and the Christian were regarded the same and were utterly detested as "the enemies of mankind;" although corruption festered the vitals of society and government, and overspread their surface as the pustules of the small pox; although the gods of the Pantheon were embalmed in classic song and eloquence, and were sustained by the sayings of sages, the statutes of statesmen, and the swords of soldiers, who, knowing the lie of their mythology, preferred, for the good of the State, any faith to infidelity; Paul would go to Rome, although there reigned there a man, of whom, when he was born, his father said, "How can he be otherwise than a monster?" and who verified the paternal prediction by the murder of his own wife and mother, and by the illumination of his garden with the blazing bodies of the disciples of Jesus, accused of the conflagration of the city, to which the monster himself had applied the brand; although he knew of the horrid dungeon of the Mamertine Prison, where the wretched Jugurtha was hurled and starved, and where the apostle himself was probably made to exclaim with new emphasis: " Oh, wretched man that I am, who shall deliver me from the body of this death?"

And executed was his high resolve, though it must be as a prisoner appealing from the procurator to the Emperor, and through the disasters of the fierce Euroclydon. His grand doctrine rang through the " Eternal City," captivated even members of the household of Cæsar, sounded forth in every direction, from this center of the civilized world, and soon resounded from the Baltic to the Sahara, from the pillars of Hercules to the Indus. Gibbon, whose ill-disguised hatred of our religion never loses an opportunity to give by his brilliant pen an infamous immortality to current slanders against the early Christians, admits that this doctrine of the Cross, preached so heroically by Paul, was an important factor in the disintegration of the Roman Empire. Though immolated on the altar of his spiritual heroism, Paul's grand achievements warranted a broader significance to his doxology with regard to the Christianized Romans: "I thank my God through Christ Jesus that your faith is spoken of throughout the world."

A modern critic says, that it is a sign of weakness, in an individual or a nation, to be given to vaticination. The friends of Rome prophesy greatly. De Tocqueville said, that America must sooner or later lie at the feet of Rome; because militia must sooner or later give way before regulars. Dr. Ewer predicted, that undisciplined Protestantism, coming in contact with well indoctrinated Catholicity, would share the fate of a glass-ball colliding with a boulder. The Poet-priest of the South said in the presence of your correspondent: " That broken phalanx standing before the body of Christ, one—indivisible, irresistible, blood-sprinkled, and God-inspired—must flee as chaff before the tornado!" But God also predicts, and predicts by his servant Daniel of something else being " broken to pieces, and becoming like the chaff of the summer threshing floors:" * * "even of that horn that had eyes, and a mouth, that spake very great things * * and made war with the saints, and prevailed against them; until the Ancient of days came, and judgment was given to the saints of the Most High; and, the time came that the saints possessed the kingdom."

And the signs of the time, do they not shed a gleam of light on the divine prediction? Ten years ago, the name of Baptist was scarcely known in Italy. Now, we have, in the very heart of Rome, a thirty thousand dollar chapel, and our little stations, with other evangelical churches, are scattered, like seeds of fire, on every hand, giving promise that, at some, perhaps not distant day, the glorious gospel of the ever blessed God, shall shine over that land of classic song and of spiritual darkness, from the Alps to the Gulf of Taranto from the Adriatic to the Mediterranean Seas.

And, how splendid the prospect, when the genius and learning, and art and science, and wealth and diplomacy, and missionary zeal of the catholic world, shall be subordinated, with the powers of the evangelical churches, to realize the grand commission of our Lord: Go and disciple the nations!

Should you, my young friend, go to Rome—and God grant that you may be led there as a missionary of the cross—you will see in the Vatican "The Transfiguration," by Raphael. On entering the apartment of this master-piece of art, you will be struck by the prominence given to the lunatic boy, at the foot of the mount. The idea of the great artist seems to have been that, the main feature of that event was not the lustrous body of the Son of man, nor the appearance of Moses and Elias as suggestive that the Christ was the end of the law and the prophets; but, that it was the amazing goodness of this being, in coming down from this splendid exhibition of his Godship to care for, and to heal a poor lunatic child. Thus would he teach his disciples in all ages, that the glory of their religion is not in their being the recipients of the divine grace, but in their being the dispensers of it—even to the demented and demoniac peoples of the earth. He expects his people to illustrate by their missionary spirit and conduct that " God so loved THE WORLD, that he gave his only begotten Son, that *whosoever* believeth in him should not perish, but have everlasting life."

Hoping that, if you have not a *distinct call to stay in this country,* you may ponder well whether you may not be the young man, whom Dr. Taylor needs in Italy.

I am yours very truly.   T.

CHINA MISSION.

BEFORE sketching our missions in China, which we propose to do in biographical outlines of our missionaries, some information of a general character may be important for our younger readers. The more we think of China, the more we appreciate the recent remark of one of our missionaries: "China only needs the gospel to be the greatest country in the world." We follow closely, and often literally, the authorities to which we have referred; and before going to press, the work was sent to China, and revised by our missionaries there.

GEOGRAPHICAL POSITION AND ARRANGEMENT.

China is that vast Empire of Asia, bounded on the north and west by the Russian Empire, on the south by the Indies, and on the east by the Pacific Ocean; and lying between lat. 20° N. and 56° 10′ N., and long. 73° 55′ E., and 144° 50′ E. Its greatest length is 3,350 miles; its greatest breadth 2,100 miles. Its area is 5,300,000 square miles.

The Empire is divided into three great parts:

First, THE EIGHTEEN PROVINCES; or China proper.

Second, MANCHURIA; or the native country of the Manchus.

Third, COLONIAL POSSESSIONS; including Mongolia, Kokonor, and Thibet.

China proper has an area of about 2,000,000 square miles, and is one-half as large as Europe. It has been described as "a broad expanse of densely populated country, forming nearly a square; two sides of which are bounded by the sea, and two by the land."

TOPOGRAPHICAL FEATURES.

Four ranges of mountains wall in the Empire on three sides. There are several lakes, but none of great importance. On the coast are the large islands of Hainan and Formosa,—the latter noted for the first settlement there of the Dutch, who were expelled about 200 years ago; and as the occasion of the recent troubles between China and Japan. The two great rivers, the Hoang Ho, or Yellow, and the Yang-tse-kiang, are only second to the Amazon and the Mississippi. Originally the Yellow River disembogued in the Pe-chi-li Gulf, to the north of Shantung Province, where we have several mission stations. Subsequently it emptied itself south of that Province, in lat. 34°. It has now returned to its old channel.

THE PEOPLE, LANGUAGE, AND RELIGIONS.

The Chinese are a mild, peaceable, industrious, and extremely conservative race; dark-skinned, black-haired, and narrow-eyed. They number about 400,000,000. Their civilization is much in advance of what our ancestors attained before they received the gospel; and is wonderful, in view of their exclusion from the rest of the world.

Their language is composed of characters variously estimated from 10,000 by the best scholars, to 40,000 in the "Imperial Dictionary." Two hundred and fourteen are called radicals, and one or more of these enter into the composition of each character of the language. The written language is understood by all the people of China, Japan, Cochin China, Loo-choo, and Corea, who can read. The dialects are peculiar to their respective provinces. Once the language was thought unattainable by the foreigner; but missionaries and merchants not only speak it, but *think* in it.

There are indications of an ancient religion of sacrifice to a (Shang-ti). "supreme ruler." *Tauism*, which is a species of materialism, has taken the place of the worship of "the heavens." *Confucianism* is the veneration and worship of Confucius, a political philosopher, who flourished about 580 years before Christ. He eschewed spiritual and future things, saying: "If we know not life, how can we know death?" but his works are full of moral maxims, among which is found in a negative form *the golden rule of the gospel.* These works are the Holy Scriptures of the Chinese; and Confucianism may be called the *State* Religion.

Buddhism is a stupid system of idolatry, imported from India, A. D. 65, by messengers sent from China—on the prediction of Confucius, that a great Teacher would come from the West—to inquire after the new religion, which was agitating the western world. The masses profess Buddhism, but the *real religion of the people is the worship of ancestors.*

INVENTIONS AND WORKS OF ART.

Printing, gunpowder, and the mariner's compass are said to have been invented by the Chinese centuries before they were known in Europe. They excel in works of nice manufacture, which, in our World's Expositions, stand unsurpassed, if not unrivalled. Their grand works of art are the Chinese Wall and the Great Canal. The former, which was built about 200 years before Christ, is twenty feet high, forty-five feet thick at the base, with towers from 37 to 48 feet in height. It spans rivers on arches, runs over mountains 5,000 feet above the level of the sea, is 1,200 miles long, employed 300,000 builders, and was an effective barrier, when built, to Tartar incursions from the north. The Grand Canal affords facilities for travel and commerce between Peking and Canton, and, intersecting the chief lakes and rivers, opens the line of intercourse with the principal cities of the provinces. It was accurately described by a Mongol historian as early as A. D. 1307. It is 600 miles long, and the longest canal in the world.

EXPORTS AND IMPORTS.

The main exports of China are silks, porcelain, and their great staple tea. The whole revenue from this last article is consumed by *their import of opium.* Vainly has the government striven against this destroyer of its people—first, by the refusal of import, on the ground that *Chinese ethics could not license what was morally wrong;* next, by the imposition of excessive customs; and, lastly, by a bloody contest with British arms.

ANTIQUITY AND DYNASTIES.

This Empire is the most ancient of the world, and was contemporaneous with the Egyptian and the Babylonian. Their *fabulous* period of history runs back into the ages previous to those empires, and bears some resemblances to biblical history. We fall in with such suggestive expressions as "dressed in leaves," the "inventors of music and husbandry," the "oldest man," nine hundred years old, the "great flood," the giant *Yu*, "nine cubits" in stature, who, assailed by his adversaries, destroyed himself. This tragedy is the subject of one of the Chinese classics, handed down by Confucius. Their *authentic history* begins with the *Chow* period, which extended to 240 B. C. This period was distinguished for the birth of Confucius, and the appearance of Laoukeun, who deified *Tou*, the god of Reason, and of Fo, or Buddh, in India. The next Dynasty was the *Tsia*, during which "the Great Wall" was built, and the works of the Chinese sages, Confucius' among them, were burnt, by an edict issued B. C. 213. Our space would not suffice even to touch the salient points of the dynasty of *Han*, from B. C. 201, to 95 B. C., when "China lost her honor" by giving her daughters in marriage to conciliate Tartar chiefs, and sent her envoys as far west as Arabia: of the *Sankwo* period, celebrated in Chinese romances and plays—one of which has been compared with the Iliad: of the dynasty of *Chin*—whence *China*—when "Queens were forbidden to reign:" and of the five dynasties from A. D. 416 to A. D. 622, when the country "was filled with crimes and contests," was divided into two kingdoms, with respective capitals at Nanking and Honan, and was ultimately united, with its capital at the latter place. During the *Tang* dynasty, from A. D. 622 to A. D. 897, "foreigners arrived with fair hair and blue eyes"—doubtless the Nestorian Christians—a monument of whom, dated 640, was discovered at Syganfoo, in Shen Si, 1625. The reign known as "The latter five successions" resembled the *feudal* system; and the Emperor of China is still regarded as the ultimate owner of all lands, from which he receives a tax of ten per cent. In the *Soong* dynasty, which started A. D. 950, the art of printing was invented, and the age of Chinese liter-

CHINA MISSION. 73

ature began; and the Tartars took possession of China under Kublai-Khan, who fixed the seat of government at Peking, and built the Grand Canal. The Tartars were driven out by the Mongols, who had conquered India, and who subdued both the Tartars and the enervated Chinese, whom they were invited to aid. "The blood of the people flowed in sounding torrents" before the Mongols, and the remainder of the Chinese Court "betook themselves to the sea, near Canton, and perished A. D. 1281." In A. D. 1366 a *Chinese* dynasty was founded, styled *Ming*. In 1405, Timour or Tamerlane died on his way to the conquest of China. In this dynasty, the Portuguese, about the middle of the sixteenth century, obtained their anomalous footing at Macao, and the Jesuits insinuated themselves into the country. The Mongols, who had been driven among the Tartars, intermarried with them. Whence the Manchow Princes, and the descent of the present reigning family from Kublai-Khan. These Princes overthrew the Ming dynasty, and the last of the Chinese Emperors fell by his own hand A. D. 1643. Thus began the *Manchow Tartar dynasty*, A. D. 1644, the ninth Emperor of which is now on the throne. In token of subjection to this dynasty, the Chinese were forced, on pain of death, to shave the head and adopt the Tartar costume, which has become the fixed *fashion* of the nation. Several of the Manchow Tartar Emperors were liberal and even great men. One of them expelled from Peking the Jesuit astronomers, who had been cherished for two centuries. The late Emperor, though a mere boy, perished the victim of monstrous debauchery, and was only worthy of the infamous distinction of some of his brutish predecessors. The present Emperor is the first of the Tartar Emperors that has appointed a Chinaman among the four members of his Cabinet.

GOVERNMENT.

With these changes of dynasties, the genius of the government has been unchanged. This passed early and naturally from the patriarchal to the purely despotic—though the name of the *parental* has been jealously maintained. The government owes its stability to the doctrines of its sacred books, the peculiar laws of the land, and the foundation which it has in the deepest instincts of our nature. Confucius teaches that the father of the family is the type for the ruler of the province and for the monarch of the kingdom. Other sacred writers show that the duties of the younger to the elder, of the citizen to the State, of the soldier to his officers, and of the subject to the Great Emperor are of the nature of filial duties. This parental idea of government is enforced by the Emperor himself doing homage to his mother, seated on a throne; by severe punishment for evil conduct of children to their parents, and for the neglect of the tombs and the worship of ancestors; and by the penalties for State crimes being made analogous to those for domestic offences. The approval by the people of the government is evinced by their contented and laborious lives, and by their undying devotion to their country. It is said that "the Emperor worships heaven, and the people worship the Emperor."

The Emperor has an "Interior Council" of two Tartars and two Chinese. There are six boards for government business: 1. A board of official appointments. 2. A board of revenue. 3. A board of rites and ceremonies. 4. The military board. 5. The supreme court of criminal jurisdiction. 6. The board of public works.

A province is ruled by a governor, and two or more provinces by a governor-general. There are 14,000 officers of the Empire, whose names are recorded in the "Red Book," and who are changed every third year. None can be an officer in his own province, or be officially connected with his father or brother. Education is commonly encouraged, because parents are held responsible for the conduct of their children; and because education is the test of official eligibility, which is decided by yearly examinations, at the "department cities" of the provinces. The standing army is 80,000; but the militia swells the nominal military force to 700,000.

The conduct of the people and their rulers to foreigners is no criterion of the home government. Mandarins and Hong-merchants regard strangers as legitimate prey. A fundamental maxim of Chinese government is thus rendered: "*The barbarians are like beasts, and not to be ruled on the same principles as citizens.* * * *The ancient kings well understood this, and accordingly ruled barbarians by misrule. Therefore to rule barbarians by misrule is the true and best way of ruling them.*"

CHINESE EXCLUSIVENESS.

The Chinese have no love for strangers. As early as A.D. 161, Marcus Aurelius, attracted by their rich silks, attempted unsuccessfully to establish commercial relations with them. Their present extreme exclusiveness, however, is not due, as is supposed, to their ignorance of the advantages of commerce. Before the seventh century, ambassages were sent to neighboring countries to propose intercourse. In the thirteenth century, Chinese junks traded as far as Calicut, on the west coast of Malabar. Jews settled in the country two hundred years before the Christian era, and the Mohammedan creed was established and protected, after the Mongol conquest in the thirteenth century. As has been seen, the Nestorians were received in the seventh century, and the English traded at Ningpo before the Tartar conquest.

The fact is, that the avarice of the Portuguese, and the equal greed of the Dutch, together with the constant hostilities between both of them and the English, as well as the misconduct of the Jesuits, who were disturbers of the peace for two centuries, have made the present Tartar government extremely suspicious of our race, and have settled the policy of exclusion, so far as possible, for the quiet and safety of their government. This policy is strengthened by their constant fear of insurgent Chinese—"*the Long Hairs*"—who, in their last attempt on the government, in connection with which our Rev. Issachar J. Roberts somewhat figured, seemed to adopt the Christian religion. British cannon may open the ports of China; but the superior conduct and character of our missionaries and merchants is a better hope of opening the hearts of this interesting and ancient people of Sinim to the religion of the Prince of Peace and the God of Righteousness.

WAR WITH ENGLAND.

A long series of troubles—arising from the attempts of England to establish trade with China, which were more easily frustrated by the intrigues of the Portuguese at Macao; from the monstrous extortions of the officers of trade; from the prohibition, and taxation, and smuggling of opium; from the strangling of smugglers and the imprisonment of the English within their factory quarters; from the broils and homicides between the marines and the natives; and from the $3,000,000 due to English merchants—was, at last, brought to a head by the overthrow in Parliament of the "East India Company" in 1834, who had the monopoly of the trade at Canton; and the attempt of the British government to establish there a "commercial commission," at the head of which was Lord Napier. After considerable skirmishing, war was formally declared, on the authority of the Crown, by the British government of India, and was successfully waged through the years 1840, 1841, and 1842. Besides the ransom price of Canton, which was $6,000,000; and that of Shanghai which was $300,000, by the treaty of Nanking, China agreed to pay before the end of 1845 $21,000,000; to cede Hong Kong to the Queen, and to open to British commerce the five ports of Canton, Amoy, Fuh Chow, Ningpo, and Shanghai. July, 1st, 1843, President Taylor, of the United States, addressed a letter to the Emperor by Hon. Caleb Cushing; and July 3d, 1844, was signed the treaty of Wanghia, by which the same privileges were granted to us as to "the most favored nations," and a qualified consent was given to the introduction of Christianity. Mr. Cushing was succeeded by Mr. Alexander Everett, who sailed from this country with our first missionaries, Messrs. Clopton and Pearcy, June 22d, 1846; and who, in a parting address made on shipboard, "gave the gratifying assurance, that whatever aid he could render to the missionaries, at any time, in his official capacity, it should be cheerfully granted." Of this gentleman, Dr. Dean, of China, remarked: "As a statesman and a scholar, he was not inferior to his brother, the Hon. Edward Everett, which is saying enough in the praise of any man."

CHINA AS A MISSIONARY FIELD.

The peculiar homogeneity of the people seems a barrier to the gospel; but when the leaven begins to work, the whole mass will move together. A common written language opens the mind of these immense multitudes to the Bible; and the grand doctrines thereof once impregnating their literature, one-third of the human family may be born to the Lord in a day. That this exclusive empire should be thrown open to

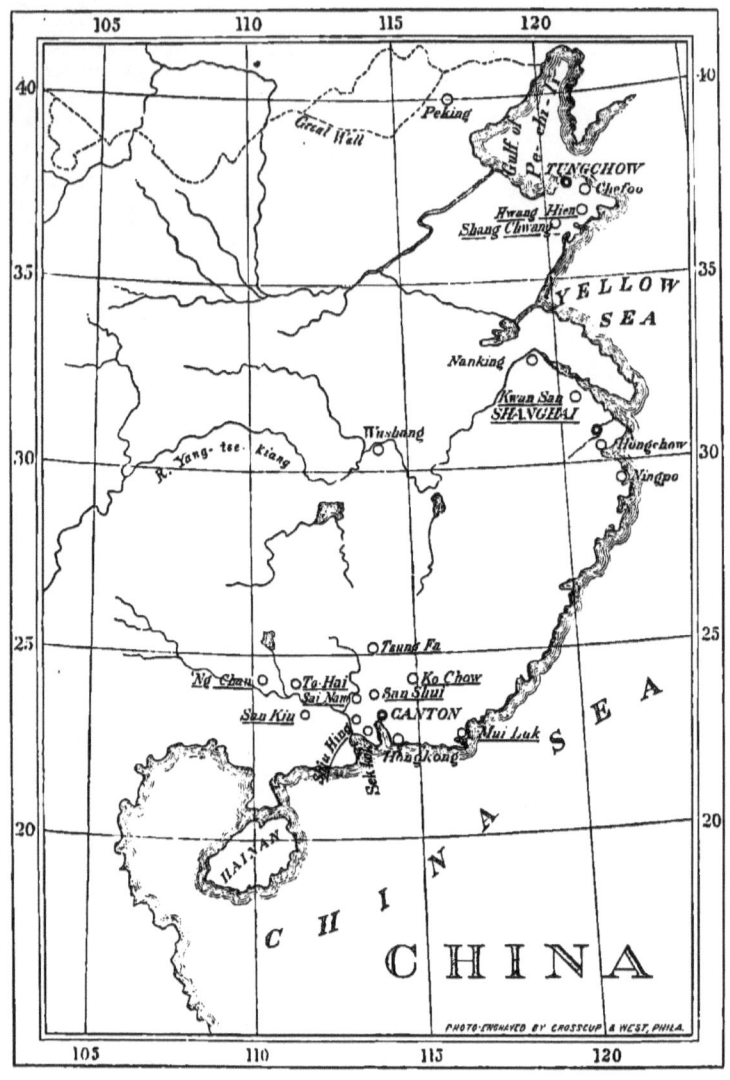

the world, in this missionary epoch of the church, is very significant as to the divine providence; and no less significant are the facts of *our* country extending to the Pacific, and the crowds of Chinese who flock to our shores. He who does not see God in the missionary work of China, has no eyes to see; and he who has no hope of this people being regenerated by the cross held up among them, does not believe the grand words of our Lord: "And I, if I be lifted up from the earth, will draw all men unto me."

PROTESTANT MISSIONS.

Rev. Robert Morrison, under the patronage of the "London Missionary Society," inaugurated Protestant missions in China by locating at Canton in 1807. He was joined in 1819 by Rev. William Milne. In 1815, two converts were baptized by Dr. Morrison. His translation of the Scriptures, completed in 1819, and his Dictionary and Grammar of the Chinese language, have been of incalculable value to subsequent missionaries, translators, and scholars. In 1830, a mission was established in Canton by the "American Board of Commissioners for Foreign Missions." And in 1835, Mr. and Mrs. J. Lewis Shuck sailed for China under the auspices of the "General Convention of Baptists of the United States."

CANTON MISSION.

CITY OF CANTON.

This is the provincial capital of the province of Kwang Tung, of which name Canton, or *Kamton*, is the Portuguese corruption. The province has the area of Great Britain, and along its great coast are scattered many islands. The city is on the Pearl River, which is formed by the union of the West, North, and East Rivers; the first two being above Canton, and the last below the city. The country drained by these rivers cannot be less than 150,000 square miles. The estuary, into which these united streams fall, might be called a gulf, but for the many islands which occupy its waters. The chief embouchure of the river is known as the Bay of Lintin—so called from the islands of that name, where the opium and other storeships formerly anchored. The inlet is the finest in the world, and forms a triangle, whose sides are about 100 miles in length.

Canton is located at the foot of the White Cloud Mountains, about seventy miles north of Macao, and ninety miles northwest of Hong Kong, in lat. 23° 14′ 10″ N., and. long. 113° 14′ 30″ E., nearly on the same parallel with Havana and Calcutta. The circuit of the city and suburbs is about ten miles, nearly six miles of which are inclosed by a wall. The population is estimated at one million and a half. It is regarded as the fourth city in the Empire for numbers, and the next to Peking in wealth. The earliest notices of the city date back to 2,000 years before Christ; but it became a regular market and port for customs A. D. 700.

The city is not so dirty as many Chinese cities, and may be said, upon the whole, to be well governed. The streets are narrow, and number about six hundred. The houses on the river are occasionally built on piles, and many parts of the city are subject to inundation "The general appearance from the hills on the north is monotonous and uninviting, being a dull expanse of black roofs, relieved by a few trees, and here and there a pole-staff, and two pagodas, which shoot up above the watch-towers on the walls."

Among the Chief Temples are the "Temple of 500 Gods," where there are 500 images of the early disciples of Buddha, and the "Five Genii Temple," where are an immense bell and five enormous stones said to be the bodies of the five rams, from which Canton takes its designation of the "City of Rams." The *Ching-hwang-miau* is one of the most important religious institutions in every Chinese city. It is a sort of palladium, in which the protecting deity of the city and the province is supposed to reside, and in which both people and rulers offer their devotions.

The area in front of the temple is filled with hucksters, beggars, and idlers, "occasionally cleared away for a theatrical performance, gotten up by the priests." The principal hall for the idol is lighted up, and enlivened by drums, bells, and other attractions.

The inner apartments are occupied by miserable creatures, almost as senseless as the idols whose altars they serve, and drawing out a vicious and misanthropic existence.

The Governor-General, and the chief officers of the province, reside in Canton. In the city are 50,000 weavers, 7,000 barbers, and 4,200 shoemakers.

For many years, Canton was the only place for traffic with foreigners. There were the principal extortions, and disturbances, and eventful scenes in the history of European intercourse with the Chinese, for several centuries. In 1802, the American flag was first unfurled in Canton. In 1822, a frightful conflagration left 50,000 Cantonese houseless. In 1838, $3,000,000 were due the English by the Hong merchants; which, as has been seen, was one cause of the war with England. There was established the first mission station of the Southern Baptist Convention; and there has been the seat of the missionary labors, in whole or part, of our Shuck, Roberts, Clopton, Pearcy, Johnson, Whilden, Gaillard, Graves, Schilling, Simmons, Williams; and of our noble missionary women, who have toiled or are toiling in Southern China for the salvation of "the middle kingdom."

Rev. JEHU LEWIS SHUCK.

Mr. Shuck was the first American Baptist missionary in China. Under the patronage of the Boston Board, he sailed in the ship Louvre, 22d September, 1835, with his wife, and a number of other missionaries. Tarrying at several points, Mr. and Mrs. Shuck arrived at Macao just one year after their departure from America. In 1842, the missionaries moved, for better protection, to Hong Kong, as that island, by the fortunes of war, had fallen into the hands of the British government. "There he was joint editor of the *Friend of China;* built two chapels; formed a school; and preached stately on Lord's Days, in Chinese and English." In 1844, the mission was signalized by a great outpouring of the Holy Spirit. On the 27th of November of that year, the lovely and beloved Mrs. Shuck fell asleep in Jesus. Her biography, by Rev. Dr. Jeter, should be read by every lover of true beauty of character, and of the cause of Christ among the nations. In the beginning of 1844, Mr. Issachar J. Roberts, who arrived in Macao shortly after the arrival of Mr. Shuck, located at Canton. The " five ports " being open, the missionaries of Hong Kong followed, with their converts, to that city. Mr. Shuck organized what was known as "The First Baptist Church of Canton." Impressed with the importance of erecting a house of worship, and desiring to commit his five motherless children to his wife's relatives, he sailed, October 21st, 1845, for the United States, where he arrived February 17, 1846. He was accompanied by his native preacher, Yong Seen Sang. Mr. Shuck was soon engaged as a missionary to Canton by our Board. With Yong Seen Sang, he attended the first anniversary of the Southern Baptist Convention, which met that year in Richmond. They made a fine impression. " Yong " (Seen Sang corresponds to our Mr.) replied to an address of the President of the Convention "with an easy grace and dignity of manner which would have done credit to the most accomplished gentleman." He had one request to make: "*that all the disciples, in their prayers, morning and evening, would remember China.*"

Mr. Shuck and Yong canvassed the South to collect funds for the Canton Chapel. In an appeal, which was published and signed by Mr. Shuck and three native assistants, appears the following : "No religion is respectable in the eyes of the Chinese, unless connected with a public building. In Canton there are one hundred and eighty heathen temples, besides pagodas and ancestral halls." Mr. Shuck received cordial welcomes. Everywhere he met large and interested congregations ready to respond to his appeals. From Nashville he wrote: "At no place has more overwhelming interest been awakened than here, and the region round about. Some brethren have come seventy miles to meet us. * * * At Enon we met, it is said, 5,000 people." At Marion, Alabama, "a wealthy deacon of the Baptist Church offered to pay $3,000 to educate, at the Judson Institute, the daughter of Yong, who has small, compressed feet, is a pretty girl, fourteen years old, and is named *Ah Wun.*" During a protracted meeting at Lancaster, Va., Dr. J. B. Jeter urged the claims of Christ upon *Mecha*, a Chinese girl, who had come as nurse with Mr. Shuck's children. On the 4th December, 1846, she was led into the baptismal waters by Rev. Addison Hall, where, fifteen years before, Dr. Jeter had led Mecha's lamented mistress, Mr. Hall's daughter, who, while living, had offered many prayers for the girl's conversion. Mr. Shuck and Yong assisted, June 15, 1846, in the designation services of Messrs. Samuel C. Clopton and George Pearcy, our first appointed missionaries to Canton. When Messrs. Thomas W. Tobey and M. T. Yates were set apart for the Shanghai Mission, it was thought that the experience of Mr. Shuck would be valuable in starting the new station; and he was transferred to that mission. He married again this year. February 20, 1847, he issued a "Farewell to the Churches," whose earnest appeal should still ring in our ears:

"The cause is yours as well as mine; yea, it is the cause of our common Redeemer, the cause of God and of universal man. I appeal for your sympathies, your prayers, and your contributions: I appeal by the last command of our ascended Lord: I appeal by the eternal interests of China's four hundred millions: I appeal by the few feeble men and women who have given up all for Christ, and are laboring in China: I appeal by the scrutiny of the final judgment, and by all the horrors which await the heathen in that fearful world of eternal night."

Appropriate services were held in the Bowdoin Square Church, Boston, of which Rev. Dr. Robert W. Cushman was pastor. On Thursday, March 11th, 1847, Mr. and Mrs. Shuck, and his little daughter, five years old, with Yong, and Messrs. Tobey and Francis C. Johnson, sailed from that city in the ship Ashburton. They arrived at Hong Kong, June 25th. Mr. Shuck, anxious with regard to his little church in Canton, made them a visit. He found things "in a better state than he feared;" for which he exclaimed, "God be praised!"

The "chapel fund" having been collected by Mr. Shuck, it was regarded right that it should be transferred with the missionary. After due publication for the assent or dissent of donors, the amount, $5,000, was appropriated to a chapel in Shanghai.

The subsequent career of Mr. Shuck, as our missionary, will be traced in connection with the mission of that city, where he published ten Chinese tracts, and labored faithfully and effectively until after the death of his second wife, which occurred in November, 1851. This affliction brought him home again, with his bereaved children. He longed to be within "hailing distance" of these tender little ones; and, at his request, his connection with our Board was dissolved July 4th, 1853. Under the auspices of the "Domestic Board" he labored in California among the Chinese. His knowledge of the Chinese language must have been accurate and extensive, as when "a committee of delegates for translating the Old Testament into Chinese was appointed in the summer of 1850, Mr. Shuck was chosen as one of those for Shanghai."

John Lewis Shuck was born at Alexandria, Va., Sept. 4th, 1812, and was educated chiefly at the Virginia Baptist Seminary, now Richmond College.

Shortly after his conversion, the following incident relating to himself occurred, and is copied from an old newspaper:

"A missionary meeting was held, and a contribution was called for. The boxes were returned and the contents counted over; bank notes, silver, and even gold. 'There is a card—who put it in?' 'A young man back in the congregation.' 'What is written on it?' 'MYSELF.'

"This was the young man's offering—*himself*. He could not give silver or gold to the mission cause, so he gave *himself*."

He was set apart as a missionary to China on the 10th of September, 1835, in the First Baptist Church of Richmond, Va.

He was married first to Henrietta Hall, daughter of Rev. Addison Hall, of Lancaster, Va., Sept. 8th, 1835, by Rev. Henry Keeling. He was married the second time in October, 1846, by Rev. M. P. Jewett, to Lizzie Sexton, of Alabama. He was married again, June 5th, 1854, in Charleston, S. C., by Dr. J. R. Kendrick, to Anna L. Trotti, who accompanied him to California. Mrs. Shuck is living with his son, Rev. L. H. Shuck, D.D., who is the pastor of the First Baptist Church in Charleston, S. C.

Mr. Shuck went to California in May, 1854. Baptized while there sixteen Chinese. The first convert was *Wong Mui*, who died recently in Canton, after years of successful service as a native preacher; and, at whose grave the First Baptist Church of Charleston has ordered a monument to be erected.

Mr. Shuck built a chapel in Sacramento; held services regularly in the Chinese language; organized a church of sixteen members; edited a Baptist newspaper; and remained there, under the Domestic Mission Board, for seven years. He returned from California in 1861 and located at Barnwell Court-house, S. C., where he died Aug. 20th, 1863. He was pastor of the churches at Blackville and Steel Creek.

Not long before his death, he said to a friend at his bedside: "Preaching the gospel has been the joy of my life." Asking for the hymn, "Just as I am," he joined in singing it to the close. He then fell into a sleep, from which he awoke with his Saviour, whom he had loved and closely followed.

Rev. ISSACHAR JACOX ROBERTS.

Mr. Roberts was born in Sumner County, Tenn., on February 17th, 1802. On March 19th, 1821, he was converted at Shelbyville, Tenn., and was baptized May 13th, 1821, by Rev. Wm. Martin. He studied in Tennessee and Kentucky, and also in South Carolina. He joined the Baptist Church in Bedford County, Mass. in 1821, was assisted in his education by the South Carolina Baptist Convention in 1827, and was ordained at Edgefield, S. C., April 22d, 1828. His first wife was Barsha Blanchard, whom he married near Augusta, Ga., January 4th, 1830. The ceremony was performed by Rev. Jabez P. Marshall, grandson of Daniel Marshall, of Virginia. She died the following year. Mr. Roberts preached in Mississippi, where he owned property said to be worth $30,000. This property, donated by him, formed the base of the "Roberts Fund Society," under whose auspices he went as a missionary to China in October, 1836. The donation proved of but little value, and Mr. Roberts connected himself with the Foreign Mission Board of the Triennial Convention.

The first six or seven years of his missionary life were spent at Macao, where he had a congregation of Lepers; and at Hong Kong, in company with Rev. J. Lewis Shuck. In May, 1844, he started a mission in Canton. He was the first *American* Baptist missionary, if not the first *Baptist* missionary in the city. Shortly after his arrival he gathered a little church, the *Uet-tung*, of six or seven members; two or three of whom became useful assistants in publishing the gospel. From the second annual report of the "China Mission Society" of Kentucky we learn that, during 1846, $3,935.63 had been expended by this church; "a floating chapel" had been procured, where regular worship was maintained; and 191,258 pages of tracts and Scriptures had been published and circulated.

Mr. Roberts offered himself to the Southern Baptist Board in a letter dated September 24th, 1845. In the meantime the Board had applied to the Kentucky China Mission Society for his transfer; and that Society, dissolving its connection with the Northern Board, advised Mr. Roberts to become our missionary. In June, 1846, Mr. Roberts wrote: "See what God has wrought in his providence for us—even exceeding our most sanguine expectations, as to openings for the reception of the gospel. Who knows whether the Southern Baptist Board has not been constituted for such a time as this.   *   *   I have leased a lot on which to build a chapel and mission house, and have $1,000 collected for this purpose." On July 21st, he wrote: "I have three promising inquirers. My chapel is nearly finished. I have just received a fine church bell from New York, and the belfry is in course of erection to-day.   *   *   I believe that all the members contribute freely, willingly and liberally, according to their means.   *   *   They have three of the assistants under their own patronage and direction." August 16th: "I made the last payment on my house, chapel, and lease yesterday.   *   *   They have been paid for by the foreign community in China through the Canton Missionary Society, and, of course, the property belongs to that Society."

The feverish state of things between the English and Chinese created hostility to all foreigners. June 29th, 1847, Mr. Roberts wrote of an assault on his house, the destruction of his records and furniture, and the sinking of the "floating chapel." The damages were assessed at $2,800. His loss of private and church papers "was irreparable." Yet he gloried in tribulation, saying: "I count all things loss that I may win Christ." Through the interposition of the American Minister, Mr. Everett, the loss was, in part, indemnified by the Chinese government.

In his journal we find: "June 2d, 1847. A contract for another lease, adjoining the one already purchased, was consummated to-day. * * * This gives me premises of more than one hundred feet long and thirty feet wide. These leases are secured in perpetuity; and the only expense, after building and keeping up repairs, besides some small government tax, will be $15 per annum. June 4th, Lye, from Hong Kong, preached as usual at the *Lune-hing-ki* Chapel."
"June 25th: The *Uet-tung* Baptist Church has been almost like sheep without a shepherd since the robbery. * * The chapel was laid in ruins and the members were scattered. But, like the apostles, they went about preaching the gospel. Met to-day in room repaired. Seven members present. All the church records entirely gone, and we began perfectly anew." June 27th: "The Chinese brethren and myself united in the Lord's Supper. There are twelve native and six foreign communicants, making the whole fraternity, male and female, eighteen—these divided between the two churches give each just nine. This is a slow progress for ten years; * * but, thank the Lord!" Among the archives of the Board of Foreign Missions is the following document: "March 19th, 1847, *Resolved*, That the Board accede to the terms on which the Executive Committee of the American Baptist Missionary Union propose to sell and transfer their premises in Canton to us, and that our treasurer be authorized to pay to treasurer of said committee, in Boston, the sum of $1,164,43½ for that object." This was the *Lune-hing-ki* Chapel referred to above.

During this year, Mr. Roberts collected in Canton and vicinity $2,930,36.

Mr. Roberts' journal, which, in many respects, is a model diary, is interspersed—we write this for our young readers—with such side-items as these: "Sent plum-pudding to Sister Pearcy, and two rattan chairs to Sister Clopton, as new year's gifts, and received pleasant letters in return. * * Saw woman beating child over the head with a club until blood ran down the face—suppose she spared the rod, when it might have done good. * * I saw the hogs drinking the blood of headless bodies just executed—some thirty of such executions, daily, in this country. * * Fell through floor of a house, over the river, with a child, into the mud waist deep. Nobody offered assistance. When extricated, I was politely asked if I would have a boat; and was then charged for the same. This is Chinese character! * * Attended party at Dr. Parker's with Dr. Happer and lady, Brother Pearcy and lady, Sister Clopton, and Brethren Johnson, French, Spear, and Bridgman, before monthly concert. Brother Johnson and myself improved a short time to-day playing ball and pitching quoits. Preached before breakfast to eighteen lepers. I would, by no means, sell my knowledge of the trade of making saddles; for it makes me independent, in my judgment, as I can thus make my own support. I feel very lonely. The missionaries seldom come to see me; and Brother Pearcy, to whom I applied for board, thinks that we can love each other better apart!"

November 24th, 1848: "I think I must return home for a season. I have but little idea of settling here—days, weeks, and months without a living soul to bear me company. It is not good for man to be alone."

His journal for this year concludes, December 31st: "Have made great progress in China in ten years. Have faith in God, and greater progress. Increase your means, brethren, and let us see whether God will not open the windows of heaven and pour you out a blessing that there shall not be room enough to receive."

In the annual report of 1849 to the Southern Baptist Convention, we find: "Three regular preaching places in Canton will be statedly occupied by our missionaries and assistants. With respect to the *Lune-hing-ki* Chapel, Mr. Roberts says: 'I have had this chapel repaired and improved. * * Being painted and whitewashed, it was opened for worship, 14th September, 1847. It will seat one hundred; and has a room suitably arranged for females."

In the same month another place of worship was opened, called *Ty-hang-how* Chapel. It is located about a half mile above the *Uet-tung*

Chapel, some one or two hundred yards from the river, on a clean street, where there are shops and families. * * Thank God for giving us such favorable opportunities!"

In 1849, in anticipation of war between England and China, during which time little could be done, Mr. Roberts returned to the United States, which the Board had authorized, April 3d, 1848. Before leaving, he effected a union between the *Uet-tung* Church, and the "First Baptist Church," of which Brother Roberts wrote, "there were only *three* members." This union bred trouble. Messrs. Clopton, Pearcy, Johnson, and Whilden had joined the mission. The first had gone to his blessed reward above, the second had been transferred to the Shanghai Mission on account of his declining health, the third had returned to the United States in ill health. Mr. Whilden remained alone, after the departure of Mr. Roberts. Though Mr. Roberts was a missionary of the Southern Baptist Convention, he retained a *quasi* relation to the Kentucky Society, and at first conducted his work independently of the other members of the mission. Subsequently, the Board requested that he should be associated with other missionaries. His residence and chapel, as has been seen, was not the property of the Southern Baptist Convention.

During his visit to the United States, he met at East Hickman, Ky., Sept., 1849, Miss Virginia Young, the daughter of John Young, Esq., Clerk of Woodford County Court, an estimable and elegant woman, to whom he was married by Rev. Wm. C. Buck, Dec. 7th, 1849. Mr. Roberts' relation to the Board of Foreign Missions was not perfectly harmonious; but he returned to China, with his wife, in 1850, as their missionary. The annual report of the mission, for that year, states: "At our several places we have had one hundred and forty-nine meetings during the last quarter, making forty-eight services per month." In the report of the Board to the Convention of 1852, we read: "The mission at Canton has been in rather a depressed condition. Since the last meeting, the relation existing between the Rev. I. J. Roberts and the Board has been dissolved." The reasons of this dissolution were investigated and published by the Convention in 1855. Mr. Roberts, however, continued independently his work in Canton.

In 1860, he went to Nanking, the capital of the insurgents, whose leader had studied with him at Canton the Christian religion. Mr. Roberts was offered the position of Minister of Foreign Affairs, and received, by royal decree, free access through the rebel territory, not only for himself, but for all religionists. By the same decree, idolatry was abolished, and provision was made for the establishment of eighteen chapels at Nanking. Mr. Roberts, December 6th, 1860, urged Rev. T. P. Crawford to join him there: and appealed with much enthusiasm to his American brethren to come up to the help of the Lord, under the protection of the rebel Emperor. In his communications he expresses kindly feelings to all, and compares himself to Joseph, whom the Lord separated from his brethren "for their good."

November 13th, 1860, Rev. C. W. Gaillard, of the Canton Mission, wrote: "Brother I. J. Roberts has gone to the north to try and teach the rebel chief the way of the Lord more perfectly. May the Lord be with him!" November 7th, 1861, he wrote: "In the month of July, the church set apart a man to the work of the ministry, and he has gone to Nanking to aid Brother I. J. Roberts." A gentleman wrote, February 6, 1862: "Mr. Roberts fled from Nanking for his life, and arrived in Shanghai last week. He has turned against the rebels with all his might, and says 'his old pupil' is crazy. He is going back to Canton." About the same date another missionary wrote from Shanghai: "Mr. I. J. Roberts has been greatly insulted by one of the kings at Nanking, and arrived here a few days ago, having barely escaped with his life. He says the rebels are a band of robbers, and should be exterminated by the foreigners. We have no hope that anything good will come out of the insurgent movement." In 1855, Mrs. Roberts, with her two children, Lillie and Issachar, returned to America, and made her residence in Rochester, N. Y. She resides now in St. Louis, Mo. Mr. Roberts returned May, 1866, and passed some time in Mississippi.

In August, 1866, he went to Upper Alton, Illinois, where he died, of leprosy, at the house of Miss Almeda Fulton. The following account of his last hours is from a letter to us, dated Upper Alton, November 8, 1875:

CHINA—CANTON MISSION.   89

"Mr. Roberts' health was failing, and he purchased a home here for his niece, who took care of him until his death, which occurred Dec. 28th, 1871. 'Let me die the death of the righteous, and let my last end be like his,' might well be the language of one witnessing his triumphant death. He used to say: 'If Christians would sing praises more for the blessings which they have, instead of complaining, and pleading for what was not best for them, we should have much more enjoyment, and set a better example to the world.' He illustrated the doctrine in his own life; for he spent most of his time singing and praying. His eyes failed, so that he read with difficulty. The morning before his death, his niece sent for me. I found him breathing with much labor. I said: 'Mr. Roberts, you are coming to the closing scenes of earth.' 'Yes,' said he, with a smile; 'but though I walk through the valley of the shadow of death, I fear no evil. Thy rod and thy staff, they comfort me.'

"After resting a few minutes, he continued: 'I shall not be five minutes in the dark valley.' I said: 'Can you see the heights beyond?' He replied, with emphasis: 'So bright that these eyes cannot behold them, until they are prepared for the sight!' The funeral was at his own house."

In his will, dated at Upper Alton, Oct. 2, 1870, he says of the church property in China: "Now this property was got up in 1844 and 1845, under the auspices of a board of local trustees, of which I was one, designed for the mission work in which I was engaged, none of us claiming any private or personal interest in the premises, excepting this small rent, named above. But the other trustees ultimately resigned their trusteeship, and turned over their responsibilities in the case entirely to me. And now, in like manner, I resign my responsibilities as trustee in favor of Rev. R. H. Graves, as senior Baptist missionary in Canton, and his successors in perpetuity."

The Board of Foreign Missions sustained no relation to this trust, and so reported to the Convention in 1873. Mrs. Roberts has laid claim to a portion of the property. The journal of Mr. Roberts, which was kept with great care, and even beauty of arrangement and chirography, manifests regularity and industry in his work; and scrupulousness in his private devotions and almsgiving, of the propriety of noting which, in view of the anticipated eyes of others, he himself expressed grave doubts. He was a man of extremes of character—like the rest of God's earthly children, made up of some gold, and of quite as much clay. Let it be remembered that he laid the foundation of our work in Canton, that during his labors vast progress was made by the gospel in China, that he displayed great liberality with his means, and was unquestionably, as his works indicate, zealous for the Master's glory. And let us rejoice in the hope that the virtues and graces which clearly appeared in his life, despite the opposing elements of frail human nature, are now expanded into a perfect and sanctified character in the presence of his Redeemer.

Miss HARRIET A. BAKER.

In the seventh annual report of the Board of Foreign Missions, we read: "In addition to the day schools which are in operation in Shanghai and its vicinity, the Board have authorized the establishment of a female boarding-school, to be placed under the care of Miss Baker. The determination to embark in this work was induced by the request of the missionaries, more or less urgently presented." Among the missionaries who desired this work, Rev. Issachar J. Roberts, at Canton, was perhaps the most urgent. On March 5th, 1849, Miss Harriet A. Baker, of Powhatan County, Va., was appointed by the Board a missionary to China, to be located in Canton. She sailed the March following, and arrived at that station in July, 1850. To the Convention of 1850, the Board reported: "Sister Harriet Baker has gone to this position for the purpose of attempting the establishment of a school for female children. This is an experiment, the beneficial influence of which remains to be tested."

A few weeks after the arrival of Miss Baker, on August 7th, Mr. and Mrs. Issachar J. Roberts reached Canton. They all made their temporary abode at the house of the Rev. James G. Bridgman, a graduate of Amherst College, an accomplished scholar, and a missionary of A. B. C. F. M., who had been until 1848 the supervisor of the *Chinese Repository*. For about six months this gentleman had withdrawn from society, and gave symptoms of a disordered mind. On December 1st, 1850, " in a paroxysm of the disease, he attempted self-destruction. Reason was restored by the loss of blood, and he was conscious during the five days he survived. A post mortem examination showed a highly congested state of the brain." Mr. Roberts was not at home at the time of the tragedy. The ladies were alone with the bleeding and demented man. Communications were exchanged with Mr. Roberts; and, in the excitement and alarm of the hour, some informality occurred with regard to a note addressed by Mr. Roberts to his wife. This occasioned an "unpleasantness" between Miss Baker and Mr. Roberts. With this trouble were connected three Presbyterian missionaries, Dr. Dyer Ball, and his sons-in-law, Rev. Dr. Happer and Rev. J. B. French, whose names revive in our mind recollections, for the allusion to which we ask pardon in advance.

Dr. Ball was the writer's first schoolmaster in Charleston, S. C. He was assisted by Fred'k D. Mills, Esq., his wife's brother, who was subsequently a lawyer in Boston. Being only seven years old, it was our lot to recite to Mrs. Ball, in their residence below the school-room, with her two daughters, Caroline and Mary. We accompanied the family to the wharf, whence they sailed for the North and China. From that time their history has been followed with more or less interest. Caroline became Mrs. Happer; and Mary, Mrs. French. These ladies have been reputed among the best American scholars of the Chinese language. In the summer of 1870, the wife of our College mate the late Dr. Knowlton, of China, entered a social circle at Hamilton, New York, who were conversing on "mutual friends." Mrs. Knowlton asked: "Whom do you know in China?" We replied: "Caroline and Mary Ball." "Caroline Happer and Mary French; why, they were among my dearest friends!" That same year, we were at Oakland, in the mountains of Maryland, sitting alone in the parlor of the Glades Hotel. A young lady of Pittsburgh came in, and remarked: "We ought to be acquainted, for I have a dear friend, whose little brother is named for you." This led to our recent conversation with Mrs. Knowlton. No sooner had the word "Caroline Ball" fallen from our lips, than she exclaimed: "Mrs. Happer! she was my mother's best friend. Dr. Happer has just visited our house, which his son, who is at Princeton, will make his *home*." This double coincidence was striking, and served to deepen our interest in these friends of our youth, with whom the missionaries of our Board in Canton have been variously and intimately associated.

These gentlemen, Messrs. Ball, Happer, and French, made earnest and persevering efforts to effect a reconciliation between our alienated missionaries. Mr. Roberts not complying with what was regarded his engagement in the matter, Dr. Ball wrote to him a letter, which seems to be touched with a little of that severity which we fancied to belong to him as our schoolmaster.

During the correspondence, Miss Baker sailed, January 23d, 1851, for Shanghai, where she arrived the 2d of February following. After her departure, a reconciliation was effected. (*Vide* Proceedings, S. B. C., of 1855.) The missionaries at Shanghai were impressed with the importance of boarding schools, not only for girls, but also for boys. The following, from the pen of Mr. Shuck, is found in the seventh annual report of the Board:

"Soon after the arrival of Miss Baker here, our mission passed a formal resolution, authorizing her to commence a *female* boarding school on a small scale, but with the view of its gradual enlargement. The general opinion among missionaries seems to be that where a mission has a boarding school for one sex, there should be in the same mission a similar school for the other sex. This is especially desirable in view of future matrimonial connections. It is the standing custom of the Chinese to betroth their children at a very early age; and for one young person, carefully brought up in a mission school, to be compelled to marry another brought up under all the influences of heathenism, would be one of the greatest discouragements and drawbacks, as well as a positive throwing away of much missionary toil, time and money. *Compulsion* is one of the main features of Chinese betrothal and marriage."

CHINA—CANTON MISSION. 93

We stop again to remark that, when our mission at Canton was left without a missionary, by the return to this country of Rev. B. W. Whilden, the interests of our Board were committed to the hands of one of the gentlemen referred to above, the Rev. J. B. French. This gentleman was described "as classical in his style; of great simplicity of taste and refinement of feeling; of sound judgment; industrious, regular, and of methodical habits; and as having a person and heart which, when nerved to defend the right and protect the injured, assumed a majesty and resistless power." He was a native of Georgetown, D. C., and lived, at one time, in Richmond, Va., where he was employed in behalf of the American Tract Society. He died at sea, coming to this country on account of his health, November 30, 1858. His biographer, after describing the burial, when the anguished widow stood on deck, with her two little boys, and saw "the enshrouded form of her loved one lifted by the strong arm of kind-hearted sailors, and then lowered into the opening waves," touchingly remarks: "No marble slab is reared there to mark his resting place or remind us of his deeds; but his name is engraved on the hearts of his compeers, in the work of disenthralling the millions of Paganism from the woes of sin; and will be remembered by many, redeemed from China, to join him in the songs of the just made perfect in heaven."

In the providence of God, Miss Baker was not allowed to labor long in her chosen work. In 1854, the Board reported to the Convention: "By the advice of Dr. Lockhart, in consequence of ill health, which threatened to be permanent, Miss Harriet Baker was induced, with the consent of the Board, December 5th, 1853, to return to this country. She expresses deep concern for the prosperity of the mission, and regrets that duty seems to demand her retirement from it."

For some years after the return of Miss Baker, the Board were opposed to single women becoming missionaries. This we had good reason to know from the vain and persistent efforts of our dear child in the Lord, Mary Canfield, afterward Mrs. T. A. Reid, who died in Africa, to go alone, under the patronage of our Board, on the mission to which she felt herself solemnly called of God.

But this policy of the Board is now changed, and they congratulate themselves and the churches because of the accomplished and efficient single women in the field, who are doing a work which men cannot do, and which will link their names indissolubly with the redemption of the greatest empire in the world.

Miss Baker is believed to be the author of "The Orphan of the Old Dominion," in which, under the name of Lumina Silvervale, she gives her own life in the character of Almaria Hobyn. The account of her conversion by reading the biography of Ann H. Judson, her early missionary impressions, and her experience and observations and performances in Canton and Shanghai, is interesting and instructive. She wields a sharp pen, and touches keenly a Mr. Hollins, of Canton, whom we recognize as our missionary, Rev. Issachar J. Roberts, as well as some other people, of whom we have only heard under the fictitious title of "The Orphan of the Old Dominion."

Miss Baker is living with her brother in one of our extreme Western States. May her life be long spared, and usefully spent to the end— no longer feeling orphanage in view of her Father's home on high. And in the sunset hour, may there shine about her glories more heavenly than the depicted beauties of her luxuriant fancy, in verification of the gracious promise: "He will beautify the meek with salvation."

Rev. SAMUEL CORNELIUS CLOPTON.

Mr. Clopton was the first missionary appointed by our Board. In reference to his decision to be our missionary, it is recorded: "We recognize in it the favorable regard of the great Head of the Church." He was assigned to Canton, August 4th, 1845. Shortly after this appointment, his friend and classmate, Rev. George Pearcy, was appointed to the same station. It was meet that these "first fruits" of the separate work of the Southern Baptists should be set apart at the first anniversary of the Southern Baptist Convention. The "designation services" were conducted, June 15th, 1846, by Dr. Jeter, who was President of the Board, and Rev. Messrs. Hinton, Bacon, Taylor, Shuck, and Yong Seen Sang. They are said to have been *profoundly impressive.* Similar exercises were held in New York, in which Drs. Dowling and Nathan Bishop officiated—brethren who were present at our last service of this kind, which was held at the Tabernacle Church, New York, January 3d, 1875, when our missionaries, David and Colley, were about to sail for Africa.

Mr. Clopton was born in New Kent County, Virginia, January 7th, 1816. In the year 1833, he was baptized by Rev. J. B. Taylor, and joined the Emmaus Church, of which his father, Rev. James Clopton, was pastor. He longed to tell the love of Jesus to others, and exclaimed, "Happy, happy time!" when referring to his first public proclamations of the gospel, which were in the summer of 1842. He spent two years at Richmond College, where he was subsequently a tutor; two years at Columbian College, where he was graduated; and two years at Newton Theological Seminary. After quitting Newton, he began to ponder whether he should not devote himself to the destitute of his native State. The Board of Foreign Missions, anxiously looking for suitable men to go to the heathen, "fixed their eye on him, and determined to invite him" to enter the foreign field. In his journal he wrote:

"How little did I think, in all my course, that the Lord was raising me up for such a work as this! I had hoped, in process of time, to be prepared for places of usefulness, but I did not expect that the Lord would call me to a work so important. Who is sufficient for such a work? The Lord strengthen and help me, and make me useful."

Finding a congenial spirit in Keziah, daughter of Rev. Miles Turpin, he was married on Tuesday, the 14th of April, 1846. Of this lady, in after life, one who knew her long and intimately says: "Mrs. Clopton was one of the loveliest women I ever met."

Mr. and Mrs. Clopton and Mr. and Mrs. Pearcy sailed June 22d, in the splendid ship "Cahota," in company with Mr. Everett, U. S. Minister to China, who, in a farewell speech on shipboard, as has been mentioned, promised to render them in China all aid "in his official capacity."

On the 9th of October, 1846, they arrived in Canton. Nov. 26th, Mr. Clopton wrote:

"On the 27th of October, we employed a teacher and have been daily studying the language with much pleasure, and some little success. * * In accordance with the wish of Brother Roberts, the ladies go alternately, once a week, to his house to attend a female congregation of some twenty or thirty persons, to whom they speak, by means of an interpreter. * * On the river are 80,000 boats, which have from ten to twenty persons each, living on them, to any one of whom we might talk of Jesus, were we able to speak the language. * * Here in this great moral wilderness, I rejoice that I am permitted to be one of the few to stand and hold up the words of eternal life."

February 23d, 1847: "We have public religious services in our chapel twice a week. * * We have, also, a conversation-meeting every afternoon, just within the chapel door. * * How much I long, on such occasions, to have my tongue loosed! * * Every Sunday morning I have a class of three persons, studying the Bible. * * Oh that God would render me useful to this truly miserable people! Let not your prayers cease to ascend to heaven for the poor Chinese!"

The following is dated June 17th, 1847: "It gives me great pleasure to say that the Lord has been pleased to stay the hand of disease, which has occasionally threatened; and has permitted me to prosecute my work without much interruption; for which I desire to record my most grateful thanks. * * We were interrupted a short time during the month of April by the appearance of the British forces in the front of the city. * * Early in the excitement I went to Hong Kong * * to refresh myself for the long, hot summer. On my return, through Jane, the nurse of our little boy, I conversed on religion with a large company. It filled my heart with gratitude thus to be able to present to their benighted minds the precious Saviour, crucified for us."

In his Journal, May 24th, are these notes: "Last night the Chinese broke into Brother Roberts' house and carried off everything." May 30th: "This afternoon I was delighted and encouraged to find myself understanding much of the remarks made to our Chinese congregation. * * Oh, do help me to thank the Lord for any progress he is permitting me to make in this strange language! Oh that he would vouchsafe the blessing that I may speedily speak to this heathen people all the words of eternal life!" June 6th: "I attended our monthly concert of prayer for missions. It was a refreshing meeting. It was pleasant to remember that we were meeting with our dear brethren and sisters in Richmond, and that we were beginning the supplications which were to be continued around the globe, in behalf of a sinful world. I hope these meetings are appreciated at home. Of all the meetings we attend, what one can surpass this, in which, with one heart, we besiege a throne of grace for a lost world? *Of all things, we need the moving power of God's Spirit on the hearts of the people!* Pray for this, and entreat the people to do the same. All are dead here. *We* cannot raise the dead."

Rev. George Pearcy conveyed the startling intelligence, July 9th, 1847: "Our dear Brother Clopton is no more. He departed this life at our residence, in this city, on the evening of Wednesday, the 7th inst., at 10 o'clock, after an illness, from intermittent bilious fever, of about ten days." Mr. Pearcy's lament was a heart-touching wail, as over the body of an own and beloved brother. Thus was snapped the thread of a beautiful and noble life.

Dr. Deau, referring to our brother, as a student at Newton, says: "He left there the reputation of a prayerful, godly young man, zealous for his Master's glory and the good of souls." He adds: "He was a man of pleasing address, and took with him to China the physical, the mental, and the Christian qualities which gave promise of a career of great usefulness."

"It was supposed that Mr. Clopton, being fresh from his native land and in the full strength of youthful manhood, had contracted a fever by exposure to the hot sun while attending the funeral services of his fellow-passenger from America, Hon. A. H. Everett, Minister of the United States to China, who," as we have seen, "died, June 29th, 1847, soon after landing at Canton."

The sad event was presented in the fourth annual report of the Board to the Southern Baptist Convention thus: "The young, ardent, and devoted Clopton is gone. He had just begun to speak in the language of the Chinese, and, by his amiable disposition and courteous manners, had secured the regard of the natives, when he was suddenly arrested by the hand of death."

Dr. J. B. Taylor, in his "Virginia Baptist Preachers," says of Mr. Clopton:

"His observation of heathenism, in all its revolting details, served only to deepen the conviction of the necessity of the gospel to bring these millions to the experience of salvation. His letters breathe a spirit of earnest devotion, to the glory of his Divine Master. * * * His brethren in this land were beginning to entertain large expectations through his agency.

"About a week after his final sickness commenced, and two days before his death, he said to his wife: 'I trust in my Saviour, and love him more than ever.' The Saviour was indeed near to him. The eye of faith discovered, as never before, his exceeding beauty and fulness. 'I would like,' he added, 'to live longer, for your sake and the little boy's; and I would like to preach the gospel to these dying heathen; but I am resigned to my Saviour's will; if he calls me, I am ready to go. Live near to God.'

"'So sudden and unexpected was the event,' wrote Mrs. Pearcy, 'we can scarcely realize that he is gone. But everything tells us that he has indeed left us. In the social circle and at the family altar, we hear not that voice with which we were so delighted to mingle ours. His seat is vacant at the table; his study is now still and lonely. Our teachers and the disciples come in, and mournfully say, 'Clopton, the teacher, has quickly ascended to heaven.' All around are sad. Sister Clopton's heart is bleeding, and we are all 'bowed down heavily, as one that mourneth for his mother.'

"The widow returned with her only son to this country. She, too, has since gone to the spirit world. May the surviving son be raised up to love the Saviour whom his father loved!"

We rejoice to add, that "the surviving son" *has* given himself to his father's God, and to the ministry of his holy word. May he follow his father's footsteps, as his father followed the Saviour! He is the pastor of the Clay Street Baptist Church of Richmond, Va., and a member of the Board of Foreign Missions.

Rev. GEORGE PEARCY.

HIS BIRTH.

This gentleman was the son of Nicholas Pearcy, a godly man of Bedford County, Virginia, of whom a friend said : "No person, we believe, ever did more to sustain a church and promote vital godliness therein." The younger Pearcy was born June 23d, 1813, in Bedford, which has given to the world many "a good minister of Jesus Christ," and where George was favored in being reared under the influence of such men as the Leftwiches and William Harris. Dr. A. B. Brown, refers suggestively to the *time* of his birth, as synchronizing with the return to this country of Luther Rice, to arouse our churches to give the gospel to the nations.

HIS CHARACTER, EDUCATION AND APPOINTMENT.

Mr. Pearcy is described as a man of sensitive feelings, modest deportment, sanguine temperament, logical intellect, great industry, strong common sense, unwavering devotion to the convictions of right, and deeply experienced Christian character.

Referring to the obstacles to an education which Mr. Pearcy had to surmount, and the manly energy with which he first made the means, and then persevered, from 1836 to 1843, through the courses at the Baptist Seminary—now Richmond College—and Columbian College, Dr. Brown pays to him this handsome tribute: "Such a hero, as he showed himself from a strong sense of duty, and from loyalty to Christ, and good will to men, has seldom been seen in an age which boasts its heroes of active courage in the charge, and of patient endurance in the bivouac, the tedious march, and the pining hospital." This heroism, however, probably sowed the disease, which brought forth his infirmity and death.

He was converted when sixteen years old, graduated at thirty, had charge of the "Valley Union Seminary," now Hollin's Institute, for two years, and studied medicine at the Richmond Medical College, after his appointment as a missionary.

Under date of November 3d, 1845, the following appears on the records of the Foreign Mission Board: "Brother Geo. Pearcy being, by request, present as a candidate for missionary appointment, made a statement of his religious experience, call to the ministry, and views of foreign labor. On deliberate consultation, Brother Pearcy was unanimously appointed a missionary to China. After which prayer was offered by Brother R. Ryland, for God's blessing upon the candidate, and the field of mission upon which he contemplates entering."

The author of the "Reminiscences of Geo. Pearcy" asks: Why did Pearcy, with Clopton alone, respond to the thrilling appeals of Judson, in 1845, to give the gospel to Asia? "The extraordinary act bespeaks the extraordinary man. He had more consecration to Christ, more deadness to the world, more courage to meet dangers, more enterprise to achieve great things, than his contemporaries;"—at least, "one or more of these qualities must have existed in him in unusual development."

MRS. FRANCES MILLER PEARCY.

On May 30th, 1846, Mr. Pearcy married Frances Patrick, the third daughter of Samuel Thomas Miller, of Pittsylvania County, Virginia, who was "for many years the most distinguished classical teacher in all that part of Southern Virginia, which lies west of Petersburg." Correcting in advance the slight and very natural error that Miss Miller had contemplated the missionary work before being addressed by Mr. Pearcy, we follow again the gifted pen, from which we have already quoted: "Finding his ideal realized, as far as a practical man could expect, in Miss Fannie Miller, of Cedar Forest, Pittsylvania, a lady of amiable disposition, handsome person, fine and highly cultivated mind, who had been cherishing purposes of kindred heroism with his own, he endowed her with all that wealth of affection which an affectionate nature, highly appreciative of female excellence, can lavish on a pure and attractive woman."

As was stated in our sketch of Rev. S. C. Clopton, Mr. and Mrs. Pearcy, after solemn designation services in Richmond and New York

City, sailed for China, where they landed in October, 1846. On the voyage was formed that tender friendship which existed between Mrs. Pearcy and the venerable Dr. Dean, who, in correspondence with her, always signed his name, "Your Papa Dean," and of whom Mrs. Pearcy admiringly said: "Would there were many such missionaries!"

THEIR SETTLEMENT AT CANTON.

On their arrival, they were kindly entertained by Dr. Devan, of the "Missionary Union." In a few days his wife, "whom the heathen revered and loved as an angel of mercy," took her flight to the spirit world. Dr. Devan being the sole representative of his Board in the city, their Mission was closed, and the premises, the *Lune-hing-Ki* Chapel, sold to the Southern Baptist Convention. The location was a miserable one, in a narrow street, between a low public house and a duck market. The effluvia arising would make our missionary, Francis C. Johnson, to say: "I must run up on the terrace to get a mouthful of fresh air." The Cloptons and Pearcys lived together as harmoniously and lovingly as the most affectionate brothers and sisters. Their mutual expressions of love and admiration were beautiful, and furnish a worthy example to missionary families who have to live under the same roof. Even now Mrs. Pearcy can say: "I love to think of Mrs. Clopton and her dear husband." "The First Baptist Church of Canton" was *hard to find;* but the few scattered members were ultimately gathered into a regular meeting, in the basement of their house.

HOW TO IMPROVE A REVIVAL.

Mr. Pearcy wrote, April 12th, 1847: "I am especially pleased to hear of the conversion of many young men in Richmond College. May they early learn to contemplate the want of the heathen, and to feel obligations to live for their Saviour. I thank God for these showers of mercy. Is it too much to hope that much prayer, and alms, and labor will result therefrom for perishing *China?* * * * *

ENGLISH AND CHINESE TROUBLES.

"A few days ago we were threatened with ruin. The British troops from Hong Kong invested this place. * * * During the row last

July, when the rabble threatened to burn the factories, they lost three of their number. The authorities, it is said, claim as many lives of English subjects. * * * The British spiked 800 guns of the forts, as they came up the river. It was supposed that they could force a way into the city, for no foreigner is permitted to enter within the walls. * * All the merchants sent off their money. * * Thousands of Chinese left, with their families and property. * * Brother Clopton took the ladies to Hong Kong. * * It was thought best for me to stand by our house and watch against thieves. * * English troops were soon on the walls, * * and stationed in our street to protect the factories. * * They were stoned from the house-tops. * * The sappers tore down two or three of these houses. * * I gave a writing to some of the peaceable citizens, for their protection, which attached the whole street to us."

The following terms were made between Governor Keying, and Sir Francis Davis:

1. City of Canton to be opened in two years from date.
2. Permission to foreigners to visit in the country and return the same day, unmolested, as at northern ports.
3. Grounds to be leased for warehouses and dwelling-houses, on the side of the river, opposite Canton, in Honan.
4. River in front of factories to be cleared of Chinese boats.
5. Ground to be leased for English churches, in vicinity of factories.
6. Burying grounds at Whampoa.

WRATH OF MAN AND PRAISE OF GOD.

In a letter dated April 24th, 1847, Mr. Pearcy says of the sentiment of the Chinese in reference to this settlement with the English: "Truly do they say, 'that the whole body of the people can only gnash their teeth with rage and indignation.'" The editor of the *S. B. Missionary Journal*, commenting on his letter, remarks: "How far the hostile movements of Sir Francis Davis are to be justified may be questionable; but the believer in divine sovereignty can easily perceive how all may 'turn out to the furtherance of the gospel.' * * * The thirst of dominion and the spirit of enterprise, so peculiar to the

British government, have broken down the wall of separation between China and other nations, through which breach the messengers of truth may enter to proclaim the tidings of the gospel." Brother Pearcy writes: "In these times of danger and commotion, we must cast our care upon God, and pray that his will may be done here as it is in heaven." Again: "Yesterday we had a crowded chapel, notwithstanding the excitement. I am happy to state that Jane, a Chinese girl, whom the late Sister Shuck reared and educated, has recently made a profession of religion, and gives evidence of true piety."

DEATH OF MESSRS. EVERETT AND CLOPTON.

Under date of July 9th, 1847, Mr. Pearcy said: "On the 28th ult., hearing of the illness of the Hon. A. H. Everett, we walked round to see him. That night, after much suffering, he departed this life." Of the last moments of the lamented Clopton he wrote, in addition to what we quoted with regard to Mrs. Clopton: "He then asked for the little boy, placed his hand upon him, looked at him long and tenderly, and, though I could not hear him speak, I doubt not but he was commending them both to God. * * * We accompanied his remains in boats to Danish Island, near Whampoa, the port of Canton, * * where we laid by the side of Sister Devan and Hon. Mr. Everett all that remained of that once manly form, there to await the resurrection of the just. Alas! my brother, I have lost a friend." Mrs. Clopton and "the little boy" sailed for America, in the Samuel Russell, February 5th, 1848. She (afterward Mrs. J. H. Pleasants) died in Henrico County, Va., May 23d, 1851.

HEALTH AND REMOVALS.

After the death of Mr. Clopton, Mr. Pearcy, it was feared, would soon follow to his "long home." Dr. Dean, of Hong Kong, had written that the only way to preserve health at Canton was by frequent visits to that island. With Mr. Johnson, who had just come up to Canton, they moved down to Hong Kong, where they met Mr. and Mrs. Shuck, and Mr. and Mrs. Tobey, who had arrived there with Mr. Johnson, June 25th, 1847. They returned to Canton the 12th of

October, 1847. But, as the warm weather of 1848 set in, both Mr. Pearcy and Mr. Johnson were attacked with fever. A large house was rented in Macao, where Mrs. Pearcy was "the housekeeper and financial secretary of a family of three Baptists, three Presbyterians, and one Methodist, who enjoyed the sea breezes, messed together like schoolboys, and divided the expenses."—Mr. Pearcy's health did not improve. The doctor said: "You will die here.' The missionaries, with one accord repeated: "We do not wish you to die; try a more northern climate." The Shanghai friends wrote: "Come up here." Ultimately, Mr. and Mrs. Pearcy concluded to go. The latter described the separation from their "home" as extremely painful; and gave, in the sadness of departure, another beautiful illustration of the ardent attachments that are sometimes formed between our missionaries in heathen lands, which make them to love their humble homes more than all the world beside.

MR. ROBERTS' DIARY.

In the diary of Rev. Issachar J. Roberts, we find many allusions to the subject of this notice. Mrs. Pearcy seems to have been a favorite of that gentleman, who permitted her to administer wholesome and well-timed counsel to him, without the least displeasure. To this lady, returning from Hong Kong to her house in Canton, which was occupied and sadly "unkept" by Mr. Roberts, he remarked: "Ah, Sister Pearcy, you will have to learn that missionaries are called to endure trials and practice self-denial." "Yes," replied Mrs. Pearcy, "but they need not enhance them, by carelessness and inattention."

The following items from his journal are taken at random:

January 9th, 1848. We attended preaching with Brother Pearcy's congregation at *Lune-hing-ki.*

May 14th. At 3 o'clock, at *Lune-hing-ki,* we partook of the Lord's Supper, Brother Pearcy officiating.

July 18th. Dr. Parker thinks that Brother Pearcy cannot live long at Canton, and that his chances for health are not very good at Shanghai. His *first* advice is, that Brother Pearcy return home; *second,* that he go to Shanghai.

CHINA—CANTON MISSION.

July 19th. Consulted Dr. Ball, who advises Brother Pearcy to go to Shanghai, which course I approved in my letter to him.

NOTES FROM MACAO.

July 17th, 1848, Mr. Pearcy wrote: "We have determined to print and circulate tracts. Brother Roberts is superintending an edition of Luke. He follows Medhurst's last edition, but inserts Goddard's words for *God* and *baptism*." Under the same date, Mr. Pearcy wrote of another severe spell of illness; also of the illness of Mr. Johnson, "who," he said, "is too feeble to take any part in our mission meetings."

The last words of the ensuing passage from his pen should not be forgotten:

"Christianity is tolerated throughout the Empire by law, so that the natives may preach the gospel without punishment. * * * Our congregations generally number thirty to seventy persons. * * * At the close of the meeting, we give each a portion of the word of God, which, on these occasions, is eagerly sought. * * * It is strange to the people to hear us pray in the name of Jesus. * * * They think we have idols also. WILL NOT THE CHRISTIANS OF HAPPY AMERICA PRAY THAT GOD WILL ENLIGHTEN AND SAVE THESE PERISHING HEATHEN BY THE GOSPEL?"

PLANS.

"Should the Lord grant us health at Shanghai, I think we shall prosecute the language in the Shanghai dialect, with the view of remaining there. Should the Board think it best to open next year a mission in *Fuh-chow-fuh*, and wish me to labor there, I will be ready to go. * * * *I want to labor and die in China.*"

FEARFUL STORM.

On the 30th of August, Mr. and Mrs. Pearcy sailed in the Hindostan for Shanghai. In a letter of Sept. 20th, Mr. Pearcy gives an account of the most terrific typhoon which had visited the coast of China for fifty years, in which their vessel was caught. It was said that a hundred vessels and a thousand lives were lost. All hope of the Hindostan and its precious freight was gone. The escape seemed "almost miraculous." Mr. Pearcy commented thus on the perils encountered: "I suppose our Heavenly Father sees that we need such discipline. There is much pride, independence, and sin in the heart, which he may intend to correct by these trials."

After the storm, they passed St. John's Island, and were shown the spot where was buried Francis Xavier, the first Jesuit missionary to China, "who preached the gospel in fifty nations, and baptized over a million of persons!"

IN SHANGHAI.

Mr. and Mrs. Pearcy got back to Hong Kong in about a month, and sailed again for Shanghai, October 1st, in the John Bunyan. They encountered another storm; but finally arrived November 19th, 1849, with improved health. As will be seen, when we sketch our SHANGHAI MISSION, Mr. Pearcy labored there for five years. The day we write these lines, our attention has been directed to a number of interesting paintings, representing the Chinese ideas of the Nemesis, which Mr. Pearcy sent to Richmond College. They are dated Shanghai, February 12th, 1853, and signed " G. Pearcy." He loved his Alma Mater, and did not forget her. The son and his work will not be forgotten by the mother. Among many valuable services at Shanghai, he originated, as one of our missionaries states, the phonetic system of reading and writing the Chinese language, which system " Mr. Crawford brought to its present state of perfection." But Mr. Pearcy's health utterly broke down. Dr. Burton said: "I take the responsibility of ordering you home." The thought of abandoning his field was worse than death itself. It was only when Mrs. Pearcy's health failed, that he would consent to return. As they were about to sail, he was seized with Asiatic cholera, and lay a day and night as if dead. Preparations were made for his interment, and the vessel waited two days for Mrs. Pearcy and her little daughter, Rebecca, to take passage after the funeral. Dr. Burton, of whom Mrs. Pearcy wrote with grateful emphasis, "I shall never forget him," adopted some violent agency, and the seeming dead was brought to life. During this state he was conscious, and feared being buried alive. Subsequently, he lay in a tranced condition, which was described as "the inexpressible transport of the spirit released from the body."

IN AMERICA.

On the 8th of January, 1855, they sailed for the United States, "bidding adieu to their Shanghai home, in the hope that the separation would not be long!" They reached Boston in April; and shortly after, Mrs. Pearcy's father's house. They felt, however, that *China* was their home. With "intense desire" he longed to return; but he yielded, with an humble spirit, to the manifest will of God. He labored as an agent of the Foreign Mission Board. Subsequently, he was commissioned, by the Domestic Board, to work among the Chinese in California. "The war put a stop to that." "His old disease, the consumption, of which his sedentary habits in earlier life, without the knowledge of hygiene," probably laid the foundation, began again to develop itself. He was forced to give himself to farming, and the registrar's office. His mind and heart, however, were not secularized. "He was punctual in all the duties of a church member, as a teacher or a superintendent in the Sunday school, unwearied in gratuitous preaching to the colored people, prompt to supply a lack of ministerial labor anywhere in his neighborhood, and very prompt, serenely and cheerful, to yield to any preacher to whom the people might prefer to listen." * * "But," continues Dr. Brown, "I should do injustice to the general Baptists if I did not add that, with his strong sense, his unbending integrity, his eminently simple and cheerful faith, his kindliness of heart, and fine social qualities, he was the object of their very general esteem, affection, and sympathy. And when skilful hands shall have brought their contributions to his monument, I suspect that few of his contemporaries will be found to deserve more honorable, and even more conspicuous mention than the humble man, who now sleeps with his children at Cedar Forest."

This faithful soldier of the cross fell asleep July 24th, 1871. Like his beloved Clopton, he passed away softly and grandly as the setting sun. To his smitten wife he said: "All is peace within; we shall not be long separated." * * "In a moment he was gone. One minute he was talking with me," says Mrs. Pearcy, "the next, in eternity!"

HIS BEREAVED FAMILY.

Our beloved sister is living at Green Hill, Campbell County, Va. Heavy has been her affliction, and Christ-like has been her resignation. In one year, she was stricken by the death of father, husband, and two children. "Even to such a proficient in submission, such a lesson was hard to master." Her remaining children, Fannie and John, this devoted mother has been striving to educate, by adding teaching to the cares of a farm. The son, who is a lovely specimen of youthful piety and filial affection, was the clerk of his church, and the assistant superintendent of the Sunday-school. He is now a student at Richmond College. Shall not our people keep alive their affection for the children, and for the relict and co-worker of Geo. Pearcy? Shall not godly men and women still rejoice to hazard all for the glory of Christ s universal dominion, having no reason to fear that their vicarious labors shall be forgotten, and that their names shall not be kept fresh and fragrant in the memory of the churches? Yet let the words of George Pearcy, which are the last that we have seen recorded of him, be engraven on every heart: "I DO NOT SEEK TO PLEASE MEN. THIS IS NOT MY RULE OF ACTION. WITH ME IT IS A SMALL THING TO BE JUDGED OF MAN'S JUDGMENT."

Rev. FRANCIS CLEVELAND JOHNSON.

HIS AUTOBIOGRAPHY.

"I was born in Greenville, South Carolina, January 12th, 1823. It was Sunday, 2 A. M. I think likely the weather was cold. I have no distinct recollection of the event itself—don't think I went to church.

"Went to South Carolina College and Brown University; graduated at neither, and learned little at either. From China, to Aiken, Marietta, Florida, Albany."

HIS FATHER—GREEK PARTICLES.

Mr. Johnson is the son of the late Rev. Wm. B. Johnson, D. D., of South Carolina, who was the first President of the Southern Baptist Convention. In his parting speech, at the first meeting of the Convention, Dr. Johnson said: "I have a dear son at College, whom I have educated for the ministry; and who, it is probable, will become a missionary in China, or some other distant land. At first, the thought was painful, but I am ready to make the sacrifice, if it please God to send him there. * * * I have yet another son, whose feelings and whose education tend to the ministry. * * * I may have to give up both."

A distinguished gentleman of the South, who was a college mate of one of these sons of the venerable Doctor, recently said to us: "The first time he came before the Greek Professor, Frank *kited* the Professor sky high on a Greek particle, to the infinite delight of the class."

Subsequently, Mr. Johnson was tutor in the school of William E. Bailey, of Charleston, S. C., where the writer, as a pupil, had the opportunity of knowing at least the *reputation* which he had for learning in the classics.

OUR HALF-FATHER IN THE LORD.

Later we had occasion to know him as something better than a pedagogue. Burdened with a load of sin piled on our conscience, under the preaching of Dr. Fuller, in the spring of 1846, we fled to Mr. Johnson to ask, *What must we do?* He turned to Rom. x. 9, and said, "Go to your closet, and on your knees, with open Bible, plead that promise; and God, who cannot lie, will save you." Thus the Lord gave us light and life; and thenceforth our soul has been knit to this man of God, as well as to the late great divine of Baltimore and of the Southern pulpit.

Such was Mr. Johnson's spiritual ardor, when he first saw his Saviour, that he went, we believe on foot, from his home at Edgefield C. H., South Carolina, to Augusta, Georgia, fully expecting, as he himself informed us, that on his publication of the gospel, the people *en masse* would turn to Christ.

THEOLOGICAL TUTOR AND MISSIONARY.

In the annual report of the Board to the Convention of 1846 the following may be found:

"The importance of securing a competent individual to give biblical instruction to native Chinese preachers, has been brought before the attention of the Board. * * * * They are not without hope that a suitable brother * * * will soon be found. They have had their eye directed to one who seems to be marked by the Great Head of the Church as eminently adapted for this position; and correspondence has been entered into with him on the subject."

The Board applied to Prof. P. C. Edwards, of South Carolina, to become their teacher of theology. At the recommendation of this gentleman and other gentlemen of his State, Mr. Johnson, who was credited with distinguished power for acquiring languages, was appointed, August 4th, 1846, as "Theological Tutor and Missionary" to China. A gentleman, present at the time, tells us that, when asked, why he entered the ministry, Mr. Johnson replied, "Why does the gosling, when hatched, go to the water?" He was ordained and set apart to the missionary work, January 31st, 1847, in the First Baptist Church, of Richmond, Va. The sermon was preached by Rev. D. Shaver; prayer, by Dr. Jeter; Bible presentation, by Rev. E. Kingsford; the right hand of fellowship, on behalf of the presbytery, by Rev. J. S. Walthall; the charge, by Dr. R. Ryland. The following points were made in the charge:—1. *Need of piety of a high order.* 2. *Importance of promotion of health.* 3. *Necessity of co-operating, in a spirit of Christian courtesy, with the brethren at home and abroad.* 4. *The value of rigid economy, in the expenditure of funds.* 5. *Obligation to honor divine truth, in all investigations and teachings.* The Doctor concludes thus: "Do not abandon this cause. Seek your grave in a heathen land. Let your epitaph be: *He died at his post.* Let converted pagans, in future ages, visit your tomb, and weeping say, with grateful veneration: This is the man, who came from the Far West, and taught our ancestors salvation through the cross of Jesus Christ."

A writer on the occasion remarked: "Mr. Johnson, by request of the presbytery, addressed the congregation. He is about 24 years old;

rather above the ordinary stature; and of good personal appearance. His manner of speaking is easy, unaffected, and entirely self-possessed. His address was distinguished by great fervor of feeling, and striking and original thought. He was heard, not only with breathless attention, but with profound and all-pervading emotion. Every eye beamed with interest, or was suffused with tears. Every bosom heaved in sympathy with the speaker. We have seen many ordination services and missionary meetings, but it has never been our lot to witness a similar service, which, from beginning to the end, was sustained with so much spirit and interest. All left the house, musing on the things they had seen and heard, and more deeply impressed with the importance of the missionary enterprise."

Farewell services for Mr. Johnson, with Messrs. Shuck, Tobey, and their wives, and Yong Seen Sang, were held in the Bowdoin Square Church, Boston. "Mr. Johnson's remarks," it was said, "were listened to with the deepest interest by all."

The party sailed on the 11th of March in the ship Ashburton. Complaint was made of "bad treatment" from the officers of the vessel. They arrived at Hong Kong, as has been seen, June 25th, 1847.

FIRST SETTLEMENT.

August 1st, Mr. Tobey wrote from Hong Kong: "Brethren Shuck and Johnson are living in a hired house, and expect to receive in their dwelling Brother Yates, on his arrival." Mr. and Mrs. Yates arrived in the "Thomas W. Sears," on the 17th of August, and left for Shanghai on the 24th, "leaving Mrs. Shuck and Mrs. Tobey sick." Mr. and Mrs. Tobey left for the same place on the 7th of September. On the 27th of September, Mr. and Mrs. Shuck sailed for Shanghai. As was said, in a previous article, Mr. Johnson stayed much of his time with the Pearcys. He would have liked to become identified socially with the Chinese. Mr. Roberts assumed the costume of the country: Mr. Johnson would, if practicable, have gone into a native family to live. He wrote:

"It is absolutely impossible to get into a Chinese family. Could it be, I would, that I might, the quicker and better, learn the language.

In this state of seclusion from the families and houses of the people, there is a great obstacle to the missionary's success."

HIS FIRST IMPRESSIONS.

August 20th. Mr. Johnson communicated from Canton: "I am now on my field. * * The living stream, which pours along the narrow streets, induces me to think its extensiveness is not exaggerated. * * I doubt whether foreigners will ever enter the walls, except at the point of the bayonet. * * No man is qualified for this work, but one eminent for prayer, holiness of life, and heavenly wisdom. He must be willing to strip off Americanism and put on Chinaism; to encounter contumely and danger, and to find in Christ compensation for the loss of all other pleasures."

SUNDRY MOVEMENTS.

Mr. Johnson arrived in China about the time that Mr. Clopton died. He wrote, Aug. 23d: "Brother Pearcy and myself left Hong Kong last Wednesday, 18th inst. Brother Pearcy will return to Hong Kong. His health demands it. I come to stay for good. * * On Saturday, Brother Roberts and I became members of the mission. As soon as this was done, we adopted resolutions concerning Brother Clopton." In the resolutions, which were probably from Mr. Johnson's pen, we find these word's: "Though his course was short, he fulfilled it well, and his works will follow him. We commend our sister, with her fatherless infant son, to the friends of missions, and to that God who is the widow's husband and the orphan's father."

The state of things at Canton being very unsettled, on account of Sir Francis Davis' recent action, Mr. Johnson, with Mr. Roberts, went temporarily to Macao, and it was thought not improbable that some other station farther north would be deemed advisable. January 9th, 1848, Mr. Roberts' journal says: "Brother Johnson and I think of departing to Macao to await the results of the anticipated war. Some think we are hasty. * * We must get another house, which we think best in Macao." Mr. Roberts labored there with the lepers, and returned to Canton, 28th April, 1848. He took the same house, *Wong Sung*

Hong, which he obtained in 1844, and opened there a room for the distribution of books in the week, and for preaching on Sunday.

CHINESE CIVILIZATION.

"My own humble opinion is, that the foreigner is vastly disposed to underrate the attainments of this people. I know, as yet, nothing of their literature by my own reading; but when I see their vast and voluminous *lexicons*, larger than most men's libraries, and their numerous works written on the origin and structure of their language, I know I am among a people who are to be accounted, not as barbarians, but as possessing a highly polished and approved language. Lexicons and other works explaining a language are the property of a nation far *advanced*. Such works exist not in unimproved languages. Just consider how recent is the oldest English dictionary of standard authority. I would your eyes could see their houses, their cities, their numerous arts, and the manifold proofs of their advanced civilization. You must not dream of any man's being fit to publish tracts here, who is not deeply imbued with the spirit of the Chinese literature—whose mind has not cast off its foreign style, speech, and thought, and put on the Chinese. By God's blessing, I myself intend to endeavor so completely to strip myself of the English language, that when I pray in private, when I meditate, I shall naturally and mechanically do it in the *Chinese* language, and not in the foreigner's language."

HOME VIEW.

Mr. Johnson was subject to glooms of despondency, occasioned in part by his ill health; but as a friend and companion, he was genial and entertaining. The diary of Mr. Roberts exposes some of their "sharp debates," as well as their friendly adjustments of disagreeing opinions. One who esteemed him highly, says of his correspondence, when away from the mission:

"His letters were very original. Sometimes he would write in a very humorous style—very much to our amusement. He was not careful of his health, or anything else. When we were away from home, the Chinese would steal his watch, his clothes, and everything they could get from him. His thoughts were not much on earthly things, and he was emphatically a man of prayer."

HIS HEALTH.

Mr. Johnson applied himself to the language with such assiduity and ability that, according to the report of the Board to the Convention, he had "begun to address the people," and according to Mr. Roberts' journal, *he kept his diary in Chinese.* His health failing, as stated in other articles, he determined, by special invitation of the Shanghai missionaries, to try there a higher latitude. Twice he was defeated in his purpose by violent storms, whereby he "gathered that it was not God's will."

November, 1848. Mr. Roberts, in Canton says: "Brother Johnson has just returned, and now thinks of trying Canton again. Dr. Parker thinks he can remove his complaint. * * He arrived here October 25th, and yesterday went to Hong Kong. He will stay there one month, and return to Canton and live in the *Lune-hing-ki* Chapel, put himself under Dr. Parker, and proceed with his studies and mission work."

This hope, however, proved illusory. It became more and more apparent that this brother, from whom so much was expected, must yield to the necessity of quitting the field.

This was the opinion of the mission, his physician, and the Board.

In 1849, the Board reported to the Convention:

"We are sorry to learn that Brother Johnson is among the number of those whose health has been impaired. As a devoted servant of Christ, his loss will be felt. Whether it may be necessary to seek another to take his place, as an instructor in theology to the native assistants, we do not advise."

He sailed for America on the 24th of August, 1849, and reached New York in December of that year.

AT HOME.

After the return of Mr. Johnson to this country, it was the privilege of the writer to hold intimate relations with him for several years; and in 1850 to unite him in marriage with Caroline Hickson, the daughter of Levi Hickson, Esq., of Aiken, S. C. He seemed to us a marvel of devotion, learning, originality, eloquence, and eccentricity, unequalled as a conversationalist, and in his best preaching hours unsurpassed, except by one, as a pulpit orator.

As he states in his *autobiography*, he was pastor in Aiken, S. C., and in Marietta, Ga. With his wife's family, he moved to Florida, where he preached and taught. July, 1872, he became the pastor of the Baptist Church at Albany, Ga. Afterwards he returned to Marietta, where he still labors, we doubt not, with zeal and power.

THE WORD OF GOD.

In a private note, protesting affectionately against being *put in printer's ink*, our beloved friend, floating into the topic of preachers caring too little for the Bible, bursts out in the following earnest strain:

"O thou Son of God, Saviour of the world, and Head of the church! Thou art still spit upon and rejected and despised; and thy priceless word is naught, while a hundred little reviews, and magazines, and novels, and theologies, and sermons are of infinite value; and poor, ignorant little preachers are told they *must* and *ought* to read this and that; and religious papers, and agents, and D.D.'s recommend this trash and that other trash, but thy word—the *only*, and to the exclusion of all else, light and life, comfort and strength, joy and solace, bread and water, wine and milk, clothing and shelter, glory and defence, all and in all to the soul—is flung away, set aside, and despised and neglected!"

AS A SCHOLAR.

Many extravagant reports are afloat of the scholarship of this gentleman. The truth is enough. An eminently learned man has just told us that he received one of his Latin letters of splendid Ciceronian phrase and period, with which he likes to test reputed scholarship, but which our learned informant was quite happy to excuse himself from answering. We only add that, through these many years of personal acquaintance with this gentleman and scholar, the question has often forced itself upon our mind: Is not a professor's chair of the ancient languages the place for Francis C. Johnson, of whom one, who was the best possible judge of his attainments, said to us, two decades of years ago: "I believe that he could address a Roman Senate as *intelligibly* as Cicero himself."

Rev. BAYFIELD WALLER WHILDEN.

PRAYERS OF A PIOUS WIFE.

Mr. Whilden is a native of Charleston, South Carolina. He was born May 29, 1819. His *second* birth was in the "Old First Baptist Church," of which his mother was a devoted member, and which has been called, "The mother of ministers." In writing these words, some twenty of such sons of the church rise up before our eyes. He was baptized by Rev. Dr. Basil Manly, Sr., in 1834, with several other young men, who became pillars of the Lord's house. He was licensed in 1838, and ordained in 1841. In 1843, he married the daughter of Mr. Robert Martin, of Union District, S. C. She was born February 13, 1821, and professed Christ in 1840. Soon after the marriage they removed to Camden, S. C., where he was pastor for four years. Subsequently, he preached at the Healing Spring Church, of the same State. Mrs. Whilden had cherished a strong desire for the missionary life, and put into the hands of her husband an article from the lamented Pohlman. In 1848, "in answer to her long-continued prayers," he offered himself to the Board; and on July 11th, of that year, was appointed a missionary to Canton.

DESIGNATION SERVICES.

On September 29th, 1848, he was formally set apart to his work in the "Old First." Said a writer, at the time: "Having pursued a course of classical and theological studies, and been a pastor for several years, Mr. Whilden now returns to the church, in the midst of which he was reared, and is by them *recommended to the grace of God for the great work* of preaching Christ among the heathen." The sermon and charge were by Rev. W. J. Hard; the right hand of fellowship, by Rev. J. H. Cuthbert; the address to the congregation, by Rev. H. A. Duncan, and Mr. Whilden closed, "with some affecting farewell remarks." The meeting was one of deep and solemn interest, and left impressions on the mind which the lapse of years will not efface. The intense feeling of the vast assembly bore testimony to the strong hold which the cause of Foreign Missions had taken upon the hearts and sympathies of the people."

Further services were held in New York, in the First Baptist Church, of which Dr. Cone was pastor, and the Tabernacle Church over which Dr. Lathrop presided. At the latter church, Mr. Whilden delivered a spirited and stirring address upon the missionary service. The following appeared in the *New York Recorder:* "Mr. Whilden appears to be gifted with more than ordinary abilities; and, from our cursory acquaintance with him and his interesting wife, we cherish strong hope of their great usefulness in China."

On Monday, October 9th, 1848, after appropriate services on shipboard, they sailed, with their three children, in the good ship Valparaiso.

ON THE VOYAGE.

On the passage, Mr. Whilden wrote: "I feel God is near me, and I trust that my interest is daily increasing in the work to which I have devoted myself. Oh that I may be found faithful in the discharge of duty!   *   *   I am endeavoring to gain all possible information about the character and manners and literature of the Chinese.   *   *   The thought that God may make me the instrument of good to the benighted will stimulate my efforts in every necessary preparation for my important and solemn work."

JOY, FAITH, LABOR.

They arrived at Hong Kong on the anniversary of Mrs. Whilden's birthday, 13th February, 1849. From that place Mr. Whilden wrote: "It is a source of unspeakable joy that I am permitted to labor *anywhere* in the Lord's vineyard.   *   *   If mountains rise before me, then there is need of stronger faith, and I may see how sweet to 'cast my burdens on the Lord.'" They landed at Canton, February 23d. From another of his letters we extract: "Mrs. Whilden and myself are making a beginning in the study of the language with teacher *Lye Seen Sang.*" Subsequently: "I began to talk to the people in such sentences as these: '*Study the Bible;*' 'the Bible says, *worship the true God;*' 'the Bible says, *believe in Jesus Christ.*' Some of them showed that they understood a part by pronouncing the words after me. * * The work mostly done is foundation work. * * Yet I feel that my labor will not be in vain. Moravians labored *five* years in Greenland before they heard of a convert; the Rangoon missionaries, *six* years; Carey and Thomas, in Bengal, *seven* years; the Moravians, in South America, *nine* years; the missionaries in Otaheite, twenty years. * * *Jehovah reigns.* The work is his. * * 'Not by might, nor power, but my Spirit, saith the Lord.'"

MISCELLANEA.

From a letter dated May 14th, we gather the following: "A great many of the Chinese near us speak English. * * They are very polite to foreigners. * * I begin with those near, and gradually distribute tracts to those at a distance. * * One of the shopkeepers said: 'Americans *good*, English *bad*, VERY BAD.' * * The *Lune-hing-ki* Chapel is located on a street running to a well known wharf, where foreigners land going between Canton and the Island of Honan. * * The people are notified of meeting by a card suspended on the door. * * After *Lye Seen Sang* spoke to the people, he gave them some tracts on 'Strive to enter in at the straight gate,' with my explanation of the text. * * I see no necessity for English schools; * * but I am highly in favor of Chinese schools. Brother Johnson expects to superintend the school at *Ti-ma-ton*, and I the one at *Lune-hing-ki*, if we succeed in commencing one.

JEWS AND PARSEES.

"The Jews in Canton are not Chinese. They came from near the Caspian Sea. Chinese Jews are found in great numbers near Peking and other places." Rev. R. H. Graves has recently seen one of their rolls of the LAW, some thirty or forty feet long. A tablet on their temple at *Kai-Fung-Fu*, visited in 1851, but now demolished, stated that they came to China 200 B. C. They were known as "*the sect that cut the sinew.*"

Mr. Whilden wrote of a *Parsee missionary*, who agreed to receive his tracts, as he wished *to learn all that is good*, on condition of secrecy; and of an intelligent hearer, who thought that Christanity would not be objected to, if the *other gods were worshipped with Christ.*

We insert here one of Mr. Whilden's missionary hymns:

THE MACEDONIAN CRY.

"Come over and help us," 'tis heard from abroad,
From nations who know not the fear of the Lord;
Who have not the book which to us has been given,
That tells of a Saviour and points them to heaven.

"Come over and help us," in darkness we stray;
The night gathers blackness, while yet you delay;
No day star illumines, no morning is nigh,
But lost and bewildered in error we die.

"Come over and help us," disease has assailed—
Disease the most fearful; for sin has prevailed;
The soul has been shattered, and daily we breathe
The poisonous damps from the regions of death.

"Come over and help us." Yes, gladly I go;
Their error, their deep degradation, I know;
And cold is my heart if I here would remain,
While millions for help are thus crying in vain.

Accept, my Redeemer, the offering sincere;
I would thy compassion, thy power declare;
And while in the mazes of error they roam,
Would bid them in thee find a refuge and home.

The following excerpts from letters of Mr. Whilden will be acceptable to those who are interested in missions, and in a missionary's views and progress.

DUTY, ENCOURAGEMENT, PRAYER.

August 20th, 1849: "Christ's command is obeyed, if the gospel is preached, even if no heart is affected. The work of the *Church* is to send missionaries; the work of the *missionary* is to sow the seed; the work of the *Spirit* is to cause the seed to spring up and bear fruit." *Macao, October 25th:* "We have distributed 1,000 tracts." *October 26th:* "I am pleased with the progress which the children have made in the catechism." *November 1st:* "After *Lye Seen Sang* preached, I closed, saying a few words on '*repentance*.' I was greatly encouraged by one of the audience, who would bow his head to show that he understood me. At night, I held family worship with the domestics. For the first time, I prayed in Chinese, repeating the *Lord's Prayer*, and added a few words at the close."

JESUS AND OTHER GODS.

November 6th: "I spoke for a few moments on 'Jesus a Jew,' as some Chinese say he was an American; others, an Englishman." *November 11th:* "The honor to false gods in heathen lands, may put to the blush the indifference in Christian lands, to the spread of the gospel." *November 20th:* "The Parsees say they do not worship the sun, but the Deity *through* the sun, as the most glorious exhibition of Deity."

DEATH OF MRS. WHILDEN.

On the 20th of February, 1850, Mrs. Whilden, at the age of twenty-nine years, was taken to her heavenly rest. Her diary is filled with earnest longings and prayers for holiness and perfect consecration to the work and the will of the Master. Her epitaph is: "*To me, to live is Christ, and to die is gain.*"

Dr. Dean writes: "She did what she could, and left behind the fragrance of a holy example and the memory of a prayerful woman, a patient mother, a pious companion, and a cheerful and consistent Christian. She enjoyed the peaceful death which God has coupled with a pious life.

"Such a death is no mean legacy for her bereaved husband and three motherless children. Her grave is on French Island, near

Whampoa, by the side of that of Brother Clopton and Mrs. Devan and others, who have, from the Middle Kingdom, gone home to the true celestial country. When from the millions of China, the purchased of the Redeemer shall be gathered home to glory, the sainted ones, who have prayed and wept and suffered and served for their salvation, shall, with no common joy, mingle with them in saying: 'Not unto us, but unto thy name will be the glory.'"

Two of these "motherless children," Mrs. N. B. Williams and Mis Lulu Whilden, have succeeded to their mother's labors, and are missionary laborers where their mother toiled and fell. Precious spot, to pious daughters!

RETURN TO AMERICA.

Mr. Roberts had gone to America. Mr. Whilden was alone in Canton. It being thought advisable, he returned with his children, August, 1850, leaving the mission in charge of Rev. J. B. French, a missionary of the American Board. At his request, as reported in 1851 to the Convention, he was transferred to the Shanghai Mission. This action was, afterward, reversed. In 1852, the Board reported to the Convention: "The mission at Canton has been in rather a depressed condition. The relation between Rev. I. J. Roberts and the Board has been dissolved. Within a short time, it is hoped that Rev. B. W. Whilden will return to this station, * * and resuscitate its languishing interests."

SECOND MARRIAGE AND RETURN TO CHINA.

Having married again, July 12th, 1852, Mr. and Mrs. Whilden sailed for China, August, 1852, and arrived at Canton, January 14th, 1853. Shortly after, he wrote: "Though no manifestation of the Holy Spirit has been visible, yet the interest seems to be increasing. May God send more laborers!" Later: "Yesterday, for the first time in China, I conducted a service *alone*. * * I am greatly encouraged in my efforts to speak. * * The name of Jesus, though not honored, is extensively known as the name of the Saviour in which Christians trust. The Sabbath, though not observed, is extensively known as the day we keep holy to the Lord. * * * Daily I distribute from 50 to 100 tracts. * * The school has *twenty* scholars. * * * *Yong Seen Sang* [who had returned from Shanghai] lectures on Bible pictures to the children. * * * Every Lord's Day the scholars are required to attend the services in the chapel. Thus we are trying to train up the rising generation in China. * * But in vain if the Holy Spirit does not accompany our labors!"

FINAL RETURN TO UNITED STATES.

The sight of Mrs. Whilden being seriously impaired, Mr. Whilden came back to America on the 19th of March, 1855. Rev. C. W. Gaillard and wife, who had arrived in China the summer before, were left in charge of the station with the native evangelist, *Yong Seen Sang*. Mr. Whilden's summary of work, given in the Board's report of 1855 to the Convention, marks great progress in our ten years of labor at Canton.

In 1855, Mr. Whilden was invited to supply the pulpit of the writer, while he visited Europe. On the pastor's return, he found that the name of "Brother Whilden" was as a sweet savor to his people. Parting with the church, he distributed among the members, as a token of *his* affection, "Jeter's Christian Mirror."

Seventeen years later, the writer having accepted his present post of labor, Mr. Whilden was called to the pastorate of the church which we had lovingly and joyously overseen for nearly a score of years. Mr. Whilden was Professor in the Cassville College of Georgia, and has published several interesting pamphlets. "A TRIBUTE TO THE MEMORY OF MRS. ELIZA JANE WHILDEN," is a touching and eloquent memorial of the life and death of a truly noble woman.

He was subsequently pastor at Jacksonville, Fla., and associate editor of the *Florida Baptist*. His present address is Trinity, Alabama. The spirit of missions still burns in his heart, as a "GOOD MINISTER OF JESUS CHRIST."

Rev. CHARLES WASHINGTON GAILLARD.

NATIVITY, MARRIAGE, APPOINTMENT.

MR. GAILLARD was by birth a South Carolinian. His name belongs to some of the best blood of the Palmetto State. His family was from the low country; but he was born in Pendleton District. He was graduated, in the class of 1853, at Union University, Tennessee, under the presidency of Joseph H. Eaton, LL.D., the honored father of Rev. T. T. Eaton, of Virginia. He lived with his widowed mother, at Starksville, Mississippi, where he joined the church. During the Baptist State Convention at Columbus, of that State, he was, at the request of the church at Murfreesboro, Tenn., ordained and set apart to the missionary work, November 12th, 1853. On the 14th of March, 1854, he was married to Miss Eva M. Mills, of Albion, N. Y. The ceremony was performed by Rev. C. C. Eager, at whose residence, in Clinton, and by whose kind offices, the young couple first met. Mr. Gaillard had been appointed by the Board on August 3d, 1853. In May, 1854, he sailed with his wife for Canton, where they arrived and were welcomed by Rev. B. W. Whilden, after a voyage of one hundred and eight days.

ALONE IN CANTON.

Referring to Mr. Whilden's contemplated return to America, Mr. Gaillard wrote: "I shall then be alone—the only male missionary of Baptist persuasion, and without a knowledge of the language. How much can be accomplished under such circumstances? Without greater effort, when will 'the heathen be given to Christ for his inheritance, and the uttermost parts of the earth for his possession?" When as much has been done for the spread of the gospel in China, as has been done and is still doing to effect the opium traffic, then will thousands of hearts and voices be raised in songs of praise to him who died to redeem a lost world. Oh, brethren, when shall that blessed day dawn on this dark land?"

EARNEST, ACTIVE, AND PROMISING.

In the report of 1854, the Board refer to Mr. Gaillard thus: "Our Brother Gaillard seems deeply impressed with the magnitude of the interests confided to him, and strong hopes are entertained that he will be eminently useful in the great city of Canton."

In the report of 1856, we read: "Mr. Gaillard and *Yong Seen Sang* have been largely engaged in the distribution of the Scriptures, not only in Canton, but in other towns, numbering from 1,000 to 3,000 inhabitants. In these excursions, they were treated with great kindness by the people, and serious attention was given to the things which were spoken. * * We have reason to expect that if Brother Gaillard is spared, he will speak the language with great fluency. The congregation, every day in the week, ranges from 50 to 100, at one chapel; and from 100 to 200, at the other."

LYE, A LOT.

April 16*th*, 1855: "Entered a town of 5,000 or 6,000 inhabitants, distributed some books, and found a disciple by the name of *Lye*, who said he was baptized by Brother J. L. Shuck, at Hong Kong, some ten years since. He appeared very glad to see us. Says he is still a disciple, and tries to teach the gospel to his townsmen; but none of them believe it. He had only a small part of the New Testament. I gave him a whole copy and some other books, and exhorted him to hold out to the end. It may be that he is a Lot in this Sodom. He says, no foreigner has ever been here before."

Their journey up the river extended 190 miles from the city of Canton. Mr. Gaillard remarks: "This is far beyond where any Protestant missionary has ever been."

MR. GRAVES AND MRS. GAILLARD.

The mission was re-enforced by Rev. Roswell H. Graves, who left this country, April 19th, 1856, and arrived in Canton, August 14th, of that year. Mrs. Gaillard, who had been taken to Macao by Mr. Graves, on account of the bombardment of the city by the British,— Mr. Gaillard having to remain to protect their property—wrote, November 11th, 1856: "Oh, if these poor Chinese had the Mighty God, even Jehovah, to fly to in the time of commotion, famine and destruction! Alas, will not the hearts of God's children be affected at the thought of their misery, as thousands go hence unprepared for eternity! * * May the church feel that her part is to pray. God has, for the present, seemingly taken the mission work in Canton from our hands. Let us pray that he may manifest his glorious majesty and power, bringing the greatest amount of good out of the least possible evil!"

THE WAR.

Mr. Gaillard wrote December 13th, 1856, that the American navy had become, through self-defence, involved in the war, and had demolished two of the Chinese forts on the river. January 13th, 1857: "The factories were all burned, and our *Lune-hing-ki Chapel.* * * The Chinese have determined to destroy Hong Kong, if they can. The Governor of Canton has issued an edict, commanding all Chinese in the employ of foreigners to leave their employers, both in Hong Kong and Macao, and forbidding provisions to be brought to Macao or Hong Kong. We are beginning to feel the effects of this. We are trying to rent a chapel here, but have not secured one yet. We have not been, however, altogether idle. I hope we may do some good. The souls of these people are worth as much as those of Canton. Macao is Roman Catholic, and may forbid our missionary work here."

SUMMARY.

Mr. Gaillard summed his work for 1856: 430 sermons, by *Yong Seen Sang*, at two chapels; 69 scholars, in three schools, who studied catechism, and compend of Scripture, both prepared by Rev. B. W. Whilden; 32,200 copies of Testaments and tracts distributed.

Mr. Gaillard remarks: "Would it not be an expenditure which God's word and providence would sanctify, to send ten men to this field, if they can be found?"

REPLY TO QUESTION.

"Yes, our now sainted brother, ten times ten might and should be sent. But are not our eyes as yet "holden?" Do we see Jesus in his providence, and hear him in his grandest and most sacred command? God grant that his people may realize why they live, and what is the world-comprehending object for which the Son of God died!

WHAT MR. WHILDEN SAYS OF HIM.

"He was one in whose society I have passed many pleasant hours—a worthy, faithful soldier of Jesus Christ, always willing to work where duty called. I love to think of my association with him. I called him 'Brother Charles,' and he called me 'Brother Bayfield.'"

WHAT HE SAID OF MISSION SCHOOLS.

"I have no school, and do not want any. * * * I do not believe that they are of any advantage to the Mission or to the scholars."

PRINTING IN CHINA.

Of B. W. Whilden's "Compend of Scripture," Mr. Gaillard wrote: "My printer prints 1,000 for $3. Other books are proportionally cheap—paper good, and printing well done. I have the blocks for John, Luke, Acts, and Genesis, and for fifteen different kinds of tracts; so that I have no trouble to get books. He prints them in our house, and all I have to do is to give him the blocks and the money, and the books are brought up-stairs in a few days.

"NANKING INSURGENTS."

Of the tract on this subject, by Mr. Whilden, "who took ground against the beneficial results of the movement," Mr. Gaillard wrote: "I think it ought to be widely circulated, if the people are as ignorant of the rebels and their religion as they were when I left America."

RETURN TO CANTON.

In February, 1858, Mr. Gaillard returned to Canton. The chapel was opened for preaching until 23d of June, when the missionaries were obliged to leave again. July and August were "spent in a wearisome captivity in Macao." They went back to Canton early in September. The Board's Report for 1858 says: "The intelligence from Canton is encouraging. The missionaries have begun regular preaching, and are importunate for reinforcements."

STREET PREACHING.

Mr. Gaillard reports: "Now, at the close of 1859, I can say my labor has not been in vain in the Lord. Assisted by *Yong Seen Sang*, I have preached daily in two chapels, and in nearly all the streets in Canton." The native brother, *Wong Mui*, who was with Brother Shuck in California, had joined the Mission, and united his labors with those of the other missionaries.

PROSPEROUS YEAR.

The year 1860 was one of great prosperity to the Mission. Mr. Gaillard wrote: "As the result of our labors, we have baptized, on profession of their faith in Christ, 37 persons—16 of whom were females. Brother Graves has also baptized three English soldiers The whole number of the church was 58." Mr. Gaillard had averaged one sermon a day, taught for six months a class in theology, and published notes on the Acts of the Apostles in thirty-five leaves, besides performing a large amount of incidental service. He said: "I try to teach that it is the duty of every member of the church to preach the gospel to their relations and friends, and all who will hear them. * * I have two men preparing for the ministry. * * We contribute monthly; each member gives something, if it is only the fourth of a cent. * * The proceeds are given to a licentiate of the church, to aid him in preaching the gospel." *December 12th*, 1860: "Our prospects for the further success of the gospel are as good as the promises of God are sure. The Spirit of the Lord has been with us all the year. We have had baptisms nearly every month this year.

THE TRUE SPIRIT.

The war in this country requiring retrenchment on the part of our missionaries, Mr. Gaillard wrote: "If necessity should compel you to call home any of the missionaries, I beg that I may be the last, though I may be the least. If you can give me $800 salary, and $150 house rent, I will remain at my post as long as the Lord will permit me. I have no desire and no idea of ever seeing America; and when I go to heaven, I want a whole army of this people to go with me."

HIS SUDDEN DEATH.

On 27th of July, 1862, a fierce typhoon swept over the city, destroying 10,000 lives. Our devoted brother suddenly ended his labors by being crushed to death under the falling timbers of his house. The Board reported to the Convention: "Brother Gaillard had become one of our most efficient and successful missionaries. He performed an immense amount of labor. The native brethren were earnestly attached to him, and much grieved at his death." In the language of Mrs. Gaillard, on another occasion: "Truly God's ways are dark and enveloped in mystery to our finite comprehension. We are taught our worthlessness, when God bids us stand by and see his salvation."

MRS. GAILLARD.

"In the middle of 1863, Mrs. Gaillard married our missionary Rev. R. H. Graves. This union promised to be eminently the means of promoting the usefulness of both the parties. But it was cut short by the hand of death. For several weeks, Mrs. Graves had suffered from feeble health, and went to Hong Kong. On the 12th of December, 1864, she passed into the presence of her Saviour." Mr. Graves wrote: "It was a bright, calm, happy death-bed.   *   *   I trust that Jesus will fill the space that she has left vacant.   *   *   I miss her much; but would not recall her.   *   *   I now look forward to the time when she will welcome me in heaven." Mrs. Graves left two little boys to weep her departure. Soon after her decease, the elder of them, under very afflicting circumstances, fell asleep.

CHRISTIAN AND CHURCH TEST.

Thus ends a bright and sad chapter in the history of our Canton sion. It suggests the joys and the sacrifices incident to the mission ary enterprise, which can only be accomplished by strong faith, and is a standing test of enlightened piety and ecclesiastic vitality.

Rev. JOHN GRIFFITH SCHILLING.

HIS ANTE-MISSIONARY LIFE.

Mr. Schilling is a native of Bavaria, Germany. He was born, January 21st, 1836, and was about a year old, when he was brought to this country. He lived in Cumberland, Maryland, where he was converted in April, 1850. He was baptized, the next month, by Rev. B. Griffith, now the Corresponding Secretary of the American Baptist Publication Society of Philadelphia. "Griffith" was put in young Schilling's name to distinguish him from his brother, also named "John." In 1856, he entered Columbian College, and went through the freshman year. In 1857, he was licensed to preach by the Baptist Church at Cumberland. He was ordained by the First Baptist Church of Washington City, at the instance of the Baptist Church of Annapolis. He supplied this church from July, 1857, and taught a district school.

In January, 1858, Rev. T. J. Bowen, missionary to Africa, visiting Annapolis, interested Mr. Schilling in the benighted sons of Ethiopia.

On March 17th, 1858, he applied to the Board for an appointment as "teacher to Central Africa." His application was accompanied by letters from Drs. J. G. Binney and G. W. Samson, of Columbian College. Dr. Binney wrote: "I have great confidence in his moral and religious character. In his natural character, he is well adapted to the missionary work." Dr. Samson, in whose family Mr. Schilling lived, said: "Mr. Schilling had a limited education, but had a vigorous constitution, an active mind, and an ardent desire to fit himself for the work of the ministry. * * He proved a close student, persevering in his efforts to sustain himself at College, and made most rapid progress, besides being a thorough scholar. * * His perfect health and sound constitution seemed to have fitted him for the field which he desires to enter. * * * He has given good satisfaction to his patrons, and has been very acceptable as a preacher, both at Washington and Annapolis. * * * I believe that, if appointed, the result would prove that he was called of God to the work."

August 18th, 1859, Mr. Schilling was unanimously accepted as a missionary; but "the designation of his field of labor was postponed." This postponement was occasioned by the continued ill-health of Mr. Bowen, and the final abandonment of his plans, in reference to a teacher for Central Africa. Mr. Schilling, though disappointed at not going to Africa, consented to enter another field. On September 14th, 1859, he was appointed to the "Canton Mission." For a while, he preached at Clarksburg, West Va., where, December 19th, 1859, he married Miss Kate Lowther. In 1860, he wrote to the Board: "My interest in the missionary work has increased very much of late. I feel that I am prompted by love of souls to go to China." In the spring of 1860, he sailed, with his wife, for Canton, where they arrived, August 3d, of that year.

LOCATING AND LABORING.

Previous to Mr. Schilling's arrival, Mr. Gaillard, of that Mission, wrote, *July* 17*th*, 1860: "We are glad to hear that Brother Schilling has sailed for Canton. We hope he may soon reach here, filled with the Spirit of Christ. There is ample room for him in Canton, if he is willing to build on other men's foundations. If not, there is a wide field before him, where the gospel has not been preached." *September 8th:* "Brother Schilling has been here about a month, and seems to be making *very good* progress in the language." *January 27th*, 1861: "Brother Schilling has written the Board with regard to *building* in a place where all the houses have been destroyed by the war." *March* 12*th*, 1861: "Brother Schilling was hunting a house and chapel in the western suburbs when you wrote of the need of retrenchment." *November 7th:* "Brother Schilling has given up his chapel, and taken one of mine. If things continue as they are, until the end of the year, we shall have to make further reductions. * * * Brother Schilling is beginning to preach, and the Chinese say he speaks very well."

The war going on in this country, the missionaries in Canton reduced their salaries *one-fifth;* and the compensation of the native assistants was reduced *one-tenth.* Early in 1862, Mr. and Mrs. Schilling removed to Whampoa. In connection with his labors among the Chinese, he preached on the Lord's Day to the foreign community. He rented a house for a chapel in one of the neighboring villages. With the aid of one of the native preachers, he prosecuted his work there and in Whampoa with encouraging success.

FIRST CONVERT.

"One man professes to be a believer. This is the first case of conversion under my care, and you may be sure I have watched it with deep solicitude. Five other men manifest considerable interest. We have retrenched our expenses as much as possible, because of the distracted state of our country. This has hindered our work to some extent, though not seriously." He baptized two native converts.

BEREAVEMENT AND RETURN HOME.

Mr. Schilling was called to drink deep of the cup of affliction. On the 24th of January, 1864, his wife was taken from him. Bitter ever, but how bitter in a heathen land such a loss! As her end drew near, she said: "I used to be afraid to die; but, now that I have to die, I have no fear at all." Mr. Schilling wrote: "I am thus left with two children—a girl three and a half years old, and a little boy about eighteen months old. What am I to do with them? The only thing I can do, is to take them home, and try to arrange for their comfort and training. This would seriously hinder my work here. My wife has several sisters, to one of whom I hope to entrust these little ones." Mr. Schilling arrived at Cumberland, Maryland, about the middle of June, 1864.

POST-MISSIONARY LIFE.

Mr. Schilling is practising law in Spencer, Roane County, West Virginia. Wishing our brother all success at the bar, we rejoice to know that his heart is still in the work of missions. He writes to us:

"I feel deeply interested in the mission work; and whenever opportunity is offered, I speak on the subject to the people of this country."

Rev. NICHOLAS BUTT WILLIAMS.

EARLY LIFE AND MISSIONARY WIFE.

Mr. Williams was born at Wetumpka, Alabama, November 18th, 1845. There he was at first under Presbyterian influence. His mother united with the Baptist Church before the conversion of her son. This eulogy has been pronounced on the young Williams: " He was noted for his energetic, studious habits, his timid, bashful manners, and his great love of truth and honesty." After the war, he was variously employed in his native State as clerk, newspaper contributor and correspondent, postmaster, and surveyor. While engaged with a company of engineers, in opening the navigation of the Coosa River to Rome, Georgia, he felt the pardoning love of Jesus, and was baptized, August, 1867, in the river, at the falls of Wetumpka. The same year, he entered the Southern Baptist Theological Seminary, where "he pursued his studies with conscientious industry and marked success, graduating in several schools." Longing to preach the gospel in "the region beyond," he was accepted by the Board, May 25th, 1871, as a missionary to Canton. On the 12th day of November of that year, he was ordained in the First Baptist Church, of Montgomery, Alabama. The ordination sermon was preached by Dr. Samuel Henderson, from Eph. iii. 8, 9, 10, 11. "He took his final leave of his native home, February 29th, 1872, reached Marshallville, Georgia, March 2d, and was married, March 4th, to Miss Jumelle Whilden, daughter of Rev. B. W. Whilden, who has been sketched in this volume. Thus the daughter, accomplished, devout, and thoroughly imbued with the missionary spirit, was to be led back to the mother's grave, in answer to that mother's dying prayer that her children 'might spend and be spent in the cause of the heathen.'" After interesting farewell services in Charleston and Baltimore, they sailed, with Mrs. Williams' sister,

CHINA—CANTON MISSION.

Miss Whilden, in company with a large missionary party, from San Francisco, on the 1st of May, 1872. They arrived, during the following month, at Canton, the home of the childhood of these missionary daughters of the sainted Eliza Jane Whilden, whose fervent prayers had led their father, also, into the same mission field, twenty-three years before. The influence of godly mothers and wives, who can estimate?

CHARACTERISTICS.

Rev. Luther Broaddus of South Carolina, to whom we are indebted for most of this sketch, says of Mr. Williams: "The leading traits of his character are great courage, inflexible firmness, sound judgment, a somewhat imaginative mind, and an enthusiastic spirit, crowned with devout piety and hearty consecration to the Master's will. In the long life which, we trust, is before him, ample opportunity will be afforded to exemplify these sterling qualities of character in making history for himself and the Church in the arduous and testing field of labor, to which he has given the energies of his early manhood."

CANTON CHURCH AND CHINESE LANGUAGE.

September 18*th*, 1872: "It is gratifying to see that every precaution is used in our mission, which prudence can devise, in the reception of members. The Chinese Christians are themselves very strict in their examination of candidates, doubtless made so by the instructions of Brother Graves and their past experience. As to vital godliness in its membership, I presume the Canton Church will compare favorably with most of our churches at home.

"The difficulties of the language would seem to give countenance to the remark of an eminent divine, that the invention of the Chinese language is one of the remarkable exhibitions of the wiles of Satan, in resisting the advance of the gospel in the world!"

"WORN DOWN."

January 9*th*, 1873: "The acquisition of the language has occupied my thoughts and time. It has been my desire and effort to show the

Chinese Christians that I am in sympathy with them." *February 27th:* "The school opened under very favorable circumstances on the 17th inst. The boys' school, of which the writer has special charge, had 25 pupils the first day, and now numbers 41. * * We are compelled to adopt the boarding-school system, in order to meet the demand made by pupils living at a distance, and to compete successfully with other Christian schools." *April* 10*th*, Mr. Hartwell wrote: "Brother Williams is hard at work studying, managing the school, and trying to preach. He has been considerably interrupted by feeble health, and looks thin and worn down to begin the summer."

POWER OF BLUE EYES.

Mr. Graves writing, *July* 16*th*, of a preaching tour of Mr. Williams and himself, says with reference to a rock, which the Chinese regard as the palladium of the town of *Szui*, that the people regarding their *blue* eyes as having the power to destroy the talismanic virtue of this stone, opposed them, and prepared to assault them, should they remain. "Brother Williams proved a congenial fellow-worker, and has in him, I think, the elements of an efficient, devoted missionary."

THE LEAVEN WORKING.

August 26*th:* "The leaven is not only working here, but *visibly* working. * * Benevolent institutions have been started by the Chinese, as an offset to those of Christianity. * * * Our teacher's love for the Scriptures is remarkable. * * * He has thrown aside the opinion that faith in Christ is alone essential, and therefore that there is no need of uniting with the church."

TRYING TO TALK ABOUT JESUS.

October 21*st:* "The *Shiu Hing* Church numbers about 20 members. Their character is at least on a par with that of the brethren in Canton. * * The hostility to Christianity is not so intense in *Shiu Hing* as in most of the country about Canton. * * * The Mahometans and the Romanists are largely represented there, which has contributed, after a fashion, to the enlightenment of the people, who, however, discriminate clearly between us and them. * * * Brother Simmons preached daily. * * * I tried several times, of course, with stammering speech, to talk about Jesus. * * * I was encouraged in my work, and was made to rejoice in the labors of others."

NARROW ESCAPES.

In 1874, Mr. Williams had two narrow escapes from death—one from a robber, who had concealed himself in his bed-room, and with whom he had a desperate struggle—the other from a typhoon, which swept over Macao, where he and his family were making a visit, and which was nigh sweeping them all into the sea. A whole night was spent in imminent danger and dreadful suspense. In the report of 1875, we read: "The mission were deeply and gratefully impressed by God's signal deliverance of Brother N. B. Williams and family, caught in a fearful typhoon on the coast of China."

RETURN HOME.

The health of Mrs. Williams failing, they returned to America, in the winter of 1876. There being no prospect of her early recovery, Mr. Williams resigned his commission from the Board. He is now the beloved pastor of the Baptist Church of Gadsden, Ala. The following sketch is from the pen of our brother:

YONG-SEEN-SANG.

This veteran soldier of the Cross and Father in Israel is one of our Chinese preachers in Canton, China. He is a native of the Heung Shan district in the Province of Canton, and is now about sixty-seven years of age.

What were the moral influences, which, in early life, tended to mould and establish the character of Yong, are unknown to the writer. There are indications, however, that he breathed a purer atmosphere than is to be found in most Chinese homes.

His educational advantages were good, and his knowledge of the curriculum taught in the schools of China, is respectable enough to give him a place among the literati. He is one of the best educated men, according to Chinese standards, ever admitted into our Canton Church.

Yong-Seen-Sang was baptized by Rev. J. L. Shuck, in 1844, at Macao. His fitting qualifications soon placed him in the ministry—a position he has since filled with honor to himself and profit to the cause. He came over to this country in 1846, with Mr. Shuck, on a visit to the churches. The influence of his presence as a Chinese convert and preacher, in awakening new interest in his American brethren towards his benighted countrymen, must have been salutary. The writer infers this, not only because we should naturally look for such a result, but from remarks made by those who met with Yong while he was in this country, and because to-day, thirty-four years since his form was seen and his voice heard in our churches, there is a band of Christian women of the First Baptist Church of Richmond, Va., who support him in his work in China. Every now and then, as the writer has been traveling about, has he met an old brother or sister who inquired after Yong-Seen-Sang. "Is he living still?" "How is his health?" "How does he look now?" are questions which are asked. And kind remembrances have been sent him, too, by the eager questioners. Only a few days ago a person in Mobile, Ala., amused the writer by describing the impression made upon another party, while listening to Yong-Seen-Sang talk. The sounds he made resembled the peculiar "gurgling noise" of water pouring from a jug.

In personal appearance Yong-Seen-Sang is tall, spare, and angular. He wears a long white beard, which, together with his height, gives a dignity to his person that a decided stoop of the shoulders cannot destroy. His countenance is open and benign, and shows a preponderance of the milder virtues—a sacrifice of strength to sweetness. In his manners he is affable and agreeable. He is never other than courteous in society. He never stoops to be coarse. An indelicate allusion on the part of another will tinge his cheek with a blush, and cover him with confusion.

From the above remarks one would infer that in character he is kind and gentle, unsuspecting and forgiving, fair and honest, modest and pure, and, with it all, possessed of a sufficient touch of dignity—if not to make him commanding—at least to inspire respect. With slight additions and alterations these characteristics are his. *He is certainly kind and gentle;* but he is more. He is, at times, timid. He lacks something of the nerve and pluck necessary to the battle of life. He shrinks sometimes when a bold unflinching front should be presented. Yong-Seen-Sang makes a better civilian than soldier, and in the "Reformation" of China, is a Melancthon rather than a Luther. (The lamented Wong Mui was the Luther of the Chinese Christians.) But it is only in times of emergency when courageous and decided action is necessary that he is wanting. *For reliability in the faithful discharge of Christian duty* he merits our warm respect. Whoever else may be absent at the prayer-meeting, in the pew, in the pulpit, he is always on hand. Yong is *unsuspecting and forgiving, fair and honest.* He possess great simple-mindedness and truthfulness, and is an easy prey to every sharper he meets. His own intentions are good, and he imagines the whole world cut from the same pattern as himself.

As a preacher, Yong is far from being either a vigorous or an original thinker. He is inclined to go in ruts, and to repeat himself. In this, however, he is not peculiar. The mental training of most of our Chinese assistants is so poor; the aids to the study of the Bible, at this stage of the work, are so few; and even the knowledge of their own written language is oftentimes so imperfect, that it is the exception to find a vigorous and original preacher among them. Then, again, the character of the preaching necessary to the uneducated, uninformed heathen mind, both as to manner and matter, the constant dwelling upon and enforcing the A, B, C's of Christianity, has the tendency to dwarf the standard and retard the growth of the preacher. But while not a vigorous or original preacher, Yong is instructive. He holds up the main facts and principles of Christianity, and presses them home, with illustrations drawn from the life of those to whom he is addressing himself. No one, from the foregoing sketch, would expect him to be a polemic. While not a decided polemic, however, he would be less a polemic than he is, if he had more ability to instruct. It is easier to tear down than to build up; to ridicule an error than to show a better way. It is a fault with our native assistants that they are rather too polemical, and, the writer thinks, perhaps Yong may be criticised along with most of them in this regard.

Yong, it has been stated, is now about sixty-seven years of age. He has reached the point so beautifully described in the 12th chapter of Ecclesiastes. It cannot be very long before "the silver cord is loosed," before "the golden bowl is broken," before "the pitcher is broken at the fountain," "the wheel broken at the cistern;" before "the dust shall return to the earth as it was, and the spirit shall return unto God who gave it." He has lived a long, a useful, and a godly life. His influence in the church and in the world has been and is a holy influence. The Christian and the heathen alike regard him with reverence. All who know him are filled with sorrow as they reflect that it is highly probable that "the time of his departure is at hand." But sorrow is turned into joy, as in imagination, they hear him catch up the triumphant language of the apostle: "I am now ready to be offered, I have fought a good fight, I have finished my course, I have kept the faith; henceforth there is laid up for me a crown of righteousness."

Rev. EZEKIAS Z. AND MRS. SIMMONS.

WHAT IS IN A NAME?

The Z. in Mr. Simmons' name stands for nothing. The owner explains the initial thus: "When I was a little boy, I received a nice book, and thinking that my name would not look well without a middle letter, I put in Z., which has clung to me ever since."

HIS FIRST TWENTY-FOUR YEARS.

Mr. Simmons was born in Tishomingo County, Mississippi, on the first day of March, 1846. He was baptized, in 1861, at Kossuth,

Mississippi, by Rev. M. P. Lowrey. For two years, he was under General Wheeler in the Confederate army. After the war, he worked hard, and studied at Georgetown and Bethel Colleges, of Kentucky. His health failing, and his means being scant, he returned to Kossuth, where he instructed his brothers and sisters. By the request of the church there, he was ordained, October 30th, 1869. Rev. J. T. Freeman preached the ordination sermon. He was appointed a missionary to Canton, in October, 1870. On the 23d of November of that year, he married Miss Maggie D. McClamroch, of Tennessee. They sailed from New York for Canton *via* Panama, December 3d, 1870; from San Francisco, December 31st; and arrived in Canton, February 6th, 1871.

STUDYING AND LONGING.

Mr. Graves having returned to America, Mr. and Mrs. Simmons were the only foreign missionaries in the mission. *Wong Mui* had charge of the churches. Mr. Simmons wrote: "We are in a good house, and have everything necessary for our comfort. I give all my time to the study of the language. I long to see the time when I shall begin to preach to the Chinese."

THE DEVIL AT WORK.

Of the *Shan-sin-fan* plot, Mr. Simmons wrote: "The shallow conspiracy to drive foreigners from the country, by circulating the report of their attempt to poison the people, only resulted in forcing them into the treaty ports. * * * It is the general opinion of the missionaries that the work has been set back several years by these troubles."

BAPTISM, COMMUNION, AND BENEDICTION.

November 17th: "We carried into the country about 5,000 tracts, and portions of Scriptures. On Sunday morning, we had service for the boat people at *San Siu.* In the afternoon we distributed books in the city. The men preached from the steps of a temple dedicated to *the ten Buddhist Hells.* The little church at *Shiu Hing* is doing tolerably well. We crossed the river and immersed two women. After preaching in the chapel by one of the assistants, we administered the Lord's

Supper. May God bless that little church, and make it a power for good in that great city!"

WORK ADVANCING.

In his report for 1871, Mr. Simmons says: "In reviewing the blessings and mercies of God last year, our hearts are made to rejoice. Surely the Lord is good—a stronghold in the day of trouble! The cause is progressing here. Our Sunday meetings are well attended. My Bible class is large and promising. The influence of the late troubles seems to have died out. We study the language with joyful hopes of soon being able to preach."

INVITED TO COME BACK.

Our assistant was ordered away from *Ngchow*, during the *Shan-sin-fan* excitement. The landlord of the chapel wants us to come back and carry on our work. It is thought safe, now, to go anywhere in the country.

MISSION RESIDENCE.

"I fear Brethren Graves and Williams will have trouble in getting houses. * * I hope the Board will build as soon as possible."

GETTING THE LANGUAGE.

February 20*th*, 1872: "The mission decided that this year I should have charge of the work at *Shiu Hing*. * * We will rent a larger house for our chapel, and improve our work in every respect. While there, I tried to preach every day. I think I shall be able, soon, to speak the Chinese without much trouble."

HOPE IN JESUS.

May 13*th*, 1872: "*Wong Mui* thought his time at hand. He said his only hope was in Jesus. * * I have not heard a prayer offered since his illness, which did not petition God for his recovery."

HEARTS STIRRED.

October 14*th*, 1872: Mr. Simmons accompanied Mr. Graves to explore a region of country hitherto unvisited by Protestant missionaries.

They went to *San Hing* City, fifty miles southwest of Shiu Hing. Mr. Graves exclaimed: "Oh, it is enough to touch any man's heart to see these eager throngs as sheep without a shepherd, and yet so willing to listen attentively to the words of eternal life!"

THE GOSPEL FELT.

February 10*th*, 1873: "The literary examinations are going on at *Shiu Hing*. Our chapel is well filled, from two to four hours, every day, except the Lord's Day. There are two or three hopeful inquirers. It is evident that the gospel and the church are being felt."

EXCEEDING EXPECTATION.

Mr. Simmons was appointed treasurer of the mission. Mr. Hartwell, writing from Canton, April 10th, 1873, remarked: "Brother Simmons is even exceeding all our expectations. He preaches regularly."

FLESH AND BLOOD.

June 25*th:* "Our mission meets weekly for prayer and the study of God's word. This gives a pleasant flavor to the other six days. * * * I weep for gratitude when I think of the hardships of the first missionaries in contrast with our privileges. * * I don't want our friends at home to think * * that we are a set of martyrs or hermits, or anything else that does not agree with common depraved nature. * * * We would be glad to begin early next fall to build our missionary residence. * * Mrs. Simmons has weekly meetings for the women, which are well attended. One of the Bible women meets with them, and does most of the talking."

A HAKKA.

"Mr. Simmons was preaching in the *Sung-shek-kosk* chapel (Mr. Roberts'), when a Hakka, who had listened very eagerly, stopped to talk with him. He had come thirteen days' journey to learn more about the truth, to which his attention had been drawn by reading a tract prepared by Mr. Graves. * * He asked Mr. Graves, 'Have you been to heaven? How, then, could you know all these things so well?'"

The Hakkas are a simple mountain people, much despised by the

Cantonese. They make predatory incursions into the plains, and have thus gained possession of a large part of two districts near Shiu Hing. One of our native assistants went among them, and they heard the gospel gladly.

AT HOME AGAIN.

January 2d, 1874: "Mrs. Simmons' health has not improved, and the doctors say we must leave here in April. We have decided to go to California and labor among the Chinese there, God willing. If our Foreign Missionary Board cannot sustain me as their missionary in California, I hope you will ask the Home Missionary Society to take me as their missionary, until the Lord makes a way for me to come back to China." Mr. Simmons worked in San Francisco among the Chinese, under the patronage of that Society. He also attended, for a while, the Southern Baptist Theological Seminary. He is now at his old home at Kossuth, Mississippi, and longs to resume his labors in China. The Board has decided that he shall return to China within "the present Conventional year."

RETRENCHMENT.

The following is extracted from an article, which appeared from his pen in the *Baptist:*

"This word, retrenchment, has been sounding in my ears for several days. A few days ago I received a letter from Brother R. H. Graves, of Canton, China, and he said that they were ordered by our Secretary to retrench in their work. And he mentioned one chapel in Canton that had been given up, and one house in Shiu Hing that had been given up, and one assistant who had been dismissed. This was sad news to us, and still sadder for Brother Graves to write it. * * * Instead of retrenchment, we should press forward and establish stations in every principal city. At least, let us, for the sake of our missionaries, and for the sake of the cause which is dear to us all, say that our missionaries shall not be forced to retrench in their work. Every pastor, every church, and every Baptist should forestall retrenchment, by sending at once a generous contribution to our Board in Richmond. It is easy to pull down what is already built up, but it is doubly hard to build again.

CHINA—CANTON MISSION.   143

I hope and pray that every one who reads this will do something for our Fóreign Mission work."

MRS. MAGGIE D. SIMMONS.

Her grandfather came from Scotland, and settled in Orange County, Virginia. Her father, David McClamroch, moved to Rowan (now Davie) County, N. C., where he married Delilah Ijams. They moved to Hardman County, Tenn., where their daughter Maggie was born, June 14th, 1843. Her parents dying while she was of tender age, she was reared by her uncle, Mr. Herndon, of Florence, Ala. In October, 1862, she professed faith in Christ, and was baptized by Mr. Essry.

"Mrs. Simmons has a lively, cheerful disposition, always looking on the bright side of life. Her work in Christ was preparatory—studying the language and the New Testament. She and a native Bible woman had semi-weekly appointments and taught the women of the neighborhood the gospel. In San Francisco, she taught in the Chinese schools. Though not robust, yet, she says: 'I wish we could start back to China to-morrow.'"

Rev. ROSEWELL HOBART GRAVES, M.D.

THE START.

The subject of these lines was born in the city of Baltimore, May 29th, 1833. He was baptized by Dr. R. Fuller, October 15th, 1848. He graduated at St. Mary's College in 1851. On May 15th, 1853, he wrote in his journal: "Brother Shuck spoke of China. My heart bleeds for the 400,000,000 still without the knowledge of Jesus! * * * Direct me, O God! Send me where thou wilt have me go." In view of the missionary work, he took the degree of Doctor of Medicine.

"*March 13th*, 1855. Mr. Graves was unanimously accepted by the Board and appointed to labor as a missionary in Canton."

"*August 6th.* The Board expressed a *decided preference* that Brother

Graves should marry; but will not *insist* upon it as *indispensable* to his going as missionary to China."

He was ordained April 12th, 1856, in the Seventh Baptist Church of Baltimore. On the 17th of the same month, there was, in the First Baptist Church of that City, a "Farewell Missionary Meeting."

UNLEARNING CHINESE.

On the 19th of April, 1856, he sailed for Canton, and arrived the 14th of August. Mr. Gaillard had been anxiously awaiting him. October 8th, 1856, he wrote: "I gained some little knowledge of the Chinese character while on shipboard; but, with regard to speaking, I have now to unlearn some things that I learned, as neither the young Chinaman, who is a native of *Fuh Chau*, nor the books which he lent me, gave the sounds of the Canton dialect."

BEGINNING OF BETTER DAYS.

In September, 1857, Mr. Graves returned to Canton from Macao, where he had been twice driven by the war. This year, the English evacuated the forts taken from the Chinese, except the *Tee-to-tune* fort. Great anxiety prevailed at Hong Kong. The imperialists had concluded a truce, for two years, with the rebel Cantonese, who had united with them to oppose the English. Mr. Graves wrote: "My congregations are smaller than they were; but most of the people remain until the end of the service. * * *Yong Seen Sang* lives in my house. His walk is that of a consistent Christian." In the report of 1860, we read: "Brother Graves has been abundant in labors. He says: ' This year has been to us the beginning of better days; for God has given to us souls for our hire.'" With Mr. Gaillard, he made frequent excursions into the country. They distributed 26,250 tracts and portions of the Scriptures, 2,500 copies of the Gospels and the Acts, and 50 copies of the New Testament, with 50 copies of Dean's Notes on Matthew. Thirteen converts were baptized. The next year was one of unusual prosperity. Among the number baptized by Mr. Graves were three English soldiers.

CHINA—CANTON MISSION.

IN THE INTERIOR.

July 17th, 1860. "Brother Graves has gone to a place where the local rebels have been, and the people there will now be more likely to hear the gospel, as they have suffered much from the rebels."

November 30th. "Brother Graves, with the approbation of the mission, has been in the country some two months, and desires to spend most of his time there."

February 27th, 1861. "Brother Graves has gone again to the country. He has his heart set on establishing a station there. I think it would be hard to find a man better suited for the work. I wish you would send us a few more such men."

He finally succeeded in establishing a station at *Shiu Hing*, formerly the capital of two provinces. He baptized several persons, founded a church, and practised medicine, prescribing to 2,620 patients. He was aided by two natives, *Luk* and *Au*. "They are good and useful men."

BRIGHT AND DARK DAYS.

After the death of Mr. Gaillard, who was pastor at Canton, Mr. Graves returned to that city by request of the church to overlook the interests there. He married, in 1863, Mr. Gaillard's widow, who died, as has been seen, December 12th, 1864. Our brother wrote touchingly and beautifully: "I feel a great void. Every now and then I see something, and say to myself: 'I will tell it to Eva.' And then I recollect she is gone!" Mr. Schilling, losing his wife, returned to America in June, 1864. Thus Mr. Graves was literally alone, as our representative in the great city and province of Canton.

LABORIOUS AND SUCCESSFUL.

Mr. Graves pressed his work with characteristic fidelity and with great success. In 1866, he had eight assistants, who aided him to carry the word far into the interior. He travelled that year about 1,600 miles on Chinese boats, and distributed 9,658 tracts. Two strong stations were maintained, the one at *Shiu Hing*, 80 miles from Canton, and another at *Wu-chau*, 200 miles from Canton, in the province of

Kwang-si. At each place he had a dispensary. They had been visited nearly 7,000 times by the afflicted. A school was opened near *Shiu Hing,* which was taught by *Seen,* deacon of the *Shiu Hing* Church, and sustained by a sum which had been set apart for the education of Mr. Graves' step-son, Chas. A. Gaillard; but which, at the death of the lad, was thus benevolently devoted by Mr. Graves. This year he lost his native helper, Luk, of whom he said: " He was full of love, was an able pioneer, has now ceased from his labors, and, I doubt not, is with his Saviour." Mr. Graves wrote: " One of the pressing necessities of this mission is a permanent chapel."

CHAPEL FUNDS AND PUBLICATIONS.

In 1867, the funds for this chapel were secured, a brother of Baltimore furnishing one-half of the amount ($1,250 in *gold*), and the Board the other half. This year Mr. Graves sent home his son, under the care of Mrs. Holmes, of the Shantung Mission. In the " Memorials of Protestant Missionaries," published at Shanghai, in 1867, are mentioned three Chinese publications of Mr. Graves: " *Important Words to Arouse the World,*" " *Questions on the True Doctrine,*" and " *Notes on Romans.*" He published also a small book on Homiletics, Notes on the Parables, and a Hymn Book. He is at present engaged on a Scripture-Geography, and a Life of Christ.

" FIRST, THE KINGDOM."

The health of Mr. Graves failing, the Board, in 1868, urged his return to America. He would not quit his post, especially as he had begun to build his chapel. The two churches of Canton, with the out-stations, were under his care. *Wu-chau* being a department city, Mr. Graves preached there to large crowds, and distributed books, with the prospect of the truth being conveyed far into the interior.

The students would cry out " Foreign Ghost," but Mr. Graves remarked: " I thought of that kingdom, whose foundations I was laying in this inland province, a kingdom which will go on increasing, when I am in the dust. I, its lonely representative, might be a gazing stock and butt of ridicule; but after awhile its glorious Head will come, and to him every knee will bow, and him every tongue will confess to be the Lord."

"THE GRACE AND COMPASSION OF GOD."

Mr. Graves' excursions into the country were marked by striking incidents of persecutions, and of conversions. In Canton, he instructed daily the native preachers. The statistics for 1868 were: Baptisms, 13; membership, 120; contributions, $58.07. In the dispensaries, 5,197 treated, and 424 vaccinated. The chapel was formally opened, 5th April, 1869, and attended by large numbers of curious Chinese. During this year, 16 were baptized. Wong Mui, who has been with Mr. Shuck, in California, was ordained, December 12th, 1869. *Au*, the worthy assistant, passed away, saying: "I know I shall see you in heaven, because I trust with my whole heart in the grace and compassion of God for my salvation."

CHEERING PROGRESS AND APOSTOLIC PLAN.

Mr. Graves remarked: "I thank God and take courage at the progress, which my eyes have seen in China. * * * Our work in Canton is set on a satisfactory basis. We have a good house for our congregations, and the living church has had an elder appointed over them, according to the apostolic plan."

RECREATION IN LABOR.

After thirteen years of faithful and exhausting toil, Mr. Graves arrived in San Francisco, March 19th, 1870, with *Fung*, a native assistant, brought to labor among the Chinese in California.

"*March 27th.* Preached at Tabernacle Baptist Church. Took rooms for *Fung* and myself, near the Chinese section of the city." *Fung* died the next year. Mr. Graves was present at the Southern Baptist Convention in Louisville, May 1870. By the invitation of the Home Mission Society, of New York, Mr. Graves, with the approval of our Board, labored among the Chinese of California. His work there was highly esteemed, and is still held, by that Society, in grateful remembrance.

WONG MUI'S REPORT.

The native pastor, who was left in charge of the two churches of Canton, reported for 1871: Baptisms, 7; members, 91. "Pray that the Holy Spirit may change men's hearts—that the true doctrine may advance, and all false systems be destroyed."

REËNFORCEMENTS.

Rev. E. Z. Simmons started for Canton in December, 1870, and arrived, February, 1871.

Mr. Graves was married by Rev. Dr. R. Fuller, in the Eutaw Place Baptist Church, of Baltimore, to Miss Jane Wormeley Norris, of that city, January 15th, 1872. On April 17th, "a Farewell Meeting" was held in Dr. Fuller's church for the missionary company, composed of Rev. J. B. Hartwell and Mrs. Hartwell, Rev. N. B. Williams and Mrs. Williams, Miss Edmonia Moon and Miss Lula Whilden, and Rev. and Mrs. R. H. Graves. They started from Baltimore the next day; sailed from San Francisco, May 1st; arrived at Yokohama, Friday, the 24th; remained there, awaiting steamer, until Monday, the 27th. The voyage had been delightful, and the two other parties were pained to say to each other *adieu.* Mr. and Mrs. Hartwell, with Miss Moon, were bound for Shantung; the others reached Hong Kong, on June the 4th, and Canton, the 5th, 1872.

REPORT AND REPUTE OF MR. AND MRS. GRAVES.

Mr. Graves resumed his usual labors in the city. The North River was ascended for 175 miles, and 25 towns were visited, where the gospel had been rarely if ever preached. The statistics of the Church were as follows: Baptisms, 16; membership, 156; native assistants, 8; Bible women, 4. One ordained native pastor, *Wong Mui.*

Visiting Canton, our beloved and lamented classmate, Dr. William Ward, of Assam, said: "I am greatly pleased with the brethren and sisters of your three mission families. No man, I believe, in the whole missionary community, stands higher than Brother Graves for excel-

CHINA—CANTON MISSION.

lence of spirit, soundness of judgment and devotion to the real marrow of the mission work."

In 1873, Mr. Graves opened a station at *Sai-Nan*, an important city at the junction of the North and West Rivers.

Wong Fung, the son of *Wong Mui*, had in charge the dispensary. "The little church at Shiu Hing shone out as a light in the midst of surrounding darkness." Young ministers were taken into the country to practise their gifts. Mr. Hartwell, on a visit to Canton, wrote: "I don't believe the missionary world contains two more conscientious, earnest, and consecrated workers than Brother and Sister Graves."

DEATH OF WONG MUI, AND CHURCH ITEMS.

In August, 1874, *Wong Mui*, the native pastor of the Canton Church, was taken to his heavenly rest. "No native can supply his place in the discipline of the church." A headstone has been provided for his resting place, by the First Baptist Church of Charleston, S. C., whose pastor, Rev. L. H. Shuck, a native of China, was a pupil of the departed man of God. Statistics of the Canton Mission; Baptized, 31; membership, 146; contributions, $90; dispensary at *Sai-Nan*, 6,500 patients; operations performed, 40; tracts and New Testaments, distributed, 17,429. Average attendance of schools, 35, and 10. Mr. Graves continues his training class, under the conviction that CHINA MUST BE CONVERTED THROUGH CHINAMEN.

MISSIONARY RESIDENCE.

The Baltimore brethren provided $4,610 for the Canton missionary residence. The Board added $2,250, the net proceeds of a bequest by the late E. Levering, Esq., of the same city. The ladies of Alabama and South Carolina contributed to the object $2,346.69. The whole amount, $9,206.69, is in the hands of Mr. Graves. May the work be soon completed!

SUMMARY.

The results of the Canton Mission from 1876 to 1880, will be found in the *Resumé* at the end of this volume.

WOMEN AND WOMEN'S WORK.

Mrs. JANE WORMELEY GRAVES.

Mrs. Graves is the daughter of George W. Norris, Esq., of Baltimore, and the wife of Rev. Rosewell H. Graves, of Canton. She was baptized by Dr. Richard Fuller. Usefully and piously was this lady engaged, as a teacher of young ladies, and as an active member of the Eutaw Place Baptist Church, when it became her duty and her happiness to unite her life with that of Mr. Graves, in the self-denying work of giving the gospel to the heathen. Her visit, with her husband, to Richmond, shortly before their departure for China, will be long remembered. Her quiet spirit, her intelligent zeal, her love of the name of Jesus, made a pleasant impression on those who became acquainted with her. Her presence, with Mr. Graves, at a prayer meeting of the First Baptist Church, when the prayers of the church were promised to them in their life-work, has been not unfrequently recalled, with the view of stimulating the members in their duty to the perishing pagans. In Canton, Mrs. Graves has superintended with Miss Whilden the education of girls, and performed missionary labor in the country, as well as in the city. Her letters are full of interest, and breathe the spirit of one who loves the cause to which she has devoted the energies of her being. Missionaries speak of her in terms of warm commendation. We pray that she may have enlarging influence for good among the women of Canton, and predict that she will gain a high place, in the estimation of God's people, among their noble women-workers for Jesus.

Mrs. JUMELLE WILLIAMS.

This lady is the eldest daughter of our former missionary, Rev. B. W. Whilden, and is a native of Camden, S. C. She is a woman of fine mental endowments, and of lovely, pious spirit. As a teacher in the Female College, of Greenville, S. C., the force of her intellectual and religious character was exerted with marked effect. While thus engaged, the acquaintance of N. B. Williams, then a student in the Southern Baptist Theological Seminary, was formed, which resulted in their marriage and her missionary life.

The health of Mrs. Williams was not vigorous in China. The climate, however, may not be regarded as unfavorable to her constitution. A photograph of herself and two children, received at the Mission Rooms, just before her return to this country, represents her as in almost the freshness of girlhood. A letter, accompanying the picture, indulges the hope that these little ones may make, in the family, the third generation of missionaries to the Cantonese. May they inherit the missionary fire of both mother and grandmother, as well as that of their father and grandsire!

Miss LOUISA WHILDEN.

Miss Whilden is the sister of Mrs. Williams. She also was born in Camden, S. C., where their father was pastor, before becoming a missionary to China. The two girls, with their brother De Leon, now deceased, were taken to Canton with their parents, and brought back to this country after their mother's death.

Miss Whilden is a graduate of the Female College, of Greenville, S. C., where she made a decided reputation by her intelligence, conscientiousness, and firmness in the cause of Christ.

Soon after her arrival in Canton, she associated herself with Mrs. Graves in the school-training of girls, and in the religious instruction of women. The neglected boat-women engaged her sympathies, and her toils have been sometimes almost beyond her strength. It has been even necessary to administer affectionate caution against the zeal which threatened to consume her. The Chinese notice her devotion, and say she works not merely from duty, but from love of their souls. Articles from her pen have excited much interest in the public mind. The name of "Miss Lula Whilden" can inspire as much enthusiasm as that of any name on our roll of consecrated missionaries of the cross. The benevolence of this lady is as conspicuous as her zeal. Often does she deny herself what seems really needful, that thereby she may gratify her Christ-like passion for doing good.

NECESSITY OF WOMAN'S WORK.

Men have no access to the families of China, to convey to them the gospel of Christ. As in all countries, the children are under the influence of the mother. The women unreached, Paganism is necessarily perpetuated by the maternal instruction of the children; and the women can only be reached by women. This woman's work is imperative, not only to elevate their degraded sex, and by that elevation to give new tone to the moral character of society; but as the rational means, under God, of undermining the fabric of heathen superstition and blasphemy. The conversion of one woman in China is worth, in its influence, as much as that of two men. The hope of China is the salvation of her women. The women of the South, therefore, are doing a divinely inspired work in supporting these women missionaries. And why may not woman's missionary societies spring up all over our land, fired with the desire to give the gospel to the women of heathen lands? Let these societies be formed; and let them band together for the simple and grand purpose of sending the ennobling and saving gospel to women, who are worse than slaves to their husbands, and better than demons to "the god of this world," in riveting the chains of darkness and death upon the nations of the earth.

Daughters of Zion, mothers in Israel, if you have love for the Saviour of your race, who has honored your sex above all humanity, in becoming the son of a woman, now is the time to show that love by making your free-will offerings to him, which, though less costly, may be no less acceptable than that which won for Mary the imperishable praise: "SHE HATH DONE WHAT SHE COULD."

THE MITE BOX.

My DEAR MADAM: I am glad that you write for more Mite Boxes.

You say: "A few of us are doing what we can." You may do much if you appreciate the importance of small contributions.

THE POWER OF PENNIES.

The woman who swept her house for the lost piece of money; and when she found it called in her neighbors to rejoice with her, believed, beforehand, in the maxim of the so-called parsimonious philosopher : " Take care of the pennies, and the pounds will take care of themselves." As the child is father to the man, so the penny is parent to the pound—a pyramid of pounds is but the product of pence. Hence, the further adage of the same sagacious sage : " He that destroys a penny destroys the thousands of pounds which might have been produced by it." And I add: " He that saves a penny for a good purpose may be laying the foundation of untold wealth, for time and for eternity." There may be such a thing as " penny wise and pound foolish ; " but there is no such thing as penny-foolish and pound-wise—at least, in the economy of him who presides over, not only the heavens and the earth, but the atoms which make up the pillars and architraves of the Temple of the Universe.

The first is that the lowest coin of all peoples is disregarded. This is true of the Cowry of Africa, the Cash of China, and the Cent of America. When you hear the rude boy say: " I do not care a cent ; " " he is not worth a cent," he means: " I care *nothing;* he is a *worthless* fellow." Was it this fact of the disregard of money in its lowest form, let me digress to ask, that suggested the policy of Sparta, which, in order to guard against the demoralizing greed of gold, restricted the State currency to an iron coinage ?

The second fact is that, in the spending of small pieces of money, however often the spending, the mind, not accustomed to the process of aggregating, is impressed as to the individual expenditures, rather than as to their sum. What lady, after shopping, has not been surprised as to " where her money is gone ?" What householder, has not exclaimed at the heavy footings of bills, made up of little purchases on the credit system ? The State of Virginia receives a large revenue from taxation of certain dime and nickle spendings, which, unconsciously, drain millions from the home to the bar-room. Many units make multitudes.

The third fact is that, in every community and country, there are more than one hundred times as many who can and will give one cent for the Lord's treasury, as there are who will give one dollar. This fact is emphasized by the consideration that God's people are generally of the poor of the earth. Paradoxical as it may seem, almsgiving is often in inverse ratio to ability; and the benevolent strength of the churches resides largely in their pecuniary weakness. The particles at the base of mountains may be smaller than those at the top; but, more numerous, and more firmly compacted, they constitute the foundations of "the everlasting hills."

The fourth fact is that giving one cent a hundred times is more than giving one dollar. The repetition forms the habit of giving, which habit is only another name for beneficent character. That was a good man who said: "Do not push the collection-basket at me every Sunday, and I will give, at any time, my share of the offerings." But he had not studied the power of habit; and the philosophy of this seventh-day contribution. Wiser was that Queen of England, who had her purse filled every day with coin to dispense with her own hand, to needy ones of her subjects.

Now, Mrs. Secretary, if you keep in mind these four facts, I think you will agree with me that any system which aims at the gathering of these unvalued, unconsciously-given, most numerous, and habit-forming pieces of money will do more for the Treasury of the Lord than any system which looks for large gifts from the more highly favored as to this world's goods. I mean to say that a general and regular collection for benevolent purposes among the millions of God's people would sum up more than all the splendid donations from the richest of the world. The principle is much the same as that by which the influence going forth from Infant Classes, like your own, is more powerful and more far-reaching than the influences of all the Seminaries, and Colleges, and Universities of the world.

By way of illustration, I may remind you of "Peter's pence," which add, by a single collection, $2,000,000 annually to the coffers of Rome; and may state that the Baptist ladies in Richmond, Virginia, agreeing to raise, in Mite Boxes, $400 for one of our missionaries' raised, the first year, $1200; that one of our Mite Box Societies, (which Societies number now at the South some three hundred), a Society composed of only thirty or forty "girls," has pledged $500 yearly for the support of a young lady in China; that the ladies of a single State raised thus for us last year, nearly one thousand dollars; and that the Christian women of our country are reported to have given to Foreign Missions, in 1878, $300,000; and, in the past five years, about $1,500,000. And what may not be done with the right spirit? The Macedonians first gave themselves to the Lord; and then, "their deep poverty abounded unto the riches of their liberality."

Let me say something now, about what I shall call,

THE MINISTRY OF MONEY.

Agassiz said that he had no time to make money. But somebody must have time to make it, and to make a great deal of it. When money making stops in the world then civilization—with its art, and science, and education; its social order, and comfort, and refinement; its civil institutions, and protection, and countless blessings—rolls back into barbaric life, and the wheels of Christianity itself, provided there be neither miracle nor Millenium, must effectually break down.

Achan's wedge of gold, and Babylonian garment were accursed, not because they were wealth, but because acquired contrary to the divine will. Balaam might have desired, without sin, Balak's house of gold and silver; but not in preference to the blessing of Israel. Ananias and Sapphira might have withheld the whole of their property; but not a particle of it, with a lie upon the lip, either to God or to man. They that *err from the faith*, in coveting after riches, are pierced through with sorrow, and drowned in destruction and perdition. Abraham was a prince among shepherds, and "the Father of the faithful." David was among the wealthiest of monarchs, and a type of King Emanuel himself. As Bouhours says: "Money is a good servant, but a poor master."

When our Saviour took that piece of money, and asked: "Whose is this image and superscription?" he did not mean to suggest that the things of Cæsar are not to be rendered to Christ. The very first offering which he received was of *gold*, with frankincense and myrrh.

Money being the representative of all earthly commodities, and the undue love of it being a specious form of idolatry, the hearty offering of it to the living and true God is one of the best tests of fealty to him, a potent means of rearing the spiritual above the carnal of our nature, and a practical exposition of the true use of the natural and circumstantial which are designed to blend with the spiritual and essential, in the reign of him whose throne is the diamond-studded heavens; whose footstool is the richly tapestried earth; and whose palace is the material as well as the immaterial universe.

If it be hard to make this offering, it was hard for Abraham to offer Isaac. But the promise made to him—"Because thou hast done this thing * * in blessing, I will bless thee, and in multiplying, I will multiply thee,"—was only one application of the general law, "Give, and it shall be given you, good measure, pressed down, and shaken together, and running over." They that make the secular secondary to the spiritual, shall secure not only life eternal, but an hundred-fold more here—at least when the saints shall ride upon the high places of the earth, and be fed with the heritage of Jacob their father, "for the mouth of the Lord hath spoken it." If a gift-test be instituted, like Prof. Tyndall's prayer-test, devoid of every element of worship, of course it will fail. But the truth still stands that "the liberal soul shall be made fat;" which was more philosophically than poetically paraphrased by the spiritual sage of the Pilgrim's Progress:

> There was a man, and all did think him mad,
> The more he gave away, the more he had.

Every penny or pound prayerfully put in the mite box or the treasury of the Lord, is something of a preacher, that proclaims a trophy from the God of this world; that predicts the enrichment, by all earthly good, of that kingdom, the gates of whose capital city are of pearl, whose foundations are garnished with all manner of precious stones, whose wall is of jasper, and whose streets are of pure gold;—a preacher that exhorts us to render our all unto him from whom are all things. The poor widow, who cast in her whole living, though but two mites, was not only wise, but prospectively rich, as faithful to the true and triumphing ministry of money.

But, to stimulate the zeal of your society, I wish to add something with regard to

WOMANS' WORK FOR THE WOMEN OF THE WORLD.

First, there is a work of sympathy. Woman's peculiar relation to human woes should make her sympathize profoundly with our human race. Especially should she feel for her sister-women, whose miseries are sometimes unutterable, and in whose endurance of them there is often more of heroism and of martyrdom than has ever been sung in epics or recorded in Martyrologies. The sacrifice of girl-children, by their mothers to save them from a worse fate, in after-life, upon the altar of human passion and hate, should sweep the whole gamut of womanly sympathy, and send out the heart, warm, and pulsating with concern, for these wretched creatures whose life-experiences are ofttimes worse than the pangs of death itself; and whose only hope is that of Sisera's mother, looking out the window and calling through the lattice: Why tarry the wheels of his chariot?—But they hope against hope—never getting anything better than they have had, until the shadows of that last solemn night close around them; and they go down to a fate more certain and more fearful than that of the victim with nail driven through his temples into the floor of the house of the seductive and murderous Jael. Our Christian women should long that these women may be elevated by the religion of him whose sole earthly parent was a woman: and who honored the sex of "the blessed Virgin Mary," not by making her an object of adoration, but by moulding from this part of man the purest, and most Christ-like type of a Christianized humanity. I covet for you, Sister Secretary, and for each of our sisters of Zion, in its broadest and holiest sense, the praise awarded to women, by the Board of Abbotsford:

> " When pain and anguish wring the brow,
> A ministering Angel thou!"

Again, there is a work of benevolent action. Christian women must go to these heathen women. They must go and look into their eyes, and down into their souls, until there is a stirring of self-respect and of that conscious dignity which belongs to womanhood. They must tell them that while in their country women are said to be incapable of education and unfit for religion, in civilized countries woman proves herself to be man's equal in intelligence, and his superior in morality and spirituality—as approximating nearer to him, who was conspicuous for the womanliness of his character, and who was of humanity the unit of which man and woman are the fractional parts. They should tell them that woman is the natural center of the domestic and social circle; that on social virtues are reared the pillars of good government; and that as a source of power she should strive to send through the radii of every day affairs a salutary influence, which may be felt to the very circumference of the society, of which she is the most formative part. They must tell them of what women have done and been—of Deborah, leading the hosts of our God; of Priscilla, teaching the eloquent Apollos more perfectly the way of the Lord; of Mary, the mother of the Saviour of the world. Our women must go to these women for the defence of their humanity, and go heroically—like Rizpah, who threw her sackcloth on the rock, and from the beginning of harvest until the waters of heaven fell upon them, watched the bodies of the sons of the departed King of Israel, against the preying birds by day and the ravening beasts by night. They must go to tell the story of Jesus and his love, and go hopefully. From the mulberry leaf come the satin and the silk. From the black of night is evolved the Aurora of day. And under the purifying and inspiring power of our religion, the despised and dejected daughter of China may rise up, the noblest thing that walks under the canopy of heaven, a true and Christian woman.

This requires sacrifice. But who so ready for sacrifices as woman? When a noble woman of our Board was going to the heathen, an admiring friend said: "What waste!" But think you, that she had any such thought? Nay, she as well as each of her sister missionaries, would esteem it honor to pour out her life as a libation upon the sacrifice of him who poured out his heart's blood for herself, her sex, and her race.

All cannot go, but all may send. It was the tear-drop on his head from his mother's eye that sent a great missionary to the East. It was his mother's prayers in the closet with him, when a little boy, that made another to shed martyr-blood in the Pacific Isles. It was his sister's piety that led to Christ the man who kindled in Persia a fire which shall never be extinguished. You know of that missionary's mother, who, when she heard that her son had been destroyed by a cannibal, said with more than Spartan grandeur: "Oh that I had another son to carry the gospel to those wicked men, who have drunk the blood of my darling boy!"

But all cannot send a living representative. Hence, I spoke of the ministry of money—a ministry well understood by women. Those women, Joanna and Susanna and Mary, who organized the first missionary society under the gospel, understood it. The "poor widow" understood it, who made the Lord the grandest contribution recorded in profane or sacred history—grander than if Queen Victoria should take her crown, and throne, and royal revenues, and palaces, and have them all re-stamped as palimpsests, with "Holiness to the Lord."

Hence, I referred also to the Power of Pennies—a power which woman, whose life is, like the earth and the sea and the heavens, made up of little things, is best adapted to generate and to control. J. Stuart Mill said he never understood Carlyle, who was so high, he could not see over him; so broad, he could not see around him; so deep, he could not see through him, until a woman gave him the key to his character. I never saw how the mass of our people could be made to work for the heathen until a now-sainted woman solved the problem by the suggestion of the Mite-Box System. Thus all may do something, and may go, by proxy, to the nations. All that this system needs is the tact, and zeal, and perseverance of our Christian women, to turn a million and a half of money into the Treasury of the Master;

which would speedily take away our reproach of giving annually "only two cents per capita for the evangelization of the pagan world;" and would send forth copious streams to convert the desert places of the earth into the garden of the Lord.

I hope that your society, and all our sister-workers for Jesus, will be encouraged in their plans. Be assured that all the wealth, and power, and circumstance of our advancing civilization will be made to contribute to the progress of Christ's kingdom—will be used as scaffolding for the up-building of God's Temple, whose foundations shall be co-extensive with our earth, and whose dome of many-colored hues —to garble Shelley's fine lines—shall tint the white radiance of eternity. Your work is sure. Heaven and earth may fail; but not one jot or tittle of the word of God, who has given to his Son "the heathen for his inheritance, and the uttermost part of the earth for a possession."

I am very truly,

Your Brother Secretary, T.

September the 15th.

SHANGHAI MISSION.

For the sake of variety, we propose to consider this Mission chronologically, under the heads of First, Second, and Third Decade, comprising the period from 1846 to 1876. The period from 1876 to 1880 will be noted in the Resumé towards the close of the volume.

Before sketching the Mission, however, we shall give some description of the City of Shanghai; also brief notices of our Missionaries, whose labors have been confined to this station. Those who labored in this Mission, but subsequently moved to Shantung, will be sketched when we consider the stations of that province.

CITY OF SHANGHAI.

Shanghai, a *Hzien*, or district city, is situated on the west bank of the Hwang-pu River, near its confluence with the Soochow Creek. It is about twelve miles from the embouchure of these united streams into the Yang-Tse-Kiang, which discharges its waters into the Yellow Sea. Its distance from the sea is about sixty miles. It is in longitude 126° 30′ E.; and in latitude 31° 24′ N., about that of Savannah, Georgia.

CLIMATE.

The atmosphere is humid, and the place is subject to very chilling winds. According to a Hospital Report of Dr. Lockhart, the sudden changes of weather, in the spring and autumn, are conducive to rheumatic and pulmonary complaints. The maximum heat is 100° and the minimum 15° F. Dr. Yates says: "I have seen here three feet of snow on the level." The average summer temperature is 80° to 93° F., by day; and from 60° to 75° by night. The thermometer ranges, in winter, from 45° to 60° F., by day; and from 36° to 45° by night. Limits in a single day are about 20°—rarely over 25°. Yet, upon the whole, the climate may be said to be salubrious.

CITY AND PEOPLE.

Shanghai is a walled town, four miles in circuit. Six gates open into extensive suburbs, which are divided from the city by a canal ten feet deep. Three canals run from the river—which is here about three-quarters of a mile wide—in transverse directions through the heart of the city. From these canals several small dykes branch off. The city stands in a wide plain of extraordinary fertility, and intersected by numerous streamlets, affording the means of navigation and communication. Its population is estimated at 6 or 700,000. The banks of the river are covered with dwellings, temples, shops, and other buildings.

The city is poorly built, when compared with some other places in the province. The houses are mostly of brick. The streets are dirty, and crowded with hucksters, chiefly of food. For a few cash (one thousandth part of a dollar), a Chinaman can dine on rice, fish, vegetables, and tea; of which he partakes, seemingly indifferent as to whether his meal is in the street, on deck, or in an eating-house. A few public edifices attract the attention, as indicating some taste and style in architecture. A foundling hospital was founded in 1707, which has been patronized by wealthy, and even royal persons. The people are quiet, but active, and respectful to strangers. The British and American Consulates tend to engender good feeling; as does occasional interchange of courteous visits. In this respect, this city is very different from Canton, where the foreigner is detested. The epithet *quei-tze*, "devil," is forbidden by public authority. There is no difficulty in securing residences; and no opposition to mission work. Adjacent to the west gate, there is a succession of gardens. A line of river-frontage, for two miles, on the northern suburbs, is appropriated to buildings for foreign merchants. The situation is good, the air salubrious, and the locality is convenient for shipping. The chief staples are cotton, rice, and wheat. There are large exports of tea and silks.

COMMERCIAL IMPORTANCE.

Shanghai is the largest seaport of Kiangsu Province. It is the *entrepot* for the commerce of Shantung and Tartary on the north; the outport of all the central provinces; the grand emporium for trade of Fokien and Formosa of the south; a usual port of access to Soo-Choo-Foo; the metropolis of Chinese fashion and literature. In position it resembles New Orleans. The native trade is probably larger than at any other city in the Empire. Nearly five thousand junks have been counted lying in the Hwang-pu, east of the town. The foreign trade will, probably, soon surpass the native in value and variety.

OPENING OF THE CITY TO WESTERN RELIGIONS.

In 1835, Messrs. Medhurst and Stephens visited Shanghai. Mr. Medhurst's Journal gives an interesting account of their interview with the native officers in a temple. In 1842, the city fell into the hands of the English, after a gallant defence of the river by General Chin, who died on the ramparts with sword in hand; and who was honored by having his image, to which incense is offered, set up in one of the temples of the city. In 1844, Dr. Medhurst and Dr. Lockhart started there the full machinery for making books. Our missions began in 1847.

In the city and neighborhood are many Romanists. The bishop is called the Bishop of Heliopolis, whose diocese is Kwansu, Shantung, and Pe-chi-li. The membership is 60,000.

Rev. MATTHEW TYSON YATES, D.D.

BIRTH AND EARLY EDUCATION.

Mr. Yates is the son of the late William and Delilah Yates, who were members of the Mount Pisgah Baptist Church, Chatham County, North Carolina. He came into the world in Wake County, near the Chatham line, January 8th, 1819. During a camp-meeting, he was baptized into the fellowship of the Mount Pisgah Church, by Rev. P. W. Dowd, on the fourth Sunday of October, 1836. "Shortly after this," writes George W. Thompson, Esq., of North Carolina, "by the advice of Brother Dowd, he became associated with me as a student, and studied the elementary branches of an English education, I believing with Brother Dowd that he was a youth of more than ordinary promise, and of exemplary Christian character. I cultivated great intimacy with him—so much so, that we would talk, without reserve, on the subject of religion and the Christian ministry."

MISSIONARY THOUGHTS—"STRUGGLES" AND LATER EDUCATION—MARRIAGE.

In a letter, dated March 17, 1846, Mr. Yates wrote: " My attention was first directed to the condition of the heathen world from reading the memoirs of Mrs. Judson, soon after obtaining, I trust, the remission of my sins. Frequently did I weep for hours, while following my plow or using my trowel, when I would reflect that the poor heathen, who knew nothing of Jesus Christ, the only Saviour of the world, must die and appear before God to be judged according to their works in this world. With my heart thus overwhelmed, rather than let my brother and dear father see me weeping, I have often left my business to go into the solitary grove for the purpose of inquiring what the Lord would have *me* to do. Thus, in my *infancy*, I had an ardent desire to do something to ameliorate the condition of the heathen. * * I told my father that, when I became a free man, I intended to go to school, if I had to make brick by moonlight to pay my way. * * At the age of eighteen I sold my horse, my only available property, which enabled me to go to an academy for one year. * * I resolved to go to College, and, by the aid of God, 'to find a way or to make one.' Very soon, however, the brethren seeing my 'struggles' came to my aid." Mr. Thompson continues: "Returning one day from the academy (Brother Yates boarded with me), he invited me to his room for a private and confidential interview. Then it was, amidst an overflow of tender emotion, he expressed to me the impressions of his mind on the subject of the ministry. Having heard him through, he asked me to advise him and tell him what to do, saying it appeared strange to him that his mind should be so strongly impressed with such thoughts, knowing that he had no suitable qualifications for such a high vocation, remarking, at the same time, he felt as though he would be willing to go to a land of heathenism to preach the gospel of Christ were he competent for such a work.

I advised him not to resist his impressions, but to pray fervently for divine instruction, and that God would direct his steps. In this interview, I asked and obtained his consent to bring his case to the notice of his pastor and Rev. Samuel Wait, then President of Wake Forest College. I invited Brother Wait to my house to make the acquaintance of our young Brother M. T. Yates, and through our joint efforts he was speedily brought to the notice of the Baptist State Convention, and was received by that body and sent to Wake Forest College, where he graduated, June, 1846, with much honor."

Under date of April 30th, 1846, Rev. John B. White, then of Wake Forest College, communicated the following to the Board of Foreign Missions: "Mr. Yates is a few inches over six feet high, straight, broad-chested, and inclined to be spare, with eyes and hair black, an agreeable countenance, and, for his opportunity, an easy and dignified manner. He has been here about six years. * * In no study was he ever *marked* below ' good ;' in most of them ' very good ;' and, in a few, ' excellent '—these marks denoting our highest grades of scholarship. * * He has a very pleasant, full voice, and possesses, indeed, many elements of a forcible and commanding speaker. I think he has a well-balanced mind."

Dr. J. B. Taylor, late Corresponding Secretary of our Board, having visited the College in February of the same year, expressed himself thus: "A young brother is there, who, in all probability, will be engaged as one of our missionaries. His name is Yates. I am much pleased with him, and cannot but hope the Lord intends him for eminent usefulness. He seems determined now to spend his life among the heathen. The Professors all speak well of him, and think him in many respects eminently qualified for the work."

Subsequently Mr. Yates wrote to Dr. Taylor: "I have with prayerful meditation looked over the globe, and there is *no field* which seems to me so inviting as China. I am now resolved—and I hope I have been guided by the Holy Spirit—that, let others say what they may about rushing into danger, I will go wheresoever God, in his providence, may direct me. * * Since coming to this irrevocable conclusion, my feelings and affections seem to have winged their way to China. This enterprise has swallowed up every other which has been concocted in my mind."

M. T. Yates and Eliza, the daughter of John and Annie Moring, were married on the 27th of September, 1846, in Mount Pisgah Church, by Rev. P. W. Dowd. Eliza Moring was born in Chatham County, North Carolina, on the 14th of December, 1821. And a help, meet for the great work of her husband, verily has she been!"

APPOINTMENT, DESIGNATION, DEPARTURE.

On the 3d of August, 1846, Mr. Yates, with Messrs. Thomas W. Tobey and Francis C. Johnson, was accepted by the Board of Foreign Missions as a missionary to China. On the 18th of October following, he was ordained at Raleigh, N. C. The services were conducted by James Dennis, Thomas Meredith, W. H. Jordan, Richard Furman, and the then Corresponding Secretary of the Foreign Mission Board. An eye-witness remarked: "This season will be long remembered. It constituted a new era in the history of North Carolina Baptists. One of their own sons was set apart to the work of preaching Christ among the heathen; and, henceforth, they are to be represented in the far distant and populous Empire of China. The brother whom they send forth is a graduate of their own institution, and enjoys in a high measure their confidence and esteem. May he long be spared, and become eminently efficient as a missionary of the cross." How literally and amply has this concluding prayer been answered!

On Friday evening, the 18th of December, Mr. and Mrs. Yates, with Mr. and Mrs. Tobey, and Dr. J. Sexton James, were "designated" to the missionary work, in the First Baptist Church of Richmond, Va. Mr. J. Lewis Shuck, who, more than ten years before, had been set apart in the presence of the same congregation, was present, with his wife, and the native preacher, Yong Seen Sang. Mr. Shuck was appointed to accompany Messrs. Yates and Tobey, who were to open the new station at Shanghai. On account of a protracted sickness, Mr. F. C. Johnson was absent from these designation services. They were described as making a profound impression on the people.

On the 15th of March, 1847, Messrs. Shuck, Tobey, and Johnson sailed from Boston, in the ship Ashburton, and arrived at Hong Kong the 25th of June. In consequence of the severe illness of his wife, Mr. Yates was compelled to defer his departure. "Our afflicted sister would have willingly been carried to her berth, and been borne from our shores with the hazard of finding a grave in the ocean; but the interdict of the physician and the advice of her friends prevented." Mr. and Mrs. Yates sailed from Boston, in the ship Thomas W. Sears,

April 26th, and, after a pleasant passage, they reached Hong Kong in August, 1847. They proceeded at once to Shanghai, on the 12th of September, and were joined by Mr. and Mrs. Tobey, September 25th; and by Mr. and Mrs. Shuck, October 27th, 1847. For thirty-three years, Mr. and Mrs. Yates have been stationed at this post; and how they have fulfilled their mission will been seen in our notice of the missionary work of Shanghai. On October 5th, 1860, Mr. Yates wrote: "I was the first to begin operations at this station, more than thirteen years ago, and I shall be the last to desert it." By the favoring providence of God, this purpose has be accomplished. Will not God's people stand by the man who has stood so steadfastly by their work, and the work of the Master?

HIS HEIGHT.

The following is taken from the *Religious Herald*, of Richmond, Va.:

"Before Dr. Yates went out to China, at the age of twenty-seven years, his height was marked on his father's door post. On his return, after a few years, he was found to be an inch higher. He went to China again, and returning, after an absence of eleven years, he had grown two inches more. The fact is remarkable. We have known no other case of the kind. The growth was evidently healthy; for his body retained its proportions, and his intellectual was quite equal to his physical development. Was the change due to climate, or to some peculiarity of constitution? Let naturalists decide."

Dr. T. H. Pritchard, President of Wake Forest College, wrote in the *Biblical Recorder* of July 2d, 1879: "The Rev. C. H. Wiley told me some time since that a Presbyterian missionary, in writing from China, said that Dr. M. T. Yates was physically, mentally, and morally at the head of the Protestant missionaries of that country, of whom there are several hundred."

Mrs. ELIZA YATES.

This lady, in the beauty of her modesty, refers to herself as "the wife of a missionary;" but, more than once, during the long absences of her husband, the whole responsibility of this mission has been thrown upon her and the native pastor, Wong Ping San; and the business-like manner in which affairs have been managed and accounts rendered has been so marked as to elicit the express commendation of the Board. J. Stuart Mill was brave enough to say, that he was indebted to a woman for his best ideas. And Dr. Yates, standing six feet, four inches, is too manly not to be equally just to his "better-half."

THOMAS WILLIAM TOBEY, D.D.

ONE OF THE FOUNDERS.

As has been stated, Mr. Tobey was associated with the origin of the Shanghai Mission. How prominent a part he took in the founding and fostering of this station appears in the published records of the Board of Foreign Missions. At present we propose only a bare outline of his *ante* and *post* missionary life.

ANTE.

Mr. Tobey was born at Fort Hill, North Providence, R. I., on the 15th of September, 1819—the same year as his missionary colleague, M. T. Yates. He professed conversion in Bristol, R. I., in February, 1837, and was baptized on the last Lord's Day of that month by Rev. Zalmon Tobey, pastor of the Bristol Baptist Church. His first collegiate year was spent in Brown University, under the presidency of Dr. Francis Wayland. He was graduated at the Columbian College, of Washington City, in 1844. In 1841, he was licensed to preach by the Lebanon Baptist Church, of Lancaster County, Va. On the 4th of August, 1846, he was accepted with Messrs. Yates and F. C. Johnson by the Board of Foreign Missions as a missionary to China. He was ordained in Washington, D. C., on August 25th, 1846, by a council called by the E Street Baptist Church, of which Rev. G. W. Samson, D. D., was pastor.

CHINA—SHANGHAI MISSION. 169

The public exercises were as follows: Rev. A. Samson offered the introductory prayer. Rev. Franklin Wilson, of Baltimore, read the Scriptures. Rev. George F. Adams offered the opening prayer. Rev. S. P. Hill preached the sermon. Rev. J. B. Taylor offered the ordaining prayer. Rev. G. W. Samson gave the right hand of fellowship. Rev. G. W. Dorrance read the hymn. Rev. C. R. Hendrickson offered the concluding prayer. Rev. T. W. Tobey pronounced the benediction.

After "farewell services" in the Bowdoin Square Church of Boston, Mr. Tobey and wife sailed for China on the 11th of March, 1847, in the ship Ashburton, with Rev. F. C. Johnson and Mr. and Mrs. J. L. Shuck. Mrs. Tobey was the sister of Mrs. Shuck, and daughter of the Rev. Addison Hall, of Virginia. They arrived at Hong Kong the 25th of June. Awaiting Mr. and Mrs. Yates, who arrived shortly afterward, Mr. and Mrs. Tobey, proceeded to their proposed station at Shanghai, where they arrived September 25th, 1847.

POST.

On account of the ill health of his wife, Mr. Tobey returned to America in 1850. In August of that year, he became the pastor of the Raleigh Baptist Church. In 1853, he accepted the pastorate of Yanceyville and Trinity Churches in Caswell, N. C. At the former place, Mrs. Tobey died. In 1858, Mr. Tobey was pastor of Sumterville and Jones' Creek Churches, in Sumpter County, Ala. In 1858, he was elected Professor of Theology in Howard College, Marion, Ala. In 1868, he moved to Paducah, Ky. In September, 1870, he entered upon his duties as Professor of Ancient Languages in Bethel College, Russellville, Ky. He made a donation of about six thousand dollars to that institution. He is now pastor of the Baptist Church at Union Springs, Ala.

MISSIONARY LIFE PREFERRED.

It will be seen that Mr. Tobey, on his return from China, entered upon the work of the ministry, and continued in the pastorate from 1850 until 1859, when he went to Marion to teach theology. The war in 1862 broke up the College, and he took the professorship of *Belles Lettres* in the Judson Female Institute, and for eight years was engaged in teaching young ladies in Marion and Paducah. Since 1870, he has been teaching young men and preaching. Thus he has been eleven years a pastor, three years a professor of theology, eight years a teacher of young ladies, and six years Greek and Latin Professor. Had it been left to his choice, he " would have much preferred to spend those twenty-eight years among the heathen; but God in his providence arranged it otherwise;" and he has cheerfully submitted to his will.

But is there not important *home*-labor in behalf of the nations? Will not Foreign Missions ever have earnest advocates in Alabama while that State includes among her citizens our three returned missionaries, Whilden, Williams, and Tobey?

GEORGE WASHINGTON BURTON, M.D.

This gentleman who occupied no unimportant place in the Shanghai Mission, was born near Murfreesboro, Rutherford County, Tenn., on the 8th of September, 1827. He was educated at Union College, located at Murfreesboro. Under date of July 1, 1850, the following record of the Board appears: "Letters were received from Brethren Whilden, Crawford, Day, Cheeseman, Bowen, and also from J. H. Eaton, recommending Dr. G. W. Burton for missionary appointment." March 17th, 1851, Dr. Burton "was duly examined and accepted as a medical missionary to labor in connection with the Shanghai Mission."

At the Southern Baptist Convention in Nashville, on the Lord's Day evening of May 11th, 1851, "Brethren B. W. Whilden, A. B. Cabaniss, T. P. Crawford and Sister Crawford, and Dr. G. W. Burton were publicly set apart to the work of Foreign Missions before a large and interested assemblage. Brother S. Baker read a portion of Scripture and prayed. Brother Taylor, Corresponding Secretary, gave the charge to the missionaries. Brother Dawson presented the Bible. Brother

Reynolds gave the right hand of fellowship, and each of the missionaries briefly addressed the assembly. The services were solemn and imposing." On the 17th of November, 1851, Dr. Burton, with Mr. and Mrs. Crawford, sailed in the Horatio from New York. They arrived at Hong Kong "in good health and after a pleasant voyage" on the 17th of February, 1852, and reached Shanghai, March 30th.

The following is from the eighth annual report of the Board: "The medical services of Dr. Burton have, without question, constituted an important item in our missionary operations in Shanghai. Not only among the poor have the remedies prescribed by him been available, but also among the better classes of society. The sick have been brought to him in great numbers. * * * May it not be hoped that he shall receive the appellation of the 'beloved physician'? If, as he dispenses to the removal of their bodily maladies, he shall also become the means of spiritual cure, he will entrench himself in the affections of the people. Certain it is that our missionaries and the doctrines they teach have been brought into more general notice by this means."

Shortly after his arrival in China, Dr. Burton was severely attacked by brain fever. A second attack made it imperative that he should return to this country the latter part of the same year. Thereupon Mr. Yates wrote: "I trust the Board will sympathize with him and us in this affliction, and render him all necessary aid to expedite his return. We can see clearly that his connection with us would, in the end, have been of incalculable value to the mission in enabling us to get a footing in interior cities. Dr. Burton has afforded relief to some sixty or more opium-eaters from *Soong Kong Foo*, a large city some thirty miles from this place. These gentlemen have urged us to go to *Soong Kong* and open a school, promising to aid us."

The Doctor's health was speedily restored, and he resolved to return at once to his abundant and useful labors. On November 3d, 1853, he married Miss Bennett, connected with the "Georgia Female College" at Madison, Ga., and daughter of Rev. Cephas Bennett, of Burmah, and grand-daughter of Rev. Dr. Alfred Bennett, of New York. They sailed from New York, December 12th, 1853, and reached Shanghai in the spring of the next year. For seven years he devoted himself to his profession. His business affording him more than a support, he labored independently of the Board.

How valuable his labors were to the mission and to the people will hereafter appear. His liberality then, and since his return to America, can be recorded only in heaven. On December 1st, 1860, Mrs. Burton, with their three children, came back to this country. Dr. Burton followed August 3d, 1861. Remaining a short time in Murfreesboro, the Doctor entered the Confederate army as a surgeon, and continued in service until the close of the war. After the war he engaged in planting. In 1869, he moved to Louisville, Ky., where, for three years, he practised his profession. Subsequently he retired into the country, while having an interest in a mercantile house of the city. Dr. and Mrs. Burton are loved members of the Chestnut Street Baptist Church of Louisville, of which Dr. Weaver—whose baptism by Dr. Boyce has made so much stir—is pastor; and are staunch friends of the Foreign Mission cause.

Rev. ASA BRUCE CABANISS.

EARLY LIFE AND EDUCATION.

The subject of this sketch was born March 12th, 1821, in Nottoway County, Va., near old Chestnut Hill, now Mount Lebanon, Baptist Church. Both of his parents died in 1829 or 1830, leaving him to the guardianship of his great uncle, Capt. P. O. Lipscomb. When only twelve years old, he was deeply impressed by the preaching of Rev. Joseph S. Baker, late of Georgia, who was then preaching, at old Chestnut Hill, as a missionary of the General Association of Virginia. The next year, attending school in Charlotte County, Va., his religious impressions were deepened under the ministry of that godly man, Abner W. Clopton. At the age of fifteen, he was put in a store as clerk at Nottoway Court-house. After twelve months, he became both book-keeper and salesman of the store. At the end of three years, he went to Petersburg, and entered the wholesale dry goods house of Edwin James & Co., as salesman. During a protracted meeting at the Presbyterian Church, of which his employer, Mr. James, was a

CHINA—SHANGHAI MISSION. 173

member, and to the choir of which Mr. Cabaniss belonged, he became thoroughly awakened, and resolved, by God's help, to acknowledge Christ and lead a Christian life. But in what church? In his own language: "The Bible compelled me to be a Baptist; for, had I followed my own inclination and sympathies at the time, I would have been a Presbyterian." He was baptized into the fellowship of the Market Street Baptist Church, in his twentieth year, by the pastor, Rev. J. P. Tustin. Within a year, he entered Richmond College, of which Rev. Robert Ryland, D.D., was President. During the three years which he spent there, the institution was visited by the missionaries, Judson, Dean, and Shuck. Their addresses and conversations took a strong hold on the mind and heart of Mr. Cabaniss, and he promised Mr. Shuck that he would go to China when he was graduated, if the Lord should open the way. From Richmond College, he went to Madison University, in the State of New York. He spent there three years, and was graduated in the summer of 1849, the year after the writer entered, who can testify to "the fragrance of his name," both among the students and among the Professors of the University.

PROVIDING FOR HIS MISSION.

On the 7th of September, 1850, "after a full and fair examination" by the Board, Mr. Cabaniss was appointed a missionary to Shanghai. The Goshen Association of Virginia, having offered to be responsible for his support in China, was visited by the missionary elect, who aroused a profound missionary spirit in the churches of the Association. "More money was collected than had ever been raised, in one year, for all missionary purposes. This generous action of the Goshen commenced an era of prosperity and active benevolence hitherto unknown to them, and scarcely equalled by any other country Association, proving that '*Religion is a strange commodity—the more you export, the more you have at home.*'"

Returning from a lecturing tour at the South, Mr. Cabaniss attended the Southern Baptist Convention at Nashville, Tenn., where, on May 11th, 1851, as has been stated, he, with Rev. T. P. Crawford, Mrs. Crawford, and Dr. G. W. Burton, was "set apart" as a missionary to

China. He was married at Mount Laurel, Halifax County, Va., to Miss M. Elvira Adkisson, by "the spiritual father of the bride," Rev. S. G. Mason. They sailed for China from New York, August the 1st, 1852, and "after a tedious voyage of five months, they landed at Macao, China, the 1st of January, 1853. Thence they went to Hong Kong, and took a steamer to Shanghai, where they were welcomed by Messrs. Crawford and Yates, and Miss Baker."

REBELS AND HYMNS.

In two years, Mr. Cabaniss had acquired sufficient knowledge of the language to begin to preach. As he already had taught in Virginia, he opened a school for native children. Besides assisting in building up the church at Shanghai, he also "frequently took tours a hundred or more miles into the interior, preaching and distributing books and tracts." The rebels being in possession of the city, and the mission houses being near the North Gate, through which they sallied to meet the besieging Imperial forces, our missionaries had fighting and bloodshed at their very door. "The Imperial party finally agreed to pay them for their houses, if they would evacuate them and let them be pulled down." At the close of the long siege, our missionaries rebuilt in the same place.

Mr. Cabaniss translated for the schools Æsop's Fables, and added, to the church hymn book, a new edition of which he issued, some of our old and familiar songs of Zion. He translated, also, the Sunday-school hymn, "There is a happy land," which "soon became as popular in China as it has been in America." Mr. Cabaniss says: "The best hymns in the book were written by the native assistant, Deacon Wong, who was a school teacher before he joined the church, and who has quite a poetical talent. He has been ordained since that time, and is now the efficient pastor of the Shanghai Church.

RETURN TO AMERICA.

On account of failing health, Mr. Cabaniss and family, by the advice of their physician, sailed for this country in the fall of 1859. They brought with them a native convert, and expected to return when their health should be re-established. Mr. Cabaniss delivered, in Virginia and at the South, a course of six lectures "On the manners and customs of the Chinese," which met with popular favor, quite complimentary to the lecturer. During the war, he and Mrs. Cabaniss had charge of the Black Walnut Academy, in Halifax County, Va. Mr. Cabaniss preached also to the Cross Roads Church. After the war, the Board of Foreign Missions being in no financial condition to send back their missionaries to their former fields of labor, Mr. Cabaniss became the Principal of the Brownsville Female College, of Tennessee. His health failing after two years' labor in the school-room, he traveled for a year, and then moved his family to Russellville, Ky. For the last seven or eight years, he has held successfully the positions of Corresponding Secretary of the Executive Board of the Baptist General Association of Kentucky, and Agent for Kentucky of the Southern Baptist Theological Seminary. Mrs. Cabaniss was a member of the Faculty of Bethel Female College, of Hopkinsville, Ky. They have the unspeakable satisfaction of seeing all of their children gathered into the fold of Christ. Dr. T. G. Keen baptized the youngest, only twelve years old, just the age at which the father was deeply if not savingly impressed with regard to his soul's salvation when a school boy, in Nottoway County, of the Old Dominion. May the children inherit the missionary spirit of their parents!

FIRST DECADE: 1846 TO 1856.

START OF MISSION.

Shanghai was selected as a missionary station, contemporaneously with Canton. The Board did not determine, however, to begin operations there until December, 1846, when Messrs. Shuck, Yates, Tobey, and James were assigned to this post. Messrs. Yates and Tobey arrived at Shanghai in September, 1847. The location chosen by them as headquarters was on a public thoroughfare, midway between the North and the East Gates, and close to the wall of the city. Mr. Shuck arrived on the 27th of October. On the 6th of November, 1847, a Baptist Church of ten members was constituted—"Yates, clerk; Tobey and Yong, deacons; Shuck, pastor." Yong and Mui, to whom reference was made in connection with the Canton Mission, moved to Shanghai, and were licensed to preach by the church there. Mr. Shuck wrote, November 7th: "We sincerely hope that it will not be long before the church and mission will have a respectable chapel. Ground can be secured, workmen are ready, and we are convinced that we can have large congregations. I feel most grateful to God for those unexpected trains of Providence, which have fixed my lot at Shanghai." As was stated in our sketch of Mr. Shuck, the five thousand dollars, collected by him for the Canton Chapel, were appropriated, with the consent of the donors, to the chapel at Shanghai. A black shadow was cast over the infant church by the sudden and shocking death, in April, 1848, of Dr. and Mrs. J. Sexton James, whose arrival at Shanghai was so anxiously looked for, as an important element of strength to this new and promising missionary interest. A sketch of them will be found among our "Lost Missionaries."

PROGRESS OF THE WORK.

The health of Mr. Pearcy failing at Canton, he and Mrs. Pearcy joined the mission at Shanghai, on the 19th of November, 1848. Mr. Pearcy wrote: "I am glad that the Board has determined not to abandon Canton. There may be a great change there for the better. * * I am inclined to think that Canton may as quickly receive the gospel as Shanghai." In a short time, Mr. Shuck became familiar with the dialect, and all the missionaries began to speak the language. Three services were held on the Lord's Day, and four during the week. A missionary sent home these cheering words: "It would encourage our brethren in America, could they peep into our meetings and see hundreds—500 or 600 natives—listening to the preaching of the glorious gospel." Several inquiries were reported; a school for girls was opened; the missionaries were hopeful; but they felt deeply, as our missionaries feel now, "the need of the prayers of God's people." The sight of Mr. Yates failing, he devoted himself to the acquisition of the colloquial language, and to the erection of the new chapel. Yong and Mui returned to Canton. In 1849, the mission was further diminished by the return to America of Mr. and Mrs. Tobey. During that year three were baptized. The next year the mission was made glad by many anxious inquirers, among whom was *See Seen Sang*, of whom Mr. Shuck said: "He talks like a lover of Jesus." In May, 1850, a station at *Oo Kah Jak*, twelve miles southeast of the city, was opened, and a building for teaching and preaching was erected there by the ladies of the mission. Twenty pupils were collected. In the city, there were three other schools.

The missionaries implored that the churches who had been praying for the opening of China to the gospel would behold the answer to their prayers, and send more laborers into the field. They concluded: "Can any turn a deaf ear to this voice from China, and yet remain guiltless of the blood of the perishing!"

REINFORCEMENT AND SEVERE LOSS.

The Board, more and more impressed with the importance of this station, were disposed to concentrate there most of their forces. At the Southern Baptist Convention, in May, 1851, as has been stated, Messrs. Crawford, Cabaniss, and their wives, with Dr. Burton, were "set apart" for the work at Shanghai. Mr. Whilden, who had returned to this country after the death of his wife, was transferred, at his own request, to this station. This action of the Board was rescinded October 24th, 1852. The reinforcement stimulated the mission. Miss Baker from Canton joined the mission, and took charge of a boarding-school for girls. A school for boys also was deemed advisable "in view of future matrimonial relations."

With regard to teaching the children English, Mrs. Pearcy expressed herself thus: "I am decidedly of the opinion that it is a disadvantage to them in a spiritual point of view, and particularly to females. In many instances it accelerates their ruin." Dr. Dean said to Mrs. Pearcy: "I hope you will never undertake to teach the Chinese English." Mr. Shuck and Mr. Pearcy reported a missionary excursion in the country, during which each of them *was presented with an idol,* which had been worshipped for many years. Another chapel was erected on the premises of Mr. Shuck, near the North Gate, so that the mission had six places of worship. At the request of some of the natives Mr. Yates began to preach at night. The meetings were well attended.

On a visit to *Oo Kah Jak,* "the people crowded around him to heal their diseases; but he preached to them Jesus—the Great Physician of souls." Alluding to this out-station, which gave cheering prospects of success, Mr. Shuck remarked: " Let the brethren bear in mind that the Foreign Mission Board of the Southern Baptist Convention was the first Protestant Board of Missions in the world, who ever held property and gained a permanent footing in the interior of China. This is decided advance in the work of missions in this land." The mission was saddened on the 21st of November, 1854, by the death of Mrs. Eliza G. Shuck, whose fall made a deep vacuum in the ranks of the little missionary band. In paying a just tribute to our departed sister, the Board added : " From the grave of the devoted and noble dead comes a voice of touching and earnest appeal to the people of God to 'go up and possess the land.' And more than the voice of the precious dead rings through the spirit of those who have ears to hear, saying: 'Go and teach all nations, baptizing them in the name of the Father, and of the Son, and of the Holy Ghost, * * and lo I am with you alway, even unto the end of the world. Amen.'"

CENTRE OF INFLUENCE.

The importance of Shanghai, as a mission station, was set forth by a gentleman of another denomination, in the following language: " The Chinese come in all directions to Shanghai. It is difficult to estimate the exact number here from other places; but some of the intelligent Chinese estimate it at one hundred thousand. Morally, though not literally, this will be like a city set on a hill. The avenues which serve for leading up hither will also serve for conducting forth the truth. As the strangers, who were in Jerusalem at Pentecostal times, could relate, when they returned, what they saw of the wonderful works of

CHINA—SHANGHAI MISSION.   179

God, so may we hope that those who gather here shall, if the Lord bless us with times of refreshing, return to their countrymen, bearing the news of salvation."

LABOR AND PRAYER.

In 1852, Dr. G. W. Burton returned to America, and, with recruited health and a pious wife, arrived again in China in the spring of 1854. A missionary describes a day's work of the doctor in the country: "Very soon the house was literally crammed, and the people clamorous for the attentions of the foreign doctor. I made a short address to the assembled crowd and offered prayer, after which the doctor began in earnest to dispense his medicines. His labors were incessant; and we, after a time, insisted on his ceasing his breaking-down exertions. Soon dinner came on, and again the doctor proceeded, until fatigue compelled him to stop, when he left for Shanghai."

At the close of 1852, Mr. Pearcy wrote: "Now, as we look over the field of our labors, and think of the religious tracts and Scriptures which have been widely circulated, and the instruction which has been imparted in various ways, we are led to believe that all has not been in vain. But our trust is in the Lord alone. Oh that the brethren at home, who help in this work by their contributions, may not forget to pray for the Master's blessing upon his word! Could I speak to them all, I would say: Brethren, *pray for us that the word of the Lord may have free course and be glorified.* I would earnestly request of the brethren, not chiefly that they may give pecuniary support, for I believe they will do that, but that they may sustain our work still more effectually by their *fervent prayers.*"

CHANGES AND CALIFORNIA.

Early in 1853, Mr. and Mrs. Cabaniss joined the mission. In December of that year, Miss Harriet A. Baker, by the advice of her physician, Dr. Lockhart, was recalled by the Board. On July 4th, 1853, Mr. J. L. Shuck was dismissed, at his own request, in order to labor among the Chinese in California, under the patronage of the Domestic Board. The health of Mr. George Pearcy seeming precarious, he was instructed by the Board to return to the United States by the way of California, where he could continue missionary work among the immigrants from China. His health improving, the Board resolved, on February 7th, 1852, to refer to the Convention the subject of establishing a station in California. The report, adopted by the Convention, advocated the proposed mission, but concluded: "Your committee feel that the suggestions in the report of the Board of Foreign Missions are not destitute of force, and yet, upon the whole, they cannot avoid the conviction that it is the appropriate work of the HOME MISSION BOARD *to provide for the spiritual welfare of all classes of population in our own country.*"

SCHOOLS, INQUIRY, REBEL CONVERT.

Mr. Crawford reported: "On the first of June, I opened a boys' school, * * and in a few days I had my complement of scholars—twenty-four interesting youths. * * Mrs. Crawford's school is still doing finely. Through these schools we are beginning to get access to our neighbors."

Mr. Yates: "You will be interested to know that there is among the people a general spirit of inquiry about our religion. Many are beginning to discriminate between the system taught by the Romanist and the religion of Christ as taught by the Protestant missionaries. All this inquiry and discrimination, however, is *head* work. Yet it is encouraging, since the mind must be informed before the heart is properly affected. Our encouragement is not founded so much on individual cases, as on the gradual enlightenment of the people generally. On this, I think, we can rest a hope of future success. * * * With the blessing of God upon our labors, *we know we shall reap, if we faint not.*"

In the latter part of 1853, *Asau*, an intelligent young relative of one of the "Insurgent Chiefs," while on his way to the Rebel Capital, was baptized into the fellowship of the Shanghai Church. When asked if he had renounced the worship of idols and ancestors, he replied, with surprise: "If one worships Jesus, he cannot worship these."

STRUGGLE FOR RELIGIOUS FREEDOM.

On March 19th, 1853, Nanking, the former Capital of China, was captured by the Insurgent *Hung-su-ch'nen* who assumed the sovereignty of the Empire as the true successor of the Mings, under the title of *T'ai-ping-tien-kwo*, or the "Peaceful reign." *Hung* was a pupil of our missionary at Canton, Mr. I. J. Roberts. The origin of the war was strictly religious. A strange dream, together with the denunciation of the Bible against idolatry, led *Hung*, while a candidate for "examination," to shatter an image of Confucius in the Examination Hall at Canton, and to urge his companions to follow his example in every direction. The move of these iconoclasts spread like wild fire through the country. Hundreds of idols were cast down, and many temples were destroyed. The authorities, attempting the arrest of *Hung*, were resisted by his adherents, who replied: "We refuse to be dictated to as to what we shall worship." "A Declaration of Rights," setting forth their right to worship the one true God, and embodying the first commandment, was drawn up, and around it the leaders knelt, with swords in hand, and appealing to God, swore to defend it with their lives. This was a bold strike for liberty of conscience. Multitudes flocked to the new standard. The Scriptures were printed and circulated among the troops. God's blessing was invoked before all meals. Idols and temples, wherever found, were demolished. Religious worship was maintained regularly in the camp. The most rigid moral discipline was enforced. "All smoking of tobacco as well as of opium, all theft, and all maltreatment of women were punished with death." Captain Fishbourne, of H. M. S. *Hermes*, visiting the headquarters of the insurgents, was told "that, in future, foreigners should have steamboats, railroads, telegraphs, and all Western appliances without restriction." They said to him: "We are going to be just as you are. We worship the same God, and would live together like brethren."

An army was dispatched against Peking; but it was repelled by "Mongolian horsemen and the rigors of the winter." Several cities fell into their hands on their way back to Nanking. The commander of this force "arrogated to himself the title of Holy Ghost, and became fanatical and even wild."

On the 7th of September, 1853, six hundred of the *hung-deu*, or red-heads, as the *local* insurgents were called from the color of their turbans, who had secreted themselves under the walls of Shanghai, near the North Gate, rushed, when the gate was opened in the morning, into the city, where there were some "80,000 Cantonese and 60,000 Fokien men, all of whom were supposed to be sympathizers with the rebels."

The Magistrate was killed, and the "great seal," with "an enormous quantity of sycee and gold bars," was captured. The Imperial forces besieged the city. Most of our fighting was in sight of the residence of our missionaries. Mr. Yates says he witnessed sixty-eight engagements. Indignities being offered to foreigners, British and American troops, after vainly warning the Imperialists to retire, scattered the besieging army. Some complication arising between the "Rebels" and the French marines, the latter battered down a part of the wall of the city, and admitted the Imperialists, who had recruited and returned to the siege. The son and nephew of *Fung*, "the Southern King"—one of the five kings under *Hung*—who had been entertained *incognito* by our missionary at Shanghai, Dr. Yates, attempted to escape to Nanking. Being foiled in the effort, one of them "went crazy." Mr. Yates says: "I took him into the city and chained him to a post in the mission school-house. He escaped, however, and was found with an axe hewing the idols and temples to pieces. * * The Rev. I. J. Roberts entered the camp, where the man was held a prisoner, and demanded him as his pupil. * * He soon recovered his senses, * * and went back to Hong Kong, where he fell ill and died." The commander of the Imperialists being killed by the explosion of one of his own mines, his troops retired, and the breach of the wall was soon repaired. The son of *Fung* was paraded in triumph through the streets. The attack being renewed, after various defeats and successes, and indescribable atrocities, on both sides, the "Long Hairs," as all the insurgents were called, shaved their heads, and escaped by night. The Imperialists took possession, and butchered all rebels who were caught in the city. During the fight our property was destroyed, for which the mission received full indemnity. "Thus ended," says Mr. Yates, to whom we are indebted for the above facts, "a useless and destructive rebellion, which, though contemporaneous with, had no connection with the *T'ai-ping* movement, having no religious character whatever."

Of the *T'ai-pings*, Mr. Crawford wrote: "They have begun in the right direction. They strike at the root of the evil. They attempt to correct the *moral sense* of the people, as well as the abuses of government. * * One hundred thousand have turned from idols." Mr. Cabaniss remarked: "The only wonder is, that they have embraced so much truth. The Chief speaks of visions; so did Constantine. He carries on a religio-political war; so did Cromwell, and so have many others. He has run into fanaticism; so have many reformers before him, the Puritans not excepted. But, notwithstanding these serious errors, we still indulge the belief that this revolution will result in great good to the Chinese. * * Whatever may be thought of their motives for embracing Christianity, the main points of the gospel are clearly set forth and strongly enjoined by them. Whether in pretence or in truth, Christ is preached, and I therein do rejoice, and will rejoice!"

IDOLS AT DISCOUNT.

The civil war in the country raging, the year 1854 was one of great trial to our missionaries. They labored, however, irregularly in the city, which was the seat of constant conflicts, and made occasional excursions into the country, where, "mingling freely with the population, and proclaiming the gospel without restraint, they were cheered with confident expectation of seeing the beneficial results of their labors." "On arriving at a town," wrote one of our missionaries, "we usually make our way into the principal temple, and there, standing up before the chief idol, sometimes making a rostrum of the table on which his offerings are laid, we tell the multitudes, as Paul did the men of Athens, of the living and true God, 'who is not like unto gold, or silver, or stone, or wood,' but who is a God of infinite power, wisdom and love. * * * Many of the people are concluding that the spirits have forsaken their gods, which renders them useless. * * Before the war, it was difficult to get an image which had been worshiped, even for a high price; now they can be bought for a trifle at nearly every curiosity shop. * * Gods, as large as men, which, but a year ago, were adored by thousands, now occupy the place of doorkeepers in the houses of wealthy foreign merchants."

SIMPLE PRAYER AND OLD-FASHIONED EXPERIENCE.

"Some twelve or more profess to pray regularly. A woman, who was asked what she said when she prayed, replied that she put her hands together and said: 'True God, Jesus, Holy Spirit.' An old man walked a mile to hear preaching, and seating himself with the apparent humility of a child, said with excitement: 'Teach *me* the way.' Sister Crawford's school teacher, Wong Ping San, (now the efficient native pastor of the Shanghai Church) has found the pearl of great price. It was really charming to hear him tell his experience, his struggles with heathenism, his efforts to make himself better, his doubts, his fears, but his final triumph, in an *old-fashioned conversion by the Holy Ghost.* God grant this may be the beginning of a general outpouring of his Spirit here!"

APPEAL FOR REINFORCEMENT.

On the 8th of January, 1855, the little missionary force was diminished by Mr. and Mrs. Pearcy being forced, by ill health, to quit the field. Mr. Pearcy wrote: "I find it a greater sacrifice to leave my field of labor than I did my native land. * * When we came out neither of us calculated on ever returning home. * * It is eight years since we arrived in China. Nearly all the American missionaries who were then in the field have either died or been compelled to return home in quest of health." This departure gave new emphasis to the following appeals from Shanghai for more missionaries:

Mr. Yates wrote: "My dear brother, the work that is looming up before us is positively bewildering. May the Lord of the harvest grant us strength, wisdom, and faith adequate for the day and times in which we live."

Mr. Pearcy pleaded: "I do most sincerely implore our churches to open their eyes and look upon this vast and waiting field, and come up and occupy it. The present plan will not at all meet the demand. Each State in the South must do more than all are now doing. Could not Maryland, Virginia, North Carolina, South Carolina, Georgia, Alabama, and all the rest, each send missionaries to occupy these great cities, and support them? Many pastors at home might give up their flocks to engage in this work."

Hear Mr. Cabaniss: "If I thought I could have any influence with my young brethren in America, I would press the Macedonian cry from this land upon them; yea, I would ring the death wail of three hundred and fifty millions of souls in their ears. But, alas! I know it would be useless, unless the love of God inspire their hearts to forsake all their fond attachments, and labor in his vineyard. Will not the churches unitedly and fervently pray that God will raise up men to supply the demand which his providence is now making in this land?   *   *   Let us pray for China, as John Knox did for Scotland; let us feel the burden of one-third of the human family pressing upon our souls, then God will hear us, and make this, indeed, a 'Celestial Empire.'"

Another misssonary cried: "Oh that there were *others* on whom we could rest the eye of hope for the future! Never did the immortal Wellington, when he exclaimed at the battle of Waterloo,' *Oh that Blucher or night would come;*' stand more in need of help than we do at Shanghai. Who will come? Is there *no* one who feels it his duty to preach the gospel to the heathen? Shall we look in vain for help? Have the perishing heathen *ceased* to awaken in the churches of Christ the deepest commiseration? *Shall not the command of Christ be obeyed?* Has his love *ceased to constrain his people?* *Whither*, then, *shall we* look for animating hope in this heavenly undertaking?"

PROMISING CONDITION OF MISSION.

In February, 1855, Shanghai fell into the hand of the Imperialists. The chapels and missionary residences, which had been injured and destroyed, were repaired and rebuilt. A missionary reported to the Board: "As regards the mission property, I can safely say it was never before in so good a condition. And never, I think, during any previous year, have we done so much effective preaching. We have four preaching places, and maintain eighteen public services per week, with an aggregate weekly attendance of 2,500 souls. We have five day schools, with an average attendance of fifty girls and fifty boys." Five were added to the church by baptism, among whom was "a literary graduate of some distinction, who, having read the New Testament three times, was brought joyfully to receive the word and to put on Christ." Ten or fifteen were inquiring the way of life. This year was signalized by the *first baptism of a Chinese woman*. The Board were greatly encouraged, and urged on the Convention renewed and enlarged efforts:

"The gospel has won glorious triumphs in China. Is it nothing that hundreds of thousands are throwing away their idols? that the Bible has been translated into the language, and is being circulated in vast numbers far in the interior? and that multitudes have already given evidence of saving faith in the Redeemer? The Board cannot but regard this part of their field as peculiarly interesting and full of promise. But we must give it a more generous and diligent culture. Our stations must be increased. More missionaries must be sent forth. With greater patience, stronger faith, more earnest prayer, and with burning zeal, must we prosecute this work."

SECOND DECADE: 1856 TO 1866.

ALMOST SUPERHUMAN LABORS.

In the eleventh annual report of the Board to the Southern Baptist Convention, we read:

"In no former year of the history of this mission has so much of effective influence been put forth. We are warranted, also, in saying that never before were the prospects of a large harvest to be reaped by our missionaries more encouraging. The health of some of the brethren and sisters has been seriously affected, and yet they have performed what might be termed 'almost superhuman labors' in the wide-spread field before them."

INS AND OUTS OF MISSIONARIES.

The earnest appeals of our missionaries for reinforcement were responded to by Rev. and Mrs. J. L. Holmes, and Rev. and Mrs. J. B. Hartwell, of whom we shall give biographical sketches, when we come to the SHANTUNG MISSION, with which their names are particularly associated. The former sailed from New York, in the ship Falconer, August 12th, 1858, and arrived at Hong Kong, January 20th, 1859. The latter embarked from the same port, on the 5th of November, 1858. In May, 1859, Mr. and Mrs. Holmes went up to Shantung, with the view of starting a mission in that province; but, as we shall hereafter see, they were soon compelled to return to Shanghai. Mr. and Mrs. M. T. Yates and Mr. and Mrs. T. P. Crawford had come back to the United States. Thus, before the arrival of the new missionaries, Mr. Cabaniss was alone at this station. The following is a memorandum of how the work stood: " Daily preaching. Preaching at night by three or four native members, who spoke very well. Three chapels inside of the city. The Sunday-school composed of all the members of the church." The health of Mr. Cabaniss and that of his family breaking down, they also were forced to quit the field, and arrived in this country, on March 3d, 1860. In a few days, their "little one fell asleep."

Mr. Yates reached Shanghai, from America, March 10th, 1860. Mr. Crawford returned by the way of California, and arrived in May, 1860. On June 2d of that year, *Suchow* fell into the hands of the *T'ai-pings,* and Messrs. Crawford, Holmes, and Hartwell, prospecting for new stations, visited that place. Mr. Holmes visited Nanking also, the capital of the Rebel King. Mr. Yates wrote: "By all means, we should have a strong mission among the rebels. The chief has invited the missionaries to come and teach his people. * * If Brother Holmes reaches Nanking, he will probably stay three months, and correct some of the errors of the rebels." Mr. Holmes returned, as did the other missionaries, unfavorably impressed by the insurgents. They brought letters from the "Rebel King" to the Foreign Ministers. Mr. Holmes wrote: "I am determined to leave Shanghai this fall, if I can find a place more to my mind." Mr. and Mrs. Hartwell, on account of the ill health of the latter, spent several months in Japan, and on December 18th, 1860, went with Mr. and Mrs. Holmes to establish an out-station in Shantung.

On August 3d, 1861, Dr. Burton, who had been practising medicine independently of the Board, returned to America. In October, 1862, he sent £200 to Mr. Hartwell. In August, 1863, Mr. Crawford, for the benefit of his health, moved to Tung Chow, in the Shantung Province. The rent of the mission house, which he had occupied at Shanghai, 1,200 *taels*, covered his house-rent and expenses at Tung Chow. Under date of February 8th, 1864, Mr. Yates made the following communications: "I also must have a change before I am too far gone. I am arranging to spend a year in Switzerland with my family. By the aid of a friend, I can do this without expense to the Board. I have offered Brother Hartwell my place as municipal interpreter. His family will remain in Tung Chow. Mrs. Holmes has an interest in her brother-in-law's business in Chefoo. We can live. Let the war of independence go on. While my kindred are shedding their blood, we should do what we can to support ourselves." Mr. Yates going to Europe, where his daughter was being educated, Mr. Hartwell returned to Shanghai to occupy Mr. Yates' post. Mr. Crawford took charge of Mr. Hartwell's church at Tung Chow. During twelve months, Mr. Crawford baptized eight persons. The membership numbered twenty-three in 1865. Mr. Hartwell was offered a lucrative position in the Custom-house at Ningpo; but Mr. Yates returning to Shanghai, Mr. Hartwell went back to his church at Tung Chow. Mr. Crawford, who had only proposed a temporary residence in the Shantung Province, resolved to remain and labor in Tung Chow, and formed there a second interest, known as the "Monument Street Church." Thus Mr. Yates was left permanently alone in Shanghai.

SHANGHAI CHURCH AND MR. YATES.

On October 20th, 1860, Mr. Yates baptized *Wong*, a prominent rice merchant. "The heathen say, 'he is a good man.'" In 1861, the church membership was twenty-two. "Two of them are preachers.

Most of them pray in public. Our church will compare favorably with churches at the South." "Yet," wrote Mr. Yates, "I doubt if a single church here would live, if all foreign laborers were withdrawn." Again: "This is a dark hour in Shanghai. At the *Sung-way-dong*, where we had two hundred hearers, now we have five to thirty. The chapel at my house, *Ki-aw-hwo*, has fifty to one hundred hearers. Living is very high—fuel thirteen cents per pound." He asked permission to sell for $4,000 the *Te-hwo-dong* house, outside of the city, as advisable, "whether missionaries stay in or remove from Shanghai." With his characteristic liberality, Mr. Yates wrote to the Board, relinquishing his salary from July, 1863, so long as certain property he had acquired would furnish him a sufficient income. He offered further to raise the funds to support another missionary, if he should be sent by the end of 1865. He added: "Cannot the young man appointed to Japan be induced to join me?"

COLLAPSE OF THE T'AI-PINGS.

In 1860, the insurgents, twenty thousand strong, marched on Shanghai, where "everybody was armed to the teeth." Mr. Crawford wrote: "The Chinese, though two millions in number, are fleeing in every direction." The *Long Hairs* came with white flags of truce, but were repulsed by the English and French forces. In the taking of the cities between Nanking and Shanghai by the insurgents, about two hundred thousand of the people perished, one-half taking their own lives. In the summer of that year, the foreign allies, who had a score or two against the Imperial government, attacked *Pai-ho* and *Ta-koo*, forts garrisoned by forty thousand troops. On the 24th of October, the treaty of *Tien-tsin*, which provided that a minister should reside at Peking, and that foreigners should have access to the whole Empire, was ratified. Mr. Crawford observed: "These fine treaties you hear of are forced by the allies, on an unwilling nation." In January, 1861, Mr. Yates observed: "The troops are still here, and we can expect to do but little for the next two or three years." The T'ai-pings subjugated the greater part of Honan, Kiangsi, Chekiang, and a part of Fokien. In taking *Suchow*, they slaughtered a large Imperial force. "Eighty thousand of the people destroyed their own lives. * * They thought that the rebels were monsters, as they were not afraid to treat the gods as they had done. * * It was found impossible to approach nearer than two miles of the city, because of the multitude of dead which filled the canal." The Imperialists were now controlled by foreigners, whose commerce demanded a cessation of hostilities. The "Long Hairs" were followed from city to city. In July, 1864, Nanking capitulated to the Imperialists. "Thus," remarks Mr. Yates, " was crushed out, by foreign aid, a rebellion, which in its beginning promised so much for Christian civilization, and the friendly intercourse of foreign nations with all parts of the empire."

MANIFOLD TROUBLES.

From 1860 to 1865, our mission struggled under the two-fold burden of the wars in China and America. The letters of our missionaries breathed the spirit of patriotism and of self-denial. By their own exertion, they largely supported themselves, although Maryland and Kentucky afforded generous aid. They felt what Mr. Crawford expressed: "War or no war, the mission must go on. We can live notwithstanding the wars of China and America." But "congregations were small, or entirely broken up; schools were dispersed; and everything wore a gloomy aspect." In 1860, our now sainted missionaries Bond and Rohrer, with their wives, were swallowed up in the "Edwin Forrest." In 1862, the Asiatic cholera raged in the city, cutting off not less than eighteen hundred foreigners, and thousands of the native population. In May of the same year, the "large chapel" was destroyed by fire; but "three-fourths of the funds, viz., 3,000 *taels*, necessary to restore it to its former condition," were secured "from the foreign community." The year 1861 also witnessed, near Chefoo, in Shantung, the horrible murder, by the rebels, of our missionary, J. L. Holmes, whose devoted wife still labors among the people that butchered her husband, and who, in love for her work, is separated from her only child—born after the death of her husband—that he may be educated in this country for the better service of the Master.

THIRD DECADE: 1866 TO 1876.

CHURCH AND CRITICISM.

The first week of 1866 was "devoted to prayer for the Holy Ghost." During the year, with the aid of an unpaid assistant, Mr. Yates "maintained seven services each week; and during a part of the year he held two services each month at an out-station." The war had demoralized the people and damaged the church. "The spirit of inquiry, which had been so manifest, was crushed out." The mission was in "a state of declension." All this was "connected more or less with pecuniary embarrassment, consequent upon the financial ruin of Shanghai." Of other interests there, Mr. Yates remarked: "The custom of some English missionaries of inducting into the church large numbers, who make no profession of conversion, has greatly injured the cause. * * * The Papists have improved the war by raising the French flag over their places of worship, and thousands have sought the protection of the Romish Church and the Virgin Mary."

RETROSPECT AND PROGRESS.

In 1867, seven were baptized. Two of the members had become useful missionaries and colporteurs. The native church contributed sixty-nine dollars. The membership was thirty-five. Mr. and Mrs. Yates had been twenty years at Shanghai. When they entered upon their work, "it was not safe for a missionary to venture far from the 'open ports.'" The opposition of local authorities, priests, and people "had to be overcome by hard knocks," and hard knocks were received in return. "One was killed, some were beaten, others were stoned, and all have been shamefully abused. *Now* what do we see," continued Mr. Yates, "as the result of our labor and sufferings? * * The country, for hundreds of miles, has been completely subdued. Missionaries may travel and preach with impunity, and reside at interior cities, without fear of serious opposition. * * With means and men, we could preach the gospel, this year, to one hundred millions of souls. * * The British and Foreign Bible Society has had two agents traveling in half of the provinces of China, selling and distributing Bibles. * * The obstacle now is that merely of the heart ossified by ages of idolatry, which can be penetrated alone by the Spirit and power of God."

LABOR AND LONGING.

On July 13th, 1868, Mr. Yates wrote: "Yesterday was the Lord's Day, and I trust eternity will show that a good day's work was done at Shanghai. * * A woman, who lived in my family seventeen years ago, was received, after a satisfactory examination, for baptism. * * This widow is the mother of an interesting family of young men, who have never been taught to worship idols. They say they must follow their mother. * * In my congregation there are nine interesting inquirers, among them two women seventy-eight years old." Mr. Yates longed for more laborers: " My dear brother, the fields are whitening for the harvest. It is impossible for any one out of the work to imagine my feelings, as I cast my eyes over this populous region, wholly given to idolatry and superstitions. How few of them know anything of the Lord Jesus Christ, and call upon his holy name! It is truly a melancholy spectacle. But how shall they call upon him in whom they have not believed? And how shall they believe in him of whom they have not heard? And how shall they hear without a preacher? And how shall they preach, except they be sent? Truly, a weighty responsibility rests upon the churches. 'Freely ye have received, freely give.'"

LETTER FROM WONG PING SAN.

SHANGHAI, CHINA, *October 8th,* 1869.

" *To the Rev. J. B. Taylor:*

"May you be filled with the blessing of God the Father, Son, and Holy Spirit.

"Your humble brother, when only seventeen years old, was a diligent inquirer after the truth; he investigated the claims of all the religions around him, but for more than ten years he found no rest for his spirit. When I was thirty-one years old, I taught a girls' school for Mrs. Crawford. I taught the girls to read the Holy Bible. While doing so I realized that the matter of that book was broad and deep—far beyond anything I had before seen. I was deeply interested in, and greatly surprised at, the wonderful revelations of that book; but I did not know that I had any sins.

"After this, Mr. Crawford urged me to pray. I did, with my wife, commence praying. Before many days had passed, light from heaven revealed to me the sins, which, up to this time, had remained concealed in my heart. Moreover, they seemed to increase day by day, till they were mountain high. I now saw that what I formerly regarded as good and praiseworthy, was false and only evil. Such a view of myself led me to pray with more earnest importunity, and to look up to Jesus for help.

"On a certain night after the people had all retired to rest, when I had prayed some time, and rose to my feet, I felt that all the enmity and ill will I had ever entertained towards others had passed away, and in my heart and whole body I felt refreshed and invigorated. Suddenly I thought and said, surely God has forgiven me my sins, or I could not so freely forgive others their trespasses against me. Thereupon I was enabled to return thanks without measure.

"In all my former life nothing that I had enjoyed, believed, or trusted in had given me anything like such joy and peace of mind. On the next day I related to Messrs. Yates and Crawford what I had felt. They both said, 'truly the Lord has not cast you off, but by the aid of his Holy Spirit, he has brought you into the family of the children of light; and now that you have obtained like grace with us, we can walk with you as a brother in Christ Jesus.' I was in due time, received into the church, and the day appointed for my baptism.

"In the spring of 1856 I was baptized in the river by the Pastor Yates. From that time my heart has been at rest; I have been able to view life and death with composure. In all times of trial and temptation the Holy Spirit has been my support and comfort. After experiences of this sort, I felt that my former trust was in an arm of strength. I read the Old Testament Scriptures and learned that the law and the words of the prophets harmonize with the teachings of the New Testament. I learned, moreover, that from old, God has desired the salvation of men. From this time forth I went into the chapel with Mr. Crawford, and spake to the people about the great mercy and salvation I had found. Within two years more than ten persons learned and believed the truth as it is in Jesus. In time the Church raised me to the office of deacon. Yates, Pearcy, Crawford, and Cabaniss, went every where preaching the gospel."

LIGHTS AND SHADOWS.

In the summer or fall of 1869, Mr. Yates *lost his voice.* This affliction broke upon him when he was peculiarly encouraged in his work. He had baptized five women within a month, and there were "several other hopeful conversions." He wrote: "I am delighted with the spirit of the new converts. * * Oh! there is joy in my little church; several of my new members are actively engaged trying to persuade their relatives and friends to come to church and become Christians." * * The prospect is in every way encouraging. My influence among the natives was never so great. * * After twenty-one years, I have touched the Chinese heart. * * I have never felt more certain of the ultimate triumph of the gospel in China. What though the laborers are few, let us not forget that it is not by might nor by power, but by my Spirit, saith the Lord? Though many have almost forgotten their missionaries, and their obligation to preach the gospel to every creature, there are a few names that have not bowed the knee to Baal; there are a few who remember the wants of the missionaries in distant lands, and pray for a blessing upon them." The native preacher, Mr. *Wong,* was ordained, and, with Mrs. Yates, was left in charge of the mission, while Mr. Yates sought, in Manchuria and America, the restoration of his voice. The new pastor baptized two persons—a woman sixty-three years old, and a native physician of Shanghai. In the confession of the latter before the church, he said: "I believe God will save me from what I fear. I put myself in his hands, and my fear left me, and I am happy." Mrs. Yates wrote: "These baptisms coming unexpectedly, when the church was mourning the absence of her pastor, encouraged the members much."

MR. YATES' VOICE RESTORED, LOST, AND REGAINED.

The voice of Mr. Yates was so recovered in this country that "he addressed large congregations with ease to himself and much gratification to his hearers. Wherever he went among the churches, a favorable impression was made on behalf of our cause." In 1870, Rev. R. S. Pritchard was appointed as a missionary to Shanghai; but was detained by ill health from starting for his field of labor. He departed this life on the 21st of January, 1872. Early in 1871, Mr. Yates turned his face towards his China home, where he arrived on the 5th day of February. He found his congregation "rallying after the fright consequent upon the *Tien-tsin* tragedy." His church was in a most healthful condition. "Oh! my dear brother," he wrote, "we have the real martyr-spirit in the infant church. The whole church is thoroughly aroused to the importance of doing something to spread the knowledge of Jesus. Many of them feel that my affliction is a loud call to them to engage permanently in the work of teaching the people the way of salvation. My chapel, which I wish to enlarge, has been *crowded* for three Lord's Days." On the 9th of July, *See*, an Amoy man, "who had never worshipped idols, as his mother became a Christian while he was quite young," was received, with his wife, for baptism. "These accessions have a tendency to stimulate the zeal of the church; and to my own soul," said Mr. Yates, "they are truly refreshing. The Lord be praised!" Two native missionaries, *See* and *Tsung*, were despatched to open a station at *Kwung San*. The people received them gladly; but the officials and literati opposed, as "they make a studied opposition to all *aggressive* missionary work."

On the 20th of September, Mr. Yates' voice was reduced to a whisper. In December, by the advice of his physician, he quitted his field again, taking the overland route for Europe and the United States. The mission was committed once more to the excellent management of Mrs. Yates, and to the native pastor, of whom Mr. Yates remarked: "Wong Ping San improves in preaching all the time. His growth in knowledge and grace is really wonderful. He is now a very good and reliable teacher of Christianity, and I trust, with the blessing of God, the church will grow in numbers and in moral power under his ministry." Mrs. Yates: "It will be my endeavor to keep up the interest and the ardor as steadily as if Mr. Yates were here. With the sound doctrine of the pastor, and the zealous co-operation of our deacon and lay preacher, *Wong Yih San*, this is not too much to hope for. From the out-station at *Kwung San*, we have reports of the speedy finishing of the chapel. Teacher *See* is a warm-hearted Christian, and we may expect good results there." During 1871, seven were baptized, making the total membership of the mission fifty-two. On the 12th of February, 1872, Mr. Yates arrived in Naples, Italy, and on the 17th of that month he wrote: "It is with pleasure and thanksgiving that I report the restoration of my voice. After whispering for months, I can speak in my natural tone of voice. Thanks unto God!"

WORK AND WORKERS.

In 1872, six converts of *Kwung San* were baptized. There were at that station ten Christians. The whole membership of the mission was fifty-eight. Mrs. Yates wrote: "*Wong* preaches regularly, and preaches well too. The members of his flock attend punctually." Our sister tried to impress on the church their obligation to be self-sustaining. Some of the members contribute liberally. "The deacon understands that nobody is to be made to give; he is simply to set it before them as a 'reasonable service.'" Mr. Yates said of *See Seen Sang*, and *Tsung Seen Sang*, at *Kwung San:* "They are both active men, and are doing a good work." In 1873, Mrs. Yates, before the return of her husband, reported: "In church matters, I hope we are making progress. Last month, our church paid the whole of Pastor Wong's salary ($15); yet only fifteen of our fifty-eight members contributed. They 'always understood that the gospel was without money and without price; that foreign Christians were to send all the money needed.'

But they are now told that it is a duty to lift the burden of their support from American Christians that they may send the gospel to other parts of the heathen world sooner."

MR. YATES' VOICE AND VICE-CONSULATE.

Though his voice did not admit of public speaking, Mr. Yates, after a short visit to this country, returned to China, *via* San Francisco. On the day of his departure, April 1st, 1873, he wrote: "On arriving in China, I shall not resume my duties, but will continue to spare my voice during the summer. America is not the place for me to rest. * * I trust all will be overruled for the best." Under date of September 11th, Mr. Yates wrote from Shanghai: "A few short talks to the church have injured my voice. I am merely superintending the mission work, and acting as door-keeper in the house of the Lord. The loss of my voice, which threw the whole of the work on *Wong Ping San*, has, under God, made him a good preacher—one of whom we are not ashamed." October 10th: "My voice is gone. To save my life, it may be deemed necessary for me to leave China again." He accepted, however, the position of Vice-Consul and Interpreter of the United States. He said: "As I need, must have, and will have a chapel, I shall proceed to do the work at my own expense, appropriating all my profits, as Vice-Consul, until the work is completed." On the 23d of February, 1874, Mr. Yates communicated the following painful intelligence: "I am sorry to have to report that my voice is much worse. I fear I shall not be able to hold on here. The Lord reigns and will direct all things for his glory."

OPINIONS OF MISSIONARIES AND STATISTICS.

In 1873, our missionaries, Mr. and Mrs. Hartwell and Mr. and Mrs. Crawford, of Shantung, visited Shanghai. Mr. Hartwell expressed himself thus: "Even in Shanghai, where wickedness so much abounds, the gospel has had its triumphs, and has erected its monuments." Mr. Crawford: "The church here is growing in grace and in numbers under the care of the venerable *Wong Ping San*, who, by the way, was my first convert in China." During this year, eight were baptized.

The membership was sixty. Eight hundred dollars, raised on the field, Mr. Yates requested to have represented in the Southern Baptist Convention of 1874. The Convention met in Texas, and the First Baptist Church of Shanghai was represented by Christian Seminoles from the Indian Territory of the United States. How suggestive of the union of "the ends of the earth," in the redeemed family of God!

MAN'S GENEROSITY AND GOD'S GRACE.

At an expense to himself of three thousand dollars, Mr. Yates erected a beautiful and substantial chapel, and also a parsonage for the native pastor, *Wong Ping San*. Messrs. Russell & Co., of Shanghai, contributed a five hundred pound Meneely bell, for the belfry. On the 14th of February, 1875, the chapel was dedicated, with appropriate services, by Messrs. Yates, *Wong* and *See*. The building was crowded morning and evening. Five persons came forward to unite with the church. Next day, they were baptized in the new baptistery, in the presence of a multitude of witnesses. In 1874, nine were baptized, notwithstanding the excited state of the public in anticipation of war with Japan. Mr. Yates wrote: "The present position of this mission for the prosecution of missionary work and for putting the church to work is most satisfactory. * * But, without the blessing of the Spirit upon our efforts, we shall see no fruit to the glory of God."

HOME AND ABROAD.

From the report of Mr. Yates, presented to the Southern Baptist Convention of 1876, we extract the following: "In December, I resigned my office as Vice-Consul General. On the death of Mr. Avery —U. S. Minister to Peking—the Consul General, George F. Seward, was appointed Minister, and the Vice-Consul General was instructed by the Secretary of State to take charge of the Consulate General. This I could not do without giving up my missionary work—my life work. I resigned, therefore, the honor and the emolument. I am happy to say that my voice seems quite restored. I have, for several months, been able to preach regularly, and labor hard on a revision of Matthew's Gospel, in the spoken language of the people of this plain—a dialect spoken by about forty millions. I have built Mrs. Yates a school-house, where, in addition to her day school, in which she is doing good service, she meets the women for Bible lessons. The congregations at the new church have been large and quite regular—three times each week. *Rev. Wong Ping San* has preached well. We have, during the year, added to our number, by experience and baptism, twenty. The present membership is seventy-two. *See Seen Sang*, stationed at *Kwung San*, has constructed a tent, which he moves from one village to another, and in which he preaches to or teaches those who call on him in his tabernacle. The prospect everywhere is good for a steady increase of the work abroad; but the apparent want of foreign missionary spirit at home causes us the deepest solicitude for the future of our life work Shall we take no part in giving Japan, and the interior cities of this great Empire, the gospel of Christ? The Lord revive his work in the hearts of his people!"

The Gospel by Matthew, referred to above, has been received at the Mission Rooms. Mr. Yates pleads earnestly for aid to circulate it. Can any lover of Jesus, who has the ability to help, review the third of a century's labor of this man of God and turn a deaf ear to his cry that the bread of life may be given to the perishing millions of China?

1876 TO 1880.

As has been stated, an abstract of the Shanghai Mission, between these dates, may be found in the *Resumé*, at the end of the volume.

SHANTUNG MISSION.

PROVINCE OF SHANTUNG.

THIS province lies south of the Pe-chi-li Gulf, and north of Kiang-si, and borders on Honan, where the Yellow River divides the two provinces. Its area is 65,184 square miles—about that of Georgia. Its population is 28,958,764—about that of Great Britain. The Grand Canal traverses the province. There is found one of the highest mountains of China, the *Tai-shan*, where every sect has its temple, and where devotees of every name crowd annually in great multitudes. A missionary tells of a company of pilgrims composed of dames, the youngest of whom was seventy-eight years old, and the oldest ninety years old, who had travelled three hundred miles to plead their long abstinence from flesh and fish, as "a reason for the happy transmigration of their souls."

"Shantung is well watered. Numerous small streams run seaward from the hills in the east; and tributaries of the Yellow and White Rivers flow through the western and southern parts. Coal is abundant, and largely exported. Iron mines are worked to a considerable extent. Millet, rice, wheat, and maize—the first of which furnishes the principal article of food—are abundant. Water-fowl and fish are plentiful. Fruits are numerous. Pears are largely exported. Their flavor is inferior. They reach the weight of eight to sixteen ounces."

This province is famous as the birth-place of Confucius, and of his disciple Mencius. The tomb of the former, who died B. C. 479, at *Kiuh-fau*, is a majestic monument, "embosomed in a forest of oaks, whose gloomy shades are well fitted to nourish the homage paid to his memory."

The coast, which is more than one-half of the circuit of Shantung, is full of indentures, some of which are excellent harbors. No large river runs through the province, and the waters on each side of the peninsula are shallow.

The capital of Shantung is *Chi-nan-Foo*. Its manufactures are coarse fabrics, made of wild silk, and ornaments of *lieu-li*—"a kind of vitreous compound made to resemble serpentine, jade, ice, and other things."

Chefoo, or Yentai, was a small fishing town on the gulf, before it was opened to foreign commerce. *Tung Chow* was the port originally ceded to foreigners; but the harbor there not proving good, Chefoo was chosen instead. Chefoo is the post-office of Tung Chow, though sixty miles distant. The scenery in the vicinity of Yentai is very beautiful, and the city is regarded as one of the most important centres for missionary labors. It was there that our beloved missionary, Rev. J. L. Holmes, settled and was murdered, and where our Brother J. B. Hartwell, who is now in this country, had a flourishing missionary station. *Tung Chow*, on the northern shore, is a prefectural city of about one hundred thousand inhabitants. It is really two walled cities, so near together that a stone can be thrown from one to the other. The houses are of brick or stone, and almost invariably one story high. The streets are wider than those of Southern China, and are paved with stones—sometimes with old mill-stones. The latitude is near that of Richmond, Va. One of our missionaries " who has lived in the States of Virginia, Kentucky, and Georgia would, without hesitation, give the preference to this climate over that of any of those three States."

Mrs. Nevius, in "Our Life in China," to which excellent work we are indebted for some of the above facts, says: "At six in the evening, we were nearing Tung Chow. I was forcibly reminded at that time, as often afterwards when approaching the city, of representations and descriptions of Jerusalem. Lying in nearly the same latitude, with hills and mountains in its immediate neighborhood, its walls and parapets running now low through a valley, now up over a hilltop, with occasional towers, and higher buildings rising above the ordinarily low structures, and particularly the clear, blue sky, against which the walls and hills stand out in bold relief, it has often suggested to my mind the Holy City, without, however, any such tender associations, as must ever cling to 'Zion the beautiful.'"

In this city, there were, "from the first, encouraging indications that the progress of missionary work would be more rapid than it had been in the older stations at the south." But before giving an account of the rise and progress of our Shantung interests, we shall present brief biographical sketches of the missionaries, who have labored there, under the auspices of the Southern Baptist Convention.

TARLTON PERRY CRAWFORD, D. D.

HIS NAME.

If we are rightly informed, by one who ought to know, this rather singular combination, in the *prænomina* of Mr. Crawford, was the result of his own juvenile choice, which suggests, if the play on words may be pardoned, that our missionary is one to *make a striking name for himself.*

BIRTH PLACE.

Mr. Crawford was born on the 8th of May, 1821, in Warren County, Kentucky. The place is midway between Bowling Green and Glasgow—"about half a mile north of the main road, and three-quarters of a mile east of the 'Pilot Knob,' which is rather an interesting and romantic spot."

HIS EDUCATION.

By the care of his mother, his primary education was prosecuted in several country schools of his native State. Subsequently he studied at Clark's Institute, in Henry County, Tennessee, and at the Academy of Rev. W. L. Slack, in Denmark, of the same State. Early in 1848, he entered Union University, located at Murfreesboro, and in 1851, "he graduated at the head of his class and with the first honors of the institution."

AS A STUDENT AND PREACHER.

Mr. Crawford was converted in March, 1837. On the 10th of July, he was baptized by Rev. Ephraim H. Owing, in Clark's River, Callaway County, Kentucky. As he appeared at Union University, over which Dr. J. H. Eaton then presided, he is thus described:

"He was of untiring perseverance in his studies, and pursued everything he undertook with the greatest tenacity. He was decided in his convictions and firm in his purposes. After having fixed upon a foreign mission he never wavered in his purpose. As a preacher, he was earnest, and soon kindled into fervent zeal in the delivery of his discourses. His sermons were good, and sometimes carefully prepared, for one of his experience and opportunity. His elocution was unattractive. Indeed, he seemed never to have bestowed a thought on the subject of *how* his message was to be delivered. Still his piety, earnestness, and zeal made him often very effective. His perseverance, and the unyielding determination that has characterized his missionary labors, are only a development of those characteristics which he exhibited in early life."

His ordination took place at the Denmark Church of the Big Hatchie Association, Tennessee, in April, 1851. Twelve ministers officiated, among whom were Messrs. Peter S. Gayle, C. C. Connor, George Day, H. L. Pettus, and Dr. Archibald Maclay, of New York. In May of that year, he, with others, was set apart as a missionary to China at the Southern Baptist Convention, which met in the city of Nashville.

HOW HE GOT A NOBLE WIFE.

" Rev. J. B. Taylor, Corresponding Secretary of the Foreign Mission Board, received a letter from Rev. E. B. Teague, of Alabama, asking if the Board would send out, as a missionary, an unmarried lady, and commending, in high terms, Miss Martha Foster, who was anxious to consecrate her life to the salvation of the heathen in China. This letter being exhibited to Brother Crawford, appeared to him a providential indication, and he immediately set out for Alabama. I first met him in February, 1851, on horseback, on this journey, within twenty-five miles of the object of his search, and answered numerous questions about the way, then somewhat obstructed by swollen watercourses, and parted with him without the slightest intimation of his name, place of residence, or purpose. Some three weeks later I accompanied him and his young bride from this county to Mobile and New Orleans, on their way to Tennessee."

Mrs. Crawford is the daughter of Deacon John L. S. Foster, of Tuscaloosa, Alabama, who fell asleep while a member of Grant's Creek

Church of Alabama, in February, 1875, and of Mrs. Susan Foster, who resides with her daughter, Mrs. E. A. Foster, in Starkville, Mississippi. The nuptials were celebrated on the 12th of March, 1851. "Whoso findeth a wife findeth a good thing and obtaineth favor of the Lord."

MOVEMENTS, LITERARY WORK, AND HONORS.

On January 6th, 1851, Mr. Crawford was appointed "a missionary to Shanghai," and " an agent of the Board, to collect funds in Tennessee, especially in the Big Hatchie Association," which had liberally offered to provide his support. On the 17th of November of that year, he sailed, with his wife, for Shanghai, where they arrived March 30th, 1852. In 1858, they returned to America. After an absence of a year and nine months, they went back in 1860 to Shanghai. In 1863, they removed to Tung Chow, in the Shantung Province. Of their labors there, we shall write in due time. Mrs. Crawford published: Book on Western Cooking; Infant's Catechism; Three Little Girls; The Chinese Bride, issued by the American Baptist Publication Society; and The Chinese Daughter-in-Law—issued anonymously by a Missionary Board of this country. Mr. Crawford published: Mandarian Grammar; Hymn Book of "Original, Translated, and Selected Hymns, with Creed"; Epitome of Ancient History; Phonetic Primer, and "The Patriarchal Dynasties, from Abraham to Adam, shown to cover a period of 10,500 years; and the highest human life only 187 years." In 1878, Mr. Crawford's health having failed, he came to this country, and attended our Convention, in May of the next year. Returning to China in July, his steamer was nearly wrecked in a typhoon. A Chinese paper, referring to the heroic conduct of those on board, says: "The Rev. T. P. Crawford came nobly to the fore." In 1879, the honorary degree of Doctor of Divinity was conferred on Mr. Crawford by Richmond College.

JESSE BOARDMAN HARTWELL, D. D.

MISSIONS IN INFANCY.

The subject of this sketch was born in October, 1835, at Darlington,

South Carolina, where his father, Rev. Jesse Hartwell, was pastor of the Baptist Church. Luther Rice was present in the family, soon after the birth of the child, and remarked: "Name him Burmah!" This suggested the name of "Boardman," which, in honor of that devoted missionary, was given to the only son of the man of God, whose spirit was ever aglow with zeal for the cause of Foreign Missions.

EDUCATION AND ORDINATION.

In 1836, Rev. Mr. Hartwell removed to Alabama. In 1843, he went to Marion, of that State, where his son, Jesse Boardman, was partly educated. In 1853, our future missionary entered Furman University, located at Greenville, South Carolina, and was graduated there with distinction, in 1856. After spending a year as Professor in Mount Lebanon University of Louisiana, he was appointed, February 1st, 1858, as a missionary to Shanghai. He was set apart to the missionary work of the gospel at Greenville, South Carolina. Dr. Jeter, of Richmond, Va., preached the ordination sermon.

MARRIAGE AND DEATH.

In September, 1858, Mr. Hartwell was married to Miss Eliza H. Jewett, of Macon, Georgia. As we have seen, they sailed on the 5th of November, 1858, and arrived at Shanghai in March, 1859. In December, 1860, they moved, with Mr. and Mrs. Holmes, to the Shantung Province, and settled at Tung Chow. We have already noticed Mr. Hartwell's return to Shanghai, during the absence of Mr. Yates in Europe, and his resumption of missionary labors in Tung Chow. There he was instrumental, as we shall see, in founding and edifying a strong church and several out-stations. A native preacher, Rev. Mr. *Woo*, was raised up under his ministry, and was left in charge of the church when Mr. Hartwell returned to this country in 1871. Until recently, *Woo* has been its efficient pastor. Mrs. Hartwell was an invaluable help to her husband in keeping up a boarding school, where the Bible was daily taught. "During six weeks of the great Chinese rebellion, Mr. Hartwell had not less than one hundred refugees on his premises, among whom he acted the triple part of surgeon, nurse, and preacher." His severe labors and exposures were followed by a long and serious illness. In a season of persecution, he was forced to seek the protection of the United States flag, and, on one occasion, he and his family escaped for their lives, on horseback, to a place of temporary security. In May, 1869, the Southern Baptist Convention received a letter, "with a *contribution*," from the North Street Church of Tung Chow, which excited much interest. In 1870, Mrs. Hartwell died, which left a fearful void in the mission work. "The infant twins she left became quite sick, and thus to all the other cares of the missionary were added those of nurse and protector for his motherless children."

REMINISCENCES OF THE HARTWELLS.

In Mrs. Nevius' "Our Life in China," she adverts, on several occasions, to our missionaries, in the following language: "Some distance from the city, Mr. Hartwell's native assistant met us. * * I was delighted to find myself at the Hartwells'. The warm, cordial welcome given us by them was truly delightful. Their house, though not at all in foreign style, was sufficiently roomy for a moderately large family, and, compared with those occupied by the missionaries at Yentai, was pleasant. * * In the meanwhile we all remained at Mr. Hartwell's. * * The chapel in his house was daily opened for services. * * Mr. Hartwell's house was turned into a hospital, and he kindly devoted himself to dressing wounds, and providing simple remedies, such as were within his reach. * * I think Mr. Hartwell's teacher and servants were all ill with the cholera; but owing, perhaps, to early remedies and most faithful nursing, they all recovered. * * Before the close of January, 1862, another little grave was made in our fast-filling cemetery. It was that of an infant daughter of Mr. and Mrs. Hartwell, 'Little Carrie,' who died, it was supposed, from the effects of cholera, which she had months before, while it was prevailing in Tung Chow."

RETURN AND REMARRIAGE.

With the approval of the Board, Mr. Hartwell, in 1871, as has been stated, brought his children to this country. He arrived in San Francisco in April of that year, and attended the Southern Baptist Convention at St. Louis, where his presence added much interest and pleasure to the meeting. "In company with two native Chinese, he passed through the country preaching the gospel with singular power, and advancing the interests of the Board. His pulpit efforts gave no indication that his ministerial life had been spent in a heathen land, but rather indicated that, had he remained at home, he would have commanded positions of high influence and power." In November, 1871, he went to the Welsh Neck Association of South Carolina, which adopted, as their beneficiary, the Chinese girl Mary, who had accompanied him as a servant to this country. She was to be educated for mission work in her native land. In December of that year, he was married to Miss Julia Jewett, of Macon, Georgia, the sister of his former wife. In April, 1872, they started, with his children—except the oldest, Jesse George—for their foreign home, where they arrived the following June. Mr. Hartwell published the "translation of a number of hymns for the use of his church."

MRS. HARTWELL AND THE CHILDREN.

Before their departure, the Board approved of Mr. Hartwell's opening a mission at *Chi-nan-Foo*, the capital of the Shantung Province. The ill health of Mrs. Hartwell and other considerations induced him to change his plan, and to open a station at *Chefoo*. His valuable work at this post shall be duly noted. To the grief of both of them, the protracted illness of Mrs. Hartwell, whose sufferings were excruciating, forced them, in 1875, to return to America, leaving their children with Mr. and Mrs. R. H. Graves, at Canton. In May, 1876, Mr. and Mrs. Hartwell were present at the Southern Baptist Convention, which met at Richmond, Va. Mr. Hartwell made a forcible speech in the interest of Foreign Missions. After medical treatment in Baltimore, Mrs. Hartwell tried the efficacy of the Hot Springs of Arkansas. Mr. Hartwell was appointed an agent of the Board of Foreign Missions, and plead ably the cause of the heathen, to whose well-being he has given the energies of his life. He is now a missionary of the Home Board, and appointed to preach to the Chinese in California. An eminent minister of the gospel has just written to us: "Brother Hartwell should have the prayers and sympathies of all God's people." Some record of his children, all of whom are in this country, will be of interest to the denomination. Jesse George was born February 3d, 1860, and was a student in Furman University of Greenville, South Carolina, where his father was graduated and ordained. Ellen Edwards, a namesake of her father's sister, Mrs. Edwards, of Society Hill, South Carolina, was born September 8th, 1863. John Holzendorf and Anna Burton were born March 6th, 1870.

The degree of Doctor of Divinity was conferred on Mr. Hartwell by Furman University. The principal facts recorded above have been gathered from an article, which appeared, several years since, in the *Foreign Mission Journal*, over the signature of T. P. L.

Rev. JAMES LANDRUM HOLMES.

HIS BIRTH AND NEW BIRTH.

Mr. Holmes was born, May 16th, 1836, in Preston County, now in West Virginia. His pious mother resides, with a married daughter, at Kinsdale, near Chicago. Reared in the Methodist faith, he united with the Methodist Episcopal Church at Morgantown, when he was about fifteen years old, although he had professed conversion some three years before. While engaged with "a Baptist friend"—who probably was the future companion of his life—in studying the nature and obligation of Christian baptism, his attention was arrested by an article from the pen of the late Rev. Dr. Richard Fuller, in the *True Union* of Baltimore, then edited by Dr. Franklin Wilson. Writing to the editor on the subject, he received from Dr. Wilson a copy of Dr. Fuller's work on "Baptism and Communion." In 1855, he was baptized in Cheat River by Rev. D. B. Purinton. From the time of his first profession of faith in Christ, he had been impressed with the duty of going to China as a missionary, and had directed his studies to that end. After his baptism, he joined the Franklin Square Baptist Church, of Baltimore, and, by the assistance of Dr. Wilson, pursued his studies at Columbian College of the District of Columbia.

STARTING IN LIFE.

In June, 1858, Mr. Holmes was graduated from that College. In July, he was ordained at the Franklin Square Baptist Church. On the 22d of that month, he and Miss Sallie J. Little, daughter of Mrs. Ann Little, formerly of Upperville and Martinsburg, Virginia, were united in the holy bands of matrimony in Cumberland, Maryland. On May the 3d of the same year, Mr. Holmes had received an appointment from the Board of Foreign Missions. With Mrs. Holmes he sailed, August the 21st, in the ship "Falcon," for Shanghai, where they arrived the February following.

ESTABLISHMENT AT CHEFOO.

Reference has been made already to their removal from Shanghai to the Shantung Province. The following is an authentic statement of the change of their abode: "In May, 1859, Mr. and Mrs. Holmes went to Chefoo, with the view of settling at Tung Chow. They were compelled to return to Shanghai until the war of China with the English and French alliance was over. As soon as possible, after peace was established, Mr. Holmes went again to Chefoo in company with Mr. and Mrs. Edkins, of the London Mission. After spending some time in securing and fitting up a house, he returned to Shanghai for his family. In December, 1860, they set sail again for Chefoo, with Rev. J. B. Hartwell and family, and Rev. G. John, of the London Mission." Under the same date, Mr. Holmes wrote: "Dr. Burton is of the opinion that it is imperatively necessary that Brother and Sister Hartwell should leave the climate of Shanghai, and, on this account, they have altered their plans about settling at *Su Chow.* * * Shanghai is a very expensive city—more so than Baltimore or Washington, D. C." "Chefoo is the port for entering Shantung, and is a place of great trade. The climate is as cold as Baltimore, Maryland." The house referred to above was secured with much difficulty, and only by an order from the Mandarins, on the ground that Mr. Holmes was an *American* and a missionary. From Chefoo he wrote, February 8th, 1861: "China is open to the preaching of the gospel in all its length and breadth. The French treaty expressly provides that their priests shall be allowed to preach and build chapels anywhere in the Empire. Under the 'most favored nation' clause, we shall claim the same privilege. * * Brother Hartwell has gone to Tung Chow to fit up a house which he has secured, and expects to move in a few weeks. Chefoo seems to me one of the most important points, if not the most important one, to be occupied in Shantung."

PERSONNEL AND EXPEDIENTS.

Mr. Holmes was possessed of a clear and strong intellect, and of an independent spirit. With regard to some policy of the Board, he did not hesitate to express very decided convictions in opposition, which, however, in no wise impaired the good understanding and perfect confidence between them. His diligence and facility in the acquisition of the Chinese language, may be inferred from his agreement in 1860 to accompany Mr. Ward, the United States Consul, to Peking, as an interpreter. The following is extracted from "Our Life in China, by Helen S. C. Nevius": "On the breaking out of the late war in the United States, the missionaries connected with Southern Societies found themselves in a most perplexing and trying position. Although in many cases, enthusiastically interested in their work, and very successful, they were, in consequence of being cut off from supplies from America, reduced to the alternative of returning home, or engaging in secular business. * * When the necessity was removed, they gladly returned to their life-work among the heathen. One of those who thus engaged in mercantile business, was the Rev. J. Landrum Holmes. He was a person whose peculiar loveliness of character made him a favorite with every one. Handsome, talented, ardent, with very winning manners, he was peculiarly fitted for usefulness among the Chinese, to whom such qualities are very attractive. The 'Amelia,' in which we sailed from Shanghai to Chefoo, had been chartered by Mr. Holmes, who, with a younger brother, not a clergyman, had already established a prosperous firm in that newly opened port of the province of Shantung. Our fellow-passengers from Shanghai were Mrs. Yates, of the Southern Baptist Board, and her daughter, Miss Annie, who had come to pass the summer at the north. Soon after the ship cast anchor, Mr. Holmes came on board to accompany Mrs. Yates to his house. * * He urged my going in company with his party, and I consented to do so. * * Mr. Holmes' house, which was rather better than the others, was a very low, one-storied Chinese building, the different rooms opening on a small enclosure or court. * * Not a tree nor shrub relieved the eye or sheltered from the heat. * * The air, owing in part to the miserable way of building without outside windows, was impure and stifling, not at all calculated to conduce to the health and vigor of those obliged to breathe it. When our fellow-passengers from the ship and ourselves were added to Mr. Holmes' family, which consisted of Mrs. Holmes and a little daughter about two years old, and two Chinese boys whom they were educating, besides servants, it seemed as if their house was already more than full. But, before night, Mr. Hartwell and Mrs. Danforth arrived from Tung Chow to seek medical aid for Mrs. Danforth. * * But warm, sympathizing hearts are always rich in expedients; the parlor had to do double duty, and was turned into a bedroom, our kind host and hostess having, however, to sleep on the floor."

MIDNIGHT GLOOM.

In September, 1861, little Anna Holmes took her flight and left the home in darkness. The ravages of the rebel banditti beggared description. Mr. Matthew Holmes, brother of our missionary, having ridden on horseback from *Tien-tsin* to Tung Chow, "spoke of the country through which he passed as one scene of desolation, the rebels having gone over the route, burning villages, capturing or killing the inhabitants, and putting to death every living thing, * * * so that he was scarcely able, in some places, to pass for the human corpses and the carcasses of beasts." Amid the horrors of the time, a Chinaman, who had received no less than twenty gashes on his head and arms, came into Tung Chow, bearing from his distant home his aged mother on his back, as Æneas bore the venerable Anchises from the flames and ruin of Troy. The name of the noble and filial *Fan-yin-tai* deserves historic immortality. But we hasten to the crisis. On the

6th of October, 1861, Mr. Holmes, with Rev. H. M. Parker, of the Episcopal Mission, went out to the rebel camp, about twenty-five miles from Chefoo, to make some terms for the safety of their town. "Mrs. Holmes had gone to pass the time of her husband's absence at Chukee, about three miles from Yentai. They did not quit their house until, one midnight, a messenger came with horses and a letter from the kind and considerate English Consul at Chefoo, begging them to leave at once, as the rebels were close at hand. They did so; but were scarcely out of the village when it was entered by the advance of the rebel army. Their house was plundered, many articles of value were carried off, and much was wantonly destroyed." Eight days after the departure of Mr. Holmes and Mr. Parker, about whose fate the most afflictive rumors were afloat, their bodies, "covered with wounds and burns," were recovered and buried on "the green island at the mouth of the harbor." "Why they were so cruelly murdered," cried Mr. Crawford, "no one knows. One thing is certain, they have slain two excellent men and missionaries of the cross in the midst of manhood and usefulness, and made the hearts of their lovely companions to mourn their irreparable loss." And though eighteen years have elapsed since the tragic event, we feel, in penning these lines, what Mr. Nevius said at the time: "Their grief is such as a stranger ought neither to 'intermeddle with' nor 'attempt to describe.'"

Mrs. J. S. HOLMES.

The subject of this sketch was the youngest child of Dr. John and Mrs. Ann Little. She was born in Upperville, Fauquier County, Va. Mrs. Little was the Principal of a Female Seminary in Martinsburg, Va., during two generations of pupils. She was a woman of devoted piety, and is still loved and reverenced by many as their spiritual mother. It is a noteworthy fact that she was one of the seven original members who constituted the Upperville Baptist Church.

Mrs. Little was an ardent friend of missions. For many years one of her sisters was an active worker in India. Thus it will be seen that our future missionary grew up in an atmosphere at once literary, religious, and missionary. In the house in Martinsburg the subject of missions was constantly discussed, and thus the minds of the children were kept turned in that direction.

When old enough she attended her mother's school, until the ill-health of the latter made it necessary to close it. Subsequently she entered the Collegiate Institute, under the charge of Mr. R. Daniel, of Baltimore, where she graduated in 1857.

Blessed with a pious mother's teachings, from early childhood her mind had been deeply impressed with serious things. As early as the age of seven years she felt that she had committed her soul to the Saviour. Yet for nearly seven years more she was kept out of a visible church by a perplexity as to the meaning of conversion. She was baptized in her fourteenth year, by Rev. Benjamin Griffith, now Rev. Dr. Griffith, of Philadelphia.

As we mentioned above, Mrs. Little was a warm friend of missions. It was not the fashion then, as it has become to some extent of late years, to set apart special objects for mission purposes, but this was one of Mrs. Little's methods. She had her "missionary bee-hive," when she lived in the country. With such deep interest in missions, it is not strange that the mother hailed with delight the daughter's expression, at the early age of fifteen, of a purpose to be a missionary. The mother spoke of the joy that David must have felt that Solomon was permitted to build the temple, and compared her own feelings to those of the royal psalmist of Israel. She herself had longed, in her younger years, to be a missionary, and it would be to her a source of great happiness if God accepted her daughter in this work. The memory of this conversation has been to the daughter as a tower of strength in many a dark and lonely hour of her life in China. Before she left America, a friend remonstrated with her on the folly of being a missionary, and, as if it were an unanswerable argument, exclaimed triumphantly: "You know your mother does not wish you to go." The reverse was true, and he was unconsciously suggesting the strongest argument against his views. She was married in July, 1858. Mr. and Mrs. Holmes "were the united offering of widowed mothers to the Lord of the harvest."

A few brief years of wedded happiness were closed by that terrible bereavement, before which we can only bow in awe at the inscrutable decrees of him whom we know to be at once All-wise and All-loving.

Now, when woman's work is one of the prominent features of Christian activity, we find it hard to realize how strange it seemed, even to some of her friends in China, that the stricken one should decide to remain at her post. As a matter of course she was expected to return to America. To give strength to her resolve to stay, there was the memory, not only of her mother's wishes, but also of a conversation with her husband soon after their arrival in China. Mr. Holmes came home one day looking very gloomy and announced the death of a fellow missionary. "If I thought I should die and leave you alone," he said, "leave you to go all that long way back by yourself, I should find it hard to say, 'Thy will be done.'" Said the brave woman, "Landrum, I would not go back; I would stay here and work."

His face, always wonderfully expressive, grew radiant. "If you feel that way," he said, "I shall have no further anxiety about the matter," and from that time his trouble was gone.

In July, 1862, Mrs. Holmes moved to Tung Chow. First, she stayed at Mr. Hartwell's; subsequently, she obtained a house on the same street. In 1867, the illness of her only child, James Landrum—born June, 1862, after the death of her husband—rendered her return to this country necessary. She brought, with her own boy, the motherless son of our devoted missionary at Canton, Dr. R. H. Graves. On November 1st, 1869, Mrs. Holmes, with her son, sailed again for China, and associated herself with Mr. and Mrs. Crawford at Tung Chow. She bought and fitted up another house—the one on North Street, previously occupied, being used as a chapel by Mr. Hartwell. She has issued several editions of "Peep of Day." Her son, Landrum, is in this country. May he fulfil the hopes of his devoted mother!

THE MISSES MOON.

These ladies are members of a well-known Virginia family, and daughters of the late Edward Harris Moon, of Albemarle County, Virginia, and of his wife, Anna M. Moon, *née* Barclay.

EDMONIA HARRIS MOON.

PATRONYMIC.

This name was given to the younger sister, at the death of her father, when she was not quite one year old. The family record indicates that her original name was "Robinett B. Moon."

EDUCATION AND GENERAL CHARACTERISTICS.

Her early education was conducted at home principally by her sister Charlotte. In November, 1866, she entered the Richmond Female Institute, of which Professor C. H. Winston, now of Richmond College, was then President. "Her standing as a pupil was excellent, and she gave evidence constantly of a strong and well-trained intellect. Her general character was marked by reserve, by independence, by much firmness mixed with proper deference, by dislike of sham and pretence, by candor and honesty. She usually thought for herself, and had perhaps a dash of originality and of romance. She was well advanced in Latin and French, and in two years graduated in mathematics, English literature, and moral philosophy." In the fall of 1870, she accepted the position of a private teacher of the children of two gentlemen near Clinton, Green County, Alabama. Her health failing as the warm weather of spring came on, she returned home the last of May, 1871.

CONVERSION AND MISSIONARY SPIRIT.

Miss Edmonia was converted under the ministry of Rev. J. C. Long —now Dr. Long, of Crozer Theological Seminary. She united with the "Hardware Church," in Albemarle County, about five miles from her home, and was baptized by Mr. Long in the summer of 1867. With regard to her baptism, Dr. Long communicated the following to the *Home and Foreign Mission Journal* of October, 1872:

"On a beautiful Lord's Day in mid-summer it was my privilege to administer the ordinance of baptism. The baptistery was in a little valley. It was an excavation made in the ground, and filled from a branch hard by. Among those who stood beneath the shade of the tall forest trees, looking on while a willing convert was putting on Christ in baptism, was Miss Moon, young but not light and thoughtless. The beauty, the solemnity, and the deep significance of the scene impressed her heart. She went home, and that very day gave herself to Christ.

"Two weeks later, her pastor met her at the church-door. Her first words to him were: 'Mr. Long, will you baptize me?' His reply was: 'Yes, Miss Eddie; when?' 'To-day,' she answered. The request was so sudden and so unexpected, that he could hardly realize that she was in earnest; but a glance at her face, all aglow with the light of pious resolution, removed his doubts. When the sermon was ended, she made known her wish to the church, and in that same baptistery in which she had witnessed the baptism of others, she was herself baptized."

Her preceptor, from whose pen we have already quoted, furnishes the ensuing testimony: "She had the ornament of 'a meek and quiet spirit,' and her piety, like her learning, would be regarded as of a solid, substantial, and useful type, without display or noise, and yet a real living power." A letter having been received from our missionary, Mrs. M. F. Crawford, of China, by the Missionary Society of the Richmond Institute, which had been founded by the liberality of Dr. W. H. Gwathmey, of Richmond, Va., Miss Edmonia Moon was selected to reply to the communication. This was an intimation of the spirit which she possessed, and may have been the means of deepening those impressions of duty which resulted in her devoting her life to the Chinese. Highly commended, she was appointed by the Board, April 9th, 1872, a missionary to Tung Chow. On the 16th of April, having declined, as unnecessary, assistance in her preparations, she started from home to join, in Baltimore, a company of our missionaries *en route* for China. Appropriate services were held in the Eutaw Place Baptist Church. In June of that year, she was settled at Tung Chow with Mr. and Mrs. Crawford, with whom she and her sister, Miss "Lottie" Moon, were identified in their valuable missionary labors. Dr. Long wrote of Miss Edmonia:

"When we heard that she proposed to go as a missionary to China, we were not surprised. We knew that she had been thinking of and pitying the Chinese, and that her heart burned to teach them the way of life. It was like her not to be appalled by the difficulties in the way. We are not surprised to learn that she has already won the respect and esteem of the people whom she has gone to teach. It is what we expected. If her life is spared, we shall be very much surprised if she does not do the work of a missionary faithfully and well. Hers, we trust, will not be a starless crown."

CHARLOTTE MOON.

RELIGIOUS LIBERTY.

As she grew up, Miss Moon was not, what is called in Sunday-school books, a pious child. She looked rather askance at things religious, and did not hesitate to make a little fun at the expense of the more sedate and less witty. The following is well authenticated: "In mid-winter, a young lady came to the school, and rather 'green.' Lottie took the new comer under her care. 'Mr. H. is a Baptist, you know, don't you?' said she. 'I know that,' said Miss Newcomer. 'And this is a Baptist school,' she added, 'and every girl that comes here has to be baptized at the Baptist Church the Sunday after arrival.' 'But,' said the girl, 'I don't want to be baptized. I don't want to join the church.' 'That don't signify,' was the reply. 'It is a rule of the school, and Mr. H., will be awful mad if you make any fuss about it. Besides, you have no time to lose. You will be baptized day after to-morrow, and you had better see Mrs. H., about what dress you must wear.' The girl was not enlightened until she sought the information."

THE MOST SCHOLARLY OF GRADUATES.

Her education was prosecuted at home, under private teachers, until the fall of 1854, when she was sent to the "V. U. Seminary," at Botetourt Springs, Virginia, now known as "Hollins' Institute," and then as now under the charge of Mr. C. Z. Cocke. She remained there two sessions. In September, 1857, she entered the "Albemarle Female Seminary," at Charlottesville, Va., which was presided over by Mr. John Hart, who was assisted by Professor C. H. Toy and other able instructors. One who had the best opportunity of forming a correct judgment on the subject has written:

"Miss Moon came to the school at Charlottesville with very good preparation as to attainments, and with unusual preparation as to natural abilities. Thus her career as a student was marked by distinguished success. It would be hard to say in what studies she most excelled. The writer, who had the pleasure of reading many of her examination papers, remembers her superlatively fine work in Latin, history, literature, and moral philosophy. He thinks that her strength lay especially in the direction of the languages and Belles Lettres studies. The Greek language was not included in the graduating course; but Miss Moon, entering on the work with her usual industry and intelligence, became a very good Greek scholar. Since that day, the writer has not heard any young ladies read with fluency and appreciation the plays of Euripides and Sophocles. Miss Moon graduated in 1861, at the end of her fourth session. It is not invidious to say that, in the judgment of many who had opportunity to know, she was the most scholarly of all the graduates of that school."

"AFTER HER CONVERSION."

Her first serious thoughts were attributed by her to the general influences in and about the Seminary. Her purposes took definite form, and her faith in Christ was declared during a time of revival, when many of the pupils of the school became members of the Charlottesville Church. She was baptized by Dr. John A. Broadus, who was then pastor of that church. One who knew her well says:

"This I do know, that Lottie Moon, after her conversion, was different from Lottie Moon before. She was not different in person, though it did seem that her face, always radiant with intelligence, had assumed a softer radiance than before. She was not different intellectually, but different in the spirit and purpose of her life—different in her influence on her fellow-pupils—different in all those details of the daily life, which at last may afford the most delicate test of the Christian character."

FRAGRANT IN THE MEMORY OF PATRONS.

Her first experience as a teacher was at home—her sister Edmonia receiving her early instructions from her. After that, she was an assistant of the Rev. A. S. Worrell, at Danville, Ky., and next of Rev. Mr. Barbour, a Presbyterian minister, who was Principal of the "Caldwell Institute," of Danville, Ky. In the summer of 1871, Miss Moon, with her intimate friend, Miss A. C. Safford, of Georgia, whom she met at Mr. Barbour's, took charge of the "Female High School," at Cartersville, Bartow County, Georgia. The pastor of the Baptist Church of that place wrote: "Miss Moon taught here for two years, and endeared herself to our entire people. She was a faithful teacher in our Sunday-school. On Sunday afternoons, she would hunt out destitute families and teach them the Scriptures. When it was announced that she was determined to go to China, many of our citizens expressed great indignation at the waste of such a noble life upon the Chinese! 'The Lottie Moon Society,' in our church, will keep her memory fresh and fragrant in the minds of our people."

REJOICING TO WIN SOULS TO CHRIST.

In February, 1873, it was proposed, by Miss Moon's pastor, to the "Ministers and Deacons' Meeting" of the Middle Cherokee Association of Georgia, to "pray the Lord of the harvest to send *then* more laborers into the harvest." On his return to Cartersville, he preached on the subject. "When you were preaching that sermon," wrote Miss Moon from China, "one at least of your hearers listened with renewed convictions of the duty to go in person to the heathen. Now here, I am more rejoiced than ever with the thought of giving my whole life to win these souls to the Saviour. I thank God that he has permitted me to come here to labor for him." Miss Moon was accepted as a missionary by the Board, July 7th, 1873; and, with her friend, Miss Safford, started from Baltimore August 18th, for China, *via* California. Miss Safford went to *Suchow*, under the patronage of the Southern Presbyterian Board. The intelligent, enterprising, and energetic labors of Miss Moon at Tung Chow will be noted, as we pursue the history of that important station of the Shantung Mission.

GOING HOME.

A. S. W., in the *Evangel*, of San Francisco, said of Miss Moon, shortly after her departure from that port:

"It was my pleasure to meet this most estimable Christian lady, in San Francisco, the 30th of August, and to have her pay a short visit to my family in Vacaville. Miss Moon was once a member of my family, and a most devoted and successful teacher in an institution with which I was connected. She now goes to China to join her sister, who, for more than a year, has been laboring among the women of China at Tung Chow, and in connection with Brother Crawford and wife of the Southern Board. It has been a cherished purpose with Miss Moon, for years past, to be a missionary to the heathen; and now that her desires in this regard are about to be gratified, she is quite happy, and says that in going to China to join her sister, she feels as if she were going home. A lady of fine intellect, of rare culture, and of splendid social gifts, she lays herself on the altar of sacrifice to glorify him who purchased her with his precious blood. Virginia never reared a truer, nobler woman. May Heaven abundantly bless her in her noble mis- sion. She sailed on the 1st of September, 1873."

RETURN.

In the fall of 1876, the health of Miss Edmonia Moon utterly failing, her sister returned with her to this country. The invalid sister, improved in health, resides in her native county of Albemarle, Va. "Miss Lottie" sailed for China, from San Francisco, November 3d, 1877, and arrived at Tung Chow, December 24th, of that year. Since that time, she has been unremitting in her labors in China, and has contributed handsomely to our missionary literature on this side of the water. The following from the pen of an honored Professor, appeared in the *Examiner and Chronicle* of October 22d, 1879 : " I scarcely remember a more clever and graphic bit of narrative than Miss Moon's journal of a visit to the interior, and every one must have acquired fresh admiration for the splendid lady who is devoting her noble talents and graces to the interests of the heathen. We are equally proud of our other missionary laborers, all of whom are persons of extraordinary force and worth—better, I often think, than we Southern Baptists are quite worthy to possess."

ORIGIN OF THE MISSION.

In a manuscript " *History of Missions in Tung Chow, for the first thirteen years, read before the Tung Chow Literary Association, July 14th, 1874,*" by our accomplished missionary, Mrs. M. F. Crawford, we find the following account of the starting of our interests in Shantung:

"Upon the signing of the treaty of Tien-tsin, in 1860, in which several new ports in China were opened to foreign trade, a number of missionaries, who had been anxiously awaiting the opportunity, immediately went forth to occupy these stations. In anticipation of this result, while the late war with China was still going on, Rev. J. L. and Mrs. Holmes were appointed by the Southern Baptist Board as missionaries to Shantung, to remain at Shanghai until the way to this province should be opened. They accordingly, on arriving at Shanghai, early in 1859, procured a *Chi-nan-Foo* teacher, and began the study of that dialect. In the summer of that year, they came to Chefoo, and remained there on board a sailing vessel for several months—Mr. Holmes frequently going ashore. He made two journeys by land to Tung Chow, and Mrs. Holmes came once by sea, not, however, landing. As there could be no foreign trade at Tung Chow, it became necessary to establish a mission or some kind of agency at Chefoo, through which a mission at the former place might be supplied. The attack upon the English at the *Taku* forts, and the consequent delay in signing the treaty, put a stop to these plans until the autumn of 1860, when Mr. Holmes, in company with Mr. and Mrs. Edkins, came to Chefoo and hired and repaired a house. By the time Mr. Holmes returned to Shanghai for his family, Mr. and Mrs. Hartwell, who had been there since the summer of 1859, and who were suffering in health, had determined to come to this more salubrious climate.

"Of the arrival of this party, Mr. Hartwell, in a communication written at my request, says: 'On the 31st day of December, 1860, after a voyage of two weeks from Shanghai, Mrs. Hartwell and myself landed, with our infant son Jesse, in Chefoo, in company with Mr. and Mrs. J. Landrum Holmes and their infant daughter Annie. Rev. Griffith John and Mr. M. G. Holmes came on the same vessel with us. *

* It was impossible to go ashore at the ordinary landing, and we were obliged to beach our boat on the French, or east shore, near the site of the present French Consulate. The waves dashed over us all the way from the ship, and froze as they fell. The prospect was cold and forbidding; but our hearts were young then and buoyant with hope. No Consul of any nationality had arrived, nor had the custom-house been established under European supervision, and the only foreigners, beside the French soldiers and those mentioned above, were one John Smith and Mr. Hyam, the Jew.'

"A few weeks later, Messrs. Hartwell and Holmes took a tour of inspection to Hwang Hien and Tung Chow, during which it was decided that Mr. Hartwell should locate at Tung Chow, and Mr. Holmes at Chefoo."

CHINA—SHANTUNG MISSION.

"At first the Shantung interests were regarded and reported as stations of the Shanghai Mission, although separated by some five hundred miles. These missionaries, who had been in Shanghai a company of 'associated missionaries,' were authorized, on their petition to the Board, to act independently of each other. In the report of the Board of Foreign Missions, presented to the Southern Baptist Convention, in 1866, we read: "Brother Hartwell refers to Tung Chow as a distinct mission, and being several hundred miles distant from Shanghai, it will most probably be hereafter thus recognized."

TUNG CHOW MISSION.

TABOOED BY THE GENTRY.

On the first day of March, 1861, Mr. Hartwell, with his family and his assistant, *Tseu Chieu T'ao*, arrived in Tung Chow. By the permission of the *Che Hien* of the city, he had hired, for a residence, a vacant "pawnbroker's establishment," near the North Gate. His literary and "buttoned" neighbors called. But they were "not at home" when he returned their visits. At this early period, these gentry fixed their resolve to oppose the gospel, which determination remains to this day, and probably has been the source of the oppositions which have marked the history of Christianity in the Shantung Province. It became impossible to rent a place for public service. A room in his residence was fitted up for the purpose by Mr. Hartwell. When Mrs. Holmes returned to America in 1867, her house, in North Street, was taken for a chapel.

COMMON PEOPLE HEAR GLADLY.

Despite this opposition of the literati, the gospel found its way to the heart of the masses. At an early date, Mr. Hartwell wrote:

"I do believe, my dear brother, that God is here, and that he is moving upon the hearts of the people, and that he intends, through our feeble instrumentality, to glorify his name among them. Blessed be the Lord Jesus who has not left us without witness of his power." In a letter of Dec. 31st, 1862, Mr. M. T. Yates, of Shanghai, wrote: "There is considerable interest at Tung Chow of the Shantung station. Several have been baptized, and Brother Hartwell mentions other interesting cases."

DURING THE WAR.

Those were "hard times." But God raised up friends in Maryland and in Kentucky, and the missionaries bestirred themselves, as we have seen, and the work went bravely on. Of Dr. G. W. Burton, now of Louisville, Ky., the Board reported to the Southern Baptist Convention: "By his munificent appropriations our missionaries were saved from absolute suffering." Mr. Crawford, who arrived at Tung Chow in August, 1863, and took charge of the mission during Mr. Hartwell's absence in Shanghai, wrote: "Our work goes on in all its departments the same as when we drew funds from the Board, except that we print no books. Of course it comes hard on us to support ourselves and the mission work, but we feel it is nothing compared to the burdens our poor brethren of the South have to bear in support of our sacred liberty." In twelve months he baptized eight persons. Mr. Hartwell wrote: "It is a great comfort to know that our brethren are determined, notwithstanding the heavy pressure that is upon them, not to abandon the missionary work. Especially do we rejoice, because this gives a pledge that we shall not be forgotten in their prayers. Pecuniarily, we have not suffered. Spiritually, we have had some things in which to rejoice. Our little church at Tung Chow, of Chinese converts, moves pleasantly on. We see some signs of growth in knowledge and grace. We have had, as yet, no reason to believe but that they are all genuine Christians. There are yet those who wish to become disciples. I hope in a week or two to baptize one or two persons." In 1865, the church numbered twenty-three native converts. There were two schools, one of which was a boarding school. From the beginning of the mission about six thousand books had been printed and distributed.

GERM OF TWO CHURCHES.

Mr. Hartwell, returning to Tung Chow at the close of 1865, took charge of the mission. In his report to the Board, 31st of December, 1866, he says: "I resumed the pastorate of the church. It was early agreed by Brother Crawford and myself that if he remained in Shantung, he should commence a new and independent interest. We have accordingly labored separately; and each will make his own report to the Board." Mr. Crawford reported at the same time: "After Brother Hartwell's return to Tung Chow, I had no chapel or certain place of abode until the first of July, when I removed to my new house, on *Che-Kya-Pai-Fong* Street, and opened regular services for the 1st, 6th, 11th, 16th, 21st and 26th, at noon, of each Chinese month—these being market days in this part of the city." This was the origin of our two churches in the city of Tung Chow—the "North Street Church," and the "Monument Street Church," of which Mr. Hartwell and Mr. Crawford were respectively the pastors.

NORTH STREET CHURCH AND OUT-STATIONS.

"The North Street Baptist Church of Tung Chow was organized on the 5th of October, 1862, with eight members, including Mr. and Mrs. Hartwell and Mrs. Holmes. On the same day three others were received and baptized. This church increased more rapidly at first than the churches in the southern ports. When Mr. Hartwell left for Shanghai, early in 1864, there were eighteen members—eight others were baptized into its fellowship by Mr. Crawford during 1864 and 1865. In 1866, *Woo Tswun Chau* was ordained deacon. In 1868, through the earnest agency of *Tsang Yuen Te*, whom Mr. Hartwell had baptized at his *Hwang Hien* station, a deep religious revival arose in the village and neighborhood of *Shang Tswong*, in *Chau Yuen Hein*, which resulted in the conversion, first and last, of about twenty persons. In the spring, a company of men and women came from that place to the city, inquiring the way to the "preaching hall,"—all but one old woman having walked the whole distance. They had prepared to bear their own expenses while here. Mrs. Hartwell spent several hours each day in instructing the women of the party, and most of them were baptized before going home. In November, 1870, in anticipation of Mr. Hartwell's return to America, *Woo Tswun Chau* was ordained pastor of the North Street Church by a presbytery, consisting of Messrs. Crawford and Hartwell. In the December following, the same presbytery, with Rev. *Woo* added, ordained *Tsang Yuen Te* and *Cheu Wun Yien* as deacons of said church, then numbering fifty-six members. Up to the present, 1874, *Woo* is pastor. The membership is sixty-three. There are two assistants. Mr. Hartwell, in coming from Shanghai, in 1861, had brought as an assistant *Tseu Chien T'ao*, who could speak Mandarin, and who was for several years an efficient helper. In 1866, he was excluded from the church. Mr. Hartwell had frequently visited *Hwang Hien* and *Shin Tien* on market days from an early period. One year he rented a chapel in the latter town. In 1867, he rented rooms in *Hwang Hien*, and stationed two men, *Sun* and *Leang*, there. He says: "This chapel was retained and constantly used until November, 1869, when, the house having been sold, I had to give it up to the purchaser and take one in the southern suburb, which was never of any considerable service. * * Up to the beginning of 1868 we had preached only on the streets in *Pe Ma*, but in February of that year I rented a house and opened a chapel, which we retained till the summer of 1873. While we held a place in *Hwang Hien*, we attended at *Pe Ma* on market days; afterwards stationed one man there. During the years 1871 and 1872 we had a small room at *Whong San Kwan;* but as this was for the most part during my absence in America, nothing was accomplished." Mr. Hartwell went to Chefoo late in 1872, and his personal labors, except a supervision of the North Street interests, are not at present a part of Tung Chow history. *Leang* is no longer his assistant. *Sun* is in Chefoo, and his other helper, *Wong*, is mostly in *Chau Yuen*. Until 1871, *Woo* occupied the place now filled by *Sun*—part teacher, part helper. The North Street Church has supported its pastor; at first at a salary of 108,000 cash per annum, afterwards 150,000 cash, part of which sum is made up of rent of property in Chefoo, given to the church by one of its members. It also pays for the benches, tables, lights, and rent of the chapel in *Shang Tswong*, kept up since 1870. Besides this, members and inquirers from the country are entertained by contributions of the church."

MONUMENT STREET CHURCH AND COUNTRY WORK.

"In December, 1866, Mr. Crawford organized the *Pai Fong* Baptist Church, composed of eight persons, including Mrs. Holmes, and Mr. and Mrs. Crawford. *Chau Ting Tsing* had been associated with Mr. Crawford, as teacher and assistant, for a year, and several preaching tours had been made in the region of *Whong Ching*. *Sun Chang Lung*, the *Whe Teu* of the neighborhood, had offered for lodging and preaching the buildings attached to *Ma Kya Miao*. A Buddhist priest had been engaged to reside there, but on *Sun's* becoming a Christian the arrangement was dissolved, and consequently the rooms are seldom used, except for preaching, or other village gatherings. Though no converts have been made in the village of *Ma Kya* itself, the truth has been extensively disseminated by the labors there. After several of the *Sun* family became Christians, *Sun Chang Lung* fitted up one of his rooms for a chapel, and Sunday services have been held there with slight interruptions for many years. Finding it burdensome for one family to entertain guests so frequently, and feeling that hospitality was a necessary part of the programme, the brethren, last year, agreed to meet, in turn, at the several villages at which the Christians live. There are nineteen church members belonging to this neighborhood. The two deacons, *Chang Yun Hwo* and *Sun Kyi Di*, lately elected, both live in this region, one of whom has rented out his farm, and has been in school three years, at his own charges, preparing for the ministry. In 1872 and 1873, the church rented a chapel, furnishing table, benches, and lights, at the village of *Mung Kya*, thirty *li* southwest from Tung Chow, to which eight brethren went, two and two in turn every Lord's Day. In the latter part of 1873, the visits became less frequent, because of the small congregations. Finally, before the end of the year, the villages by common consent refused to attend the services, and they were discontinued. *Chau* was dismissed from his place, and from the church, in 1869, for gross crimes. Since 1871,

Lieu Bu Yun has occupied the position of teacher. He and other brethren have frequently gone on voluntary preaching tours, either with or without Mr. Crawford. Some of them have also been diligent in going from village to village in their own neighborhood to preach the gospel. Mr. Crawford has throughout adhered to his plan, adopted soon after entering on his work in Shanghai, of having no paid assistants. During this spring, the church sent out a couple of brethren on a preaching tour in the borders of *Hwang Hien, Chi Hia* and *Chau Yuen*. In 1867, Mr. Crawford rented a chapel on South Street, but the effort was a total failure. The present church membership of the Monument Street [in 1874] Church is fifty-four."

The above account of the two Baptist Churches of Tung Chow is taken from Mrs. Crawford's " History of the Tung Chow Mission."

RAIDS AND RELIGION.

Previously, we noticed the havoc of the "Long-hair" marauders. For the following we are indebted to the pen of our missionary, Mrs. M. F. Crawford, of Tung Chow:

"In the fall of 1861, the approach of the robbers sent terror to the hearts of the natives. The mandarins characteristically closed the gates of the city, shutting out the frightened country people, who came running hither for safety. Thousands, of all classes and ages, cowered under the city walls. Persons within drew up by ropes friends they saw outside. * * This raid forms a memorable epoch in the life of these people. Thousands of men and boys were carried off, who have never returned. Traces of the depredations may still be seen in the ruined houses, and the widows and orphans found in almost every village in the surrounding region. Great numbers of women jumped into the wells, after throwing their children in, or hung themselves in their own houses. * * * In the summer of 1867, the robbers made another raid. The people again flocked in multitudes to the city for protection. All the spare rooms of the several mission houses were crowded with the relatives and friends of servants, and with the Christians from the country. The refugees, having nothing to do, came to us for medicine, or through curiosity, or to pass away the time. An opportunity was thus afforded for preaching to thousands who would perhaps never otherwise have heard the gospel. Regular instruction, as far as practicable, was given to those who found temporary homes with us, and visitors were taught daily, as they crowded in, to the utmost limit of our strength, for about two months."

GETTING A HOUSE UNDER DIFFICULTIES.

"On Mr. Hartwell's return to Tung Chow, in December, 1865, Mr. Crawford committed to his teacher, *Chow Ting Ching*, the matter of purchasing a house for him. Chow bought it in his own name and rented it to Mr. Crawford, as had been stipulated. Notwithstanding our treaty rights, this seemed the only way of securing a home. * * Placards were immediately posted in different parts of the city calling upon both gentry and people to rise up and prevent the occupancy of the house by foreigners. There was so much excitement that after a vain appeal to the *Che Hien*, a special messenger was dispatched to E. T. Sanford, Esq., at that time United States Consul at Chefoo. Mr. Sanford came promptly in person and informed the mandarins that he would take possession of the property next day. Early the following afternoon, Mr. Sanford, in company with Messrs. Mills, Crawford, and Hartwell, with one or two Chinese attendants, entered the house, posted on the door a notice, with the seal of the United States attached, and hoisted the American flag. A crowd began to collect, a gong was beaten, and the excitement became general. Messrs. Crawford and Hartwell going on the street to inquire by whose command the gong was beaten, the mob closed in upon them. The sight of pistols caused the crowd to fall back, and the two gentlemen regained the door. Before midnight, an agreement was entered into between Mr. Sanford and the *Che Fu*. A week later Mr. Crawford was put in possession. Some time after, Mr. Sanford came up in the Wachusetts, commanded by Capt. Townshend, who demanded the punishment of the chief instigators of the riot. The United States Minister did not approve of the steps taken, but whether from the visit of the Wachusetts, or from the determined spirit of the Consul and the missionaries to maintain their treaty rights, certain it is that the back of the opposition to foreigners having houses was broken by our victory and its accompaniments."

SERIOUS AND SILLY VENTS OF VENOM.

"On the 21st of June, 1870, occurred that horrible tragedy, which startled not only all the foreign residents in China, but the whole civilized world—the massacre at Tien Tsin. The causes which brought on this calamity had been at work for years. There are men among the officials and gentry who are bitterly hostile to foreigners, and who strive, by all the means in their power, to annoy and drive them away. * * In 1863, the whole city was alarmed by stories that foreigners had poisoned the wells. Mr. Hartwell, writing of this period, says: 'I remember that the excitement ran very high, and was kept up by designing men who actually threw drugs into wells, and then had the wells cleaned out, triumphantly exhibiting what they found, which, however, always proved to be Chinese drugs, and were always tied up in Chinese cloth. The reports began as early as 1861.' * * In 1864, during the excitement in regard to foreigners getting homes, it was proposed by the gentry to exterminate us. * * In the winter of 1867 and 1868, it was confidently asserted that, at the new year, we were all to be murdered. * * Foreigners were accused of kidnapping women and children for the purpose of getting their eyes and hearts for medicinal uses. All manner of atrocities were attributed to us. * * The reports caused no especial uneasiness until after the massacre at Tien Tsin. Then our enemies became bolder, and meetings were held by the gentry with reference to what should be done with us. * * Letters were sent to S. A. Holmes, Esq., acting United States Consul at Chefoo, through whom two British men-of-war were dispatched to convey us away. This flight was, probably to the majority of us, one of the most trying acts of our lives. From the 1st September to the 20th October, we were in Chefoo, leaving our houses in charge of trusty servants, under the Mandarins' protection. After our return in an American man-of-war, the people seemed more friendly. Stories about exterminating us and attributing vile things to us were revived in the summer of 1873, when the visit of the provincial governor to review the troops gave another pretext to them. * * A note was found in our yard, warning our teachers, servants, and pupils to leave us, as we were doomed to be slaughtered by a certain day specified. * * When the governor left, it was said there was some delay in the arrangements; but on the 15th day of the 8th month, the feast of the harvest moon, a day still kept in remembrance of the destruction of the Mongols, our doom was to be sealed. This period passing quietly, the excitement died a natural death."

WOMAN'S WORK.

Before noting the work of our women in this mission, a glance at the *native* women, as presented by Mrs. Nevius, of the Presbyterian Church at Tung Chow, and by Mrs. Crawford, may not be uninteresting:

AT HOME AND ABROAD.

"Women, when at leisure, or when unengaged in serving, usually sit *à la Turk* on their 'kangs;' and they are apt to take their meals there. The 'kang,' which is their bed at night and the divan and lounging-place for the whole family by day, is a platform of mason work about two feet high, six feet wide and twelve feet long. It is so constructed that, in winter, fire can be kindled below, with a flue for carrying the heat and smoke to every part, so that it becomes thoroughly warm, though not hot.* * 'Women's talk' is very different from men's, and it is much harder for us to understand them, or they us. I can speak 'Mandarin' pretty well, but make wretched work with these Tung Chow women. * * The customary questions to strangers are: What is your name? How old are you? Are you married? How many children have you? etc., etc. * * The daily employments of Chinese ladies of wealth or rank are embroidery, making their toilet, chit chat, and games of chance. Not a little time is expended in the selection of materials for dress, articles of jewelry, etc., which are sent from the shops to the house, for their inspection before purchasing." Mrs. Crawford tells of an elegantly dressed woman who called upon her to "hear of Jesus," who was on her departure met at the door by her heathen husband and shamefully knocked down and beaten on the ground—the poor creature only wringing her hands and crying: "*How many people saw him do it!*"

HOW THE LADIES REACH THEM.

Mrs. Nevius writes: "The experiment" of visiting the women "has been tried by various missionary ladies, who have 'Bible women,' as they are sometimes called, under their superintendence, and it has been found to succeed well. I know of no other way in which Chinese women, in the seclusion of their homes, can be reached. Either foreign or native women must go to them with the 'good news' of salvation, or the great majority can never hear it."

Mrs. Crawford says: "The ladies have visited from house to house, taught visitors, instructed classes, as far as they have been able to gather them without pecuniary inducements, used their influence in bringing women to attend public services, and superintended schools, besides aiding in the country work. In the itinerant labors our women have participated. * * To fully appreciate the work of visiting from house to house in this city, it is necessary for one to understand the peculiar difficulties through which it has been prosecuted. The houses here, unlike those in the Southern ports, which have doors standing open and many of the occupants exposed to view, have dead walls on the street, with closed entrance. To gain admittance one must either knock and wait the pleasure of the inmates, or open the door and walk unbidden in, possibly to be rudely or coldly received. While we were all strangers, and the people shy and suspicious of us, this was no easy matter, and required great ingenuity, tact, and persistence. After acquaintances were formed it became comparatively easy, but it is still one of the most difficult departments of labor."

VARIED EFFORTS TO EDUCATE.

We copy again from Mrs. Crawford: "At an early period Mrs. Hartwell opened a boarding school for girls. There were not many pupils, for the Chinese were suspicious of the 'outside barbarians.' This school was disbanded in 1864, when Mrs. Hartwell went to Shanghai. A day school of small boys was begun in 1863, supported mostly, at first, by the North Street Baptist Church. Its superintendence was soon handed over to Mrs. Holmes. It was afterwards removed to rooms in her house. The support was assumed by herself, and it was thus carried on, with the exception of one interval, until the spring of 1867. She had brought two boys from Chefoo. They remained in her school as members of her family and learned English. Mrs. Hartwell opened a second school in 1868, only taking promising girls of more than twelve years old, upon whom she bestowed much labor. It was continued until September, 1870, several months after her death. In 1867, when Mrs. Holmes left for America, I took her school of six little boys, securing a new teacher. The number gradually increased, and it soon became a boarding school, supported by the mission, and still continues such. Mrs. Holmes, on her return in 1870, opened a boarding school for girls at her new residence, which is growing gradually in numbers, as the people gain confidence in us. In 1872, she began a day school for boys, which, in 1873, she transferred to Miss Edmonia Moon. Efforts for girls' day schools have thus far proved unsuccessful. The first, opened by myself in 1865, consisting of five girls from eight to twelve years old, soon died. Efforts, however, to teach girls and women to read, at their own homes, have not been altogether without encouragement, and are prosecuted with untiring diligence by the missionary ladies. Most of the Christian women, also, have been taught to read. In the autumn of 1872, Mr. Hartwell opened a boys' boarding school on North Street, which, after his absence, was carried on by Pastor *Woo* and the native teacher. So far as I know, the only attempt to have a school at an out-station was the one by the Presbyterian Church in 1867, which proved a failure."

MONUMENT STREET INTEREST.

In addition to the general view of the two churches which had been given, a few details may serve to make the sketch more complete.

1871.

Mr. Crawford wrote: "I am contracting for a lot on which to build a chapel. I must have three thousand dollars for the work. I cannot afford to stop labor for the want of a cheap chapel. I shall confidently expect the Board to furnish the means. Twenty years of constant labor in China entitle me to a chapel in which to train the congregation, which from nothing I have gradually built up to its present number.

"I have a class of five studying for the ministry. They come about once in three months; remain as my guests for a week or ten days, studying the Scriptures; then they go home and study the lessons I give them; and thus they are to go on studying and preaching without *money*, till they are ready to be ordained and settled as pastors over the churches which they themselves are to establish, (at least such is the theory of the plan,) and look to their own people for support.

"Never relax your work in China. It is one of your most promising fields. Christianity gains ground day by day and year by year. The government and people all feel that their ancient strongholds are giving way before its onward march. They will make one final and feeble effort to preserve them, and then all will be over, and China will fall into line and voluntarily follow in the wake of Christendom."

1872.

In "Proceedings of Convention of 1873," we find: Brother Crawford's chapel at Tung Chow has been completed and dedicated. He writes: "Everybody, both native and foreign, says it is a most beautiful structure. The acoustic properties are fine. The whole cost has been some three thousand dollars."

"Miss E. Moon is making rapid progress in the language. She promises to be a *real missionary*. Only send out another of the same character to live and labor with her. The *women* of China must be converted to Christ. Mrs. Holmes is well, and is driving on with all her might. At times she seems to overtax her strength."

"At the beginning of the year we had forty-five members; five have been added by baptism, so that we now number fifty persons. We have contributed twenty dollars by monthly collections."

Mrs. Crawford wrote: "At our annual examination the boys displayed considerable proficiency in Mathematics, Astronomy, Evidences of Christianity, Scriptural History, New Testament, and their own classics. There was a debate between two champions from each school. The question selected by themselves was: 'Is Christianity profitable for *this* life?' The speakers were from seventeen to twenty-three years old. I was not ashamed of the manner in which my two handled the affirmative. All four are professed Christians. These examinations and exhibitions are quite a stimulus to both the schools, giving to them a variety, which schools among the natives never have."

1873.

Mr. Crawford: " Miss Lottie Moon enters on her new life with firm and sober delight. She will prove a true missionary. The two sisters are of one purpose and one heart; and if God grants them health and strength, we may reasonably expect them to make a deep impression on the hearts of these heathen women. I do trust the sisterhood will prayerfully, conscientiously, and constantly take a lively interest in their mission."

Miss E. Moon: "I have had a severe spell of sickness, and though still not strong, yet am well enough to attend to school duties in the morning, and to visit and teach from house to house in the afternoon. Sometimes I take the field and give the people a long talk; some listen eagerly to the story of the cross, but, alas, how few feel the need of a Saviour! I would not leave the work for all the world. I believe that God will bless his word, even though proclaimed by so unworthy an instrument as myself. Has he not said, 'My word shall not return unto me void, but shall accomplish that whereunto it is sent'?"

Miss C. Moon: "I have been with my sister on some of her visits to the native women. Some would not admit us at all; others listen coldly and with evident restraint; only a few hear the word gladly. Nevertheless, we must 'sow beside all waters.' We wish to have, as soon as possible, a boarding school for girls. Two thousand dollars are needed for the building. The greatest blessing we can bestow upon the people is Christian education for wives and mothers."

Mrs. Crawford wrote: "Mr. Crawford's health is giving us great uneasiness. Some missionary should be in the field, preparing to take up our work, should we be called to leave it." A Presbyterian missionary wrote to our Board: "Mr. and Mrs. Crawford need rest and recreation. It would inspire them with new energy and strength, and, humanly speaking, would add many years to their useful lives. But how can they leave the church without a pastor, the school without a superintendent, the mission without a man?"

1874.

"The services in the church and the little chapel in the city have been regularly sustained. The Sunday-school has grown in numbers and interest. The theological class has been taught one week in each quarter, and a good deal of preaching done in the study and on the streets. The ladies have labored almost incessantly, superintending their schools, teaching women and children, and visiting from house to house.

"Public sentiment seems more favorable than at any previous period, and we hope that the Spirit of God is beginning to move on the hearts of the people at large, though the great majority of the inhabitants of Tung Chow continue as hard as the nether millstone.

"We have never paid native preachers with mission funds. We believe the system will retard the growth of vital Christianity in China and all other heathen lands. We desire to see the church grow from the healthy root of faith in Christ and love for his cause."

"Mrs. Holmes' lungs are weak, and she may have to go south. Miss Eddie Moon is now under medical treatment."

"Church members, fifty-seven; baptized, seven. Mrs. Crawford's boys' boarding school, sixteen pupils. Mrs. Holmes' girls' boarding school, fourteen pupils. Miss Eddie Moon's boys' day school, ten pupils. Sunday-school, about fifty pupils."

1875.

"The health of all our missionaries, except Miss Eddie Moon, has been more than ordinarily good. Means sufficient for all our wants have been furnished by the Board, and we have every reason for gratitude and praise. Every department of our work has been kept in full vigor throughout the year, and all appointments, both in the city and country, sustained without special interruption. Much seed, on old and new, good and bad, ground has been sown. God's word never returns unto him void. The results cannot be reduced to figures.

"The ladies, besides their daily work in their schools and in the city, have visited about two hundred villages, varying from one to twenty-five miles from this place, thus: Mrs. Crawford, 131; Mrs. Holmes, 128; Miss Lottie Moon, 88; Miss Eddie Moon, 30.

"Mrs. Crawford's boy boarding school has averaged 18 pupils; Mrs. Holmes' girl boarding school, 15; Miss Eddie Moon's little boys' day school, 10; the Sunday-school about 60.

"Congregations in the large chapel are still rather floating and uncertain. The people having no church-going habit or ability to listen to a public discourse, it is exceedingly difficult to build up an orderly congregation. We have no paid native assistants.

"We enter the new year with the same hardened heathen world before us, and the same work to be done over and over again. With confidence in the protection of God, the power of the gospel, the support of the Board and the churches of Christ, we shall continue to batter these ramparts of sin and Satan. Thanking the Board for their aid and generous sympathies, I pray for the blessing of God on all his faithful people."

NORTH STREET INTEREST.

1871.

A letter from the North Street Church, to the Southern Baptist Convention, dated February, 1871, gave the following statistics: "In 1869, we contributed to the girls' school, $37; to the Hwang Hien Chapels, $34; to the Chau Yuen Station, $29.60; and in 1870, to the

Hwang Chapel, $12; Chau Yuen Chapel, $13; Chefoo, $2—making a total of a little over $127. * * We have commenced holding service in Chefoo two nights every week, under the preaching of Brother Ki Tong Tai, whose services are gratuitous. * * This year we have collected for the purchase of a Christian burying-ground $55, and our monthly contributions amount to $36.95. We have called to the ministry our brother, *Woo Tswun Chau*, and invited him to be our pastor in 1871, we ourselves paying his salary. * * * Our present number of members is 56."

1872.

Mr. Hartwell returned to China this year, and moved his residence, as shall be seen, to Chefoo. With regard to Pastor *Woo* and his church at Tung Chow, Mr. Hartwell wrote: "Woo Tswun Chau has shown himself equal to the responsibility placed upon him, and has managed the church with a great deal of discretion and propriety. Some of the members seemed to think that I would at once assume the pastorate, and that they would be relieved of the necessity of sustaining the pastor; but I was glad to see the spirit with which Woo met this feeling and combated it. He told them that he was very ready to resign the charge, but that he would never be sustained in the ministry by funds drawn from foreign churches; that they were indebted to the foreigners for the introduction of Christianity and the founding of this church; that they were indebted to them also for the use of the house in which they worshipped, but that they had no right to expect or to ask foreigners to sustain a pastor for them. They were now already an organized church, which he hoped would continue till the second coming of Christ. Instead of their being dependent upon the missionaries, the missionaries ought to be dependent on them."

1873.

Mr. *Leang*, who had labored at Pe Ma, and Hwang Hien, having gone to Chefoo to assist Mr. Hartwell, these stations were unoccupied. The statistics of the church and stations were as follows: "Baptized during the year, four; expelled, one; present membership, sixty-three;

CHINA—SHANTUNG MISSION. 239

total number connected with us, from the first, eighty-one; contributions for the year, $110; total income of church from all sources, $224. The church bears its own expense, except the chapel rent. Native Pastor Woo maintains himself well."

1874.

From the Board's report to the Southern Baptist Convention we quote: "The salary of the native pastor, Rev. Woo Tswun Chau, is paid by the church, but the rent of the house, the expenses of the school, the salary of the assistant preacher and teacher, are covered by the appropriation to the Chefoo Mission."

1875.

We copy the following from the "Proceedings of the Southern Baptist convention, 1876:" "The North Street Church is composed of native members, and is attempting to be self-sustaining. Rev. *Woo* is pastor; but Brother Hartwell, though living in Chefoo, kept an advisory relation to it, and aided it by his constant counsels and occasional presence. The church has written a strong letter to the Board, on China churches being independent of foreigners, while there should be all sympathy and affection and co-operation between the races. A school is attached to this church, and also an out-station."

The occasion of this letter was a proposed unification of the Shantung interests, which was contemplated by the Board, and to which reference will be made in our next and last article on China Missions.

CHEFOO MISSION.

The history of the mission at Chefoo has been brief and sad, although relieved by a few bright pages. As has been already seen, scarcely had our missionary, J. L. Holmes, who made his first visit there in 1859, fairly begun his work, early in 1861, when he was smitten, October, 1861, by a murderous death. In 1862, Mrs. Holmes moved to Tung Chow. In the North Street Church, of that city, which was organized that year, there were several members who resided in and about Chefoo. This, together with the fact that Chefoo is the post-office of Tung Chow, kept constantly in the mind of the mission and of the Board this site of our earliest missionary work in the Shantung Province, which site had been hallowed, also, by the blood of our now sainted Holmes.

In 1869, Mr. Hartwell wrote to the Board: "Our members living at Chefoo are still agitating the question of my having an assistant and a regular appointment there, and I am now, more than I have ever yet been, disposed to yield to their wishes."

As has been stated, when our missionaries had been driven from Tung Chow, in 1870, they labored, for a short time, in Chefoo. Mr. Hartwell reported: "I think I did not mention that I was stopping in Chefoo, in the home of one of our native members. Ten years ago, when he was baptized, I suppose a hundred dollars would have bought all he was worth. He is now the head of a hong, owns an ocean steamer or most of it, and carries on three hongs—one at Tien-tsin, one in Chefoo, and one at Shanghai. His wife was a pupil in one of the mission schools in Shanghai. I think he remembers and tries to act upon a sense of his obligation to God in the use of his property. It was he who built the chapel in Chefoo and presented it to our church. One of my chief objects in moving to his place, instead of stopping with our English Baptist friends, as I have usually done on my short visits to Chefoo, was that I might be near the chapel, and maintain, during my stay, some extra services. I preached regularly every Tuesday and Thursday nights, and every Sunday afternoon. Brother Crawford preached also several nights a week, so that the chapel was kept pretty constantly open." In the winter of 1870, our missionaries returned to their churches in Tung Chow. In 1871, the North Street Church, of Tung Chow, wrote to the Southern Baptist Convention: "We have commenced holding service in Chefoo two nights every week, under the preaching of Brother Ki Tong Tai, whose services are gratuitious."

In 1872, the year that Mr. Hartwell returned to China, the Board reported to the Convention: "Brother Hartwell proposes to establish a mission at Chi-Nan-Foo, the capital of the Shantung Province. The Board authorizes it if, on consultation with Brother Crawford, it is deemed wise. In that event, his chapel will be erected in that city. This will be an approach toward the great capital, Peking."

In 1873, the Board informed the Convention: "Since his return to China, Brother Hartwell has become so convinced of the advantages, as a centre of missionary influence, of this station, which is the port of entry on the Pe-chi-li Gulf, that, instead of going to Chi-Nan-Foo, as he designed, when in this country, he proposes to make his residence at Chefoo. He says of the place: 'It grows every year in commercial importance. Since I first knew it, it has sextupled itself. From the vast extent of territory which trades here, missionaries think it the best point in the country for preaching to the heathen. Another consideration is, that while it is far enough from Tung Chow for establishing a separate interest, and yet near enough for me to overlook the church there, it is not so distant from our out-stations as to render them inaccessible. A number of our members are here. I therefore earnestly request the Board to appropriate $4,000 for a dwelling-house, and $4,000 for a chapel at Chefoo.'"

From the report of 1874, Mr. Hartwell is quoted: "I have rented a house in Chefoo, which is large, commodious and airy, but quite separate from the native population. Sometimes, however, we have at our evening family prayers a company of twenty Chinese."

"I availed myself of the kind offer of Dr. William Brown, of the English Baptist Missionary Society, to use the chapel connected with the hospital he has just opened in Chefoo. I conduct services in the morning, and the native assistant in the afternoon, except on Sundays, when I take both services. I am gratified by the attendance at the chapels in the place, and am very hopeful of good results from our labors."

"Mr. Leang, who was at work in Pe Ma and Hwang Hien, which stations are not now occupied, is with me here. Our assistant, Shang Tswang, has been constant and zealous in his labors, and the brethren there accord him confidence and affection."

"Brother Hartwell's congregations," says the report of 1875, "are good, and he thinks the people are receiving the ideas of the gospel. The population is a floating one, which may account in part for only a few professing Christ. Many Mohammedans from Chi-Nan-Foo attend his services. They deny that they are Chinese, and claim that their ancestors were from Mecca. They worship one living God; practice circumcision; observe Friday as their worship day, and know of Jesus, as a prophet, under the name of Yee Zoo. They have an excellent tract on the Divine Unity. At first they seemed cordial, and almost ready to call our missionaries coreligionists, but they are full of inveterate prejudice against the religion of Christ. Brother Hartwell says that whosoever shall go to Chi-Nan-Foo will have much to do with these Mohammedans, and adds: 'Would to God that I could go.'."

In 1873, the Board reported to the Convention: " Our Sister Hartwell has been an invalid since July last, enduring through protracted periods intense suffering. Several times she has been 'at death's door.' That she may be near her physician at Chefoo, is an additional reason for Brother Hartwell's removal to that city. This beloved sister, from whom so much was and is hoped, is affectionately commended to the sympathies and supplications of the Convention and churches."

Under date of January 21st, she writes: " I have assuredly had to undergo a severe ordeal in this long and trying illness, and I know not as yet what lessons our dear Lord has designed to teach me in visiting me thus with this rod of affliction. Trials are often, I know, ' levers in God's hands to raise us up to heaven.' Oh that I may be enabled to await the issue, and feel entirely submissive to the Divine will! Will you not, then, give me an interest in your prayers, that I may be taught to feel in very truth that

> ['However dark my way, or prospects be,
> All, all is right, since overruled, my God, by thee.' "

In 1874, Mr. Hartwell wrote: " Mrs. Hartwell has been ill for many months. By the doctor's advice we took a trip to Canton. The change apparently did good, but the good was only apparent. She suffers as much as she did a year ago, and she desires the prayers of God's people for her speedy and entire restoration."

1875. The Board reported: "So intense and protracted has been the suffering of his wife, that Brother Hartwell was forced reluctantly to apply for permission to return with her to America, in hope of more successful medical treatment. In January last, the Board authorized the return, and Brother Hartwell may possibly be at the Convention."

1876: "The station at Chefoo, where Rev. J. B. Hartwell made his residence, has been closed since Brother Hartwell's return to this country. Should our brother be permitted, by the restored health of his wife, to go back to China, he will probably make his home at *Chi-Nan-Foo*, to which city his mind and heart have been earnestly directed, as one of the most important fields in China for missionary labor."

PROPOSED UNION OF THE TUNG CHOW INTERESTS.

REPORT OF BOARD.

The following is extracted from the proceedings of the Southern Baptist Convention of 1876: "*Tung Chow.* There are two stations in this city of the Shantung Province—the North Street Church, and the Monument Street Church. For apparently good reasons, the Board deemed a consolidation advisable. After a conference between the churches, at which Rev. M. T. Yates, of Shanghai, presided, the unification was found to be impracticable, if not, under all the circumstances undesirable."

1876 TO 1880.

SEE RESUMÉ AT END OF VOLUME.

JAPAN MISSION AND OUR LOST MISSIONARIES.

JAPAN.

LOCATION AND CLIMATE.

JAPAN is composed of about 3,850 islands, lying off the eastern Coast of Asia, between 129° and 146° Longitude east from Greenwich, and between 31° and 46° north Latitude. It is divided into Japan Proper, which is composed of three large islands; and the dependent islands. The whole Empire contains 160,000 square miles and 30,000,000 of people. The climate is said to be not unlike that of England. The heat of summer which averages at Nagasaki 98° Fahrenheit, is much modified by the sea-breezes. "The rainy season" is June and July. * * "No part of the ocean is subject to heavier gales. The hurricanes are terrific. Earthquakes are not uncommon. Yeddo, on the island of Niphon is the Capital, the residence of the Emperor, and is more populous than Peking of China. The principal commercial city is Osaka, whose streets are intersected by numerous canals, which are spanned by more than one hundred bridges."

ORIGIN AND DISCOVERY.

The authentic history of the country begins B. C. 660, with the reign of Zin-muten-Noo, "The Divine Conqueror," who conquered Nippon, and built there a temple palace, dedicated to the Sun Goddess, which continues the patron divinity of the people. According to the most approved conclusions of Comparative Philology, the Japanese are not Chinese, but Tartar in origin. They have also the Tartar complexion, and physiognomy. Their introduction to Europe was by Marco Polo, a Venetian traveller, whose maps and descriptions of Japan, called by

JAPAN MISSION AND OUR LOST MISSIONARIES.

JAPAN.

LOCATION AND CLIMATE.

JAPAN is composed of about 3,850 islands, lying off the eastern Coast of Asia, between 129° and 146° Longitude east from Greenwich, and between 31° and 46° north Latitude. It is divided into Japan Proper, which is composed of three large islands; and the dependent islands. The whole Empire contains 160,000 square miles and 30,000,000 of people. The climate is said to be not unlike that of England. The heat of summer which averages at Nagasaki 98° Fahrenheit, is much modified by the sea-breezes. "The rainy season" is June and July. * * "No part of the ocean is subject to heavier gales. The hurricanes are terrific. Earthquakes are not uncommon. Yeddo, on the island of Niphon is the Capital, the residence of the Emperor, and is more populous than Peking of China. The principal commercial city is Osaka, whose streets are intersected by numerous canals, which are spanned by more than one hundred bridges."

ORIGIN AND DISCOVERY.

The authentic history of the country begins B. C. 660, with the reign of Zin-muten-Noo, "The Divine Conqueror," who conquered Nippon, and built there a temple palace, dedicated to the Sun Goddess, which continues the patron divinity of the people. According to the most approved conclusions of Comparative Philology, the Japanese are not Chinese, but Tartar in origin. They have also the Tartar complexion, and physiognomy. Their introduction to Europe was by Marco Polo, a Venetian traveller, whose maps and descriptions of Japan, called by

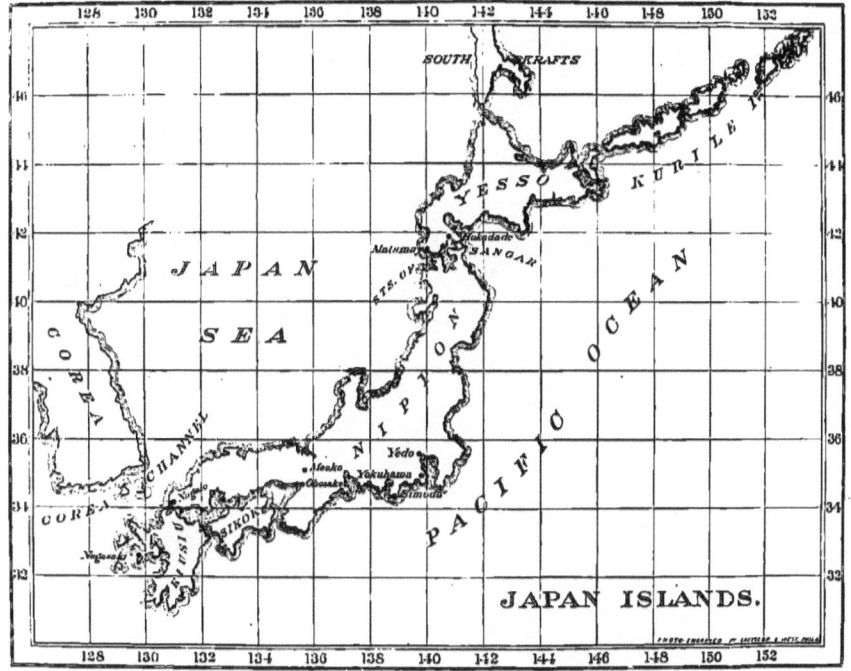

him Cipango, were published in 1295. They confirmed the conjectures of Christopher Columbus, who, when he arrived in Cuba, supposed that he had reached that country as the goal of his long cherished hopes.

GOVERNMENT.

There are two Emperors—one secular, the other ecclesiastical—and a Grand Council of State, composed of thirteen members. The main feature of the government is a combination of feudalism, and of checks and balances. "The code is the bloodiest in the world. Death is the prescribed punishment for most offences. The government proceeds on the principle that he who violates one law will violate all, and is unworthy to live. * * The Japanese doctrine is that if the man of wealth or influence is a criminal, he has no right to fare any better than the poorest man in the kingdom who commits a crime. Therefore all shall be treated alike." One reason of the past excessive conservatism, which precluded innovations, was that the failure of any project brought before the Grand Council was capitally punished.

PEOPLE, LANGUAGE, AND COMMERCE.

The Japanese are a more vigorous and better educated people than the Chinese. They have made great progress in the industrial and fine arts. Paper was made in the seventh century, and printing with blocks was practiced as early as A. D. 1200. In the manufacture of silks, crapes, and porcelain, they are unsurpassed. An old Spanish writer in the seventh century, says: "The palaces of the Emperor, and of some of the nobles, were literally covered with plates of gold." Woman is regarded as a social companion. Polygamy is unknown. As to the language, there are three dialects: First, the *Yomi*, the primitive language, in which the poetry and light literature of the country is written: Second, the *Koye*, a modification by "the ideographic cypher of the Chinese," introduced A. D. 290, in which the sacred books are written. Third, a mixture of the two, which constitutes the common language of the Empire. The chief productions are rice and tea. The main article of food is fish. The Portuguese were admitted to the country for trade in 1543; the Dutch, in 1600; the English, in 1613;

the Russians, in 1792. The first year of the commerce with the Dutch, £840,000 were exported, and in sixty years, the amount of gold sent out of the kingdom was £25,000,000 to £50,000,000. In 1831, a Japanese junk was blown to our western coast. In 1837, the crew was taken back to their country, in a man of war, dismantled of her armament. Our vessel was fired upon, and retired. After several other efforts to get access, the Expedition of Commodore Perry opened negotiations, and "it was reserved for our own, the youngest of the nations, to break down at last, the barriers with which this singular people had surrounded themselves, and to be the first in modern times, to establish with them a treaty of friendship and trade." Since that time, the Japanese have made wonderful advancement by the introduction of the ideas and improvements of our western civilization. They are now educating a number of their young men in our country. Their common school system is extensive, and they covet the possession of our best gifts in art and science. They are in the van of eastern progress.

THEIR RELIGION, AND CHRISTIANITY.

Their original religion, called *Sin-syn*, meaning Gods and Faith, was devoid of idolatry. The only decorations of their old temples were a mirror, the emblem of purity of soul, and strips of white paper, also an emblem of purity. As to the *Sin-too* creed, its leading features, according to Siebold, are some vague notions of the immortality of the soul, of rewards and punishments, a paradise, and a hell. Its five great duties, are, 1st: Preservation of pure fire as an emblem of purity. 2d: Purity of soul, heart, and body. 3d: Observance of festivals. 4th: Pilgrimages. 5th: The reverence of Kami, of whom the greater are canonized men. * * The only object of worship is the Sun-Goddess, Ten-sio-dai-zin, who is the patron divinity of Japan. Christianity was introduced by the Portuguese in 1550. In 1597, the Dutch, it is said, assisted in persecuting native Christians. The crucifix was called "The Devil of Japan," on which traders were required to trample. Recently a flood of light has broken over the country, which is wide open to the missionary laborers of the cross of Christ.

See "Commodore Perry's Expedition to Japan, by Francis L. Hawks, D.D., LL.D."

OUR LOST MISSIONARIES.

Rev. JOHN QUINCY ADAMS ROHRER AND MRS. SARAH ROHRER.

HIGH COMMENDATION.

Mr. Rohrer, who, with his wife, went down into the deep, in the ill-fated "Edwin Forrest," was born at Rohrersville, Washington County, Maryland, on the 16th of August, 1831. After his death, his aged father, Mr. David Rohrer, wrote: "John Quincy's moral character and deportment were always good, and, indeed, I may add, second to none in this community. I say so, not because he is my son, but of a truth." The deceased was studying medicine, when he felt called of God to carry the gospel to the heathen. The late Dr. T. F. Curtis, Professor of Theology in Lewisburg University, where Mr. Rohrer was graduated in 1857, said of him: "His manners were exceedingly gentle, manly, and pleasant. * * * All his influence was for good. * * * Of his piety, there could be no doubt. * * * I formed a higher and higher opinion of his character and qualification for that great work in which he steadily prepared to engage." Professor J. R. Loomis, of the same University, writes to us: "Mr. Rohrer was a member of the 'Church of God,' or Winebrennarian Church. As their views are substantially like the Baptists', he felt no hesitation in joining our church in Lewisburg, which he did soon after coming here. He was a superior student, and one to whom I was personally very warmly attached, and I am glad that an effort is making to gather and make permanent what may be known of him."

MISSION TO JAPAN.

In the report of the Board, in 1860, to the Convention, we read: "Three missionaries are now under appointment for Japan. This band of brethren, J. Q. A. Rohrer, Crawford H. Toy, and J. L. Johnson, will, we hope, ere the close of the year, be upon their destined field. The first of these will probably sail in a few weeks—the two others, with Brother J. William Jones for the Canton Mission, some time in the fall." In the same month and year that Mr. and Mrs. Rohrer sailed for Japan, Mr. Yates, of Shanghai, wrote: "In Japan the people dare not listen to the name of Jesus." At his own request, Mr. Rohrer was assigned to that field. "He was the first missionary of our denomination to that strange people. He was evidently impressed, deeply impressed, with the magnitude of the work and the dangers attending it." When asked of these dangers, he replied, with a radiant smile: "God has said, 'Lo, I am with you.'" Dr. Jno. W. M. Williams, of Baltimore, to whose eloquent discourse, delivered December 8th, 1861, in commemoration of the life and death of "The Lost Missionaries," we are indebted for the principal facts of this sketch, and the one immediately following, says: "There was that polished patience about his manner, combined with an inflexible adherence to Christian principle, that would have seemed eminently adapted to such a sphere" as the work among the Japanese. Mr. Rohrer was baptized by Rev. William Moody, of Shippensburg, Md., in 1853. He married Miss Sarah Robinson, of Montrose, Pa., on the 26th of April, 1860. In June, 1860, he and his wife joined, by letter, the First Baptist Church of Baltimore, in order "to be members of a church connected with the Southern Baptist Convention, and to leave their membership with those who, they felt assured, would give them their sympathies and prayers. He was publicly ordained and set apart to the work of missions," in that church, "June, 1860. * * They came among us utter strangers, but the few who made their acquaintance were charmed with their lovely Christian character, their meekness and gentleness and godly sincerity." When objection was made to his going to Japan, while his relatives were unconverted, Mr. Rohrer answered: "The Japanese have no Moses, nor the prophets, nor Jesus, whom to hear." Before his departure, he delivered a farewell address in the Church of the United Brethren of his native town. "His remarks to his associates were very impressive and solemn. Many were the tears shed on the occasion."

Mrs. ROHRER.

Sarah was the only child of Major Sidney T. and Mrs. L. Robinson, and grand-daughter of the Hon. Tracy Robinson, of Pennsylvania. She was born in Montrose, Pa., July 7th, 1836. She was baptized by the Rev. A. L. Post, April 12th, 1856. At one time, she proposed to unite with the Episcopal Church, "but her honest convictions of the truth, as taught in the New Testament, would not permit her to neglect the solemn and impressive ordinance of baptism. * * When she returned home from the baptismal waters, she rejoiced and said *she was so happy that no language could express it.*" She received the earlier part of her education at a female seminary at Binghampton, her father's native place, whither she moved, with her mother, in the fall of 1840. In 1855, she took charge of the musical department of "Laurel Bank Seminary." She gained a high reputation as a pianist. She went, then, to Musical Vale Seminary, in Connecticut, "where she completed her thorough bass and musical education." Her piano and guitar were sent to Japan, in hope that they would " win the Japanese females to civilization and religion, and also be a source of living, if anything should deprive them of support." She was described by her mother as "winning, obedient, patient, pious, benevolent, and true in friendship. She was studious to the last, and reviewed the French and German languages, with the view of speaking them in Japan. * * In Mr. Rohrer and Sarah was a union of piety, benevolence, education, and refinement seldom equalled."

THEIR DEPARTURE.

Mrs. Robinson, who expected to follow her daughter to Japan in the next vessel which sailed with missionaries, accompanied Mr. and Mrs. Rohrer on board the "Edwin Forrest." Before taking their final adieu, the mother, in the agony of her soul, knelt by her daughter's side, and prayed that God would forgive her for consenting to the bitter separation from her only and darling child. Mrs. Rohrer replied: "Mother, with the exception of parting with you, this is the happiest day of my life. If we are lost at sea, death will find us in the path of duty." Mr. Rohrer had written: "Our Heavenly Father is said to notice the falling sparrow, and much more does he mark the fall of his servants. * * If there is no place on earth for us to labor for God, then, I trust, we may say with Paul: 'I am now ready to be offered, and the time of my departure is at hand.'" Dr. Williams concludes his funeral sermon thus: "Was the 'Edwin Forrest' burnt at sea? Did the flames gather around these disciples—they fell into each other's arms, and looked up through the burning mass, and saw *Jesus standing* to welcome them into his presence. Did the ship founder and go gradually down—they embraced each other, and thought of Jesus, and as the waters gathered around them, they looked up and saw Jesus standing to give them an abundant entrance to heaven. They *lived well:* I am sure they *died well;* and though their bodies lie entombed in the great ocean, yet they rest as sweetly in the bosom of God as if they had breathed their last under the parental roof, reclining upon a mother's loving arm. * * They were lovely and pleasant in their lives, and in their death they were not divided."

Rev. ALFRED LUTHER BOND AND MRS. HELENA DAMERON BOND.

BIRTH, CHILDHOOD, AND YOUTH.

Alfred Luther Bond was born of Methodist parents, Dr. A. J. and Mrs. P. Bond, in Athens, Ohio, July 2d, 1833. "From a child," his mother writes, "he was noted for his kind and affectionate disposition. He was truthful, highly sociable, and generous in his disposition. * * He was slow to believe without evidence; he was firm in what he did believe, and persevered in whatever he undertook and felt to be right." At an early age, he went to Baltimore, and was employed as a clerk on Baltimore Street. "He seems never to have forgotten the discipline of home. The prayers and solicitude of pious parents followed and restrained him in the hour of temptation."

CONVERSION AND CHRISTIAN CHARACTER.

As a seeker after truth, he was "straightforward, calm, earnest, and honestly inquired: 'What must I do to be saved?'" Dr. Williams further says: "I was favorably impressed with his fine personal appearance, and his kind and manly bearing. * * Being reared in the faith of the Methodist Church, it cost him a mighty struggle to adopt the doctrines of any other church. * * He took the word of God alone for his rule of action. * * This reverence for the Scriptures characterized his whole future life, * * and all who conversed with him were astonished at his fund of religious information and familiarity with the word of God." He was baptized by Dr. Williams into the fellowship of his church, on the 5th of February, 1854. "From the beginning of his Christian life, his aim was 'soul prosperity,' and he set his standard high." He seemed to be deeply impressed with the brevity of life, as if coming events were casting their shadows before. Six truths he desired to realize. The first two were: "1. Time is quickly passing away. 2. Life is short at best." A series of *Rules of Action Conducive to Progress in the Christian Life*, adopted by him, soon after he made a profession of religion, opens thus: "Time is precious, and must be husbanded." His mother observes: "Another item I find in all his letters. He is impressed with the truth that time is short, and that whatever he does, must be done quickly." His life appears to have been in harmony with his pious and prayerful utterance: "Jesus, Master, I dedicate myself unreservedly unto thee. Oh, give me wisdom and strength to honor thee always."

MINISTRY, MISSIONS, AND MARRIAGE.

Sustained by his church, he entered Columbian College, D. C., to prepare himself for the ministry, to which "it was evident," said his pastor, "God had called him." In all his studies "he stood among the first." But it was as a man of God that he was "a shining light." A fellow-student says: "His constant cry was, 'Oh, that I could approximate nearer to the character of Jesus!'" His last vacation, he spent as a colporteur in Virginia. Dr. Binney, when President of the College, said that "he was worth his weight in gold to the institution, so excellent was his moral influence upon the students." With regard to the heathen, he said: "Shall I not go? Is it not my duty? Shall I not do as much as possible for my Saviour, when he has saved my soul!" After he resolved to go, he became a *one-idea-man*. Dr. Williams says: "I do not suppose that any one ever gave more thought to the heathen, and especially those of China, than he did." Proffers were made him to settle in North Carolina, where he preached during one of his vacations, but he exclaimed: "I'm going to China. God calls, and I must go." He wrote to the Board, saying, "Here am I, send me.". After an interview and examination, which he describes as "a very pleasant one," the Board accepted him in April, 1860, as a missionary to Shanghai. In the following June, he was graduated from the Columbian College. In July, 1860, he was ordained and married in the First Baptist Church, of Baltimore.

MRS. BOND.

Helena Dameron, the wife of Rev. A. L. Bond, and the daughter of William and Adaline Dameron, was born in Baltimore, December 20th, 1840. She united with the First Baptist Church, of that city, on the 10th of February, 1856. This high encomium is pronounced upon her: "She was never known to disobey her parents. * * In the home circle, she was a beautiful Christian character." Her preceptor, Professor Thayer, Principal of the Eastern Female High School, of Baltimore, says of her: "She was eminently mild and amiable in her disposition, and far from being opinionated and dogmatical; yet, when in the path of duty, she was steadfast and immovable. Anxious only to know the will of God, she stopped not in the path of duty to consult her own ease or comfort. * * Her native ability, untiring industry, and assiduous attention to instruction secured her at once a high scholastic position; and ever maintaining this rank, as well as a continuance of conduct which was enriched by every principle of disposition and of action that could render a pupil admired as well as beloved, she deservedly graduated among the most distinguished in her class." When "comparatively a child," she took a school in

Virginia. The gentleman, who engaged her services, wrote: "She is a true woman—we are pleased with her, and could not be better suited." She formed a Sunday-school in her "log school-room." The servants, to whom she would read and explain the Bible, called her "The little missionary." With regard to becoming a foreign missionary with Mr. Bond, she wrote to a friend: "I feel my obligations to that Saviour who has done so much for me. I would thus show my gratitude by consecrating my life, my all to his service, and do my part, however *humble* it be, to promote his cause, to disseminate his glorious gospel among the poor heathen. * * We know for whom we should go, and who has said, 'Go ye into all the world and preach the gospel to every creature,' and who has promised, 'Lo, I am with you alway.' For *his sake* we would go, and in obedience to his command; who, then, and what shall 'hinder?'"

COSTLY SACRIFICE.

On the 3d of August, 1860, they sailed from New York, with Mr. and Mrs. Rohrer, in the "Edwin Forrest," which, to this day, has never been heard of. Referring to the elevated spirit which Mr. Bond assumed and maintained after fixing the purpose of devoting his life to the cause of missions, Dr. Samson, one of his Professors at Columbian College, wrote: "Always peculiarly manly and noble in bearing, as he was in form, there was a radiance of countenance and a general air of devotion to some high and holy service that made him seem a marked man, even in the recitation room and in the circle of friends, as he was in the College prayer-meetings, and in the pulpit. There could hardly have been a costlier sacrifice to missionary zeal than God required, when Brother Bond and his companion, with their wives, were, far off on the ocean, taken by their Heavenly Father to himself."

Doctor JOHN SEXTON JAMES AND MRS. ANNE PRICE JAMES.

MISSIONS, MEDICINES, MARRIAGES.

Dr. James, the eldest son of Israel E., and Elizabeth James, was born in Philadelphia, July 10th, 1818. He was baptized by Dr. J. H. Kennard early in 1837. "From the time of his conversion he had a strong desire to labor among the heathen as a missionary physician, and had correspondence and personal interviews on the subject with the late Corresponding Secretary of the Missionary Union, Dr. Solomon Peck." He was graduated at Brown University in 1842, and then entered Newton Theological Seminary. A fellow-student of his, at both places, describes him to us, as "of small stature, light complexion and blue eyes, good-tempered, animated in face and movement, unusually active and energetic, and an excessive lover of law and order, a fair student and a good man." On Sunday evening, August 25th, 1844, he was married to Elizabeth Rotzel, in the Tenth Baptist Church of Philadelphia, by the Rev. Joseph H. Kennard. His wife was the daughter of Joseph and Mary Rotzel, and was born at Hilltown, Bucks County, Pennsylvania, January 24th, 1824. Annie Tolman James, daughter of J. Sexton James and Elizabeth R. James, was born at Sommerville, a country seat, near Rising Sun Village, Philadelphia County, April 17th, 1845. The child died August 5th, 1845." The health of Mrs. James was so feeble that her physician forbade her to go to Burmah, where her husband had thought of laboring. He then gave up the idea of being a missionary. Mrs. James died at Sommerville, September 11th, 1845, aged 21 years, 7 months and 18 days. "After her death, her husband felt that Providence had called him to missionary work, and he offered himself to the Southern Board. Dr. Taylor suggested China as a field where a missionary was wanted, who could add to his influence over the natives by skill in medicine." In the spring of 1846, he graduated in medicine at the Jefferson Medical

School of Philadelphia, and practised the profession a few months at Sommerville. On November 2d, 1846, Dr. James was invited by the Board of Foreign Missions of the Southern Baptist Convention "to confer with them, with reference to his appointment as a physician at one of the mission stations in China." November 16th, after the usual examination, the candidate having retired, it was unanimously

1. *Resolved,* That Brother J. Sexton James be accepted as a missionary physician to China.

2. *Resolved,* That the Board accede to the request of his father that Dr. James should have the privilege, if desired by him, of returning at the end of five years, "on the condition that his return shall not be an expense to this Board."

On the 15th of January, 1847, it was

"1. *Resolved,* That Brother J. Sexton James be appointed Treasurer of the Shanghai Mission.

2. *Resolved,* That the Treasurer of the Board be authorized to pay to J. Sexton James, Treasurer of the Shanghai Mission, —— dollars to defray the expenses of said Mission."

"J. Sexton James and Annie Price Safford were married Tuesday morning, June 15th, 1847, in the First Baptist Church of Salem, Massachusetts, by Rev. Thos. D. Anderson." His wife was the daughter of Joshua and Sarah B. Safford, and born in Salem, December 22d, 1824, the same year as his first wife, Elizabeth Rotzel. As has been stated, on the evening of December 18th, 1846, "designation services" for Messrs. Yates, Tobey, and J. Sexton James were held in the First Baptist Church of Richmond, Virginia. Mr. Tobey, with Messrs. Shuck and Johnson, sailed on March 11th, 1847, and reached Hong Kong on the 25th of June. Mr. Yates sailed in the *Thomas W. Sears,* the 26th of April, and on arrival at Hong Kong, proceeded with Mr. Tobey to Shanghai. Mr. and Mrs. James sailed from Philadelphia, Nov. 11th, 1847, in the ship *Valparaiso.*

LETTER EXTRACTS.

From Hong Kong, Mr. Shuck wrote: "We are anxiously wishing for Dr. James' arrival. The last three overland mails all brought me letters from him." On ship-board, Dr. James noted: "We have observed the monthly concert, and have our meetings for conference and prayer. * * Many of the crew have been under my professional care. * * While attending the sailor in sickness or dressing his wounds, the missionary physician can, with propriety, introduce the subject of religion, and that under the most favorable circumstances." On landing, Mrs. James sent home the following: "Saturday afternoon, March 25th, 1848, we took our Chinese pilot, and 9 o'clock P. M. found us safely moored in Hong Kong harbor. The city presented a fine appearance from the deck. It was brightly illumined with its many lanterns, and being built on the side of a hill, showed to great advantage. Precious home letters greeted us, and our hearts did burn within us as we thanked our kind Preserver for all his rich mercies. * * After breakfast, we went into the dear little Baptist Chapel, and our hearts inwardly exclaimed: 'What hath God wrought.' Eighty souls, sitting in their native costume, listened to the news of salvation. A native preacher read to them the Holy Scriptures. The songs of Zion were sung by lips attuned to praise. Brother Dean addressed them earnestly. We could not understand, but we felt that it was good to be there. Pray that the Spirit of the living God would bless these efforts, and crown them with success to his own glory."

THE CATASTROPHE.

No vessel sailing for their destination, Shanghai, Mr. and Mrs. James, in company with Dr. Dean, went up to Canton in the Valparaiso, in which they had gone to China. They arrived, and were welcomed at the house of our missionaries, Mr. and Mrs. Pearcy, on the 1st of April. Mr. Pearcy wrote: "Friends and the missionaries called to see them, and they visited all the mission families, and several temples and places of interest. * * They were highly delighted with their visit to Canton, and it afforded us great pleasure to enjoy their society and to mingle our supplications with theirs at a rich throne of grace. * * But they felt that they had not reached their field of labor, and desired to embrace the first opportunity for Shanghai." Dr. Dean preceded them to Hong Kong. On the 13th of

April, they took passage in the schooner "Paradox," chartered for the occasion by gentlemen who thought it "perfectly safe and more pleasant" than the "Fast Boat," in which they did not embark, on account of the crowd of Chinese passengers. On the 15th of April, entering Hong Kong Harbor, the schooner was capsized by a sudden squall, and our beloved missionaries, who were in the cabin, went down with the vessel, to rise no more until the trumpet shall sound, and the sea shall give forth her precious treasures. It was reported at Canton that their bodies had been recovered. Mr. Issachar J. Roberts, as is stated in his diary, took down coffins for their interment; but all efforts to raise the "Paradox" had failed. Mr. Roberts also notes: "The vessel was commanded by Mohammed, a larker, with a crew of the same kind, who all swam out."

REFLECTIONS.

At this mysterious dispensation, the missionaries were startled and cast down; the kindred and friends of the deceased were well nigh heart-broken; the Board passed appropriate resolutions, and sought consolation in *the doctrine of the Divine Sovereignty;* and the Southern Baptist Convention "was compelled to be dumb." Mr. Pearcy wrote: "They lie buried beneath the billows, and it is not likely that they will be raised till the morning of the resurrection. I almost rejoice that they were not divided in their death." Dr. Dean remarked of them: "Not recalled, but *promoted;* not dead, but *translated;* not lost, but *living.* The shock to us has been overwhelming; but the transition to them, though unexpected, has been peaceful and glorious."

Mrs. Safford, the mother of Mrs. James, referring to the bitter affliction, observes: "How many plans I have heard them make, and how many resolutions form, for the advancement of Christ's cause, in connection with the mission at Shanghai. Dear, precious ones! God knows—and they know *now*—why they were not permitted to carry out their wishes." The following is taken from Mrs. James' journal: "It is a delightful thought that we have a Friend always near us, and one whose listening ear is ever open to our cry. Those are sweet words that came to my mind this afternoon:

> In the loneliest hour there is a helper nigh :
> Jesus of Nazareth passeth by.

"How unsearchable are the ways of the Lord, and how little can we foresee of our own movements. God reigneth—let the earth rejoice. My destiny is in his hands, who seeth the end from the beginning. Nowhere else would I live: blessed be his holy name!"

Dr. J. Sexton James was the brother of Charles Sexton James, the able Professor of Mathematics and Natural Philosophy of the University at Lewisburg, Penn.

DOES IT PAY?

RICHMOND, VA., *October 8th.*

MY DEAR SIR: Bishop Pierce, of Georgia, when asked: "Will the heathen be saved, if we do not send the gospel to them?" replied: "Shall WE be saved if we do not send it to them?" There is something about this preaching to the nations, which, I judge from your letter, you have never considered. Who is a child of God, but one that is born into the image of him who was self-denying for the world's redemption? What is a gospel church, but a company of baptized believers, organized for their development, by obedience to the behests of him, who commanded: "Go ye into all the world, and preach the gospel to every creature?" Hence, the church is called "the Light of the *world*." Judson had the right view when he told the King at Ava, that he had come to preach to his people to save them, and to save his own soul. Max Müller says: "The Church is missionary, progressive, world-embracing. When it ceases to be missionary, it ceases to exist."

Riding on the cars, I heard a Papist say to a Baptist: "The difference, sir, between us, is this: You object to my having one Pope, and I object to your having as many Popes as there are members of your churches." That was a severe thrust at a people, who boast that their Shibboleth is "Thus saith the Lord;" and who appropriate largely to themselves the grand words of Chillingworth: The Bible, the Bible, is the religion of Protestants.

Yet, is it not in the face of God's plain commands, that you ask, whether it is not a waste of time, and money, and life, to give the gospel to the "imbruted pagans?" Is there not in such arraying of your judgment against the divine word more of Popery than in the Papist; yea, than in the Pope of Rome himself? Do you not at least give fearful occasion to the biting sarcasm of that Romanist? Suppose it does seem a waste. What has the servant to do with that, when the Master says: Go?

But from your own calculating stand-point, "does it" not "pay" as much as to preach the gospel in this country? I clip from a periodical of high authority the following, changing the figures to agree with more recent statistics:

COMPARATIVE VIEW.

1. *Relative success.*—Ordained Baptist ministers in the United States, 14,954; Baptisms last year, 102,736, or over *seven* to each minister; ordained Baptist missionaries in Asia, 234; baptisms last year, 17,000, or *seventy-two* to each missionary.

"It is calculated that, in the last fifty years, the average annual number of converts of the Home Missionary Society has been *nineteen;* and that, during the same period, the average annual number of heathen converts of the Missionary Union and Free Mission Society has been *forty-three.*

"2. *Relative Expenses.*—In the Associations of New York, Long Island, and Black River, the expense per convert is $430. Under the Baptist Missionary Union the expense per heathen is $55, or *eight to one* in favor of the Missionary Union. In the mission station where there has been the largest number of converts, the expense per convert is $24: in the church of these Associations, where there has been the largest number of converts, the expense is $115, or *five to one* in favor of the missionary work. In the largest mission, the expense has been $43 per convert: in the largest church of these Associations, the expense per convert is $751, or *eighteen to one* in favor of the foreign missionary work. This calculation is made by an experienced *lawyer,* and not by an enthusiastic preacher." That it *does* pay, may be inferred from the regular increase of men and money invested in the enterprise. When Andrew Fuller tried, in the city of London, to get money enough to pay William Carey's way to India, he had to go into the lanes and alleys to hide his disappointment and chagrin.

At the first meeting of the Triennial Convention, $25.00 was raised for Foreign Missions. Now about fifty grand Protestant organizations are engaged in the work, with 11,040 Christian laborers, 761,388 communicants, 229,058 scholars, and 350,000 adherents, who have adopted the Christian name; and this work is supported at an annual expenditure of $6,531,930. "In more than 300 isles of Eastern and Southern Polynesia, the gospel has swept heathenism away," says the Secretary of the London Missionary Society. Of the 1,350,000,000 of the earth, 360,000,000 profess faith in Christ.

You suggest doubts as to African evangelization. Philip had no doubt when he preached Jesus to that Cushite, or black man, whose people, ruled by queens called Candace, according to ancient writers, lived "south of Egypt." Witness African evangelization in America. Are Africans more degraded than the Fijis? At a recent anniversary of the Wesleyan Missionary Society, the Governor of Fiji said that of the 120,000 Fijis, 100,000 were regular church-goers; that the natives themselves had built 800 church-houses.

On the progress of the work, Rev. J. H. Boothe says, in 1879: "During six years, the Protestants of Japan have increased from 13 to 12,000. The leading paper in Japan, speaking of Christianity, said not long ago, 'It is astonishing how this way is spreading.'

"The Hon. Wm. Ware has lately visited the Sandwich Islands, and he reports that no land is now better supplied with schools and churches, and says: 'There are in Worcester County, Mass., more persons who can neither read nor write, than in the Sandwich Islands. Sixty years ago the people of these islands were cannibals. On the monument of Dr. John Giddis, who labored as a missionary in one of these islands, is engraved the sentence: When he came here there were no Christians: when he went away there were no heathen.

"The Presbyterians of this country report 600 converts at their missionary stations during the past year; the Congregationalists 1,225, while the Baptists report 17,000. The Presbyterians spent $461,686, the Congregationalists $482,204, and the Baptists $278,823.

"The various Missionary Societies of the world have put in circulation one hundred and fifty millions of copies of the Scriptures in heathen lands, and the Bible is now printed in 230 modern languages and dialects.

Hear what the Secretary of the Missionary Union says, in his Annual Report of 1879: "Especially do we find ground for encouragement in the wonderful successes of Christian missions hitherto. At the close of 1877, British India, including Burmah and Ceylon, contained 500,000 Christian natives, with a nominally Christian population of at least 2,000,000 more. And, at the same ratio of increase which has prevailed during the last twenty years, fifty years more will make the whole vast region as really Christian as Great Britain is to-day. Then look at China, with its 14,000 converts, mostly gathered since the opening of the treaty ports. If any one should be inclined to regard this as a small number to be gathered out of the 350,000,000 or 400,000,000 of China, let us remind him that, if conversions go on in the same ratio in the future as in the past, thirty-five years from to-day will see 26,000,000 of professing Christians in China, with a nominally Christian population of 100,000,000 more.* Then look at Africa with its 180,000 Christians on the south-eastern coast, between the Cape of Good Hope and the Zambesi, besides the thousands on the southern and western coasts; and four, perhaps five, of the noblest missionary societies are pushing on to occupy the region around the great central lakes. See Polynesia with 68,000 converts, and a Christian population of more than 100,000. Think of Japan, which stands in the van of heathen civilization, and inquires for the true religion,—the authoritative system of God, and the all-sufficient religion for humanity. Though the open converts to Christianity are not numerous, yet the labors bestowed upon the people have resulted in more than the average success in other lands. Consider how many Christian schools

---

* Dr. Legge says, "The converts have multiplied during thirty-five years at least two thousand-fold, the rate of increase being greater year by year. Suppose it should continue the same for other thirty-five years, and in A. D. 1913, there will be in China 26,000,000 of communicants, and a professedly Christian community of 100,000,000."—*Conference on Foreign Missions*, p. 171.

there are in all those lands training the children of the converts for usefulness among their countrymen, and how native evangelical agencies are multiplying. Think of the missionaries and their native assistants, numbering not less than 10,000, who are sowing beside all waters, and what harvests are being gathered. Think of the Bible translated into 230 heathen languages and dialects, and actually printed and circulated in the tongues of more than three-fourths of the inhabitants of the globe. Think how mission presses are multiplying Bibles, tracts, treatises, and hymnals, all of them teaching the way of salvation, or the means of Christian growth, or the claims of Christian duty.

"But what are we to think of the new epoch in missionary progress which began with 1878? The record of revivals during the last year, both in Great Britain and America, when carefully made up, will prove to be a marked one. And the report which is laid before you to-day gives an account of 113 baptisms in a single station in China, as a result of a movement which began last year, when, in the same station, 169 were baptized. The like of this has never been known in China before 1877, except among the early Jesuit missions. Sweden reports for 1878, 2,600 baptisms in our own missions. And other societies and the Evangelical Lutherans have reaped harvests nearly equal to our own. The baptism of 10,500 converts in our mission to the Teloogoos sets the stamp of wonder on the year under review. And the wonder increases when this work is seen to be only a small part of a wider and more comprehensive movement. The Church of England missionaries in the district of Tinnevelly have gathered more than 30,000 converts. The work is moving southward from Ongole, and northward from Tinnevelly, and promises to envelope all the intermediate territory. The Tamils, under the care of the American Board of Commissioners, are beginning to come in flocks to confess Christ. More than 70,000 people in that portion of India south of the Deccan have cast away their idols, and professed their belief in one living, eternal God, who made heaven and earth.

"The numbers thus added to the mission churches in other parts of the world confound all previous ratios, and point to a movement wider, deeper, more pervading, than we have before experienced in the history of modern missions. It is the Lord's doing, and it is marvellous in our eyes. Prophecy foretells just such results as these. The Spirit was sent forth into the world to produce them. The Church has been praying for them. If they are not to be given, our presence in heathen lands is simply impertinence and folly. If the heathen do not come in this multitudinous way, the work never will be done, and the world will never be brought to Christ."

But the world will be brought to Christ. And wherever the word goes among the nations it proves itself the power of God unto salvation—"the sword of the Spirit" having the two-fold qualities of the keen scimetar of a Saladin, slicing into pieces the most abstruse subtleties of East Indian philosophy; and of the huge battle axe of Richard Cœur de Lion, hewing down, and hacking to pieces the most monstrous devil-worship of Central Africa. All it needs is to have free course, that it may go through the nations, refreshing and revivifying them, as if the limpid Jordan were invested with ten thousand-fold more volume, and should burst through the bosom of the Dead Sea, and bear onward to the ocean its stagnant waters.

But there is much to be done. The number of pagans who have never heard of Jesus is so vast, that if they were to file before us, one in every five seconds, it would take over one hundred years to count them; and the number of missionaries sent to them by the million and a half of Baptists of the South is so small, that were each of our missionaries to preach to eight hundred of them every day of the week, it would take over two hundred years to tell them but once that Jesus died for their souls! As stewards of the manifold grace of God, how can we justify the disparity of retaining in our Southern States one minister to every one thousand souls, while we send out one missionary to every forty millions of the heathen? As the servants of Jehovah, must we not press forward more vigorously the chariot of light, that our earth may be baptized into its rays, and come forth a new earth, wherein dwelleth righteousness?

Much is to be done at home. But the power of the gospel cannot be localized. The son of Manoah was not born to be bound to a treadmill, but to bear away the brazen gates of Gaza, and to scatter single-handed the compacted forces of Philistia. Luther said that the doctrine of Justification by Faith, was for the standing or falling of the church. But faith is manifested by works. However true to the ordinances and the doctrines, our people must come down from their position and power if they fail in this great essential duty of Christianity. The hero of the Iliad was invulnerable, save as to his heel; and he fell before the shining shaft from the twanging bow of Priam's wily son.

And God's people will arise under the smitings of the truth and of conscience, in the day of God's power, as Peter was aroused by the angel of the Lord. They will go forth as Joshua and as Gideon, relying on the word of God; and every opposition shall fall flat, and every enemy shall be put to confusion. The work is virtually done. What year is this? 1880 of what? The earth's foundation? The Grecian Olympiads? The building of Rome? The Mohammedan hegira? No, no! 1880 of Christ's advent for the world's salvation. Thus the very wheels of nature, which mete out the ages, move in commemoration of the Saviour of Mankind. His name and insignia are emblazoned on the folds of time, which, like a banner, floats over all, and publishes to the universe, that the nations are captured by our Lord. The movement of worlds is but a triumphal procession toward the glorious consummation, when, in the name of Jesus, every knee shall bow, and every tongue confess that Jesus Christ is Lord, to the glory of God the Father. Already the cry is gone up into the ear of him, with whom there is no time, "The Kingdoms of this world are become the Kingdoms of our Lord, and of his Christ."

That you may be among the earnest few who do not ask: "Will it pay?" but who say to their great Leader in the language of the followers of an ancient worthy: "Ready in heart and hand,"—which by the way, is in its original Latinity, the motto of your own beautiful " city by the sea "—is the sincere desire of

Yours very truly,

T.

AFRICAN MISSIONS.

AFRICA AND LIBERIA.

AFRICA.

IN our introductory notes on this continent, as was said in the opening of this volume, "I only aim at a compilation."

GEOGRAPHY AND TOPOGRAPHY.

"Africa," says the learned Prof. Guyot, "is the most singular in its form of all the continents. Its mass, nearly round, or ellipsoidal, is concentrated upon itself. It projects into the ocean no important peninsula, nor anywhere lets into its bosom the waters of the ocean. It seems to close itself against every influence from without. Thus the extension of the line of coasts is only about 14,000 geographical miles for a surface of 8,720,000 square miles; so that Africa has only one mile of coast for 623 miles of surface." Its area is now estimated at nearly eleven million square miles, which is three times the surface of Europe. It extends from latitude 37° 21' N. to 34° 52' S., which makes its length nearly 72 degrees, or 5,000 English miles. Its breadth at the equator is computed at 4,760 English miles. There are two great physical divisions of the continent: The great plain of Northern Africa, comprising the Sahara Desert, the Lake Tchad region, and the valley of the Lower Nile; and the great Table-Lands, with their numerous ranges and groups, of Central and Southern Africa. The former division contains mountains 5,000 feet high, and is only denominated *plain* to distinguish it from the more elevated region of the South. From the Cape of Good Hope three successive terraces of table land extend northward for a thousand geographical miles, and rise into mountains of great height—into one peak of 20,000 feet. The system of the Atlas Mountains, which occupies the northwestern region of Africa, is distinct from these two divisions, and consists of several ranges, the highest point of which has an altitude of 15,000 feet.

LAKES AND RIVERS.

North of the equator, the principal lakes are Tchad, with its one hundred islands, and Demboa, on the table lands of Abyssinia, which is 6,110 feet above the level of the sea. On the equator are lakes Albert Nyanza and Victoria Nyanza; and south of the equator, Tanganyika, Bangweola, and "the great lake" Nyassa, 2,825 feet above tide, which was discovered by Livingstone in 1859. The five rivers, Nile, Niger, Zambesi, Senegal, and Orange, aggregate over 10,000 miles of water-course. Stanley has recently discovered that the Congo and Lualaba are one river, forming a highway across the continent from Lower Guinea, the greater part of the distance, to Zanzibar. The Nile, 3,600 miles long, drains an area of 2,000,000 square miles.

CLIMATE.

"The general climate of Africa," says Malte Brun, "is that of the torrid zone; more than three-fourths of the continent being situated between the tropics. The great mass of heated air, incumbent on these hot regions, has ready access to its northern and southern parts, situated in the zones called temperate, so that the portions of them adjoining the tropics are equally torrid with the regions actually intertropical." In Upper Egypt and Nubia, eggs may be baked in the hot sands, and the saying of the Arab is: "In Nubia the soil is like fire, and the wind like a flame." In the day-time the soil of the Sahara rapidly absorbs the solar rays, but during the night it cools so rapidly that ice is sometimes formed. The regions along the Atlantic and Mediterranean coasts are rendered more temperate by the influence of the sea. In northeastern Africa, are ranges of mountains covered with perpetual snow.

PEOPLE.

The population of Africa is estimated at 200,000,000, and may be divided into two general classes, viz., the foreign, or mixed, and the Ethiopic, or negro, races. Of the former, who extend from the Mediterranean coast to about 20° N. latitude, are Turks, Arabs, Jews, French, and Moors. The Berbers of the Atlas region, the Tuaricks and Tibbous of the Sahara, and the Copts of Egypt, whose ancestors intermarried with the Greeks, Nubians, and Abyssinians, may be regarded as descendants of the primitive stock, while the Moors are of mixed descent, native and foreign. From the region occupied by these mixed races southward to Cape Colony, the negro family is found. Their principal nations are the Mandingoes, in Senegambia and farther inland; the Yolofs, "who are the handsomest and blackest of all negroes," and dwell along the Atlantic coast between the Senegal and the Gambia; the Fellatahs, who are black, with a striking copper hue, occupy the central parts of Soudan, and are one of the most remarkable nations in Africa, being industrious, living in commodious and clean habitations, and being mostly Mohammedans; the Guinea nations, whose negro type is particularly distinct; and the Galla tribes, who occupy Eastern Africa from Abyssinia to the Portuguese possessions in Mozambique, south of the equator. The Kaffres, Hottentots, and Bushmen form a distinct variety, closely resembling the Mongolian races of Asia, and occupy the greater portion of Southern Africa.

LANGUAGES, RELIGIONS, MORALS, GOVERNMENTS.

The Arabic is the language of the North, and the Mandingo is used from the Senegal to the Niger. But the languages of the negroes are as numerous as the nations. Seetzen says, "the languages of Africa must amount to a hundred or a hundred and fifty;" but some trace them to a common origin. Dr. John Leighton Wilson, late missionary of the American Board, writes: "In the northern half of the continent, or that portion of it inhabited by the black races, the different languages show little if any affinity for each other; while in the southern division one great family prevails over nearly the whole of it, even to the Cape of Good Hope." As to the social and religious condition of Africa: polygamy is common in the country; cannibalism exists in some parts; and human blood is sometimes mixed with the mortar used in the construction of temples. Mohammedanism prevails in the northern countries; Christianity is professed in Abyssinia and in Egypt by the Copts, though little understood; but the natives generally are abandoned to the most debasing superstitions and devil-worship. The governments are excessively despotic.

EXPLORATIONS.

The Arabs penetrated Northern Africa, passed across the Sahara Desert to the centre of the continent, then along the western coast as far as the Senegal and Gambia, and thence to Sofala on the east. The Portuguese circumnavigated the continent, and gave an accurate outline of the coast. The discovery of America and the West Indies, and the slave trade, afforded means of a more extended knowledge of the coast between the Senegal and the Cameroons, and of the manners and customs of the people. With the English and French settlements in Africa began a systematic survey of the coasts and portions of the interior. In 1788, a Society was formed in London for the exploration of Inner Africa. Under its auspices important additions were made to the geography of Northern, Western, and Central Africa by Houghton, Mungo Park, Hornemann, Denham, Clapperton, and Burckhardt. In 1831, this association was merged into the Royal Geographical Society. "In the last eighty years, more has been done to develop the geography of Africa than during the whole of the seventeen hundred years since Ptolemy." Among the most distinguished explorers of the Nile are Bruce, Brown, Buckhardt, Cailliaud, Rüppell, Russeger, Speke, Baker, Burton, Grant, and the Egyptian expeditions up the Nile.

The Dutch settled South Africa in 1650; but not much information of the interior of that portion of the continent was gained until the close of the eighteenth century, when a series of journeys was begun by Sparman, and continued by Le Vaillant, Barrow, Trutter, Somerville, Lichtenstein, Burchell, Campbell, Thomson, Smith, Alexander, and Harris. In 1847, Messrs. Krapf and Rebmann, missionaries of the *East African Mission* of England, began a series of explorations from Zanzibar, which are full of interest. Dr. Krapf came to the conclusion that " from the Galla boundary down to the Cape of Good Hope there is one family of languages, which he calls the Suahili stock; which stock, he thinks, from specimens of West African languages, begins on the southern bank of the Gaboon River." The explorations and discoveries of the lamented David Livingstone, which have been followed up by the lauded Henry M. Stanley, have excited so much interest in this field of research that the Royal Geographical Society of England, says the *Saturday Review*, is raising an " African Exploration Fund " for several expeditions " to explore or examine seven distinct routes." This fund, says Sir Rutherford Alcock, " will be devoted to the scientific examination of Africa—the physical features and resources, and the best route to the interior." What effect the present war between England and the Zulus will have on the exploration and civilization of Southern Africa remains to be seen. We only add, that while immense treasures and noble lives are consecrated by science to the physical development of this great country, why should the saints of the Lord withhold their means and men to secure the spiritual transformation of the people of whom it is divinely written: " Ethiopia shall soon stretch out her hands unto God ? "

WESTERN AND CENTRAL AFRICA.

EARLY DISCOVERY.

This part of the continent belongs to that division of Africa called Negritia by the Latin geographers. It extends eastward across the continent, north of the equator, into the valley of the Nile. Its inhabitants were known to the ancient Egyptians, as is attested by their monuments. Necho, a king of Egypt, employed Phenician navigators to explore the coast. The true shape of the continent was delineated by these explorers. This knowledge was lost. The oldest maps represent the coast as running eastward from Cape Palmas, and sweeping round to the Red Sea. Nearly six hundred years before Christ, the Carthagenians explored the western coast, some suppose, as far as Sherboro Island, near Liberia. The inhabitants were carried across the Great Desert and sold to the Carthagenians. After the fall of Carthage, the Romans became acquainted with the countries beyond the Sahara. This is indicated by their remains and remnants of their language among the people. When the Saracens arrived in Northern Africa, the routes to Soudan were probably as well known to the Moors as to us. In the tenth century, these hordes, which spread desolation in many parts of Europe and Asia, came down upon the fertile table-lands of Central Africa. They conquered, imposed their religion and laws, and established kingdoms, which were highly lauded by Arabian writers of that age. They were absorbed by the millions of negroes, and retrograded into semi-barbarous Africans. As effects of the invasion, most of the people are Mohammedans, a knowledge of the written Arabic is extensively diffused, and there is among them an obvious mixture of Shemitic blood. The Arabs, Moors, and mixed races on the Desert have enslaved the inhabitants, in whom the form, features, and characteristics of the negro are perfectly developed.

LATER DISCOVERIES AND SLAVE TRADE.

The Portuguese were the next adventurers in these African waters. Antonio Gonzales took slaves from the coast of Western Africa as early as 1440. In 1462, Piedro de Cinta, in the employment of the King of Portugal, to whom Pope Martin V., had given all the territories he might discover from Cape Bojador to the East Indies, to be conquered and "recovered to Christ and his church," made the first discoveries on the coast, of which we have any distinct and authentic account. For nearly a century and a half the Portuguese were masters of the coast. The slave trade to the West Indies was begun in 1503, and encouraged by edicts of Ferdinand V. of Spain in 1511, and of Charles V., in 1515. Procuring slaves and selling them to the Spaniards was a principal trade of the Portuguese. Their language was commonly used in business, and was understood by the natives, who traded with foreigners. The English, by Thomas Windham, visited the whole coast from Cesters to Benin in 1553. In 1554, Captain John Lok, with three ships, reached Cape Mesurado, and brought home "certain black slaves," which were probably the first ever seen in England. In 1588, the English "African Company" was incorporated. The Portuguese resisted vigorously these encroachments. But by 1604, they were driven from all their posts, from Cape Mesurado to Cape Palmas. A few years later the Dutch, who had entered the list of traders despite the grant of Pope Martin V., had possession of Cape Mount, and the English of Sierra Leone. The Portuguese retired inland, and were lost by amalgamation with the natives. From about 1600, pirates and unscrupulous traders began to scourge the coast. From 1688 to 1697, the "Buccaneers" in the West Indies were broken up, and spread themselves, as elsewhere, along the western coast of Africa. For thirty years, they were one of the powers. Several times they plundered Sierra Leone, and for seven years they held the bay next south of that cape. In 1730, they were dispossessed by the French. Meanwhile, the Genoese first, and then the French, obtained the exclusive privilege of furnishing slaves for the Spanish colonies. In 1713, the English Government, by the famous Assiento treaty, obtained it, for the South Sea Company, for thirty years. In 1739, England sold out the remaining four years to Spain for a hundred thousand pounds! In 1730, not a European factory was in operation where Liberia now is. The testimony laid before the British Parliament from 1791 to 1807, showed that, on the "windward coast," where is Liberia, "every tree was a factory," and ships stopped and traded wherever a signal was made. The more recent discoveries of this part of Africa have been previously mentioned. On March 23, 1850, Mr. James Richardson, of England, started from Tripoli, accompanied by Drs. Barth and Overweg, for a journey as far as Lake Tchad. They were reinforced on February 20, 1852, by Dr. Vogel and two sappers and miners. The valuable results of their explorations of Lake Tchad and the surrounding country may be seen in the new edition of the Encyclopedia Britannica, and in Dr. Barth's volumes on Central Africa. An interesting and reliable work is "Central Africa," by our own missionary, T. J.

Bowen, who sailed from this country on the 17th of December, 1849, for Liberia and Yoruba, under the auspices of the Southern Baptist Convention; and who, after doing a good work in Africa, fell asleep in this country in November, 1875. Let Southern Baptists pray that the mantle of their pioneer Bowen may fall on their missionaries David and Cosby, and that their lives may be long spared for the evangelization of the great continent of Africa.

LIBERIA.

PHYSICAL FEATURES.

Liberia extends along the western coast of Africa from Manna Point, latitude 7° 25' N., longitude 12° 34' W., to the river San Pedro, latitude 4° 44' N., longitude 6° 37' W. The length of the sea coast is about 520 miles. The extent of the territory inward is from ten to forty miles. The country contains probably 17,270 square miles. It was composed of four separate colonies. The population is some 10,000. They are blacks from the United States and their descendants, with some civilized natives. Monrovia, the principal town, carries on a considerable coasting trade. The country is well watered. The coast is deficient in harbors. It is, however, a continuous roadstead, where ships may lie at anchor within a mile or two of the shore. Landing-places for boats occur every five or ten miles. The products are those of tropical climates. Palm oil is made in large quantities. Cam-wood and ivory are brought from the interior for exportation.

ABORIGINES OF THE COUNTRY.

The territory of the Bassas extends from the Junk River to the Cesters, about ninety miles on the coast, and inward perhaps seventy miles. Mr. Ashman estimated their number at 125,000. They are ignorant and degraded. They have no written language, and no knowledge of art or science. There is no individual property in the land.

Bowen, who sailed from this country on the 17th of December, 1849, for Liberia and Yoruba, under the auspices of the Southern Baptist Convention; and who, after doing a good work in Africa, fell asleep in this country in November, 1875. Let Southern Baptists pray that the mantle of their pioneer Bowen may fall on their missionaries David and Cosby, and that their lives may be long spared for the evangelization of the great continent of Africa.

LIBERIA.

PHYSICAL FEATURES.

Liberia extends along the western coast of Africa from Manna Point, latitude 7° 25' N., longitude 12° 34' W., to the river San Pedro, latitude 4° 44' N., longitude 6° 37' W. The length of the sea coast is about 520 miles. The extent of the territory inward is from ten to forty miles. The country contains probably 17,270 square miles. It was composed of four separate colonies. The population is some 10,000. They are blacks from the United States and their descendants, with some civilized natives. Monrovia, the principal town, carries on a considerable coasting trade. The country is well watered. The coast is deficient in harbors. It is, however, a continuous roadstead, where ships may lie at anchor within a mile or two of the shore. Landing-places for boats occur every five or ten miles. The products are those of tropical climates. Palm oil is made in large quantities. Cam-wood and ivory are brought from the interior for exportation.

ABORIGINES OF THE COUNTRY.

The territory of the Bassas extends from the Junk River to the Cesters, about ninety miles on the coast, and inward perhaps seventy miles. Mr. Ashman estimated their number at 125,000. They are ignorant and degraded. They have no written language, and no knowledge of art or science. There is no individual property in the land.

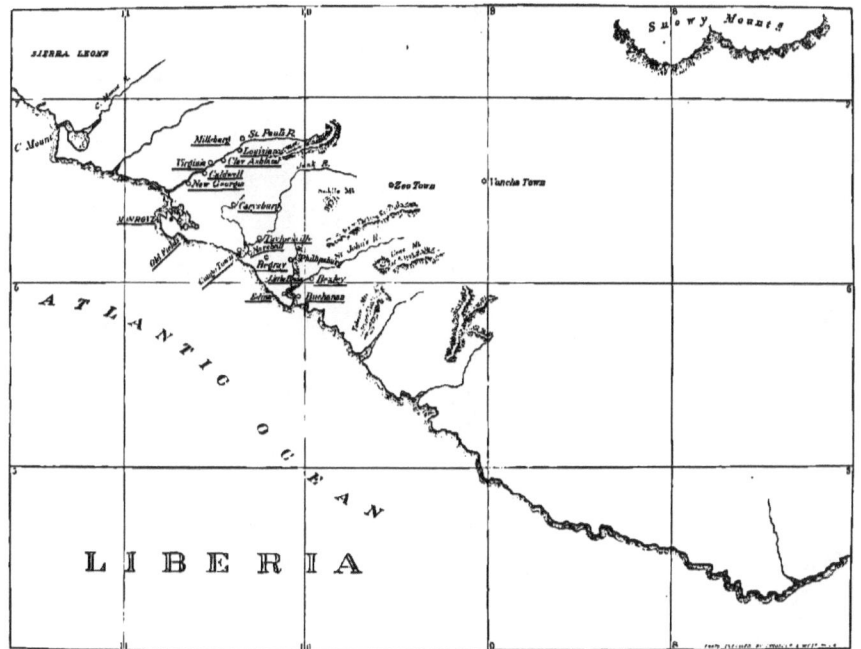

They work the ground for three months, and are idle the rest of the year. They are hired by the colonists. They live in small villages of twenty to two hundred houses—usually some eight feet square. Their domestic utensils are a pot, a bowl, and sometimes a wooden spoon. Their wardrobe is a yard of cloth. Bassa women dress like Grebo men at Cape Palmas; and Grebo men, like Bassa women. They eat cats, dogs, snakes, frogs, and fish, with rice, cassada, palm oil, bananas, and green corn roasted. Their principal amusement is dancing. They seem to have no system of religion. They believe in witchcraft and the efficiency of charms furnished by *Gre-gree* men. They have some vague notion of future existence, and throw food on the graves of deceased relatives years after their death. Some think the dead returns in the infant, whose identity the *Gre-gree* man determines. The tribes are divided into petty kingdoms, and these are sub-divided into districts. The *Devil-laws* are the high laws; and the *Devil-Bush* is the supreme court. "No man is regarded a gentleman who has not ten or twenty wives. Some men of influence have fifty or sixty."

ORIGIN OF THE COLONY.

In 1787, Granville Sharp and other British philanthropists started on the west coast of Africa the colony of Sierra Leone. This is a peninsula about twenty-five miles in length, washed by the Atlantic on the northwest and south, and partly bound on the east by a bay formed by the Sierra Leone River. The colonists were about 1,200 negroes, who had joined the English forces in the first American Revolution. At the close of the war, they went to Nova Scotia. Thence, with some Maroons from Jamaica, they were transported, in 1792, to Sierra Leone. Negroes captured from slave-vessels were added to the colony In 1856, they numbered about 50,000 inhabitants in the enjoyment of many advantages, educational and religious. The chief city is Freetown. In 1789, Dr. Samuel Hopkins, of Newport, R. I., who had been since 1773 in correspondence with Rev. Ezra Stiles, afterwards President of Yale College, and others, on the subject of forming in Africa a settlement of negroes from this country, wrote to Granville Sharp to learn whether colonists from America would be received at Sierra

Leone. In 1787, Dr. William Thornton, a Virginian, had been in Newport, proposing to form such a settlement "with free blacks from New England." On December 31, 1800, the House of Delegates of Virginia requested the Governor of the State to correspond with the President of the United States, for the removal of certain colored people from the State. In 1805, Africa was determined for the settlement, "to include free blacks and slaves who might be emancipated." The President, Mr. Jefferson, applied to the Sierra Leone Company to receive the proposed colonists, but was refused. In December, 1816, Gen. Charles Fenton Mercer renewed the subject in the House of Delegates of Virginia. His resolution was passed on the 23d of the same month. The same day a meeting was held in Washington City, under the influence of Dr. Robert Finley, of New Jersey, who had, the year before, written on the expediency of forming such a colony, and was visiting Washington to confer on the subject with his brother-in-law, Elias B. Caldwell, and Francis S. Key, to whom Gen. Mercer had communicated his intention in 1815, and who had pledged to him their co-operation. The constitution of the Colonization Society, which owed its origin to these various influences in different parts of the country, was adopted December 28, 1816, and the officers elected January 1st, 1817. ↳ January 21, 1820, the first colonists, eighty-nine in number, embarked on the Elizabeth from New York. Cape Mesurado was purchased December 15th, 1821. On January 7, 1822, the colonists landed on the island. In a few months, under the conduct of Elijah Johnson, they removed to the Cape, where was started the germ of the Liberian Republic.

DIVISIONS OF TERRITORY, AND PRINCIPAL SETTLEMENTS.

R. B. Medberg wrote: "The northerly portion of Liberia, including Marshall, is called Monrovia, and is under the jurisdiction of the American Colonization Society. Bassa Cove Colony, including Edina and Bassa Cove, is under the patronage of the New York and Pennsylvania Colonization Societies. The colony at Sinou or Greenville was settled by the Mississippi Colonization Society; and the Maryland

Colony at Cape Palmas, seventy or eighty miles eastward of Sinou, was founded by the Maryland Colonization Society.

Monrovia, in Monrovia County, is situated on the left bank of the Mesurado River, on ground which rises into a lofty promontory. New Georgia is five miles northward from Monrovia, and composed of some three hundred recaptured Congos and Elbos. In 1842, the Baptist Church there had seventy members. Caldwell, on the St. Paul's River, is eight miles from Monrovia. It once had 600 or 800 inhabitants. The location is unhealthy. Millsburg, on the same river, is twelve miles from Caldwell, and is a comparatively healthy place. Thirty-five miles down the coast from Monrovia is Marshall, an agricultural town, near the mouth of the Junk River. Seventy miles southeast of Monrovia, in latitude 6° N. and longitude 10° W., is Edina, a pleasant village of 300 or 400 people, having the ocean on the southwest, and on the east a broad expanse of water formed by the union of the St. John's and Mecklin, or Bensen, Rivers. On the opposite side of this basin stands Bassa Cove, containing some 300 inhabitants. About seventy miles from Edina, on the Sinou River, is Sinou. Among the colonists are some 1,500 native Africans, who have come into the colonies to learn 'Merica fash.'

CHANGE OF GOVERNMENT.

At first the government was administered by officers appointed by the Colonization Society. By the advice of the Society, the colony proclaimed its independence on August 24, 1847. The Republic of Liberia, with a constitution similar to that of the United States, was organized at the beginning of the next year. It has been recognized by the principal nations of Christendom. "Some 300 miles of the coast, from St. Paul's River to Calvary River, belonged to this Republic, and the remainder to Maryland in Liberia, which in 1854 passed from a colonial State into national independence."

A HAPPY PEOPLE.

A United States officer, writing from Liberia, May 12th, 1848, says: "The people are moral and religious, and, to judge from what I saw at Monrovia, I do not think, for the number of the inhabitants, there is a greater amount of human happiness to be found in any part of the world."

A PEOPLE PREPARED FOR THE LORD.

"Contiguous to these communities are unnumbered native towns, containing in all a vast number of souls. These are under the pious watch-care of the colonies, and are gradually becoming assimilated to them in manners and customs. They are a people prepared for the Lord. Their head men will give encouragement to the evangelist, and call the congregations together to hear the word. Their sons will be gladly brought to the schools to be taught the elements of knowledge, and to receive instruction in spiritual things. Very important facilities may be furnished by the churches already formed in the colonies. Every consideration connected with the subject invests it with a solemnity and interest which language is too feeble to describe."

OTHER MISSIONS.

IN WESTERN AFRICA.

In Western Africa, as in Southern Africa, the Moravians were the earliest evangelical missionaries. In 1836, they began work on the Gold Coast. Since that time, stations have been established by English and Scottish Societies (1795 and 1797); The Wesleyan Missionary Society (1796); the American Presbyterian Mission (1832); the American Board (1833); The American Episcopal Mission (1822); the Methodist Episcopal Church in the United States (1833); the Basle Missionary Society (1826); and the Triennial Baptist Convention in 1821. Details are impracticable. Some 80 stations have been established; 13,154 church members baptized; and 12,877 pupils gathered. The influence has been potent and far-reaching. The expense, in more than silver and gold, has been great; but has not the gain been greater? "Many valuable lives," remarks Rev. Henry

Newcomb, "have been sacrificed in attempting to plant the gospel on these inhospitable shores. But they have not been sacrificed in vain. If more than 13,000 souls, or a moiety of them, have been saved, it would be worth the sacrifice of every missionary who has landed there. But the results of the self-sacrificing labors reach far beyond what appears in statistical tables." As the work of the Triennial Convention is cognate to our own, we shall trace its Mission in Liberia and among the Bassas, as far as the origin of the Liberian Mission of the Southern Baptist Convention.

MISSION OF THE TRIENNIAL CONVENTION.

At the "Missionary Jubilee," Deacon William Crane, of Baltimore, said: "I assisted in November, 1813, to organize the Richmond Foreign Missionary Society, probably the earliest missionary body in our denomination south of Philadelphia.

In 1815, I was engaged in a gratuitous colored tri-weekly night school in the now Old African Church, of Richmond, with Lott Carey and fifteen or twenty more of the leading members. The same year, the Richmond Baptist Missionary Society was originated, with a view solely of missions in Africa, but auxiliary to this body. They made me President, or Corresponding Secretary, for fifteen or twenty years, and also repeatedly sent me as their delegate to the old Triennial Convention.

In January, 1821, Lott Carey and Colin Teage were sent to Liberia as missionaries of our Convention, with a considerable number of colonists. It devolved on me to superintend their outfit." These first missionaries were colored men. In February, 1822, they went from Freetown, of the English colony of Sierra Leone, to Monrovia. In 1823, a church was formed and six were baptized. In 1824, nine more were added by baptism, and a house of worship was erected. Mr. Carey, who was a man of unusual intelligence and energy, became its pastor. Mr. Teage returned to Sierra Leone. In 1825, Rev. Calvin Holton joined the Mission; but soon died. The same year, Mr. Carey was appointed Vice-Agent of the Colony of Liberia, and soon after, Vice-Governor. At his death, the church numbered one hundred. Mr. Teage was made pastor, and soon the membership was nearly doubled. In 1830, Rev. Benjamin Skinner was appointed a missionary, and arrived with his family in December. In six months, all had fallen victims to the climate. For five years the work was prosecuted by pious emigrants. Among them were Rev. A. W. Anderson, Rev. John Lewis, and Rev. Hilary Teage, son of Colin Teage. In 1834, Dr. Ezekiel Skinner, who was a preacher and physician in Connecticut, and the father of the missionary, went to Liberia to reside. In 1835, Rev. William G. Crocker and Rev. W. Mylne were appointed missionaries. They selected Edina as their station. At Bassa Cove a church-house was erected, and in 1836, sixteen were baptized. Mr. Mylne was *pro tempore* the pastor. Mr. Crocker published, in 1836, a spelling-book and vocabulary of the Bassa language. In 1837, the Edina Mission houses were completed and occupied. Among the pupils of the school was an intelligent son of King Kober, who subsequently became an assistant of Mr. Crocker. In May, 1838, Mr. Mylne returned to the United States with hopelessly shattered health. The same year, Rev. Ivory Clarke and wife reinforced the Mission. Mr. Clarke took the pastorate of the Edina Church, and Mr. Crocker went to Madebbi. In September, 1839, Miss Rizpah Warren arrived as a teacher and married Mr. Crocker. She died on August 28th, 1840. Mr. Crocker, who had been very sick, went to Cape Palmas. In July, 1841, his illness forced him home. In December, 1840, Messrs. Alfred A. Constantine and Joseph Fielding, with their wives, arrived with the view of going into the interior. In six weeks, both Mr. and Mrs. Fielding were dead. Mr. and Mrs. Constantine, unable to stand the climate, returned to America in June, 1842. The health of Mr. Crocker improving, he returned to Africa in February, 1844, having married Miss Mary B. Chadbourne, of Newburyport. While occupying the pulpit in Monrovia, the second day after his arrival, he had an attack, from which he died in two days. "He was a missionary of truly apostolic stamp, and deserves to be enrolled among the foremost of the heroic men who have braved every peril and sacrificed life itself for the benefit of the benighted children of Africa." Mrs. Crocker joined Mr. and Mrs. Clarke.

Her health failing, she returned to the United States. In January, 1845, the principal station was moved from Edina to Bexley. The young chief, Kong Kober, took charge of an out-station at Little Bassa, and assumed the name of his lamented teacher, Lewis Kong Crocker. Mr. and Mrs. Clarke carried forward the work—translating, preparing books, and teaching. "The morals and manners of the people were greatly improved. All the interests of civilization were promoted, and many of the natives embraced the gospel and were baptized according to its requirements." Mr. Clarke's health succumbed. He longed for reinforcement. He quitted the field in April, 1848, and died at sea on the 26th of that month. Kong Crocker was faithful at Little Bassa. Rev. Jacob Vonbrunn, assisted by two teachers, had charge at Bexley. On January 15th, 1852, Messrs. Henry B. Goodman and J. S. Shermer, with their families, who sailed from Norfolk, Va., arrived at Bexley. Mrs. Shermer died in September, 1853; and Mrs. Crocker fell on sleep at Monrovia in November of the same year. Mr. Shermer was constrained by failing health to return to America —leaving Mr. and Mrs. J. S. Goodman, both enfeebled, to prosecute the work which had cost so many sacrifices, but which was so full of hope. For the further labors of the Missionary Union, we must refer to the publications of that Society.

ORIGIN OF OUR MISSION IN LIBERIA.

THE BOARD AND CONVENTION.

The Mission of the Boston Board was traced by us to the year 1853. In 1854, our Board reported: "14 stations; 11 churches; 153 communicants; 80 additions during the year previous; 11 schools; and 30 pupils." The work originated eight years before. On February 2, 1846: "It was moved that the Board deem it expedient, as soon as practicable, to establish a mission on the coast of Africa." In their first report to the Convention, held in Richmond, Va., June, 1846, the Board said: "Africa is doubtless to be evangelized. * * * The most encouraging prospects of success urge the immediate occupancy of the field." A committee reported and the Convention adopted as follows: "Twenty-five years ago, a little church of only seven members, with Lott Carey as pastor, was organized in an upper room of a private dwelling in this city. That church is now the first Baptist Church of Monrovia. It has become the mother of some seven to ten churches, and also of the Providence Baptist Association of Liberia. Since that period, hundreds of colored Baptists have emigrated from this country, and settled permanently in the land of their forefathers. They will gladly coöperate with the Board of this Convention, and particularly with the vast numbers of their colored brethren in the Southern States, in spreading the gospel over that benighted country. * * Your committee deem it peculiarly important that at least two well-educated, well-qualified missionaries, fitted for the work, should be employed there as leaders in the African mission." In the fall of the same year, Rev. John Day and Rev. A. L. Jones were appointed our missionaries, the one at Bexley, the other at Cape Palmas.

TRANSFER DISCUSSED.

As early as the fall of 1845, the Boards of Boston and Richmond had corresponded on "the transfer of missions." A report, offered by Dr. Francis Wayland, and adopted in Philadelphia, October 24, 1845, by the Northern Board, was sent to our Board. This report held that "no transfer could be made without the full consent of the missionaries;" but that the "missionaries should have the choice of the associations; * * * * and if any of them should prefer to change their relation from us to the Southern Board, they should, in the spirit of fraternal regard, be allowed every facility for doing so." In the *Missionary Journal* of July, 1846, the following appeared: "It is known to our readers that the question of transferring the African Mission from the Boston to the Southern Board has been, for some time past, under serious consideration. It is not probable that any transfer will be made. If our brethren at the North deem it best * * to continue their operations on the coast of Africa, we shall pray for and rejoice in their success. At the same time, the Southern Board are contemplating the vigorous prosecution of the work in that field. Rev. J. Clarke, of the Northern Board, wrote from "British Akrah, April 3, 1846: Of late our attention has been several times directed to the subject of transferring the African Mission to the Southern Board, and at last to that of abandoning the mission. We have consented to the transfer, provided it be found best for the cause of missions on the whole. But to abandon it, would be wicked in the extreme. * * * How many of the poor, benighted Africans are looking to the Baptists of America to give them the only thing which will save them from an awful hell, while these same Baptists are deliberating whether they shall recall their missionaries, and abandon the field on which the beloved Crocker, Fielding, and their wives fought and fell. * * Oh, let it not be named among you; publish it not to the world; let it no more come into your holy convocations; but declare to the world and the church that you are ready to send men to Africa, and clear your garments of the blood of these poor heathen."

THE CHURCHES ALMOST FORSAKEN.

The *Journal* of September, 1847, says: "Brother Day represents these missions as containing rather more than three hundred members, nearly all destitute of pastors, and in a feeble and declining condition. He exclaims: 'Will the Lord cast us off forever? Is his mercy clean gone? Hath God forgotten to be gracious? * * Whichever way I look I find cause of grief, whether to the churches, the colony, or the poor heathen. The churches are in a state so low, they seem almost forsaken. * * Of what can I write good news? All the good I know is prospective. I look forward to a better time * * when undefiled religion will exert its influence."

RELIGION IN MONROVIA COUNTY.

The following, from Brother Hilary Teage, son of Colin Teage, and editor of the *Liberian Herald*, under date of November 17th, 1847, gives a more cheering view of things in Monrovia County, Liberia: "In this county are nine villages—Farmington, Marshall, Monrovia, New Georgia, Caldwell, Virginia, New Orleans, and Millsburg. In each of these villages, except Farmington and New Orleans, is a Baptist Church. At New Orleans we expect to institute one next week. In the county are nine Baptist preachers. Of these, two, Brother F. S. James, at Virginia, and myself, are ordained. Brother Smart, a native African, but for a long time a resident of Charleston, S. C., preaches for the church at Junk. There are three preachers at Monrovia, John T. Richardson, A. B. Henderson, and myself. We minister to the churches here. The church at New Georgia numbers sixty-three members. All but five are native Africans. A more intelligent church is not found in the colony. All our churches have six meetings for worship during the week. Regular contributions vary in the churches. In Monrovia, each male is required to give twelve and a half cents, and each female six and a quarter cents, per month. Brethren James and Underwood labor at Virginia, where most of the members at Caldwell have attached themselves. There are two preachers at Millsburg, Brethren David White and Adam Luckburt, both zealous and good men. I feel safe in putting down two hundred and eighty as the regular communicants in the county."

CHRIST'S VISIBLE BODY.

"A fundamental article of our creed is, that the church of Christ is a *spiritual* building, and we hold to none but *believers'* baptism. A girl whom I rescued from slavery about twelve years ago is a member of Christ's visible body. She is married to L. K. Crocker, of the Baptist Mission at Bassa. In the number and conduct of our converts, we would compare favorably with any other mission on this coast."

WITHDRAWAL OF THE UNION.

July 7th, 1856: "A letter was received from Rev. J. G. Warren, Corresponding Secretary of the American Baptist Missionary Union, informing that they had decided to withdraw their missionaries from Liberia, and inquiring if this Board would purchase their mission premises at Bassa."

BIRD'S-EYE VIEW.

In order to avoid, in the earlier biographical sketches which will follow, references to persons, places, and things, of which the reader may not have heard, we shall present a bird's-eye view of our work in Liberia during the first decade from 1846 to 1856: .

NEW VIRGINIA.

This station is on the St. Paul's River, a few miles from Monrovia. In 1848, Rev. F. S. James was located there as pastor and teacher; and reported "nearly one hundred additions to the church" within the year. He preached also at New Orleans, and at several native towns. He died in 1849, greatly lamented. In September, 1851, Rev. Jos. M. Harden was settled at Virginia. The school numbered, that year, one hundred and eighteen pupils. He had charge also of four other churches. In 1854, twenty-two were baptized. He was a valuable missionary; and, in 1855, was transferred to Lagos, in connection with the Yoruba Mission.

BEXLEY.

From 1846 to 1854, this station was under the charge of Rev. John Day, and enjoyed a course of uninterrupted and increasing prosperity. In the Board's report of 1848, Mr. Day is quoted as saying: "The work I call *yours*, as I believe it will be the glory of the *South* to prove themselves the great benefactors of the negro race." In 1850, the Board say: "Our missionary writes, I am not discouraged, for I have never witnessed such bright prospects for the mission." Mr. Day was a great sufferer in person and family; but he humbly said: "I murmur not." He tells of the death of a Bassa headman, baptized in 1846, who was remarkably fond of the Bible, and read and expounded it to his countrymen. Dying, he said: "I am going to heaven." "That," says Brother Day, "that cry I 'am going to heaven' from the dying Bassa headman rewards me for all my toils, and pays a thousand-fold for all the expenditures of the mission." In 1854, he says: "The natives are becoming more and more enlightened, see more clearly that God controls the affairs of men, and that they are accountable to him and must appear before his righteous bar." In 1855, twenty-four were baptized. "On my own land is a village of say thirty inhabitants. You would suppose them Christians. They solemnly attend the reading of the word, and kneel reverently in prayer."

Mr. Day opened in Bexley "a manual labor school." In 1849, there were forty-five boys in the school. In 1850, the school contained fifty pupils. Mr. Gurley, Secretary of the American Colonization Society, said: "The school presented scenes to awaken gratitude in every pious heart." In 1851, our missionary said: "The intelligent, easy demeanor of these native youths would readily make them pass for colonists. I hope that most of my large boys are thinking of eternity."

BASSA COVE.

In 1848, the Board stated: "At Bassa Cove is a flourishing school under the care of Brother Elkins. The captives and the natives are doing well, and are deriving' great benefit from the school. Brother A. P. Davis was preaching here, at Edina, and in the adjacent native towns, with good success. In 1849, Brother Davis was the missionary. Besides attending to the school and church at Bassa Cove, he made frequent preaching excursions among the natives" as far as Cape Palmas, and among the churches and stations on the St. Paul's River. In one of these towns, he baptized John B. Davis, his interpreter, of whom more will be said. For some years, there was no missionary at Bassa Cove. The Board reported in 1853, Charles Henry as the teacher. The church had twenty-three members. Missionaries of other stations rendered aid as they could. In 1855, Brother Davis is again at the station. He says: "The indications are highly favorable. I have baptized seven, and have nine to baptize. I can have as many in my school as I can attend to."

EDINA.

In the notice of Bassa Cove, it was stated that Brother Davis preached at Edina. In 1849, the Board reported Rev. J. H. Cheeseman as appointed to this station. 1850: "The Board have a flourishing station and school of sixty pupils under Rev. J. H. Cheeseman. Brother Cheeseman, besides being preacher and teacher here does missionary and superintending work in the region around. Last spring he opened a school ten miles up the Mecklin River." In 1851, nine baptisms were reported. In 1852, "continued prosperity and encouragement." Baptized a native who "gave evidence in his own vernacular that he is born of God." 1853: Gracious revival after most discouraging season from wars between colonists and natives. In 1854, several baptized. 1855: The schools at Edina and Buchanan very encouraging, and number over eighty. Ten baptized. Edina is a very important field.

MONROVIA.

In 1849, the church there having no pastor, the Board reported that B. J. Drayton had been directed to devote a part of his time to them. This he did with success. At length, as stated in the report of 1851, A. T. Wood was stationed there. He was under the patronage of the Board only a short time. In the report of 1853, H. Teage was missionary there. More than fifty had been added to the church, and the school was flourishing. Death took our brother away in the midst of great usefulness and bright prospects. His place was temporarily filled by J. T. Richardson, under whom the cause prospered. In 1854, it was stated that he had baptized twenty-seven. During that year, Rev. John Day removed from Bexley to Monrovia. He exerted a healthful and widespread influence, and enjoyed a gracious revival. Much will be seen hereafter of his work here and in the "Day's Hope" schools.

CAPE PALMAS.

In 1849, B. J. Drayton is reported at this station. 1850: "Brother Drayton preaches regularly, superintends the schools, and visits from house to house. Congregations large. The labors of our missionaries are highly appreciated by the natives." 1851: The natives are still calling for the God-man to come and teach them. Native fields are opened a hundred miles back. 1852: Seventeen additions to the church; Sunday-school, one hundred and two; day-school, thirty-one. In 1853: The church and school still progressing; one hundred and thirteen in the Sunday-school. A school was established in the house of a native headman, William Davis. Four baptisms. 1854: The work advancing. Revival enjoyed. Davis Town continues to observe the Lord's Day. Four baptized. Influence of the station good on colonists as well as natives.

JUNK

is about forty miles south of Monrovia, on the river of the same name. Marshall is the county town. A small church and school have been sustained since 1850. They have had occasional labors from the missionaries.

NEW GEORGIA.

This settlement is composed chiefly of re-captured Africans. More than forty years ago, in 1836, a Baptist Church was established, which enjoyed the labors of Lott Carey, Colin Teage, Waring, and other efficient ministers. In 1849, a flourishing school is reported under William A. Johnson. In 1850, the school was under W. H. Stewart. It numbered sixty-eight. Several unordained members aided in divine services, and our missionaries gave occasional attention. In 1850, Brother Day baptized there thirteen persons. He said: "It is a heavenly place." In 1854: "The church and school are prospering. In the school, under W. H. Stewart, are fifty-one: in the church, eighty-four." 1855: Prosperous. Brother Joseph M. Harden missionary. Fourteen baptized. Brother W. H. Clarke, visiting this station, wrote: "I saw a native boy about twelve years old, a member of the church, who is quite a prodigy. His answers struck me with astonishment. To hear him talk, you would forget you were in Africa. Since Brother Harden's removal to Lagos, the station prospers under Brother Underwood."

NEW ORLEANS: LOUISIANA.

In 1849, there was a school here under W. H. Stewart. In 1852 Brother Harden was preaching at the station. He wrote: "The church at Louisiana, constituted last November with eight members, numbers nineteen. I visit them as often as I can, and feel greatly interested in their spiritual welfare. I would be thankful for any assistance in building their house of worship." 1853: "This station is supplied by Brother Richardson. The prospect of building up an efficient church is cheering." 1855: "The church in Louisiana is increasing in numbers and influence. Five baptisms during the year." The progress during 1856 still encouraging.

SINOU.

This county is on the coast above Cape Palmas. The Board state in 1850 that it had recently been adopted as a station, and Rev. R. E. Murray appointed missionary. The prospect was encouraging. 1851: Missionary, R. E. Murray; teachers, Mr. and Mrs. Lewis. The church numbered "more than eighty;" the school, ninety-nine scholars. 1852: Rev. J. Roberts had been added to the mission. There were two chapels—one at Greenville, and one at Reidsville. Everything prosperous; several had been baptized. 1853: Preaching "regularly kept up at Greenville, Farmersville, Middle Settlement, and Lexington." Several baptisms. 1854: Rev. Mr. Batteese had been associated with the mission. Brother Murray wrote: "The conduct of the converted Africans is so correct, * * and their influence on their heathen brethren is so good, that my heart is filled with strong desires for operations on a more extended scale." 1855: *Lexington*, Israel Mason and J. Strother, teachers. This station in Sinou County has engaged the labors of Brethren R. E. Murray and Israel Mason, and during the past year shared in the manifestations of the Lord's power and grace. Two baptized." *Greenville:* "Missionaries, R. E. Murray and J. Roberts. Here the sway of truth is beginning to be felt. The church has increased much. Baptisms, twenty-three. *Farmersville:* A church was constituted April 9th with twenty-three members by our missionaries, Murray and Roberts; four baptisms. In Sinou, much is done for the salvation of the natives. It is an important point, "offering great facilities for labor among both colonists and natives."

MILLSBURG.

This town in Mesurado County had been frequently visited by our missionaries, and "quite a number were added to the church." In 1850, it is mentioned as of sufficient importance to be occupied as a station. 1851: Edward Paul, teacher; scholars, thirty-eight. The church occasionally supplied by missionaries, and "Brother R. White, who resides in that region." 1853: R. White, missionary. 1854: Brother Richardson wrote, "Our Zion is on the march." Sixteen or more baptized. 1855: Besides Mr. White's labors, "two licensed preachers of the church are active in spreading the gospel." Brother White wrote: "Everything appears to be progressive." Eleven baptized. This church shared in the gracious revival of 1855.

CALDWELL.

For some years this station had no settled missionary. The report of 1853 says: "Caldwell—J. T. Richardson, missionary. The number and efficiency of the church is increasing." 1854: "Our cause is gaining ground. The wild men of the woods bow before the Lord, confess their sins, and acknowledge that there is no other name given whereby they must be saved but the Lord Jesus Christ." 1855: "The church, though small, is having many additions and otherwise improving. Baptisms during the year, four."

CLAY ASHLAND.

Missionary, J. T. Richardson. This town bids fair to be one of the most influential on the St. Paul's River. The Church has a new and neat house of worship. The school, forty-two pupils. Our missionary says: "The heathen say, 'bring God-palaver to our towns; take our children into your schools and teach them God's book.'" Brother Clark, on the way to Yoruba, preached the opening sermon in the new church. During 1854, five were baptized.

NEW KENTUCKY.

A new church was constituted here by Brethren Davis, Roberts, Cheeseman, and Richardson, with some thirty members. About forty or fifty Christians are found in the settlement. J. T. Richardson, missionary.

NEW STATIONS AND LABORERS.

At Careysburg: J. Woodson, preacher; Julia Hazzard, teacher. At Vonbrunnville: Jacob Von Brunn, preacher and teacher. At King Graystown: James J. Powell, teacher.

SIERRA LEONE MISSION.

This mission was organized in 1855 by the appointment of George R. Thompson as missionary. The Board reported that from the representations of Brethren Bowen, Kingdon, and Day, "it is one of the most inviting fields on the African coast." In 1857, twenty baptisms were reported.

BAPTISMS.

In Liberia and Sierra Leone not less, probably, than three hundred have been baptized.

ELI BALL AND JOHN KINGDON.

Mr. BALL'S APPOINTMENT AND IMPRESSIONS.

On the 8*th of April*, 1851, a proposition of Rev. Eli Ball, to visit our stations on the coast of Africa, " with a view to his own usefulness" was accepted by the Board. Mr. Ball sailed from Savannah, about the middle of December, 1851, " to secure definite information, and to learn the best means of conducting our operations." The Convention pronounced "the visit of Brother Ball to Liberia, well timed and fitted to do much good." The impression made by most of the Missionaries and Stations was favorable.

Mr. Ball related this incident: "Wm. Davis, the head man, is brother to the King of the Grebos. He has begun a Reformed town. He allows no work on the Lord's Day, no sassy wood, and no *gre-gree.* The following is the agreement between him and Brother Drayton: This certifies that, I, William Davis, head man of this town, do agree and promise to sustain the Southern Baptist Mission in my town, and also to support preaching and to encourage it by my example. I will also give my house for the use of the school. I agree to have no labor on the Lord's Day; my children and people shall attend teaching and preaching. I will take care of all books put into my care.

"*April 8th,* 1852." An interesting scene at Bexley, the residence of our Missionary Day, is thus described by Mr. Ball: "In company with Brother Marshall, Brother Davis, and a Brother Shackelford, from the Northern Neck of Virginia, I went up to meeting. After a sermon the wife of Brother Day was received by the church for baptism, and I had the pleasure to baptize her in the beautiful river St. John's, that flows along by his door. How cheering the event! how delightful the scene! Never shall I forget that day—that soul-reviving meeting. While I stood among the evergreen trees that lined the bank, and saw the still broad river flowing by in noiseless grandeur, I thought of Jordan, of John and of Christ, and primitive days seemed present. Strange, it appeared to me, that, any Christian who admits that the immersion of a believer in water, to make a profession of religion, is Christian baptism according to the New Testament, should try to make something else do."

Brother Ball reported to the Board, that "the missionaries, though none of them had received the advantages of thorough mental training, were in advance of the people in piety, talents, and knowledge, and that they should be retained in their work. The schools, though susceptible of great improvement, are doing much good, and, in a survey of the whole field, he found much to excite joyous and grateful feelings." The effect of Brother Ball's visit upon the missions seemed happy.

A member of the Monrovian Church wrote: "I think it advisable to send out a brother yearly to meet with us in our Association, and confer with us about matters pertaining to the general spread of the gospel in this land. I had the pleasure of Brother Ball's company in visiting some of our missions up the St. Paul's. I am happy to say that, every heart seemed cheered, and every thing, in a spiritual sense, wore a cheerful aspect. Oh, that the Lord may bless the feeble means used for the salvation of the tens of thousands of Africa's sons and daughters around us, who are without hope!"

Brother R. E. Murray, who with J. Roberts is located at Sinou Station, which "is in a very encouraging condition," wrote: "Brother Ball arrived here in company with Brother Cheeseman. He has taken the hearts of the brethren. His visit will be attended with the most important and lasting effects. It has animated my own soul, and imparted life to the church. It will give spirit and energy to our operations here and throughout Liberia."

HIS DEATH.

January 11th, 1853—Rev. Eli Ball was re-appointed "as a suitable delegate to the Liberian Mission, to sail in November of that year.

August 1st, 1853, his decease is recorded by the Board, with the consolation that "Providence permitted him to close his days so peacefully in the midst of his family and friends." In 1854, the following was reported to the Convention: Rev. Eli Ball had indicated his willingness to repeat his visit to the Coast of Africa, and the Board gladly availing themselves of his services, re-appointed him to this special agency. He was arranging to leave by the earliest opportunity, when his work on earth was cut short by the mandate of his Divine Master, whose will was that the toils of earth should be exchanged for the employments of the heavenly world. His death was a sad event to the friends of missions, and especially to the cause of African Evangelization. The consolation of the Board was that "he who reigns over all, when he takes away one instrument can provide others, and that he will make all things work together for good to them that are called according to his purpose."

MR. KINGDON'S BRIEF MISSION.

On June 14th, 1854, Rev. John Kingdon was appointed temporary Agent and Superintendent of the Board to visit the Liberian Missions, with a view to their enlargement and increased efficiency * * and was authorized, July 3d, "to make the most economical arrangement for reaching the colony of Liberia, by the way of London."

On the 23d of April, 1855, the tidings were received that this brother also had fallen asleep. Under date of the 30th April, is *this* record: "Brother John Kingdon of Baltimore volunteered his services to fill the place left vacant by the lamented Ball, to visit our stations in Liberia and Yoruba. In the prosecution of this perilous duty he fell, but not until he had performed good service for his Divine Master. The Board deplore his death as a calamity: but in it they still recognize the hand of God." * * * Mr. Kingdon had been connected for several years with the English Baptist Mission on the Island of Jamaica, and his experience in the missionary work qualified him to perform the duties of the special agency. He was requested, on his way, to go to London, to secure ready transmission of supplies to Yoruba. He visited Sierra Leone, and most of our stations in Liberia, attending the Association at Edina; and had returned to Monrovia to take the steamer down to Lagos, the seaport of our Yoruba Mission. He was stricken with fever, and in a few days borne to the grave. His heart was in the work. It was difficult for him to repress the purpose to do more than his strength allowed. His appointment was not in vain. He infused new life into our missionary work and cheered the hearts of our brethren toiling in the field."

GRANDEUR OF THE FIELD.

In their Annual Report of 1853 the Board said: "There is perhaps no portion of the world where, on a larger scale and at less cost, the blessings of salvation may be communicated. * * It would not be saying too much to aver that tens of thousands of heathen are now immediately accessible to evangelic influence. * * It would not be an unreasonable expansion of our work, if from Cape Mount to Cape Palmas, about five hundred miles, the number of laborers were trebled, and all the appliances of Christian effort were brought to bear with greatly increased power upon the different stations."

LIBERIA AND SIERRA LEONE MISSIONS.

OUR COLORED MISSIONARIES.

Rev. JOHN DAY and Rev. A. L. JONES.
THEIR APPOINTMENT.

John Day was born at Hicksford, Va., February 18, 1797; baptized in 1820; licensed to preach, 1821; and went to Liberia, 1830. On February 2d, 1846, "It was moved that the Board of Foreign Missions deem it expedient, as soon as practicable, to establish a mission on the coast of Africa; and that the Corresponding Secretary be instructed to make inquiries concerning suitable persons for missionaries for the African Mission." On the 7th of September, of the same year, "The following resolutions were adopted:

"1st. *Resolved,* That Brother John Day be appointed a missionary to occupy a mission station at Grand Bassa, on the western coast of Africa, and labor among the natives in its vicinity.

"2d. *Resolved,* That Brother Alexander L. Jones be appointed a missionary to labor at Cape Palmas, on the western coast of Africa, and among the natives in that vicinity."

QUALIFICATIONS OF BROTHER JONES.

"Mr. Jones is a native of Richmond, but has spent the greater part of his life on the coast of Africa. His educational advantages have been good. He speaks the language of those among whom he will labor with fluency, and is regarded as in every way well qualified for the office of a Christian missionary."

APPROPRIATION TO THE MISSIONARIES.

On November 2d, 1846, the following was adopted by the Board: "Salary for John Day, six hundred dollars per annum; for A. L. Jones, five hundred dollars per annum. The above amounts are for their entire expenditures. In case of the death of a missionary, leaving a family of children, the Committee recommend an appropriation of forty dollars per annum for each child up to seven, and fifty dollars from the age of seven to thirteen."

PAINFUL REVERSE.

In 1847, the Board reported to the Convention that they had "appointed Brother John Day, who has been, for several years, in the employ of the Boston Board, to labor among the Bassa tribes; and A. L. Jones, a young and talented minister, residing at Cape Palmas, to be engaged within the limits of the Maryland Colony. It was considered a favorable indication of Providence that such men could be secured; but the Board were required to suffer a painful reverse in this their first effort to bless the tribes of Africa. Before the notice of our appointment reached the coast, Mr. Jones had been called to mingle in higher and happier employments in the world above. His loss will be painfully felt, and to human view, it might seem that it could not be easily repaired; but God seeth not as man seeth. He can raise up other and better instruments, even by means of this afflictive bereavement. The Lord reigneth; let his people still trust and rejoice in him."

MISSIONARY, AND LIEUTENANT GOVERNOR.

Brother Day wrote: "I had recommended the appointment of Brother Jones; but a few days after was called to mourn his death. When I wrote I thought I would do what I could in the service of your Board, and support myself. When, however, the intelligence came of my appointment, I took the subject more fully into consideration, and have determined to give the remainder of life to the work of a missionary, under the patronage of your Board. My mercantile business I close, so as to commence unencumbered the first day of next month. The office of Judge I resign, and would immediately resign the office of Superintendent of public affairs; but, without being consulted, I was elected Lieutenant Governor, and as I cannot resign that office without some little inconvenience to the people, I have concluded to retain the office of Superintendent, as I am paid one hundred dollars for the little service I render, and apply that to procuring an interpreter."

DIVISION OF THE FIELD.

"Brother Day has been for many years," reported the Board, "connected with the Colony, and enjoys the confidence and esteem of all who know him, as a man of discretion and piety. Communications have been received informing us that he commenced his labors with the beginning of the present year.

"The Rev. Mr. Clark, of the Boston Board, is also laboring among the Bassa people; an arrangement has been made with Mr. Day to divide the field between them."

RESOLUTIONS ON BROTHER JONES' DEATH.

On March 19th, 1847, the following was adopted by the Board:

"*Resolved*, That the Board have heard with deep concern of the death of Brother A. L. Jones, who was our appointed missionary at Cape Palmas, on the western coast of Africa; and while with all due submission we bow to this mysterious dispensation, we cannot forbear expressing our anxious solicitude that the vacancy thus created may be speedily filled.

"*Resolved*, That we sincerely sympathize with the family of our deceased brother, and with the church with which he was connected; and pray that God may overrule this event to the good of his own cause at Cape Palmas, and the surrounding country."

SUPERVISOR OF THE FIELD.

August 2d, 1847, Brother Day was made Treasurer of the Mission, and was subsequently appointed, with Brother John H. Cheeseman, Executive Committee and Supervisor of the Field.

In 1848, Brother Day wrote: "I am preparing for a tour of one or two hundred miles into the interior that I may see the extent and prospects of the great work you have to accomplish." We give an item or two from his journal: "The old King of Tattou's town agreed, in behalf of his people, to relinquish the superstitious customs of the Bassas, and I agreed, in behalf of his Excellency, J. I. Roberts, that his people should enjoy all the rights and privileges of colonists. I preached on Repentance, in a small town, and the men stared me in the face, as if I were deranged, and asked, 'Are these things so?' The people of Dyemes said: 'We think man lives, but cannot tell where he goes. Sometimes we think he is like a goat. We are troubled about these things, and go to play.' At Blackwell's, the King, in his surtout of scarlet and gold, received me most kindly. His china and glass and cutlery, from Liverpool, were of superior quality. His many slaves love him for his great kindness. I promised to send a missionary. He said: 'The news is too good to be true.'" In the Missionary Journal, of November, 1848, he wrote: "The cordiality with which I am everywhere received by the natives, the attention they give to the word, their apparent desire for instruction, the readiness with which men who are worthy enter our houses, greatly encourage me. * * I may be a little enthusiastic, but I can see no reason why, under the blessing of heaven, my highest expectation may not be realized." Again he wrote: "Since the Cesters affair"—a fight between the Liberians and the native tribes in March, 1849—" thirteen of the head men about Bexley have put themselves under the protection of the Republic. * * * They say they are perfectly convinced that there is a God, and that he controls the affairs of men." In February, 1850, he thus appeals for Africa: "Shall the heathen of other countries be more cared for because their missionaries are better able to plead for them? Are they on that account nearer the Saviour's heart? No: 'though black, in his eyes these Bassas are comely.' For them he left the courts of heaven, for them he died, for them he rose, for them in heaven he intercedes. For them a special prophecy goes forth: 'Ethiopia shall soon stretch out her hands unto God.' 'Behold Philistia, and Tyre, and Ethiopia!' This is a ruined race; gone forever, unless God and his people lend a helping hand. Africa, bleeding, dying, ready to be buried, I leave thee in hands more able to plead thy cause." Again he writes: "The earth does not afford a better scope for the display of goodness, love, mercy, and power, than does the colored race. As long as I live I shall contribute to the great object of Africa's salvation. Those who bless Africa, God will bless, and those who curse Africa, God will curse." The work of organizing the forces at command was begun and carried forward with the promptness and vigor of able generalship. His reports of how he sent one missionary here, and another there; and directed one to do this, and another to do that, sounds more like an Apostle's words than those of a Baptist Bishop. Yet he felt the position too much for him, and he moderately but significantly wrote to the Board: "A talented, well-educated white man would not possess too much ability for your purposes."

TEACHING AND PREACHING.

Mr. Day had a manual-labor school at Bexley, which almost supported its boarding department. "Many of the boys," said he, "are the sons of head-men and petty kings, who were brought naked and untutored, and placed under these benign influences. The religious instruction they have received shows itself in their good behaviour. Messrs. Rambo and Hoffman examined some of my pupils and seemed delighted with their improvement, and the general prospects of our mission. My education, with the exception of two or three years in a common school, has been the result of my own efforts. I find it easy to grasp the principles of things, and I think I could write some little books which might be of some use to the Bassas. Mr. Crocker laid the foundation, why may I not build upon it?" "My school, of some fifty scholars," he wrote October 6th, 1849, "I flatter myself is not excelled by any native school in the Republic. * * * I am enjoying the luxury of doing good. I am preparing mothers to raise their children in the nurture and admonition of the Lord; young kings to rule in righteousness, and a large company to carry the word abroad. The young head men Benya and Howes are now itinerating in the country, reading and expounding the word of God, praying and exhorting among the natives." Of his own preaching tours, which extended from seventy-five to one hundred and fifty miles in the interior, he wrote: "I have preached to a thousand natives, and speaking low could be heard by the whole. Not a whisper, not a stir, until I had done. Every ear attention; every eye fixed. They knelt solemnly before their Master. A stranger would have thought them fit for the ordinances of the gospel." Rev. Mr. Gurley, Commissioner of the United States to Liberia, wrote January 20th, 1850: "Mr. Day and his associates in Christian labors appeared to me eminently devoted to the cause of the Redeemer: and the native school of the Superintendent, presented scenes to awaken the gratitude and joy of every pious heart. Mr. Day observed: 'In our schools are taught say three hundred and thirty children, ninety-two of whom are natives. To more than ten thousand natives the word of life is statedly preached, and in every settlement in these colonies, we have a church, to whom the various means of grace are administered, and in every village we have an interesting Sunday-school. In our Sunday-schools are taught, say four hundred colonists and two hundred natives; and all has been done at an expense of $4,680. We have baptized this year eighteen natives and seven colonists, besides those baptized by Messrs. Murray and Drayton, who have not reported. Although we cannot boast of many conversions, yet the regular progress of improvement in divine knowledge, both of colonists and natives, is truly encouraging."

"I cannot express too strongly my confidence in the great benefit to be anticipated from an earnest prosecution of our holy work in Africa. *All Africa is open to benevolent labors*, and I hope and pray that your Board will increase ten-fold their noble exertions to gather the poor children of the African forest into the fold of the Great Shepherd and Bishop of our souls."

HEALTH AND BEREAVEMENT.

"In the 1st Lord's Day of July, 1849," wrote Mr. Day, "after preaching, I was taken with a severe ague. My lungs were badly inflamed, and I discharged so much blood that I thought my appointed time was come." In 1850, Mr. Day was ill with lung fever for a month: and experienced a bitter affliction in the loss of his wife and daughter. In his anguish he cried: "I would not give a straw for life. But who will care for the poor heathen? I have worn out myself and can rest in peace. God is too wise and too good to do wrong: but, oh that dart, its wound it would seem will never be healed. That embrace, that look haunts me like a ghost. Asleep, awake, I see her smile in death. But I murmur not." Later he wrote: "Let me but be in the path of duty, with the promises of God to sustain me, and I can hope against hope and persevere, though mountains of difficulty oppose me. God is omnipotent, and he who has promised is faithful."

DAY'S HOPE AND MONROVIA.

"At their annual meeting at Norfolk, in 1852, the Board, after addresses by J. B. Jeter, B. Grimsley and W. F. Broaddus, resolved that a high school, or incipient college, should be established in connection with our mission in Africa. In February, 1854, Mr. Day, at the request of the Board, moved from Bexley to Monrovia, where the school was established under the name of Day's Hope." From that place he wrote: "There never has been, since my connection with the mission, a brighter prospect. If men of good moral character, enlarged minds, good common sense, and warm hearts, well acquainted with human nature, could be sent among the natives, glorious results might be expected. Few of the natives are so reckless as to stand up in defence of their superstitions. The knowledge of a God has spread through this country, so far as I have been. The way is now prepared for the faithful, the pious, the prayerful minister. I wish, sustained by my great Leader, never to cast away the shield, but twelve years of unremitted toil makes my constitution to quail, and admonishes me of the necessity of prudence—alas! a lesson I have too slowly learned."
* * * October 11th, 1856, he wrote: "Last Sunday one hundred and twenty children attended Sunday-school in the school edifice. Monday I found not a boy prepared to enter the higher department. The teacher had attempted to teach sixty-four boys, without classification. I organized the school and took the superintendence. The girl school, under Miss Lewis, is far in advance of the boys. I took in five

young preachers. I put them on the study of the Bible, English grammar, and history. I shall aim to make them acquainted with church history, evidences of Christianity, systematic divinity, and, if they can lay hold readily, the Greek language. To keep them from ranting, I shall teach a little pulpit oratory. The whole range of science would fit them better to preach the simple and sublime gospel of the Son of God. * * Could you hear the sagacious questions often propounded by the poor heathen, and the difficulties raised by the Mohammedans, you would see at once that a missionary needs a well furnished mind. The mind should have the grasp of the lion and the tongue of the child." Brother I. T. Richardson had written, August 13th, 1856: "The school edifice will reflect great credit on the denomination." And, Mr. Day, on September 9th: "The seminary is not equalled in symmetry and good workmanship in Monrovia." A little human nature appears in the following note from Brother Day: "Day's Hope, Monrovia, December 6th, 1856. My brethren here are whispering round, 'Day is getting up a separate interest; Day is about to establish another church.' No, Day is a servant of the most high God, and wishes to show to poor heathen the way of salvation. But, I shall not cease to cry until this is a complete missionary establishment, with its common, classical, and theological departments. I have a personal interest in it. How? *My soul is in it.*"

The church, under Brother Day, was signally blessed. The baptisms reported in 1857 for two years were thirty-four, and the church membership two hundred and twenty. "One object of Day's Hope was the training of young men, who might be indicated by the churches as qualified and called of God to preach the gospel."

The following is from the *Liberian Herald* of Monrovia: "The seminary is under the immediate care and superintendence of the Rev. John Day. A much better man for strict moral and Christian character cannot be found. We have been acquainted with the reverend gentleman for several years. The even and unassuming manner of his life has gained for him a general feeling of respect and esteem. Mr. Day's church in Monrovia excels those of any other denomination. Without disparagement to other congregations we may say, the Providence

Baptist Church is the best attended of any in this city; and we judge there must be more religion among them too." In *The Commission* of October, 1858, appears the following, evidently from Dr. A. M. Poindexter: "*Day's Hope.* The school at Monrovia is doing a good work under the superintendence of Brother Day. It has fully equalled our expectations thus far. But in the feeble state of his health, we feel some anxiety as to its failure. If a suitable *white man* could be found to take charge of it and to give a general supervision to the mission work in Liberia, great good would probably result. * * Brother Day has more than once suggested the propriety of sending one to take charge of the seminary. * * Is there any one who for the love of Christ and souls is willing to encounter the risk? We would suggest that unmarried white men are better suited than those who are married. We think the climate less dangerous to the male than the female. We simply express our own views."

PREMONITIONS.

May 8th, 1858, Mr. Day wrote: "Bishop Payne stopped at Bassa and to my grief he told me to-day that my moving from there had much broken that mission. * * I have wished to see the Board before I die that I might suggest many things which would be service to them." July 30th 1858, Mr. Richardson wrote: "Brother Day is too feeble to do anything in the way of traveling or labor." Our brother himself wrote: "What is to become of 'Day's Hope?' you ask. I had hoped you would send some one to take charge of it more capable than myself. This school is the hope of the mission. * * The Methodists have trained missionaries here, whom they would not fear to send anywhere. Our schools are eclipsed by the superior qualifications of their teachers. But don't despair. All is not gone. * * Send books! Philosophical, Theological, Historical, Classical, Scientific. Send books! I can safely say, the progress of my young men has equalled that of either of the other schools."

GATHERED TO HIS FATHERS.

In the Report of the Board in 1859, is this brief but mournful record: "Our brother, John Day, has been gathered to his fathers.

This event, of which we have been in painful expectation for some time, owing to the age and frequent sickness of our brother, must deeply affect the interests of our mission. Brother Day was the Superintendent of the Missions of Liberia and Sierra Leone. Upon information received from him, and his judgment as to men and measures, the Board have, to a considerable extent, relied. We trust that God, who gave him to us, and who has now called him to himself, will give others to perform the labors from which he has been called."

EXTRACTS FROM Prof. E. W. BLYDEN'S EULOGY.

LOVE OF METAPHYSICS.

Rev. John Day entered a theological class directed by Rev. Mr. Clopton. Rev. J. B. Jeter, of Richmond, Va., then quite a young man, also frequented Mr. Clopton's study. From Mr. Clopton, Mr. Day acquired that love for metaphysical discussion and research which those who attended his preaching could not fail to discover.

BURNING ZEAL FOR THE GOSPEL.

While pursuing his studies under Mr. Clopton, Liberia began to attract the attention of the people. He made up his mind to cast in his lot with those who were laboring to establish a home for themselves and their children. Coincident with the desire for a land of liberty, there was a burning zeal to preach the gospel to the degraded Africans who roam these forests.

GRAVE OF THE FAMILY.

Having sacrificed his property, he embarked in December, 1830, with a most amiable wife, and four interesting children, for this land, which so soon was to be the grave of the affectionate group.

A HOUSEHOLD WORD.

For hundreds of miles into the interior he preached to the people. Take the city of Buchanan as a center, and with a radius of 60 or 70 miles describe a semi-circle, and there is no point to which you can go within that semi-circle where the name of John Day is not a household word; and at many points you will readily recognize precious evidences of his toils and efforts.

AS JUDGE AND STATESMAN.

He studied closely and patiently the science of Jurisprudence, and the general principles of statesmanship. In 1853, he was placed, as the succesor of Chief Justice Benedict, at the head of the Judiciary, which position he held with dignity and credit until his demise. His charges and decisions discovered a deep insight into legal principles. In the Legislative Hall, his counsels were wise and judicious. He boldly advocated the Declaration of Independence and the establishment of the Republic; and rode triumphant over the exasperated populace who threatened him. He was elevated to the National Convention, and was one of the signers of the Declaration of Independence.

THE GOOD PHYSICIAN.

He acquired a sufficient knowledge of pathological principles and of therapeutics to be a very useful practitioner among the poor of his neighborhood. Not a little of his earnings was expended in unwearied services among the sick. By his well-bred gentility, the cordiality of his manners, and his sympathy with their griefs, he won the esteem and love of all around him. The needy knew that he was their friend: and in their humblest tenements he was met with the warmest welcome.

AS A SOLDIER.

Mr. Day was also a soldier of no ordinary courage. On several occasions has he risked his life among uncounted numbers of the enemy, accompanied by only a few men—others refusing to follow, regarding his undertakings, from their boldness, as the result of some mental disorder.

HIS MORAL AND RELIGIOUS CHARACTER.

No one could have intercourse with him without perceiving prominent features of character formed by the combination of virtue, courage, assiduity, perseverance, with natural talents and genius of no inferior order. There was such a frankness and sincerity in his words and actions that no one could for a moment suppose he was not what he seemed to be. There was in his life a beautiful consistency and harmony. His piety was genuine. He had clear and distinct apprehensions of the great truths of salvation; and a thorough persuasion that the promises of God recorded in the Bible are yea and Amen in Jesus Christ. He had strong faith in the assurance that "Ethiopia shall soon stretch out her hands unto God."

EDUCATOR AND THEOLOGIAN.

Mr. Day was untiring in his efforts to promote the educational interests of Liberia generally, and of the Baptist Church particularly. He did not relax his efforts until he succeeded in establishing Day's Hope Academy. Day's Hope! Significant appellation! It indicates the deep sentiment of his heart, that intellectual and moral culture was the hope of Liberia, and of the church. May his hopes not be disappointed! He entertained the greatest reverence for the old theological and metaphysical writers. One line, he would frequently say, from Edwards or Butler or Leighton or Fuller is worth pages of the light productions which the steam press so rapidly throws off. He often referred to Paley's Natural Theology as having arrested his fearful career, when he was nearing the rapids of skepticism and infidelity.

HIS LIFE AND DEATH A LEGACY.

He has left us an illustrious example. We have reason for congratulation in view of the lasting influence for good, of a long life of self-denial and usefulness, closed with a beautiful serenity—a dignified calmness and peace. Such a life, such a death, constitute a legacy richer than the silver mines of Peru, and more valuable than the sparkling deposits of Australia or California.

Rev. FREDERICK S. JAMES.

NATIVITY AND EMIGRATION.

Mr. James was born on the 8th of March, 1817, in Bertie County, North Carolina. He was the son of Jonathan James, who emigrated with his wife and five children to New Virginia, on the coast of Africa, in the year 1826, on board of the ship "Indian Chief."

HIS AUTOBIOGRAPHY.

"Father died at Monrovia, in 1832, leaving me, his eldest son, then about sixteen years old, to provide for mother, and the rest of the family. I cultivated the ground, and carried on business as a joiner. I soon built a small house for mother, and with the other children, put myself out as a hireling. I was converted in November, 1834, under a sermon preached by Rev. F. C. Teage, from Jer. viii. 20. In the year 1840, I married Priscilla Carter, a member of the Baptist Church, and a daughter of Brother James and Sister Virginia Thomas, who were residents of Richmond, Va. They are both deceased. In 1842, I was made a deacon. In 1845, I was licensed by the same church. At the Providence Association, in 1847, I was ordained by Elders John Day, J. Clarke, and A. P. Davis."

HIS APPOINTMENT AND ACCLIMATION.

On June 14th, 1847, the Board "*Resolved*, That Frederick S. James, of the Liberian Colony, be appointed a missionary of this Board, to preach to the destitute churches of New Georgia, Caldwell, Millsburg, and the surrounding towns, at a salary of $400 per annum. Having been for some time, a resident of Liberia, he is acclimated, and in a measure, prepared to commence efficient operations, as a Minister of the cross.

HIS ACCEPTANCE.

Mr. James replied: "I assure you I cordially accept the appointment extended in your letter of the 22d July, hoping, with divine assistance to be of some use, in the missionary cause. I began my labors here—in New Virginia, when Brother Day, with confidence in the Board, thought fit to authorize me to take charge of the station, on the first of April. I completed the houses in three months, and opened a common day-school on the 19th of July. The number of pupils is thirty-eight. Twelve read well in the New Testament. The little church numbers eighteen members. I have received five by experience, and four by baptism. I visit occasionally Millsburg, New Orleans, New Georgia, and Monrovia."

MISSIONARY SOCIETIES.

Mr. James wrote: "In my humble opinion, our first effort is to cultivate the minds, and awaken the conscience of our own people, whose conduct has a bad effect upon the natives. When we can get the Christian community to co-operate with us, by circumspect deportment, the work of civilizing and Christianizing the heathen will prosper. All the converts seem to be progressing in the divine life. We hope the day is not far distant when we shall be able to inform you of the formation of Missionary Societies to assist you in this good work. In the churches under my charge, as well as in all others here, a regular monthly contribution of an amount, regulated by rule, or conscience, is enjoined upon every member, which defrays a great portion of the expenses of the church."

GREAT REVIVAL.

In their Report of 1848, the Board quotes, with regard to the state of things at New Virginia, from a Missionary not in our employ: " We are now enjoying the most extensive and I believe the most genuine revival and reformation I have ever witnessed in the Colony. The Lord is manifesting his power, and grace, in a most wonderful manner. As we put down such large numbers of candidates as are now baptized, some may fear that the terms of admission are more facile than the Scriptures warrant. To ease such minds, we will state as a fundamental article of our creed, that the Church of Christ is a spiritual building; and we hold to none but believers' baptism."

"Mr. James, our Missionary, says: 'Since I wrote you, it has been my unspeakable privilege to baptize in the Mesurado, on the 5th inst., thirty-three candidates, who, with the twenty-four baptized by Mr. Teage, makes in all forty-seven souls added to the church at Monrovia since the revival commenced. In addition to the seven candidates for baptism at New Virginia, of which I informed you, I have received thirteen others. There are also seven candidates at New Georgia."

Nearly one hundred have been added to the churches within the limits of this station since the last Annual Report. To God be all the glory."

HOPEFUL PROSPECT.

The following was adopted by the Southern Baptist Convention in 1848:

"At no period since Christians have been laboring to evangelize and civilize Africa has the prospect that 'Ethiopia shall soon stretch out her hands unto God,' appeared so bright as at present. During the twenty-five years which have passed, since the first Baptist Colored Missionaries were sent from this country, scenes of prosperity and of adversity have alternately cheered and depressed the struggling band of Christ's servants in Africa. But now the clouds have been scattered, the Sun of Righteousness has begun to shine upon our efforts, and nothing but energetic labor and fervent prayer seem wanting to gather a rich harvest for God. * * Let our churches and pastors weigh well their responsibilities in regard to Africa, listen to God's voice calling for her evangelization, and hasten to the work in view of the judgment seat."

A GOOD MAN FALLEN.

In the Report of the Board, in 1849, we find under the head of "Mournful Bereavement:" The Board are compelled to record the sudden removal on Nov. 9th, 1848, of F. S. James, of New Virginia. He was a good man. In the language of one of his co-adjutors 'he was pious, amiable, laborious, self-denying, beloved by his people and all who knew him. He sought not his own, but his Heavenly Father's glory. Filled with the spirit of his station, he carried blessed influences wherever he went."

HIS WORKS DO FOLLOW HIM.

The Board passed the following, February 5th, 1849: "*Resolved*, That while the Board regard the unexpected death of Rev. F. S. James, their Missionary at New Virginia, as deeply afflictive to them and the Mission, they cannot but rejoice in the evidence given by their brother of an unaffected love to Christ, and laborious, successful devotion to his work as a Christian Missionary. He rests from his labors and his works do follow him."

PENSION AND RESCINDMENT.

"August 22d, 1849. *Resolved*, That an allowance of $40 be paid to Mrs. James, widow of our Missionary, F. S. James, for support of her child, in accordance with a rule adopted by the Board in the commencement of the African Mission.

"*Resolved*, That the regulation providing for orphans of Missionaries in Africa be rescinded, leaving it discretionary with the Board to make special grants in extreme cases."

AN EVEN-SPUN THREAD.

"Mr. James was truly beloved by all who knew him. He maintained the best moral character. As a Christian he was able to stop the mouth of the gainsayer by his common deportment. His life was an even-spun thread. As a Minister, he was interesting and spiritual. He was a brilliant star in our Mission. He has gone from a large field of labor and, I trust, to reap a large reward."—*Jno. Day.*

THE LORD DELIGHTED TO BLESS HIM.

Mr. Day wrote, December 6th, 1848: "I found the school at New Virginia highly interesting. The stamp of Brother James' meekness seemed deeply impressed on the whole school. I found the members of the church in a devout and heavenly frame of mind. 'Oh,' said a poor old woman, 'I had thought we were forsaken. Blessed be the name of our Heavenly Father, who never leaves nor forsakes.' It required nerves of sterner stuff, a heart more flint-like than mine, to say to these despairing children of my Heavenly Father, 'we cannot help.' I overlooked Brother James' accounts, took charge of the deed for the lot of New Virginia, and talked with his disconsolate widow. I went ashore at King Broomley's town, and preached. Before I rose to preach, one said: 'Where is the king's *dash?*' I told him I had nothing to give.

Brother James had been in the habit of preaching in this town long before his death; but still they had not forgotten a custom which our Methodist brethren in their zeal to do good, had adopted—they *dashed* head men; *dashed* new converts, which, while money abounded, were numerous. It is clear that when the natives have not been paid to hear, their reformation is more obvious." Speaking of Mr. James' success, Mr. Day says: "At New Virginia is a school of sixty-two children, a most interesting Sunday-school, and a church of eighty to one hundred members, built up principally by his indefatigable labors. Besides, he preached in several native villages. At New Orleans, he laid the foundation and built up a church. Everything in his hand prospered as if the Lord delighted to bless him."

DEAD, YET LIVING.

Rev. A. P. Davis, in one of his missionary tours, wrote: "But of all the churches I visited, none appeared to me to exhibit such order as that at Virginia. This station was occupied by our much lamented brother James. Here we have a consistent, plain, whole-hearted, well-taught Christian church; a resolute, firm set of faithful brethren. They seem to have drunk deep into Brother James' spirit, and in every house his name lives. They talk of his plans, and seem to be as much determined to follow them now as when he was living in person among them."

APPROPRIATE EPITAPH.

A paper, with some statistics of the life and labors of our deceased brother, from the pen of our late Corresponding Secretary, Dr. Taylor, is endorsed with these six words, which are an appropriate epitaph of Frederick S. James: "A Good Man; and Faithful Missionary."

Rev. J. H. CHEESEMAN.

HIS FIELD OF LABOR.

Referring to the station at Edina, the Board reported to the Convention in 1849, as follows: "The Board were induced by his own solicitation and by the recommendation of .Brother J. Day, to appoint (March 5th, at $450 per annum) at this place, Brother John H. Cheeseman, who will labor as their missionary in the circumjacent region. He will itinerate among the Bassas, by whom he is much beloved, preach to the church at Edina, and visit the destitute churches on the coast; inspect the schools connected with our mission, etc., etc. He has experience in this work, having been for some time in the employ of the Baptist Missionary Union."

THE LORD DOING GREAT THINGS.

"*February 25th*, 1849. As I rose (at New Georgia) to introduce divine service," wrote Mr. Cheeseman, "I could not but pause for a moment's reflection. Here, thought I, is a congregation of Christians, who, but for the light of the gospel, might like their brethren, be groping in darkness. In front of the desk, sat thirteen candidates for baptism. Surely the Lord is doing great things for us, for which we are glad."

THE COUNTRY AND THE CHURCH.

"*February 26th*. To-day, His Excellency, the President, reported his doings in England and France, before the Senate and House of Representatives. He has done honor to himself and his country."

"*February 28th*. I had the pleasure of baptizing two young men, who, I hope, will prove useful members of the church.

SOLOMON PAGE.

"*Edina, April 27th*, 1849. In January last, I organized a school here, which numbers now about sixty pupils, many of whom are very interesting, and are progressing rapidly. I have employed a young man, Solomon Page, as assistant teacher. He is not a professor of religion, but strictly moral, and a close student. When at home, I take charge of the senior class.

AMONG KINGS.

At Kingdon, ten miles up the Mechlin River, I started a school, which is in full operation. I have much conversation with the old king. He acknowledges the truth of God's word, and expresses a determination to make an effort to secure the salvation of his soul. I arrived at King Bais'. The king expressed himself gratified. His people were assembled, and I preached. All were attentive. At Dyemes' town, I was introduced to the head-man, as a God-man. He said: "You be God-man, eh? You can talk my people God word? I tank you. I be glad too much." The whole town assembled, and I preached with some liberty, on "There is but one God." One said audibly, "True." I addressed them next day on "Repentance, and Faith in our Lord Jesus Christ."

October 12*th*. Old King Tattou is an interesting man, and possesses a goodly share of natural abilities. He remarked that he regretted, above all things, that in his youth he had not been favored with the advantages now afforded his countrymen. I told him, his age would be no excuse, if he neglected the word of God: that God was willing to save all who came to him by his Son Jesus Christ. The old man replied: "True, true, I be old; I have no time to lose. I must pray one time."

SOLEMN ENTREATY.

This part of Africa is greatly improved in the last twenty years. What has God wrought for us! I entreat you in the name of God the Father, in the name of God the Son, who gave himself for poor Ethiopia; in the name of our holy religion; and in consideration of the multitudes on the coast sinking into eternal woe, to send us men and means; and with God's blessing, large returns will be made in a few years.

EXECUTIVE COMMITTEE AND SUPERVISORS.

The following is copied from the Board's Records: "January 7th, 1850. *Resolved* that, John Day be appointed Treasurer, and J. H· Cheeseman, Secretary of the Mission. * * * That each missionary will be expected to devote himself wholly to his work, and that a faithful report of services rendered, shall be forwarded, each quarter, to John Day, and John H. Cheeseman, as the Executive Committee of the Mission. June 24th. Brethren Day and Cheeseman are appointed Supervisors over the Mission, and are empowered to suspend unworthy missionaries, until they can report to the Board."

NOT SHADOW FOR SUBSTANCE.

Referring to a revival in his church, during which five were baptized, Brother Cheeseman says: "Our most sanguine expectations are more than realized. Natives baptized, give very intelligent views of the work of grace wrought in the heart. I regard it of the highest · importance, that in the great doctrine of regeneration, they be correctly taught, lest they mistake the shadow for the substance."

HIS SCHOOL.

With regard to his school of sixty—native pupils, Brother Cheeseman wrote: "I would support them out of my own means; but with a wife and five children, I cannot do it. I have selected a youth, sixteen years old, five feet high, and intelligent, to be supported by the E. Street Baptist Church, Washington. My native youths are improving finely."

BOARD'S SUMMARY OF THE WORK.

"We have fifteen missionaries and assistant missionaries, under our direction; and from the last summary of their labors it appeared that for the preceding twelve months there were taught in our schools, an average number of 420 children: baptized at the different stations sixty-four or sixty-six. Our Sunday-schools are generally filled; the average number 440. Cape Palmas, Sinoe, Edina, and Bexley Churches enjoyed refreshing seasons, and were generally encouraged.

These results furnish ground for gratitude to God, who has wrought all our works in us, and for us. The providence of God is calling loudly for expanded operations. The Board invoke the aid of their brethren throughout the South, in this enterprise. Brother Cheeseman wrote December 20th 1850: 'Our statistical table shows an aggregate of 522 members of the churches.'"

IMPORTANT ACTION OF BOARD.

Again we copy from the Records: *August 2d*, 1852. "In reference to the suggestion of superseding the Executive Committee, we recommend that Brethren Day and Cheeseman be retained as our financial agents for the present; and that, for the purpose of an advisory council, and to recommend suitable fields and laborers, the missionary preachers together with five lay brethren, be appointed by the Board, viz.: B. P. Yates from Mesurado, etc., etc.

November 6th, 1854. " Referred, with a letter of J. H. Cheeseman, the question of changing the location of the Financial Committee of the Liberian Missions from Bexley to Monrovia."

December 4, 1854. " In their estimate, the Committee have omitted the names of J. H. Cheeseman, of Edina, and Robert F. Hill, of Bexley, believing that, for the present, at least, it will be proper not to make any appropriations on their behalf. They also recommend the following: 1. *Resolved,* That the Financial Committee consist of Brethren John Day and B. P. Yates. 2. *Resolved,* Where a full support is allowed, the entire time of the missionary shall be employed in the work; and that one-third of his time shall be given to the spiritual benefit of the natives. 3. *Resolved,* That the Financial Committee be requested to hold each missionary and teacher to a rigid accountability, in assigning drafts for their benefit."

April 30th, 1855. "*Resolved,* That $500 be allowed for the continuance of Rev. J. H. Cheeseman and his interpreters at Edina and vicinity; and that he be urged to devote as much time as practicable to labor amongst the surrounding tribes."

APOLOGY FOR MR. DAY.

"Since I have resided in Monrovia," Brother Day wrote, "I found a Krootown of some sixty or seventy men, besides women and children. I have been there frequently and talked with them. Other missionaries tell me efforts have been made without effect. I am not the least discouraged. I shall tell them of the love of God, of a bleeding Saviour, of the worlds of bliss and of woe, and beseech them to be reconciled to God by Jesus Christ."

The following record of the Board appears, November 5th, 1855: "Brother Day having without authority from the Board, employed Brother Josiah Neyle as school-master at Bootan, and also a female teacher in a Krootown, the appropriations ($400) were sanctioned, but Brother Day must be cautioned against such expenditures in the future."

Brother Cheeseman wrote: "I regret very much that Brother Day entered into any arrangement without consulting the Board, after knowing the amount appropriated. But his great anxiety to do good, I suppose, induced him to do it, presuming the Board would approve of it. * * I shall suggest to him the propriety of drawing bills of exchange only when they are due, and in no case to transcend the appropriation, which will save him the disagreeable necessity of having his drafts returned protested."

THE LORD OF HOSTS IS WITH US.

In the year 1856, the Republic of Liberia was in a state of war-confusion. Brother Cheeseman wrote: "Our friends and relatives were called to leave us to engage against the hostile natives of the Blubarre, Sinoe, and Butan tribes; while those at home trembled, knowing that the menacing conduct of surrounding tribes too clearly indicated what would be the result, did our army fail to be successful. The Lord of Hosts was with our forces, as he has ever been in every engagement (since the foundation of our infant government) with the aborigines; and peace with her balmy wings again hovers over us."

INVARIABLY OWN A BIBLE.

April 29*th*, 1858. Brother Cheeseman wrote: "If the Board will allow me to establish a school at Bexley, one at Farmersville, and two on the Mechlin River among the natives, I really believe they would be productive of much good. The natives are anxious to be taught. I see boys who have been taught to read at school, and they invariably own a Bible, which they read at times.

DEATH OF J. H. CHEESEMAN AND J. T. NEYLE.

Very soon after the meeting of the Convention, when the death of our senior missionary, Brother John Day, was reported, the Board were called upon to mourn another severe trial, in the death, by drowning, of the next oldest missionary, Brother J. H. Cheeseman, and one of our best teachers, Brother J. T. Neyle. They were crossing the river St. John's, in a small boat, which capsized, and all on board, four in number, perished. The Board were deeply affected by the removal of such men as Day and Cheeseman.

ABLE MINISTER, GOOD SHEPHERD, AND SENIOR SECRETARY.

Dr. A. M. Poindexter, introducing to the readers of *The Commission* an obituary notice of Brother Cheeseman, which appeared in the Liberian *Herald*, from the pen of Rev. Z. B. Roberts, of Greenville, testified: "Brother Cheeseman was a good man, a devout Christian, and an able minister. In his death our mission sustained a great loss." Brother Roberts said: "I have lost a father, brother, and a true friend, in the death of our well-beloved and distinguished fellow-citizen, Rev. J. H. Cheeseman. My acquaintance with Brother Cheeseman has been for eight years: six of which I was under his special care, and enjoyed his liberality. I feel a deep sense of my indebtedness to him for many kindnesses. I was one of the sheep of his flock, and feel justified in saying that his only thought, with a few exceptions, was for the salvation of sinners. Oh, how can I forget his sweet counsels, his warning voice, whenever my feet would go astray? As a good shepherd, he would say with the poet:

> 'Don't graze too near the bank, my gentle sheep,
> The sand is quick beneath thy feet—the pit is deep.'"

Brother S. S. Page writes from Marshall, August 30th, 1859: "In the death of Brother John H. Cheeseman, the denomination in Liberia has sustained a loss as great, if not greater than ever before. Brother Cheeseman was a devoted missionary, a successful and faithful preacher, a pious Christian. Our Association has lost her Senior Secretary; the denomination, one of her best and most influential preachers."

PRESENTIMENT.

"On the 19th of June, 1859, the Rev. John H. Cheeseman preached in his church at Bexley with unusual unction: and in administering the Lord's Supper, he called attention to the Lord's words: 'I will drink no more of the fruit of the vine with you, until it be fulfilled in the kingdom of God.' He remarked, I am informed, "We all shall not meet again in this chapel: I know we shall not." On Monday, he retired as usual to his office for prayer and meditation. With the gloom of death before him, he prayed most earnestly. Every action indicated his approaching dissolution. He said to his wife: 'I must go; my hour is come.' Crossing the river St. John with my dear cousin, Joseph T. Neyle, together with poor little Charles Washington, the boat was turned over, and they sank to rise no more alive. Five days before his death, Brother Neyle wrote to me: 'A gloom passes over me. I have witnessed more of the power of the Spirit of God lately than ever. I cannot last long.' Thus it was with our beloved friends. The hovering shades at the entrance of the dark door did not affect them, for it was irradiated by the beams of the Sun of righteousness. Their hope of salvation rested on the atonement of their Saviour and the immortality of his love.

FUNERAL.

"His funeral sermon was preached in his church, on the 24th of last month, to an overflowing crowd of attendants, by Rev. A. P. Davis. This good old Baptist preacher did justice to his text, which was the words of Paul to Timothy, 2d Tim. iv. 7, 8. 'I have fought a good fight, I have finished my course, I have kept the faith; henceforth there is laid up for me a crown of life which the Lord, the righteous judge, shall give me at that day.' It was a solemn occasion, and the tolling of the bell, which preceded the services, reminded us of our approaching dissolution. Upon the whole, it was a meeting long to be remembered."

Rev. A. P. DAVIS.

ACCLIMATED.

In the July number of the *Southern Baptist Missionary Journal*, of 1847, the following appeared: "At a recent meeting of the Board, June 14th, A. P. Davis and Frederick James, ministering brethren of color, were appointed to labor in preaching the word on the coast of Africa. Having been for some time residents of Liberia, they are acclimated, and in a measure prepared to commence efficient operation as ministers of the cross. Arrangements have also been made for the organization of a Manual-labor School; and the publication of suitable books and tracts for circulation among the people. It is the design of the Board to extend, as fast and as far as possible, the blessings of the gospel among the tribes of the coast."

BIRTH AND EMIGRATION.

This brother was born in Culpeper County, Va., November 15th, 1805; was baptized, May, 1824; licensed, 1829; removed to Africa, 1834; ordained, 1836.

TO MEET THE CRISIS.

The September Journal says: "Mr. A. P. Davis appeals in earnest and plaintive tones that vigorous measures may be adopted by us to meet the crisis which seems to have been reached by the churches of our denomination in Africa, and to spread among the heathen the knowledge of the true God and his Son Jesus Christ."

NATIVE CONVERTS.

In 1848, Mr. Davis preached at Bassa Cove and Edina, and in five native towns. He reported: "I have baptized seven: five at home, and two while travelling. Among the last named, is my interpreter, whose name is J. B. Davis. He has made several tours among his countrymen alone. Many admire his improvement; some are enraged. They feel that there is a reality in the religion of Jesus to which they are strangers. * * * Very high views of religion seem to be entertained by many of them. They believe when a person goes into the water, he has tested his religion, or belief in the true God. My interpreter conducts public prayer whenever we stop in the country, in his own language; and I have never seen him eat a meal without publicly giving thanks. He is quite a young man, and commands attention and respect. He attends church and Sunday-school regularly. His wife says she wishes to do likewise, but is ashamed on account of her want of clothing. In our Sunday-school are from fifteen to thirty Congos. Mr. Purvis, whom Mr. Day has employed to preach among the natives, is a Congo, and preaches to them in their own language. "He tells me," says Mr. Day, "very interesting things of those among whom he labors."

Visiting several of the churches, Mr. Davis writes as follows: "June 15, 1849, I reviewed the school at Junk, taught by Mr. Richardson. Their pronunciation was good. Children, as small as I ever heard recite, went through the whole multiplication table without missing a word. The church had a two days meeting, and seemed to be comforted.

"I learned with regret, at Millsburg, that Mr. Willis, whom in company with Mr. Cheeseman, I ordained deacon, was dead. The church has sustained a loss in this event, not to be supplied among our present inhabitants. The community at large mourn his death. At New Virginia, it was truly a high day to the disciples of Jesus; and the exercises were a feast of fat things to them.

"At Monrovia, I preached to one of the largest and most respectable congregations. Nearly all the principal men—the President among them—were present. All appeared at the river to witness the baptism of two candidates. Between one and two hundred were at the Lord's Table. What but an adamant could fail to be moved? All was joy and gladness, and the effect was seen in the conviction and conversion of sinners."

Mr. Day of Bexley writes: "Multitudes of poor natives looked on with solemn awe. In the presence of that large concourse, I baptized ten professing Christians." Another says of the scene: "Oh, delightful sight! Brother Day, assisted by Brother Davis, baptized, while the banks of the river literally resounded with the praises of God. Brother Cheeseman preached in the afternoon, and the candidates were received into full fellowship. It was truly a melting season." Edina also has been blessed. Mr. Cheeseman exclaims: "How good is the Lord! Oh, that I could praise him as I ought!"

INCONGRUOUS STATE OF THINGS.

In 1849, Mr. Davis wrote from Bassa Cove: "The meeting-house is always filled to overflowing. There is nothing I see to hinder the prosperity of our cause, or to extinguish the fire already kindled. The natives are inquiring after the word of God. They need it; their condition is heart-rending. Men and women are almost naked. My heart bleeds. Continually are they dancing and killing each other in the use of Sassy-wood. These are the best pleasures they know."

DISMISSED AND RESTORED.

On January 7th, 1850, Mr. A. P. Davis was dismissed, and the Bassa Cove Station discontinued—"to equalize our appropriations along the Liberian Coast, especially as Bassa Cove is near Edina, where we have a station and a school."

On February 6th, 1854, the following resolution was passed by the Board:

"*Resolved*, That one hundred and fifty dollars be appropriated to A. P. Davis of Bassa Cove, with the understanding that he report regularly to the Board, as their missionary."

June 12th, 1855: "*Resolved*, That if the erection of a house at Davis' Town will insure the labors of Brother Davis at that place, fifty dollars be allowed for that purpose; and that Brother Davis be instructed to unite if possible, the school at Nimbly's Town with that at the Settlement. But, the Board direct that the school at Nimbly's Town be abandoned; and that unless the above arrangement be carried into effect, the appropriation of two hundred dollars for the school at Davis' Town be withdrawn.

OLDEST MISSIONARY INSPIRED.

Mr. Davis then of Buchanan writes, July 6th, 1860: "I arrived in Liberia nearly twenty-six years ago. * * * I am now the only missionary living, who was appointed when Brother Day first received his appointment, after he left the Northern Board. So I am the oldest missionary, now belonging to our Board, in Africa." August 16th: "I preached at Brother Von Brunn's station last Sunday. Six chiefs were in the congregation. Some came a hundred miles; and some had never heard of Jesus. They listened with breathless attention. I never felt more inspired to preach Christ crucified."

FAITHFUL UNTO DEATH.

Mr. Davis writes December 5th, 1860: "Brother John B. Davis, the first fruit of my labors, among the Bassas, is dead. He died last October. He continued firm in the faith and practice of Christianity to the day of his death. He stood high, not only with the church, but with the Government. His services were largely sought as an interpreter, and he was often sent for, to settle difficulties between it and its allies."

THE COMMAND AND THE PROMISES.

"I, at times, have been brought to wonder, as you seem to have anticipated, what it is that prevents my success; as I make it a rule to do nothing, in conversation or in contracts or in visiting places or in giving countenance to any cause, that would interfere with my influence as a minister. I often have to lay aside my feelings, and take the commands and the promises as the rule of my action." *December 5th*, 1860.

DURING AND AFTER THE WAR.

In 1861, Mr. Davis is reported at Buchanan, as pastor and teacher, assisted in the school by Mrs. S. A. Davis. In 1863, he was still at Buchanan, but the Board reported: "From the various Mission Stations in Liberia, but little information has been received. Our churches have been more or less visited by the divine blessings. There have been numerous baptisms. All the missionaries are at their posts." Mr. Davis shared the fate of our other missionaries during the war: of which more will be said hereafter. The last record of him is in 1867, as follows: "The Baptist churches held their regular Annual Meeting Association with the Baptist Church of Buchanan (Grand Bassa). Brother A. P. Davis presided as moderator, who for thirty years has been prominent in our missionary record." In the re-organization of the Mission in 1872, his name does not appear on the list of Missionaries.

REV. BOSTON J. DRAYTON.

This brother was born in South Carolina, August 11, 1817, and was baptized in Richmond, Va., in 1847.

FIRST APPLICATION.

The following record of the Board appears April 5, 1847:

"The committee on the African Mission, without recommending as candidates for missionary appointment Brethren Boston J. Drayton and Jordan Smith, colored men, introduced them to the Board for their examination. The Board voted to enter upon their examination; and after a thorough inquiry into their religious experience, theological views, and call to the missionary work, on motion the following resolutions were adopted:

"*Resolved*, That it is inexpedient to employ Brother Boston J. Drayton as a missionary of the Board.

"*Resolved*, That the case of Brother Jordan Smith be laid on the table, and that the committee on African Missions be instructed to inquire into the lawfulness and expediency of appropriations being made by the Board, as cases may arise requiring such assistance, for the purpose of educating colored missionaries."

SECOND APPLICATION AND APPOINTMENT.

On December 6th, 1847: "An application of Brother Boston J.

Drayton, a colored brother, for missionary appointment was referred to the Committee on African Missions." On January 3d, 1848, the following was adopted, on recommendation of the Committee on African Missions:

"1. *Resolved*, That Brother Boston J. Drayton be appointed a Missionary on the coast of Africa, his particular location to be fixed by the Mission in Africa.

"2. *Resolved*, That his salary be fixed at $350 per annum, and the necessary outfit."

On February 7, 1848: *Resolved*, That $119.31 be appropriated for the outfit and passage of Brother Drayton, Missionary to Africa," who sailed from Baltimore in the brig *Amazon* 5th February, 1848.

THE DIMES AND DOLLARS.

The Missionary Journal of February, 1848, noticing the appointment of Brother Drayton, says: "We have now four missionaries in Africa, and the hope is entertained that the number will be doubled. The attention of pastors is called to this subject. In their meetings for colored people, by presenting the claims of the African Mission and allowing them an opportunity of aiding in the work, their dimes and their dollars will be cheerfully contributed."

DESIGNATION SERVICES.

"On Sunday morning, January 30th, 1848, the designation of Brother B. J. Drayton, as our missionary to Africa, took place at the First African Church, of Richmond. It was a deeply solemn occasion. Opening prayer, by Brother Drayton; sermon and instructions to the missionary by the Corresponding Secretary; prayer for the blessing of God upon our brother, by Brother Ryland, pastor of the church. The assembly was then addressed in a sensible and pathetic manner by the candidate. Weeping and sobbing in various parts of the house, indicated that a deep tide of feeling had been produced. A collection was taken amounting to $27.33. After this the congregation, with peculiar fervor, united in singing familiar hymns, and the parting hand was given to him whose face in the flesh they expected to see no more."

FAREWELL MEETING.

"In the afternoon a farewell meeting was held in the Second African Church. Our esteemed brother, Heman Lincoln, of Boston, who was providentially present, expressed his high gratification in witnessing the services of the day. A collection was taken, amounting to $7.57. All found it good to be there. An impression was made which we trust may be beneficially felt among the African churches for years to come."

DEPARTURE AND PASSAGE.

Brother Drayton sailed from Baltimore in the brig Amazon, on Saturday, February 5th, with forty or fifty emigrants for the colonies. On the passage their vessel collided with another. Brother Drayton wrote: "Thank the Lord, all is safe, and we are now making our way. The passengers all appear to be in good spirits. I hope the Lord of the sea will smile upon us, and bless us with a safe and speedy passage."

THE BIG BOOK.

Brother B. J. Drayton, who with the consent of the Board, was called to the temporary pastorate of the Monrovia Church, writes, June 1st, 1848: "This country is growing daily by the influx of natives from the interior, who come wishing to learn the 'Big Book.' My church numbers 167 members, of whom twenty-three are natives, who exhibit much piety. They will be of great use to me in preaching to the surrounding tribes. I have re-organized the Sunday-school and have a very fine Bible Class. I am pleased to see every Lord's Day, the natives as well as the colonists trying to learn wisdom's way."

A NATIVE AND THE GREAT PHYSICIAN.

"You talk about the Lord Jesus Christ—him the Doctor for the heart-sick people. Oh, these words make me glad! You talk plenty about the medicine he give, and that he take no money, he give it freely. Oh, Massa, that make me so glad! That time me go home, me comfort very much. Thank God, the Lord Jesus Christ take his own blood for medicine, and take all my sin away."

KING BROMLEY AND FUTURE LIFE.

Brother Drayton writes, July 11th, 1878: "Brother James and I stopped at King Bromley's town. We prayed for an interview with the present King recently crowned, in regard to our preaching among his people. He was somewhat reluctant at first, but after a while consented to give us an audience. We took a survey of the mementos that were about the grave of the deceased king. At his head was a dark granite stone, all stained with blood. They said that they had killed a chicken and sheep for the king's breakfast. They had been doing so ever since his death. There was a gun also at his head. They said: 'He be great war-man in his time, he lib kill too much in war, he be great man, dat gun lib tell whar he be.' Brother James mentioned our desire to preach to them once a week. The King agreed and told us we could come at any time, and he would gather his people to hear us. They all followed us to the water's side. We proceeded up the river to Millsburg, and stopped at Brother White's, a licentiate of our church."

THREE MONTHS' WORK.

"*Monrovia*, 1848. The last three months I have travelled 120 miles; preached 37 sermons; lectured 7 times; attended 15 prayer-meetings; visited 178 families; distributed 215 tracts, and attended 4 concerts of prayer for the spread of the gospel. My Bible Class contained thirty-four males and twenty-seven females. The Sunday-school is in a healthy condition. Much interest seems to be manifested in this department of my labor. Pray for me."

REQUEST DECLINED.

On the 24th of June, 1849, the following record was made by the Board: "The request of Brother B. J. Drayton to allow him to receive his salary direct from the Board, instead of from Brother Day, was declined. But the Secretary was ordered to instruct Brother Day to make the transmission of his salary as convenient for Brother Drayton as possible."

CAPE PALMAS AS A FIELD OF LABOR.

The church at Cape Palmas also being without a pastor, Brother Drayton, by direction of the Board, moved down to this point on the coast. "As a field of labor among the natives," says one of our brethren, "a more interesting need not be desired. There are large native towns in the midst of the American settlements—one of five hundred houses—and the number of natives within or directly about the settlement is at least 5,000. The women appear the most degraded I have ever seen. * * If a heart can be affected, deep feeling will be experienced in visiting Cape Palmas."

ALL ARE BENT ON WRONG.

"*Cape Palmas:* I arrived here on 17th December, 1848, with my family, all in good health, and pleased with the location. I thank the Lord who has been with me all the time with his goodly providence. My daily prayer is: 'Lord, take away self-will, self-dependence, pride, and carnal ambition.' I see a living mass, enveloped in the grossest darkness. To elevate them appears almost impossible. Yet it will be done. I have the word of God on my side. This encourages me to labor in this sultry climate, to enter with all my heart and strength upon the work. The natives are guided by the devil. He sits upon the throne wielding a universal sceptre. All are bent on doing wrong. They have strong confidence in their 'Devil's Bush,' the *gre-gree*, and other heathenish rites. These keep them buried in the mire of degradation. But I believe a radical change will be brought about."

LOST IN WONDER: BOOKS, BOOKS!

Cape Palmas is in the jurisdiction of the Maryland Colonization Society, and is the most Southern of the Liberian stations. Of a revival, Brother Drayton writes, in 1850: "Two years ago we could scarcely raise a congregation, but now our house is crowded. They seem anxious to follow in the good old way. All are alive to their duty. I am lost in wonder at the goodness of God in raising the drooping head of his people." Ten or fifteen were baptized. In the Sunday-school, were 102 scholars. With regard to a day school, which

Mrs. Drayton taught, Brother Drayton wrote: "Davis, a very intelligent native, requested me to open a school, and he assured me that I should have from 70 to 100 children. If you establish it, it will be the only general native school among 2,000 natives. The natives I have are from Yabboo—none from Cape Palmas." In 1851, thirty-one were in the school. Receiving some books, Brother Drayton wrote: "Please remember me in this particular always. Books! books! books!"

THE WORK ADVANCES.

Attending the Association at Monrovia, Brother Drayton baptized thirteen persons, eight of whom were natives. In 1852, he baptized seventeen persons.

In 1853, he wrote from Cape Palmas: "Davis' Town adheres to observing the first day of the week as a season of rest from labor, and for receiving regular Christian instruction. Ten families are expected to remove into the town this year."

In 1854: "The work still advances at Cape Palmas."

CÆSAR AND CHRIST.

In 1857, it was reported that "B. J. Drayton was elected Governor of the Maryland Colony. Our chapel has been burnt, and the schools temporarily suspended. The native school was conducted by James Moore, and the colonial by Hanson W. Motton. The Sunday-school has 65 in attendance; the church, 89 members, one licentiate, and two exhorters. It is hoped that Brother Drayton will be able soon to resume his full missionary work."

Mr. Drayton wrote to the Board in 1857: "I was elected almost unanimously Governor of the Colony of Maryland. It appeared to me, after consultation and prayer, that under the existing circumstances of the State, I would pursue the path of duty to accept the office. But with a heart actuated with the warmest emotions for the prosperity of your interest, I consider it to be my duty to sustain the same unbroken relation to you, and to employ my leisure moments, and best endeavors, for the furtherance of the Redeemer's kingdom."

INQUIRING ABOUT JESUS.

In February, 1859, Brother B. J. Drayton wrote from Cape Palmas: "Within the last two years, more inquiries have been made about Jesus than ever have been in years past. This interesting people must have the gospel; they must be taught prayerfully and systematically, and I know the harvest of the Lord will be abundant and joyful. * * I have had with me Brother Richard H. Stone and wife, who were waiting the steamer from England to convey them to Lagos. They left here on the 28th of January, in good health and spirits. Brother Stone preached for us the Sunday previous. I admire him much. He seemed anxious to enter upon his labors, and much devoted."

REQUEST OF BROTHER B. J. DRAYTON.

"CAPE PALMAS, September 16th, 1859.—Since the affliction in the death of Brethren Day and Cheeseman, I have had solemn thoughts respecting our operations, and my own responsibility to God and the church. * * The motto of the few remaining in Liberia should be: 'Go forward.' * * I would request you to allow me to take a tour throughout the whole field, to ascertain the true state of affairs, as well as to encourage, by the help of the Lord, those who may feel to be called of the Lord to preach the gospel. We are in want of men. The loss of those who have gone to the church triumphant, is a keen stroke to the church here."

January 4th, 1860: "My visit to Monrovia, is simply to attend the session of the Supreme Court, of which I have been appointed Chief Justice, to fill the vacancy occasioned by the death of our lamented Brother John Day. I have preached at the church, which should be second to none in the city or country. My prayers are that Day's Hope may be indeed a hope to the church. Of Brother Fitzgerald, I can only say, he is apparently a fine man, and will possibly be of eminent service to the cause of the country."

COMMENDATION OF BAPTISTS.

Brother B. J. Drayton writes September 17th, 1860: "Every Baptist minister in Liberia, so far as I know, does his duty. They go farther than any other sect, and are willing to sacrifice more, and have done more work with less means and encouragements. The denomination numbers over 1000 communicants, and is growing, and does not feel second to any in point of energy and interest in the cause of Jesus. The people in Liberia are doing a good work. The Lord is certainly with them. They have contributed, and will contribute, to every good work as their means and circumstances justify. They are grateful for favors, and will not compromise principle for gain. I mean Baptists."

CALLED TO THEIR ACCOUNT.

In 1866, the Board reported: "Brother B. J. Drayton, who at the time, was Chief Justice of the Liberia Colony, and who for many years, was missionary of this Board, has recently been drowned. He sustained an approved character, and we cannot but lament his death. Brethren James Bullock of Millsburg, and S. W. Britton of New Georgia have also, within the last three years, been called to their final account."

Rev. J. T. RICHARDSON.

"On October 2d, 1848, the appropriation by Mr. Day of $100, to Brother J. T. Richardson, for services, as our Evangelist, was confirmed by the Board." August 22d, 1849: "*Resolved*, That the recommendation of Brother Day to dismiss for the present from the service of the Board J. T. Richardson and Smart Purvis be concurred in."

REVIVAL.

After the death of Mr. James, Mr. Richardson and Mr. White gave a part of their time to the towns of Mesurado County. On November 24th, 1849, Mr. Richardson wrote:

"I will now inform you, that there has been a glorious out-pouring of the Holy Spirit among all the churches in this county. Among the five churches, fifty persons were added, two-thirds of whom are natives. Ten were added to the Monrovia Church, seven of whom are natives. May the Lord carry on the glorious conquest of the gospel of his Son!"

WILD MEN BOWING BEFORE GOD.

The Board reported: "Since the death of Mr. Teage, in 1853, the church at Monrovia has been supplied by Mr. J. T. Richardson, to whom God has vouchsafed his special blessing. At one time six were baptized by our missionaries; and at another twenty-one." At Millsburg, Mr. Richardson writes: "Eight souls were happily converted to God, and received for baptism. More recently sixteen have been baptized." At Caldwell he writes: "With us are seen the wild men of the woods bowing before the Lord, confessing their sins, and acknowledging that there is no other name under heaven given among men whereby they must be saved, but the name of the Lord Jesus Christ."

DISCOVERY ABOUT BAPTISM.

Mr. Richardson writes: "In reading my Greek Testament, I have found the wide difference in regard to baptism. In the English translation, it reads, 'I indeed baptize you with water.' But in the Greek I find in, which means *in*, instead of with. I shall plod on, until I am able to read in the original the Lord's word.

CHURCHES VISITED BY THE SPIRIT.

Mr. Richardson wrote in 1854: "Since my last, we have witnessed a powerful revival. The Spirit seems to have visited most of the churches. The baptisms were as follows: At Millsburg eleven; Caldwell four; Louisiana five; Clay Ashland five; New Virginia seven; New Georgia fourteen; Monrovia thirty-one; Bassa Cove eight; Edina ten; Bexley twenty-four; Lexington two; Greenville twenty-three; Farmersville four; Cape Palmas twenty-eight; Sierra Leone one."

WHITE FOR THE HARVEST.

In the report of 1855, the Board says: "This prosperity has continued from year to year, and now it is our privilege to report more than ordinary manifestation of the divine regard. This field furnishes the largest opportunity of diffusing the influence of the gospel. Mr. W. H. Clarke, when passing on the way to his field in Yoruba, remarks: "My brother, if you wish to be useful in gathering many sheaves into the garner of the Lord, come here, come to a land where arms are outstretched to receive you. Leave the land most blest of heaven, and come to a region only dark, because there is no gospel light. * * I don't think I ever addressed a more interesting audience. While I was speaking to them of Jesus they paid the profoundest attention. The field seems to be already white for the harvest."

ON THE BANKS OF THE ST. PAUL.

Clay Ashland: J. T. Richardson, Missionary; School, with forty-two scholars. This is a new town on the St. Paul's River, and bids fair to be very influential. Mr. Clarke writes: "It was my pleasure to preach the opening sermon in the nice frame house just built by the industry, and at the expense of the prosperous and zealous little church. It was filled to overflowing. After preaching, I baptized four youthful converts, who, as they rose from the water, came up straightway singing praises unto God. Ah, my brother, it is not often we witness just such a scene, in our favored land, * * as transpired in the wilderness of dark, benighted Africa, on the banks of the St. Paul, Lord's Day, about one o'clock, July 30th, 1854."

CONSTITUTION AND ORDINATION.

New Kentucky. J. T. Richardson, Missionary. "The members at Kentucky have constituted themselves into a church with, I believe, thirty or more members, and some forty or fifty children are found in the settlement. Brethren Davis, Roberts, Cheeseman, and myself attended to the constitution of the church, and the ordaining of three deacons."

ROD OF CHASTISEMENT.

Mr. Richardson wrote, May 22d, 1858: "The Rev. Richard White fell at his post, on Monday, the 3d of this month, and Adam Locket, on the 1st. The latter was carried to the house for all the living on

Sunday, and the former on Monday. It seems the blessed Lord is holding his rod of chastisement, over his churches and people, for one after another is called away continually of late."

MR. DAY TOO FEEBLE.

Mr. Richardson writes, July 30th, 1858 : "The surrounding villages are filled with the Mandingo, the Vey, the Golah, the Dey and the Ressiah tribes. The time has come for us to put forth our best efforts to excite an interest in them. I learn from my visits among them, that good has been done. * * Since the death of Brother White, I have done what I could to supply Millsburg and Louisiana, which are important points. Brother Day is too feeble to do anything in the way of travelling or labor."

TO TAKE CHARGE AT MONROVIA.

As has been seen, on the death of Rev. John Day, January 30th, 1859, Rev. J. T. Richardson was requested to take charge of affairs at Monrovia, until instructions might be received from the Board. He writes, March 26th : "On the 25th, I baptized seven hopeful converts; one was a little boy about eleven years old, who has been trained for the last five months by our missionary, Brother Britton. Brother Britton is much beloved by the people of New Georgia."

ANOTHER SON CONVERTED.

May 14th, 1859. "Our Zion is travailing. The Holy Spirit is in the midst of it, causing stony hearts to feel, and opening the eyes of poor sinners, who are crying for mercy. Eighteen have been received from the water. Five of the young men of our High School are hopefully converted, and are sitting at the feet of Jesus, in their right mind. Blessed be the name of God! I have another son converted, who is a student in our High School. The work goes on with increased interest." Thus writes Mr. Richardson.

BASSAS NOMINAL CHRISTIANS.

Mr. Richardson says, December 30th : "I visited all the stations in Bassa County. The prospect of each is bright. Brother Hill's church, at Grand Bassa, is in a thriving condition. Also, Brother Von Brunn's, who has forty native Christians, who nearly all read the Holy Scriptures. * * He is a perfect gentleman and Christian in his conduct, which makes all love him. He has great influence among the natives; preaches and prays in the Bassa tongue. To Edina, we shall send Brother Fitzgerald, who, I believe, will be useful. I called by Brother L. K. Crocker's station, and was highly pleased with his scholars. He is doing a good work among his native brethren. His heart seems fixed on their salvation. I visited Brother Herndon's station. I think he is not suited for the heathen. We have agreed to let Brother Crocker have the entire field, and put Brother Herndon where he can likely do more good. Missionary influence in the Bassa country is great. You may safely put down the Bassa people as nominally Christian."

REPORT FROM THE STATIONS.

Isaac Roberts, at Greenville, Sierra Leone, reports his field " very encouraging." James Bullock, at Williamsburg, says: " I am much encouraged in the work of the Lord." Adam White, of Marshall, writes: " Small pox has broken up several native towns in our neighborhood, but we have reason to thank God that no death has occurred in our church. Wm. C. Burke, of Clay Ashland, reports: " Twenty-five hopeful converts have been added to the church by baptism. Our little Zion numbers now 103." R. F. Hill, of Bexley, who preaches also at Edina and Farmersville: " Our House was finished, and dedicated on Wednesday, December 7th, and the Association convened on the eighth. Since then, I have been preaching at Bexley." S. W. Britton, New Georgia: " We have lost a good number of members during the epidemic of small pox. I did not budge an inch, and was the instrument in God's hands of doing much good. We lost two deacons. Our prayer is that God would sanctify this dispensation of his providence." Jas. H. Wilson, of Grand Cape Mount: " The people show much interest in having a missionary. Made forty-six family visits. Have thirteen candidates for baptism." J. T. Richardson, Monrovia: "My church is now in a fine state. Schools at all the stations from Junk to Grand Bassa, are in a healthy condition, especially Von Brunn's, Mrs. Cheeseman's, and Hill's. The schools at Day's Hope are moving on finely." F. Richardson: "I have preached fourteen sermons at my native stations—at Bromley's and Javerstown." A. P. Davis reports his station at Buchanan: "Prosperous, and the schools increasing in interest."

SIERRA LEONE.

"The stations at Sierra Leone have been attended with about the usual degree of prosperity, and the missionaries write happily as to the future."

SUMMARY.

Baptisms during the year, 113: Church members, 1,064: Pupils, 512.

NOT RE-ENROLLED.

In 1860 and 1863, Mr. Richardson is reported as our missionary in Liberia. In the re-organization of the Mission, in 1872, he was not re-enrolled as one of our missionaries.

Rev. R. E. MURRAY.

AUTOBIOGRAPHY.

Mr. Murray was a South Carolinian by birth, and spent much of his time in Charleston. In 1843, he emigrated to Liberia. He states that he arrived at Monrovia on September 4th of that year. On the 5th, the church letter of himself and wife was handed to Rev. Hilary Teage, then pastor of the Providence Baptist Church of that place. In May, 1844, he received the office of Superintendent of Emigrants for Sinoe, which was then attached to Grand Bassa County. He sailed from Monrovia, May 10th, 1844, and arrived at Sinoe on the 16th inst. "I discovered but two Baptists in the place. On August 22d we opened a house of worship. Only three Baptists were present. Sister

Peel, an old acquaintance of mine from Charleston, did not unite with us until 1847. We were evil spoken of, ridiculed, and people were taught by an apostate Baptist that we were a dangerous set; that any who followed us would go to hell, as we placed our hope of salvation entirely in water baptism. On the first Lord's Day in June, 1846, two were baptized by Brother Jones, of Cape Palmas, and on the same day a church of five members was organized. In May, 1848, another was added to us, and was baptized by Brother A. P. Davis. On the 12th of July the "Colonel Howard" arrived, bringing us a fine company of emigrants, and added fourteen members to our church. This was life from the dead. From that time, until 1853, the increase of the church has been rapid, both by letters and baptism. Our denomination has now, August 26th, 1856, two independent churches—one in Greenville, and one in Farmersville, (organized April 9, with 29 members) under the pastoral charge of Rev. J. Roberts. Besides, there are a number of brethren in various parts of the country. I can confidently say that there is not a tribe within a circuit of 70 miles, some persons of whom have not heard the gospel. Since the declaration of peace, the natives of Sinoe and Butan have requested that teachers and preachers be sent them. Since the revival of 1850 in this place, there have been ten natives baptized.

NOTES FROM REPORTS AND OTHER SOURCES.

On August 22d, 1849, Mr. Murray was appointed missionary at $450 per annum, and Mr. Day was authorized to expend for schools, $400 in addition. In 1850, the schools consisted of ninety-nine pupils, with Mr. Lewis and Mrs. Morel, as teachers. "Our meetings at Fishtown are held under a large India-rubber tree. Large numbers from seventy to eighty miles distant attend." "When I came to this place in 1844," writes one of our brethren, "I found a *gre-gree* house, a little to the back of Fishtown. In 1845, all the chiefs united in repairing it. Now it is going to ruin and no man regards it. I am astonished at the respect evinced for the Lord's Day. Natives refuse to trade because it is God's day. Upon the whole, I believe that their superstition is already beginning to decline." Instead of

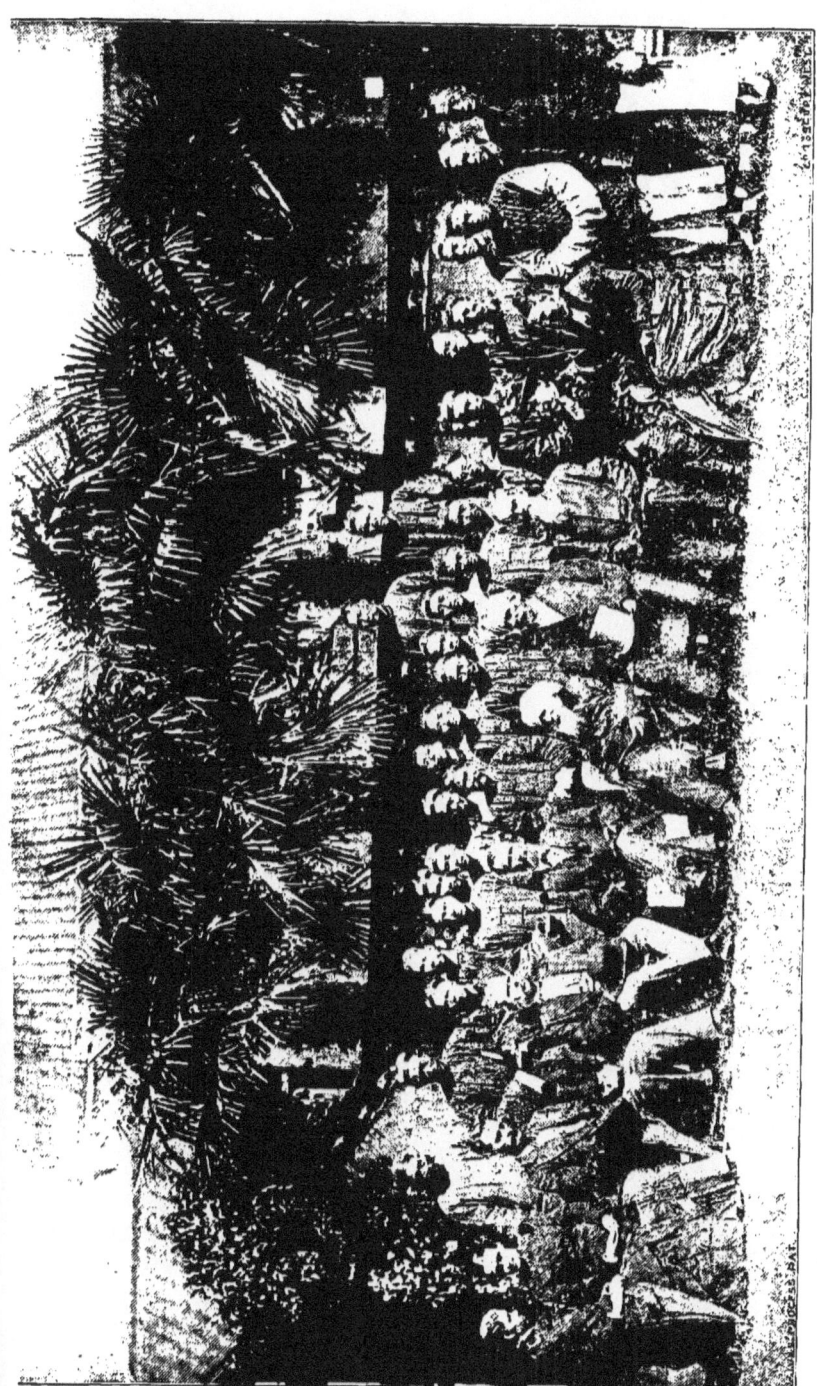

Miss F. B. Lightfoot.   Rev. J. R. Goddard.   Rev. Wm. Dean, D.D.   Rev. T. P. Crawford, D.D.   Mrs. Mason.
                                                  (Siam.)   (Southern Baptist.)
Miss E. Inveen.   Rev. G. L. Mason.   Rev. H. Jenkins.   Rev. M. T. Yates, D.D.   Mrs. Yates.
                                                  (Southern Baptist.)

CHE-KIANG AND KIANG-SU BAPTIST ASSOCIATION, SHANGHAI, OCTOBER, 1881.

using the Sassy wood, "they have discovered the advantage of going before civilized tribunals." In 1851, Brother Murray says: "Our prayers have been heard and answered. The Lord has restored the joy of his salvation, and sinners are inquiring what they must do to be saved." Brother Cheeseman writes of this station, July 3d, 1850: "They have eight or ten candidates for baptism. Brother Murray complains of the rainy season, but every missionary can find abundant work in the rains if he will look for it."

Rev. Mr. Batteste was appointed, February 6th, 1852, to labor at Sinoe with Brethren Murray and Roberts.

Mr. Murray says: "On the part of the young natives, there is a strong disposition to throw off the shackles of heathen customs and superstitions. But they are opposed by the old people, who work on their fears by stories invented for that purpose." Brother H. Teage wrote: "While at Cape Palmas, I asked the old King, if he did not see that 'Merrica man passed him and his people.' He said, 'Yes.' I told him 'it was God palaver, made Merrica man pass him.' He said: 'True, I took dat, all we old man go die, den dem chicks [children] go make God palaver; den Merrica man no go pass him agen.'"

In October, 1856, Mr. Murray wrote: "An important station has been opened at Grand Butan. Brother Neyle has been appointed by Brother Day. Brother Britton fills the place of Brother Batteste, and has a better education than our deceased brother. I shall be able to devote much time to the natives. I have much to do with them since my residence here, and often lament their degraded condition. They are dying for lack of knowledge. I am aware of the difficulties before me, but I believe the Great Head of the Church will give success to his own work."

DECEASE AND OBITUARY.

On the 14th of November, 1856, Mr. Murray passed to his reward. Thus it was recorded: "The indefatigable labors of R. E. Murray, have done much to diffuse the gospel at Sinoe, and to establish there the cause of truth. It is the painful task of the Board to record his removal by death. A vacancy has been thus created which will not easily be filled. He was a good man, and his death will be mourned by many."

The following appeared in *The Commission* of February, 1857: "R. E. Murray was one of the best men connected with our Coast Missions. With him, would seem to have died the hope of a successful mission. Brother Murray was eminently a man of peace—a conscientious, good man. He was Judge, Superintendent, and Missionary. He lived in a hut, and died with $28 in hand, leaving an almost helpless family, because of his large benevolence to his fellow-men."

REV. JOSEPH M. HARDEN.

APPOINTMENT.

On December 2d the following record of the Board appears: "Immediate action with regard to the appointment of Joseph M. Harden, a young colored brother of Baltimore, as a missionary to Africa, was laid on the table, and Brother Crane was requested to inform Brother Harden of this action. On December 11th, 1850, the following is recorded: "A statement having been made by the Corresponding Secretary, in regard to the health of Brother Harden, and also of other circumstances in connection with his case, the resolution declining his appointment was rescinded, and then on motion, the said Harden was appointed to labor as a missionary on the Coast of Africa, under the direction of Brethren Day and Cheeseman."

A RIGHT SPIRIT.

Shortly after arriving in his field at New Virginia, Brother Harden wrote: "I have passed through the acclimating fever, and have in a great measure recovered from the symptoms with which I was afflicted in America. With a dependence on the Holy Spirit, I am endeavoring faithfully to discharge my duty in a meek, patient, and humble manner. Your advice as to the cultivation of a right spirit, I appreciate. My education, I know, is defective; and, as Brethren Day and Cheeseman both can tell you, I have seized upon every opportunity to improve my mind. To sit down contented would be foolish and wicked. The church here has suffered greatly for want of a pastor. Often I adopt the language of Paul: 'Who is sufficient for these things?' But like the same Apostle, 'I can do all things through Christ who strengtheneth me.'" "I have suffered the heavy loss of my only daughter and four barrels of provisions. Like Jacob, all these things seem against me, but they teach me not to set my affections on things below the skies."

AS A BISHOP.

After the death of the lamented James, it was hard to find a suitable man to fill the pastorate at New Virginia. Brother Harden, a man of kindred piety, entered that field on the 21st of September, 1851. Before his ordination he wrote: "Brother Richard White baptized seven at my station; at another time, fifteen were added to the church." He preached also at Caldwell, Louisiana, New Orleans, and Millsburg. He wrote: "Since I have been in Africa I have preached twenty-five sermons. I have five churches to attend to, besides looking after the schools. * * I expect to die preaching the glad tidings of salvation. I shall consider it an honor to die in such a cause." In 1851, one hundred and eighteen were in the school; in 1853, ten were baptized; in 1854, twenty-two put on Christ by baptism. He wrote: "The school under P. M. Page is in a flourishing condition. One of the scholars, ten years old, died in the fall of last year, giving evidence of deep interest in spiritual things. In Stewart's excellent school are fifty-one pupils."

REMOVAL TO LAGOS.

On page 11 of Vol. 11 of *The Commission*, appears the following: "Brother Jos. M. Harden was transferred, in the winter of 1855, to Lagos, because he was fully acclimated and believed to be adapted to the work assigned to him. His time has been engaged in acquiring the language and in giving instruction to the people. By his own liberal contribution, he has, without expense to the Board, secured the erection of a chapel which has been opened for worship. Brother Harden has rendered most efficient service to the Yoruban Mission by superintending the passage of our missionaries, and the transmission of supplies from the coast to the interior."

HORSE-RACING.

May 4, 1858, he writes: "To-day, the first horse-race came off at Lagos. * * The chief cook and bottle-washer of this wicked business calls himself a preacher of the gospel. * * I would rather be the pastor of the three members that I now have than to be the pastor of all the other professors of religion in this place in their present state."

Mrs. HARDEN AND HER SON.

Hereafter Mr. Harden will be noticed in connection with the Yoruban Mission, in which he was eminently useful. When that mission was closed, he betook himself to brick-making for a living. After his death, which we believe was on May 13th, 1864, his wife continued that business. Subsequently she engaged in merchandizing, by which the family was sustained, and the house of God aided. During the long dark period between the close and the re-opening of the Yoruban Mission, the church at Lagos was largely maintained by the intelligence, piety, and generosity of this woman of God. Her maiden name was Sarah Marsh. She was born in Sierra Leone about the year 1835. A member of the Church of England, before her marriage, she was a teacher in the school of that church at Abbeokuta. Three children were born unto them. Only one survives, Samuel Murray Harden. He was born June 12th, 1859, and was baptized at Lagos by Rev. W. J. David, September, 1875. He studied in the "Church Missionary Society Grammar School" at Lagos, in which he was a teacher for twelve months. In 1877, he entered the Richmond Institute of Richmond, Va., as a student for the ministry. Having graduated there with distinction, he is now studying at the "Worcester Academy," Mass.

Rev. J. J. FITZGERALD.

INDEFINITELY POSTPONED.

"*August 4th*, 1851: A letter was received from Rev. J. J. Fitzgerald, of Madison, Georgia, with reference to his appointment as a missionary to Africa. The Corresponding Secretary was directed to reply that, for reasons mentioned in his own communication, it is deemed expedient to postpone indefinitely action in the case."

APPOINTED AND COMMENDED.

"J. J. Fitzgerald (of Illinois) was appointed missionary to Liberia, November 9th, 1859 (J. B. Jeter, the President of the Board, entertaining a high opinion of him, from personal acquaintance). One hundred dollars were appropriated to pay passage of himself and family." The Board, referring, in 1860, to the death of Mr. Cheeseman, say, by way of consolation: "We are favored by finding Brother J. J. Fitzgerald, who has entered upon his labors." Mr. Day wrote: "Brother Fitzgerald is much delighted with his appointment to Grand Cape Mount."

KING SANDFISH.

Grand Cape Mount is on the coast above Monrovia. Brother Kingdon wrote: "I have been gratified by the reception given to us by King Sandfish, who reigns over a most extended district, north of Grand Cape Mount. After a statement of the gospel, and the desire of the Southern Baptist Convention to establish missionaries among the natives, he said he would take great care of any missionary or teacher; would give two hundred children to be instructed, and do all he could to forward the object. This James Sandfish has had a decent education, and acts well as an interpreter. Chief George Cain, close to Cape Mount, received us equally well."

ONLY SAVED BY GOD'S MERCY.

From Cape Mount, Mr. Fitzgerald wrote, September 3d, 1860: "On the twelfth of July, I arrived here, with my family. Attempting to get ashore, our surf boat swamped and capsized, and my wife, child, and myself were only saved by God's mercy and the help of friends. The accident caused Mrs. Fitzgerald a severe spell of fever. The people of this settlement are perhaps the poorest on the coast, because, first, most of the emigrants are sent to Caryburg; second, the Veys and Golahs, who inhabit this part of the country, have been in constant wars. I found the church in a state of confusion. Harmony has been restored. I protracted a meeting, and fifteen or sixteen have professed conversion. I preached on the design and mode of baptism to a crowded house of Methodists, Presbyterians, and Baptists. A class-leader of the Methodist Church, his wife, and another lady, all members of high standing, joined our church. We have twenty-nine candidates for baptism."

THE CHIEF OF SINNERS.

"I must say that the power of the Holy Ghost and the majesty of the gospel have been displayed in our midst. Christ has verified his word, that he can save the chief of sinners. Two of Satan's most notorious servants have been the subjects of Christ's saving grace, and many other hardened sinners." September 3d, 1860.

WHY SILENT.

"The death of our little Edwin, and the illness of my wife, who has not been able to sit up more than three or four days at a time for the last two months, will be deemed I hope, a sufficient excuse for my silence." November 7th, 1860.

SWEET AND HEAVENLY TIME.

"The Lord seems still to be gracious. We are enjoying a sweet and heavenly time. In addition to twenty baptized some time ago, I shall baptize ten more next Sunday, if there be no preventing providence.

SOMETHING NEW ACCOMPLISHED.

"A Church almost dismembered, has been united; confidence has been restored to the doubting and despairing; the energies of the church have been called out to erect a substantial place of worship: and more than thirty have united with us. At the last conference we passed a resolution, to take collections once a quarter for the Board."

WORTHY OF HELP.

"We have commenced our new brick church. We are poor but willing. One of the members, in Conference, said, that he would do all he could; and, if God would let him see the church completed, and hear one sermon in it, he would be willing to depart. Such a people are worthy of help. Will you help us? It is endangering not only my life, but the lives of my congregation to preach where I now do. If you would send a few Sunday-school books, they would be gratefully received." November 7th, 1860.

EMBARRASSED BUT BLESSED.

Brother Fitzgerald wrote in 1862 of "serious embarrassments from the failure to receive funds." But "religiously speaking," he says, "Cape Mount is in a prosperous state. In October, I baptized thirty-seven converts."

RETURN AND DEATH.

In 1867, the Board reported as follows: "Rev. J. J. Fitzgerald, one of the most worthy of our missionaries, of the Grand Cape Mount Mission, having come to this country, on account of his wife's feeble health, was contemplating a return to his field during the present year. But the decision of the Divine Master has interposed, and he has been called to another sphere. He died at Paducah, Ky., on the 15th January. He was a man of superior preaching ability, and an excellent worker. His death will be seriously felt in Liberia. May the Lord of the harvest raise up many others for this field"!

W. W. STEWART.

Rev. John Day wrote: "March 10th, 1849. I preached in New Georgia, where we have a most interesting school of Congoes, Ebos, and Veys, under William W. Stewart. I wish I could speak of all our teachers as I can of Stewart. He appears in his glory with these poor, ragged children around him. Stewart said to a little boy, who came in entirely naked : 'You cannot remain here, in that state.' The little fellow, with a heavy heart, left the house. Stewart then said to me: 'That poor little fellow is very anxious to learn, and learns fast, but he cannot attend school regularly, for want of clothes· * * My eyes were filled with tears. * * I said: 'I shall try to do something for such children.'"

Mr. Stewart became a teacher at Day's Hope; and died in 1857.

REV. ISAAC ROBERTS AND REV. CÆSAR FRAZER.

In 1851, Isaac Roberts and Cæsar Frazer, both from the State of Georgia, were appointed missionaries. The latter was sustained by the Rehoboth Association. He was a native African, having been brought to this country in his youth. His emancipation was voluntarily effected by his master, with special reference to the devotion of his life to the interest of his father-land. As to the former, he began his labors in Farmersville, Sinou County, January 1st, 1852, where he labored faithfully and well, in connection with Rev. R. E. Murray, whom he survives.

December 26th, 1856, Brother Roberts wrote: "On the 2d of November I preached at Farmersville, baptized four persons, and administered the Lord's Supper. * * On the 14th, I preached the funeral sermon of Brother R. E. Murray."

April 19th, 1858, Brother Roberts wrote from Greenville: "I have baptized eight persons for my son, B. B. Roberts, who has been called to the pastoral charge of the Greenville Church. At my little church at Farmersville, I baptized four. * * A poor woman earnestly asked, what she must do to be saved. I pointed her to Jesus. Every mark of penitence was seen in her. * * After the sermon, a doctor asked me to show him how to be saved. I thanked God that I could teach him the way of life. * * I pray God that I may be called away from the midst of the heathen preaching to them Jesus. Then shall I be able to say: 'Now lettest thou thy servant depart in peace, for mine eyes have seen thy salvation.'"

Rev. LEWIS KONG CROCKER.

CHANGE OF NAME AND MARRIAGE.

In 1836, Mr. W. G. Crocker, missionary of the Triennial Convention entered the newly built premises of Edina. Among his pupils was the intelligent and admirable son of King Kober. Afterward, the young chief became an assistant of Mr. Crocker. In 1845, he took charge of an out-station at Little Bassa, and assumed the last name of his lamented teacher, He was faithful at his station; and married a pious girl, "who had been rescued from slavery by Mr. Hilary Teage" in 1835.

EVANGELIZING HIS PEOPLE.

August 19*th*, 1859: "Since I have been connected with your Board, my constant prayers have been to him who heareth prayers, to enable and prepare me fully for this great work of evangelizing my countrymen. * * The change of the people's habits and customs convinces me that the cloud of superstition and heathenism will be cast away by the knowledge of the gospel of Jesus Christ. * * The Bassas to which I belong, need to be taught as well as to be preached to. Though having a vague notion of immortality, they have really no worship. * * I have a school of twelve promising young Bassas, which I sustain from my own little means. Will you please make a small appropriation for their support?"

PERFECT FISHERS OF MEN.

Our native Prince, preacher L. K. Crocker writes: "Mount Hope, October 1st, 1860. If our brethren in America, could see the changes which are taking place among the natives, they would, instead of being disheartened, be more fervent in prayer, that the Lord would hasten the time, when the heathen shall be given to his Son, for an inheritance. * * Missionaries ought not to confine themselves to formal preaching. To be a perfect fisherman, one must understand the management of the seine, the cast-net, and the hook. To the large congregation, I deliver a sermon; to a less number, I use the catechetical method; when I meet one, conscience will not permit me to part without a word about his never-dying soul. Since our children are clothed, a new aspect is thrown around our labors in school. We have a larger number than formerly to our Lord's Day meetings. The natives come of their own accord.

RE-APPOINTED AND DEPARTED.

When the Mission was re-organized in 1872, Brother Crocker as shall be seen, was re-appointed, and did faithful service. He is now in the midst of his heavenly reward.

Rev. MELFORD D. HERNDON.

A STUDENT AT DAY'S HOPE.

Rev. John Day wrote September 25th, 1858: "Mr. Herndon is attending school at Day's Hope, four hours in the day, and makes rapid improvement. It is a pity that such a mind could have had no early advantages. I have great hopes of him. His habits of ranting have been formed for want of better direction. His abundantly good sense, with the grace of God, will put all right. He is beginning to read so as to be understood; and seems as in a new world. For knowledge, he is like a hungry man. He is meek and docile as a child.

MISSSIONARY OF OUR BOARD.

On the recommendation of Doctor Howard Malcom, of Philadelphia, Mr. Herndon was appointed a Missionary by our Board; but his services were discontinued on account of sundry statements received from Africa by the Board. Returning to this country, he issued on the back of his photograph the following:

"Melford D. Herndon was born near Russellville, in Logan County, Kentucky, 1814. He was emancipated in 1852 by the will of James Herndon, of Simpson County, Kentucky. In 1854, he went to Liberia, in Africa, with his brothers, Solomon and Robert, who had been set free at the same time with himself. He learned to read and write at a Mission School, called 'Day's Hope,' taught by Rev. John Day, in Monrovia, and having a missionary spirit, he was appointed a missionary among the Bassa people. For fifteen years he was aided by the Missionary Board at Richmond, Va. Owing to the lack of funds, the salaries of the missionaries in Africa were suspended, August 31, 1872. Anxious to save the souls of the heathen and to teach the children, he has come here to obtain pecuniary aid. He desires to secure thirty dollars per annum to sustain fifteen boys and girls. 'It is more blessed to give than to receive.'"

OTHER MISSIONARIES AND TEACHERS.

Prepared sketches of Robt. F. Hill, A. T. Wood, Wm. A. Johnson, Edward Paul, Samuel P. Day, S. S. Page, W. Moore, Smart Purvis, H. Teage, Richard White, Henry Underwood; and of Brethren Brock, Button, Von Brunn, and others, are omitted for lack of space.

B. P. YATES.

One of the most valuable men connected with our work in Liberia is the brother whose name heads this article. He is not a preacher nor a teacher; but he has often taken a fraternal oversight of the work, especially in the time of its severe need, and managed the finances of the Mission for over twenty years. On June 12th, 1855, it was, "*Resolved*, That B. P. Yates of the Financial Committee be appointed Secretary of the Committee." At our request, he has furnished the following

AUTOBIOGRAPHICAL OUTLINE.

"I was born in the city of Richmond, September 2d, 1809, of free parents. I received a common-school learning, such as was granted to colored children in the city of Richmond at that time. I was not apprenticed to any trade or handicraft. Mr. Robert Sharp took me when young, and kept me in his office on Carey Street, where I did the work of a clerk until I left for Liberia.

"On my arrival in Liberia, upon recommendation, I found immediate employment in a mercantile house, which employment I held for several years. On the dissolution of the firm, I was able to set up business for myself.

"I left the city of Richmond 10th of January, 1829, for Norfolk; left Hampton Roads, 9th of February, and arrived at Monrovia, 18th of March, 1829.

"I was married January 2d, 1832, to Miss W. N. Payne, daughter of Rev. David Payne, of the M. E. Church, Liberia. She is now living and in good health. We have had four children, only one of whom is now living.

"I was baptized by Rev. Colson M. Warring, of the Providence Baptist Church, Monrovia, January 3d, 1831. I then joined the above-named church, in which I was ordained deacon, 1840, and still hold that office.

"My employments have been various. I have served in the army as private in the line, and now hold the rank of Brigadier General. I was Vice President of the Republic, Judge of the Court of Session nine and a half years, and am now Judge of Probate Court. I have been the servant of the Southern Baptist Mission in Liberia, as their Financial Agent, under their appointment dated 1854."

SUPERINTENDENCY.

B. P. Yates was appointed Superintendent of the Liberian Mission *Pro Tem.*, on the death of John Day, April 2, 1859. On September

14, 1859, he was appointed Permanent Superintendent, with J. T. Richardson associated with him.

TOUR OF INSPECTION.

Brother B. P. Yates wrote August 24, 1859: "I had commenced a visit to all the various stations in this and Bassa County, and got as far as Marshall Junk, when I was seized with a severe attack of ague and fever. * * From what I have seen both of churches and schools, I am fully satisfied, that they came up to the standard of their several reports without any embellishment.

BRIGHT NUDE BOY.

"Jack Powell found a book on my counter. He read so clearly as to attract the attention of Rev. Mr. Payne. A man standing by said: 'Is that boy positively reading?' He was almost in a state of nudity, one handkerchief around his loins. Mr. Payne said: 'Where did you learn to read?' The boy replied: 'Mr. Powell, who keeps the Baptist Mission School near my father's town, taught me.' Mr. Payne asked me, who paid Mr. Powell for teaching them? I answered—God."— *B. P. Yates*, of Monrovia.

MR. YATES' REPORT ON CHURCHES AND SCHOOLS.

"July 13th, 1860. The church at Careysburg has received some fifty or seventy-five additions by the ship M. C. S.—Millsburg is moving on as usual.—Both the church and school at Louisiana are on the march.—Clay Ashland holds her own.—At Virginia, H. Underwood has been visited with an abundant out-pouring of God's goodness, 13 to be baptized next Sunday.—At Caldwell, with F. Richardson, as pastor, the church begins to hold up its head, though few in numbers.—New Georgia, F. W. Britton as pastor, is not on the mountain-top, but is holding on the even tenor of her ways.—The church at Monrovia has been cold, and dull, but there is a sound in the tops of the mulberry trees. Our hearts are warmed; the schools are in a healthy state.—King Gray's district school is in a fine condition. The boys surpass anything I have ever known, so far as learning to read goes.—The church at Marshall is on the forward march. Brother White, from ill health, resigned the pastorate. The church called Hugh Waller, who seems destined to do much good. The school is in a flourishing state. Brother Page is a worthy man.—At Edina, the school continues under the instruction of Mrs. Cheeseman. Brother Roberts still preaches there and at Bexley. Both churches are in a healthy state.—Von Brunnsville Church and school move on steadily. Buchanan Church has been visited by an out-pouring of God's blessing.—Sinoe: Brother Roberts is very acceptable to the church and the natives.—Since the death of Brother Morrill, Brother Monger has taken charge of Farmersville.—I am heavily taxed when I visit the native schools. The children feel their advancement in civilization, and beg me to clothe them. Can any aid be given for this specific purpose? May our happy lot be to see Ethiopia stretch forth her hand unto God!

RETRENCHMENT.

The war being upon us, the Board reported, in 1861: " In the retrenchments to which the Board felt themselves compelled, nearly all the teachers employed in this Mission have been dismissed, so that during the coming year, but little can be expected in this department. The measure was adopted with reluctance, and only from a felt necessity. Great good has been done by the schools. But the Board must retrench and could do so as effectually at no other point."

NOT FORSAKEN BY GOD.

The Board reported in 1863: " From the Mission Stations in Liberia, but little information has been received. The Superintendent of the Mission, Brother B. P. Yates, writes: ' I am glad to say that notwithstanding our many impediments God has not forsaken us. Our churches have been alive in spiritual matters. They have been more or less visited by the divine blessing. There have been numerous baptisms. A large proportion are native converts; the majority are of the Congo Tribe. Through deep waters we have been called to pass, but our Heavenly Father has not suffered them to overflow us.' "

MISSIONARIES STILL AT THEIR POSTS.

In another letter, he says: " Our Missions are still in active operation. All the missionaries are at their posts. The schools, except those taught by the pastors of the churches to which they belong, have been discontinued except two native schools, one in this country and one in the Bassa country."

DAY'S HOPE.

Brother Yates wrote September 28th, 1865: "The Liberian College, with twelve students in the college proper, is the only reliable means of education among us, and it admits only such boys as have made certain progress. Since the commencement of the war, Day's Hope has been suspended. Our denomination is behind in the means of intellectual culture. It will require at least $1,000 to put the premises in proper condition. A competent teacher for the higher department will devote a portion of his time for $400. It is my earnest prayer that Day's Hope in its Primary and Higher departments will be re-opened."

IDENTIFIED TO THE END.

Brother Yates having been identified with our Liberian Mission to its final close in 1875, will be referred to in our subsequent history of that Mission. He still lives in Monrovia, honored by the State, and beloved by the church.

REV. J. JAMES CHEESEMAN.

"Mr. Cheeseman was appointed by the Board, through their General Superintendent, Rev. A. D. Phillips, on his visit to Africa, in January, 1871. "The American Settlement at Edina, on the Sea Coast and on the west bank of the Saint John's River, together with Buchanan, on the east bank, have the most flourishing Baptist Churches of any in the Colony. Brother J. J. Cheeseman, at the former place, is doing a good work. His father, Rev. J. H. Cheeseman, of whom a sketch has been given, was our missionary at the same place. He taught school, and also gave instruction to a class of young men, looking to the ministry. The son, the subject of this notice, has the best Sunday-school in the Colony, and, I believe, the best working church. During the years that our work has been suspended there, he has kept steadily on, supporting himself and family, preaching every Sunday, and giving instruction in the week to young men preparing for the ministry. These young men are sent out every Lord's Day to the villages and towns of the native heathen, where regular service is held."—*Home and Foreign Journal, March,* 1872.

It is not saying too much to affirm that Mr. Cheeseman was perhaps the most polished and accomplished Colored Missionary, who has ever been connected with our African Mission. His chirography was elegant; his letters were finely written; and his reports of the stations were models of accuracy and business-propriety.

The following description is from the pen of a gentleman well acquainted with Mr. Cheeseman.

"Our Missionary, Rev. J. J. Cheeseman of Edina, Liberia, is about medium size, easy and ready in conversation, rather polished in manners, fine-looking, with a pretty well developed head, and in many respects is superior to his fellow-men. His educational advantages in early life were inferior, but because of close attention to his well selected library, he has obtained a pretty good stock of general information, which, in the possession of a practical mind like his, is well calculated to bring him to the front rank of his countrymen, where he stands.

"As a business man, he is shrewd, careful, and successful. As a book-keeper, he is a good accountant, and has almost perfect chirography. As a politician, he enjoys the confidence of his constituents, and his judgment is highly regarded by his colleagues in the Legislature.

"As an earnest, practical, exhortative preacher, probably he has not an equal, and certainly not a superior, in Liberia. He has considerably more executive ability than is characteristic of his race. His church is the largest and most prosperous in the country; and has established two or three mission stations among the Americo-Liberians and aborigines. It has built two or three chapels, besides assisting in the erection of several churches in other sections of that country."

The following picture of the native women from his pen, under date of February, 1872, indicates something of humor: "After many civilities had been extended to Sister Liberty, and she had been greeted as the missionary lady, I was surrounded by a group of would-be handsome ladies, clothed with no more than two yards of cloth each. These ladies not only had on all this cloth, but were decorated in the most elaborate manner with paintings of chalk, and on the whole presented an appearance not at all agreeable. They began a minute examination of my person, and finally got around to my watch-guard. After begging for it, which, of course, was refused, they then became desirous to know what was at the end of it in my pocket. I took out my watch and showed them the works, at which they expressed much surprise and wonder. They concluded this inspection by complimenting me with a pat, first on the breast, then on the shoulder, and calling me *Khahnay*, viz.: sweet-heart. * * * At half past seven o'clock P. M. I assembled the town-people for worship. During the services, a female was seen all the while melting in tears, whom I afterward found to be one of the King's women, or wives. She expressed the desire to become a Christian. * * * The melody of the congregation could not be compared with our best choirs: but they showed a willing mind and made a noise."

The valuable services of Mr. Cheeseman are elsewhere referred to. His connection with the Board ceased, in 1875, under circumstances explained by the following correspondence:

MONROVIA, LIBERIA, *May* 25, 1875.

REV. J. J. CHEESEMAN.

My Dear Brother:—Having been informed that you have entered upon the political arena, which is contrary to article 1 of instructions to ministers, we deem it to be our imperative duty to ask you to send us your resignation as Missionary of the F. M. B. S. B. C., the discontinuance of your connection with the Board to begin July 1st, 1875. You will draw your regular salary up to June 30th, the end of the second quarter.

The article above referred to reads thus: "They (the missionaries) shall not engage in any secular pursuits or trade for themselves, or act as agents for others," &c. My brother, we regret exceedingly to have you leave our ranks, for the laborers are few. More men are needed: souls are perishing. And oh that the ministers could pity these men and women as our Saviour did! Being enthused with this spirit, we would go as he did about our Father's business.

We could write more, but must forbear, trusting the Lord will be with you, and hoping to hear from you soon, we remain,

Yours, in Christ,

(Signed) W. J. DAVID,
B. P. YATES.

Reply.

EDINA, BASSA, *June* 20, 1875.

MESSRS. YATES & DAVID, MONROVIA.

My Dear Brethren:—Your letter under date of 25th May is to hand, and in reply thereto I beg to say that I do not recognize your authority to ask my resignation nor to dismiss me from the service of the Board. Because: In view of my official relation to the Board as Spiritual Advisor to missionaries in general and Superintendent of missionaries in particular within this (my) district, I hold that any charge against me must first be brought to the notice of the Board; that action may be taken thereupon. And, until this is done, I shall rely upon the honesty and integrity of the Board for an impartial decision in the premises. Meanwhile, I shall claim every privilege guaranteed to me. Yours truly,

(Signed) J. JAS. CHEESEMAN.

EDINA, BASSA, *June* 20, 1875.

REV. H. A. TUPPER, D.D., *Cor. Sec'y*, &c.

Dear Brother:—I very much regret to have occasion to call your attention to some unpleasantness which has come up between Brethren Yates and David and myself, particulars of which you will gather from enclosed copies of correspondence which has passed between us.

You well know my relation to the Board, and as such I think I am answerable only to the Board for any departure from its rules. Not being a missionary employed among the heathen, but being employed to overlook those thus employed, I do not conceive it to be a departure for me to follow secular pursuits, so long as I discharge faithfully the duties of my official relation to the Board.

I do not know that it will be amiss to say that, in view of the relative position I hold with Brother Yates, I have as much right to follow legitimate secular pursuits as for him to be serving as Judge of Courts. Do not understand me as using this against Brother Yates. I rather commend him more to the confidence of the Board, as I believe he has been and is still a faithful servant. This present action I look upon as merely an oversight as to extent of authority.

Respecting Brother David, I do not recognize in him any further authority than conferring with us in re-organizing the Mission work here. I am rather impressed that he has wilfully transcended his authority. I hope, however, that I am in error and that I am charging him wrongfully.

Until action is had by the Board through you, I shall not respect the action of Brethren Yates and David, and with perfect willingness to submit to the impartial decision of the Board, I remain,

Yours, faithfully,

J. J. CHEESEMAN.

OUR COLORED MISSIONARIES OF SIERRA LEONE,

H. P. THOMSON AND J. J. BROWN.

MISSION AT SIERRA LEONE.

The Board "*Resolved* (April 3d, 1855), That five hundred dollars per annum be appropriated for the establishment of a mission at Sierra Leone, and that our Financial Committee at Monrovia be authorized to secure the services of Rev. H. P. Thomson as our Missionary there, should they on examination deem it appropriate."

THE PROSPECT ENCOURAGING.

Sierra Leone is one of the most inviting fields on the coast of Africa. Rev. Mr. Thomson, residing at Freetown, who "earnestly desires to leave his position as First Clerk in the Government Post Office, that he may give himself wholly to preaching the gospel," will take charge of the Mission. Brother Day represents the prospect as most encouraging.

SUPERVISION.

June 9th, 1856.—The Committee on the African Missions of our Board recommended that the stations at Freetown and Waterloo of Sierra Leone be under the supervision of the Financial Committee at Monrovia, and that the travelling expenses of Mr. Day in visiting the Sierra Leone Mission be allowed by the Board.

GREAT ENCOURAGEMENT.

H. P. Thomson writes, Waterloo, June 23d, 1856: "We need a good chapel. We have only a shabbily built house of sticks and mud, which can hardly hold fifty persons. * * But I can exclaim with wonder: 'What hath God wrought?' Jesus' love for poor sinners has filled them with amazement, and many ask: 'What shall I do to be saved?' * * Those who were formerly content to live without marrying are now earnestly desiring it: those who were willing to serve idols are forsaking them, and flocking to the house of God. Is this not great encouragement?"

NEW APPOINTMENTS.

Brother Day wrote from Freetown, May 6th, 1857: "I have appointed Leigh Richmond as teacher of the school here. Educated in the Church of England; baptized some ten years ago, he was long a teacher in the Methodist Mission, and has good recommendations. * * Cosso, where our chapel is, is a native town. The eight to be baptized now, will make twelve at Cosso. I have employed a young man, highly recommended, by name George Weeks, and sent him there to preach, catechize, and devote himself to the work of the Mission. I allow him two hundred dollars. Mr. Brown, whose labor is beyond his strength, having two congregations in Freetown, I employ to devote all his time at Waterloo. I allow him two hundred dollars. I also allow one hundred dollars to the teacher at Waterloo. They have a very poor teacher at Freetown."

Under date of January, 1858, Mr. Brown writes: "Now we have employed one Mr. Daniel W. During, who we believe is both able and competent to discharge that duty with credit, and believe also that in course of time the school will be enlarged. It now numbers fifty-eight."

Mr. Weeks writes: "During divine service, a great many are obliged to sit or stand outside, whether it rains or not."

NO DEW: GRACIOUS SHOWER.

Freetown, June 19th, 1858. Rev. J. J. Browne wrote: "The church here is not progressing; no convert in six months. Why should the dew of heaven fall copiously, while we are dry and barren? We want more faith, more prayer, more wrestling with God for the outpouring of his Spirit.

Waterloo is twenty-three miles from Freetown; a mighty revival is agitating that place. When Brother Weeks first entered the town, there were five members; in eighteen months they have increased to thirty-five. The small chapel is generally full, and the people attentive. We must watch and pray to God, and the people will forsake dumb idols, and crown Jesus Lord of all."

EXHIBIT 1858.

This Mission was in charge of Rev. J. J. Browne at Freetown, and George S. Weeks at Waterloo, with the teachers, D. W. During and Leigh Richmond. November 17th, 1858, Brother Browne made the following exhibit: "From January to September 30th inclusive, thirty-six persons were admitted into church fellowship by immersion. The total number of Baptists in connection with the Southern Board is one hundred and sixteen; viz., at Freetown, seventy-two; at Waterloo, forty-four. The school under D. W. During, numbers eighty-four, who are taught Reading, Writing, Arithmetic, English Grammar, Geography, etc. The day-school at Waterloo has twenty-nine children under Mr. Leigh Richmond. The Sunday-school numbers forty, and, as at Freetown, consists of children and adults. The means of grace have been well attended."

Sierra Leone, February 1st, 1859. "Mr. Windham was an incompetent teacher," writes Mr. Day, "whom I advised to be dismissed so soon as a man could be obtained. James Early died last night. On the 27th December, the son of the Elder Richmond was baptized at Freetown with eight others. The ministry is greatly assisted by Mr. Barrett, a native of this place, who returned home from America, a preacher, licensed by the African Baptist Society of that country." In a previous letter, Mr. Day mentioned the death of W. H. Stewart, the teacher of the boys' school at Monrovia.

DENIED BUT NOT DISCOURAGED.

April 18th, 1859. Mr. Browne wrote: "Though the Board do not think it right and proper to comply with my suggestions as regards the appointment of a Sub-agent of the Colony, yet the promptness and Christian-like manner of your correspondence encourages me as well as my laboring brethren not a little."

THE COSSO PEOPLE.

March 31st, 1860. "Oh that some of you were present to hear our Cosso brethren and sisters offering prayer! It would make you weep to consider that some years back they had no one to tell them about their souls; but now the Lord has sent help from a country far beyond the sea, to instruct them to escape from hell, and flee to heaven. * * Oh! if you were here to hear the Cosso children spelling, reading, and singing, it would astonish you. Some years past they were running mad in the streets; now I bless the Lord they can read the Bible clearly and distinctly." W. S. Browne, Waterloo, Sierra Leone.

NOT SO WELL IN SIERRA LEONE.

J. J. Browne writes: "Freetown, October 21st, 1860. We have a new teacher, Richard J. Hayeley. The church at Waterloo and school are not so well as I wish. The people are not satisfied with Brother W. S. Browne. They still wish Brother Weeks to return to them. He has agreed to go up at the end of the quarter. I hope the next quarter to write you better news. I am still sick."

TROUBLES AND CLOSE.

STATISTICS OF MISSION.
1860.
LIBERIA AND SIERRA LEONE.

Churches and Stations.	Pastors.	Baptized during the year.	No. of Members.	Teachers.	No. of Scholars.
Monrovia,	J. T. Richardson,		194	High School, H. R. N. Johnson,	12
				Primary, W. W. Stewart,	59
				Congo School, J. N. Brander,	12
Grand Cape Mount,	J. J. Fitzgerald,	26	48	P. B. Anderson,	55
Careysburg,	A. Woodson,	2	42	John R. Freeman,	32
Millsburg,	James Bullock,	1	26	R. F. White,	29
Louisiana,	F. Richardson,	5	35	P. M. Page,	20
Clay Ashland,	Wm. C. Burke,	9	110	Wm. C. Burke,	21
New Virginia,	H. Underwood,	11	73	D. L. Leiper,	42
Caldwell,	F. Richardson,		10		
New Georgia,	S. W. Britton,	7	93	S. W. Britton,	37
				Mrs. G. A. Britton,	
Marshall,	Hugh Walker,		26	S. S. Page,	38
Edina,	R. F. Hill,	3	52	Miss M. A. Cheeseman,	22
Bexley,	R. F. Hill,		36		..
Vonbrunnsville.	J. Von Brunn,			Jacob Von Brunn,	40
Buchanan,	A. P. Davis,	4	40	A. P. Davis,	39
				Mrs. S. A. Davis,	
Greenville,				Jas. N. Lewis,	49
Farmersville }	Isaac Roberts,		258		
Lexington,					
				Wm. H. Monger,	29
Cape Palmas,	B. J. Drayton,		68	H. W. Motton,	28
				G. H. Jordan, (native pupil,)	12
Little Bassa,	L. K. Crocker,			Geo. B. Peck,	14
" " Interior,	M. D. Herndon,			M. D. Herndon,	
King Grey's Town,				J. J. Powell,	17
Congo Town,				Moore Worrell,	20
Free Town, }	J. J. Browne,			Richard James Hayeley,	38
Waterloo, }	Wm. S. Browne,		147	Wm. S. Browne,	
24	18	68	1258	26	665

LIBERIAN MISSION.

DURING THE WAR.
1863 to 1866.

ON THEIR OWN RESOURCES.

In 1866, the Board reported: "For the last three or four years, the stations on the coast, eighteen or twenty in number, have been thrown on their own resources, with the hope that at no distant period they might, as formerly, be vigorously sustained. Remittances have been made for services performed in 1860 to 1861, and there are a few claims yet to be met by the Board."

LEAST EXPENSIVE AND MOST REMUNERATIVE.

"In these fields, more than a thousand believers in Jesus have been baptized by our missionaries. For the number of the stations and the extent of the field, these missions have been less expensive, and, in the number of accessions to the churches, more remunerative than any other under our control. It has been difficult to bring into operation the self-sustaining principle among the churches; but that difficulty may more or less be overcome."

THE CHURCHES AND SCHOOLS.

"The people and their pastors have manifested a commendable zeal in keeping together their respective churches, in the absence of pecuniary aid from the United States. They have all been blessed with seasons of revival. Brother H. Walker is the Stated Supply at Junk. He has been remarkably active. The ordinances have been administered there by Brethren Hill and Davis as occasion requires. A very promising young Brother Gibson of that church will probably be or dained at the next Association. The churches at Monrovia, on the St. Paul's River, and at Careysburg, have been blessed; but the unvarying cry is, 'The laborers are few.' In the church at Monrovia there are two young brethren looking forward to the ministry. Our day schools have all gone down."

RESOLUTION OF THE BOARD.

March, 1866. *Resolved*, That, in view of the divine care of our missionaries during the past four years of frightful war, we are under renewed obligations to cherish an humble and grateful spirit, and to prosecute our work with renewed diligence."

Their report of this year concludes thus: "Let us, then, go forward, inscribing on our banner: 'Jesus and the gospel proclaimed to all nations.'"

The Convention adopted the following resolution:

"*Resolved*, That the Board be instructed to consider the expediency of an early resumption of the Mission Stations on the African Coast."

DISMAL INTERREGNUM.

1866 TO 1870.

VAIN APPEAL.

The Board reported in 1867: "The condition of the Treasury has forbidden any attempt during the year to resume our work on the Coast of Africa. The appeal has come to us from that quarter imploring aid; and had the means been within our power, it would have met with a favorable response."

REPORT OF FINANCIAL SECRETARY YATES.

Association: This body, "The Baptist Association of Liberia," had its annual meeting (1867) with the Baptist Church at Buchanan. Brother A. P. Yates was Moderator. The churches were properly represented. The Cape Palmas Church petitioned the Association, and the Providence Baptist Church at Monrovia for aid, and for brethren "to ordain Brother Milton, if found worthy, to the work of the ministry." The minutes of the last Association have not been printed. The churches are on the onward march.

"*Monrovia:* In November, December, and January, the church immersed twenty-four candidates. To the two young men training for the ministry, the church has appropriated $150. Cannot the Board lend a helping hand? Unless Day's Hope be repaired before the dry season, it will be a shameful waste of means. I am unable to do more until I am reimbursed for what I have done in keeping it up for the last five years. The Mission Cause here languishes for lack of men and means."

Representative but not responsible: "I gave notice to the Brethren, that as Agent to the Board, I could not hold myself responsible for their salaries, but I would represent their services to the Board. Brother A. Woodson has given his undivided attention to the church at Careysburg. If the Board can remunerate him, it will be the redemption of the pledge I made."

INSTRUCTION REQUESTED, AND ADVICE GIVEN.

1868: "The Board have under consideration the expediency of commencing their operations anew on the coast, where so many seals of the divine blessing have already been found. Is it the desire of the Convention that this field shall be re-opened? Special instructions on this question are desired."

The Convention replied: "So soon as the discretion of the Board shall dictate it, and the receipts of the Treasury will justify it, they would advise the re-opening of the Liberian Mission."

BRIEF AND DISMAL.

1869: "The Board have not been indifferent as to the resumption of our Liberian Missions; but the resources have not at any time been sufficient to warrant a serious consideration of the subject."

A RAY OF LIGHT.

1870: "Funds have been received during the year, from colored brethren in the South, and the time may not be distant, when both men and money will be furnished for this field in abundant measure for our African churches."

BASE OF OPERATIONS IN LIBERIA.
1871 TO 1876.

VISIT AND RETURN OF REV. A. D. PHILLIPS.

Mr. Phillips, who had been identified with the Yoruba Mission for some twelve years, returned to America at the close of the year 1868; and in 1871, was reported by the Board to the Convention, as having been commissioned, according to his wishes, to visit the Coast of Liberia, with the view of securing a good base of operation, for establishing missions among the contiguous tribes, and for carrying forward the work of missions into the interior of the country. At Sierra Leone he found the churches "walking in the truth," and recommended our former missionary, Brother Weeks, for re-appointment. He appointed in Liberia, subject to the approval of the Board, eight or ten men to labor "among the native tribes." The Convention adopted the view that, "the exploration of Brother Phillips, in Sierra Leone, and the Bassa Country, will serve to prepare the way into the interior for the gospel." Mr. Phillips, believing that the missions of Africa could be superintended from America, returned to the United States, about the time of the death of Dr. Taylor; and for several weeks conducted affairs in the office of the departed Corresponding Secretary.

MISSIONARIES AND STATIONS.

A. D. PHILLIPS, *White Missionary.*

Old Fields—Fifteen miles from Monrovia—H. Underwood, Missionary.

Congo Town—On Junk River, near Marshall—E. Waughn.

Taylorsville—Between Junk and Farmington Rivers—Teacher, Josephine Early; Preacher, G. Tytler.

Herndonville—Between Marshall and Little Bassa—M. D. Herndon, Missionary, and Gibson, Teacher.

Little Bassa—On the coast, sixty miles below Monrovia—L. K. Crocker and Tate.

Phillipsburg—On Mechlin River, twenty miles interiorward—M. D. Liberty.

Donogba—Near Bexley, on St. John's River—J. Cook.

Zeo's Beir Country, 100 miles interior—G. F. Gibson and Cuthbert.

B. P. Yates, Financial Agent, and J. J. Cheeseman, Superintendent.

MR. PHILLIPS' REPORT CONDENSED.

I arrived in Monrovia on Sunday, the 22d of January, 1871. I visited Marshall, where I found a feeble church. Several native towns offer inviting fields. All the converts at "Old Fields" signed a letter begging me to send them regular instruction. From Mt. Olive, on the Farmington River, I went some ninety or one hundred miles in a northeasterly direction to King Zeo's territory and town, called the Beir Country. They are a savage race. But King Zeo received me graciously and treated me hospitably. His influence extends over all the surrounding Bassa tribes, who number some two hundred thousand, and speak the same language. Some of these people are very anxious for us to send them missionaries. I entered into a written treaty with King Zeo, he binding himself to protect our missionaries and teachers, and I, that *only* those should be sent who would devote themselves *exclusively* to preaching and teaching. Returning to Marshall, I set out for Grand Bassa, Little Bassa, and Edina. I suffered much for water. Finding it impracticable to walk farther, and having seen enough to form a judgment about the points to be occupied, I appointed eight preachers and teachers, and returned to Marshall and Monrovia, quite broken down. I took steamer to Lagos, where I was quite pleased with the progress of the little church. They are willing to make any sacrifice to secure preaching. I would suggest that a suitable man be sent to them. Also, that a training school be established at Edina, under Brother Cheeseman.

RULERS AND PEOPLE.

The missionary wrote cheeringly of the gratitude, improvement, and earnest desire for instruction manifested by the natives; and gave encouraging instances of the interest which the rulers evinced in our work.

Sister Early of Taylorsville, wrote: "The King has given me three of his daughters for the school."—Brother Cook, who is from Columbus, Ga., said: "The King at Donogba has learned to read the Scriptures, and says he wants to be a Christian."—Our native prince missionary, L. K. Crocker, urged that as the people believe in God as the Creator of all, but that there is no mode of worshipping him, they need to be taught concerning the Lord Jesus Christ, the Son of God, and the Mediator between God and man.—Of Zeo's town in the Beir country, Brother Gibson writes: "The natives seem to be growing into reverence for the gospel, and respect for the Lord's Day. They attend meetings regularly twice on the Lord's Day. Vonkra, the ruler now since Zeo is dead, seems willing and tries to lend all his influence in favor of the gospel. Brother Cuthbert's school is progressing finely. I believe that if we undertake great things for God, we may expect great things from him."—Brother Cuthbert wrote: "Some of the principal men in the town are becoming much concerned about the salvation of their souls. Some have come to us privately, making anxious inquiries about this salvation of Jesus Christ."—Brother Yates says: "Vonkra writes me there is no fear that the missionary operations will be interfered with."—Brother Cheeseman: "Several of the natives have told me that they desire to quit their heathen practices and serve our blessed Jesus."

EYE ON YORUBA.

As has been stated, the stations in Liberia were re-established with the view of extending work into the interior. Our Missionaries had been driven out of Yoruba, but the Board entertained the hope of re-entering that country, possibly from the North, and probably, in time, as formerly, from the South. Hence they report in 1872: "Lagos ought to be occupied as the key to the Yoruba country. The little band in Abbeokuta are unmolested in their weekly services; and though the white man is excluded, we should stand at the door, ready to enter as soon as an opening is granted."

SUPERINTENDENCY.

In the report on African Missions, adopted by the Convention, we find the words: "The Mission should be, for the most part, conducted by colored men * * but, in organizing this mission, and establishing it upon a permanent basis, at least one white man should be employed as Superintendent." The Board had reported in 1872, to the Convention: "Whether the work in Africa can be accomplished without a resident Superintendent of our race, is a question which experience has not yet decided."

LOSS BY DEATH AND WITHDRAWAL.

In 1873, the Board reported that Brother H. Underwood departed this life in July, 1872, and that Brother T. Early preached occasionally in his place at "Old Fields:" also that Brother E. Waughn, of Congo Town, which Brother Tytler and Gibson occasionally supplied, had, in August of the same year, gone to his reward. These humble laborers of Christ had no place among the distinguished of earth, but they may wear a bright crown among the redeemed of heaven." They also reported that: "Brother Phillips, so long identified with, and so laborious and successful in, our missions, thinking it not best to return to Africa to live, withdrew in May, 1872, from the employment of the Board. It is a cause of congratulation that his valuable services are still secured to the Convention, in behalf of Domestic and Indian Missions.

A WHITE MAN NEEDED.

On the death of King Zeo of the Beir Country, a conflict arose in his family with regard to the succession; and notwithstanding the assurance of Vonkra, the brother of the late King, that our missionaries would not be interfered with, they were warned to quit the country; and consulting their apprehensions perhaps somewhat unduly, they retired into Liberia. The Board, confirmed by this circumstance in previous convictions, reported, in 1878, to the Convention: "The Board is convinced that while most of the labor in Africa must be done by colored missionaries, a superior man of our race is needed on the field as an enlightened instructor, a wise counselor, and a bold leader. No suitable person has been found."

SUSPENSION OF MISSIONARIES.

Not proposing to maintain missions in Liberia, except as posts to carry the gospel into the interior, and our country being in the midst of one of the most fearful money-pressures and panics which was ever known, the Board reported thus to the Convention: "When the news came that our missionaries had been driven out of the Bier Country by intestine troubles, which news synchronized with the cramped condition of our treasury, it was thought prudent to suspend the missionaries and teachers, excepting Brethren Yates and Cheeseman, until a suitable white missionary could be secured, and the necessary funds should be raised."

NOBLE CONDUCT.

The distress of the missionaries and teachers was extreme, and their piteous appeals were most touching. Extracts from their letters are found in the Report of 1873. But they "resolved that the work should go on at their own expense, until the patronage of the Board might be again extended." Mr. Gibson wrote: "With one accord, and without communication with each other, we have concluded to go on with the work, and trust to God, who has promised to be the hope and strength of his people."

FOREIGN MISSIONS.

BRIGHTENING PROSPECTS.

Brother B. P. Yates, under date of November 2d, 1872, reports "a glorious revival" among the churches. At New Georgia, eighteen were to be baptized. He says: "The candle of the Lord is once more shining on the heads of his people." December 16th, he wrote: "Brother W. F. Gibson, one of the missionaries driven from the Beir Country, informs me that he has just received a messenger from one of King Zeo's sons, saying that the disturbances would soon be settled, and that he would come down in a short time to carry our missionaries back."

IS A WHITE MAN ESSENTIAL?

The Board reported: "The Convention must decide whether the resumption of the Mission shall depend or not upon securing a suitable white man for the field." The Convention responded: "We cannot but commend the wisdom and fidelity displayed in the conduct of this Mission."

APPEALS, APPROPRIATIONS, AND APPLICANTS.

In the Report of 1874, the Board presented an appeal from Africa, in which our missionaries say: "The suspension reduced us and our families to the point of nakedness and starvation; but we do not deem it right to omit duty, because the Board have neglected us: and again, Woe is us if we preach not the gospel." Brother B. P. Yates also addressed the colored people of this country: "The first church established in Liberia is the present Providence Baptist Church of Monrovia. From this germ have originated about twenty churches and the Liberian Baptist Association. A peculiar claim rests on us. The efforts of white men to introduce the gospel in this land have been devoted and self-denying; but they have been a series of disasters and death. The work must be done by us, and by you, who are enjoying the glorious advantages of education." The Board reported that two colored brethren of the Richmond Institute, H. B. Bunts and W. W. Colley, had applied to be sent to Africa; also Brother W. J. David, whom the Board had appointed "to excite interest and raise funds in behalf of African Missions, as preparatory to such further appointments as may be deemed advisable." The following is also copied from their report: "The Board appropriated $500 to meet the present distressed condition of our suspended missionaries;" and Brother B. P. Yates, of Monrovia, was directed to draw for $115, which was all that our Treasury contained specifically for African Missions."

ACTION OF THE CONVENTION.

The Convention endorsed the sentiment that, if Africa is evangelized, colored men must do the work. * * And that the Board should look out and appoint some suitable white brother, who shall give counsel and take the lead in the movement of missions in Africa, if, after due deliberation, the Board in its wisdom may deem such appointment advisable.

CHANGE OF BASE: CLOSE OF THE LIBERIAN MISSION.

Departure of Missionaries: On the 8th of January, 1875, Brethren W. J. David and W. W. Colley, after appropriate services in the Tabernacle Church, New York City, sailed for Monrovia, and on the 8th of February arrived at Sierra Leone.

Instruction of the Board: Brother David was instructed, if he saw no prospect of re-entering the Yoruba country, to make another attempt in the Beir territory, east of Liberia, from which our missionaries were driven in 1872.

Good News from Yoruba: From Sierra Leone, Brother David wrote, February 15th: "Missionaries can enter Yoruba. Mr. and Mrs. Townsend, white missionaries of the English Church, have gone to Abbeokuta by invitation of the King. The people there say that the white man's God has killed all of their princes who were concerned in driving away our missionaries. Bishop Crowther has visited Ogbomishaw and addressed thirteen of the native Christians, whom he found in worship on the very spot where our chapel stood. Mr. Nicholas, who, as Secretary, spent several years at Lagos, says the prospect was never so bright as now, and he thinks that the authorities of the above places will be glad to give up the mission premises so soon as we get there. Truly I am cheered by these wonderful works of Providence. Let God be praised! After arranging business at Monrovia, I shall proceed to Lagos."

From Sister S. M. Harden, of Lagos: "Some converts from Ogbomishaw have come down to look for missionaries. You see how welcome a missionary would be. How anxiously the people must have prayed and waited before they came to Lagos for a missionary. I hope our good friends will not be discouraged, but will take pity on us and help us."

PRESENT AND FUTURE OF THE MISSION.

Brother B. P. Yates wrote, October 27th, 1874: "I am sorry I can not say anything as to the growth of our churches. Our regular and stated meetings are properly and fully attended. The Sunday-schools are in a most healthful condition." The Board remarked: "Whether our missions in Liberia shall be prosecuted, will depend on prudential indications with regard to other fields in Africa." They were mindful of the words of the noble Melville S. Cox: "Though a thousand fall, let not Africa be given up."

Liberian Mission closed: In the report of 1876, we find the following: "Brother David visited the Vey people, living northward from Liberia, and was impressed with the favorable opening for missionary effort. He baptized two persons. Remaining awhile in Monrovia, the capital of Liberia, he, according to the instructions of the Board, sailed June 21st for Lagos, and entered Yoruba, the field from which our missionaries were driven many years ago. Satisfied with the good prospect of renewing our labors in that country, he returned to Monrovia, settled all accounts, and closed the Liberian Mission, and, with Brother Colley, went back to Lagos. They arrived October, 1875."

Change of base: Thus was changed the base from which to operate on the interior of Africa, from Liberia to Lagos. This involved the closing of the Liberian Mission, which had been prosecuted for thirty years. The future work of Brethren David and Colley is identified with our Yoruban Mission, which will be next considered.

there. Truly I am cheered by these wonderful works of Providence. Let God be praised! After arranging business at Monrovia, I shall proceed to Lagos."

From Sister S. M. Harden, of Lagos: "Some converts from Ogbomishaw have come down to look for missionaries. You see how welcome a missionary would be. How anxiously the people must have prayed and waited before they came to Lagos for a missionary. I hope our good friends will not be discouraged, but will take pity on us and help us."

PRESENT AND FUTURE OF THE MISSION.

Brother B. P. Yates wrote, October 27th, 1874: "I am sorry I can not say anything as to the growth of our churches. Our regular and stated meetings are properly and fully attended. The Sunday-schools are in a most healthful condition." The Board remarked: "Whether our missions in Liberia shall be prosecuted, will depend on prudential indications with regard to other fields in Africa." They were mindful of the words of the noble Melville S. Cox: "Though a thousand fall, let not Africa be given up."

Liberian Mission closed: In the report of 1876, we find the following: "Brother David visited the Vey people, living northward from Liberia, and was impressed with the favorable opening for missionary effort. He baptized two persons. Remaining awhile in Monrovia, the capital of Liberia, he, according to the instructions of the Board, sailed June 21st for Lagos, and entered Yoruba, the field from which our missionaries were driven many years ago. Satisfied with the good prospect of renewing our labors in that country, he returned to Monrovia, settled all accounts, and closed the Liberian Mission, and, with Brother Colley, went back to Lagos. They arrived October, 1875."

Change of base: Thus was changed the base from which to operate on the interior of Africa, from Liberia to Lagos. This involved the closing of the Liberian Mission, which had been prosecuted for thirty years. The future work of Brethren David and Colley is identified with our Yoruban Mission, which will be next considered.

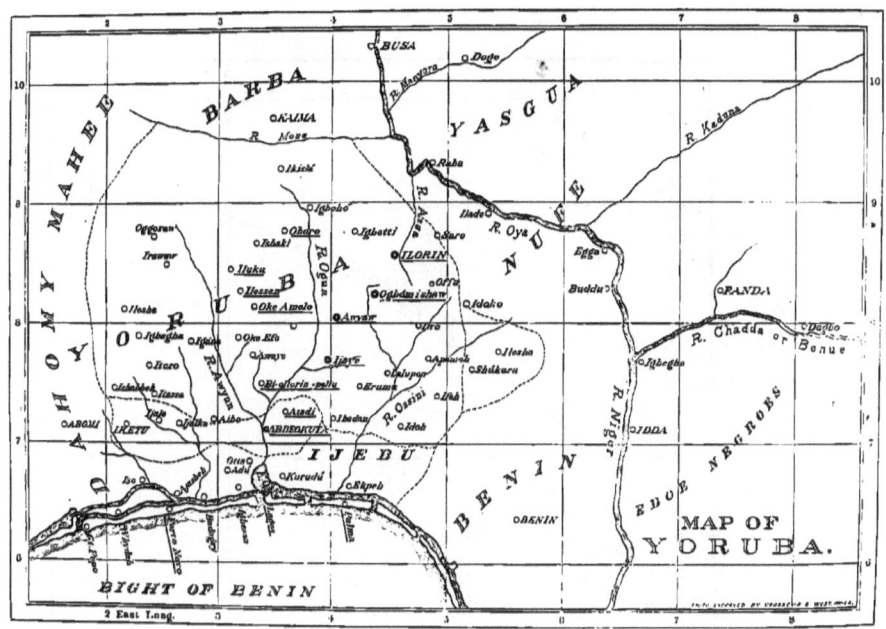

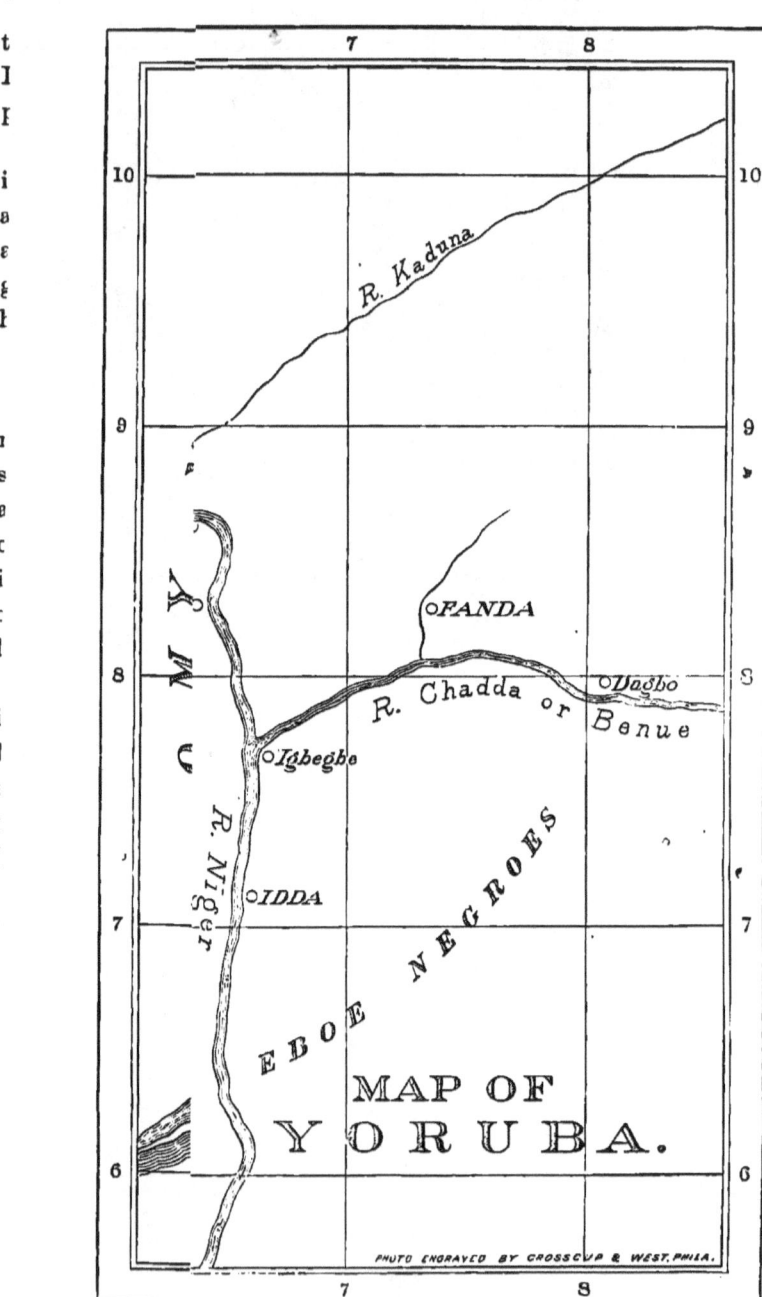

YORUBA MISSION.

YORUBA.

GEOGRAPHY.

YORUBA belongs to that part of Central Africa known as Soudan, which extends across the Continent, from Senegambia on the west to Abyssinia and Nubia on the east. In 1817 or 1818, it was one of the most powerful kingdoms in Western Africa; but, by intestine wars, a once richly cultivated and prosperous country, comprising 145 towns, was reduced, (about 1825), to a barren wilderness. The Yoruba country is located about 60 miles inward from the Bight of Benin, and is bounded by Dahomey and Mahee on the west, and the river Niger on the east and north. This definition comprehends several other tribes, as the Iketu and Egba, and others on the south, and Effong, Ifeh, and others on the east; but, these all belonged to the Yoruba family, and speak varieties of the same language. The Yoruban is spoken by some 4,000,000 of people. In 1857, our late missionary, T. J. Bowen, estimated the population of the nineteen chief cities. Those with which our missions have been chiefly identified, are as follows: Lagos, the seaport, 20,000, Abbeokuta, 60,000, Ibadan, 70,000, Awyaw, the capital of Yoruba, 25,000, Ogbomishaw, 25,000. Present estimates would more than double these figures. Abbeokuta is some 567 feet above the sea, and Ogbomishaw 1305 feet. The soil is various; and the streams generally clear, when not swollen. In some places they have a milky color, from the potter's clay, which abounds in the country. The water in Africa is always warm. "When the thermometer stood at 85° in the shade, it sank to 75° in a bold stream at the foot of mountains 1500 feet high. By exposing it to the wind, it becomes a little cooler. Yoruba proper is entirely free from swamps. The only lake is Ossa, which Rev. W. J. David, our missionary to Yoruba, writes, "extends along the sea-coast a distance of two hundred miles, varying in width from one quarter of a mile to a mile, and occasionally opening into the sea. There is no continuous mountain range, although huge rocks and occasional mountains rise up abruptly from the plain. The whole country is an open prairie, scattered over with small spreading trees. There are some forests on the rivers, where trees may be found ten feet in diameter." Mr. Bowen remarks: "Its position in regard to the sea and the Niger, its healthiness, and the facility with which roads may be constructed, all conspire to make Yoruba one of the most important portions of the African Continent. If colonized by civilized blacks from America, and properly conducted, it would soon command the trade of all Central Africa, to which it is the natural key."

SEASONS AND CLIMATE.

There are two seasons, the *dry* corresponding with our winter, and the *wet*, corresponding with our spring, summer, and autumn. Four inches of rain is considered a remarkable shower, and more than twenty inches is bad weather in the wettest month, which is June. No torrents fall in Yoruba. The average heat, in the dry season, in the shade, is about 80° or 82° F. The mercury does not rise higher, in the shade, than 93° or 98° F. Yet the weather is hot, especially in the sun. There is no cool, bracing season to invigorate the system. A damp south-west wind comes in from the Atlantic. Excessive dews make the mornings chilly. The best time for travelling is August and September, when the air is comparatively cool and there is little rain. The bane of African residents is *debility*. Hence missionaries should return home, occasionally, and re-invigorate their constitutions. "In Central Africa there may be good climate; but, great care must be taken against the common malaria of the country, which, though not injurious to the natives, may be fatal to the un-Africanized system of other races. Fortunately, several laws of malaria are so well known that we may measurably guard against it by availing ourselves of this knowledge."

SOMETHING ABOUT THE PEOPLE.

The Yorubans, who are a mixed race, probably of Asiatic descent, are gentle, not lazy, reverential to parents and rulers, remarkably cleanly, having a "strong current of public opinion against vice, and in favor of executing the laws, and not more covetous than other people."

But, they are seemingly devoid of conscience, and destitute of modesty. They have a good share of common sense, and are shrewd observers of character and motives. Their language is rich in abstract terms: and their government and laws indicate that they have studied out and reduced to practice what is called the balance of power by checks and limits, long before the barons of England extorted the great charter from King John." Polytheism has no existence in Yoruba. They make God the efficient, though not always the instrumental, Creator and Controller. The *Orisha*, or idol, is esteemed and called an *Intercessor*. Their idols are some three or four hundred. The images are only symbols. No sacrifices are made to God: all gifts and offerings are made to their idols. They believe in "the Furnace-world," but have no fears of being lost. They make offerings to Satan, under the name of *Eshu*, "the ejected," to conciliate him. Mr. David says: "They do not worship Satan." They pour oil on his altar, as if to mollify his evil disposition. The government is conducted by a King and his counselors: and by governors and their counselors in the various towns. Neither the King, nor any governor or chief is above "the common law of the land." Judicial proceedings are before the ruler of the town and his council, "according to law and testimony": and, before the *Oboni*, which is a secret Institution, connected with the government, and with the religion of the country. Its business is always secret. This court is feared by the mightiest men in the land. The capital offences are murder, treason, and arson; in some places, robbery and adultery. Prisoners taken in war are slaves. But four-fifths of the people are free. They live in walled towns and cultivate the surrounding country. Every man has his own farm; but there is no property in land. The women do most of the trafficing, but do not work on the farm. The streets of the best and largest cities are narrow and intricate. The most curious object of each town is the *market*, where everything is sold, from the native rat to velvets and other imported articles from the four quarters of the globe. The houses are one story, with from ten to fifty rooms opening upon a court, which is entered by a single gate, prudently guarded by the horse-shoe or other amulet, to defend the premises against "ghaists, spirits, and devils." They sit and sleep on mats. The men wear trousers, and the women wrappers. All are fond of ornaments. They are eminently social and polite and quite ceremonious. Equals kneel to each other; inferiors prostrate themselves before superiors. Polygamy is universal.

There is no science, and all the arts are in a rude state; yet, there are iron smelters, and carpenters, and leather dressers, and saddle-makers, and barbers, besides professional hunters and fishers. The women spin, and sell to the weavers, who are men. "The peculiar glass-manufacture of Central Africa is confined to three towns in Nufè. The art is a profound secret. The porcelain-like appearance of the glass would indicate that feldspar, which abounds in the country, enters into its composition." The affinities of the Yoruba language with the Greek, Saxon, French, Spanish, Portuguese, Welsh, Latin, and English, Hebrew and Sanscrit, which have been traced by Vidall, Kalle, and our lamented missionary Bowen, are striking. Bowen's "Grammar and Vocabulary of the Yoruban-Tongue," published by the Smithsonian Institute, is an admirable contribution to Philology. As to the origin of this people, Bowen quotes from an old Arabic work, in which the author refers familiarly to African Chronicles written long anterior to the presence of Arabs in Soudan, and says that the Copts, who settled Burnu, wrote a history of Takrour, or Central Africa. The writer, the Puloh King, Bello of Sokoto says of Yoruba: "The inhabitants of this province, it is supposed, originated from the remnant of the children of Canaan, who were of the tribe of Nimrod. The cause of their establishment in the west of Africa was, as it is stated, in consequence of their being driven by Yaarooba, (Yaruba), son of Kahtan (said to be the first who wrote the Arabic language, and, according to an Arabic history a great king of Arabia in the days of the prophet Heber) out of Arabia to the western coast between Egypt and Abyssinia. From that spot they advanced into the interior of Africa, till they reached Yarba, where they fixed their residence. On their way, they left in every place which they stopped at, a tribe of their own people. Thus, it is supposed that all the tribes of Soudan, who inhabit the mountians, are originally from them, as also the inhabitants of Yauri." For preceding and following about Africa, see *Bowen's Central Africa.*

FIRST DECADE—1848–1858.

THOMAS JEFFERSON BOWEN, AND HENRY GOODALE.

BIRTH, EDUCATION, AND EARLY LIFE OF MR. BOWEN.

MR. BOWEN was born in Jackson County, Georgia, January 2d, 1814. His early education was limited, but "having a great thirst for knowledge, and an excellent memory, he continued his studies after he left school, diving into every subject in search of truth or something new, until he became a man of extensive and varied information—a self-educated man." How well disciplined and furnished was his mind is attested by his "Central Africa," to which we are indebted for most of our knowledge of Yoruba; and his quarto work on the Yoruban Language, to which reference has been made. From his pen we copy these words: "I was baptized by Elder John Rasberry, about October 1, 1840; and began to preach about a year after.—T. J. B." In 1841, he abandoned the law for the ministry, and "spent eight years travelling in S. W. Georgia, S. E. Alabama and Florida, as a self-sustained missionary, but occasionally engaging in teaching."

EXTRACT FROM HIS PRIVATE DIARY.

"In some respects I am glad, in others I deeply regret, that my feelings and conduct have been peculiar. When very young, about twenty-one years old, I debated within myself whether I should labor and strive as other men do to become rich and great. I was thought to be a young man of talents and of honorable character. My relatives and friends (it was in Stewart County, Ga.,) had money and influence, with which they were willing to assist me. Jesse Bull, the brother of Judge Bull, offered me his office and practice at law. People held out to me the tempting bait of wealth and honor, as a lawyer and politician. But something within me said: 'What is the use?'

In a hundred years, it will not matter whether I have been rich or poor, great or little. My chief concern ought to be the salvation of my soul. Eternity! boundless, fathomless Eternity! To be lost! Oh, what can compensate for the loss of the soul? But to secure salvation I felt assured that I must renounce my natural ambition, which I confess was very great. For this reason, I refused the kind offers of my friends, and turned away from an alliance in marriage with a girl, because she was rich and belonged to a thoroughly worldly-minded family, ensnared by the sophisms of Universalism. * * Notwithstanding all this, although I verily believe I was perfectly sincere, I found it impossible to surrender my heart and life to God.

"In the spring of 1836, I plunged into the Creek Indian War. Friends said, 'Poor Tommy is sure to be killed.' Indeed, on one occasion, May 29, 1836, I escaped by a miracle, running the gauntlet for a hundred yards or more through a shower of bullets from the rifles of about seventy Indians. Those nearest to me were not twenty yards off. Yet only one bullet struck me, which was the first fired, while I was standing and looking out intently for the foe, whom I had heard. Mr. Jackson, the only man with me, was killed, being shot in eight places. In December, 1836, I started alone for Texas, to aid in repelling the Mexicans who were seeking to oppress and subdue our countrymen in that portion of Mexico. About November, 1839, I reached home again, having seen my desire accomplished in the independence of that country. Six days after my arrival at the headquarters of the Texas army, I received a commission, which I neither sought nor expected. While in the army, I commanded Company B, Second Regiment of Infantry; then Company C, First Cavalry; and, for a brief time, this latter regiment. I resigned my commission from a deep-seated conviction that I could not become a Christian while my life and heart were devoted to military service.

"I must confess that I resigned with no little regret, and that I have never seen the day when that regret had wholly disappeared. Yet I have always been glad that I had strength to relinquish a pursuit to which I was so much attached, and sorry that my heart was so evil as to love that service, and especially to look back upon it with regret that I must leave it. Oftentimes I have said to myself: 'What profit would it be to my soul in eternity even if I had risen to be the greatest general of the age? The glory of this world passeth away, but the love of God—our love of God—abideth forever.'

> In hope of that immortal crown
> I now the cross sustain,
> And gladly wander up and down,
> And smile at toil and pain.

"Truly my share of toil and pain has been very abundant. But, if I know my own heart, I bear it all willingly, not so much for the sake of being saved, but for the sake of serving him, who is worthy of ten thousand times all the service we can render to him.

"In October, 1840, after a long, long period of seeking, I obtained hope in Christ, and soon after was baptized in the name of the adorable Trinity. My happiness in those days was more than language can express. About September, 1841, I began to preach, and about a year after I was called to ordination. I then resolved that, until I should marry, which I scarcely expected to do at all, to give *all* my earnings, except a bare support, to the poor and to the spread of the gospel. This I think was wrong, and I am now suffering want, because I have not been sufficiently mindful of myself."

ORIGIN OF THE MISSION.

On October 2d, 1848, a communication from Mr. Bowen on the establishment of a Mission in Central Africa, was received by the Board. In the November number of the Southern Baptist Missionary Journal of that year, appeared a valuable article from the same gentleman on "Central Africa." In this paper was shown the practicability and advantage of a Mission there. A committee, of whom Rev. J. L. Reynolds, D.D., was chairman, presented an elaborate and crudite report, which was published in the March, 1849, number of the Missionary Journal, advocating the proposed Mission, and recommending, January, 1849, that Mr. Bowen be requested to appear before the Board. On February 22d of that year, Mr. Bowen, having been examined "in relation to his religious experience, call to the ministry, and practical views in regard to Central Africa as a field of missionary labor, the Board unanimously appointed him as a missionary to that country."

OTHER MISSIONARIES.

Rev. B. W. Whilden, of the China Mission, was invited to accompany Mr. Bowen, but on August 22d he declined the invitation. October 18, 1849, Rev. Henry Goodale, who had been appointed to China, January 3, 1848, but whose wife, Mrs. M. J. K. Goodale, had died suddenly a short time before their expected departure, was, with Mr. Bowen, present at the meeting of the Board, when the following resolution was adopted: "*Resolved*, That Brother Goodale be transferred to the Central Africa Mission, provided that, after due consideration, he may feel it to be consistent with a sense of duty." On August 22d of that year, a colored brother, Robert F. Hill, who had been recommended by Rev. Mr. Reynoldson, being present, and having been examined, the following was adopted:

"WHEREAS, Brother Hill expresses his earnest desire to accompany Brother Bowen to Central Africa; therefore,

"*Resolved*, That, when Brother Hill shall have procured his freedom by purchase from his present owners, he shall be appointed as an assistant in that Mission."

DEPARTURE AND ARRIVAL.

Designation services took place in the Grace Street Baptist Church, Richmond, Va., on the 7th of September, 1849. On December 17th, Messrs. Bowen, Goodale, and Hill sailed from Providence, R. I., in the "Smithfield," and arrived at Mourovia, in Liberia, on the 8th day of February, 1850.

SAD VISIT TO GOLAH.

"The young colored brother, Robert F. Hill, not answering the purpose for which he was attached to the Yoruba party, was detached from them."

Having heard of a town, some 150 miles interiorward, which was ruled by a civilized king, Mr. Goodale concluded that a Mission there would be more favorable than one in Central Africa. Mr. Bowen undertook the journey with him, in hope of finding there Pulohs to teach the Fellatah language, which is spoken on the Niger. They arrived, March 6th, at Sama, the seat of government, and had a "palaver"— which was really a "squabble"—with Lansanna, who had succeeded "the civilized king," Boatswain. The sequel is mournful and dismal enough. Mr. Goodale, who had brought four American boys from Monrovia as servants and students, opened a school with six scholars, including a Golah boy, who could speak English, and one of the Vey tribe. He obtained a grant of land from the King, and began preparations to sow rice. On Sunday the missionaries preached. Mr. Goodale was taken sick on the same day, and, "in spite of our utmost care and attention," says Mr. Bowen, "he died about a month after. His zeal continued unabated to the last. Not choosing to bury him in the heathen grave-yard, we prepared his grave under a tree on the Monrovia road, only a few yards without the gate of the town." Mr. Bowen adds: "Almost every one knows what it is to mourn the death of a friend, but there are not many who can fully appreciate the sorrow and loneliness of a man who buries his beloved and only companion in the wilds of Africa."

REV. HENRY GOODALE.

Mr. Goodale was born at West Boylston, Massachusetts, on the 22d February, 1822. At the age of fourteen he professed conversion, and joined the church at Winchendon, where his friends had moved. In 1841, he began a course of study in reference to the ministry. His health failing in 1843, by the advice of his physician, he removed to Maryland, where he taught a school. Afterwards he went to Kentucky. In 1844, he was employed by the Young Men's Tract Society of Louisville as a Colporteur. His journal from August 9th, 1844, to December of the same year, was kept with great regularity, entries being made nearly every day, describing his efforts and success in his field of labor, with frequent reference to his personal religious feelings, often complaining of himself, and again giving utterance to expressions of thanksgiving to God for the unspeakable peace with which he was favored. In 1845, he entered Georgetown College, and passed through a limited course of study, remaining there until the middle of 1848.

His missionary appointments have been noticed. He died in April, 1850. The late Corresponding Secretary says of him: He was "conscientious, energetic, spiritual-minded;" had "medium mental powers," and "education not thorough."

MR. BOWEN'S ROUGH EXPERIENCE.

Finding no Pulohs at Sama, Mr. Bowen resolved to return at once to Monrovia, and sail for Badagry. His experience in getting back, is thus summed up: "The various difficulties and adventures, which I passed through before I could regain the Coast; how the negroes appeared determined to have the remnant of my goods:—how I was bullied, and threatened by Lansanna, and a personage called a Golah King, who was chief of all the Golahs in Sama;—how I had to quarrel and almost fight for seven days, before I could obtain permission to leave the town;—how the surly Golahs, on the road almost starved me, as I returned through the country;—how I visited Gebby Island, and found the eastern branch of the river beyond it more than a quarter of a mile wide;—how my carriers tore open my packages, and robbed me of several dozen knives, and my bottle of Cologne-water;—and how I finally arrived at Monrovia, hungry, weary, and glad, about 9 o'clock at night—all this need not be related. After some delay at Monrovia, during which I visited Grand Cape Mount and Gallinas River, I finally sailed for Cape Coast Castle, about the 20th of June, 1850."

BADAGRY AND THE SLAVE COAST.

On the 5th of August, Mr. Bowen arrrived at Badagry, after having stopped on the coast at El Mina, which was settled by the Portuguese in 1481, and now belongs to the Dutch, who permit no missionaries to live there; and at Cape Coast Castle, of which we have given some information, and where our missionary remained about three weeks, with the family of Rev. T. B. Freeman. Mr. Freeman was the Superintendent of the Wesleyan Missions, which were begun in 1835, and "have penetrated into the interior to Kumasi, the capital of Ashantee, and to Abbeokuta, the capital of Egba." Mr. Bowen visited at Cape Coast the grave of the gifted, but unhappy Miss Landon, the poetess "L. E. L.," who married a government officer and died on the Coast of Africa.

Badagry contains about 10,000 inhabitants. The houses are built of bamboo. The streets are narrow and tortuous, and filled with "thieves and drunkards, whose only object in life is sensual gratification, and who are the most impudent and shameless beggars." When a missionary preached, they would reply "by laying their hands on their stomachs, and saying, 'White man, I am hungry.'" An English missionary remarked of the people, "their cup of iniquity is full, and they are ripe for destruction." Hearing a great uproar one day, Mr. Bowen asked: "What's the matter? Oh, they have caught a witch, and they are going to kill her."

The market is crowded daily with people, buying and selling every manner of thing from rum to royal purple. The currency of the Slave Coast is the cowry, a small shell, brought by the English from India and Zanzibar, 2,000 of which make a dollar. The Yoruban language is spoken here and along the Slave Coast, which is so named "because it afforded the most intelligent, and docile, and industrious negroes for the American plantations." "In 1850, nearly all the Slave Coast, led by Gezo, the King of Dahomey and Kosokkoh, the Usurper at Lagos, were in favor of the slave trade, and opposed to lawful commerce and missionaries. Only Abbeokuta, and a minority at Badagry were opposed to the slave trade, as contrary to the best interests of the country." Mr. Bowen was informed that Gezo and Kosokkoh were concocting a plan to destroy Abbeokuta and Badagry, so as to expel the English merchants and missionaries, and restore the slave trade, as in former days. More of this anon.

ABBEOKUTA.

Being informed that he could not get to Bohoo, for which he had started, Mr. Bowen, after staying eight days in Badagry, started on the 14th of August, for Abbeokuta, " the capital of a very small, independent kingdom of Egba, which is numbered among the countries of Guinea, but in character is more nearly allied to Soudan. * * The

Yoruban country begins about twenty miles north of Abbeokuta, or eighty miles from the sea-coast." On the 18th of August, "we suddenly emerged into an open country, and my eyes were greeted with a more lovely scene than I ever expected to behold in Africa— a vast expanse of undulating prairie, scattered over with palms and groves, and bounded in the distance by blue and lofty hills. Passing through this lovely country, we arrived at the Ogun River, which flows by Abbeokuta. We entered the city by twilight."

The wall of Abbeokuta is some fifteen miles in circuit, and the city contains about 100,000 people. "Fifty years ago the Egba kingdom contained some three hundred towns."

Desolation has followed wars, which swept away 200,000 people. Abbeokuta was settled by the refugees of a hundred towns, who fled to the high rocks of that place, which means *under the Rock*.

VISIT TO IKETU.

On the 3d of September, Mr. Bowen obtained permission from Sagbua, the Chief of the Egbas, to go as far as Iketu, some sixty-five miles west of Abbeokuta, though he would not allow him to go to Bohoo, or Igboho. On the way at Aibo he preached to an *Albino*, or white negro, and a crowd which had collected around him. The Albino said: "My heart holds all you have said." Failing to get permission to go to Iketu from the king of the place, Mr. Bowen was forced to retrace his steps to Abbeokuta.

Some months after, the King of Iketu prematurely sent for Mr. Bowen. On his arrival he found some of the chiefs greatly opposed to it. The king's house was fired, and an attempt was made to poison Mr. Bowen. The king requested him to keep "in-doors," but Mr. Bowen was soon preaching to the people, saying. when the king objected to it, "You must not forbid me to deliver the message of the King of kings, who sent me to Iketu." Matters became so serious that the king advised Mr. Bowen to return to Abbeokuta, which he did on foot, after having remained about a month in Iketu.

Finding it impracticable to proceed to Bohoo, which he earnestly desired, he remained eighteen months in Abbeokuta, engaged in the study of the Yoruban language, which he could speak well in about that time. The Wesleyan Mission had started there under their Superintendent, Mr. Freeman, in 1838; and the Episcopal under Messrs. Townsend and Crowther—now Bishop Crowther—both native Yorubans, in 1846. When Mr. Bowen wrote in 1857, there were some six hundred communicants of the two churches.

WAR AND SLAVE TRADE.

On the 3d of March, 1851, the King of Dahomey appeared before Abbeokuta with 10,000 men, and 6,000 women. The Egbas marched out 15,000 strong. Mr. Bowen stood on the wall and gave some direction to affairs in which his military experience came into play. The enemy were routed " with 2,000 slain and several hundred prisoners." Gezo's defeat did not deter Kosokkoh, who burnt Badagry a few weeks after the battle of Abbeokuta. In November, 1851, Consul Beecroft, with a part of the British Squadron, went to Lagos "to make a treaty" with Kosokkoh, who, under the advice of several Brazilian and Portuguese slavers, met the English with powder and shot, and on the second day defeated them. Thirty days after, however, the English returned, and drove Kosokkoh and his party from the town. In 1855, they made peace with the English, and "agreed to abandon the slave trade." January 2d, 1857, Mr. Bowen heard that the King of Dahomey had sent word to the Egbas, and Kosokkoh had sent word to Lagos, to prepare again for war. In the meantime "the missions were in a very flourishing condition, and by a royal proclamation at Lagos the Lord's Day was generally and carefully observed."

TRIP TO YORUBA AND RETURN TO AMERICA.

"In October, 1851," said Mr. Bowen, "about twenty months after my arrival in Africa, I received the first letters from home. * * This joy was speedily followed by an increase of funds, and to crown all I now at last heard of an open road to Isehin, in the heart of Yoruba." Having sent messengers in advance to get permission to enter the country, which is ever indispensable, he, " a little more than two years after landing in Africa," was ready to proceed with a fair prospect of success. On the way from Eruwa to Bi-olorrun-pellu, two women meeting them, rushed into the woods exclaiming: 'Emaw!' Monster! On which Brother Bowen remarks: " No philosophical ethnologist ever doubted the proper humanity of Africans more sincerely than some of the Africans doubt ours." At Bi-olorrun-pellu the king showed him his Bible, which he regarded in perhaps superstitious reverence, and Mr. Bowen preached to him Jesus. A woman begged to be baptized, which was not granted. A company of Mohammedans heard him for several days courteously and with interest, and departing said: "You have smitten us with the sword, but we are not offended."

His daily habit was, he says, to spend the mornings " in the piazza of my house, sitting on a mat, and preaching to the people who sat around me." Mr. Bowen says: "Everybody in that country believes in one true and living God, of whose character they often entertain surprisingly correct notions. Most of the people worship certain imaginary creatures as mediators between God and men; but some reject such mediation, and attempt to hold direct communication with God himself."

After several vain attempts to push forward towards Ishakki in the West, he was forced by a train of irresistible circumstances to go backward to Ijaye. He stopped at Awaye, where he was cordially greeted. " My ardent hopes and too precious hopes were blighted, and the disappointment preyed so on my feelings in spite of my better reason, that I fell into a dysentery, which came near endangering my life. Kumi, the chief at Ijaye, had sent him word, says Mr. Bowen: "If I had come to preach, I had gone far enough to begin; but if I would build a house in Ijaye, and if some of the white men would live there, Areh (Kumi's title as Generalissimo) would give me permission, and messengers to go, wherever I might choose, at some future time." Accordingly, Kumi received him very cordially, and bade him select a site for a house. Mr. Bowen writes: "Having no money to build a house, I resolved to return to America, and report progress." It was June, the wettest month in the year; but I was too impatient to wait for better weather." He returned to Bi-olorrun-pellu, and thence to Abbeokúta, and down the Ogun to Lagos, despite the hostility of the

Ijebus, "who were in the habit of shooting people in the canoes." "Hoisting the Stars and Stripes on a bamboo staff, and laying six loaded guns at my feet, we pushed off into the rapid current, and were soon gliding through the hostile district." The second day, he arrived at Lagos; and after coasting about a month, he embarked on a Hamburg brig, and had a disagreeable passage of one hundred and three days to London. Thence he proceeded to the United States.

MRS. L. H. BOWEN.

Lurenna Henrietta Davis was reared and educated in Greensboro, Georgia. She was graduated from the Georgia Female College, under the Presidency of George Y. Browne, in the class of 1850.

Her parents moved to Georgia from North Carolina in 1813, shortly after their marriage. Mrs. Davis professed Christ in early life. "She was quiet and unobtrusive, but always exerted a strong influence for good. The great anxiety of her heart was the conversion of her husband and children. Before she departed, on May 29th, 1866, she saw them all in 'the ark of safety.'"

Mr. Davis was over fifty years old, when he was baptized by Rev. Dr. P. H. Mell, of Georgia. He went to rest on September 7th, 1875, at the age of eighty-eight years. Two of their daughters became missionaries. When Lurenna spoke to her parents of going to Africa with Mr. Bowen, they with sweet resignation replied: "It is a severe trial to give up a daughter to go so far away; but if you feel that the Lord calls you to the work, we dare not refuse. God will be as near you in Africa as here, and we can pray for you just the same."

She was married to the Rev. T. J. Bowen, May 31st, 1853, by Rev. C. M. Irvin.

MR. BOWEN VISITS ABBEOKUTA.

On July 6th, 1853, Mr. and Mrs. Bowen, with Rev. J. S. Dennard and Rev. J. H. Lacy and their wives sailed for Africa. On August, 28th, they landed at Lagos "for the purpose of proceeding to Ijaye in Yoruba.' Kosokkoh had gathered his forces to re-take Lagos from the English, and the lake and river were infested with hostile parties.

So soon as the lake was cleared by the English, they started to Abbeokuta. "Mr. Dennard and myself," writes Mr. Bowen, "thought it lawful to charge our double-barreled guns with heavy shot." Soon after arriving in Abbeokuta, "the remainder of our party were laid up with fever."

PROSPECTING AND OPENING STATIONS.

About two months after their arrival at Lagos, Mr. and Mrs. Bowen proceeded at once alone to Ijaye. Kumi welcomed them. Mr. Bowen began at once to build himself a mud house, which was entered February 1st, 1854. In June he erected a chapel 20 by 30 feet. In July, he baptized a man and soon after a woman. In September, Mr. William H. Clarke, a missionary of our Board, arrived. Not long after, he baptized a man; and Mr. Bowen another. In April, 1855, Mr. Bowen visited Ilorin. The king promised to give land for a station. In Ijaye the labors of Messrs. Bowen and Clarke consisted of building, preaching, and travelling. They built a large mission house, designed, in part, to accommodate new missionaries, until they should pass through the acclimation fever. Mr. Bowen says: " Our preaching labors were incessant and arduous, so that every corner of Ijaye heard the gospel. Many times the people heard it with such rapt attention that a stranger would have thought the whole town was on the point of turning to God. Others opposed with equal ardor." In the autumn of 1855, Mr. and Mrs. Bowen moved to Ogbomishaw, and began another station. Mrs. Bowen had to cross the Obba River by embracing one end of a huge calabash, and the ferry-man the other, and locking arms, which is the mode of ferrying in that country. After renting a house and making all arrangements for Mrs. Bowen's comfort, Mr. Bowen started for Ilorin to make a second effort to settle as a missionary in that Mohammedan town. That year the mission was reinforced by the arrival of Mr. and Mrs. A. D. Phillips, and Mr. J. F. Beaumont. Mr. Philips remained at Ijaye, where his wife fell a victim to the fever of the country. Mr. Beaumont went to Ogbomishaw.

Subsequently the mission was strengthened by the addition of Messrs. Trimble, Priest, and Cason, and their wives. "Our whole force," wrote Mr. Bowen, "consists of eight men, five of whom are married. The first station is at Lagos, on the sea-coast, in charge of Mr. Harden, a colored man from Liberia; and the most interior station, is Ogbomishaw, which stands at the point where the Fauna and Flora of Guinea begin to give place to those of Soudan. The distance from Lagos to Abbeokuta, by the river Ogun, is ninety miles; thence by the road to Ijaye, sixty miles; thence to Ogbomishaw, fifty miles; thence to Ilorin, twenty-eight miles; thence to Ilade on the Niger, about fifty miles, so that in going from Lagos to Ijaye, we travel one hundred and fifty miles; to Ogbomishaw, two hundred miles; to Ilorin, two hundred and thirty, and to the Niger, two hundred and eighty miles. By a direct road, the whole distance would be less than one hundred and fifty miles."

VISIT TO ILORIN, AND RETURN TO AMERICA.

Ilorin belonged once to Yoruba. It is now an independent city, governed by a king, and composed of Pulohs, Hansas, Kanikès, and Yorubans. When Mr. Bowen proposed a visit there in 1855, it was regarded as a wild attempt. He was hooted at by some, and sought to be discouraged by others. He boldly, however, marched through two gates of the city, without saying "By your leave," and was only halted at the third. When asked why he had sent no messenger to get permission of the king, he replied: "I am myself a messenger of a King." After a courteous semi-imprisonment, he was brought before the king, closely interrogated as to his purposes, and invited to preach. To his surprise and delight, he found himself in high favor. The king promised to give him on his return a house in "Feda," which is the aristocratic part of the city. This, however, he promptly declined, as "the poor were to have the gospel preached to them." When he made his second visit, in the autumn of that year, he found that a change had come over the spirit of their mind; or what is more probable, their former professions of good will were only "make believe." The authorities complained that since his visit other white men had been there who were "stern and unsocial," and that permission could not be given "to white men to live in Ilorin." The king said, curtly: "It won't do; we do not reject God, but we are Mussulmen."

On his return to Ogbomishaw, the king gave him a beautiful building site. In three months, he completed "a comfortable cottage of three rooms, a servants' house, kitchen, etc.; and surrounded the whole with a wall five feet high, enclosing some fifty yards square." The gospel made a good impression here, and the people listened with interest. Some professed to abandon idolatry, and to pray to the true God. "When we left Ogbomishaw, a crowd of people followed us some distance on the road, expressing many wishes for our safety during the journey."

"In the spring of 1856, various causes," writes Mr. Bowen, "required my return home." That year the Board reported: "Brother Bowen may be soon invited temporarily to return to this country for the purpose of superintending the publication of the grammar, and vocabulary, and portions of the Scriptures, which he has been preparing. This will also allow the opportunity of recruiting his exhausted energies, which have been affected by excessive labors."

Mr. and Mrs. Bowen visited on their return, Sierra Leone, where in 1851, Messrs. Bowen, Dennard, and Lacy ordained Messrs. Browne and Thompson; and which colony, Mr. Bowen says, is "one of the greatest triumphs of modern benevolence." In 1857, the Board reported Mr. Bowen in our country, and express their earnest sympathy with his sufferings—"especially in the great heart-pain of being prevented from returning to his chosen and loved field of labor."

DEATH, AND THE BEAUTIFUL CITY.

After Mr. Bowen's return from Brazil, to which reference has been made, such was his nervous state, that at times he lost all self-control. This part of his history is too painful to recall. From 1868 to 1874, he travelled in Texas and Florida. He returned to Georgia, and on the 24th of November, 1875, away from his family, he was taken to his "long home." His smitten wife exclaimed: "Oh, Brother Tupper, this blow has fallen hard upon my heart! To think, I was spared to come from Africa to soothe the dying pillows of both my parents, and was denied the privilege of attending my dear, suffering, heart-broken husband in his last moments! But it is all right with him now. I am left to toil on, and battle with life awhile longer. Pray for me, that I may have grace and strength for every duty, until the Lord shall call me to join the loved ones in the 'Beautiful City.'"

Messrs. DENNARD, LACY, AND CLARKE.

REPORTED TO THE CONVENTION.

In 1853, the Board reported to the Convention: "It was the happiness of the Board to examine and appoint to this field Rev. J. S. Dennard, by birth and education a Georgian, but more recently a resident of Alabama, and Rev. John H. Lacy, formerly of Virginia, but now of Alabama. Subsequently Rev. W. H. Clarke of Georgia was also received."

EARLY AFFLICTIONS.

As has been seen, Messrs. Lacy and Dennard sailed with Mr. Bowen from Boston on the 5th of July, 1853, via England, for their chosen field. On the 28th of August, the missionaries arrived at Lagos, "after a pleasant voyage," and "passed on to Abbeokuta.' It was deemed wise by them for Mr. Dennard to return to Lagos, Mr. Lacy to remain at Abbeokuta, and Mr. Bowen to pass on to Ijaye." The Board advised that "all should locate at Ijaye, a higher and comparatively healthy latitude, until they should become perfectly acclimated."

In the meantime Mr. Dennard had gone down to the coast and was called to drink the bitter cup of affliction in the death of his wife, which occurred January 4th, 1854. She calmly and quietly fell asleep in Jesus, after an illness of five days. Her disease was African fever of the most aggravated form. It was attended with all the symptoms of yellow fever, except the black vomit. Most of the time she was delirious and unconscious of pain. She was buried in the grave-yard of Rev. Mr. Gollmer. Her smitten husband exclaimed: "The Lord gave her to me. In the short space of six months and a half he took her from me. It is the Lord's doings. Be still, my bleeding heart, and know that God has done this. Just and true are thy ways, O thou King of Saints!" * * He continued: "If the dear brethren at home will only hold the rope for me, I will descend the dark mine of heathenism and dig and toil and suffer, until my Master calls me home, and then again I shall hold communion sweet with my own dear sainted Fannie in that land of eternal love. O, blessed Saviour, give me grace and strength to labor successfully in thy cause so long as I live!"

In their Report of 1854, the Board says: "They are also deeply afflicted in the return of Brother Lacy to this country. The reason assigned by him in taking this step, was the inflamed condition of his eyes."

The same year, another event of the most afflictive character occurred. Mr. Dennard had entered upon his work with the intrepidity and faith of one who counted not his own life dear unto himself. He longed to minister to the tribes of Yoruba in spiritual things, and was willing to suffer the loss of all things. Strong hope was entertained that he might be permitted to see his cherished wishes gratified in the conversion of many under his ministry. But God had otherwise determined. Very soon after the death of his wife, and while his lacerated heart was yet bleeding with the separating stroke, he was himself carried away from his work on earth, to enter upon the rest of heaven. This event occurred on the 17th of June, 1854. That he was eminently qualified for his position, appeared from all his history before he entered our service, and from his communications written after his entrance upon the mission-field. He longed for more laborers—"Send us," said he, "this year, as many single men as you can get to come, and three or four house carpenters, (colored men.) These single men can remain here four or five years, and then go home and get married if they wish. By next year you can send us as many married men as you can get to come. If I live, by that time I will have one or two comfortable houses completed."

In December of 1854, Rev. W. H. Clarke arrived in Africa, and located in Ijaye.

From Lagos he wrote:

"It may seem a little strange to you that I should be at this place.

But my brother, you have no idea of our trouble and embarrassments in the prosecution of our labors. Agents we have, it is true, but you must recollect they are of an African stamp, slow, careless, and negligent; and this is not the first time that one of us has been necessitated to leave home, that our building operations might be carried on. When I left Ijaye our cowries were nearly exhausted, though we had a good supply sixty miles distant, at Abbeokuta. Our foundation wall had been laid, and must we stop? Under the circumstances, it being necessary for Brother Bowen to superintend the buildings, I soon determined to make a visit to Abbeokuta, and if necessary to Lagos' to settle our unfinished business, and I am now happy to state that our affairs begin to assume a straightforward appearance. These labors, however, have not been attended without some risk.

"I have made considerable proficiency in the language. I have read nearly through Matthew, and can talk something intelligibly about the cross. One great difficulty with the learner is in securing a good interpreter, without whom, he may learn and unlearn much to his disadvantage.

"I have preached considerably in the streets to the people of Ijaye many of whom, under all the circumstances, paid remarkable attention. Some of the crowds manifested an interest that you seldom witness in our American congregations. In a word, it is a still under-current that in some future day, under the blessing of God, will burst forth over the whole city. I have never yet been unkindly received or treated by a single crowd. Though the people are idolaters of some kind, orisha, thunder, or heat worshippers, they are not bigoted, will acknowledge your message is kind and good, and sometimes express the belief that the people will, by-and-by, 'little by little,' believe the word. They will argue and urge objections, but seldom are they of a nature that cannot be easily answered or refuted. From my short acquaintance, I think them quite a hopeful people, and I feel somewhat prepared to answer Brother Taylor's inquiry with regard to sending out missionaries."

In 1857, the Board reports, with regard to Ogbomishaw: "This station is at present occupied by Brother Clarke. Here our Brother and Sister Browne were located." The letters of Mr. Clarke, which were published in *The Commission*, are full of interest. They will repay the reader for a careful persual. In 1858, the Board say: "Brother Clarke has made a trip through Ilorin to the Niger. In giving some account of the excursion, he notices several important towns, which it is desirable to occupy, and pleads earnestly for more laborers.

In 1859, Rev W. H. Clarke of the Yoruba Mission returned to this country, under a provision of the Board, permitting the missionaries of this mission to return within four-years, for the re-invigoration of their constitution. Brother Clarke was not sick, but he felt it to be necessary, to prevent breaking down of his strength, to avail himself of this permission. He expects to go back to Yoruba, during the year."

In 1860, the Board reported: "Brother Clarke has determined to remain in this country, and the relation between him and the Board has ceased."

Rev. J. S. DENNARD.

"Mr. Dennard was born August 27th, 1817, in Twiggs County, Georgia, and was the oldest of seven children." "He was educated in Jeffersonville, Twiggs County, under Milton A. Wylder, and completed the study of the languages under Miller of Perry, Houston County, Ga. As a boy, he was spirited, self-confident, and exceedingly enthusiastic, very active and energetic, but fonder of books than play. In school, he was ambitious. At the age of sixteen, he often delivered original addresses. He was affectionate and kind in his family, especially to the domestics, and to inferior animals. He was admitted to the Bar in 1839, and practiced law in Houston, and the adjoining counties. In Florida, where he went, in the spring of 1845, for health and recreation, he was convinced of his sins, while in conversation with some young ladies and gentlemen. He took the position of an infidel, and was so overwhelmed with guilt in his denial of the God to whom he had so often heard his mother pray, that he retired to spend a night in agony and remorse. On his return home in October, he professed religion during a Methodist revival. In the winter following, he connected himself with the Baptist Church in Perry, having been baptized by Rev. A. T. Holmes.

In 1848, he visited Alabama, where he was pastor over the following churches, Enon, Glenville, Ramah, Mount Moriah, and New Harmony (now Pine Grove). In Georgia, he preached at Fort Gaines, and Cotton Hill. He was married to Miss Fannie Smith of Cotton Hill, Georgia, June 18th, 1853, by Rev. A. T. Holmes. They sailed for Africa the next month; and, in less than a year, they both were in Heaven.

REV. J. H. LACY.

Mr. Lacy was born in Halifax County, Virginia, December 15th, 1821. He was baptized on the fourth Sunday in November, 1842, into the fellowship of Millstone Baptist Church, of Dan River Association, by Dr. A. M. Poindexter. He wrote: "I am under obligations to Brother E. Dodson, for my first lessons in Greek. I also taught, and studied with Brother J. J. James, of North Carolina, for several years, and spent six months at the Baptist Seminary at Richmond, in 1843. These are about all the opportunities I ever had." He was married to Miss Olivia E. Barkley, daughter of Elder J. G. Barkley, of North Carolina, May 1st, 1853, by Rev. M. R. Forey of Murfreesboro, North Carolina. The certificate of ordination, dated Milton Baptist Church, N. C., July 1st, 1850, is signed by the brethren following: Stephen Pleasant, Samuel Wait, Elias Dodson, Isaac Mirriam, John S. Pritchard. He left Boston, as has been said, July 5th, 1853, and arrived at Lagos the last of August. Returning, by the advice of the Surgeon of the English Navy, he reached New York, March 4th, 1854. Since his return, he has been preaching in Halifax and Pittsylvania Counties of Virginia. He says: "I am much interested in missions, for they are the sum and essence of Christianity. Every prayer and sermon should have the spread of the gospel as their main object, and every life should be conformed to the same end."

REV. W. H. CLARKE.

Mr. Clarke was born in Eatonton, Putnam County, Georgia, in 1826. He was educated in Putnam County and at Mercer University, where he graduated in July, 1848 or 1849. He taught school, after he graduated, in Houston County, for one year, during which time he was licensed to preach the gospel. The Lumpkin Baptist Church called him to the pastoral care of the church. Mr. Bowen, our missionary to Africa, returned to his own home in Stewart County, full of ardent devotion to the work. Mr. Clarke suddenly came to the conclusion of identifying himself with Mr. Bowen's work. When Mr. Bowen returned from Africa the second time, Mr. Clarke was left alone in this missionary field.

On his return to this country, he commenced lecturing in favor of the African Mission. He married within the first year after his return an estimable lady, now living in Newton, Ga. He studied medicine, taking two courses of lectures, and graduated, but never practiced. He continued in the ministry, and was to the last a friend to the African Mission. But, as the result of his more mature reflection, he believed that it was attended with too many dangers to the health and life of the white man, for him to continue to labor in this field. He thought that it was emphatically the field for the colored missionary, and was a strong advocate for fitting and qualifying colored men for missionary labors in Africa. He died at Albany, Georgia, November 12th, 1871, uttering these words: "Blessed Jesus, come quickly."

MESSRS. TRIMBLE, PRIEST, CASON, AND BEAUMONT.

FAREWELL OF MR. AND MRS. PRIEST.

In their "farewell" to the Alabama Association, by whom they are sustained, the following is found, expressive of their reliance on the Divine Arm for support:

"When we are on the calm or turbid bosom of the ocean, or in the far-off land of Africa, we will fondly remember that we have a home in the hearts of *Alabama Baptists*. We were both brought up by widowed mothers, who were both members of the Methodist Church. We are, with *two exceptions*, the only Baptists of all our connection. You have adopted us as your missionaries, and, indeed, we feel that we are your children. We know that you will supply our every want. But we want you to think more of the cause of the blessed Lord than of us. We beg you to pray and weep for us in connection with the church of Christ and the salvation of benighted Africa. Nothing in this world can make us happier than to know that your heaving bosoms are bedewed with prayerful tears for our success. For the God of all grace has promised to hear you—yes, brethren, *think* of it—*your* prayers. Some of your faces we hope to see once again before we leave our 'own native land ;' but, the next time we meet with the most of you will be at the judgment day."

ORDINATION OF MR. PRIEST.

Mr. Priest and wife were set apart as missionaries to Yoruba, in the Baptist Church of Montgomery, July 15, 1856. In the morning, Dr. A. M. Poindexter, Secretary of the Foreign Mission Board, preached the ordination sermon from Matthew xxviii. 19-20. After the discourse, the services of the Lord's Supper were conducted by Elders J. D. Williams and D. Lee. At night the ordination services were continued. Prayer, by Elder J. D. Williams. Ordaining prayer, by Elder D. Lee, accompanied by the imposition of hands by the Presbytery. Charge, by Elder P. H. Lundy. Presentation of Bible, by Elder Tichenor, pastor of the church, in some appropriate remarks. Elder Poindexter spoke of the relation of the missionaries to the Board, to that church of which they were members, and to the Alabama Association. He gave them his hand, and proposed that, while the hymn "Blest be the tie that binds" was sung, any one might extend to the missionaries his hand in token of affection and pledge of remembrance. "It was a solemn and melting time. All seemed to feel the tenderness and grandeur of the occasion."

SUPPORT OF MR. AND MRS. TRIMBLE.

The Goshen Association, of Virginia, through the Board, arranged for the support of Mr. S. Y. Trimble and wife in Yoruba. They also liberally contributed to aid in the expense of their outfit, passage, etc. Their example was worthy of universal imitation.

PUBLIC FAREWELL MEETING.

On the 7th of September, a meeting was held in the Tabernacle Church of New York City, in reference to the departure to Central Africa of Rev. S. Y. Trimble, of Kentucky, Rev. J. H. Cason, of Tennessee, and Rev. R. W. Priest, of Mississippi. Dr. E. L. Magoon and Rev. Dr. E. Lathrop conducted the opening exercises. Rev. Dr. Jas. B. Taylor, Corresponding Secretary of the Board, gave a brief account of our fourteen stations, in successful operation, in Africa, which had been lately greatly blessed of God, and of our missionaries finding in Central Africa " a salubrious climate and a superior people dwelling in walled towns and cities, where a series of labors had been begun which promised the most benign results." After remarks by each of the missionaries, the Missionary Hymn was sung, and the congregation gave the parting hand to the missionary company. On the 19th of September, the party sailed in the bark Heritage, followed by the prayers and blessings of a multitude of loving hearts.

ON THE WAY AND ARRIVAL.

October 21st and November 20th, Mr. Trimble sent notes by passing vessels, in which he gives the state of health of the company. On December 7th, they were at El Mina, and on the 12th they landed at Lagos.

EARNEST BEGINNING AND EARLY RETURN.

Leaving Lagos on the 15th of January, 1858, in canoes, they arrived in Abbeokuta on the 19th of that month. " The sail was very pleasant, and all our things are safe." Brother Priest wrote on the 21st: " We feel resigned to the providence of God, but we feel desirous, if it be his will, to live long among these people, and hold up Christ as the only way of salvation." " OGBOMISHAW, March 10.—Truly the Lord has been merciful   *   *   in leading us to a land of idolatry and superstition, and in permitting us to point the poor heathen to the Lamb of God that taketh away the sin of the world. We feel that we would spend our last breath in telling sinners of Jesus, our precious Saviour. * * About the health of this country, I see nothing to prevent a *healthy man* from enjoying health, with prudence and care. * * The gospel must be preached in faith. The missionaries must have faith, the Board must have faith, and all the churches must have faith, before God will bless their efforts, here and elsewhere. * * I am full of hope, though I may live to see but little of the fruits of the gospel."

"*May* 13*th:* We have large congregations at this station now, and most of them seem very much interested in the cross of Christ. At the old station, our congregations are small, but there are some very hopeful cases. I believe that there are two or three with whose hearts the Spirit of God is at work. * * Mrs. Trimble has two girls to teach."

August 10*th:* " Our conviction increases that God, some day, will have a great and zealous people in Africa. * * *We will labor for it, we will pray for it, we will expect it.* * * The people say that they are glad that I have come among them—that the word of God is good. * * Many of them have noticed already the change in the people since the missionary came among them. Mrs. Trimble and I are both quite well; have had no fever in ten months. * * We are unworthy of such a trust as God has committed to us. * * The people are afraid to let us have their children to live with us. The bigots laugh at one who does it, and call him the white man's slave. * * I do not believe in the propriety of missionaries teaching school. They should preach the gospel, and make that their great work. * * Our new house will soon be finished, and our yard and garden fenced and fixed off, after which we would be glad to have you come and see us."

"*April* 30*th, Steamship Armenian:* This letter will inform you of our departure from our *very dear African home* in Ogbomishaw, the 26th of January: sailed from Lagos in the steamship Gambia, on the 7th of February: broke down at Bathurst, in the river Gambia, on the 24th; were towed back to Sierra Leone by steamship Candace, where we remained until the 1st of April; and expect to reach Plymouth, England, to-morrow. * * Mrs. Trimble's health continued to fail until we were advised by all to go to a more healthy climate. * * We fear that her spine is affected by that fall from her horse in March, 1857; and many other symptoms have followed, which reduced her so much that she could not walk when we sailed from Lagos. * * I had some fears that I should be called upon to bury my dear companion in the bosom of the restless deep. * * Mrs. Trimble has borne all her sore affliction with much patience. * * We do not wish any to think that we left Africa forever—but only until health be regained and time to return." The simple and sad report of the Board of the Southern Baptist Convention, May, 1859, was: "Rev. S. Y. Trimble and wife have returned to this country, on account of the failure of Mrs. Trimble's health."

Rev. SELDEN Y. TRIMBLE.

Mr. Trimble, who died of pneumonia, October 4th, 1873, at his residence, in Parkersville, Lyon County, Kentucky, was born in Logan County, Kentucky, the 17th of September, 1827.

"His parents being poor and having a large family, were not able so much as to give him a good common education. They were not religious, and he received from them no special training for the great work to which he afterwards consecrated himself.

"Being accustomed to the hardships of a constant laborer on the farm he was the better fitted to endure the toils and privations of a missionary life. At the age of twenty-one he made a profession of conversion, and was baptized by Rev. Thomas Felts. He was licensed to preach by the Baptist Church at New Hope, Logan County, Kentucky, in January, 1850. About this time he entered Union University, Murfreesboro, Tenn., where he remained until he graduated in 1854. While in college he was impressed with a desire to become a Foreign Missionary, and offered himself to the Board at Richmond, Va., to go to Central Africa.

"In 1856, he was appointed to this work. Having incurred considerable expense in educating himself, he engaged to act one year—1855—as missionary in Little River Association. During this year he was instrumental in the establishment of the Church at Canton,

Trigg County. The 10th of July, 1856, he was married to Miss Mary E. Morehead, of Logan County, Kentucky. In company with Revs. R. W. Priest and J. H. Cason and wives, they embarked in September of the same year for the field of their labors in Africa. They were out about six months.

"They commenced their work under favorable auspices. All had to return in about two years on account of the health of their wives. Mr. Trimble's wife, who lives at Princeton, Kentucky, has never recovered, and is now an invalid with six orphan children. In the year 1859, he took charge of Canton and Donaldson Creek Churches, in Trigg County, Kentucky. Afterwards he was pastor of several other churches, and was also missionary for the Association. On the evening of the 25th of September, 1873, he preached from the words: 'According to your faith, so be it unto you.' The next morning he was taken sick and died the 4th of October.

"Mr. Trimble had great force of character and untiring energy. He was sometimes abrupt and exceedingly severe in his reproofs. Perfectly fearless, he never swerved from the convictions of his judgments. He cared but little for public approbation. In preaching he was bold, pointed and plain, instructive and earnest. In labors he was abundant. Whatever he did, he did with all his might. He wore himself out and fell at his post.

For months before his death he seemed to be impressed that his days were almost numbered, and spoke often in his sermons of the uncertainty of life. His last sermons were more earnest and powerful than usual. I suppose he baptized about five hundred persons, among the number three of his own children. He never was very well remunerated for his services. But he provided well for his family, and left them a competency."

His last words were the same as those of the lamented Clarke: "Come, Lord Jesus, come quickly."

Rev. R. W. PRIEST.

FEVER.

Mr. and Mrs. Priest arrived in Ijaye on the 25th of February, 1857. From that place, Brother Priest wrote: "By the time we had ourselves a little fixed up, we all began to have the fever, except Mrs. Priest. I do not know that I suffered more than some of the others; but about the transactions of two nights and a day, I know but little, for I slept all the time.

PREACHING JESUS.

"After I recovered, I began to preach in the market-places. I felt quite well, and was careless about my health. One evening, after preaching the third time that day, I was followed by four or five elderly-looking men, who said they wished to hear me tell about my religion. Though my interpreter was quite hoarse, I tried to preach to them Christ, the Saviour of sinners. A large crowd had gathered, and there was much good attention. The men appeared thankful, and said: 'The word is sweet.' The next day I preached three times, and the *next* I had the fever again. Since then I have not tried to preach in the markets much. But I have visited families, and preached to visitants. Oh, brethren, unite with us in fervent prayer for the power of the Holy Spirit to open the hearts and understandings of these poor, benighted sons of Ham."

PERSECUTION AND SNAKE WORSHIP.

On April 9th, Mr. Priest wrote: "Here I have the pleasure of going from house to house every day to preach *Christ* to benighted heathen. I have the privilege of weeping with those who weep, of rejoicing with those who rejoice, and of praying with and for the *persecuted in Christ*. One of the native converts was whipped by her husband's mother for coming here. Still, she came the next day to our prayer-meeting. When we gave her our hands as a token that we would constantly pray for her, I felt that I was living in *another age*. When Opheka, who had been beaten for serving Christ, gave her hand to the persecuted sister, her words of exhortation and consolation were enough to melt the hardest heart to tears. I wept; but wept tears of joy. I comprehended the expression: 'They departed from the council, rejoicing that they were counted worthy to suffer shame' for Christ's name." * * "I saw two women begging. Each of them had a large snake about her neck. These were the poor women's gods! * * I talked kindly to them, and told them that that was by far the worst thing I had seen in Africa, though I had just seen a human skull upon the altar of the idol."

MOVED TO ABBEOKUTA.

On September 12th, 1857, Brother W. H. Clarke wrote from Ijaye: "Brother Trimble and myself are here, in consultation with Brethren Phillips and Priest on the interests of the mission. Under all the circumstances, it has appeared to us very desirable that one of our number be stationed forthwith at Abbeokuta. The losses we have sustained between Lagos and this place, in the way of theft and otherwise, leave us no alternative. In conformity with these views, we have stationed Brother Priest at Abbeokuta, who leaves this morning for that place."

BAPTISMS, AND GOD WITH HIS PEOPLE.

December 29th: "On the 16th of April, I baptized my interpreter, with a woman. The first day of November I baptized our teacher, who made a profession of religion in Ogbomishaw. Last Lord's Day, I baptized our cook and his wife. I hear that two others intend applying soon for baptism. I trust the day is not distant when we shall be strong enough to organize ourselves and transact our religious affairs systematically. At the prayer-meeting, Monday and Friday evenings, every one tries to pray, and every evening I endeavor to give some religious instruction. Pray that we may live humbly and rely on the Lord for strength and blessing." * * "You very correctly say, Mrs. Priest joyfully shares all the toils and sacrifices. She *is* faithful. I know no one better capacitated to win the affections and confidence of the heathen. If the Board says we must leave here, we shall be glad; if the Board says, we must remain here, we shall be glad. God directs the counsels of his people."

DEATH OF Mrs. REID—LITTLE ROBERT.

On September 21st, 1857, our missionaries, Rev. T. A. Reid and wife, arrived in their field of labor. On May 26, 1858, Brother Priest wrote: "You will receive by this mail the sad news of the death of Sister Reid. Yes, she has gone to her reward. She did all that she could. She gave her life for the cause! One month ago, when we thought Mrs. Priest standing in the twilight of eternity, Sister Reid was enjoying good health. Surely, man knows not what a day may bring forth. * * Will the Board give us $250 to build a wall around the house, or shall I live exposed to the heathen, the cows and sheep, and the goats, for some time to come? * * * I have much to do, and have to do it myself, as the money for the building is expended, and I cannot go in debt. Mrs. Priest and little Robert Warner send much love. He weighs twenty pounds, and will be a year old the 10th inst. God has been very merciful, for which we can never feel as humble and grateful as we should feel."

GRACE NOT TO WITHDRAW THE OFFERING.

"August 28. Mrs. Priest is not able to be up one day out of a week, but she has never expressed a willingness to leave the field. She says, nothing but death can separate her from this people. She offered herself on the altar of Foreign Missions, and when the flame of God's love begins to consume her, her greatest desire and most earnest prayer is that God would give her grace not to withdraw the offering. I think it was well enough for me to express a willingness to carry her home. Now I assure you, it is not painful for us to feel that we shall, in all probability, meet you no more in the toils of time.

"September 2d. Since writing the above, I have passed through a severe attack of fever. * * * Mrs. Priest says she now feels as though she would get well. But our feelings are so delusive here."

THE IMMUTABLE PROMISES OF GOD.

From letters dated September 30th and November 24th and 29th, the following extracts are made: "I have not seen Mrs. Priest more cheerful and encouraged since we have been here. She has health now, so that she can be in school amongst her children.—I have taken one room of the mission building for a house of worship. Notwithstanding we are in a city of not less than a hundred thousand inhabitants, our little house is seldom half filled.—The only source of our encouragement is the eternal truth, in the immutable promises of our blessed Master.—I have been quite ill since the 23d."

FAITH IN "POOR, FRAIL WOMAN."

In appealing for Mrs. Priest's school, the following letter from one of her little scholars to his heathen mother, is given by Brother Priest:

"My Dear Mother:—Wishing you are quite well, in these few lines, with all my friends, and with all my family, my mother, I want you to trust in the Lord, for he is your help. I want you to went to church every Sunday, with Ege, and pray to your Master, and say 'Have mercy upon me, and forgive all my sins.' If you will not do what I told you, if you die, you will go to hell-fire, then you will live in everlasting fire—the fire cannot go out. But if you do what I told you, if you die, you will go to your Master; there you shall live forever, and praise unto the Lord in joy, and peace, and strength.—You can't get any quarrel there. I remain,
"Yours truly, Son,
Ed. Gabbidon."

"I am firmly of the opinion," says Mr. Priest, "that no man should go alone, as a messenger of God, to a nation of heathen. There is more faith and unyielding perseverance in the bosom of one poor frail woman than in that of the stoutest giant-hearted man."

NO END TO WORK.

"Mrs. Priest has suffered a great deal of late, with pain in her side, and for days at a time she has been kept in her bed.—Our little Robert is a hearty child, and is beginning to talk Egba.—I have been laboring hard in Abbeokuta for more than a year. When we first came to this town, I felt much like working for the souls of the people; but I have had to make doors, windows, and lay floors myself, to get a house to live in. I have labored so constantly, that there was little time for preaching, and in fact, I had but little desire to preach.—Now we have one room 20 by 14, and one 14 by 14 finished, and one 12 by 14 with a floor laid, but no covering overhead but grass.—There will be a wall to build around the houses soon; and then the old houses will be to repair, and then something else will have to be done. And I see no end to such work."

BRIGHTER DAY FOR YORUBA.

"You know I have never been over-sanguine in my letters about African conversion. I have even been slow to express what I did hope for Africa. I do not think you have ever read my urgent appeals, or *even a request*, that the Board would send out more missionaries. The reason has been because it appeared to me that we had things mixed up here, somehow; and the more coils there are in a tangled rope the harder it is to get it straight. But now, dear brother, I assure you with the candor of a far-off brother, that I am confident I have never seen a brighter day for the Yoruba Mission. The mission is a unit, and our united prayers go to the mercy-seat of the Lord as the prayer of one man."

RETURNED.

In the annual report of the Foreign Mission Board, of 1860, is recorded: "Brother R. W. Priest has returned to this country, and not contemplating a continued connection with the work in Africa, is no longer a missionary of our Board. * * Abbeokuta, left by Brother Priest, is unsupplied. It is a city of about 70,000 people, and ought to have a good Baptist missionary. Temporary arrangements have been made to keep up the missionary premises, until they can be permanently occupied by a missionary." Mr. Priest is now laboring in Texas.

REV. J. H. CASON.

On the 8th of January, 1857, Mr. and Mrs. Cason arrived at Lagos. Mr. Cason wrote, with regard to the commerce and character of the place: "I was surprised to see the great number of vessels here, and to find trade so brisk. American vessels bring rum, tobacco, powder, and cloth. These articles are in demand at very exorbitant prices.

* * Rum is the curse of the negro here, and our American and other merchants administer it to them. * * It would surprise you to see the loads of ivory the native merchants collect. * * The rich generally speak English, and many of the poorer classes speak so as to be understood. The rich men, who have been engaged in commerce, are as polite and obliging as men in the States. We see some high-toned gentlemen, whose morals, character, and reputation are unimpeachable. On the other hand, many—yes, the masses, are low, ignorant, and superstitious. Yet, they can and will be elevated. * * * * On the 12th, Brother Harden wrote for us to land. * * The surf, though pretty bad, became as gentle as a river while we were crossing. This was enough to make us thankful, since we are told that fifty persons have lost their lives there in the last year. We found Brother Harden well, who received us with open arms and heart. He is well situated here, and can do great good. He is prompt to attend to business, and well fitted to manage the affairs of his position. * * His house is square, with a hall of six feet through, and four comfortable rooms, one of which is a store-room. Some of our goods have been started to Abbeokuta. * * We are in good health, and I hope somewhat prepared for the climate—having been so long on the coast. * * A doctor from an English man-of-war, who has been in practice here for a long time, says Dr. Ford's little book on African fever is the best thing he ever saw on the subject, and advised us to follow him attentively. * * * We are well and anxious to start. Brother Harden's house seems like home. The King sent his staff to congratulate us, and to extend the right hand to us. He sent for us, but Brother Harden said we had no time, as we were getting ready to start to the interior."

On February 12th, Mr. Cason wrote from Ijaye: "Our purpose is, through the Lord, to Christianize and civilize the masses. The opposition is great. * * To change their religion, their laws, customs, and institutions must all be changed. This, in all probability, will be the work of ages, as well as the Lord's work. Jeremiah said: 'Pass over the isles of Chittim and see, and send unto Kedar, and consider diligently and see if there be any such thing. Hath a nation changed their gods, which are yet no gods?'

"You will conclude that I am low-spirited; but you are mistaken. If my heart does not deceive me, I am glad to be here, and am resolved to labor with as much earnestness as though these people were informed and ready to embrace the truth. * * * The people must be instructed orally, for Brother Phillips says, not one in ten thousand can read a word. Even the interpreters can scarcely read or understand when any person else reads either English or Yoruba."

In *The Commission*, of September, 1857, appears the following, from Brother Cason's pen: "If it is the Lord's will for me to labor in laying the foundation for others to build on, there shall never a murmur be heard, though I never see any of the fruits of my labor. Some person must do the first work. * * As long as there is an exaggerated report about Africa, men who are unprepared for the field are liable to come, and as a natural consequence the climate, or something else, will disagree with them, and they will return, having cost the Board two or three thousand dollars; and, in addition to this, they will tell an unfavorable tale. The Board cannot exercise too much caution in sending out men. * * In a word, they should be MEN as well as Christians."

On September 29th, 1857, Mrs. T. A. Reid wrote from Lagos: "We left Sierra Leone on the 13th of September. On Monday we cast anchor off Monrovia. * * Mr. Reid brought me a flower. It was a simple Four O'Clock; but it was clothed with attractions, being the first flower that I had seen that had been nurtured in that dark land. Early on the following morning we were not a little surprised at seeing Brother Cason, who, with his wife, had arrived that morning in the Candace. We were glad to see him, and sad too, that it was under such circumstances. His wife's failing health demanded an immediate return to America. May the Great Physician heal her, and spare her life many, many days, that she may labor for the Lord. She can work at home, if she cannot in Africa. Mrs. Cason's ill health is not attributable to the climate of this country, Brother Cason told us. He gave us very cheering accounts, indeed, of the health of the other missionaries, and told us that we 'need have no fears, only be prudent.'"

After their arrival in Richmond, Va., the following was officially published: "Brother and Sister Cason are in our city. They had just fairly entered upon their work in Africa, when they were reluctantly compelled to leave, by the state of Sister Cason's health. It is gratifying, however, to be able to state that the climate of Africa had no influence in producing this necessity. But her condition required medical aid, which could not be had in the missionary field. We stated in the *Journal* that exposures in a journey from Ijaye to Ogbomishaw, and a fall from a horse, may have somewhat injured her. But, neither Brother Cason nor his wife thinks that these circumstances affected her injuriously. We understand that her physicians expect Sister Cason to be restored to health, but that some months will elapse before she can safely visit her friends in the West. Brother Cason's health is very good." Mr. Cason was the Pastor of the Baptist Church at Columbus, Mississippi, and for many years, has labored in sundry capacities, in the State of Tennessee. His Post-office is Nashville.

Mr. JOHN F. BEAUMONT.

On the 4th of October, 1856, Mr. Beaumont sailed in company with Mr. A. D. Phillips, from New York, for Africa. Mr. Beaumont, not a minister, was appointed to assist in the preparation of books, and otherwise to aid in the spiritual instruction of the people. Under date of March 8th, 1857, Mr. Beaumont wrote from Ogbomishaw: "The surface of this country in many respects resembles some portion of the Western States; the composition of the soil, however, is very different. This country consists of vast prairies, stretched out as far as the eyes can reach, with here and there a gentle undulation. The country appears to me to be most admirably adapted to grazing, and the people about here have some of the finest cattle I have ever seen. Cotton is cultivated in many places. They manufacture a kind of coarse cloth out of the cotton they cultivate, which is much worn by the natives.— A person who has never seen any trees except those in the United States, would not readily credit an account of the astonishing magnitude to which some of these trees attain.—The town in which I am located is situated on an inclined plane. It is well supplied with water by several small streams of water around and in the town. It has the appearance of being healthier than Ijaye; the country around is not so low and flat, and the nights are not so cool and chilly."

Again he writes from Ogbomishaw: " From the progress I have made in my studies I am inclined to flatter myself that by the blessing of God I shall be able to talk Yoruba before many more months shall have rolled over.—I can now rejoice that I am engaged in a work in which both my heart and soul can participate to the fullest extent. I feel an humble confidence that we shall finally succeed in this glorious work, if we only closely follow Jesus Christ.—The people are always ready to hear the word of God, and generally all that the white man has to say is assented to with marked approbation.—One of the officers came to see me one day, and after talking with him for some time I concluded by repeating the Ten Commandments. He replied, 'May God grant me power to keep those commandments.'—The people have no idea of a change of heart, and they look upon the gospel as being the white man's fashion. They need line upon line and precept upon precept."

We quote again from Mr. Beaumont: " I am making some progress in learning the Yoruba language, and am looking forward to the time when I shall be able to talk to these people in their native tongue concerning the redemption purchased by Christ, as the happiest of my existence. A want of thought and a love of freedom from care lead them, when in conversation, readily to assent to almost anything you may happen to say. In my opinion, it is owing to this and not to a love for the gospel, that they so readily sanction its precepts and teachings.—When beholding interesting looking groups of these people engaged in their superstitious ceremonies, I have had to turn away from them, in order to prevent their seeing me shed tears.—Many professing attachment to the word of God, are like those that followed after Christ, because they had eaten of the loaves and fishes. They either expect employment and good pay or presents from the white man."

From the February number of *The Commission*, 1857, we clip the following: "We regret to learn by a letter from Brother Beaumont, that he expects to return to this country, his health being so seriously affected that he regards it unwise to continue upon the field. It is known that he went out principally with a view to the preparation of books for the Yoruba people. He is not an ordained minister of the gospel, but it was believed he would be eminently useful if the specific work for which he was sent could have been completed. A letter, dated December 1, informs us that he had left Ogbomishaw, and was at Lagos, on his way to the United States. We regret that he did not remain longer at his post, giving more time to the process of acclimation." The Board reported, in 1857, "Brother John F. Beaumont remained in Africa about twelve months, but his health being in his estimation seriously affected, he returned to this country."

Rev. A. D. PHILLIPS.

Mr. Phillips was born in North Carolina, Moore County, near Carthage, August 6th, 1827. His parents were both pious. His father often talked to his children on religion, making it a personal matter with each of them. Mr. Phillips professed faith in Christ at a very early age. While quite young his father moved to Mississippi, and there, at the age of eighteen, on his birth-day, young Phillips was baptized. "Not many days after," he says, "I had a great longing to preach, or in some way to tell others of Jesus. But when I began to consider seriously about it, I tried to think it was the work of Satan. I said to myself, 'I have no education, and it would be wicked in me to try to talk or do anything.' Hence, so far as possible, I drove the thought away." With commendable earnestness, he entered an academy. Soon he began to teach a little school. Then he took charge of an academy in a flourishing town. "While teaching," says he, "I conducted a prayer-meeting in the neighborhood. My church heard of me, and without my knowledge licensed me to preach. I felt very awful about it. I was offered a place in Mercer University, Georgia, where I finished my education. I was strangely impressed that it was my duty to go to Africa. Through Rev. T. J. Bowen, the Board heard of me, and opened a correspondence. Finding Brother Clarke, they advised me to prosecute my studies. After Brother Lacy returned, the correspondence was renewed, which resulted in my being called to Richmond, to be examined by the Board. Rev. S. Y. Trimble was examined at the same time, and we were both appointed to Africa in July, 1854. As an agent of the Board, I visited all the churches of the Columbus Association, in Georgia, which body adopted me as their missionary. The last day of August, 1855, I married Miss Fannie C. Williams, of Georgia. On the 4th of October of the same year, we, in company with Mr. Beaumont, sailed from New York, with five Presbyterian missionaries, in the bark "Mende," for Africa. The 1st of December, of the same year, we anchored off Monrovia, Liberia—the first land we made; and the next day, Sunday, I preached my first sermon in Africa. After going to Lagos, I went to Ijaye, where Brother Clarke was, and where I, with Mrs. Phillips, was to remain. Mr. Beaumont went on to Ogbomishaw, where Brother Bowen and his wife were. Mr. Beaumont was a fine scholar, and was sent out to teach."

Mrs. Phillips having died, and the country being in confusion by war, Mr. Phillips returned to this country. In 1871, he went back to Africa, as has been seen in our sketches of the Liberian Mission.

Having re-organized the work in that part of Africa, he returned to America. Having a settled conviction that the white man should not labor in Africa, he has remained in this country. He is at present the beloved and useful pastor of the Baptist Church at Gallatin, Tennessee.

REV. T. A. REID.

"I was born in Hall County, Georgia, twelve miles north of Gainesville, November 23d, 1828. I had little opportunity of education, beyond the common county school, till I was nearly grown. My father was a Baptist minister, having a large family, and receiving little or no salary. In 1849, I went to Pickens Court House, South Carolina, and spent one session in a good school, beginning the first of January. The remainder of the year I taught school, so as to be able to continue my studies. In 1850, or 1851, I went to an Academy, opened by my former teacher at Williamston, in Anderson County.

In 1852, I took charge of the Academy in Gainesville, Hall County. At the close of this school, and year, I had made money enough to pay my board, tuition, and other expenses at Williamston, the two previous years, and this year too. I went to Mercer University, the beginning of February, 1853, having but ten dollars in gold to meet the necessary expenses of tuition and board.

"That great and good man, Rev. P. H. Mell, D.D., entered my room, for I was his guest, and said, that he and his wife had decided to take me as a member of their family, and incur all my college and other expenses. Here was a realization of what God had promised, when he said 'Commit thy way unto the Lord; trust also in him; and he will bring it to pass.' On the second Lord's Day in November, 1846, my father baptized myself, two brothers, and a sister, into the fellowship of the Macedonian Missionary Baptist Church, in Lumpkin Co., Georgia. The ordinance was administered, in a beautiful mountain stream, in the presence of a large congregation. From the time I exercised faith in Christ, July, 1845, I felt impressed to preach. I told Dr. Mell the whole story. He took steps in my behalf. On Wednesday night before the second Lord's Day in April, 1853, I delivered my first public discourse before the church at Penfield. On the following Saturday, the church, on motion of that venerable man, Dr. John L. Dagg, licensed me to preach. Dr. Mell arranged with the Executive Board of the Baptist State Convention, to pay all my expenses. In September, 1856, I was adopted by the Rehoboth Association of Georgia as their missionary to Africa. I was called to ordination by the Executive Board of that Association, with the consent of the Macon Baptist Church. The ordination took place at Fort Valley, so as to be most convenient to the Association, on the 31st of May, 1857."

Mr. Reid was married to Miss Mary E. Canfield, May 26th, 1857. They left Georgia the last of July, 1857; and sailed for Africa from New York, in the schooner Hanover, August 7th, 1857. They reached their field of labor 21st September following. Mrs. Reid died in Ogbomishaw. Mr. Reid left Africa June 10th, 1864; stopped one year in England; arrived in New York 25th August, 1865; and reached his home in Georgia October 2d, 1865.

Mr. Reid writes: "In November, 1865, I went to New York City to have a book published, and to raise funds for the purpose of carrying some religious colored families back with me, to the Yoruba Country. I failed to get my book published. In October, 1867, the Georgia Association adopted me as their Foreign Missionary. The first of January following, I went to Augusta, Georgia, and spent two months, attending Medical lectures. On the 17th of March, 1868, I married Miss V. T. Ammen of Fincastle, Va. During the fall, I received calls to the Fellowship Church, near Ninety-Six, South Carolina, and Cedar Grove, twenty-one miles east of Greenville. I had entered the Seminary September, 1868. In January, 1870, I was called to Virginia, by the illness of Mrs. Reid, which made it necessary to go to Baltimore, and thence to New York for medical treatment. During 1871 and 1872, I preached in protracted meetings, where I saw glorious works of grace. On the 15th of October, 1872, I went to the Pine Bluff Church, Arkansas, as Pastor. On the 13th October, 1874, I moved to Red Bluff. I am now laboring in Mercer County, Kentucky."

Messrs. PHILLIPS AND REID.

The labors of these gentlemen in Africa will be more fully reviewed in the next decade. But, they began in this period of our Yoruban Mission. For the sake of convenience, biographical outlines of them have been given, although with the disadvantage of anticipating somewhat our detailed account of their honorable and successful works.

SHE WILL NOT LOSE HER REWARD.

In 1857, the Board reported: "Brother A. D. Phillips has enjoyed almost uninterrupted health, and has been able to continue in the acquisition of the language and in the performance of other missionary service. But his excellent lady, very soon after their arrival at Ijaye, was stricken with African fever, and passed to her home in heaven. Her heart was in the work, and she was cheerfully awaiting the will of her Divine Master, to live and labor, or to fall in the field she had chosen. She will not lose her reward."

INDUSTRIOUSLY AND HOPEFULLY ENGAGED.

The Board also reported Brother Phillips at Ijaye, where "he will be joined by one or more of the recently arrived families. Houses for the comfortable accommodation of the missionaries have been erected, and a chapel, in which regular religious services are held. A church has been constituted, and five of the people of the town, giving evidence of a change of heart, have been baptized." In 1858, the Board report: "The missionary labors of Brother Phillips, during the year, have been very much interrupted by his having to superintend building at Abbeokuta and by sickness. At latest information, he had recovered his health, and was industriously and hopefully engaged in endeavoring to instruct the natives, publicly and privately."

REINFORCEMENT.

In 1857, the Board reports: "Rev. T. A. Reid, of the Rehoboth Association, Georgia, has been appointed missionary to Yoruba to fill the place of the lamented Dennard, and has entered upon his work at Abbeokuta. Before their arrival, Brother Priest had been located by the Mission at Abbeokuta. It was at one time contemplated by them both to remain there and to establish two stations. But the necessity of occupying Awyaw led the Board to direct that Brother Priest should locate at the latter town." Subsequently Mr. Reid moved to Ogbomishaw.

AFFLICTED BUT NOT FORSAKEN.

The Board reported:

"We advert to the death of Sister Reid with feelings of profound grief. Her exalted piety, cultivated, intelligent, and earnest devotion to the work of missions, had greatly endeared her to our hearts, and led us to hope for a bright career of usefulness for her in the chosen field of her Christian toils. But he who ' seeth not as man seeth,' was pleased to disappoint our expectations. She was taken with malignant fever, and died at Ogbomishaw, after a short illness, on the 17th of May, 1858. This was an overwhelming affliction to our beloved brother, but the Lord wonderfully sustained him.

"The labors of Brother Reid at Ogbomishaw were blessed. He baptized two females before he left on an excursion for the benefit of his health, and several others, especially an old man who had not been baptized because of sickness, gave hopeful evidence of interest in the truth."

SUMMARY.

From Mr. Phillips' summary of the labors of the year 1858, we make the following extract:

"It is with profound gratitude to God that I recount the mercies and blessings of the past year. I have baptized one heathen convert, and seen all those formerly baptized making as fair advances in a divine life as could be expected. * * Everything seems to be moving smoothly on, and to my vision the clouds in our horizon are fast dispersing; and we even now imagine we feel the genial rays of the glorious Sun of righteousness. Lord grant it may be so. I have been here nearly three years, and have endeavored to observe very closely the signs of the times, and I *think*, at no time of my stay here there has been more to encourage. And I am looking forward to the year 1859 with interest, and *do* believe that the Lord will bless us.

"Our weekly prayer-meetings are interesting and encouraging. In one of these prayer-meetings I called upon a mother to pray: and oh, what pleadings on behalf of her *children*, her husband, and all her country people! Then she begged God to give health and ability to the white man in this country to *preach Jesus*, and to put it into the hearts of *many* of his white children to 'come over and *help us*.'"

THE SECOND DECADE.

1858 TO 1868.

This period will be sketched along the line of the biography of Rev. R. H Stone; then by the reports of his work, and of that of Rev. T. A. Reid and Rev. A. D. Phillips, given together, under their plans of labor.

Rev. R. H. STONE.

Mr. Stone was born in Fauquier County, Va., on the 17th July, 1837. Having first obtained some knowledge of the elementary branches of learning at an "old field" school, he was educated at "Black Hill Seminary," in Culpeper County, a boarding school conducted by A. G. Simms, Esq., and at "Kemper's University School," at Gordonsville, Va. He was baptized by Rev. Silas Bruce in the summer of 1866, and connected himself with the Salem Church of the Shiloh Association of Virginia.

He married Miss Susan J. Broadus on the 22d of October, 1858, and sailed for Africa, from Baltimore, on the 4th of November of the same year. He sailed from Africa on his return in the middle of December, 1862, having passed *four* years in the interior of Africa. He was detained four months in England, and arrived in this country in 1863. He reached Culpeper Court House on the 2d of July, just in time to see his mother-in-law die.

He went out again in October (*via* England and Madeira), and returned by the same route in the summer of 1869.

Excepting a short time that he was in the army as a missionary chaplain, just before the close of the war, he has been preaching and teaching. At present he is the Principal of the Culpeper Graded School, and pastor of *Lael Church* of the *Shiloh Association of Virginia.*

The sketch of Mr. Stone's missionary experience will be given in his own language:

" We went out in the Colonization ship, M. C. Stevens, and touched at Sierra Leone, Cape Mount, Mourovia, and Cape Palmas, passing a month in Liberia. From Cape Palmas he went on to Lagos, about 900 miles farther South. Here we were compelled to land, by crossing a most dangerous bar, swarming with sharks, but got safely through, and were made comfortable by Brother J. M. Harden, our colored missionary, stationed at that point especially to receive missionaries and forward them to the interior. Brother Harden had many excellent moral and intellectual characteristics, that made him a very agreeable companion for even the white missionaries. His excellent widow is still living in Lagos. Brother Harden forwarded me by canoe to Abbeokuta, which is 60 miles by land, but which is farther by water.

"After five days, we reached Abbeokuta, and were received by Brother Priest, who was then living in an unfinished mission house. We found Abbeokuta very different from Lagos, in many important respects. The situation of the latter is not so healthy, and provisions there were very inferior, scarce and dear. The appearance of the native population of Lagos did not impress me as favorably as those of Abbeokuta. But Abbeokuta had no marks of civilization anywhere, and in Lagos a few foreigners had settled for purposes of trade, and their foreign-built houses were a great comfort to the eye of the *new* missionary. Abbeokuta was situated amidst isolated granite cliffs, and surrounded by vast, beautiful, and palm-dotted plains of grass and jungle. It extended seven miles in one direction.

"Having rested a few days, we proceeded by land to Ijaye. This town was surrounded by a dense forest which the governor would not allow to be disturbed. It was therefore the lair of hyenas, leopards, and other wild beasts, which howled and prowled about the streets all night. But this forest and the outside jungle forest furnished the people with the greatest abundance of the largest and best game. We lived mostly on game, milk, and butter, but all kinds of provisions were very abundant, of the best quality, and exceedingly cheap.

"The elevation above the sea-level is greater than that of Abbeokuta, and we would have enjoyed most excellent health here if we had had a better house.

"The population of Ijaye was about 75,000; perhaps 100,000. It was free from the scorpions and other reptiles which infested the rocks of Abbeokuta, and the centipedes which infested the sands of Lagos. Besides, the *government of the city* and the *character of the people* were better.

"I lived here *two* years. In the beginning of the second year (1860) I was captured by a party of Ibadans and taken to their town and tried for my life on the charge of being a *spy*. This capture and its attendant circumstances revealed to us the fact that formidable preparations were being made for the destruction of Ijaye, and that the whole of the kingdom was combined against that city because the governor, Areh, would not acknowledge the authority of a new king just come to the throne.

Having escaped my captors, I reached Ijaye in time to see a large army approach and attack it. Every five days there was a pitched battle. The Abbeokutans came to the assistance of the Ijayans, but this only prolonged the war, and the town was taken and completely destroyed. During the siege, many of the starving (hundreds died around our house from starvation) people brought their children to us. These we sent to Abbeokuta—that is, Mr. Phillips, who had charge of the Ijaye station when I came, took them safely down, and took care of them in Abbeokuta, having obtained an appropriation for that purpose.

"I remained in Ijaye until the end of the year, or rather until the spring of 1861. When all was lost, I came down to Abbeokuta, bringing what children we had left and all our effects. All the converts except two had preceded me, and we established a flourishing school of seventy children and a church of thirty converts at Abbeokuta. The refugees from Ijaye gathered around us, and we had a much more flourishing mission than we had before the war began.

"In January, 1861, Brother Phillips was compelled to go to England for his health. I was again left alone—Brother Priest having gone home and Brother Reid being shut up in Awyaw. After eight months, Brother Phillips returned, and as my wife's health had completely failed (December, 1862,) I came down the river to Lagos, on my way home. I found the place very much changed in the four years of my absence in the interior. The people had become somewhat civilized and I was regarded as a sort of pioneer.

"I returned in 1867 to relieve Brother Phillips. We succeeded in rallying our broken ranks in Lagos, and I was again left in charge. This is a sad and joyful period of my missionary life. The Lord worked with me and gave me encouraging success, but I was compelled to leave the field and return to this country in 1869. Whether I shall be permitted to go out again the Lord only knows.

"Let me add: I went to Awyaw, when I escaped from Ibadan, to put myself under the protection of the King, and I recollect that it was an open country, and that Brother Reid had a pretty little mission-house there. As to *Ogbomishaw*, when on the painful and perilous journey above mentioned I reached that place in the night, after a ride of sixty miles that day, I was in great danger from wild beasts, and was also sick, hungry, and distressed, and in no mood for observations. I spent the whole of next day in Brother Clarke's deserted house, which I found to be well furnished and the prettiest and best arranged house in the mission, both for convenience and health. Such surroundings rather aggravated my grief, and I spent most of the day in wandering about the house and premises, and in prayer over my own desolate situation, as well as the desolation of this station.

"I remember to have come on a grave in the tangled grass in one corner of the mission premises, and on examination, found that it was Sister Reid's grave. Over this I prayed that her work might *still remain*. Altogether, I think Ogbomishaw is the most inviting field of missionary labor in Yoruba. In one little room of the house, I found a splendid library, all the books having Brother Clarke's name in them. This library, together with the entire premises, were carefully protected by the chief in the hope that Brother Clarke would some day return."

This outline of Mr. Stone's work will be "filled out," as we proceed now chronologically, at the expense of retracing our steps somewhat.

1858 TO 1861.

LAGOS.

In 1858 the Board said: Brother Harden still continues in Lagos in the faithful discharge of his duties as Missionary Agent of the Board. He has preached regularly in the chapel and from house to house, but as yet has not been permitted to witness the success of his efforts in the conversion of his hearers. We trust it may not be long before the seed which he has sown in tears shall spring up a gospel harvest." The Board said, in 1859: "Were it not necessary to keep an agent in Lagos for the transmission of supplies to our interior stations, it may be doubted whether it would be advisable for Brother Harden to remain there. The field seems peculiarly sterile and uninviting. Our brother writes, at times, as if almost discouraged, but, again, relying upon the power of the gospel and the promises of God, he seems to expect a blessing upon his labors. He—as indeed do all the missionaries—earnestly pleads for an interest in the prayers of the brethren." 1860: "Brother Harden has, with little interruption, preached the word to such as could be induced to hear. * * His wife conducts a school, which appears to be doing well." 1861: "The labors of Brother Harden have been attended with more encouraging results than heretofore. His congregations are larger. Two have been baptized and two excommunicated. There are now eight church members. Sister Harden has a school of nineteen, who, in addition to books, are instructed in needle work and other useful employments. If they had means to provide for children, she could have a much larger school. But the Board, with the limited means at their disposal, and the urgent demands of other departments of the work, have not deemed it judicious to make an appropriation for this object."

1859–1860.

AWYAW.

Our lone missionary, T. A. Reid, was here. He wrote: "That we need a strong reinforcement, none will doubt or deny; yet we hear of no one buckling on the armor of the gospel, and heeding the Macedonian cry: 'Come over and help us.' Brethren, is this right in the sight of God? Are you content to lave your brows in the waters of forgetfulness, till every missionary impression is forever extinguished?

The duties which now devolve upon the present missionaries are truly arduous, but must be borne, however debilitated our frail constitutions are, or the cause of our blessed Master must languish. Although our number is so much lessened, and no visible prospects of any additions, yet we are not without hope; because we believe that it is the cause of God, and he will, in his own good time, make it prosper and rise in majestic triumph over all opposition.

"We need more missionaries here than in China, according to population, or any other field which has a written language through which to operate. Here, all instruction has to be conveyed orally, or not at all. Hence, the reason of the slow progress of the gospel, and the intense labor which devolves upon the missionary."

IJAYE.

Brother Stone wrote: "I have had no reason to regret so long a journey, nor to regret coming to this land of 'the shadow of death.' Experiences of divine goodness have continually attended my steps, since I bade adieu to my native country, and 'the Lord will provide,' appeared written on all the dispensations of Providence which have befallen me in this country. Our temporal wants have been much more abundantly supplied than we expected, and in our souls, the Lord has not left us comfortless, but has appeared exceedingly near and dear to us."

Writing again on the subject of reinforcements, he says: "I cannot yet agree with Brother Clarke in regard to white men living here. * * The Israelites did not stand still and see the salvation of the Lord, when the way was opened, nor should we, when God has supplied us with so many convenient means of sending abroad the gospel. The way is already open, and the enemy hard upon us."

Brother Phillips regarded the prospects of the mission as hopeful. He said: "We are all getting on very well here. I hope we grow in favor with the people every day. I am looking with interest to several, who attend our services on the Lord's Day, and give some signs of interest. I have had very interesting conversations with Mohammedans, of late. I seldom preach through an interpreter."

1860–1861.

WAR.

The Board reports: "The missionaries in the interior have been surrounded throughout the year by all the horrors of war. The details of this deadly strife, as they have been given from time to time in the letters of the missionaries, and published in our periodicals, are appalling. Thousands upon thousands have been slain; famine and disease have added their desolations. But, amidst all, God has graciously preserved the lives of the missionaries. The chief scene of conflict has been at Ijaye. At its commencement, Brethren Phillips and Stone, and Sister Stone, were there. They have at no time felt apprehensive of personal danger, except while Brother Stone was, for a short period, a captive to the Ibadan people.

"By their attention to the sick and wounded, and to the children thrown on their care, our brethren believe they have gained the confidence and respect of the natives to an extent beyond what could have been attained in peaceful times; and they think that, when peace returns, their labors will be greatly facilitated, and their prospects of success increased from this cause."

'TURNED SCHOOL-MASTER.

Mr. Phillips was temporarily at Abbeokuta. Mr. Phillips left Ijaye on the 29th of July for Abbeokuta. There, with the children brought from Ijaye, and others placed under his care, he soon had a large school. On the 16th of January, 1861, he says, "At present, the children with me, who are clothed, fed and taught in school, are *forty-four!* Two died with me; one was carried away. I found it was not much use to try street preaching here, so I turned *school-master*. I am carrying on a fine agricultural school.—Some of the oldest seem deeply impressed with the news of salvation, and I pray the good Lord will soon give us souls among them."

THE GREAT SALVATION.

As Mr. Stone stated, he and Mrs. Stone continued at Ijaye. They have been diligently engaged in attention to the sick and wounded, teaching the few children that remain with them, and imparting a knowledge of the gospel at every opportunity, to those around them. In general, they have enjoyed good health, but at last advices both had been sick—Sister Stone very ill. Brother Stone had recovered; and Sister Stone was decidedly convalescent. Brother Stone writes most hopefully. There was, with some, evident interest in the "great salvation."

LONELY, BUT HOPEFUL.

Mr. Reid continued at Awyaw. He suffered a great deal from a local disease, aggravated by the absence of judicious medical advice, and the want of attention. His situation was lonely, as all communication between him and the other missionaries was cut off. He was still hopeful. He baptized one, and had hopes of others.

STATE OF THE MISSION.

In his Annual Report, Brother Phillips thus sums up the results of the year: "There has been one baptized [above Lagos] this year—that was at Awyaw. Two have been dismissed from fellowship and three restored. Total membership above Lagos thirteen. I have now with me two ready for baptism. One is a young native man, who has been with us several years; the other is a Mr. West, from New York, a carpenter. Though our additions have been few, I contend our advance has been great. We never before had such influence with the people, or such a deep hold upon their affections."

NEED OF MORE LABORERS.

"Brother Phillips urges very earnestly the importance of reinforcing the mission. The need is pressing. He contends that his own experience, and that of others, demonstrates the practicability of *efficient and continued labor by white missionaries*, and appeals affectionately and solemnly for such to go. Suitable colored missionaries, also, are needed."

1861 TO 1863.

WAR CONTINUES.

The terrible war which for several years desolated the Yoruba country still continued. Mr. and Mrs. Stone, who were then at Ijaye, found it necessary amid the fearful collisions at that place, to remove to Abbeokuta.

As the prospect of securing and remitting funds was not favorable during the condition of the war in our country, Brother Harden, from the 2d of April, 1862, engaged in brick making at Lagos, thus securing all that might be necessary for the support of his family. Subsequently he writes: "I feel considerably encouraged, just now, having a pretty good attendance at church on Sunday. The people seem to be awakening from their slumbers. Some of the women come regularly on Saturdays to scour the benches, and the roof being leaky, one of the men came of his own accord to repair it. There is one attendant whom I believe to be converted."

The mission at Abbeokuta was largely favored of the Lord. More were baptized within two years than during the whole preceding history of the mission. Mr. Stone and his wife, in conjunction with Brother Phillips, labored with indefatigable zeal in the prosecution of their work. But the health of Mrs. Stone failing, they were compelled to return home.

Brother Phillips' health being somewhat affected, by long continued labors at his post, he visited England for a short period. He embarked from Lagos on the 22d of January, 1862, and having spent several months at London and other places, he returned to his station with greatly recruited strength.

"During the year," wrote Mr. Phillips, "we have received more encouragement than ever before. We baptized twenty in 1861, and Brother Stone has baptized five since I left. We feel that a great work of grace is going on in our congregation."

1866–1876.

A GOOD MAN FALLEN.

On the 15th of May, 1864, Rev. Joseph M. Harden was taken away, after a severe and protracted illness of congestion of the liver. He was a good man, and in many respects mentally cultivated beyond the usual standard of colored men. His widow received some assistance from the committee in Baltimore.

POWERFUL INFLUENCE.

Brother Phillips, in a letter dated October 1st, 1864, said: "I am getting on as well as I could expect in my hampered circumstances. I manage to keep the children fed, and in some way clothed. In the beginning of the year, I sent the largest boys to work for themselves, but they still live here, so I have not lost them in my congregation. My congregation is good; more than my room will seat. I have this year reclaimed a few and excluded a few, and now have four candidates for baptism. We have a very powerful influence over our people in this country, so much so that they are afraid to go contrary to us. This proves to me, more and more, how important it is to have the right men over the churches.

Awyaw was under the care of Brother Reid until the spring of 1864, when his failing health compelled him to leave. His circumstances during the war in Yoruba were peculiarly embarrassing, and it was at the risk of his life that he at length passed amid the contending hosts down to Abbeokuta. We had not heard of him, nor had Brother Phillips received information from him, for more than two years, so completely was he cut off by the destructive wars of that country. He wrote: "I was very loth to leave my post till the war was over, but necessity seemed to demand it. I was destitute of almost everything. My clothing was worn out, and no food but native, and that not good, because of the scarcity of cowries to buy food with. Many times, for several days, I have lived on *one cent's* worth of food per day. Sometimes, for five or ten days, I did not taste meat of any kind. At one time I was twenty-seven months without seeing the face of a white person. Thus I have gone on until I came down to Abbeokuta." During all this time he had funds, but not in the currency of the country. He says: "Sometimes I could change a few dollars for cowries, but not often." He left the station at Awyaw in the care of a native assistant. The same is true at Ogbomishaw. He returned to America.

VIOLENCE AT ABBEOKUTA.

Rev. A. D. Phillips remained at his post during the entire period of the war, though cut off most of the time from his brethren. His church of native members, about thirty in number, seemed revived, and an increased interest in the public services of the Lord's house was manifested.

Mr. R. H. Stone, who had been in this country for several years, determined to return to his field. He sailed from this country in 1867, leaving his family to follow at some more favorable opportunity. But before his arrival a sad calamity had been sustained by the mission, requiring its removal, at least temporarily, from Abbeokuta to Lagos. An excited mob, without restraint from the authorities, surrounded the premises occupied by Brother Phillips, and by violence robbed it of all the money, clothing, provisions, and furniture it contained. The building itself was nearly destroyed. The mission-houses of several of the English Boards were also broken to pieces and their contents taken away. Brother Phillips was thus left with no clothing but such as he had on his person, and without resources was compelled to leave Abbeokuta.

He arrived at Lagos but a short time before Brother Stone entered upon his work. These two brethren were thus unexpectedly placed in circumstances of peculiar peril.

Mr. Stone wrote: "In regard to what I propose to do, I will say that I hope to gather together here nearly if not quite all our Abbeokuta and other interior converts and children, and to instruct and train them, and to labor in connection with them, among the purely heathen population of this place. I also hope to have a good school here next year. Sister Harden is a most valuable acquisition to us for this purpose, and will prove a great service in this thing. I also expect to assist in teaching during the heat of the day, when I cannot be safely doing anything else. Sister Harden will keep the girls at her house, and I will keep the boys with me. In all these things I can only trust the Lord to direct me.

"I find that this station will not only be an important one, but an *expensive* one. The white missionary cannot possibly live on the salary allowed to an interior missionary. Everything is very dear. Besides, as there are several hundred white people here, and among them several resident missionaries and their wives, the man who lives here will have to occasionally exchange the ordinary courtesies of civilized life, and live in rather different circumstances to those of interior missionaries. The Church Missionary Society allow their married missionaries £250 per annum, but we have always managed to live on less than they do, and we can do it still, I believe."

RETURN OF BROTHER PHILLIPS.

Mr. Phillips had been, without interruption, diligently engaged in his missionary work for twelve years. A communication signed by the English Missionaries at Abbeokuta, urged that for the prolongation of his life, and the interest of the Mission, it would be wise to take a temporary absence from the field. In reference to his expected departure, he wrote:

"I feel it will be best for me to leave for a little while, as I can now easily be spared from the mission. In the meantime, I am hard at work, trying to get up a little chapel. Our own people have contributed liberally for it, and I have received £10 sterling from a friend in England, which I intend to put in it, and so hope to complete it before I leave. We have a fair prospect of doing good, and collecting together a larger congregation than we have ever had in Lagos. As I have often written you, I believe an energetic white man in Lagos will get a large congregation, but we can only get on very poorly, except we are properly supported. But I am so tired, and so ashamed of always writing about money, I wish to never mention it again. The brethren in the South ought to be sufficiently acquainted with our condition by this time, and if they want *their* mission to be a poor 'underling' let them say so. As for myself, I have nothing to live for but the mission, and I very much regret having to spend two or three months on board a vessel doing nothing."

THE THIRD DECADE: 1868 TO 1878.

THE LONE MISSIONARY.

After the departure of Mr. Phillips from Lagos, Mr. Stone writes thus: "I continued to teach several hours of the day until my health became seriously bad, and I determined to get a teacher, and devote myself entirely to the more important parts of the work. It then numbered nearly forty scholars, and continues about as I left it, for though several more have been received, others have been dismissed. I continue to exercise diligent care over the children, especially in their religious education, and give the teacher to understand that he is only an assistant in their secular education, and that I alone am their religious teacher. No expense attends the school except the salary of the teacher, and a house and support for the Abbeokuta children. Sister Harden teaches the girls sewing.

"During the last four months twelve persons have been received for baptism. Of these, I have already baptized nine, and the others await the administration of the ordinance next Sunday. The greater portion of the new converts are interior natives, who are relations and acquaintances of the members of the church here, and who previously heard the gospel from us in the interior. Last Sunday evening I baptized three non-commissioned officers of the regular troops stationed here.

"In addition to the persons received for baptism, and including two who were restored before Brother Phillips' departure, six persons, who had been excluded, have been restored to full fellowship, making eighteen additions to our new church here.

"Since the completion of our chapel, we have a service every Saturday evening. Besides this, we have service morning and evening on the Lord's Day. The service in the evening is always in Yoruba. The Spirit of the Lord seems to be among us. Our Sunday-school is prospering, but the want of efficient teachers has compelled me to divide it into five large classes. My day-school has run up from the original *three* that I had in the house with me, to *thirty-five*, and they still come."

HIS RETURN.

The return to this country of Mr. Stone, in 1869, is thus explained by himself: "A protracted illness, during which I was incapable of any business, finally culminated in brain fever. As the Colonial Surgeon declared my case was incurable without a change of climate, the Wesleyan Missionary, Mr. Rhodes, kindly transferred me, with my baggage, to the English steamer, where Mr. Roper assisted me in the remaining things connected with my passage. Though still afflicted with chills and fever while in England, I was able to get immediately aboard another steamer leaving for America. My health improved very rapidly in the latter part of the voyage, but I am not yet able to read without being made quite dizzy and sick. I have not enjoyed this precious privilege of reading for several months. I feel as one waked from an unpleasant dream. Though somewhat bewildered by the apparently circuitous movements of the Shekinah of my faith, I still feel assured that it will lead me to the place where the ark will go over before me. Fully assured that it is the will of the Lord, the same grace enables me to return that enabled me to go. I left funds in the hands of Mrs. Harden to carry on the school until you could send her instructions. Mr. Rhodes, assisted by an ordained and experienced native preacher, will preach for the converts twice on every Sunday. Twenty were baptized during the year, one candidate remaining."

By a letter from the mission the Board learned that the school at Lagos was still continued, and that the church were anxiously waiting for the return of Brother Phillips. Funds were sent to meet the liabilities of the mission.

SUBSEQUENT HISTORY.

1870–1875.—In consequence of the continued hostility of the king and head men in the interior, it was impracticable to re-enter upon our mission-work in Yoruba. In our sketch of the Liberian Mission, an account is given of the return of Mr. Phillips to Africa, and his re-establishment of our missions in Liberia and the Bier Country. But, better days were dawning.

1875 to 1876.—The appeal of the Board of Missionaries for Africa, as has been stated, was responded to by Rev. W. J. David, of Mississippi, and Rev. W. W. Colley, a colored brother of the Richmond Institute, of Richmond, Va. After appropriate services in the Tabernacle Baptist Church, of New York, of which Rev. J. B. Hawthorne, D. D., was pastor, the missionaries sailed for Liberia, as has also been mentioned, on the 8th of January, 1875, and arrived at Sierra Leone on the 8th of February. But, before we proceed, a brief sketch of these brethren, and our native preacher, Moses L. Stone, may be in place:

REV. WILLIAM J. DAVID.

Mr. David was born near Meridan, Lauderdale County, Mississippi, September 28th, 1850. He was baptized by Rev. J. B. Hamberlin, into the fellowship of the Meridan Baptist Church, August, 1867. He attended school at that place, and went to Mississippi College, at Clinton, to prepare for the ministry, under the recommendation of the Meridan Church, by which he was licensed to preach. After some missionary labors, he went to Crozer Theological Seminary, at Upland, Pennsylvania. He was ordained in Meridan, at the Bethlehem Association, September 25th, 1873, by Rev. Messrs. Columbus Smith, J. B. Hamberlin, T. J. Walne and L. M. Stone.

The Superintendent of the Meridan Sunday-school adds: "May the Lord indeed make Willie David a great blessing: his first missionary work was done here, in connection with our school, having gathered in twenty-four scholars in the space of three months!"

REV. W. W. COLLEY.

Mr. Colley was born in Prince Edward County, Va., February 12th, 1847. He was baptized by Henry Fults in September, 1870, and united with the Gravel Hill Church. He entered Richmond Institute in the fall of 1870. The vacations of 1871 and 1872 were spent preaching in Louisa County. Thirty professed conversion. He was ordained at Alexandria, Va., in May, 1873. The vacations of 1873 and 1874 were spent at Norwich, Conn.—Here he baptized eighty persons.—He sailed for Africa as missionary of our Board, January, 1875, and returned to this country, in the fall of 1879.

MOSES L. STONE.

The following is from the pen of Rev. R. H. Stone; "The Macedonian cry from the young native Yoruban, Moses L. Stone, is especially worthy of notice, as all his antecedents indicate that he is *perfectly sincere*. Besides this, his letter indicates a most remarkable proficiency in English for one so young. He was one of the school children at Abbeokuta when our station was destroyed there in 1867. When I began a station and school at Lagos in the beginning of the year 1868, I found it convenient to take him into my household together with several other boys. In a few months he gave such evidence of genuine piety that I baptized him. From the first, he exhibited an unquenchable thirst for knowledge. I remember that I once found him prostrate on the floor at one o'clock at night studying by the aid of a little native lamp. He, of course, made rapid progress in general knowledge. I gave him such instruction as I could in the Scriptures for more than a year. After sickness compelled my return, his unassuming piety and superior intelligence led the other converts to make him their religious teacher and adviser in conjunction with the Wesleyan missionary. One so well reported of by all, should, I think, receive some notice from the Board. I hope that when he is ordained, the Board will sustain him in Ogbomishaw. I believe that he will yet become as great a blessing to Yoruba, as Bishop Crowther, if he receives anything like the aid and encouragement that Crowther did from his own denomination."

Messrs. David and Colley arrived in Lagos, October 14th, 1875. Mr. David wrote: "Brother Colley and I are pleased that we are to go to Lagos and Yoruba, instead of Liberia, as our *hearts* have been there all the while. Lagos and its environs number some 65,000 inhabitants. It is called the 'Liverpool of Western Africa,' and is becoming one of the most healthful towns on the coast. Yoruba is a vast and promising field. It is believed that more than 4,000,000 of people speak the Yoruban language."

Health of Missionaries. Under date of December 3d, Brother Colley wrote from Lagos: "My first spell of fever was on the 15th of May. I have been able to work only at intervals. Since our arrival here I have had four attacks. Brother David does not suffer much from fever. Recently, however, Mr. David has been attacked with dysentery, occasioned by the use of improper food."

First reception at Lagos. From a letter of Mr. David, of September 8th, we make the following excerpts: "Soon after I went ashore I was visited by about forty-five of our members—some from the interior. I do not think I ever saw people so rejoiced. Immediately they had a meeting in their bamboo chapel to thank God, who had answered their prayers. It was a mutual thanksgiving. Though we did not understand each other's language, except through an interpreter, our Heavenly Father knew our hearts. I baptized three candidates. Others applied, but I advised them to await my return."

Churches of the Interior. "I reached Abbeokuta, a city of about 175,000 souls, July 15th, and was cordially received by the King and elders. I found there sixteen of our members. I heard directly from Ogbomishaw, where there are some eighteen more, who do not neglect 'the assembling of themselves together,' besides several converts. These brethren have often travelled twelve days journey to Lagos to inquire if 'God's men had yet come.' "—Truly the labors of our former missionaries are not lost.—" I had permission to go to Ogbomishaw, but returned to Lagos after spending nine days in Abbeokuta. The head men were quite anxious that I should make my home there. They would say 'the wicked men who drove away the missionaries are dead. White men can come and live among us in peace.'"

Organization of Lagos Church. From Lagos, Mr. Colley wrote, March 7th, 1876: "On January 1 we organized the church here with twenty-four members, and the next day baptized twenty into the church. We have three young men with us—one an interpreter; another training for usefulness; and the third, the son of our late missionary, Mr. Harden."

As the chapel was in a dilapidated state, for the repairs of which Brother David asked an appropriation, a house was secured at £75 per annum, "which," he says, "has a hall as large as our chapel, where we hold night services, and preach and teach when it rains."

Another Man Needed. Mr. David writes: "I hope the Board will send out another man, that Lagos, Abbeokuta, and Ogbomishaw may each be occupied."

Mr. Colley wrote: "I hope the colored brethren will begin their work in Africa this year, either by sending a man or supporting one in the field. This is *their* field of labor. I ask when will they obey their Saviour's commission? Now is the time for the churches to offer their *centennial* sacrifice to God, by sending the 'Bread of Life' to the heathen of Africa." "We have been exceedingly anxious to reach the interior stations before the rains. Now they have commenced. We have the work here as properly arranged as we can get it for the present. We have just this moment talked with members from Abbeokuta, who have information from places beyond. They want to know '*when are we coming to their towns to preach Christ?*' Such cries come with almost every man and woman who comes from the interior."

1876–1877.

THE WORK AT LAGOS.

Of 65,000 inhabitants, about 4000 have professed Christianity. "The rest have to learn the first principles of life in Christ."

Our Chapel, a brick building, 30 by 48 feet, which will accommodate between three and four hundred persons, was, on March the 2d, nearly completed, at an expense of some $1,300. Brother Colley says: "Our burden now is a Mission-House to save heavy rent."

Native Teachers. "Your heart would rejoice," adds our missionary, "to hear the young men teach Christ. When I am prostrated by fever, they preach to me in broken English, and on Sunday, they preach to the people from the same texts, in Yoruban. The church supports one of these young men who study with us."

The Church has doubled itself in eight months—having fifty-eight members "who show their faith by their works." On February 11th, seven were baptized; previously, four were reported. An old Ijaye chief, for whom prayer had been long offered, fell down in one of our meetings, and worshipped the Christian's God. "When the Lord shall convert this pagan," says Brother Colley, "there will be a grand ingathering of heathen souls, who are restrained by his influence."

The Sunday-school numbers eighty-five; the day school forty. "We strive to reach the parents through the children."

Thanks and Astonishment. "All join in hearty thanks to the Board for what God has enabled it to do in this field during the past year. Will not the churches pray the God of missions to bless us equally the next year? Brother David and I were thunderstruck at your letter on retrenchment."

Mr. David writes: "Brother Colley and his three young men are doing well at Lagos."

ABBEOKUTA AND THE INTERIOR.

From Lagos Mr. David wrote, June 19th, 1876: "My heart swells with joy at the thought of starting to-morrow for the regions beyond."

Mr. David's Appeal: "The cry in all the towns, large and small, that I have visited, is for teachers. I shall not beg the Board to manifest more interest in this field. When you remember that five of our faithful band fell in Yoruba; that scores of towns have gates open to the men with the gospel; that millions of men and women are perishing, and but few there are to break to them the bread of life,— there is no need of any words from me to kindle that fire in your heart that has enveloped mine—though I would to God we had more men. For the sake of the blessed Jesus send us two. The work is too great for Brother Colley and myself; but we dare not abandon a single place. We will struggle on, hoping and praying that help will soon come. Our motto is, 'Go forward.' I have lost my right arm by sending my interpreter, Moses L. Stone, to Ogbomishaw, where he began work on the 23d of January. Brother Colley pushes the work here. Thus we have three important stations occupied. If we get the two men we ask for, then Ibadan and Oyo will be occupied, and we shall have a line of stations two hundred miles towards the interior. I feel a greater need than ever before of the Holy Spirit."

1877—1878.

W. J. DAVID.

Ill Health.—Smitten by disease and sun-stroke, and assured by an experienced physician that his life was in imminent peril, this brother left his station at Abbeokuta on the 2d of August last; and sailed from Lagos on the 7th of the month for Liverpool, where he arrived on the 4th of September. After submitting to medical treatment in England, and traveling on the continent at the expense of a liberal friend from South Africa, he started back on the 23d of February, improved in health, but not fully restored. Under that date he wrote from Liverpool: "It is with a joyful heart I bid adieu to civilized and Christian England to return to my work among the converts and chiefs, the peasants and beggars, who are anxiously awaiting my return. Perhaps I am returning too early for my good, but my desire and anxiety are too great for me to remain any longer. Once more I cast myself on the bosom of my loving Father. My heart is fixed, my hope is bright, and as I know in whom I believe, I can cheerfully bid you farewell."

The latest news from him was from Madeira. On March the 2d, he wrote: "We have had a splendid voyage, thus far; we are now one-third the distance and one-fourth the time on our way to Lagos. I am better than when I left Liverpool."

THE WORK BEFORE HIS DEPARTURE FROM AFRICA.

"This Mission," he wrote from Abbeokuta, "is on an encouraging foundation—encouraging to the laborers here, to the converts, to the heathen, and should be to the Christians at home. We have in our schools sixty children. There are three churches, where scores of men and women are learning the way of life; and two Mission houses, healthful and comfortable."

Of Ogbomishaw, our native laborer, Moses L. Stone, remarked: "Surely the Lord is working among us both to will and to do of his good pleasure. I have some one hundred and forty every Sunday to hear about our blessed Saviour. From these he will, no doubt, choose his own. I go on Saturday to prepare the people for Sunday, and go on Monday to impress what they heard on Sunday."

Subsequently Brother David wrote: "The school teacher and interpreter will do all they can in teaching the people during my absence, with occasional help from Brother Colley. I had not heard from Ogbomishaw for several weeks previous to my departure, owing to troubles of long standing between the Egba and Yoruba governments. In fact an Ibadan army was marching against Abbeokuta when I left. There was hope that other tribes would interfere and settle the difficulty. With disappointed hopes and bitterness of grief I left the mission, just as it was put in readiness to work, and when danger was threatening the country."

At Abbeokuta, he arrived on the 25th of June, and was cordially received by rulers and people. For presents, worth twenty-five dollars, he secured a site, and ordered a chapel. "I determined," he wrote, "to build the Lord's house and to trust him for the means. Imagine my delight, when a few minutes after the orders were given, your letter, with £100, was received. This chapel and the one at Ogbomishaw, will cost some seventy-five pounds. Our stations will be then in working order. We must go forward."

In the Church, we cannot count on more than four or five of the old members. The interpreters and teachers of our former missionaries are polygamists; and others are living, in other respects, disorderly. May the Good Shepherd help us to lead these wanderers home! Yet the prospect is bright.

Interiorward. On the twelfth of August, after many vexatious delays, Brother David started for Ogbomishaw *via* Ibadan and other large towns of Yoruba. He wrote: "I have good health and good spirits, and I trust I shall have the presence of the Lord by day and by night. If you do not hear from me, be assured that I am about my Father's business." On the way the people gave profound attention, and many exclaimed, "we will worship the true God!" Privately some inquired the way of life.

Ibadan, a city of two hundred thousand souls, was reached the third day. "As I stood," writes our missionary, "upon the western spur of the Kong Mountains, and looked upon the thousands of houses at my feet, and remembered the myriads of flaming altars, all reeking with bloody sacrifices, I could not refrain the thought: Oh that I had the tongue of an angel! As I walked through the winding alleys, and beheld those sons and daughters of Ham, as they go with their offerings from one idol-shrine to another, seeking peace and finding none, living and dying, without God and hope, the pent-up sigh broke out: 'How long, O Lord, how long will thy servants delay their coming to the rescue of this people!' The head chief, who is a Mohammedan, received me kindly, and asked me to select a mission lot, and live among them."

Ijaye. The ruined city of *Ijaye*, one day's journey northward from Ibadan, was visited in honor of a precious sleeper there. "There was no loving one to point the weary traveller to her resting place, beneath the heavy jungle. But in that day, when India and China and the sea shall give up the bodies of their faithful missionaries, Mrs. A. D. Phillips, too, will come forth from the ruins of Ijaye, to receive her crown of unfading glory."

At Awyaw, where our old mission buildings lie in ruin, the King, surrounded by his eunuchs and forty or fifty of his eight hundred wives, gave our missionary a grand reception. The King expressed himself greatly pleased; and proposed to aid in the erection of houses, if a mission would be established there. "What more encouragement," asks Brother David, "do Christians want, when a heathen king proposes to help them to build, if they will send the men?"

Ogbomishaw. On his arrival at this place, the people, who expected him, cried out, "God be praised! He has heard our prayers which have continued these many years." There had been misinformation about the number of Baptists there. "Only one," Brother David writes, "had been baptized. Twelve or fifteen others had heard the gospel from our missionaries. Some of them had learned to read.

Though persecuted, they had met and heard the Bible, from the time our missionaries left them until my return—a period of about eighteen years." During his stay of two months, our brother collected under the branches of the trees planted by our former missionaries, a regular congregation of one hundred and twenty-five hearers; baptized three; instructed six or eight other inquirers, and built a chapel of 23 by 37 feet, in which were used "the doors, windows, and benches of our old mission-house." Many other articles, left by our former missionaries, had been sacredly preserved.

A second attack of illness prostrated Brother David at Ogbomishaw. "So sure," says he, "were my interpreter and many others, that they would have to dig a grave for me, that they gave vent to their feelings in sobs and tears. I do not think I ever heard more earnest prayers than those for my recovery. Again, the Lord heard. I shall not say how much I suffered."

The Grave of Mrs. T. A. Reid. "Long since her lips ceased to warn that people. As I stood alone and thought of the faithful missionary, I felt that if she could speak, she would say: 'Though I have fallen, let not Yoruba be given up.' I cut the brush from over the grave and replaced the head and foot-boards—the stones have been stolen. I hoped that when death calls for me, I too might be found pointing the same people to the same Saviour. The silent voice from that grave has inspired me with greater desire and determination to labor while it is day, for the night cometh."

On his return to Abbeokuta, Brother David found that his chapel had been completed and "dedicated to God in a prayer-meeting held by two old women, who were the first converts of our missionaries." To recruit his health, he returned, after an absence of five months, to Lagos. "Our meeting with Brother David, on his return from the interior," writes Brother Colley, "was one of greatest interest I ever witnessed in Africa. As he told the story of the interior, the hearts of the many who heard him could not conceal their sobs. We know that God went with him, and we congratulate the Board on the complete re-opening of Yoruba, though by so much suffering of our brother." "While here," writes Brother David from Lagos, "I am preparing mud and thatch for a mission house in Abbeokuta." From Abbeokuta he writes, March 1st: "The mission house is nearly finished. The work on the wall-enclosure will begin at once. The mission house in Ogbomishaw will be finished so soon as the rains, which begin in March, supply water. I have here a school of fifteen, a congregation of 120, and a church of five members."

At *Lagos*, the new chapel was dedicated on the 10th of May. Brother Colley wrote: "The amount raised among the people was £75, or $360 of hard money of this place. The missionaries here think the house should have cost £450, while it has only cost £321 7s. 8d. God has shown his approbation of our movements. The day-school is doing well. The Sunday-school is well attended and interesting. Many of the men and women have learned in six months to read the New Testament in their vernacular. Some are so moved upon that they come at once for baptism and church membership."

Brother David's Condition. Again Brother Colley wrote: "On the 12th of June, I left Lagos for Abbeokuta, where I remained about twenty days, which did me some good, and gave me an opportunity of watching Brother David's double complaints, and helping him all I could with his work in that very large town. On the 25th of June, Brother David moved into the new mission-house, which stands on the same lot with the chapel, in the Ijaye part of the town. The house is a good one, and the locality I believe to be the best, both for work and for health. I write to beg the immediate action of the Board to call Brother David from Africa, that his life may be spared, or at least prolonged. All the missionaries agree with us that he ought to go away from Africa at once. The great trouble with him is to get his consent to quit his station with the work so well begun."

Work in Brother David's Absence.—Under date of October 23d, Brother Colley writes from Lagos: "Yours of July 20th found me in Abbeokuta again busily arranging the work to suit the war raging between Abbeokuta and Ibadan. The effect of the war is not to drive us out of the respective countries, although we are cut off from our Ogbomishaw station. Our young man, Moses L. Stone, is there, and from all I can hear is doing well. The war is very much in the way of missionaries and their work. At Abbeokuta there were some forty-seven in the Sunday-school, and ninety on the day-school list. I left one of the young men in charge, with promises from several of the chiefs that they would ' go to church, send their children to school, and help the young man to take care of the station until our Brother David should return.' At Lagos I am much pleased and encouraged with the work. The congregations are increased and increasing. The day-school has an average attendance of thirty-eight children. The wars are much felt. We know it is very hard with our Board; still, the men on the field must be aided to keep up."

W. W. COLLEY.

In the absence of Brother David, Mr. Colley sent this statement of the condition of the mission:

"*The War.*—The war in the Yoruba country continues with no signs of its end. Our young brother, Moses L. Stone, from that place, arrived here on the 18th of February, after travelling twenty days to evade the armies, having passed through the Ijesa country.

"*Our Work at Ogbomishaw.*—The present success of the work at Ogbomishaw is equalled only by the tenacity with which that people held on to the teachings of our missionaries for nearly twenty years, during which time they had no leader. There are eighty or one hundred attendants on the church services, and sixty regular attendants on the Sunday-school, seventeen of whom can read the psalms or any part of the New Testament in their native tongue. There are forty converts. Fifteen or twenty are praying for baptism, having given up their heathen practices and friends for Christianity. They would have been baptized if I could pass the armies to enter that country. The day-school numbers twenty-three. We have there a lot of land with mission house and chapel. We must have a wall around the premises, and we join Moses in begging $75 for that purpose. Who will give it? To Ogbomishaw is 200 miles.

"*Our Abbeokuta Station.*—The young man in whose care is the station, was here in January. The chiefs stand to their promises. The work goes on. The attendance in the church is very good. The day-school is nearly the same. The Sunday-school numbers twenty-five to thirty. The membership grows slowly. There are some waiting for baptism. "*Lagos.*—Death has made his visits, many and horrifying, not only to the interior of the Yoruba country, but on this island. He has compelled the government to open a new grave-yard—the old one, which is quite large, having been buried over more than twice. The small-pox is rapidly filling the new burying place. Many Christians and some of our very best and most useful people have been cut off. On Sunday, the 24th of February, I baptized eight of twelve converts. About forty took the communion after the baptism. The membership· is sixty—thirty-eight having been baptized since we came to Yoruba—two expelled, one married out, and one dead; leaving fifty-six as a total for Lagos. The Sunday-school is doing well. The day-school has fallen off owing to the hard times, but will average thirty attendants

"*License to Preach.*—The Christians were so rejoiced to see and hear how God had blessed the work of Moses at Ogbomishaw, that they voted unanimously to give him license on the 22d of February, as a means of encouragement. The little Baptist Church at Lagos, West Coast of Africa, gave in hard money to Missions last year £21 6s. 8½d., or $102.41. I hope Dr. Tupper will show at the Convention what could be done for our Missions if each Baptist Church South would give just half of that amount."

1878—1879.
JOINT ARRANGEMENT.

The Foreign Mission Board of the Colored Baptist State Convention of Virginia, having appointed Rev. Solomon Cosby their missionary to Africa, our Board agreed with that Board that, for the present, their missionary might use our chapel in Lagos while our missionary, Rev W. W. Colley, should go to Abbeokuta, and supply the place of our returned missionary, Rev. W. J. David. Brother Colley writes: "I am glad of the plan agreed upon by the Boards, although it will be quite difficult, on account of the unsettled state of the country and the breaking up of my work here, to carry out the plans as completely as the Boards and I desire. Anyhow, Brother Cosby will greatly help me, and I shall be of much help to him."

LAGOS.

A recent baptism, when five converts "put on Christ," is described as witnessed by "thousands of Christians, Mohammedans, and Pagans," who were eagerly awaiting the impressive ordinance. The day-schools, Brother Colley says, are not doing as well as he desires, in view of the fact that "out of them must come the future interpreters, teachers, and preachers for the far interior." He is encouraged in church matters. During the year their little band contributed to various objects $122.60, "which," writes our missionary, "is nearly enough money to support a native missionary to their interior brethren." Should not our churches be aroused by the depths of such poverty abounding to the riches of liberality?

ABBEOKUTA.

Brother Colley reports: "Abbeokuta is greatly in need of a white man." Brother David is fully persuaded that the black man cannot do all the needed work of Africa. Of a recent visit to Abbeokuta with Brother Cosby, our missionary, Colley, writes: "We have just spent eight days in that town, where we labored with much success among the people, from the old tyrant, Oguelipe, down to the poor naked boys and girls in the streets. We baptized three happy souls in the presence of all the rulers and the people. The Governor attended service at the chapel. He, and many of the chiefs, gave close attention, and knelt with us in prayer. In the afternoon, the house could not hold one-third of the people. Several expressed themselves willing to be Christians. Of these we formed a class for instruction and prayer with the brethren. The chiefs led the procession to the brook to see the 'death and resurrection' of the converts baptized into Jesus Christ. Thus you see that we are not without encouragement, even in these war times."

OGBOMISHAW.

"We received a letter from Brother M. L. Stone, of this station, in which he states that he had been badly treated, beaten and cut, and a part of his means taken from him by the Ondo people. He says he is in want of funds to carry on the work." The full appropriation to the mission has been received at Lagos. All communication with this station is now cut off. Brother Stone, who is not ordained, asks Brother Colley: "May I baptize the waiting converts, as it is impossible for you to enter the far interior at present?"

The following is the last communication from Mr. Stone:

OGBOMISHAW, *February 19th,* 1879.

DEAR MR. DAVID: Since my arrival I have written four letters to you, telling you how great were my troubles, pains, and fears on my journey to this place—how I would have been drowned in the deep because of the rain and tornadoes, and how the savages would have killed me after plundering my goods, had it not been for the mercies of God. I suffered twenty-one days of virtual imprisonment and almost starvation in Aye. I met with trouble from town to town. I was severely beaten, and had wounds made in my flesh with the points of their knives. Oh, I cannot tell of all our troubles, pains, and fears, with pen and ink!

A few days after our arrival I had an attack of rheumatism, which confined me to my bed for many days. As soon as I began my work, I gave the members their new hymn-books and Testaments, and the children their slates, all of whom were very glad.

Our congregation is very good every Sunday. The Lord has blessed us with an increase of ten heathen regular attendants on preaching.

I have received six sets of Ifa gods, besides eight different other gods, given up by the new comers.

The owner of the converted slave refuses to take money for him, and says we must buy another slave in his stead. My wife's mother has been redeemed for 28 bags of cowries, ($70.00,) and is living with us and attending church.

Barika and I undertook the expenses of repairing the chapel, which is about ready for use again.

The Governor is well and is trying to make friends with us. He visits me occasionally.

The school is getting on well. The members and candidates for baptism beg you, in the name of God, to "come over and help us."

Yours affectionately. M. L. STONE.

LAST MOVEMENTS.

Rev. W. J. David arrived in Richmond on October 17th, 1878.

On November 17th, 1878, he married Miss Nannie W. Bland, daughter of the late Rev. W. F. Bland, of Chesterfield County, Virginia. With grave doubts as to the wisdom of a woman-missionary going to Africa, the Board, induced by the earnest petition of Mr. David, resolved that he and his wife might go, so soon as funds should be provided.

Rev. W. W. Colley wrote May 22d: "All the missionaries here tell me to leave at once for a change. I would be glad to be able to remain until next spring; but, if I am compelled to leave, Brother Cosby has consented to take care of our work."

Again he wrote, as follows, from Baptist Mission House, Agajaiye Station, Abbeokuta, under date of July 3d, 1879:

H. A. TUPPER, D. D., *Cor. Sec.*

My Dear Doctor:—I am now in the act of putting the houses here in temporary repair, that they may withstand the heavy rains of this season. As we have the corrugated iron ready to cover the chapel, we need only the timbers for the roof, which we can get ready by the next dry season. For the want of a good corrugated covering, the Mission House is a constant exposure. At present, both the chapel and the house are untenantable. I was unable to look after things from bad health; and now, in the midst of the rains, I am compelled to undergo some expense to save the buildings.

While the roads to the far interior are closed, there are scores of small, accessible towns, where we could labor with greater success than in the larger towns. In large communities, for the sake of Christ, wives are slow to leave their husbands, servants their masters, and people their chiefs.

Brother Cosby loves his work. He has just recovered from another severe attack of fever.

Yours very truly,
W. W. COLLEY.

On the 15th of August, Mr. Colley sailed from Lagos. He arrived in the United States, the middle of November. On the 17th of November, the Board accepted his resignation as their missionary to Africa.

Mr. and Mrs. David sailed from New York for Africa, December 8th, 1879, followed by the prayers of many anxious and loving hearts that they might abide under the shadow of the Almighty.

MISSION TO THE JEWS.

ANTI-TYPE OF JUDAIC TYPOLOGY.

October 12th, 1879.
To Rabbi E. S. L. of A. G.:

Respected Sir:—When in your city, last spring, I was struck with your remark, made somewhat in pleasantry, that you intended to put a Baptistery in your Synagogue " to teach people the meaning of baptism," as derived from the ancient practice of the Jews, who always introduced the proselyte into their congregation by immersion. This came to my mind, as my eye fell recently upon the following testimony of Isaac M. Wise, the learned editor of *The American Israelite*, of Cincinnati, in criticising a work of Rev. Isaac E. Heaton on the Mode of Baptism:

" Mr. Heaton confounds baptism with the sprinkling of the ash of the red heifer, diluted in water, upon the person or thing which had come in contact with a dead body. * * * Any child, however, can see that there is also a sanitary cause involved in this law, and there is no passage on record to show that John the Baptist thought of this law. The very fact that he went to the Jordan suggests that the case of Naaman with his leprosy, and the command of the prophet Elisha, were in the mind of the Baptist; and Naaman undoubtedly submerged his body seven times in the Jordan.

" If Mr. Heaton, instead of quibbling on words and consulting dictionaries, would have inquired after facts and would have looked up the matter in the *Mishna* and other Jewish codes, he would have discovered that the Jews had no idea of sprinkling—they knew the bath and submersion. Consequently, John the Baptist submerged his converts in the Jordan.

"We know exactly what John did at the Jordan, and all the dictionaries cannot change the fact. John sent his candidates into the Jordan to swim and be cleansed of their moral leprosy, like Naaman, exactly as the modern rabbi sends the proselyte penitent to the *Mikrah*, 'the ritual bath.'

"Sprinkling holy water on persons to drive out evil spirits was a pagan custom, noticed frequently in Jewish literature; but the Jews were not guilty of that folly, and Mr. Heaton ought not to be guilty of the folly of challenging a world on the strength of his dictionaries and cyclopædias.

"Verse 18 (of Num. xix) proves that *Tabal* signifies to submerge in water; 2 Kings v. 10, 14, proves—in spite of Mr. *Heaton's* definitions —that *Rahaz eth besaro* means to bathe by submersion."

To-day, while talking to a company of Bible-students on the Types of the Old Testament, as suggested by the ix. Chapter and vs. 1-12, of what is called in our Testament "Hebrews," a gentleman remarked: "I think the pious Jew must see that Christianity is referred to by the Ritual of the Judaic Economy."

These circumstances have led me to address this letter to you, which I do with greater confidence, as a mutual friend writes to me of yourself: "The Rabbi admires Jesus."

I ask your attention, Rabbi, to some views on the Typology of the Old Testament, as bearing upon our religion, which we desire to promote among your people, not only in this country, but in Jerusalem, and all over the world. For wherever our missionary goes—whether to Italy, or China, or Liberia, or Central Africa, there the Jew, who is the only true cosmopolite, is found.

In presenting the subject as it passed through my own mind, I must beg that you consider several prefatory points, though of a very elementary nature:

The first is that there are inner and outward parts to all organic things and beings. In material organism, there are not only substance and form and color, and other properties; but there are laws and functions which generate and support and regulate these properties. In intelligent beings, there is what is called the subjective part, and also its expression in the part objective. There is the spirit world and the natural world; and these constitute the one perfectly organized universe.

The second point is that the material and the immaterial world, however intimately connected, are far sundered by diverse natures. Matter can never be so refined as to make any approach to mind; and mind can never be so materialized as to be any nearer to matter. The chasm between the world of sense and the world of spirit may be bridged over, and the two be so closely united as to defy the discrimination of the astutest mortal vision; but the chasm is there still, and as deep as the opening between the hemispheres of a cleanly rifted globe.

The third point is that order and adaptation pervade all the works and systems of God. So universal are these principles, that order is called heaven's first law; and upon the general adaptation of means to ends in Nature—especially the adaptation to discover the great First Cause—is framed a conclusive argument for the divine existence, which has been called "the soul of the Universe." Humboldt defines Nature as "a unity in diversity of phenomena blended in one grand whole ($\tau\grave{o}$ $\pi\tilde{a}\nu$) animated by the breath of life."

The fourth point is that, in this two-fold world, the parts of which are so orderly and reciprocally and usefully related, there is a widespread, if not universal, feature of resemblance or correspondence or representation between things seen and unseen, present and future, human and divine. All phenomena represent internal laws; all expressions are more or less representative of inward states or real nature. The whole external world, in its more than myriad parts and relations, is a grand figuration—a pictorial representation of the grander spiritual world, and of the attributes of God himself. Did not Plato approach the truth in his great doctrine that the Divine Ideas of creation are patterns of all things that are made?—

The fifth point is that based upon this general order and adaptation and analogy between the inner and outer works of nature, and between the varied kingdoms of creation and the mind and attributes of the Creator—although the two are entirely and eternally distinct and separate one from the other—there are special figurative representations pointing to the future and to the Messiah found in the Holy Scriptures, which representations, though given directly by divine authority and interpreted sometimes by divine inspiration are, as founded on these elementary facts of Nature, subject to the laws of reason and common sense for interpretation which are applicable to similar classes of figurative representations found in other writings. These special figures are what I call the Typology of the Old Testament.

Now, let us see some of those laws, elaborated in Lord's Theological and Literary Journal, which, founded in reason as well as deduced from divine interpretations of types, are applicable to many kinds of emblems and symbols—among them, our Baptism and Lord's Supper —and to all of the types of the Jewish Religion and State:

The first law is that *the type implies the thing typified.* This law is axiomatic, and is applicable to all symbolic representations. The sign of mathematics implies the thing signified. The figure of speech, the idea or the thing figured. The prophetic image, the event or the object prophesied. Correlation is essential to typology. A type, without something typified, is an absurdity; it is to a divine type as inarticulate sounds are to human speech; as the ravings of the Pythoness to the inspired oracles of God. Hence our Baptism and Lord's Supper, which are respectively symbols of dying to sin and rising to holiness; and of faith which feeds on our Lord and grows up into him, imply the existence of this life and of this growth in those that are baptized and that come to this Supper.

The second law is that *the type must be fixed in its form and the antitype fixed in its character.* (1) The letter A of any given alphabet must always be A, and never B or C. The figure 2 of any system of numbers must always be 2, and never 3 or 4. The lamb of any system of types must be always a lamb, and never a goat or an ox. (2) And the sounds represented by A must never be those of I or U. And the value of 2, at one and the same time, never that of 3 or 4. And the anti-type of the lamb must never have, as the thing typified, the nature of the goat or the ox. (3) Without this law, there would be no intelligibility in language; no reliability in mathematics; and all systems of figurations or typical adumbrations would be confusion worse confounded. Hence, baptism is baptism, and nothing else. It is not either baptism or rantism or affusion. Hence the thing signified also must be fixed. It cannot be either dedication or profession or purification or something else. It must be always and only death to sin and life to holiness. So the Lord's Supper: it must be the Supper instituted by our Lord, at which each communicant is to partake himself of both the bread and the wine, not to represent this or that or something else, but, communion with the Saviour for the development of the spiritual nature of the communicant.

The third law is that *the type and the thing typified must be of different orders or kingdoms of nature.* In natural figuration, the more distinct the one is from the other, the better. The fox is a better representation of human cunning than the thief; the lion, of man's strength or courage than the athlete or the hero. Hence, in the prophetic figuration of Joseph's superiority, the sheaves and stars are of different kingdoms from his brethren and his parents; and so likewise, the rams of Daniel, which represented kings, and the bear and fat kine, which represented the years of famine and of plenty. And this law involves two minor laws: 1st. That the type is always the literal thing. 2d. That the main points of the type must correspond with the main points of the anti-type. Hence, again, the Water of Baptism must be literal water; and the going down into the water and the coming up out of the water must be these very acts, as the things signified are not material, but spiritual. So the bread and the wine are literal bread and wine, and nothing else, as the thing symbolized is the spiritual communion of the soul with the Lord.

The fourth law is that *the essence of typology is in the resemblances between the type and the anti-type.* This principle holds in many other figurations—as in the Portrait or the Parable. Destroy the likeness and you destroy the portrait or the parable. If the resemblance between the type and the typified be removed, the type, as a type, is immediately destroyed. I repeat, that resemblance is the essence of all typology. Hence, the resemblances to the moral states and acts symbolized is the essence of Baptism and the Lord's Supper. Take from Baptism the resemblance to death and to resurrection, and the Baptism is destroyed. So in the Lord's Supper. Mass, for instance, destroys the resemblance, and with it the ordinance.

The fifth and last law is that, *the order of any set of related types must be the order of the corresponding things or states or persons typified.*

This law is founded in the main idea of figuration, which is to represent resembling things of different natures: for, the natural and divinely appointed order of things is an essential condition of the things themselves. Hence, law, by which all things, physical and moral, exist, is defined as *"The Order of Sequence."* Take away the order in which faculties or organs of man or beast are constituted, or of the functions or properties of the plant or the stone, and you destroy the nature of the thing. Remove the order of the seasons, the planets, the framework of nature, or the relations of the seen and the unseen, the human and the divine, and you ruin them at once. Man tried it, and he died. Angels, also, and were damned. Hence, if the order of Baptism and the Lord's Supper is destroyed, the ordinances are destroyed. If the Lord's Supper is put before Baptism; or either of them be put before the spiritual state designed to be represented, the divine order is violated, and the soul and the church are put in jeopardy. The relation of the Symbols is essential to the Rites. Sanctification necessarily comes after regeneration. Hence, Communion must come after Baptism. This order is as fixed as that old age follows infancy; that, the meridian or setting sun follows the morning dawn. In a word, in order to preserve what is called gospel order, the symbolic act of burial and arising with Christ must be prior to the symbolic act of communion with and growing up into the Lord.

Fearing that I may have presumed too far on your expressed interest in our Church Ordinances, I beg now that I may be allowed to make an application of these laws, to the end that we may discover to which the types of the Old Testament point. I might take in detail such types as Melchisedec; the Passover; the Serpent in the Wilderness; the Temple. But, for the sake of brevity, I take, in a general view, the whole Jewish Ritual—with its divinely fixed institutions, its scrupulously observed order, and its minutely adjusted relations, which the author of the "Hebrews" calls "the substance of good things to come," and I ask, what, according to the laws announced, is the Anti-type of this Divine Type?

1. Is Judaism the anti-type? This Ritualism was identical with this Theocratic System and State; and, hence, by Law I. and Law V. which require that, the type and the typified should be neither identical nor of the same nature, Judaism itself cannot be the Anti-type. Such an application would be also in opposition to the rule that the anti-type is future to the type.

2. Is Skepticism the Anti-type? According to Law II. the fixed type implies the Anti-type fixed. But, doubt is the essence of Skepticism; and doubt is damned in the religion anti-typical to the Judaic ritual.

3. Is Materialism or Rationalism the true anti-typical religion? According to Law IV. and Law V., where in these sciences is the resemblance to the institutions, and where the correspondence to the order of the service of the Jewish Ritual? Where is the great end foreshadowed—the God of Nature and Revelation? As without hope and without God, neither of these systems can be the anti-type and the truth.

4 Is Christianity, then, the Anti-type of the Typology of Judaism? Let us apply the laws:

1st. In answer to the Jewish Type here is a system clearly defined distinct in its institutions and doctrines, and claiming and worthy to be the Anti-type of the Jewish economy.

2d. As to its fixedness, the law of the New Testament is as binding as that of the Old; and the great works of Repentance, Faith, Redemption, Sanctification, are fixed in our Christ, according to eternal decrees, so that the gates of hell cannot prevail against the kingdoms of which these works are constituent and fixed elements.

3d. Again, compare this spiritual and gracious economy with the formal and legal economy of Moses, and could systems be more diverse in nature? Though counterparts of each other, they are essentially and entirely and eternally dissimilar and separate. One the letter, the other the spirit: one grievous and destructive, the other joyous and life-giving. Between the natures of the two, might be exchanged the language of Abraham and Dives; "Between us there is an impassable gulf fixed."

4th. As to the Resemblance and Correspondence of the main parts, look at the Temple and the Church; the High Priest and Jesus; the Priesthood and God's people; the Altar and Calvary; the Paschal lamb and the Lamb of God that taketh away the sin of the world; the varied offerings and church services; and, could type and anti-type be more perfectly ordered and adjusted? The type is the literal things, and the anti-type the spiritual significance and eternal reality. "Church-Order" is the felicitous title given to gospel representations of spiritual states and acts, corresponding wonderfully to the order and necessities demanded by the Judaic Typology. Its harmony with the elements of nature is perfect; and it is alone adapted to the exigency of the fallen and lost state of our race. As thus founded in nature, as well as in the word of God, is not Christianity the great Anti-type, which commends itself as worthy of all acceptation?

Now, my Jewish brother, put that Baptistery in your synagogue. But, remember that Baptism is not a Jewish rite. It is an institution of Christ, which sets forth the cardinal doctrines of his religion. You "admire Jesus;" believe in the Lord Jesus Christ, and be baptized. The Reformed Israelites believe, I understand, that there will be an ultimate union between them and Christians. This looks a little hopeful. Our Jesus is your Messiah. Confess him; teach him; preach him. Go yourself first into that baptistery, believing and being baptized; and, what a change might be wrought in your people! Your synagogue may be converted into a Baptist Church; and you and yours would strike hands with us in the great work of presenting the Christ to God's ancient people the world over. The Southern Baptist Convention expressed its conviction, in 1877, that they should extend the gospel among the Israelites. A noble friend of Foreign Missions sends statedly a gold piece of money for the First Baptist Church of Jerusalem. We must have that church. Would that you, honored sir, might be prepared to be our missionary to establish that church in the City of David! I long to see our peoples with one faith, one Lord, one baptism. I long to see the world under the banner of Jehovah Jesus.

Begging pardon for this trespass on your valuable time, I am,
With sentiments of the highest consideration,
Yours, T.

JESUS—THE MESSIAH OF THE JEWS AND THE DESIRE OF ALL NATIONS.

TO THE CONGREGATION OF THE HEBREW TEMPLE (SHAAR EMETH) OF S. L. M.

FELLOW TRAVELERS TO THE ETERNAL WORLD:

Sitting in the private room of your splendid Temple with Rabbi S. who was engaged with a class in the study of the Hebrew Scriptures, my heart went out toward him who seemed to me as that distinguished man reading the Book of Isaiah, into whose chariot the humble Philip stepped and " preached unto him Jesus." And I longed to preach to him and to you this Jesus—the Alpha and the Omega of gospel preaching, of whom a profound spiritual metaphysician said: " He is a child of God, who can say from his heart ' Blessed Jesus.' "

And to whom did Philip preach Jesus? To one—please read Acts viii. of our New Testament—who is assumed to be a Jewish proselyte, and a native courtier of a Gentile government, who had just asked with regard to a certain prophecy of Isaiah: " Of whom speaketh the prophet this? Of himself or of some other man?"

And here let me remark that it is a good thing that the great subject of the gospel, instead of being an idea or a doctrine, is a Man. For, while to the refining and speculative mind there may be more in the ideal than in the real; more in principles than in persons; to the simpler and more practical intelligence of the majority of mankind, that which is manifest and sensuous is always the most attractive and important; and, of all outward things, nothing is so interesting to, or influential over, the heart of man as man himself—humanity, I mean—in loveliness or greatness of character. Hence the works of literature which survive the ages are those that most faithfully delineate human nature; and the works of art that are of the most world-wide renown are those which represent human beauty, or power, or passion, as the Apollo Belvidere, the Dying Gladiator, the Laocoon of the Vatican at Rome. It was wise, therefore, when God would make a supreme revelation of himself, to make it in the person of a man—a man of heavenly wisdom and divine love, who as the perfection of humanity and the natural object of human aspiration and hope, would be as a kind of magnet to the world; so that he could say with a deep significance: "And I, if I be lifted up from the earth, will draw all men unto me." When that Procurator of Judea said, "Behold the man!" he little knew that he was dealing with the most potent law of the moral universe, which was destined to absorb the Jewish polity, supplant the schools of Pagan wisdom, and overthrow the empire of error and evil, and on its widespread ruins to erect, as an imperishable monument to the wisdom and power and grace of God, the kingdom of the man Christ Jesus, whom Philip might well preach to this proselyte pagan prince, as the Messiah of the Jews and the Desire of all Nations.

The Messiah of the Jews. And how simply might the Evangelist have proven to the Ethiopian that Jesus was the Christ, by an argument as wide as the range of honest skepticism itself. As an intelligent visitor at Jerusalem where he had gone to the Passover, and probably staid over to the feast of Pentecost, the Chamberlain of Candace, if he did not see Jesus who was the absolving topic of the Capital of Judea, received, no doubt, some right impression with regard to him; which impression may be emphasized by the preaching of Peter, under whose pungent criminations he also may have been pricked in heart, though having too much self-control to cry out with the multitude: "Men and brethren, what shall we do?"

He betook himself to the Jewish Scriptures. Philip finds him searching a Messianic prediction. And why not, under the teaching of the Evangelist and the influence of the Spirit, some right idea of the Christ promised? Which idea would render imperative the question: Whence the correspondence between the living man and the prophetic picture? A satisfactory reply to which would be as the voice of God himself: "This is my beloved Son, hear him."

Can there be a miracle? Here is one for all time—Jesus seen alike by the Prophet and the Ethiopian, separated by seven centuries! One has dared to say that there was collusion between the sick man of Bethany and the wonder-worker of Nazareth. But there could be no collusion between Isaiah and the Eunuch, sundered by the ages of time!

Can there be a revelation? Let the skeptical inquirer answer this: How the pencil of prophecy could have traced this life-like portrait of this man, which portrait, as the scholarship of the Ethiopian might have attested, was published in his country nearly three hundred years before the man portrayed was born?

The day will come when the rejecting Infidel shall look upon him whom he has pierced, and shall be in bitterness for him as one is in bitterness for his first-born; and when the believing Jew shall exclaim with a joy and emphasis which the Gentile convert can never know: "My Lord, and my God!" And with burning zeal and missionary toil your "peculiar people" shall compass the earth, until there shall be "life from the dead"—the resurrection of our ruined race!

Jesus is also "the Desire of all nations," as the Light of the world, the Lord of glory, and the Friend of sinners.

He is the Light of the world. Paul preached Jesus on Mars' Hill. The smoke that struggled upward from that altar dedicated to the "Unknown God" was a fit emblem of the intellect of man vainly striving after the True, the Good, the Absolute. Mr. Gladstone says, that Grecian philosophy tended to the Truth. But, if so, it tended only as the earth's shadow on the moon tended to the discovery of the new world; and not as the Star of Bethlehem which actually brought men to the feet of the Saviour of mankind—" Whom, therefore, ye ignorantly worship, him declare I unto you," exclaimed the Apostle to the Stoics and Epicureans, as he preached unto them Jesus—the risen Jesus, in whom are all the treasures of wisdom and knowledge; and from whom if any man lack wisdom and ask of him, may be received that wisdom which is from above, which is " first pure, then peaceable, gentle and easy to be entreated, full of mercy and good fruits, without partiality and without hypocrisy," than the which the light of heaven could not photograph a more perfect likeness of this Jesus, who is the essence—the very quintessence of wisdom itself.

He is the Lord of glory—misnomer as this may seem of one who in his day was spit upon and hung up between two thieves, and who in our day is slandered by lofty intellects, making learned and determined efforts to reduce him to a hero of history, because he cannot be proven to be a myth! But these polite and erudite strictures of gentlemen of science, who hold nothing too sacred for the knife of their criticism; and who think that they concede much when they tell us that Jesus was indeed a great man, having the genius to conceive and the boldness to undertake the establishment of a universal empire—these assaults, like those of other centuries, equally subtile and more malignant, will pass away in their turn, like the evening eclipse—like the meteor that flashes across the firmament, only to sink into darkness, leaving untouched and undimmed the fixed lights of heaven.

The antecedents of Jesus suggested that he was the Lord of glory—his antecedents in those very ideas of human wisdom with regard to the essence and expression of moral good, which never had any realization, except in the two-fold nature of this mysterious personage; ideas which were lingering echoes of this being who once tenanted the Temple of human nature before its downfall and ruin—ideas, which were nature's prophecies of the return of this being as necessary to satisfy the notions ever flitting before the human mind in reference to "the supreme good:" his more distinct antecedents in the Messianic predictions which culminated in those extraordinary appellations: "Wonderful, Counsellor, Mighty God, Everlasting Father, Prince of peace."

When he came into this world he proved himself the Lord of glory.

In reply to Renan, Roussell says, that Jesus led a life, not only of self-sacrifice, but of disinterestedness; that he not only taught the purest religion, but he practised all he taught. This, I say, raised him above the plane of humility; and above that plane why not into the plane of divinity? But, shall the Creator serve the creature? Why not? Whether is more glorious, the sun pouring out himself to beautify and beatify worlds around, or wrapped up in his splendid glory, pursuing a solitary way through the trackless regions of space?

As the dispenser of nature's glory, Jesus is the Lord of glory. Who paints the flower that smiles on the face of the earth? Who makes to glow the stars in the coronet of night? Who moves the panorama of this world's history and the heavens' revolutions? The Second Person of the adorable Trinity is placed on the throne of the Universe to create and to control, in order to the revelation of the Divine Nature, specially in the reclamation of a fallen race; and all these works around and above us, visible and invisible, are but mirrors set up in the palace of the Great King to reflect the excellency of the Lord of glory.

And the day cometh when the mind that criticises, and the heart that hates and the tongue that curses will bring their acknowledgments, with the tributes of kings, and the acclaims of angelic and redeemed hosts, all of which shall be as a royal diadem to crown him who is the Lord of glory, the Lord of all!

And "the Friend of Sinners." Lord Bacon says that there is no friendship between equals. Certainly the highest friendship is between this exalted being and the fallen children of men. I mention two familiar facts to establish that he is the "Friend of Sinners."

The first is that Jesus took our nature upon him after man had fallen by sin. I say "after man had fallen," because, before his fall he was in the image of God. Nor did Jesus take upon himself humanity as a prince may put on the garb of a peasant, or an angel may assume the conditions of man. He entered into the vitality and consciousness of our nature, and bound himself to it as one is bound to his own created self; and thereby he pledged himself to love and support, and honor and immortalize it, even as he is immortal. Twain were made one in the incarnation of the Lord Jesus Christ. Great was the humiliation of our Lord: but it was the humiliation of one who quits his home to share the fare and the pallet of an incarcerated brother; the humiliation of the mother, like Augustine's, who follows her erring boy by day and night, through heat and cold, over land and sea, if by her prayers and tears and agonies, she may only win back the darling of her bosom; the humiliation of that one who stands by the bedside of that wasted, wasting form, loved more than life itself, if by any service, however menial, he may restore or alleviate. Deep was the humiliation of the Son of God: but, the glories of heaven could not keep him from it. Tearing away from those shining ranks and "brushing aside suns and stars" he sped to our world of woe, and, anticipating the self-destroying way of man, he cast his own body over the abyss of death that man might have a living way, by which to pass into an inheritance incorruptible and undefiled, and that passeth not away, in the heavens.

The other fact is that he died for us. The sinlessness of Jesus was the antipode of death. Hence we need seek no further exposition of his cry on Calvary—"Eli, Eli, lama sabachthani?"—than the instinctive shrinking of an immaculate nature from the least contact with the idea of sin. Yet, he who knew no sin was made sin for us, that we might be made the righteousness of God in him. His assumed nature was laid on the altar of divine decrees and human necessities. Thereby he erected a platform for increasing intercession, and purchased a warrant for the most extended overtures of mercy. What more could he do for me and for you, fellow-sinners? What is the language of the cross of Golgotha? I know that the Jew, unlike yourselves, looks and says, "Bold blasphemer!" the skeptic, "Poor fanatic!" the pseudo-philanthropist, "Blessed martyr!" But the Spirit of God teaches: "Behold the Lamb of God, that taketh away the sin of the world!"

And this truth is God's fire and hammer, by which he burns and heats the hardened heart of man. The most obdurate have been overwhelmed by the doctrine of "Christ and him crucified," and from the deepest penitence have arisen with joyous and regenerate heart to cry: "Blessed and Divine Friend of sinners!" Do you not, my beloved brethren, feel the need of such a friend?

"I need thee, precious Jesus,
  For I am full of sin;
My soul is dark and guilty,
  My heart is dead within:
I need the cleansing fountain,
  Where I can always flee;
The blood of Christ most precious—
  The sinner's perfect plea."

And I shall always need him. Often have I tried to satisfy my mind and heart without him; but as often have I had to return, and to say:

"Continually to thee, my Saviour and my song,
  My heart returns from far unsatisfied;
Stay thou with me the while, my pilgrim heart along
  The weary way has none beside—
    Stay, stay continually.

"My hands had gifts, my Lord, too fondly counted o'er,
  And loved too well for loving only thee;
See one by one they are gone, I hold them now no more,
  That thou mightest all my treasure be—
    Mine, mine continually."

But, not only I need him, my friends. He is equally needed by you, and all your people, and the whole world. He is the desideratum of our race, the desire of all nations, the true substance, of which wealth and wisdom, pleasure and power, love and life, are but the attractive shadows. Hence his last and sublime command: "Go ye into all the world, and preach the gospel to every creature."

But, "as a man thinketh in his heart, so is he." Let me, brother man, come close to you, and ask, What are your heart-thoughts of Jesus? In our Scripture there is a dreadful passage: "If any man love not the Lord Jesus, let him be Anathema, Maranatha"—*accursed when the Lord cometh.*

When he cometh,
    'Mid the horror and confusion
    Of that sorrowful conclusion
    Of each miserable delusion,

oh, where will you stand? What will you say, if you have not Jesus as your friend? Were you to step on an acorn, and it should spring up into an oak of a hundred years; were you to turn aside the oozing spring, and it should burst forth a roaring, rushing cataract; were you Alypius, the minion of the apostate Julian, whose silver and sacrilegious pickaxes, driven into the God-sealed foundations of Jerusalem, brought forth scathing and scattering balls of fire, your dismay would not be one-half that it will be, if in this day of God's gracious visitation you trample on this holy thing, and wave away the offers of his mercy, and tear open afresh by your sins the wounds of the sacred Crucified, when, on the morrow of eternity, your vision will be startled by the great white throne on which shall be seated this same Jesus, to dispense the destiny of your soul, and of all souls, world without end.

> "The world is very evil,
> The times are waxing late,
> Be sober and keep vigil,
> The Judge is at the gate:
> The Judge who comes in mercy,
> The Judge who comes in might,
> To terminate the evil,
> To diadem the right:
> When the meek and gentle Monarch
> Shall summon from the tomb,
> Let man, the guilty, tremble,
> For man the God shall doom."

But, my believing brother—for is there not one secret heart-believer in the congregation?—what are your heart-thoughts of Jesus? You look up and say: "Lord, thou knowest all things: thou knowest that I love thee." Then saith the Lord: "If ye love me, keep my commandments."

1. Be good. It is not enough to hope that you shall rest in the bosom of Father Abraham. As in the Gothic architecture, the parts are not only the strongest but are marked by the greatest ornamentation; so, not only is your faith to rest on the rock of ages, but you must seek to adorn the profession of the Messiah by the beauty of holiness.

2. Do good. There is a law of reciprocity in the kingdom of grace, as well as in the kingdom of nature. As the shell on the sea-shore voices back the murmurs of the great deep; as the earth puts forth her fruit and flowers in response to the sunshine and flowers of heaven; as the torches of night catch the rays of the departing god of day and scatter them upon the ways of erring man; so, as by faith which is described as "the substance of things hoped for, the evidence of things not seen," we realize the invisible and the eternal, our soul should swell in profounder praises to God; as the bounties of heaven are dispensed upon us, our lives should abound in the fruits of holiness; and, as we are enlightened, so we should enlighten others by holding forth the word of life, whose rays are to reach as far as the death-shades of sin itself. "Footprints on the sands of time" do not represent the work of an earnest soul in this world. As the blue current of the Rhone may be tracked through the waters of Lake Leman, so there should go forth from every believing heart and from every congregation of God's people, influences for the saving and sanctifying of others, which may be traced through the boundless expanse of eternity itself.

3. And how good and great the work of giving Jesus to the ancient people of God! "My heart's desire and prayer to God for Israel is that they may be saved." And I long that my people should have great heaviness and continual sorrow in their hearts, as did Paul, who could wish himself accursed for his "kinsmen according to the flesh, whose are the fathers, and of whom, as concerning the flesh, Christ came, who is over all God blessed forever." The eyes of the world are fixing on your wonderful people. A Jew holds a deed of trust on the land of the prophets and the Apostles. A Jew controls the exchequer and the armies and the diplomacy of the greatest empire on earth, whose escutcheon we are now told is embossed with the prophetic unicorn, and the lion of the tribe of Juda, and whose navies at Cyprus, as the ships of Tarshish, await the coming of him, of whom certain men in white, said to his troubled disciples on the Mount of Olivet: "This same Jesus which is taken up from you into heaven shall so come in like manner as ye have seen him go into heaven." Jesus, to whom all the world is converging, was an unmixed Jew. "Salvation

is of the Jews." Would that my people, who are laboring to spread the religion of Jesus over the earth, could see their obligation to the Israelites, and the adaptedness of your people to disseminate a universal religion. The scattering of the Jews among the nations is a solution of the three great difficulties of giving Christianity to the human race, viz.: the difficulties of language, of climate, and of aversion to strangers. The Jews are at home, and acclimated in, and speak the tongues of, every nation under the sun. All they need is to see the Christ in Jesus—to see that that star which rested over the manger of the Son of the humble Mary was pointing to the firmament above, as an appropriate canopy, all overwrit with the ancient hieroglyphs of his wisdom and power and goodness—yea, pointing to a world of glory beyond, every ray of which was publishing him its maker and its God. And Israel shall recognize the fact that Jesus—"the end of the law for righteousness to every one that believeth"—came into this world to change it from a dark and disgraceful thing into a reflector of the divine attributes—from a broken and dishonored vessel of sin into a censer of Jehovah to diffuse the incense of his praise as far as the uttermost limits of the intelligent universe. Yes, he came to put his hand upon our world, to ordain it, and to commission it, and to send it forth as a missionary among all inhabited worlds to fulfil the end of the world's creation, which was "to the intent that now unto the principalities and powers in heavenly places might be made known by the church the manifold wisdom of God, according to the eternal purpose which he purposed in Jesus Christ our Lord, of whom the whole family in heaven and earth is named."

The Jew is to be the grand missionary of the cross which is superscribed with the motto, THIS IS JESUS, THE KING OF THE JEWS.

Concluding with the quaint lines:

> "What think ye of Christ? is the test
> To try both your state and your scheme.
> You cannot be right in the rest
> Unless you think rightly of him."

I am, with sincere love and earnest desire,

Yours,   T.

RICHMOND, VA., *November* 5, 1879.

ORIGIN AND FOREIGN WORK OF SOUTHERN BAPTIST CONVENTION.

ITS ORIGIN.

DEAR HENRY: You say that, as a young pastor, you are "painfully ignorant of the results of modern missions, and know very little about the birth and parentage of the Southern Baptist Convention." I shall borrow your *homely* figure, "birth and parentage," in writing of the origin of our Convention; and shall give you a summary of our work, and the foreign work of the other evangelical denominations. I hope that the more you know of missions, the more you will love the cause and instruct your people in regard to it; and that the more you think of our Convention, the more you will realize its necessity for Southern Baptists. A distinguished gentleman, living in a northern state, has just written to me: "Do keep up and extend the work of the Southern Board. If Southern Baptists give up their Southern Boards, it will result in their abandonment of all general missionary work. Helpless, hopeless, they will look idly on, and trust to the 'wealthy North' to do what they themselves ought to be doing for Christ."—THERE IS NO IDEA OF "GIVING UP." I am,

Yours affectionately, T.

Richmond, November 6th, 1879.

P. S.—In what I write, I shall follow, sometimes literally, the best authorities, taking the liberty of making changes to adapt them to the present writing. T.

GRAND-PARENT OF THE CONVENTION.

British rule in India, which divided that country into three Presidencies, of Madras, Bengal, and Bombay, over each of which presided a British Governor, though tyrannical and anti-Christian, as conducted by the "East India Company," brought to the attention of Christian philanthropy in England the great peninsula of Hindostan, lying in Southern Asia between the parallels 8° and 33° north latitude; and bounded on the north-west, north, and north-east by the Himalaya Mountains and the Indus River, and on the other sides by the Indian Ocean and its bays. My space would not suffice to give the most cursory view of this vast and ancient Empire, with its 1,600,000 square miles; its great rivers, the Brahmapootra and the Ganges; its diversified climate, ranging between 100° Fahrenheit, in summer, and the freezing point in winter; its three dead languages, and its fifty spoken tongues; its poetic literature, and its sciences of astronomy, geometry, algebra, and arithmetic—to the last of which we are indebted for *our* system of notation, borrowed from the Arabs, who borrowed it from the Hindoos; and especially of its 195,000,000 of immortal and deluded spirits, bowing down to the religions of Brahminism, Buddhism, Jainism, Seckism, or to the equally fatal system of Mohammedanism, which numbers among its devotees not less than one-seventh of the whole population.

William Carey, born in the county of Northampton, England, a shoemaker and schoolmaster and Baptist preacher, may be called the father of modern Baptist Missions. The fearful state of the heathen preyed on his heart; and the longing for their salvation became the passion of his soul. While teacher and preacher at Moulton, he wrote as an essay: "An inquiry into the obligation of Christians to use means for the conversion of the heathen," which produced a profound impression. In 1784, the Northampton Association appointed the MONTHLY CONCERT OF PRAYER, which has been just re-organized by the Baptist women of Richmond. At the same association, in 1792, Mr. Carey preached a powerful sermon from the words of the Prophet Isaiah: "Enlarge the place of thy tent, and let them stretch forth the curtains of thine habitations: spare not, lengthen thy cords, and strengthen thy stakes; for thou shalt break forth on the right hand and on the left; and thy seed shall inherit the Gentiles, and make the desolate city to be inhabited." Chap. 54: 2, 3. In treating the subject, he made as his points: 1st. *Expect great things from God*—2d. *Attempt great things for God.* This led the Association to organize "The English Baptist Missionary Society," which we have called the "Grand-Parent of the Southern Baptist Convention," on the 2d of October following, at which meeting was collected £13 2s. 6d.

The Rev. John Thomas, who had been a surgeon in the East Indies, was invited by the missionary committee to accompany Mr. Carey to India. Mr. Carey's words to the committee are well known: "From Mr. Thomas' account there is a gold mine in India; but it seems almost as deep as the centre of the earth. Who will venture to explore it?" asked Mr. Fuller. "I will go down," said Mr. Carey; "but remember, brethren, you must hold the ropes." They sailed with Mrs. Carey, who at first refused to go, in a Danish ship, the Kron Princessa Maria, June 13th, 1793, and arrived the 7th of November at Balasore Roads in Bengal.

In 1796, Mr. John Fountain reinforced the mission. In April, 1799, Messrs. Ward, Brunsden, Grant, and Marshman sailed for India; and arrived at Serampore, a beautiful and healthy Danish town on the river Hoogly, some fifteen miles from Calcutta, on the 12th October. Mr. Carey joined the mission at this place, famous in the history of Baptist Indian Missions, January 10th, 1800. On December 28th was baptized the first Hindoo convert, Krishnu, the author of that precious hymn,

> "O thou, my soul, forget no more
> The Friend who all thy sorrows bore:
> Let every idol be forgot,
> But, O my soul forget him not."

The excitement incident to this conversion and baptism was said to be the occasion of the derangement of Mr. Thomas, whose mind, long bent in anxious desire for some fruit of their labor, yielded under the pressure of the overjoyous occasion.

Through floods of affliction from England and from India this little mission had to pass; but their triumphs of faith and labor, of which there is no space to write, superabounded all their sorrows. Before the death of Mr. Carey, which occurred June 9th, 1834, the

ORIGIN AND FOREIGN WORK OF THE CONVENTION. 463

Scriptures had been translated into forty languages, and issued in 210,000 volumes to upwards of 270,000,000 of souls; to which work the noble triumvirate, Carey, Ward, and Marshman, had devoted £50,000 of their own hardly-earned means. Before the golden rays of gospel truth, first shed on it by this Society, the thick gloom of East India Paganism, though still resisting, is daily receding; and shall be, sooner or later, scattered as night shadows are driven before the rising day.

Babu Keshub Chunder Sen, the head of the Brahmo Somaj, the Theistic Church of India, in an eloquent lecture on "Christ," recently delivered, paid this tribute to the Christian missionaries:

"Christ, and not the British Government rules British India. England has sent us a tremendous moral force in the life and character of that mighty Prophet, to conquer and hold this vast Empire. None but Jesus, none but Jesus, none but Jesus, ever deserved this bright this precious diadem—India; and Christ shall have it. If, then, India is encompassed on all sides by Christian literature, Christian civilization, and a Christian government, she must naturally endeavor to satisfy herself as to the nature of this great power in the realm which is doing such wonders in our midst. India knows not yet this power, though already much influenced by it. She is unconsciously imbibing the spirit of this new civilization, succumbing to its irresistible influence; therefore, India ought to be informed as to the real character of the source of this reforming influence—Christ. It is not the British army, I say again, that deserves any honor for holding India. If unto any army appertains the honor of holding India for England, that army is the army of Christian missionaries, and headed by their invincible Captain, Jesus Christ. Their devotion, their self-abnegation, their philanthropy, their love of God, their attachment and allegiance to the truth—all these have found and will continue to find a deep place in the gratitude of our countrymen; therefore, it is needless, perfectly superfluous, for me to bestow any eulogium upon such tried friends and benefactors of our country. They have brought unto us Christ; they have given us the high code of Christian ethics; and their teachings and examples have secretly influenced and won thousands of non-Christian Hindus."

The mistake will not be made of supposing "the English Baptist Mission Society" the mother of modern missions. The Reformation

464 FOREIGN MISSIONS.

had sown the seed of new life to our religion; and between 1556, when the Swiss sent out fourteen missionaries to South America, and 1792, some six or seven missionary Associations and enterprises, organized by Reformed churches and zealous individuals in Europe and America, had proclaimed the gospel to the four quarters of the earth. Bartholomew Ziegenbalg and Henry Pultscho, sent out in 1705 by Frederic the Fourth, King of Denmark, to Tranquebar, on the Coromandel Coast, may be regarded "the parents of Eastern missions." The most noted and praiseworthy of these enterprises was that of the Moravians, who, in 1741, when they sent out their first missionaries to Greenland, numbered only 600; and who, ten years after, had their heralds of the cross not only among the icebergs of the Arctic Circle, but under the scorching sun of the Torrid Zone, as well as among the red men and the black men of America, and the tawny sons of Asiatic heathendom. The Moravians, as appears from their statistical report, just published, number in all 30,619. Of these 8,278 are in Europe, 5,705 in Great Britain, and 16,236 in the United States, besides 400 missionaries and their children. Their average contribution to Foreign Missions is four dollars per member. "How do you account for this missionary spirit of the Moravians?" asked the writer of one of their former missionaries, who promptly replied: "They teach their children that this is the religion of Jesus." If Baptists would be like the Moravians, in missionary zeal, they must teach their children at the knee, and around the hearthstone, and in the Sunday-school, that *the missionary spirit and enterprise is the religion of Jesus.*

The epitaph indited for himself, by William Carey, is worthy of the founder of modern Baptist missions:

"*A wretched, poor and helpless worm,
On thy kind arms I fall.*"

PARENT OF THE CONVENTION.

"The General Convention of the Baptist Denomination in the United States" was an offspring of the "English Baptist Missionary Society," and the parent of the Southern Baptist Convention. The letters and appeals of Carey, Ward, and Marshman were widely circulated, and read with deepening interest in this country. "*The Star of the East*," preached and published in England, in 1808, by Dr. Claudius Buchanan, the Scottish chaplain to the East India Company, who gave to the world, in 1804, the first translation of the New Testament in Persian and Hindostanee, had also stirred the souls of the lovers of Jesus all over the land. As early as 1802, the Massachusetts Baptist Missionary Society was organized to preach the gospel in the new settlements of the United States, "and *further* should circumstances render it proper." But now "Mite Societies" for missions were formed in the larger churches. In November, 1811, the Boston Association of Baptist ministers recommended contributions to the "*Eastern Translations;*" and offered to transmit funds contributed for the object. In 1812, $4,650 was given for this purpose in Boston and Salem alone.

In 1812, Adoniram Judson, with his wife and Luther Rice, sailed for India from this country—the one on the 19th of July, from Salem, and the other on the 24th of the same month, from Philadelphia—as missionaries of the "American Board of Commissioners for Foreign Missions." This Board had been organized in 1810, to take care of these young gentlemen who, with other students at Andover Seminary, had devoted their lives to the work of saving the heathen. On their passage, while studying and translating the word of God, Mr. and Mrs. Judson became Baptists in sentiment. A few months after, Mr. Rice adopted the same views. They were baptized by Mr. Ward, in the chapel at Serampore. Letters with regard to this event having reached this country, in February, 1813, a meeting of Baptist ministers was held at Dr. Baldwin's, in Boston; and the "Baptist Society for propagating the gospel in India and other foreign parts" was formed. This Society requested of the "English Baptist Society" that our missionaries, although located in Burmah, and supported by the Society in America, might be associated with the mission in Serampore.

With the same good judgment that prompted the "London Missionary Society" to deny any assistance to the American Board when Mr. Judson and his colleagues were adopted by them, the "English Baptist Missionary Society" declined this co-operation; and urged through their Secretary, Mr. Fuller, the independence of the missions of this country.

Shortly after their arrival in India, Mr. Judson and Mr. Rice were driven from the country by the tyranny of the Directors of the East India Company, and took refuge in the Isle of France. It was agreed that Mr. Rice should return to America to arouse the churches on the subject of missions. War going on between England and the United States, he sailed by the way of St. Salvador, and arrived in this country, September, 1813. Mr. and Mrs. Judson, resolved not to abandon their work, sailed for Madras, where they met the increased hostility of the Company, and on the 22d of June, 1813, they set sail for Rangoon, the chief seaport of Burmah. In 1807, the English Baptists had formed a mission there, but before this time it had been abandoned by all the missionaries. Mrs. Felix Carey, the wife of one of them, was still living in the city, and received the strangers.

The arrival of Mr. Rice in the United States gave a new impulse to the growing missionary feeling and enterprise. He was employed by the Society to visit the Middle and Southern States to invite co-operation in the glorious work; and the whole country was inflamed in zeal under the power of his vivid descriptions and eloquent appeals. Various associations had been formed, and it was proposed that there should be some general missionary organization. In May, 1814, twenty-six ministers and seven laymen, from eleven States and from the District of Columbia, met in Philadelphia as the place agreed upon; and then and there was organized, "The General Missionary Convention of the Baptist Denomination in the United States of America," and with Dr. Richard Furman, of South Carolina, as President, and Dr. Thomas Baldwin, of Massachusetts, Secretary, and Dr. William Staughton as Corresponding Secretary. This organization was commonly known as the "TRIENNIAL CONVENTION." The grand history of this body is inseparably connected with the Baptist missions of Burmah, China, and Africa, and with the imperishable fame of Judson, Boardman, Kincaid, Wade, and hosts of others whose names and deeds of glory for Christ's sake are recorded in the Lamb's book of life. The organization, undergoing several constitutional changes, continued until 1845, when the "*Southern Baptist Convention*" was formed; and the remaining part of the Triennial Convention passed into the present "*American Baptist Missionary Union.*" The labors of this latter organization have been abundant and most successful, and their laborers have been among the noblest of the messengers of the churches, whom Paul calls "the glory of Christ"—not the least among them, the dear friends and college mates of the writer, the late lamented Dr. William Ward, of Assam, and Dr. Miles J. Knowlton, of China.

The following facts and figures may some day be of use to you:

FOREIGN WORK AND LIABILITIES OF THE BAPTIST GENERAL CONVENTION, APRIL 1, 1846.

Missions, 16; stations and out-stations, 143; missionaries and assistants, 99, of whom 42 are preachers; native preachers and assistants, 155; churches, 82; members of churches, 5,373, including ·604 baptized past year; schools, 54; pupils in attendance, 2,000.

Receipts, $100,219.94, including $29,203.40 toward debt. Remainder of old debt, $10,985.09. Total liabilities, $34,835.09.

Before the organization of the Southern Baptist Convention, 257 missionaries had been sent into the field—213 from the North and West, and 23 from the South; the others, not of this country. The contributions to the Triennial Convention from 1814 to 1845 were $874,027.92.

The *Memorial* of August, 1846, referring to the South, used this language: " In the thirty-three years of the operations of our Foreign Mission organization, these slave-holding States have paid into the common treasury $215,856.28, or less than one-fourth of what has been contributed for this object."

BIRTH OF OUR CONVENTION.

The following is extracted, with the consent of the author, from the "HISTORIC SKETCH" of Rev. Wm. Williams, D. D., published by request of the Southern Baptist Convention, 1871:

"The Southern Baptist Convention was organized in the city of Augusta, Georgia, in the month of May, 1845. It originated in a withdrawal of the Southern churches from union and co-operation with 'the General Convention of the Baptist Denomination in the United States,' popularly known as the Triennial Convention. This body was organized in Philadelphia, May 21st, 1814. It had at first one object, the prosecution of Foreign Missions.

"This work was confided to a Board of Commissioners, styled 'The Baptist Board of Foreign Missions in the United States,' and located finally at Boston. At the first Triennial session, in 1817, the one object of the Convention was enlarged so as to embrace Domestic Missions—both objects being entrusted to the one Board until an experience of several years showed that it was wiser to confine the labors of the Board to the one object of Foreign Missions. Domestic Missions being withdrawn from the Convention and its Board in 1826, and there being a growing desire and demand for benevolent effort in this direction—a natural result of the Foreign Mission work—'The American Baptist Home Mission Society' was organized in Philadelphia in 1832. If it seem desirable to any, on the score of economy, to merge our Foreign and Domestic Mission Boards into one, let us profit by the experience of our brethren in past years, and hesitate to sacrifice efficiency to a mistaken economy. The constitution of the Triennial Convention, as well as the history of its proceedings from the beginning, conferred on all the members of the Baptist denomination in good standing, whether at the North or the South, eligibility to all appointments emanating from the Convention of the Board. Unmistakable indications, however, not necessary or profitable to speak of particularly, prompted the Alabama Baptist State Convention, in 1844, to adopt a preamble and resolutions, to be submitted to the Board of Foreign Missions of the Triennial Convention—the second of the resolutions being as follow:

"'That our duty at this crisis requires us to demand from the proper authorities in all those bodies, to whose funds we have contributed, or with whom we have in any way been connected, the distinct, explicit avowal, that slaveholders are eligible and entitled equally with non-slaveholders to all the privileges and immunities of their several unions, and especially to receive any agency or mission, or other appointment which may run within the scope of their operations or duties.'

"To this the Board, in the course of their reply, frankly and explicitly said: 'If any one should offer himself as a missionary, having slaves, and insist on retaining them as his property, we could not appoint him. One thing is certain, we can never be a party to any arrangement which would imply approbation of slavery.'

"When this reply was made known, the Board of the Virginia Foreign Mission Society addressed a circular to the Baptist churches of Virginia, communicating this decision of the Board of the Triennial Convention, and containing, among others, a resolution 'that this Board are of opinion that in the present exigency it is important that those brethren who are aggrieved by the recent decision of the Board of Boston, should hold a Convention to confer on the best means of promoting the Foreign Mission cause and other interests of the Baptist denomination in the South,' and suggesting Augusta, Georgia, as a suitable place for holding such Convention, and Thursday before the second Lord's Day in May, 1845, as a suitable time. Both at the North and the South a separation seemed inevitable. At the North it was desired by many, regretted by a few, and expected by all.

* * * * * * * *

"Before the proposed Convention in Augusta could meet to deliberate upon any course for the future, a separation had virtually been made by the Home Mission Society, at its meeting in Providence, April, 1845. At that meeting, Dr. John S. Maginnis, of New York, proposed the following preamble and resolutions:

"'*Whereas*, The American Baptist Home Missionary Society is composed of contributors residing in slaveholding and non-slaveholding States; and, whereas, the constitution recognizes no distinction among the members of the Society as to eligibility to all the offices and appointments in the gift both of the Society and of the Board; and, whereas, it has been found that the basis on which the Society was organized is one upon which all the members and friends of the Society are not now willing to act; therefore,

"'*Resolved*, That, in our opinion, it is expedient that the members now forming the Society, should hereafter act in separate organizations at the South and at the North, in promoting the objects which were originally contemplated by the Society.

"'*Resolved,* That a committee be appointed to report a plan by which the object contemplated in the preceding resolution may be accomplished in the best way, and at the earliest period of time, consistently with the preservation of the constitutional rights of all the members, and with the least possible interruption of the missionary work of the Society."'

"This was adopted by a considerable majority, and in pursuance of the second resolution a committee was appointed, which reported that 'as the existing Society was planted in the North, has its Executive Board, and there received a charter of incorporation, which it seems desirable to preserve, and as a separation seems to many minds inevitable, owing to the strong views of churches and individuals against the appointment of slaveholders to serve the Society, and as such views prevail principally at the North,' it was, therefore, recommended 'that the existing organization be retained by the Northern and other churches, which may be willing to act together upon the basis of restriction against the appointment of slaveholders.' This was adopted by an almost unanimous vote.

"At the call of the Board of Managers of the Virginia Foreign Mission Society, there assembled in Augusta, May 8, 1845, three hundred and ten delegates from the States of Maryland, Virginia, North Carolina, South Carolina, Georgia, Alabama, Louisiana, Kentucky, and the District of Columbia. Owing to the short notice of the meeting of the Convention, other States were reported only by letter. Rev. William B. Johnson, D. D., was chosen President. It was resolved 'that a committee of two from each State represented in the meeting be appointed to prepare and report a preamble and resolution for the action of the Convention.'

"The resolution reported by the committee is as follows:

"'*Resolved,* That for peace and harmony, and in order to accomplish the greatest amount of good, and for the maintenance of those scriptural principles on which the General Missionary Convention of the Baptist Denomination of the United States was originally formed, it is proper that this Convention at once proceed to organize a Society for the propagation of the gospel.'

"This was unanimously adopted, and the same committee, with some additions, was appointed to prepare a constitution, which, after some amendments, was adopted unanimously. In the address of the Convention 'to the brethren in the United States, to the congregations connected with the respective churches, and to all candid men,' it is said: 'The constitution we adopt is precisely that of the original union; that in connection with which, throughout his missionary life, Adoniram Judson has lived, and under which Ann Judson and Boardman have died. We recede from it no single step. * * * We use the very terms, as we uphold the true spirit and great object of the late General Convention of the Baptist Denomination of the United States.' It would seem, then, from the resolution above given, and from this extract from the address of the Convention, that the Southern Baptist Convention, formed upon the constitution of the Triennial Convention, and 'for the maintenance of the scriptural principles' on which it 'was originally formed,' is the real and proper successor and continuator of that body, which, at a special meeting held in New York, November 19th, 1845, was 'dissolved,' and the American Baptist Missionary Union, with an entirely new constitution and a different basis of membership, organized in its stead.

"At the meeting in Augusta, a Board for Foreign Missions was appointed, to be located in Richmond, Va., and one for Domestic Missions, to be located in Marion, Ala. Before the adjournment of the Convention, it was resolved 'that with profound gratitude to the Great Head of the church this Convention recognizes the harmonious and unanimous action to which it has arrived, and that we regard the exhibition of the spirit which has governed its deliberations as a pledge of the divine blessing in the origin and prosecution of this organization.'"

Thus was started into existence the Southern Baptist Convention, which gathered around itself the enthusiastic support of the Baptist churches of the South; received the "God-speed" of Judson, in an address made by him at Richmond, shortly after its formation; and the wisdom of which formation has been vindicated by the fact that, while Southern Baptists contributed to the Triennial Convention from

1814 to 1845, $212,000, they have contributed to the Southern Baptist Convention, from 1845 to 1879, for Foreign Missions alone, $939,377.23. In the last seven years $284,010.99 have been given for Foreign Missions, which is $72,000 more than the whole amount raised during the thirty years of our connection with the Triennial Convention.

Should the churches rise up to a due appreciation of their sacred obligations to this body, and of the noble services which it has rendered to Christianity and to the world, its future influence will be measured only by the important part it shall perform in leading the nations into the glorious liberty of the children of God, and in edifying the human race into a body meet for its great and Divine Head, Jesus.

SUNDRY ITEMS.

BOARD OF GENERAL CONVENTION.

At the first meeting of the Southern Baptist Convention, May 8, 1845, "By request, Brother J. B. Jeter gave a short statement of the proceedings of the General Board of the Baptist General Convention, at its late meeting in Providence, R. I., which meeting he, with some other brethren from Virginia, Maryland, and Georgia, had attended."

The following appears on page 154 of the "Life and Times of J. B. Taylor:" "On April 21st (1845), in company with Mr. Jeter, he started to attend the meeting of the Foreign Mission Board in Providence, R. I. While there, they were the guests of Dr. Wayland, and were treated with great kindness. Mr. Taylor found the interview with President Wayland and his family 'peculiarly pleasant.' The discussions in the meetings, however, were 'far from pleasant.' But he and his associates were enabled to maintain a quiet spirit in the midst of these trying scenes. Referring to this, Dr. Gillette, soon after, wrote to him: 'The mild, kind, gentlemanly, Christian spirit manifested by yourself and other brethren from the South won upon many hearts.'"

Our Convention directed the Board of Foreign Missions to correspond with the Boston Board with regard to mutual claims; and authorized the Board "to make any equitable and prudent arrangement with that Board to take a portion of its missions under the patronage of this Convention."

OBJECT OF SOUTHERN BAPTIST CONVENTION.

The preamble of the Constitution declares that the Convention is a plan " for eliciting, combining, and directing the energies of the whole denomination in one sacred effort for the propagation of the gospel." Let two things be noticed as in the minds of the founders of the Convention: 1. The advantage of *united effort* to save the world—"in one sacred effort." 2. The *eliciting* of the benevolence of the churches, as well as combining and directing it. The ablest churches or bodies, which might carry on their own mission work, have an important office in the Convention of eliciting the benevolence of feebler bodies, for the 'one sacred effort" to propagate the gospel.

FORM OF BEQUEST.

I hereby give and bequeath unto the Southern Baptist Convention, formed in Augusta, Ga., in the month of May, 1845, and chartered by the Legislature of the State of Georgia, by an act passed and approved December 27th, 1845, (here insert the amount of money, or subject, if other property, either real or personal,) for the purposes of Foreign Missions.

FIRST APPOINTMENTS AND ACTS.

Rev. J. B. Jeter, D.D., was the first President of the Board of Foreign Missions. Rev. Wm. B. Johnson, D.D., then President of the Southern Baptist Convention, was appointed General Agent to collect funds for the Board.

Rev. James B. Taylor was elected Corresponding Secretary, December 1st, 1845, and served until December, 1871, when he ascended to the rewards of a faithful and noble life.

Prof. John S. Maginnis, of Hamilton, N. Y., wrote to inquire whether young men of the North would be appointed by our Board. The Board replied that "suitable men would be appointed irrespective of geographical distinctions."

At the suggestion of the Boston Board, through Dr. Francis Wayland, it was agreed that "the property and liabilities of the General Convention should remain with that body;" and that "the missionaries should have the choice of the Associations with which they would be connected."

RESUMÉ OF OPERATIONS OF THE BOARD.

FROM LIFE AND TIMES OF J. B. TAYLOR, BY G. B. TAYLOR.

FROM 1845 TO 1863.

China Mission. Twenty-two missionaries had been appointed, most of them being married. Of these, five had fallen—viz.: Clopton, James, Gaillard, Holmes, and Bond; as, also, four missionaries' wives —viz.: Mrs. Shuck, Mrs. James, Mrs. Whilden, and Mrs. Bond. Mr. Roberts had been dismissed. Eight had returned permanently to this country—viz.: Messrs. Tobey, Whilden, Johnson, Shuck, Pearcy, Cabaniss, Burton, and Miss Baker; three had been prevented by the war from going out. Five missionaries remained upon the field—viz.: Messrs. Yates, Crawford, Schilling, Hartwell, and Graves, all but the latter being married and their wives actively engaged. Mrs. Gaillard and Mrs. Holmes were also laboring as missionaries. Besides, several native assistants had been employed. Stations had been maintained all the time at Canton and Shanghai, and new ones had been established at Shiu-Hing, Che-Foo and Tung Chow. Schools had been kept up, several chapels had been erected, the word of God and religious tracts had been scattered far and wide, and the missionaries had preached to tens of thousands in the interior of the Empire. Considerably more than one hundred converts had been baptized, most of whom were holding out well, and, in the judgment of the missionaries, broad and deep foundations for future labor had been laid.

Yoruba Mission. Originated in 1849. Sixteen missionaries had been appointed, including Mr. Harden, a colored man, at Lagos; most of them being married. Of these, Messrs. Goodale and Dennard had died; Mrs. Dennard, Mrs. Reid, and Mrs. Phillips had also died. Two, appointed as missionaries, had been prevented from going out. Eight had returned permanently to this country, leaving Messrs. Harden and Stone and their wives, and Messrs. Reid and Phillips, still identified with the mission. Stations had been maintained at Lagos, and, with more or less interruption, at Abbeokuta, Ijaye, Ogbomishaw, and Awyaw. Though many disasters had been encountered, some fifty converts had been baptized, and the missionaries were sanguine of ultimate and enlarged success.

Brazil. A mission in Brazil had been commenced, and Mr. Bowen sent out; but his health had broken down, and for that and other reasons the mission had been abandoned.

Japan. A mission in Japan had also been determined on, and Messrs. Toy, Johnson, and Rhorer had been appointed as missionaries. The two former had been prevented by the war from going out, and the last named had, with his companion, perished at sea. The mission had been abandoned, at least for the time.

The Liberia Mission. This mission was established soon after the Board began operations. It was conducted by colored men, though two white ministers, Elders Ball and Kingdon, had gone out as special agents of the Board, and the latter had fallen a victim to the fever of the country. Some twenty-four stations were maintained, twenty pastors and twenty-six teachers being employed. There were about twelve hundred church members, and seven hundred pupils at the schools, while more than one thousand converts had been baptized. A most happy influence had been exerted by this mission, both upon the infant colony and upon the uncivilized natives within a few miles of the coast.

Total receipts of the Board from its formation to the Convention in 1863, $437,037.

FROM 1863 TO 1872.

China. In this Empire thirteen missionaries had labored at eleven stations and out-stations, viz.: Mr. and Mrs. Hartwell, Mr. and Mrs. Graves, Mr. and Mrs. Crawford, Mr. and Mrs. Schilling, Mr. and Mrs.

Yates, Mr. and Mrs. Simmons, and Mrs. Holmes. Of these, two had died, and one had returned to this country, leaving ten either on the field or temporarily absent. Four missionaries had been appointed, but one had been prevented by death from going out. Besides, three native pastors had been ordained, and twelve unordained assistants and four Bible-women had been employed. A chapel had been erected in Canton. Between two hundred and two hundred and fifty converts had been baptized.

Yoruba. Stations had been kept up for several years at Lagos, Abbeokuta, Ogbomishaw, and Awyaw. The number baptized cannot be stated with accuracy—probably forty. The present status of the African mission appears from the reports of 1871 and 1872.

Hayti. A mission to Hayti was determined on in 1867, but abandoned on account of the death of the missionary.

ITALIAN MISSION.

This had been wonderfully blessed. The Board had now at Rome one missionary, Dr. Cote, three native evangelists, and one colporteur, and six stations were occupied, at each of which there was a Baptist Church, the total membership being two hundred and seventy-one. At the meeting of the Convention of 1872, twenty thousand dollars were pledged toward building a chapel in Rome.

Receipts for this period, $144,159; but this is exclusive of what was sent out by the Baltimore Committee, and of collections in Confederate currency during that portion of the war embraced in this resume.

SUPPLEMENT BY PRESENT CORRESPONDING SECRETARY, 1872 TO 1879.

CHINA MISSION.

Canton. Reinforced by Rev. N. B. Williams and wife, Miss Lula Whilden, and Mrs. R. H. Graves. Rev. E. Z. Simmons and wife transferred to American Baptist Missionary Union to labor with

ORIGIN AND FOREIGN WORK OF THE CONVENTION. 477

Chinese in California, on account of ill-health of Mrs. Simmons. Nine thousand dollars contributed for missionary residence. Death of native pastor, Wong Mui. Six new cities opened in China for foreigners, in 1876. Rev. N. B. Williams and wife return to America. Wong and Fong set apart to the gospel ministry. Member Lough Fuh pastor of church of 100 Chinese converts in British Guiana, of whom 52 were baptized in 1876-7. Student Dong Gong, pastor of 12 or 15, in Oregon. Brother Graves published "Notes on Parables." Native Missionary Society opened station at San Kiu. Chinese Demerara brother opened self-sustaining chapel in 1878. Chapel and school-house built in To Hai. Dr. Graves writing books on "Life of Christ," and "Scripture Geography." Since 1875, 18,508 patients attended. In last three years, 36,000 tracts distributed; $450 contributed by native members; 129 baptized. Present number of pupils 107. Church membership 191. Rev. E. Z. Simmons and wife, with Miss Sallie Stein sailed from San Francisco for Canton February 1, 1880.

Shanghai. Rev. M. T. Yates loses his voice, and makes trip to United States to restore it. Great efficiency of native pastor, Wong Ping San, and Mrs. Yates in absence of Dr. Yates. Chapel remodelled for $3,000 at the expense of Dr. Yates, acting as Vice-Consul of the United States. He also built school-house for Mrs. Yates. Resigned Vice Consulate in December, 1875. New Chapel dedicated February, 1876. Dr. Yates gives $500 as "Centennial offering." Endowed school of 20 boys for life. Translated part of New Testament and published several thousand copies. Grand Conference of Missionaries, at which our missionaries presented valuable papers, 1877. The 12th September of that year, 30th anniversary of Mr. and Mrs. Yates' arrival at Shanghai. At own expense went to California in 1878 for his health. In 1879, Mrs. Ling, noted for her "power in prayer," in charge of station. Native contributions this year, $333—$3.66 per member. Mrs. Yates' school flourishing. Earnest spirit of members. Baptized in four years, 50. Present membership 91. Dr. Yates says: "The work of last year (1878-9) the most successful which we have done in China." November 1, 1879, a church of sixteen members was constituted at Kwin San, fifty miles from Shanghai.

SHANTUNG.

Reinforced by the Misses Moon and Mrs. J. B. Hartwell. Station reëstablished at Chefoo by Mr. Hartwell. Ladies of Georgia and Virginia collected $2,382.63 toward house for the Misses Moon. Return of J. B. Hartwell and wife, on account of illness of the latter. It is our sad duty to report that she died in San Francisco, December 3d, 1879. Chefoo station closed. The Misses Moon return to the United States on account of illness of Miss Edmonia. Mr. and Mrs. Crawford spend three months in Japan. Miss L. Moon returned December 24th, 1877. Great Famine. Proposed union of churches. Mr. Crawford returns to America, on account of his health, and sails for California July, 1879. In four years the ladies made 1027 visits to country villages. In schools 56. Church members 115. Great Revival in the provinces. "1500 awaiting instruction to enter the church."—J. H. Eager appointed missionary.

AFRICAN MISSION.

Missions of Bier Country, opened by Rev. A. D. Phillips, suspended on account of internal war. Rev. W. J. David.and Rev. W. W. Colley reinforce work, and directed to re-open mission at Yoruba, as country now accessible to missionaries. Stations opened at Lagos, Abbeokuta, and Ogbomishaw. Mr. David goes to Europe and to America, for his health. Married and returned to Africa in 1879. Mr. Colley returns to the United States the same year, leaving the work in the hands of Mr. Solomon Cosby of the colored Baptist State Convention of Virginia. Eighty members. Three missionaries and seven assistants.

ITALIAN MISSION.

Serious troubles, and dismissal of Messrs. Cote and Gioja; $20,000 for chapel sent to Rome, and returned as chapel could not be secured. Reinforced by Rev. G. B. Taylor, D.D., and wife, and several evangelists. Native pastor at Rome, Prof. Cocorda, of Milan. Death of Giannini: defection of church at Bologna. General prosperity in provinces. Eligible *locale* in Rome. Dr. Taylor baptized fifteen persons at ancient Puteoli. Great enlargement of the work in the provinces and strong additions to membership and evangelists. Cost of Chapel $34,821.94. Dedicated November, 1878. Dr. Taylor comes with family to America to collect funds. Quite ill. He expects to sail for Italy February 7th, 1880. Church members, 134; stations, 11; Evangelists, 9.

BRAZILIAN MISSIONS.

Reorganized in 1879, at Santa Barbara, province of San Paulo, with Elder E. H. Quillin as Missionary.—On Lord's Day, December 7th, 1879, "The Station Church" was constituted with twelve members, near Santa Barbara Station, on railroad leading into the interior.

Receipts for this period $284,010,99.

VIEWS SOUTH AND NORTH.

ACTION OF SOUTHERN BAPTIST CONVENTION.

"The Committee, to whom were referred the resolutions on co-operation with our Northern brethren, have had the same under consideration, and instruct me to report the following resolution:

Resolved, That five brethren be appointed by this Convention to bear to our Baptist brethren of the Northern States, at their approaching anniversaries, expressions of our fraternal regard, and assurances that, while firmly holding to the wisdom and policy of preserving our separate organizations, we are ready, as in the past, to co-operate cordially with them in promoting the cause of Christ in our own and foreign lands.

On motion, the chair appointed the following Committee, under the above report:

J. B. Jeter, Virginia; George B. Taylor, Italy; H. A. Tupper, Virginia; H. H. Tucker, Georgia, and R. M. Dudley, Kentucky."—*Proceedings,* 1879.

NORTHERN VIEWS AND SOUTHERN COMMENT.

Dr. Tucker of the delegation to the Northern anniversaries at Saratoga, 1879, having presented a paper setting forth reasons why our missionary organizations, North and South, should be preserved separate and intact, the following comments were made:

"Scarcely any Northern Baptist needs to be convinced that it would be wholly unadvisable to try to bring about organic union between the Baptists of the North and the South."—*Examiner and Chronicle*, June 5, 1879.

"The editor of the *National Baptist* says: 'I quite agree with Dr. Tucker as to the practical bearing of the matter of organic union. How much would the 966,191 Southern white Baptists contribute to the Union having its seat in Boston? How much to the Home Mission Society having its seat in New York? And on the other hand, such an organic union would make the income of the Union and of the Home Mission Society appear even more humiliating than now. It is bad enough when we divide, perhaps, less than $40,000 among 634,798 Baptists. When we come to divide the contribution among 1,600,939 white Baptists what will the quotient be?'

"This settles, at least for years, the question of organic union between the churches of the two sections. The next question will be on the division of the work North and West."—*Biblical Recorder*, June 11, 1879.

RECEIPTS OF FOREIGN MISSION BOARD
FROM 1845 TO 1879.

	1845 to 1846	1847	1848	1849	1850
Alabama	2441 10	1368 60	1049 16	1595 33	914 49
Am. Tract Society			500 00		600 00
Arkansas					
Bible Board					
Bible Society (A. F.)					
Bequests					
Canada					
California					
Connecticut					
District of Columbia		130 16	50 00	55 00	35 00
Delaware					
England and Scotland					
Florida					256 27
Georgia	1920 33	2151 87	2449 75	1632 33	4137 20
Indiana					
Illinois					
Indian Territory					
Interest		1854 04	222 20	1026 29	693 39
Kansas					
Kentucky	392 00	933 56	1101 44	607 55	1049 05
Louisiana	5 00	95 60		30 00	
Michigan					
Maryland		1533 29	807 26	823 23	293 96
Maine					
Massachusetts					
Missionaries and Missions					
Mississippi	283 83	1039 44	1279 56	1073 84	1804 25
Miscellaneous Receipts					
Missouri				99 42	158 00
Nebraska					
New Jersey			10 00		
New York		118 05	150 00		
North Carolina	251 92	833 47	1406 58	880 78	1003 82
Nova Scotia					
Ohio					
Oregon					
Publication Account			10 60	56 00	
Pennsylvania			6 09		10 00
Returned and Exchanged			9 00		
Rhode Island		20 00			
South Carolina	2660 87	2591 92	2221 48	2736 56	3250 19
Southern Baptist Convention					
Tennessee		765 25	273 65		1032 00
Texas				28 00	22 50
Virginia	3734 00	4525 38	7861 56	6083 60	7756 55
West Virginia					
Totals	**11,089 05**	**17,964 97**	**19,503 73**	**16,727 93**	**23,016 67**

FOREIGN MISSIONS.

RECEIPTS OF FOREIGN MISSION BOARD—[Continued.]

	1851	1852	1853	1854	1855
Alabama	2000 00	1398 48	1687 54	2615 51	2513 57
Am. Tract Society	300 00	201 00	200 00	200 00	100 00
Arkansas	7 00	1 90		50	
Bible Board		100 00	1700 00	1700 00	548 75
Bible Society (A. F.)					
Bequests					
Canada					
California					
Connecticut					
District of Columbia	77 10	71 65	57 03	46 66	231 46
Delaware					
England and Scotland					
Florida	233 00	242 22	15 75	316 88	54 00
Georgia	4565 77	3480 98	5545 93	3363 48	8299 52
Indiana					
Illinois					
Indian Territory					
Interest	463 90	697 21	596 46	355 05	261 65
Kansas					
Kentucky	689 13	917 85	437 84	98 37	600 03
Louisiana					101 00
Michigan					
Maryland	974 32	1551 29	959 83	1581 98	812 72
Maine					
Massachusetts					
Missionaries and Missions	7 00	858 37	165 00		
Mississippi	1539 31	1140 50	857 82	1108 16	997 90
Miscellaneous Receipts		664 74			
Missouri	591 05	245 00	235 57	199 00	1141 00
Nebraska					
New Jersey					
New York					
North Carolina	1234 23	1559 23	1577 49	1291 31	1820 45
Nova Scotia					
Ohio					
Oregon					
Publication Account		29 80			
Pennsylvania					
Returned and Exchanged		286 53		15 00	300 00
Rhode Island					
South Carolina	2598 77	3490 59	1620 14	2907 48	3932 96
Southern Baptist Convention					
Tennessee	814 77	1575 18	1825 31	1201 65	909 04
Texas	38 25	37 00	45 00	35 00	45 80
Virginia	5655 41	5989 73	3911 74	5705 89	7396 75
West Virginia					
Totals	21,789 01	24,548 30	21,438 45	22,741 92	30,066 60

ORIGIN AND FOREIGN WORK OF THE CONVENTION. 483

RECEIPTS OF FOREIGN MISSION BOARD—[Continued.]

	1856	1857	1858	1859	1860
Alabama	2904 15	4081 03	4902 55	5474 00	7536 10
Am. Tract Society		200 00		401 00	
Arkansas		11 00	50	5 00	27 60
Bible Board	200 00	1000 00			1023 40
Bible Society (A. F.)					
Bequests			500 00		
Canada					
California					
Connecticut					
District of Columbia	116 18	88 69	88 40	56 85	158 42
Delaware					
England and Scotland					
Florida	139 70	13 00	84 50	624 98	154 37
Georgia	4821 00	6283 97	5293 51	8696 14	6463 10
Indiana					
Illinois			5 00		
Indian Territory					
Interest	13 13	34 12	6 00	402 90	592 04
Kansas					
Kentucky	2174 08	2150 28	3202 47	3566 80	4497 78
Louisiana	30 00	152 00	340 49	758 32	435 22
Michigan					
Maryland	2085 99	975 88	1041 30	1222 73	869 87
Maine					
Massachusetts					
Missionaries and Missions					
Mississippi	609 30	1418 26	1088 57	539 07	1827 29
Miscellaneous Receipts					
Missouri	497 21	468 25	411 75	206 72	283 60
Nebraska					
New Jersey					
New York		70 00			
North Carolina	1272 84	2772 67	2152 28	2164 40	2582 73
Nova Scotia					
Ohio					
Oregon					
Publication Account			423 31	319 79	
Pennsylvania		50 00			
Returned and Exchanged	200 00			101 18	
Rhode Island					
South Carolina	2140 24	2962 08	4264 08	4849 98	5120 63
Southern Baptist Convention					
Tennessee	1638 33	1049 47	1871 33	1074 06	1074 05
Texas	13 00	10 25		27 00	275 13
Virginia	7648 69	8141 29	8726 51	9332 95	7673 74
West Virginia					
Totals	26,503 84	31,932 29	34,402 55	39,823 87	41,195 07

484 FOREIGN MISSIONS.

RECEIPTS OF FOREIGN MISSION BOARD—[Continued.]

	1861	1862	1863	1864	1865
Alabama	5042 49	4118 21	245 50	2224 55	
Am. Tract Society	300 00	207 00			
Arkansas	20 00				
Bible Board	100 00	100 00			
Bible Society (A. F.)					
Bequests			500 00		
Canada					
California					
Connecticut					
District of Columbia	87 79				
Delaware					
England and Scotland					
Florida	154 89	30 30	6 00	172 69	
Georgia	6965 77	5844 25	1223 22	15,425 04	9299 31
Indiana					
Illinois					
Indian Territory					
Interest	744 41	376 47	387 90	1407 80	3429 78
Kansas					
Kentucky	1516 74	2639 93			
Louisiana	522 50	351 50	231 00		120 00
Michigan					
Maryland	894 84	763 09			
Maine					
Massachusetts					
Missionaries and Missions	1529 33	393 82	5 00		
Mississippi					
Miscellaneous Receipts	233 50	758 67		90 00	100 00
Missouri	733 90	25 75			
Nebraska					
New Jersey					
New York					
North Carolina	2243 02	1569 47	782 64	3003 87	3800 76
Nova Scotia					
Ohio					
Oregon					
Publication Account			279 91		
Pennsylvania					
Returned and Exchanged	949 32	39			
Rhode Island					
South Carolina	3795 98	1997 64	1723 63	7187 14	5774 13
Southern Baptist Convention					
Tennessee	688 00	49 05		250 00	
Texas	276 50	45 00	5 00	10 00	
Virginia	6026 60	5076 54	3244 63	10,528 62	6256 07
West Virginia					
Totals	32,886 47	24,347 08	8,634 43	40,299 71	28,680 05

ORIGIN AND FOREIGN WORK OF THE CONVENTION.

RECEIPTS OF FOREIGN MISSION BOARD—[Continued.]

	1866	1867	1868	1869	1870
Alabama	554 40	1458 42	415 95	1656 98	1320 90
Am. Tract Society					
Arkansas			7 00	15 00	52 90
Bible Board					
Bible Society (A. F.)			300 00		
Bequests					
Canada					
California				5 00	
Connecticut		10 00			
District of Columbia	91 97	63 54	134 17	114 99	15 00
Delaware		5 00			
England and Scotland				2151 85	
Florida		1 00	15 00	21 50	127 15
Georgia	447 00	4468 17	1491 40	2294 99	3552 01
Indiana		2 00	5 00	10 00	9 15
Illinois	20 00	15 00			8 50
Indian Territory					
Interest					
Kansas					
Kentucky	3522 99	5014 02	1337 92	4720 55	5560 32
Louisiana		885 55	280 00	294 95	496 87
Michigan					
Maryland	646 79	2280 61	3437 54	2537 42	1694 62
Maine					
Massachusetts					10 00
Missionaries and Missions				237 80	
Mississippi		183 10	196 41	432 50	701 65
Miscellaneous Receipts					1398 31
Missouri	563 30	1337 15	1106 45	531 60	1485 06
Nebraska					
New Jersey		20 00			
New York			25 00	10 00	65 00
North Carolina	114 09	1187 85	1173 40	494 52	1107 07
Nova Scotia					
Ohio		5 00			
Oregon					
Publication Account					
Pennsylvania	10 00				
Returned and Exchanged	126 64				
Rhode Island					
South Carolina		727 55	502 50	834 70	1225 09
Southern Baptist Convention					
Tennessee	182 90	1031 65	782 01	669 60	684 45
Texas		495 02	621 48	86 23	242 79
Virginia	237 45	2166 66	2858 39	1866 37	1804 90
West Virginia	113 00	310 65	141 82	205 86	376 29
Totals	6,630 53	21,667 94	14,831 44	19,192 41	21,938 03

RECEIPTS OF FOREIGN MISSION BOARD—[Continued.]

	1871	1872	1873	1874	1875
Alabama	1720 79	1977 86	2301 97	1477 39	1029 03
Am. Tract. Society	100 00	200 00			
Arkansas	82 50	118 90	145 55	53 03	124 80
Bible Board					
Bible Society (A. F.)					
Bequests	100 00				
Canada			10 00		
California					
Connecticut	25 00				
District of Columbia	21 01	3423 85	279 10	29 26	89 48
Delaware					
England and Scotland		358 40	1298 29		
Florida	26 40	46 55	100 97	36 68	20 10
Georgia	2527 53	3227 48	6836 51	5808 19	5119 32
Indiana	13 00	2 00	19 75		1 00
Illinois	7 00	10 00	367 00	16 00	16 00
Indian Territory					
Interest		150 03	280 02		
Kansas				5 70	
Kentucky	5609 55	2470 00	8842 56	7210 00	5015 70
Louisiana	106 05	318 60	58 00	254 34	269 35
Michigan			3 00		
Maryland	2952 44	2121 35	4535 29	2987 49	6337 68
Maine	6 50		7 50		
Massachusetts			1838 74	402 40	12 00
Missionaries and Missions		945 00	10 00		1061 97
Mississippi	1136 70	991 35	1254 27	1596 06	
Miscellaneous Receipts	830 57	885 09	2817 22		
Missouri	2844 08	1199 52	966 22	792 55	523 00
Nebraska					
New Jersey		150 00	15 15		
New York	175 00	25 00	1437 00	935 00	210 00
North Carolina	1329 65	1788 69	2805 25	1420 62	1195 15
Nova Scotia					
Ohio		4 00	100 00		17 15
Oregon			10 00		
Publication Account					
Pennsylvania	20 50	3 00	120 0(		50 00
Returned and Exchanged			12 0(	18,054 01	
Rhode Island					
South Carolina	898 51	1629 18	3563 18	4302 74	2033 77
Southern Baptist Convention	251 45	279 30	100 00		
Tennessee	636 38	744 87	1510 22	996 65	795 35
Texas	736 52	518 86	504 69	129 15	1007 05
Virginia	3093 35	4902 37	8608 09	6072 63	5571 89
West Virginia	498 82	411 36	266 17	191 79	348 79
Totals	25,749 30	28,905 55	51,023 62	52,841 68	30,848 58

ORIGIN AND FOREIGN WORK OF THE CONVENTION. 487

RECEIPTS OF FOREIGN MISSION BOARD.—[Concluded.]

	1876	1877	1878	1879	Totals.
Alabama	1371 13	1315 54	1153 46	1381 35	73,247 58
Am. Tract Society					3509 00
Arkansas	192 00	462 75	265 82	119 31	1713 05
Bible Board					6472 15
Bible Society (A. F.)					300 00
Bequests	2417 50		99 58	74 58	3691 66
Canada				1 00	11 00
California	2 00	5 25	10 00	10 00	32 25
Connecticut				39 00	74 00
District of Columbia	272 80	188 25	16 00	260 75	6350 50
Delaware					5 00
England and Scotland					3800 54·
Florida	62 78	47 10	77 80	82 39	3163 96
Georgia	7174 70	4344 68	4728 11	4176 98	164,148 54
Indiana		2 00			63 90
Illinois	18 00	19 40	31 10	68 00	601 01
Indian Territory				1 00	1 00
Interest	1245 80	1190 28	1122 95	1100 00	18,640 68
Kansas				1 00	6 70
Kentucky	5924 87	5024 00	5297 69	4846 81	96.981 70
Louisiana	499 15	316 25	630 65	404 15	7985 94
Michigan					3 00
Maryland	2252 95	2196 51	2099 37	2296 36	55,567 96
Maine					14 00
Massachusetts		22 40		473 40	2758 94
Missionaries and Missions			76		3285 90
Mississippi	1628 00	2010 27	2132 32	1871 70	32.669 58
Miscellaneous Receipts		14 37	5 00		9215 15
Missouri	710 63	1269 37	1888 39	2433 62	22,947 16
Nebraska			1 00		1 00
New Jersey				206 06	401 21
New York	61 00	190 00		484 62	3955 67
North Carolina	2681 03	2245 49	3277 38	3394 90	58,624 10
Nova Scotia		124 48			124 48
Ohio			2 40	2 40	130 95
Oregon					10 00
Publication Account					1214 81
Pennsylvania	5 50			5 00	280 09
Returned and Exchanged					20,154 07
Rhode Island				125 77	145 77
South Carolina	6088 86	3026 98	3284 75	4006 54	100,010 82
Southern Bapt. Convention	60 00	341 75	52 50	45 00	1130 00
Tennessee	1548 02	771 27	1148 77	917 95	27,438 08
Texas	1689 62	895 95	561 45	1052 81	9354 96
Virginia	9263 61	6116 01	5110 22	6482 93	195,431 11
West Virginia	476 91	146 99	66 97	152 84	3708 26
Totals	45,646 86	32,287 34	33,064 45	36,578 22	$ 939,377 23

FOREIGN MISSIONS.

SUMMARY OF MISSIONS.

Missions Commenced.	NAMES OF PROTESTANT FOREIGN MISSION ORGANIZATIONS.	Number of Ordained Missionaries.	Native Laborers.	Number of Church Members.	Number of Pupils.	Approximate Annual Income.
	American Organizations.					
1810	American Board of Foreign Missions.	131	....	28,737	14,410	$482,204
1814	Baptist Missionary Union	141	984	80,475	7,397	278,723
1819	Methodist Episcopal Church Missions.	298	290	23,477	19,158	268,077
1832	Presbyterian Church Missions	120	64	10,391	10,059	463,851
1832	Reformed Dutch Church Missions.	17	....	1,123	2,341	59,504
1846	American Missionary Association.	16	....	550	329	191,604
1845	Board for Foreign Missions of So. Baptist Convention.	14	44	750	477	35,000
1845	Methodist Episcopal Church South Missions.	7	24	70	32	62,157
1859	United Presbyterian Church Missions.	16	130	1,056	2,735	74,000
1859	Nova Scotia Presbyterian Church Missions.	5	....	1,000	1,500	1,500
1859	American Woman's Union	....	....	....	....	....
1876	American Bible Society	....	....	....	....	....
1867	American Southern Presbyterians.	20	15	1,260	550	56,000
	British Organizations.					
1701	Society for Propagation of the Gospel in Foreign Parts.	464	....	30,000	....	742,000
1800	Church Missionary Society	329	181	27,080	57,145	1,115,000
1795	London Missionary Society	230	4,300	101,928	38,231	546,740
1792	Baptist Missionary Society	290	....	29,496	15,079	250,344
1842	Primitive Methodist Missionary Society.	211	3	147,000	....	32,000
1769	Wesleyan Missionary Society	1,071	....	147,103	....	730,085
1816	General Baptist Missionary Society	23	15	884	6	42,006
1860	United Methodist Free Ch. Missionary Society	40	....	5,656	3,951	11,770
1860	Methodist New Connection Missions.	4	....	284	....	2,500
		3,447	6,050	638,320	173,400	5,445,065

PROTESTANT MISSIONS.

Summary of Protestant Missions.—(Concluded.)

Missions Commenced.	Names of Protestant Foreign Mission Organizations.	Number of Ordained Missionaries.	Native Laborers.	Number of Church Members.	Number of Pupils.	Approximate Annual Income.
	Brought forward.............	3,447	6,050	638,320	173,400	5,445,065
1840	{ Welsh Calvinistic Methodist Missions.......................... }	4	....	211	714	5,500
1824	Church of Scotland Missions....	11	....	218	2,800	10,000
1843	{ Free Church of Scotland Missions....................... }	28	....	3,171	14,100	247,144
1847	{ United Presbyterian Church Missions................... }	47	300	8,427	10,741	212,130
1844	{ English Presbyterian Ch. Missions..................... }	12	....	1,000	....	58,500
1840	{ Irish Presbyterian Church Missions................... }	11	70	223	1,300	3,000
1845	British Society for the Jews.....	....	....	....	....	8,378
1844	{ South American Missionary Society......................... }	14	....	....	....	9,352
1855	Turkish Missions Aid Society...	....	....	....	....	4,500
1836	{ British Foreign and Bible Society....................... }	....	....	....	....	....
1837	English Episcopal..................	....	....	....	....	....
1863	{ Scotch National Bible Society.......................... }	....	....	....	....	....
1457	United Brethren Foreign Board.	....	....	70,646	....	130,000
	Continental Organizations.					
1732	Moravian Missionary Society....	156	....	20,742	....	24,500
1822	{ Paris Evangelical Missionary Society..................... }	21	....	1,500	900	8,500
1828	Rhenish Missionary Society......	56	....	4,656	4,000	12,000
1833	Berlin Missionary Society.........	35	....	2,000	1,500	10,000
1813	Basle Evangelical Missions	186	275	5,850	3,218	175,290
1797	Netherland Missionary Society..	20	....	....	13,057	8,000
1852	{ Hermansburgh Missionary Society..................... }	44	....	....	....	7,700
1842	Norwegian Missionary Society..	19	....	114	150	4,000
1860	Utrecht Missionary Society.......	10	....	4	60	4,000
1860	Danish Missionary Society........	2	....	....	....	1,500
	Totals............................	4,123	6,695	757,282	225,949	6,395,059

SYNOPSIS OF SOUTHERN BAPTIST MISSIONS.

AFRICAN MISSIONS.

LIBERIA AND SIERRA LEONE MISSIONS.

NAMES OF BAPTIST WORKERS.

ANDERSON, P. B., teacher.
BALL, Rev. ELI.
BARRETT, Rev. Mr.
BATTESTE, Rev. Mr.
BENYA.
BOWEN, Rev. T. J.
BRANDER, J. N., teacher.
BRITTON, Rev. S. W.
BRITTON, Mrs. G. A.
BROCK, ———
BROWNE, Rev. J. J.
BROWNE, Rev. W. S.
BULLOCK, Rev. JAMES.
BURKE, Rev. WILLIAM C.
CHEESEMAN, Rev. JOHN H.
CHEESEMAN, Mrs. SARAH MARSH.
CHEESEMAN, Rev. J. JAMES.
CHEESEMAN, Miss M. A., teacher.
CLARKE, Rev. W. H.
COLLEY, Rev. W. W.
COOK, J.
CROCKER, Rev. LEWIS KONG.
CUTHBERT, ———
DAVID, Rev. W. J.
DAVIS, Rev. A. P.
DAVIS, J. B.
DAY, Rev. JOHN.
DAY, SAMUEL P.

DRAYTON, Rev. BOSTON J.
DURING, DANIEL W., teacher.
EARLY, J.
EARLY, JOSEPHINE, teacher.
EARLY, Rev. T.
ELKINS, ———
FITZGERALD, Rev. J. J.
FRAZER, Rev. CÆSAR.
GIBSON, G. F.
HARDEN, Rev. JOSEPH M.
HARDEN, Mrs. J. M.
HAYELEY, RICHARD JAMES, teacher.
HAZZARD, JULIA, teacher.
HERNDON, Rev. MELFORD D.
HILL, Rev. ROBERT F.
HOWES, ———
JAMES, Rev. FREDERICK S.
JOHNSON, H. R. N., teacher.
JOHNSON, WILLIAM A.
JONES, Rev. ALEXANDER L.
KINGDON, Rev. JOHN.
LEWIS, J. N., teacher.
LEWIS, Miss, teacher.
LIBERTY, M. D.
MASON, ISRAEL, teacher.
MONGER, WILLIAM H.
MOORE, JAMES.
MOORE, WORRELL.

490

SYNOPSIS OF SOUTHERN BAPTIST MISSIONS. 491

MOREL, Mrs., teacher.
MORRILL, Rev. ———.
MOTTON, HANSON W., teacher.
MURRAY, Rev. R. E.
NEYLE, J. T., teacher.
PAGE, P. M., teacher.
PAGE, SOLOMON S.
PAUL, EDWARD, teacher.
PECK, G. B., teacher.
PHILLIPS, Rev. A. D.
POWELL, J. J., teacher.
PURVIS, Rev. SMART.
RICHARDSON, Rev. F.
RICHARDSON, Rev. J. T.
RICHMOND, LEIGH, teacher.
ROBERTS, Rev. ISAAC.
ROBERTS, Rev. Z. B.
STEWART, W. H., teacher.
STEWARD, W. W., teacher.
STONE, Rev. R. H.

STROTHER, J., teacher.
TATE, ———.
TEAGE, Rev. HILARY.
THOMPSON, Rev. G. R.
THOMPSON, Rev. H. P.
TYTLER, Rev. G.
UNDERWOOD, Rev. HENRY.
VON BRUNN, Rev. JACOB.
WALKER, Rev. HUGH.
WAUGHN, E.
WEEKS, Rev. GEORGE.
WHITE, ADAM.
WHITE, Rev. RICHARD.
WILSON, JAMES H.
WINDHAM, ———, teacher.
WOOD, Rev. A. T.
WOODSON, Rev. A.
WOODSON, Rev. J.
YATES, B. P.

PLACES OCCUPIED OR VISITED.

BASSA.
BASSA COVE.
BEXLEY.
BLACKWELL'S.
BUCHANAN.
BUTAN.
CALDWELL.
CAPE PALMAS.
CAREYSBURG.
CLAY ASHLAND.
CONGO TOWN.
DAVIS TOWN.
DONOGBA.
DYEMES.
EDINA.
FARMERSVILLE.
FREETOWN.
GRAND BASSA.
GRAND BUTAN.
GRAND CAPE MOUNT.
GREENVILLE.
HERNDONVILLE.
JAVERS TOWN.
JUNK.
KING BROMLEYSTOWN.
KING GRAYSTOWN.

LEXINGTON.
LITTLE BASSA.
LOUISIANA.
MARSHALL.
MARSHALL JUNK.
MESURADO.
MIDDLE SETTLEMENT.
MILLSBURG.
MONROVIA.
NEW GEORGIA.
NEW KENTUCKY.
NEW ORLEANS.
NIMBLY'S TOWN.
OLD FIELDS.
PHILLIPSBURG.
REIDSVILLE.
SIERRA LEONE.
SINOU.
TATTOU'S TOWN.
TAYLORSVILLE.
VIRGINIA.
VON BRUNNSVILLE.
WATERLOO.
WILLIAMSBURG.
YABBOO.
ZEO'S BEIR COUNTRY.

YORUBA MISSION.

NAMES OF BAPTIST WORKERS.

Beaumont, John F., teacher.
Bowen, Rev. Thomas J.
Brown, ———.
Cason, Rev. J. H.
Clarke, Rev. W. H.
Colley, Rev. W. W.
Cosby, Rev. Solomon.
David, Rev. William J.
Dennard, Rev. J. S.
Goodale, Rev. Henry.
Harden, Rev. Joseph M.
Harden, Mrs. J. M., teacher.
Lacy, Rev. John H.
Phillips, Rev. A. D.
Priest, Rev. R. W.
Reid, Rev. T. A.
Reid, Mrs. Mary E.
Stone, Moses L.
Stone, Rev. R. H.
Trimble, Rev. Selden Y.

PLACES OCCUPIED OR VISITED.

Abbeokuta.
Agajaie.
Awyaw.
Awaye.
Badagry.
Bi-olorrun-pellu.
Eruwa.
Ibadan.
Ijaye.
Iketu.
Ilorin.
Lagos.
Ogbomishaw.

BRAZIL MISSION.

NAMES OF BAPTIST WORKERS.

Bowen, Rev. Thomas J. | Quillen, Rev. E. H.

PLACES OCCUPIED OR VISITED.

Santa Barbara. | Station Church.

ITALIAN MISSION.

NAMES OF BAPTIST WORKERS.

Basile.
Bellondi.
Berruati.
Brachetto.
Cocorda, Professor.
Columbo.
Cote, Dr. W. N.
Cossù.
Ferraris.
Gardiol.
Garuti.
Giannini.
Gioja, G. B.
Guerrini, Rosa, Bible woman.
Laura, Secundo.
Martinelli.
Mollo.
Papengouth, Count.
Paschetto.
Pinelli.
Revelli.
Taylor, Rev. Dr. Geo. B.
Torre, Count.
Volpi.

PLACES OCCUPIED OR VISITED.

ACQUAVIVA.
BARI.
BARLETTA.
BOLOGNA.
CAGLIARI, ISLAND OF SARDINIA.
CARPI.
CIVITA VECCHIA.
GRUMO.
LA TOUR.

MILAN.
MODENÀ.
NAPLES.
POZZUOLI (PUTEOLI).
ROME.
SAN PASSIDONIA.
TORRE PELLICE.
TURIN.

CHINA MISSIONS.

CANTON MISSION.
NAMES OF BAPTIST WORKERS.

AU, Assistant.
BAKER, Miss HARRIET A., teacher.
CLOPTON, Rev. SAMUEL C.
CLOPTON, Mrs. KEZIAH TURPIN.
FUNG, or FONG, assistant.
GAILLARD, Rev. CHARLES W.
GAILLARD, Mrs. EVA M. MILLS.
GRAVES, Rev. ROSEWELL H.
GRAVES, Mrs. JANE W. NORRIS.
JOHNSON, Rev. FRANCIS C.
LUK, assistant.
LYE SEEN SANG, teacher.
PEARCY, Rev. GEORGE.
PEARCY, Mrs. FRANCES MILLER.
ROBERTS, Rev. ISSACHAR J.
ROBERTS, Mrs. BARSHA BLANCHARD.
ROBERTS, Mrs. VIRGINIA YOUNG.

SCHILLING, Rev. JOHN GRIFFITH.
SCHILLING, Mrs. KATE LOWTHER.
SEEN, deacon.
SHUCK, Rev. J. LEWIS.
SHUCK, Mrs. HENRIETTA HALL.
SHUCK, Mrs. LIZZIE SEXTON.
SIMMONS, Rev. EZEKIAS Z.
SIMMONS, Mrs. MAGGIE D. CLAMROCK.
STEIN, Miss SALLIE.
WHILDEN, Rev. BAYFIELD W.
WHILDEN, Mrs. ELIZA JANE MARTIN.
WHILDEN, Miss LOUISA.
WILLIAMS, Rev. NICHOLAS B.
WILLIAMS, Mrs. JUMELLE WHILDEN.
WONG FUNG, assistant.
WONG MUI.
YONG SEEN SANG.

PLACES OCCUPIED OR VISITED.

CANTON.
HONG KONG.
KAI FUNG FOO.
KO CHOW.
MACAO.
MUI LUK.
NGCHOW.
SAI-NAN.

SAN HING CITY.
SAN KIU.
SAN SHUI.
SHIU HING.
TO HAI.
TSUNG FA.
WHAMPOA.
WU CHAU.

SHANGHAI MISSION.

NAMES OF BAPTIST WORKERS.

BAKER, Miss HARRIET A.
BURTON, GEORGE W., M. D.
CABANISS, Rev. ASA BRUCE.
CABANISS, Mrs. M. E. ADKISSON.
CRAWFORD, Rev. TARLETON P., D. D.
CRAWFORD, Mrs. MARTHA FOSTER.
HARTWELL, Rev. JESSE B.
HARTWELL, Mrs. ELIZA H. JEWETT.
HOLMES, Rev. J. LANDRUM.
HOLMES, Mrs. SALLIE J. LITTLE.
JAMES, Rev. J. SEXTON.*
JAMES, Mrs. ANNIE P. SAFFORD.*
JOHNSON, Rev. FRANCIS C.
LING, Mrs., teacher.

PEARCY, Rev. GEORGE.
PEARCY, Mrs. FRANCES P. MILLER.
SEE SEEN SANG, teacher.
TOBEY, Rev. THOMAS W.
TOBEY, Mrs. —— HALL.
TSUNG.
WHILDEN, Rev. BAYFIELD W.
WHILDEN, Mrs. ELIZA J. MARTIN.
WONG MUI.
WONG PING SAN, Rev.
WONG YIH SAN, deacon.
YATES, REV. MATTHEW T., D. D.
YATES, Mrs. ELIZA MORING,
YONG SEEN SANG.

PLACES OCCUPIED OR VISITED.

SHANGHAI.
FUH-CHOW-FUH.
KI-AW-HWO.
KWIN SAN.
KWUNG SAN.
NANKING.

NINGPO.
OO KAH JAK.
PEKING.
SOONG KONG FOO.
SUCHOW.
SUNG-WAY-DONG.

SHANTUNG MISSION.

NAMES OF BAPTIST WORKERS.

CHEN WUN YIEN, deacon.
EAGER, Rev. J. H.
CHANG YUN HWO, deacon.
CHAU TING TSING or CHOW TING CHING
HARTWELL, Rev. JESSE B., D.D.
HARTWELL, Mrs. ELIZA H. JEWETT.
HARTWELL, Mrs. JULIA JEWETT.
HOLMES, Rev. J. LANDRUM.
HOLMES, Mrs. SALLIE J. LITTLE.
KAI TONG TAI, assistant.
LEANG, assistant.

LIEU BU YUN, teacher.
MOON, Miss CHARLOTTE, teacher.
MOON, Miss Edmonia H., teacher.
SUN, assistant.
SUN CHANG LUNG.
SUN KYI DI, deacon.
TSANG YUEN TE, deacon.
TSEU CHIEN T'AO, assistant.
WOO, Rev.
WOO TSWUN CHAU, deacon.

* Lost at sea on their way to Shanghai. See page 257.

SYNOPSIS OF SOUTHERN BAPTIST MISSIONS.

PLACES OCCUPIED OR VISITED.

Chau Yuen Hein.
Chefoo, or Yentai.
Chi Hia.
Chi-Nan-Foo.
Chukee.
Hwang Hien, or Whong Ching.

Mung Kya.
Pe Ma.
Shang Tswong.
Shin Tien.
Tung Chow.
Whong San Kwan.

JAPAN MISSION.

MISSIONARIES.*

Bond, Rev. Alfred Luther.
Bond, Mrs. Helena Dameron.

Rohrer, Rev. J. Quincy Adams.
Rohrer, Mrs. Sarah Robinson.

* Lost at sea on their way to Japan. See pages 247-253.

GENERAL INDEX.

ABBEOKUTA, 364, 367, 369, 379, 401, 402, 403, 411, 414, 419, 421, 429, 430, 431, 432, 433, 436, 437, 439.
    violence at, 423.
Abyssinia, 6, 369, 372.
Acquaviva, 59.
Adams, Rev. G. F., D.D., 169.
Africa, 261, 265.
   " Central, 269.
   " climate of, 405.
   " languages of, 267.
   " rivers of, 266.
   " explorers of, 268.
   " tribes of, 267.
   " Western, 269, 276.
African Missions, 265-441, 474-478.
Agajaiye Station, 441.
Ah Wun, 81.
Aibo, Africa, 380.
Alabama Baptist State Convention, resolutions of, 468.
Albert Nyanza Lake, 266.
Albino, an, in Africa, 380.
Alcock, Sir Rutherford, 269.
Amazon, 4, 5.
American Baptist Home Mission Society, 468, 469.
American Baptist Missionary Union, 56, 61, 467, 488.
American Baptist Publication Society, 18, 129.
American Board of Commissioners for Foreign Missions, 77, 488.
American Israelite, 442.
American Missionary Societies, summary of, 488.
American Tract Society, 18.
Ammen, Miss V. T., 410.
Amoy, 76.
Ancona, 17.

Anderson, Rev. A. W., 278.
Anderson, Geo. W., D.D., 22.
Anderson, P. B., teacher in Africa, 357.
Anderson, Rev. Dr. Thos. D., 255.
Andes, 4, 5.
Anti-type of the Jewish Ritual, what is it? 448.
Apollo Belvidere, 451.
Arabia, 6.
Areh, Yoruban title, 382, 415.
Asau, 180.
Ashantee, 378.
Ashman, Mr., 272.
Ashmore, Rev. Dr. William, 39.
Assiento, Treaty of, 271.
Atlas Mountains, 266.
Au, 145, 147.
Augustine's mother, 455.
Awaye, 382.
Awyaw, 369, 411, 415, 416, 417, 420, 422, 434.
Aye, 440.

BABU Keshub Chunder Sen, on Christ, 463.
Badagry, 378.
Bagna di Lucca, 42.
Bais, King, 311.
Baker, Miss Harriet A., 90-94, 177, 179.
Baldwin, Rev. Dr. Thomas, 466.
Ball, Dr. Dyer, 91, 92.
Ball, Rev. Eli, 289, 290, 291.
Bangweola Lake, 266.
Baptism, water of, must be literal water, 446.
Baptism and the Lord's Supper, essence of, 447.
    relative position of, 447.
Baptistery in Synagogue, 442.
Bari, 22, 26, 37, 48, 52, 58, 59.

Barika, 440.
Barletta, 52, 53, 58.
Barrett, Rev. Mr., 356.
Barth, Dr. Henry, 271.
Basile, Signor, 25, 26, 36, 40.
Bassa, country, 349, 361.
" Grand, 363.
" Little, 363.
" Mission station, 362.
" tribes of, 362.
Bassa Cove, 275, 284, 329.
Bassa Cove Colony, 274.
Bassas, the, 272, 273.
Batteste, Rev. Mr., 287, 335.
Beaumont, John F., of African Mission, 384, 405, 408.
returns to America, 406.
Beecroft, Consul, 381.
Beir Country, Africa, 362, 363, 365, 366, 367, 478.
Bello, King of Sokoto, 372.
Bellondi, Signor, 47, 48, 51, 52, 58.
Benedict, Chief Justice, 303.
Bengal, 460.
Benin, Bight of, 369.
Bennett, Rev. Dr. Alfred, 171.
Bennett, Rev. Cephas, 171.
Bennett, Miss, 171.
Benya, 297.
Bequest to Southern Baptist Convention, form of, 473.
Berruati, Signor, 52.
Bexley, 283, 329, 348.
Bi-olorrun pellu, 382.
Binney, J. G., D. D., 129, 251.
Bishop, Dr. Nathan, 93.
Black Hill Seminary, Va., 413.
Blackwell's, 296.
Blanchard, Miss Barsha, 83.
Bland, Miss Nannie W., 441.
Bland, Rev. W. F., 441.
Blyden, Prof. E. W., 302.
Board for Domestic Missions, of Southern Baptist Convention, 471.
Board for Foreign Missions of Southern Baptist Convention, 471.
Board of General Missionary Convention, the meeting at Providence, R. I., 1845, 472.

Boardman, Rev. George Dana, Missionary to Karens, 466.
Bohoo, or Igboho, 380.
Bologna, 17, 21, 26, 36, 58.
Bombay, 460.
Bond, Rev. A. L., 190, 250, 253.
Bond, Dr. A. J., 250.
Bond, Mrs. Helena Dameron, 252, 253.
Boothe, Rev. J. H., 260.
Bowen, Rev. T. J., 9, 12, 129, 272, 289, 369, 370, 407.
death of, 386.
sketch of, 373.
Bowen, Mrs. L. H., 9, 393.
Brachetto, Signor Barnardo, 46, 51.
Brahmapootra River, 461.
Brahmo Somaj, 463.
Brander, J. N., teacher, 357.
Brantly, Rev. Dr. W. T., 56, 57.
Brazil, 3-8.
Brazil Mission, 3-15.
" Resumé of, to 1863, 475.
" in 1879, 479.
Bridgman, Rev. J. G., 90, 91.
Brindisi, 17.
Britton, Rev. S. W., 328, 331, 332, 335, 345, 347, 357.
Britton, Mrs. G. A., teacher, 357.
Broadus, John A., D.D., 16, 17, 56, 219.
Broaddus, Rev. Luther, 133.
Broaddus, Rev. Dr. William F., 45, 299.
Brock, 345.
Brodnax, R., 10, 11.
Brown, Dr. A. B., 99, 107.
Brown, Dr. Wm., 241.
Browne, Rev. J. J., 353, 354, 355, 356, 386.
Browne, Rev. W. Y., 351, 356.
Browne, Pres. Geo. Y., 383.
Brunsden, Rev. Daniel, English Baptist Missionary to India, 462.
Bruce, Rev. Silas, 413.
Buchanan, African Station, 285, 320, 348, 349, 359.
Buchanan, Rev. Claudius, 465.
Buck, Rev. W. C., D. D., 87.
Buddhism, 71.
Bullock, James, 328, 332, 357.
Bunts, H. B., 366.

498 GENERAL INDEX.

Burke, Rev. W. C., 332, 357.
Burton, Geo. W., M.D., 170-172, 179, 224.
Burton, Mrs. G. W., 171, 172, 179.
Butan, 314.
Butler, Rev. D. E., 61.

CABANISS, Rev. A. B., 172-175, 179, 185.
Cabaniss, Mrs. M. E., 174, 175, 179.
Cæsalpinia Braziliensis, 3.
Cagliari, 51, 59.
Caldwell, African Station, 274, 281, 288, 329, 347.
Caldwell, Elias B., 274.
Calicut, 75.
California, 82, 147, 207, 478.
Calvin, 65.
Canfield, Miss Mary E., 409.
Canton, 71, 73, 76, 77, 84, 112, 126.
" chapel, 80.
" church, 133.
" investment of, 101, 102.
Cape Coast Castle, 378.
Cape Horn, 5.
Cape Palmas, 285, 293, 294.
" church at, 325, 329, 360.
Cape St. Roque, 5.
Carey, Rev. Lott, 277, 280, 286.
Carey, Rev. Dr. William, 259, 461.
" epitaph of, 464.
" death of, 462.
Careysburg, 289, 347, 359, 360.
Carlyle, 64.
Carpi, 25, 35, 47, 58.
Carthage, 65.
Cason, Rev. J. H., 384, 394, 402, 403, 404, 405.
Cason, Mrs., 402, 404.
" return to America, 405.
Chamberlain of Candace, 451.
Chapel of First Baptist Church, Shanghai, dedication of, 198.
Charles V., 270.
Cheeseman, Rev. J. H., 285, 289, 291, 295, 310-317, 327, 329, 330, 335.
Cheeseman, Rev. J. James, 349-353, 362, 363, 365.
Cheeseman, Mrs, teacher, 333, 348.

Cheeseman, Miss M. A., teacher, 357.
Chefoo Mission, 239.
Cheu Wun Yien, 226.
Chillingworth, 258.
Chi-Nan-Foo, 207, 242, 243.
Chin dynasty, 72.
Chin, General, 163.
China, 69, 261, 262.
China Mission, 69-77.
" Resumé of, 1845-1863, 474.
"   "   " 1863-1872, 475.
"   "   " 1872-1879, 476.
China, Provinces of, 69.
Chinese, the, 70.
Chinese civilization, 113.
Chinese Jews, 118.
Chinese Missionaries, Grand Conference of, in 1877, 477.
Chinese Wall, 71.
Ching-hwang-miau, 78.
Chow period, 72.
Church Missionary Society, 424, 448.
"Church Order," what it signifies, 449.
Cinta, Piedro de, 270.
City of Rams v. Canton, 78.
Civita Vecchia, 17, 25, 35.
Clarke, Rev. Ivory, 278, 281.
Clarke, Mrs. I., 278, 279.
Clarke, Rev. W. H., of Yoruba Mission, 286, 288, 384, 387, 388, 408, 416.
" sketch of, 391.
Clay Ashland, 288, 329, 347.
Cleveland, Ohio, 56, 57.
Clopton, Rev. Abner W., 172.
Clopton, Rev. Samuel C., 76, 79, 81, 87, 94-98.
Clopton, Mrs. Keziah T., 95.
Clopton, Rev. James, 95, 96.
Cocorda, Prof., 32, 33, 35, 37, 39, 40, 41, 42, 43, 48, 49, 50, 51, 52, 54, 58, 59, 60, 62.
Cocorda, Mrs., 59.
Cœur de Lion, 263.
Cocke, Mr. C. Z., 218.
Colley, Rev. W. W., 366, 367, 368, 428, 430, 435, 436, 437, 438, 441.
" sketch of, 427.
Colonial Possession, 69.

GENERAL INDEX.   499

Columbo, Signor, 48, 51, 52, 59.
Columbus, Christopher, 4.
Committee from Southern Baptist Convention to Baptist Brethren of Northern States, 1879, 479.
Concert of Prayer, Monthly, 461.
Cone, Spencer H., D.D., 117.
Confucianism, 70.
Confucius, 71, 72, 73, 200.
Congo Town, African Station, 362, 364.
Congo Tribe, 348.
Constantine, Rev. Alfred A., Missionary to Africa, 278.
Constantine, Mrs. A. A., 278.
Convention in Augusta, 469, 470.
Cook, J., 362, 363.
Cosby, Rev. Solomon, 272, 438, 441.
Cosso, 354, 356.
Cossù, Signor, 35, 40, 59.
Cote, Rev. C. H. O., M.D., 15, 29.
Cote, Rev. W. N., M.D., 15, 22, 23, 27, 28, 29.
Cowry, value of, 379.
Cox, Melville S., 368.
Chefoo, or Yentai, 190, 200, 207, 209.
Crane, Deacon Wm., 15, 277.
Crawford, Rev. T. P., D.D., 88, 170, 180, 202–204, 224.
Crawford, Mrs. Martha, 203, 204, 228, 231, 232, 235.
Crocker, Rev. L. K., 279, 332, 343, 344, 357, 362, 363.
Crocker, Mrs. L. K., 282.
Crocker, Mrs. Mary B., 278.
Crocker, Mrs. Rizpah W., 278.
Crocker, Rev. Wm. G., 278, 281, 343.
Crowther, Bishop S., of Yoruba, 367, 381, 428.
Crozer Theological Seminary, Upland, Pa., 427.
Crystal Palace, 18.
Culpeper Graded School, 413.
Curry, Rev. Dr. J. L. M., 39.
Curtis, Thos. F., D.D., 247.
Cushing, Hon. Caleb, 76.
Cushman, Rev. Dr. R. W., 81.
Cuthbert, Rev. J. H., 117.
Cuthbert, ———, 362, 363.

DAGG, Rev. Dr. John L., 409.
Dahomey, 369.
Dameron, William, 252.
Danforth, Mrs., 211.
Danish Missionaries to India, 464.
D'Aubigné, 33, 39.
David, Rev. W. J., 53, 272, 338, 352, 353, 366, 367, 368, 369, 427, 428, 430, 432, 435, 436, 438, 440, 478.
Davis, Rev. A. P., 284, 285, 289, 305, 315–321, 330, 333, 334, 357, 358.
Davis, Mrs. A. P., 320.
Davis, D., 10, 11.
Davis, Sir Francis, 102.
Davis, John B., 284, 318, 320.
Davis, J. Staige, M.D., 62.
Davis, Noah K., LL.D., 43.
Davis, William, head man, 290.
Day, Rev. George, 203.
Day, Rev. John, 280, 281, 283, 284, 285, 286, 289, 290, 293–304, 305, 308, 309, 310, 311, 313, 318, 319, 324, 327, 335, 341, 344, 345, 346, 353, 354, 355.
Day, Mrs., 290, 299.
Day's Hope School, 299, 327, 333, 344, 349, 360.
Day, Samuel P., Liberia Mission, 345.
Dean, Dr. William, 76, 97, 177.
Demboa, 266.
Demerara, 14.
Dennard, Rev. J. S., 383, 411.
  sketch of, 390.
Dennard, Mrs., death of, 387.
Desire of all Nations, Christ the, 450.
De Souza, 7.
De Toqueville, 66.
Devan, Rev. Dr. T. T., 101.
Dey tribe, 331.
Dieppe, 20.
Dobbs, C. E., 56.
Dong Gong, Chinese pastor in Oregon, 477.
Donogba Mission Station, 362.
Donogba, King at, 363.
Dorrance, Rev. G. W., 169.
Dowd, Rev. P. W., 163.
Dowling, Rev. Dr., 95.

Drayton, Rev. Boston J., 285, 290, 321 -328, 357.
Drayton, Mrs. B. J., 326.
Dudley, Rev. Dr. R. M., 479.
Duncan, Rev. H. A., 117.
During, D. W., teacher, 354, 355.
Dutch, 75.
Dyemes, 296, 311.
Dying Gladiator, 451.

EAGER, Rev. C. C., 123.
Eager, Rev. J. H., Missionary to Shantung, China, 478.
East India Company, 76.
tyrannical and Anti-Christian rule of, 461.
opposition to Missionary Settlements, 466.
East River, 77.
Eastern Translations, contributions for, recommended by Boston Association of Baptist Ministers, 465.
Early, Jas., 355.
" Josephine, teacher, 362, 363.
" Rev. T., 364.
Eaton, Jos. H., LL. D., 123, 202.
" Rev. T. T., 123.
Edina, 274, 278, 284, 285, 329, 343, 348, 349, 350, 363.
Edkins, Mr. and Mrs., of London Mission, 209.
Edwards, Prof. P. C., 110.
Effong, 369.
Egypt, 51, 372.
Egba, 369, 379, 401, 433.
Elkins, teacher, 284.
El Mina, Africa, 378.
English, The, 75, 79.
English Baptist Missionary Society, organization of, 462.
parent of Triennial Convention, 464.
summary of, 488.
Enon, 80.
Epicureans and Stoics, Paul Preaching to, 453.
Eschman, Rev. John, 15.
Eshu, Yoruban Satan, 371.
Eruwa in Yoruba, 382.

Europe, 15-68.
Everett, Hon. Alex. H., 76, 85, 95, 103.
Everett, Hon. Edward, 76.
Ewer, Dr., 66.
Examiner and Chronicle on Organic Union, 480.
Explorers of Africa, 268.
of the Nile, 268.

FAN-YIN-TAI, 211.
Farmersville, 287, 329, 332, 334, 342, 348.
Farmington River, 362.
Fellatahs, Africa, 378.
Feller, Madame, 15, 29.
Felts, Rev. Thos. 396.
Ferdinand V., 270.
Ferraris, Missionary, 26, 34, 40, 58.
Fielding, Rev. Joseph, 278, 281.
" Mrs. Jos., 278, 281.
Fiji, Governor of, 260.
Fijis, 260.
Finley, Dr. Robert, 274.
First Baptism of a Woman in China, 186.
First Baptist Church at Jerusalem, Contribution for, 450.
Fishbourne, Capt., 181.
Fishtown, 334.
Fitzgerald, Rev. J. J., 327, 332, 339-341, 357.
Fletcher, 8.
Florence, 17.
Fo, or Buddh, 72.
Fokien, 162.
Ford, Dr., Book on African Fever, 403.
Foreign Mission Board, 61.
receipts of, from 1845 to 1879, 481.
Formosa, 70, 162.
Foster, Dea. J. L. S., 203.
Fountain, Rev. John, English Baptist Missionary to India, 462.
France, 16, 34.
Frazer, Rev. Cæsar, 342.
Frederick IV. of Denmark, sends Missionaries, 464.
Freeman, J. R., teacher, 357.
Freeman, Rev. T. B., Wesleyan Missionary to Ashantees, 378.
Freetown, 353, 354, 355, 356.

GENERAL INDEX. 501

French, Rev. J. B., 91, 92, 93, 121.
Friend of Sinners, Christ the, 454.
Fuh Chow, 76.
Fuh-chow-fuh, 105.
Fuller, Rev. Andrew, 259, 462.
Fuller, Richard, D. D., 109, 143, 208.
Fults, Henry, 427.
Fung, 147, 182.
Furman, Rev. Dr. Richard, 466.
Furnace World, of Yoruba, 371.

GABBIDON, Edw'd, letter of, 401.
Gaillard, Chas. A., 146.
Gaillard, Rev. C. W., 79, 88, 122, 123–128, 130.
Gaillard, Mrs. Eva Mills, 123, 125.
Gainesville, Ga., 409.
Gallatin, Tennessee, 408.
Gallinas River, 378.
Ganges River, 461.
Gardiol, Signor, 19, 25, 27, 40.
Garuti, Signor, 47.
Gaussen, 33.
Gayle, Rev. R. S., 203.
General Missionary Convention of the Baptist denomination in the United States, 464.
   first object, Foreign Missions, 468.
   formation of, 466.
   undertakes and gives up Home Missions, 468.
   liabilities of work in 1846, 467.
Genoa, 17.
Gezo, King of Dahomey, 379.
Giannini, evangelist, 18, 26, 36, 52, 53.
Gibbon, 66.
Gibson, G. F., 358, 362, 363, 364, 365, 366.
Giddis, Dr. John, 260.
Gillette, Rev. Dr. A. D., 16, 20.
   extract of letter to Dr. J. B. Taylor, 472.
Gillette, Mrs. A. D., 20.
Gioja, Rev. G. B., 22, 23, 24, 28, 29, 478.
Gladstone, on Grecian Philosophy, 452.
Golahs, Africa, 331, 378.
"Gold Mine in India," 462.
Gollmer, Rev. Mr., 387.
Gonzales, Antonio, 270.
Goodale, Rev. Henry, 373. Life of, 377.

Goodale, Mrs. M. J., 376.
Goodman, Rev. J. S., 279.
Good Hope, Cape of, 265.
Goshen Association, Va., 393.
Gospel, its great subject, 450.
Grand Canal of China, 71, 73.
Grand Cape Mount, 378.
Grand Conference of Chinese Missionaries, 1877, 477.
Grant, Rev. William, English Baptist Missionary to India, 462.
Graves, Rev. R. II., M. D., 14, 79, 89, 118, 124, 127, 141, 143–149.
Graves, Mrs. Eva M. Mills, 128, 145.
Graves, Mrs. Jane W. Norris, 148, 150.
Grecian Philosophy, Mr. W. E. Gladstone on, 452.
Gre-gree men, 273.
Greenville, 287, 329, 342.
Griffith, Benjamin, D. D., 129, 213.
Grimsley, Rev. B., 299.
Grumo, 59.
Guerrini, 42.
Guerrini, Rosa, 33.
Guicciardini, Count, 47.
Gurley, Mr., 284, 298.
Guyot, Professor, on Africa, 265.

HAGUE, Dr. Wm., 30, 56, 57, 61.
Hainan, 70.
Hakkas, 141, 142.
Hall, Rev. Addison, 81.
Hall, Miss Henrietta, 82.
Hamberlin, Rev. J. B., 427.
Han dynasty, 72.
Hannibal, 65.
Happer, Dr., 86, 91, 92.
Hard, Rev. W. J., 117.
Harden, Rev. Jos. M., 283, 286, 287, 336–338, 385, 403, 413, 416, 421.
   death of, 422.
Harden, Mrs. J. M., 338, 368, 414, 417, 423, 425, 426.
Harden, Samuel M., 338, 429.
Harris, Prof. H. H., 57.
Hart, Mr. John, 218.
Hartwell, Jesse B., D. D., 11, 187, 188, 201, 204–208, 209, 211, 240, 241, 242, 243.

GENERAL INDEX.

Hartwell, Mrs. J. B., Missionary to Shantung, death of, 478.
Hartwell, Mrs. Eliza H., 187, 188, 205, 206.
Hartwell, Mrs. Julia J., 207, 242, 243.
Hawthorne, Rev. J. B., D. D., 427.
Hayeley, R. J., teacher, 356, 357.
Hazzard, Julia, teacher, 289.
Heaton, Rev. Isaac E., on mode of baptism, 450.
Heber, Arabian Prophet, 372.
Hebrew Scriptures, Jews studying, 450.
Hebrew Temple, Letter to congregation of, 450.
Heliopolis, Bishop of, 163.
Henderson, A. B., 282.
Henderson, Rev. Dr. Samuel, 132.
Hendrickson, Rev. C. R., 169.
Henry, Charles, teacher, 284.
Herndon, James, 345.
Herndon, Rev. Melford D., 332, 344, 345, 357, 362.
Herndonville Mission Station, 362.
Hickson, Miss Caroline, 114.
Hickson, Levi, 115.
Hill, Rev. R. F., 332, 345, 357, 358, 376.
Himalaya Mountains, 461.
Hindostan, extent, 461.
  literature, 461.
  population, 461.
  religions, 461.
  rivers, 461.
Historic Sketch by Rev. Dr. William Williams, 467.
History of Tung Chow Mission, by Mrs. Crawford, 221, 228.
Hoang Ho, or Yellow River, 70.
Hoffman, Mr., 297.
Holmes, Rev. A. T., 391.
Holmes, Rev. J. L., 187, 188, 190, 201, 208-212, 214.
Holmes, Mr. Matthew G., 211, 222.
Holmes, S. A., U. S. Consul, 230.
Holmes, Mrs. Sallie J., 187, 188, 190, 209, 212, 214, 234.
Holton, Rev. Calvin, 277.
Holy water, Sprinkling of, 443.
Honan, 72.

Hong Kong, 76, 78, 79, 103, 111.
Hong Merchants, 74, 79.
Hoogly River, 462.
Hopkins, Dr. Samuel, 273.
Horace, 48.
Howes, 297.
Hoyt, Rev. Dr. Wayland, 38.
Humboldt, his definition of Nature, 444.
Hung-su-ch' new, Chinese insurgent, 181.
Hwang-pu River, 161.

IBADAN, 369, 416, 432, 434.
  Ibadans, 414.
Ifeh, 369.
Igboho, or Bohoo, 380.
Ijaye, 382, 384, 388, 389, 403, 406, 408, 411, 414, 415, 417, 419, 421, 434.
Ijaye chief, 431.
Ijesa country, 437.
Iketu, 369, 380.
Ilorin, 384.
India, 73.
  " British, what rules it, 463.
  " its three Presidencies, 460.
  " Scriptures in, 463.
Indus River, 461.
Irvin, Rev. C. W., 383.
Ishakki, in Yoruba, 392.
Italian Mission, 16-68.
  Resumé of, 1872, 476.
  " from 1872-1879, 478.

JAMES, Prof. C. S., 258.
  James, Rev. F. S., 232, 283, 305-309, 317.
James, Israel E., 254.
James, John Sexton, M.D., 166, 254-258.
James, Jonathan, 305.
James, Mrs. Priscilla Carter, 305.
James, Mrs. Elizabeth Rotzel, 254.
James, Mrs. Annie P. Safford, 255, 256, 257.
Japan, 244-246, 261.
  " Protestants of, 260.
Japan Mission, 244-253.
  " " Resumé of, 475.
Jefferson, President Thomas, 274.
Jeremiah, 403.

Jerusalem, contribution for First Baptist Church in, 450.
Jesus, King of the Jews, 459.
" sinlessness of, 455.
" The Messiah of the Jews and the Desire of all Nations, 450.
Jesuits, 73, 75.
Jeter, Rev. Dr. J. B., 24, 25-29, 80, 81, 110, 299, 472, 473, 479.
Jews, 75.
" eyes of the world fixed on, 458.
" scattering of, its probable results, 459.
" Southern Baptist Convention on, 449.
John the Baptist, submerged his converts, 443.
John, Rev. Griffith, of London Mission, 209, 222.
John VI, King Dom, 6.
Johnson, Mrs. Caroline H., 114, 115.
Johnson, Rev. F. C., 79, 81, 86, 108-116.
Johnson, H. R. N., teacher, 357.
Johnson, William A., 286, 345.
Johnson, Rev. Dr. William B., 109, 470. General Agent, 473.
Jones, Rev. A. L., 280, 293, 294, 295, 334.
Jones, Rev. Dr. T. G., 34.
Judaic Typology, 442.
Judson, Rev. Dr. Adoniram, 258, 465, 471.
goes to Isle of France, 466.
to Madras, 466.
to Burmah, 466.
Junk, 282, 286, 318, 333, 358.

KAI-FUNG-FU, 119.
Kamton, v. Canton, 77.
Keen, Rev. Dr. T. G., 175.
Kennard, J. H., D.D., 254.
Key, Francis S., 274.
Keying, Governor, 102.
Khahnay, 351.
Ki-aw-hwo, 189.
Ki Tong Tai, 240.
Kidder, S.
Kincaid, Rev. Dr. Eugenio, Missionary to Burmah, 466, 468.

King Gray's District School, 347.
King Graystown, 289.
King of the Jews, Jesus the, 459.
King of Yoruba, 426, 434.
Kingdon, Rev. J., 289, 292, 339.
Kingsford, Rev. E., 16, 110.
Kober, King, 278, 343.
Kokonor, 69.
Kong Mountains, 434.
Kosokkoh, of Lagos, 379, 381.
Knowlton, Rev. Dr. Miles J., Missionary to China, 467.
Krapf, Dr., 269.
Krishnu, first Hindoo convert, 462.
Kublai-Khan, 73.
Kumasi, capital of Ashantee, 378.
Kumi, Chief of Ijaye, 382, 384.
Kwang-si, 146.
Kwang Tung, 77.
Kwin San Church constituted in 1879, 477.
Kwung San Mission Station, 195, 196, 109.

LACY, Rev. J. H., 386, 388, 389, 391.
Lacy, 408.
Ladies of Georgia and Virginia, Collection of, for house for the Misses Moon, 478.
Lagos, 283, 337, 367, 368, 369, 402, 404, 414, 415, 416, 421, 428, 429, 430, 435, 436, 437, 438, 439, 474, 476, 478.
new chapel at, 436.
the Liverpool of Western Africa, 436.
Lake Leman, Rhone current in, 458.
Lansanna, 378.
Laocoon, 451.
Laoukeun, 72.
La Plata, 5.
La Tour, 26.
Laura, Secundo, 46-51.
Lathrop, Edward, D. D., 117, 394.
Leang, 226, 238, 241.
Lee, Elder D., 393.
Legge, Dr., 261.
Leghorn, 17.
Leiper, Dr. L., teacher, 357.
L. E. L., Miss Landon, grave of, 379.

Leo XIII., 65.
Lepers, congregation of, 84, 112.
Levering, E., Esq., 149.
Lewis, J. N., teacher, 257, 334, 357.
Lewis, Miss, teacher, 299.
Lewis, Mrs., teacher, 257.
Lewis, Rev. John, 278.
Lexington, 257.
Liberia, 265, 272.
   Republic of, 275, 276.
Liberia Baptist Association, 366.
Liberia Mission, 353-368.
   Resumé of 1845 to 1862, 475.
   suspension of, 365, 368.
Liberia and Sierra Leone, Statistics of, 357.
Liberian *Herald*, Editor of, 251.
Liberty, M. D., 362.
Liberty, Sister, 351.
Light of the World, Jesus the, 452.
Little Bassa, 343.
Lincoln, Heman, 323.
Ling, Mrs., of Shanghai Mission, 477.
Lintin, Bay of, 78.
Lipscomb, Captain, P. O., 172.
Livingstone, Dr. David, 269.
Locket, Adam, 330.
Lockhart, Dr., 161.
Lok, Captain John, 271.
"Long Hairs," 75.
Long, J. C., D, D., 216, 217.
Loomis, Prof. Justin R., LL.D., 247.
Lord of Glory, Christ the, 453.
Lord's *Theological and Literary Journal*, 445.
Lorimer, G. C., D. D., 23, 24, 56.
Lough Fuh, Chinese pastor, Demerara, S. A., 14, 477.
Louisiana, 347.
London Missionary Society, 77.
Luk, 145, 146.
Lundy, Elder P. H., 393.
Lune-hing-ki Chapel, 85, 86, 101, 104, 118, 125.
Luther, 65, 264.
Lye Seen Sang, 118, 120, 124.

MACAO, 78, 75, 78, 79, 80, 84, 112, 125.
   "Macedonian Cry," 119.

McDonald, Rev. Dr. Henry, 56.
McDougall, Dr., 63.
Madeira, 432.
Madison University, 15.
Madras, 460.
Maginnis, Rev. Dr. John S., 469.
   inquiry of Southern Board, 473
Magoon, Rev. Dr. E. L., 394.
Mahee, 369.
Malabar, 75.
Malcom, Rev. Dr. Howard, 344.
Mamertine Prison, 66.
Manchow Princes, 73.
   Tartar Dynasty, 73.
Manchuria, 69.
Mandarins, 74.
Mandingo Tribes, 331.
Manly, Rev. Basil, D. D., 55, 116.
Marcus Aurelius, 75.
Marion, Ala., 80.
Marshall, 274, 281, 362, 363.
Marshall Junk, 347, 348.
Mars' Hill, Paul on, 452.
Marshman, Rev. Joshua, English Baptist Missionary to India, 462.
Martin V., Pope, 270.
Martinelli, Signor, 21, 25, 35, 36, 40, 47 53.
Martyn, Rev. Henry, English Missionary to Persia, 8.
Mason, Israel, teacher, 257.
Massachusetts Baptist Missionary Society, 465.
Maury, Commodore, 5.
Mazzarelli, 50.
Mecha, Baptism of, 81.
Mecklin River, 285.
Medburg, R. B., 274.
Medhurst, Dr., 162.
Melancthon, 65.
Mell, P. H., D. D., 388, 409.
Mencius, Chinese Philosopher, 200.
Mende, Ship, 408.
Mercer, Gen. C. F., 274.
Mercer University, Georgia, 407, 409.
Meriwether, R., 10, 11.
Mesurado, Cape, 274.
Middle Settlement, 257.
Mikrah, the Jewish ritual bath, 443.

GENERAL INDEX.   505

Milan, 17, 32, 33, 35, 46, 58.
Millsburg, 274, 281, 288, 324, 329, 347.
Milne, Rev. Wm., 77.
Milton, 360.
Ming Dynasty, 73.
Mishna, 443.
Mississippi College, 427.
Mite Box, The, 152.
Mite Societies formed. 465.
Modena, 25, 33, 35, 47, 53.
Mohammedans, 75, 418.
Mollo, Signor, 25.
Monger, W. H., 348, 357.
Mongolia, 69.
Mongols, The, 73.
Monrovia, 272, 274, 276, 277, 281, 324, 326, 328, 329, 332, 333, 347, 362, 363, 368.
    Church at, 359.
Monte Casino, 49.
Monte Citorio, 52.
Monthly Concert of Prayer, 461.
Monument Street Church, Tung Chow, 227, 233.
Moody, Rev. Wm., 248.
Moon, Miss Charlotte, 217-221, 235, 237, 478.
Moon, Miss Edmonia H., 143, 215-217, 221, 234, 235, 236, 237, 478.
Moore, Jas., teacher, 326.
Moore, Worrell, 345, 357.
Moravians, contributions to Missions, 464.
    missionaries, 464.
    numbers of, 464.
Morel, Mrs., teacher, 334.
Morrill, Rev. ——, 348.
Morrison, Rev. Robert, English Missionary to China, 77.
Motton, Hanson W., teacher, 326, 357.
Mount Hope, 343.
Mount Olive, 362.
Müller, Max, 258.
Murray, Rev. R. E., 287, 288, 291, 333-336, 342.
Mylne, Rev. William, 278.

NANKING, 72, 76, 88, 181.
    Napier, Lord, 75.

Naples, 17, 37, 49, 51, 52, 59.
Nashville, 80.
National Baptist on organic union of Southern and Northern Missions, 480.
Necho, King of Egypt, 269.
Nestorians, 72, 75.
Nevius, Mrs. Helen S. C., 206, 210.
New Georgia, Africa, 274, 275, 281, 286, 329, 341, 347, 357, 366.
New Kentucky, 289.
New Orleans, Africa, 281, 287.
New Testament in Persia and Hindostanee, 465.
New Virginia, 281, 282, 283.
Neyle, J. T., teacher, 314, 315, 316, 335.
Ngchow, 140.
Nice, 17.
Nicholas, Mr., on prospects in Yoruba, 367.
Niger, River, 369.
Nina, the, 4.
Ningpo, 75, 76.
Nubia, 369.
Noel, Rev. Baptist W., 40, 49.
Northampton Association, England, 461.
Northern Views and Southern Comment on organic union of the missionary organizations, 480.
North River, 77.
North street church, Tung Chow, 226, 227, 237.
Nyassa Lake, 266.

OBBA River, Africa, 384.
    Obidos, 4.
Oboni, Secret Institution of Yoruba, 371.
Ogbomishaw, 367, 368, 369, 384, 405, 406, 408, 409, 411, 416, 423, 428, 429, 430, 433, 434, 436, 437, 438, 439, 476, 478.
Oguelipe, 439.
Ogun River, Africa, 380, 385.
Old Fields, African Station, 362, 364.
Oliver, Edward James, Esq., Treas. of English Bap. Tract Society, 45.
Ondo People, 439.

GENERAL INDEX.

Oo Kah Jak, 177, 178.
Organic Union of the Missionary Organizations South and North, 479.
   Rev. Dr. H. H. Tucker on, 480.
   Biblical Recorder on, 480.
   Examiner and Chronicle on, 480.
   National Baptist on, 480.
   Northern Views and Southern Comments on, 480.
Orinoco, 4.
Orisha, Yoruban Idol, 371.
Ossa, Lake, 369.
Overweg, Dr., 271.
Owing, Rev. Ephraim H., 202.

PAGE, S. S., 310, 311, 315, 345, 348.
   Page, P. M., teacher, 337, 357.
Paiho, Fort of, 189.
Panbrazil, 4.
Pantheon, 55.
Pappengouth, Count Oswald, 40, 49, 51, 52.
"Paradox," the schooner, 257.
Parents of Eastern Missions, 464.
Parker, Rev. H. M., of Chinese Episcopal Mission, 212.
Paschetto, Enrico, 35, 40, 46, 51, 58.
Patton, Mrs., 20.
Paul, 65.
   On Mars Hill, 452.
Paul, Edward, teacher, 288, 345.
Payne, Rev. David, 346.
Payne, Bishop, 301.
Payne, Miss W. N., 346.
Pearcy, Rev. George, 76, 79, 81, 86, 87, 94, 95, 97, 99–108, 176, 179, 184, 185, 256.
Pearcy, Mrs. F. M., 95, 98, 100, 104, 108, 177.
Pearl River, 77.
Peck, G. B., teacher, 357.
Peck, Solomon, D. D., 254.
Pe-chi-li Gulf, 70.
Pedro I Dom, 6.
Pedro II, Dom, 6.
Peel, 334.
Peking, 71, 73, 78.
Penfield, 409.
Père La Chaise, 46.

Peru, 4.
Pettus, Rev. H. L., 203.
Philadelphia, 3.
Philip and the Eunuch, 450.
Phillips, Rev. A. D., 349, 361, 362, 364, 384, 404, 405, 407, 411, 415, 418, 419, 420, 421, 422, 423, 424.
Phillips, Mrs. F. C. Williams, 408, 410.
   grave of, 434.
Phillipsburg, African station, 362.
Piazza Navona, 21.
Pierce, Bishop, 258.
Piles, Mr., 11.
Pinelli, Signor, 19.
Pistoia, 17.
Plato, his divine ideas, 444.
Po, 46, 51.
Poindexter, Rev. Dr. A. M., 301, 315, 393.
Polo, Marco, 244.
Polynesia, 260, 261.
Portuguese, 4, 73, 75.
Post, Rev. A. L., 249.
Powell, J. J., teacher, 289, 347, 357.
Powell, Jack, African boy, 247.
Pozzuoli, Ancient Puteoli, baptism at, 479.
Preble, Mr., 27.
Priest, Rev. R. W., 384, 394, 398, 402, 411, 414, 415.
Priest, Mrs. R. W., 398, 400, 401.
Prime, Dr., 54.
Pritchard, Rev. Dr. T. H., 169.
Pritchard, Rev. J. S., 391.
Pritchard, Rev. R. S., appointed missionary to China, death of, 195
Protestant Missions, Summary of, 488, 489.
   AMERICAN:
   American Baptist Missionary Union, 488.
   American Bible Society, 488.
   American Board of Commissioners for Foreign Missions, 488.
   American Missionary Association, 488.
   American Southern Presbyterians, 488.
   American Woman's Union, 488.

GENERAL INDEX. 507

AMERICAN:
Board for Foreign Missions of So. Baptist Convention, 488.
Methodist Episcopal Church Missions, 488.
Methodist Episcopal Church South Missions, 488.
Nova Scotia Presbyterian Church Missions, 488.
Presbyterian Church Missions, 488.
Reformed Dutch Church Missions, 488.
United Presbyterian Church Missions, 488.
BRITISH:
Baptist Missionary Society, 488.
British and Foreign Bible Society, 489.
British Society for the Jews, 489.
Church Missionary Society, 488.
Church of Scotland Missions, 489.
English Episcopal, 489.
English Presbyterian Church Missions, 489.
Free Church of Scotland Missions, 489.
General Baptist Missionary Society, 488.
Irish Presbyterian Church Missions, 489.
London Missionary Society, 488.
Methodist New Connection Missions, 488.
Primitive Methodist Missionary Society, 488.
Society for Propagation of the Gospel in Foreign Parts, 488.
Scotch National Bible Society, 489.
South American Missionary Society, 489.
Turkish Missions Aid Society, 489.
United Brethren Foreign Board, 489.
United Methodist Free Church Missionary Society, 488.
United Presbyterian Church Missions, 489.

BRITISH:
Welsh Calvinistic Methodist Missions, 489.
Wesleyan Missionary Society, 488.
CONTINENTAL:
Basle Evangelical Missions, 489.
Berlin Missionary Society, 489.
Danish Missionary Society, 489.
Hermansburg Missionary Society, 489.
Moravian Missionary Society, 489.
Netherland Missionary Society, 489.
Norwegian Missionary Society, 489.
Paris Evangelical Missionary Society, 489.
Rhenish Missionary Society, 489.
Utrecht Missionary Society, 489.
Providence Church, Monrovia, 360, 366.
Provinces of China, 69.
Pulohs, African tribe, 378.
Purinton, Rev. D. B., 203.
Purvis, Rev. Smart, 318, 345.
Puteoli, now Pozzuoli, baptism at, 479.
Pultscho, Henry, Danish, missionary to India, 464.

QUILLEN, Elder E. H., Missionary, Brazil, 3, 12, 13, 479.
Queen of England, 76.

RABBI E. S. L., letter to, 442.
Rabbi S., 450.
Rambo, Mr., 297.
Rams of Daniel, 446.
Randolph, Warren, D. D., 18.
Raphael, 67.
Rasberry, Elder J., 373.
Ratcliff, Rev. Richard, 10, 11, 12, 13.
Rebellion in China, End of, 190.
Receipts of Foreign Mission Board, S. B. C., 1845-1879, 481-487.
   from 1845-1863, 475.
   from 1863-1872, 476.
   from 1872-1879, 479.
Red Book, the, 74.
Reformation, The, its results, 464.
Reformed Israelites, 449.

GENERAL INDEX.

Reid, Rev. T. A., 400, 408, 411, 415, 416, 417, 420, 422.
Reid, Mrs. Mary Canfield, 93, 404, 410.
 death of, 400, 409, 411.
 grave of, 416, 435.
Renan, Roussell's reply to, 454.
Ressiah tribe, 331.
Revelli, Signor, 33.
Reynolds, Rev. J. L., D. D., 375.
Rhodes, Mr., 426.
Rhone, current of in Lake Leman, 458.
Rice, Rev. Luther, 465.
 returns to America, 466.
Richardson, Rev. F., 333, 347, 359.
Richardson, Mr. James, 271.
Richardson, Rev. J. T., 282, 285, 287, 288, 289, 300, 301, 323-333, 347, 357.
Richmond, Baptist Women and Concer of Prayer, 461.
Richmond Institute, 366, 427.
Richmond, Leigh, 354, 355, 356.
Rio de Janeiro, 3, 5, 7.
Roberts, Rev. B. B., 342.
Roberts, Rev. Isaac, 287, 289, 291, 330, 334, 335, 342, 348, 357.
Roberts, Rev. Issachar J., 75, 79, 80, 83-90, 96, 104, 105.
Roberts, President J. T., 296.
Roberts, Rev. Z. B., 315.
Robinson, Major Sidney T., 249.
Robinson, Hon. Tracy, 249.
Rocca Imperiale, 48.
Rohrer, Rev. J. Q. A., 190, 247-250.
Rohrer, Mrs. Sarah R., 248, 249, 250.
Roman Chapel, cost of, 479.
Rome, 15-68, 476, 478, 479.
Roper, Mr., 426.
Rosa, Signor, 19.
Rotzel, Joseph, 254.
Roussell, reply to Renan 454.
Ryland, Rev. R., D. D., 100, 110, 173.

SAGBUA, Chief of Egbas, 330.
 Sacramento, Cal., Rev. J. L. Shuck builds chapel at, 83.
Safford, Miss A. C., 219, 220.
Safford, Joshua, 255.
Safford, Mrs. Sarah B., 256, 257.
Sahara Desert, 265.

Sai-Nan, 149.
St. John's River, 349.
St. Paul's River Church, 359.
St. Peter's, Rome, 19.
Salminici, Signor, 53.
Sama, in Yoruba, 377.
Samson, Rev. Dr. G. W., 16, 253.
Samson, Rev. A., 169.
Sandfish, King James, 339.
Sandwich Islands, 260.
Sanford, E. T. Esq., 229.
San Germano, 49.
San Hing City, 141.
San Kiu, native Missionary Station at 477.
Sankwo period, 72.
San Passidonio, 35.
San Paulo, 3, 6.
Santa Barbara, Brazil, 3, 13, 479.
Santa Cruz, v. Vera Cruz.
San Siu, 139.
Saratoga, 62.
Scattering of the Jews, its probable results, 459.
Scipio, 65.
Schilling, Rev. J. G., 79, 129-132.
Schilling, Mrs. Kate Lowther, 130.
Scriptures in India, 463.
Sea Coast settlement, 349.
Secchi, Father, 49.
Seen, 146.
See Seen Sang, 177, 195, 196, 198, 199.
Senegambia, 369.
Serampore, 462.
Seward, Geo. F., American Minister to China, 193.
Shanghai, 76, 106.
Shanghai, City of, 161-163.
Shanghai Mission, 81, 160-199.
Shanghai, Romanists in, 163.
Shangti, 70.
Shang Tswong, revival in, 225.
Shan-sin-fan, 139, 140.
Shantung Mission, 199-243.
Shantung, Province of, 70, 199-201.
Sharp, Granville, 273.
Sharp, Mr. Robert, 346.
Shaver, Rev. Dr. D., 110.
Shen Si, 72.

Shermer, Rev. H. B., 279.
Shipton, Miss Anna, 47.
Shiu Hing, 134, 139, 140, 145, 146.
Shuck, Rev. J. L., 77, 79-83, 92, 111, 124, 136, 176.
Shuck, L. H., D.D., 82.
Shuck, Mrs. A. L. Trotti, 82.
Shuck, Mrs. E. G. Sexton, 82, 178.
Shuck, Mrs. Henrietta Hall, 77, 80, 82.
Siebold, on Japan, 246.
Sierra Leone, 353, 361.
 Colony of, 273.
 Mission, 289, 329.
Simmons, Rev. E. Z., 79, 138-143.
Simmons, Mrs. M. D. Clamrock, 139-143.
Simms, A. G. Esq., 413.
Sinim, 75.
Sinlessness of Jesus, 455.
Sinoe, 333.
Sinoe Church, 348.
Sinou, 275, 287.
Sin-syn, Original Japanese Religion, 246.
Sin-too, Japanese Creed, 246.
Skinner, Rev. Benjamin, 278.
Skinner, Rev. Ezek., M.D, 278.
Slave Coast, 378.
Slave Trade, 381.
Smart, Mr., 282.
Smith, Rev. Columbus, 427.
Smith, Jordan, 321.
Snake Worship in Africa, 399.
Soo-Choo-Foo, 162.
Soong Dynasty, 72.
Soong Kong Foo, 171.
Soudan, 369, 372, 379.
South America, 3-15.
 Swiss Missionaries to, 464.
Southern Baptists, increased contributions for Foreign Missions since 1845, 472.
Southern Baptist Convention, Birth of, 467.
 first appointments of, 473.
 grandparent of, 460.
 parent of, 464.
 object of, 473.
 origin of, 460.

Resumé of Operations of, 474.
Synopsis of Workers and Places, 490.
Southern States, contributions to General Missionary Convention, 467.
Sprinkling Holy Water, 443.
Sprinkling, Jews no idea of, 443.
Stanley, Henry M., 269.
"Star of the East," 465.
Staughton, Rev. Dr. William, 466.
Stephens' visit to Shanghai, 162.
Stewart, W. H., teacher, 286, 287, 356, 362.
Stewart, W. W., teacher, 337, 341, 342, 357.
Stiles, Rev. Ezra, 273.
Stoics and Epicureans, Paul preaching to, 453.
Stone, Rev. L. M., 427.
Stone, Moses L., 427, 428, 431, 433, 436, 440.
Stone, Rev. R. H., 327, 412, 413, 418, 419, 421, 423, 425, 426, 428.
Stone, Mrs. S. J. Broadus, 413, 415, 419, 420, 421.
Strother, J., teacher, 287.
Suchow, 187, 189, 209.
Sun Chang Lung, 227.
Sung-way-dong, 189.
Sung-shek-kosk Chapel, 141.
Sweden, 262.
Swiss Missionaries to South America, 464.
Switzerland, 15, 34.
Syganfoo, 72.
Synagogue, Baptistery in, 442.
Sziu, 134.

TABAL, meaning of, 443.
 Tai-pings, 183, 187, 189.
Ta-koo, Fort of, 189.
Takrour, or Central Africa, 372.
Tamils, the, 262.
Tanganyika Lake, 266.
Tang Dynasty, 72.
Taranto, 48.
Tartars, the, 73, 75.
Tate, 362.
Tattou's town, King of, 296, 311

Tauism, 70.
Taylor, Rev. Geo. B., D. D., 35, 36, 37, 38, 40, 41, 42, 43, 51, 52, 54, 55, 57, 58, 59, 60, 62, 64, 65, 479.
Taylor, Mrs. G. B., 59.
Taylor, Rev. Dr. J. B., 30, 98, 165.
  at Board of General Missionary Convention, 1845, 472.
  chosen, Corresponding Secretary of Foreign Mission Board, S. B. C., 473.
  death of, 361.
Taylor, President, 76.
Taylorsville Mission Station, 362, 363.
Tchad Lake, 266.
Teage, Rev. Colin, 277, 286.
Teage, Rev. Hilary, 278, 281, 285, 329, 333, 335, 343, 345.
Teague, Rev. E. B., 203.
Tee-to-tune Fort, 144.
Te-hwo-dong, 189.
Teloogoos, 262.
Ten-sio-dai-zin, Japanese Sun Goddess, 246.
Thayer, Professor, 252.
Thibet, 69.
Thomas, Rev. John, English Baptist Missionary to India, 462.
Thomas, Rev. R., 11.
Thompson, Rev. H. P., 353, 354.
Thompson, Geo. W., Esq., 163.
Thompson, Rev. Geo. R., 289, 386.
Thornton, Dr. Wm., 274.
Thurber, Hon. Chas., 60.
Tiber, 51.
Tichenor, Elder, 393.
Tien-tsin, massacre of, 195, 230.
  " treaty of, 189, 221.
Ti-ma-ton, 118.
Timour, or Tamerlane, 73.
Tinnevelly, 262.
Tobey, Rev. T. W. D. D., 81, 111, 168-170.
Tobey, Rev. Z., 168.
To Hai, chapel & school house built, 477.
Torre, Count, 33, 47, 58.
Torre Pellice, 58.
Tosti, 49.
Tou, Chinese god of reason, 72.

Townsend, Rev. H., Episcopal Mis sionary to Yoruba, 367, 381.
Townsend, Mrs., 367.
Toy, Prof. Crawford H., 218, 248.
"Triennial Convention," See Gen. Miss. Conv. of Bap. Denom. of the United States. Division and change of name, 467.
Tranquebar, missionaries to, the "Parents of Eastern Missions," 464.
Trastevere, Rome, Baptist Church at, 21. 23, 27, 33, 37-42.
Trimble, Rev. S. Y., 384, 395, 408.
Trimble, Mrs. Mary E. Morehead, 395, 397.
Trotti, Miss Anna L., 82.
Tsang Yuen Te, 225, 226.
Tseu Chien T'ao, 226.
Tsia dynasty, 72.
Tso Sune, 14.
Tsung Seen Sang, 195, 196.
Tucker, Rev. Dr. H. H., 20, 21, 22, 27, 479.
  paper of, on preserving both Southern and Northern Missionary Organizations, 480.
Tung Chow, 188, 200, 201, 205, 209, 210, 211, 224, 228, 229.
Turin, 17, 46, 51.
Tupper, H. A., Cor. Sec'y., 12, 20, 23, 56, 57, 352, 438, 441, 479.
Tustin, Rev. J. P., 173.
Typology, Judaic, 442.
  laws of, 445.
  what it is, 445.
Tytler, Rev. G., 362, 364.

UET-TUNG Church, in Canton, 84, 85, 86, 87.
Underwood, Rev. H., 282, 286, 345, 347, 357, 362.
  death of, 364.
Underwood, John L., 10.

VAN METER, Rev. W. C. 23, 42, 50, 54, 57.
Vatican, The, 23.
Vatican School, 57, 59.
Venice, 17, 51, 58, 47, 48, 51.

GENERAL INDEX.   511

Vera Cruz, 4.
Vey Tribe, 331, 368.
Via della Croce, 17.
Via Theatro della Valle, 55.
Victor Emmanuel, 16.
Victoria Nyanza Lake, 266.
·Viey, 5.
Vincent Yanez Pinzon, 4.
Virginia, 347.
"Virginia Baptist Preachers," 98.
Virginia Foreign Mission Society, circular of Board, 469.
Vogel, Dr., 271.
Volpi, Signor, 52, 58, 59.
Von Brunn, Rev. Jacob, 279, 239, 332, 345, 357.
Von Brunnville, 289, 320.
   Church and School at, 348.
Vonkra, 363, 365.

WADE, Rev. Dr. Jonathan, Missionary to Burmah, 468.
Wait, Rev. Samuel, 164.
Waldensian Valley, 25.
Walker, Rev. Hugh, 348, 357, 358.
Wall, Rev. J, 18, 26, 27, 42, 49.
Walne, Rev. T. J., 427.
Walthall, Rev. J. S., 110.
Wanghia, Treaty of, 76.
Ward, Rev. Dr. William, American Baptist Missionary to Assam, 467.
Ward, Rev. William, English Baptist Missionary to India, 462.
Ware, Hon. Wm., 260.
Warner, Robert, 400, 401.
Warren, Rev. Dr. J. G., 282.
Waring, Rev. ——, at New Georgia, Africa, 286.
Warring, Rev. Colson M., pastor at Monrovia, 346.
Waterloo, Africa, 354, 355.
Waughn, Rev. E., 362, 364.
Wayland, Francis, D. D., 168, 280, 472.
Weeks, Rev. George S., 354, 355, 356, 361.
West, Mr., Yoruba, 420.
West River, 77.
Whampoa, 131.

Whilden, Rev. B. W., 79, 87, 116–122, 123, 125, 126, 376.
Whilden, Mrs. E. G. Martin, 116, 120, 122, 133.
Whilden, Miss Lulu, 121, 133, 148, 150.
White Cloud Mountains, 78.
White, Adam, 332.
White, Rev. John B., 165.
White, Rev. R., 288, 329, 330, 337, 345, 348.
Williams, Miss Fannie C., 408.
Williams, Elder J. D., 393.
Williams, Dr. J. W. M., 248, 251, 252.
Williams, Rev. N. B., 79, 132–135, 148.
Williams, Rev. Dr. William, his Historical Sketch, 467.
Williams, Mrs. Jumelle Whilden, 121, 132, 135, 150, 151.
Williamston, S. C., 409.
Willis, Mr., 318.
Wilson, Rev. Dr. Franklin, 16, 169, 208.
Wilson, Rev. Dr. John Leighton, 267.
Wilson, J. H., 332, 333.
Windham, teacher, 355.
Windham, Thomas, visits African Coast in 1553, 271.
Winston, Prof. C. H., 215.
Winkler, Rev. Dr. E. T., 51.
Wise, Isaac M., Editor of *Am. Israelite*, 442.
Woo, Pastor of Church in Tung Chow, 205.
Woo Tswun Chau, Rev., 225, 226, 235
Wong, 188.
Wong Fung, 149.
Wong Mui, 83, 127, 137, 139, 140, 147, 148, 149, 176, 177.
Wong Ping San, Rev., 168, 184, 192, 194, 196, 197, 198, 199.
   letter from, 192–194.
Wong Yih San, 196.
Wood, Rev. A. T., 285, 345.
Woodson, Rev. A., 357, 360.
Woodson, Rev. J., 289.
Worcester County, Mass., 260.
Worrell, Rev. A. S., 219.
Wu-chau, 145, 146.
Wylder, Milton G., 390.

XAVIER, Francis, 106.

YAAROOBA, Son of Kahtan of Arabia, 372.
Yang-tse-kiang River, 70.
Yates, B. P., 313, 345-349, 352, 353, 359, 362, 363, 365, 366, 367, 368.
Yates, Rev. Matthew T., D. D., 20, 21, 22, 81, 111, 163-167, 180, 188, 191, 192, 195, 197, 198, 199.
Yates, Mrs. Eliza, 165-167, 191, 194, 196, 199, 210, 211.
Yong Seen Sang, 80, 81, 95, 122, 124, 125, 127, 135-138, 144, 176, 177.
Young, Miss Virginia, 87.
Yoruba, 364, 367, 368, 369, 402, 426, 427, 428, 429, 431.

climate of, 370.
government, 433.
language, 372, 406.
mission in, 283, 288, 330, 361, 375.
Resumé of, from 1849-1863, 474.
Resumé of, from 1863-1872, 475.
Resumé of, from 1872-1879, 478.
people of, 370, 372.
·Yu, the Giant, 72.

ZEO, King, 362, 363.
sons of, 366.
Ziegenbalg, Bartholomew, Danish Missionary to India, 464.
Zin-muten-Noo, Japanese " Divine Conqueror," 244.
Zwingle, 65.

ERRATA.

PAGE.
82, for John L. Shuck, read Jehu L. S.
157, for Board of Abbotsford read Bard.
212, for Mrs. J. S. Holmes read Mrs. S. J.
279, for Henry B. Goodale read J. S. G.
for J. S. Shermer read Henry B. S.
334, for J. Roberts read Isaac Roberts.

PAGE
336, for W. F. Gibson read G. F. G.
345, for Button read Britton.
347, for F. W. Britton read S. W. B.
348, for H. Waller read H. Walker.
359, for A. P. Yates read B. P. Y.
365, 478, for Bier County read Beir.

www.ingramcontent.com/pod-product-compliance
Lightning Source LLC
Chambersburg PA
CBHW031942290426
44108CB00011B/642